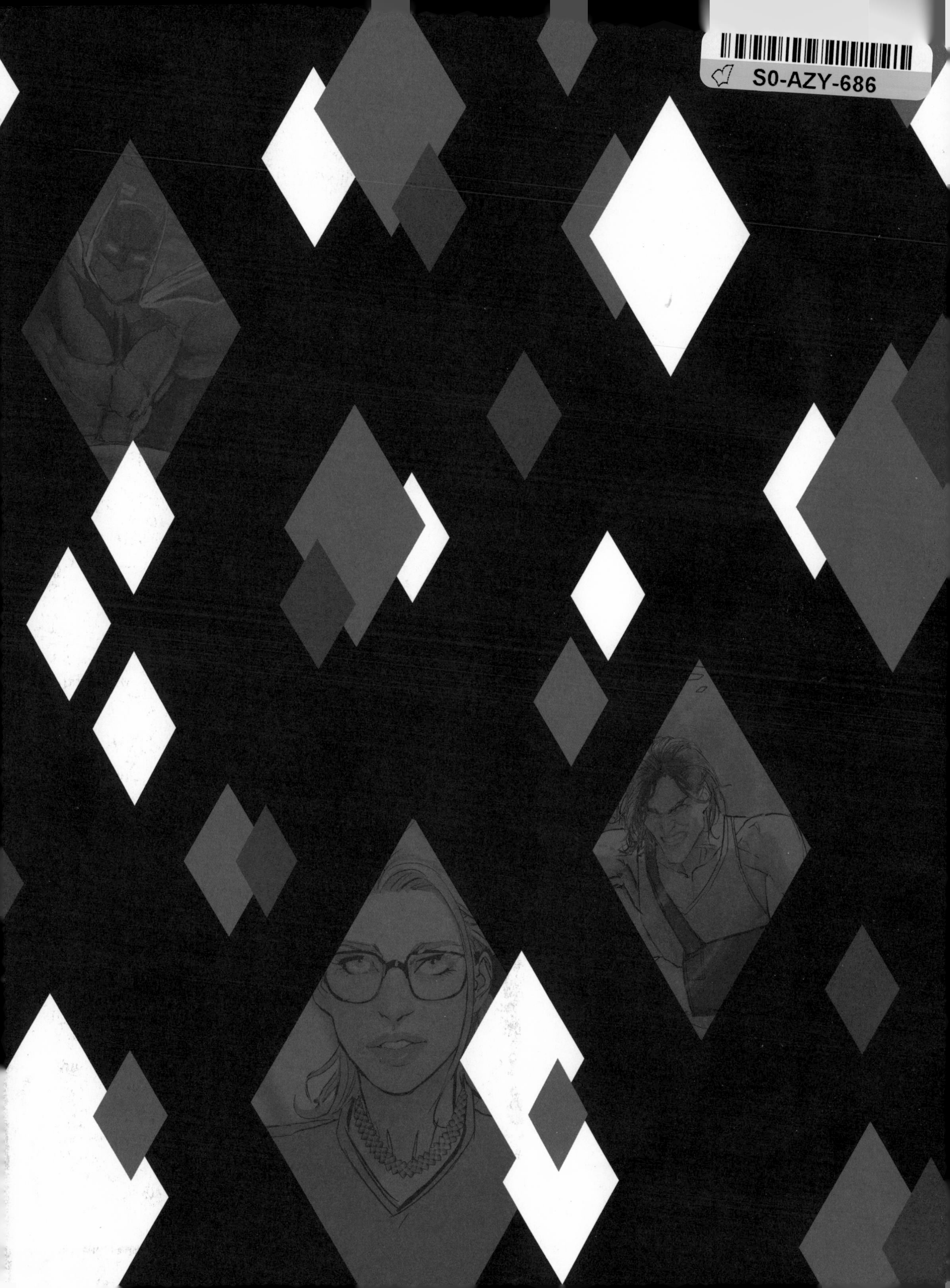

HARLEEN

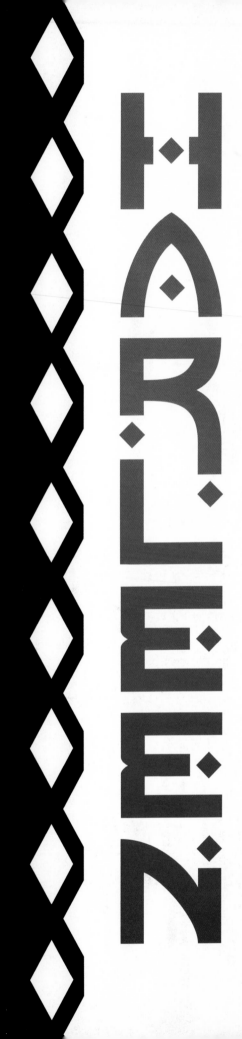

Story and Art by
STJEPAN ŠEJIĆ

Lettering by
GABRIELA DOWNIE

Cover Art and Original Series Covers by
STJEPAN ŠEJIĆ

HARLEY QUINN created by PAUL DINI and BRUCE TIMM

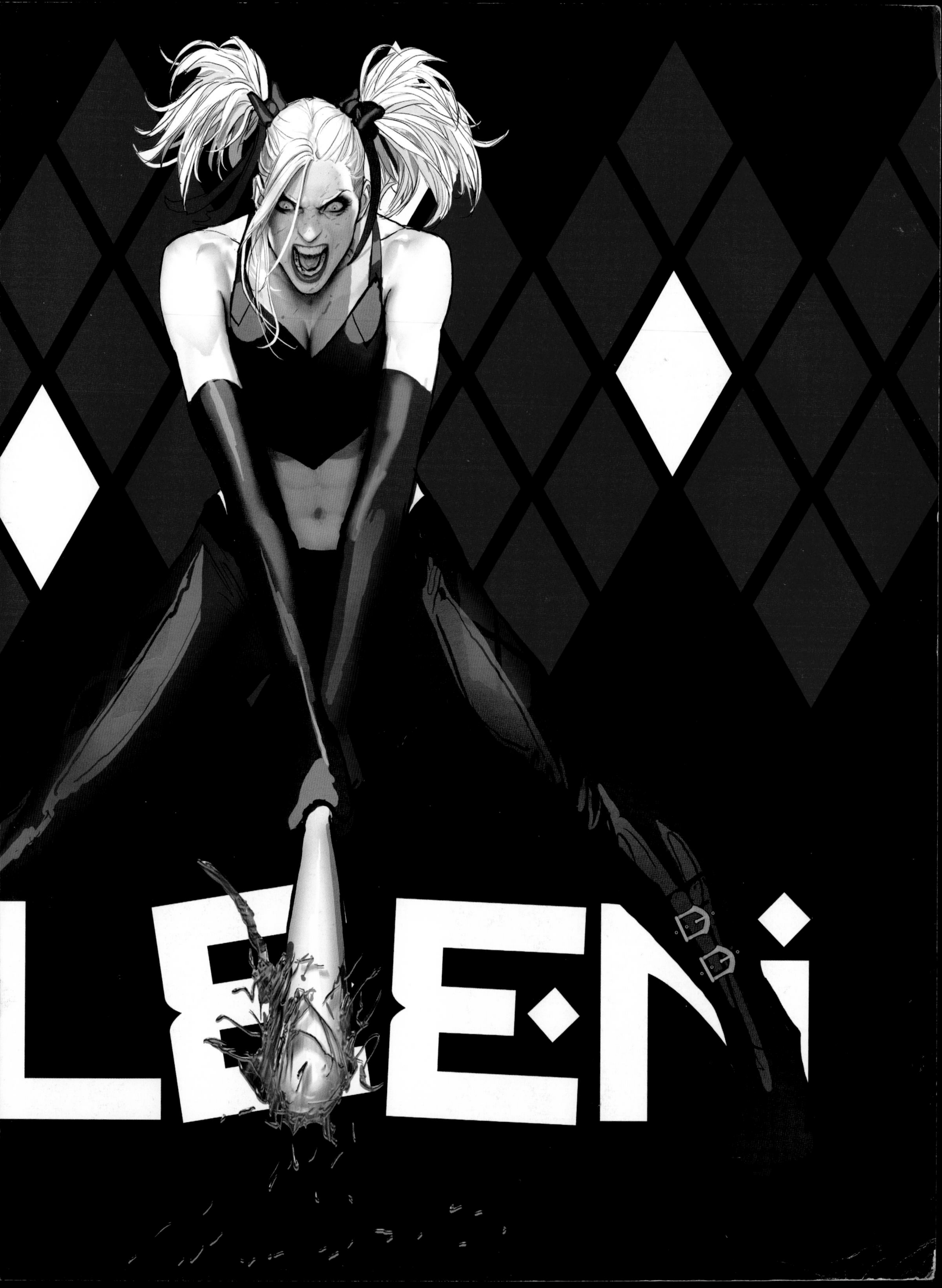

HARLEEN

DC Comics, 2900 West Alameda Ave., Burbank, CA 91505
Printed by Transcontinental Interglobe, Beauceville, QC, Canada. 1/3/20. First Printing.
ISBN: 978-1-77950-111-0

Library of Congress Cataloging-in-Publication Data is available.

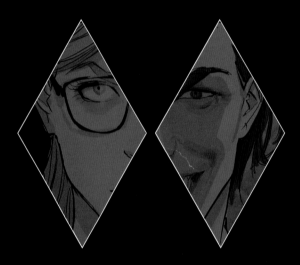

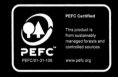

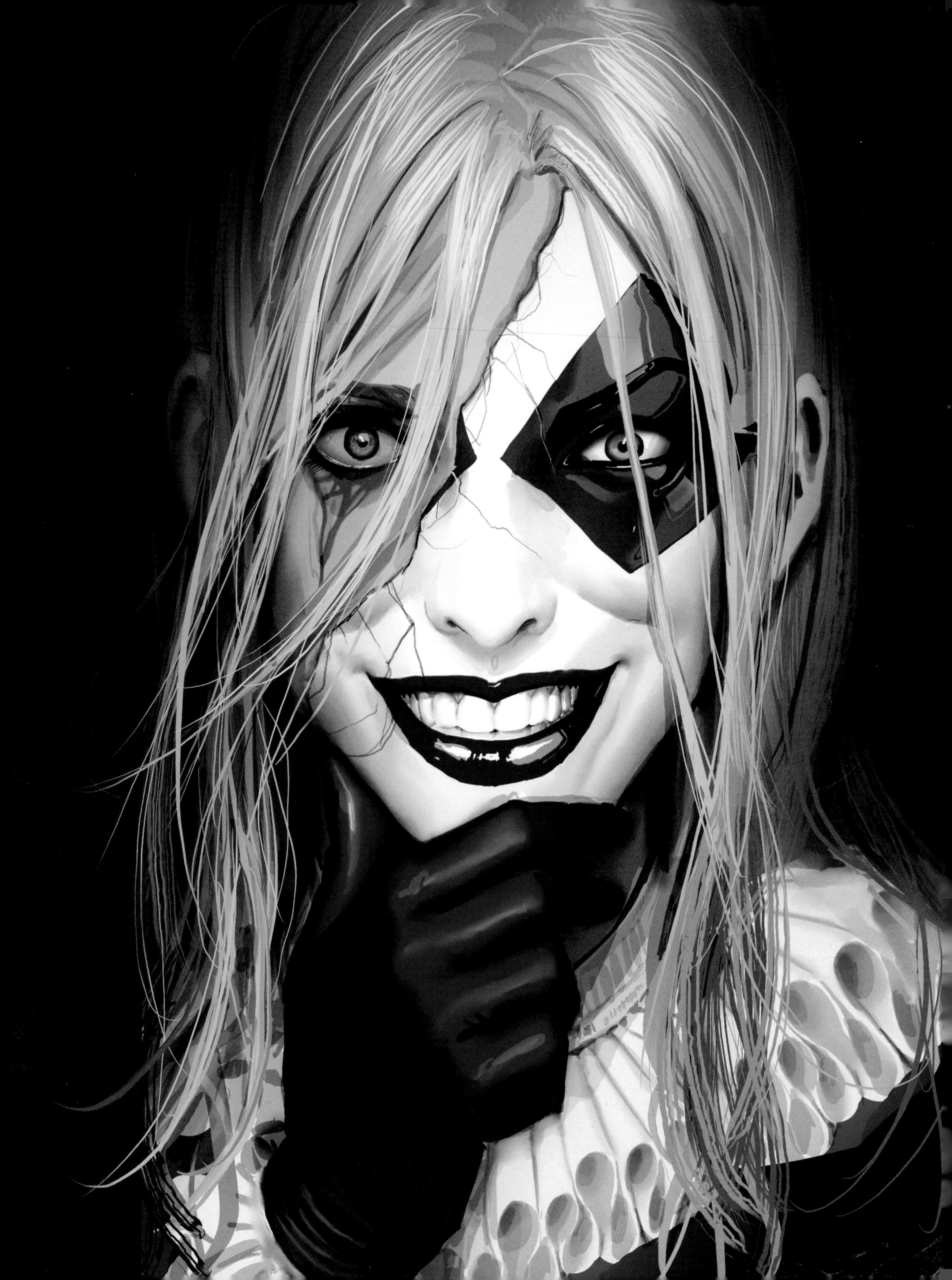

BOOK ONE

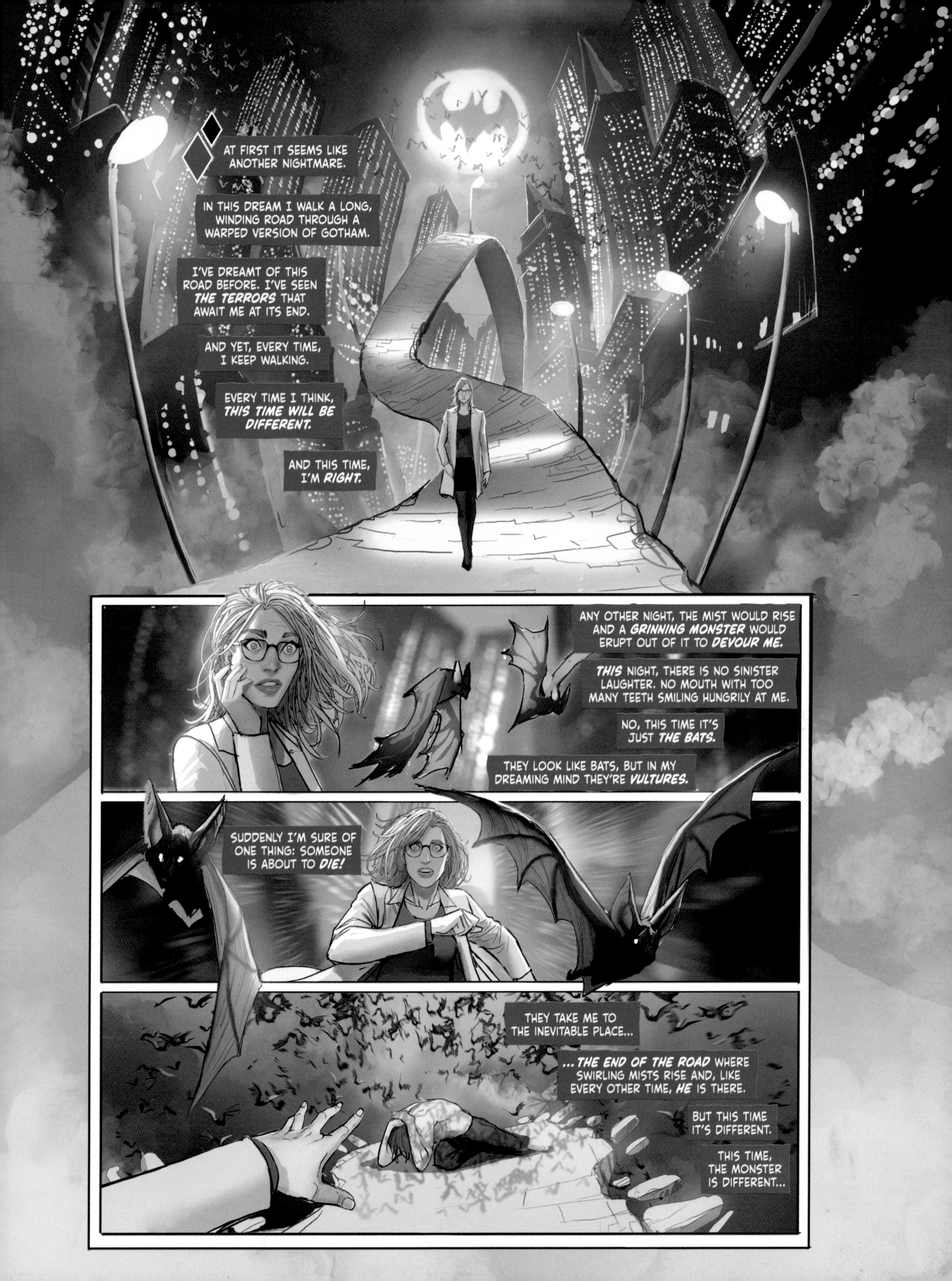
AT FIRST IT SEEMS LIKE ANOTHER NIGHTMARE.
IN THIS DREAM I WALK A LONG, WINDING ROAD THROUGH A WARPED VERSION OF GOTHAM.
I'VE DREAMT OF THIS ROAD BEFORE. I'VE SEEN THE TERRORS THAT AWAIT ME AT ITS END.
AND YET, EVERY TIME, I KEEP WALKING.
EVERY TIME I THINK, THIS TIME WILL BE DIFFERENT.
AND THIS TIME, I'M RIGHT.
ANY OTHER NIGHT, THE MIST WOULD RISE AND A GRINNING MONSTER WOULD ERUPT OUT OF IT TO DEVOUR ME.
THIS NIGHT, THERE IS NO SINISTER LAUGHTER. NO MOUTH WITH TOO MANY TEETH SMILING HUNGRILY AT ME.
NO, THIS TIME IT'S JUST THE BATS.
THEY LOOK LIKE BATS, BUT IN MY DREAMING MIND THEY'RE VULTURES.
SUDDENLY I'M SURE OF ONE THING: SOMEONE IS ABOUT TO DIE!
THEY TAKE ME TO THE INEVITABLE PLACE...
...THE END OF THE ROAD WHERE SWIRLING MISTS RISE AND, LIKE EVERY OTHER TIME, HE IS THERE.
BUT THIS TIME IT'S DIFFERENT.
THIS TIME, THE MONSTER IS DIFFERENT...

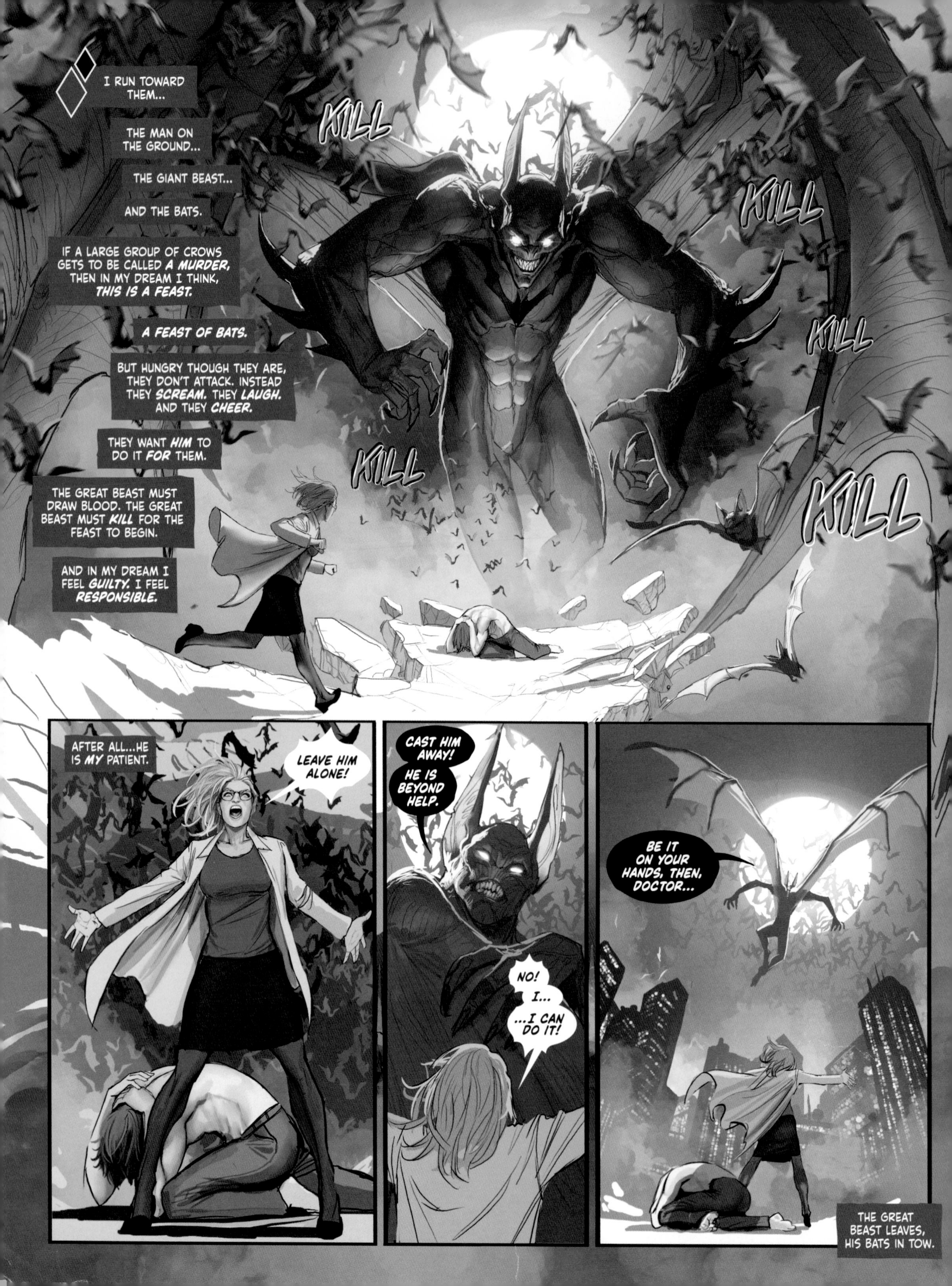
I RUN TOWARD THEM...
THE MAN ON THE GROUND...
THE GIANT BEAST...
AND THE BATS.
IF A LARGE GROUP OF CROWS GETS TO BE CALLED A MURDER, THEN IN MY DREAM I THINK, THIS IS A FEAST.
A FEAST OF BATS.
BUT HUNGRY THOUGH THEY ARE, THEY DON'T ATTACK. INSTEAD THEY SCREAM. THEY LAUGH. AND THEY CHEER.
THEY WANT HIM TO DO IT FOR THEM.
THE GREAT BEAST MUST DRAW BLOOD. THE GREAT BEAST MUST KILL FOR THE FEAST TO BEGIN.
AND IN MY DREAM I FEEL GUILTY. I FEEL RESPONSIBLE.
KILL
KILL
KILL
KILL
KILL
AFTER ALL...HE IS MY PATIENT.
LEAVE HIM ALONE!
CAST HIM AWAY!
HE IS BEYOND HELP.
NO!
I...
...I CAN DO IT!
BE IT ON YOUR HANDS, THEN, DOCTOR...
THE GREAT BEAST LEAVES, HIS BATS IN TOW.

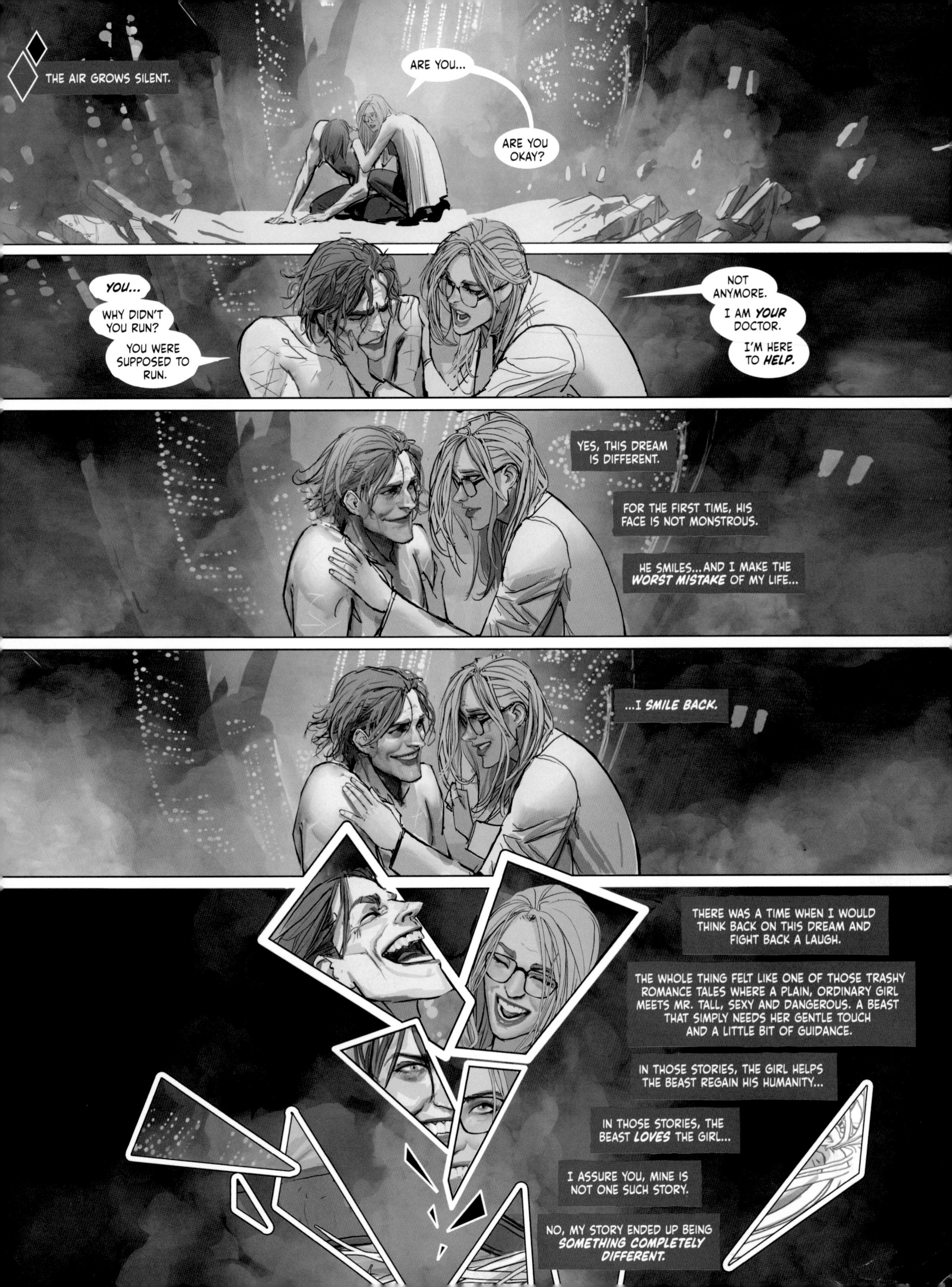
THE AIR GROWS SILENT.
ARE YOU...
ARE YOU OKAY?
YOU...
WHY DIDN'T YOU RUN?
YOU WERE SUPPOSED TO RUN.
NOT ANYMORE.
I AM YOUR DOCTOR.
I'M HERE TO HELP.
YES, THIS DREAM IS DIFFERENT.
FOR THE FIRST TIME, HIS FACE IS NOT MONSTROUS.
HE SMILES...AND I MAKE THE WORST MISTAKE OF MY LIFE...
...I SMILE BACK.
THERE WAS A TIME WHEN I WOULD THINK BACK ON THIS DREAM AND FIGHT BACK A LAUGH.
THE WHOLE THING FELT LIKE ONE OF THOSE TRASHY ROMANCE TALES WHERE A PLAIN, ORDINARY GIRL MEETS MR. TALL, SEXY AND DANGEROUS. A BEAST THAT SIMPLY NEEDS HER GENTLE TOUCH AND A LITTLE BIT OF GUIDANCE.
IN THOSE STORIES, THE GIRL HELPS THE BEAST REGAIN HIS HUMANITY...
IN THOSE STORIES, THE BEAST LOVES THE GIRL...
I ASSURE YOU, MINE IS NOT ONE SUCH STORY.
NO, MY STORY ENDED UP BEING SOMETHING COMPLETELY DIFFERENT.

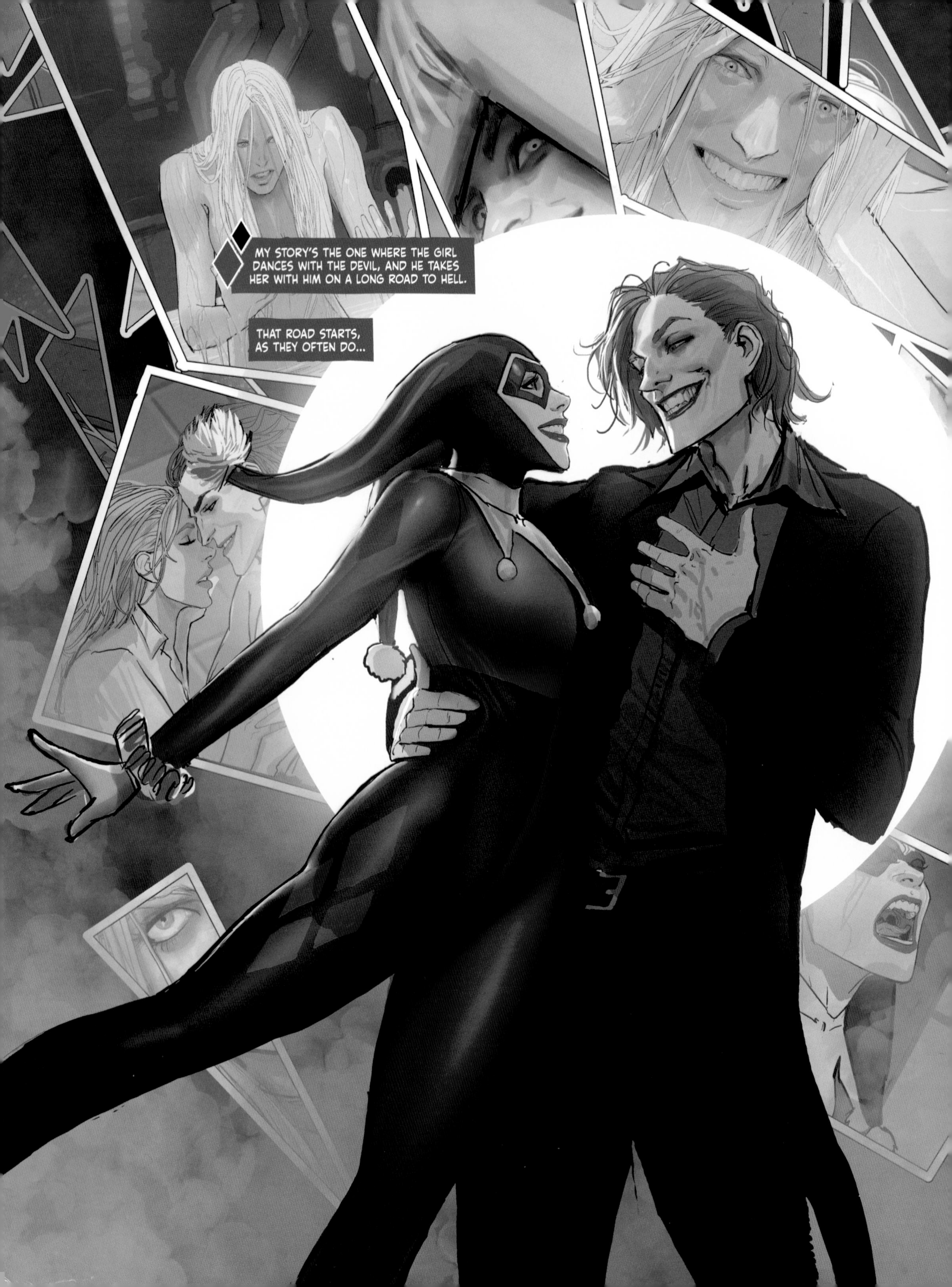
MY STORY'S THE ONE WHERE THE GIRL DANCES WITH THE DEVIL, AND HE TAKES HER WITH HIM ON A LONG ROAD TO HELL.
THAT ROAD STARTS, AS THEY OFTEN DO...

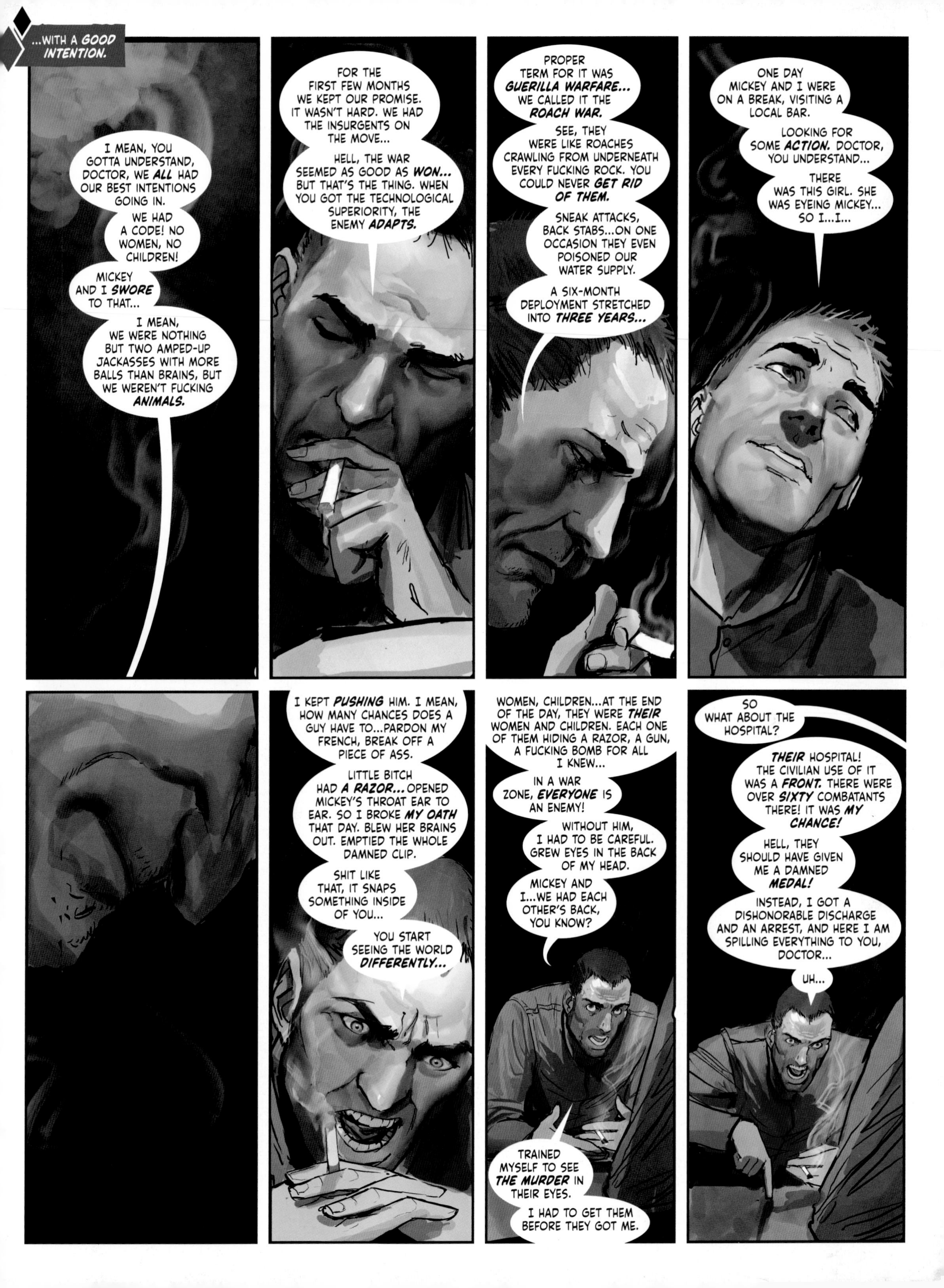

...WITH A GOOD INTENTION.
I MEAN, YOU GOTTA UNDERSTAND, DOCTOR, WE ALL HAD OUR BEST INTENTIONS GOING IN.
WE HAD A CODE! NO WOMEN, NO CHILDREN!
MICKEY AND I SWORE TO THAT...
I MEAN, WE WERE NOTHING BUT TWO AMPED-UP JACKASSES WITH MORE BALLS THAN BRAINS, BUT WE WEREN'T FUCKING ANIMALS.
FOR THE FIRST FEW MONTHS WE KEPT OUR PROMISE. IT WASN'T HARD. WE HAD THE INSURGENTS ON THE MOVE...
HELL, THE WAR SEEMED AS GOOD AS WON... BUT THAT'S THE THING. WHEN YOU GOT THE TECHNOLOGICAL SUPERIORITY, THE ENEMY ADAPTS.
PROPER TERM FOR IT WAS GUERILLA WARFARE... WE CALLED IT THE ROACH WAR.
SEE, THEY WERE LIKE ROACHES CRAWLING FROM UNDERNEATH EVERY FUCKING ROCK. YOU COULD NEVER GET RID OF THEM.
SNEAK ATTACKS, BACK STABS...ON ONE OCCASION THEY EVEN POISONED OUR WATER SUPPLY.
A SIX-MONTH DEPLOYMENT STRETCHED INTO THREE YEARS...
ONE DAY MICKEY AND I WERE ON A BREAK, VISITING A LOCAL BAR.
LOOKING FOR SOME ACTION. DOCTOR, YOU UNDERSTAND...
THERE WAS THIS GIRL. SHE WAS EYEING MICKEY... SO I...I...
I KEPT PUSHING HIM. I MEAN, HOW MANY CHANCES DOES A GUY HAVE TO...PARDON MY FRENCH, BREAK OFF A PIECE OF ASS.
LITTLE BITCH HAD A RAZOR... OPENED MICKEY'S THROAT EAR TO EAR. SO I BROKE MY OATH THAT DAY. BLEW HER BRAINS OUT. EMPTIED THE WHOLE DAMNED CLIP.
SHIT LIKE THAT, IT SNAPS SOMETHING INSIDE OF YOU...
YOU START SEEING THE WORLD DIFFERENTLY...
WOMEN, CHILDREN...AT THE END OF THE DAY, THEY WERE THEIR WOMEN AND CHILDREN. EACH ONE OF THEM HIDING A RAZOR, A GUN, A FUCKING BOMB FOR ALL I KNEW...
IN A WAR ZONE, EVERYONE IS AN ENEMY!
WITHOUT HIM, I HAD TO BE CAREFUL. GREW EYES IN THE BACK OF MY HEAD.
MICKEY AND I...WE HAD EACH OTHER'S BACK, YOU KNOW?
TRAINED MYSELF TO SEE THE MURDER IN THEIR EYES.
I HAD TO GET THEM BEFORE THEY GOT ME.
SO WHAT ABOUT THE HOSPITAL?
THEIR HOSPITAL! THE CIVILIAN USE OF IT WAS A FRONT. THERE WERE OVER SIXTY COMBATANTS THERE! IT WAS MY CHANCE!
HELL, THEY SHOULD HAVE GIVEN ME A DAMNED MEDAL!
INSTEAD, I GOT A DISHONORABLE DISCHARGE AND AN ARREST, AND HERE I AM SPILLING EVERYTHING TO YOU, DOCTOR...
UH...

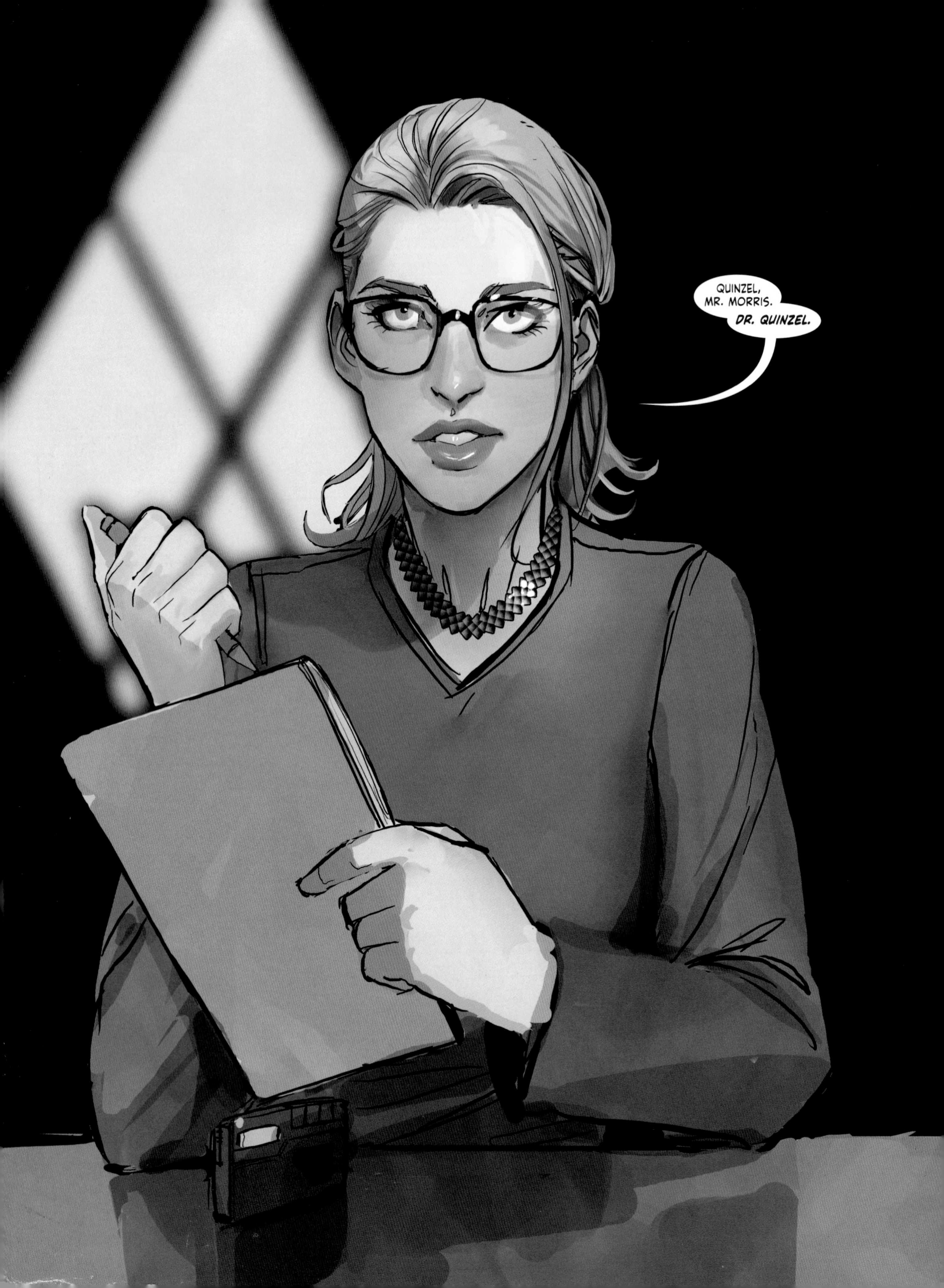
QUINZEL, MR. MORRIS.
DR. QUINZEL.

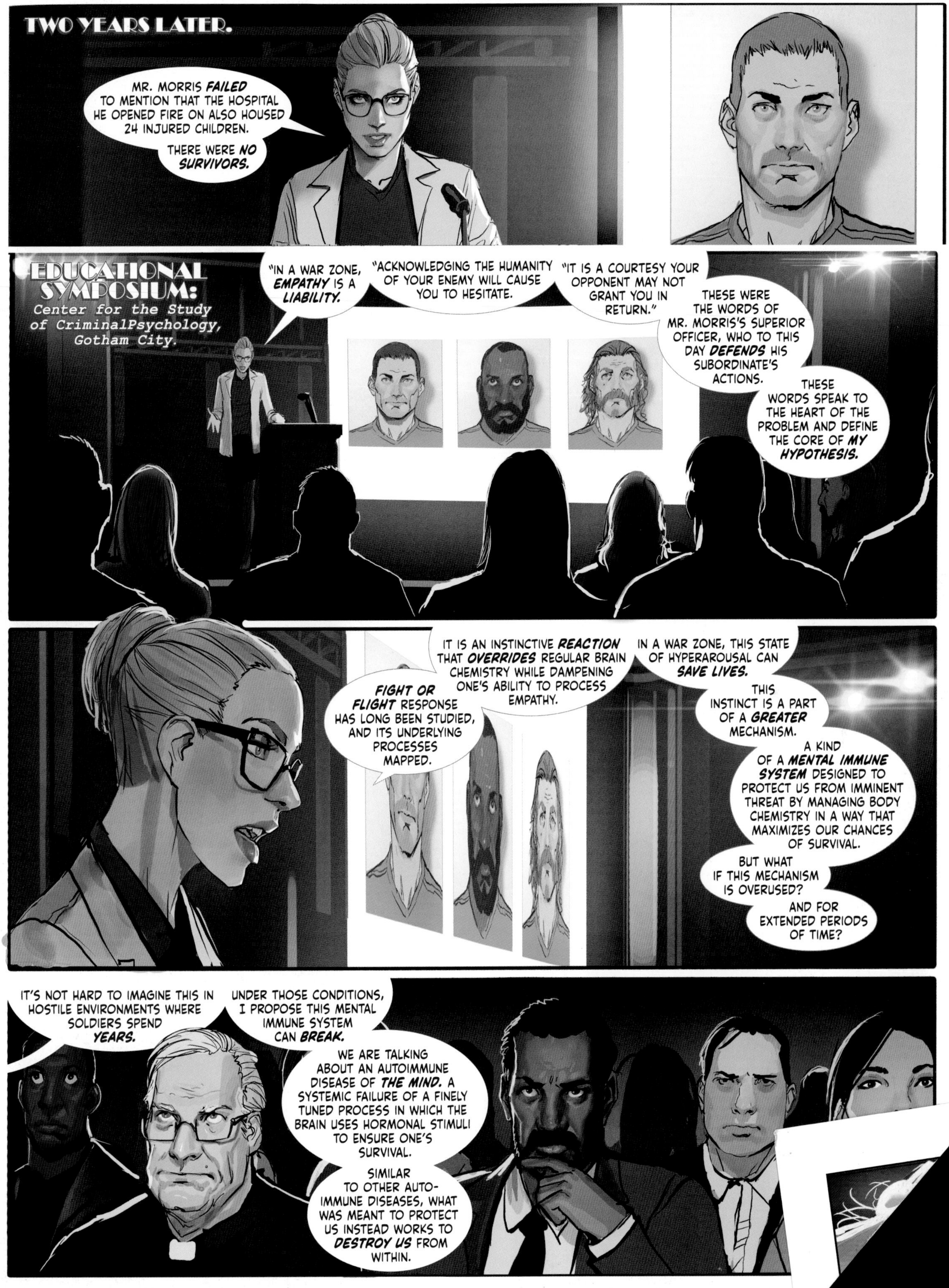
TWO YEARS LATER.
MR. MORRIS FAILED TO MENTION THAT THE HOSPITAL HE OPENED FIRE ON ALSO HOUSED 24 INJURED CHILDREN.
THERE WERE NO SURVIVORS.
EDUCATIONAL SYMPOSIUM: Center for the Study of CriminalPsychology, Gotham City.
"IN A WAR ZONE, EMPATHY IS A LIABILITY.
"ACKNOWLEDGING THE HUMANITY OF YOUR ENEMY WILL CAUSE YOU TO HESITATE.
"IT IS A COURTESY YOUR OPPONENT MAY NOT GRANT YOU IN RETURN."
THESE WERE THE WORDS OF MR. MORRIS'S SUPERIOR OFFICER, WHO TO THIS DAY DEFENDS HIS SUBORDINATE'S ACTIONS.
THESE WORDS SPEAK TO THE HEART OF THE PROBLEM AND DEFINE THE CORE OF MY HYPOTHESIS.
FIGHT OR FLIGHT RESPONSE HAS LONG BEEN STUDIED, AND ITS UNDERLYING PROCESSES MAPPED.
IT IS AN INSTINCTIVE REACTION THAT OVERRIDES REGULAR BRAIN CHEMISTRY WHILE DAMPENING ONE'S ABILITY TO PROCESS EMPATHY.
IN A WAR ZONE, THIS STATE OF HYPERAROUSAL CAN SAVE LIVES.
THIS INSTINCT IS A PART OF A GREATER MECHANISM.
A KIND OF A MENTAL IMMUNE SYSTEM DESIGNED TO PROTECT US FROM IMMINENT THREAT BY MANAGING BODY CHEMISTRY IN A WAY THAT MAXIMIZES OUR CHANCES OF SURVIVAL.
BUT WHAT IF THIS MECHANISM IS OVERUSED?
AND FOR EXTENDED PERIODS OF TIME?
IT'S NOT HARD TO IMAGINE THIS IN HOSTILE ENVIRONMENTS WHERE SOLDIERS SPEND YEARS.
UNDER THOSE CONDITIONS, I PROPOSE THIS MENTAL IMMUNE SYSTEM CAN BREAK.
WE ARE TALKING ABOUT AN AUTOIMMUNE DISEASE OF THE MIND. A SYSTEMIC FAILURE OF A FINELY TUNED PROCESS IN WHICH THE BRAIN USES HORMONAL STIMULI TO ENSURE ONE'S SURVIVAL.
SIMILAR TO OTHER AUTO-IMMUNE DISEASES, WHAT WAS MEANT TO PROTECT US INSTEAD WORKS TO DESTROY US FROM WITHIN.

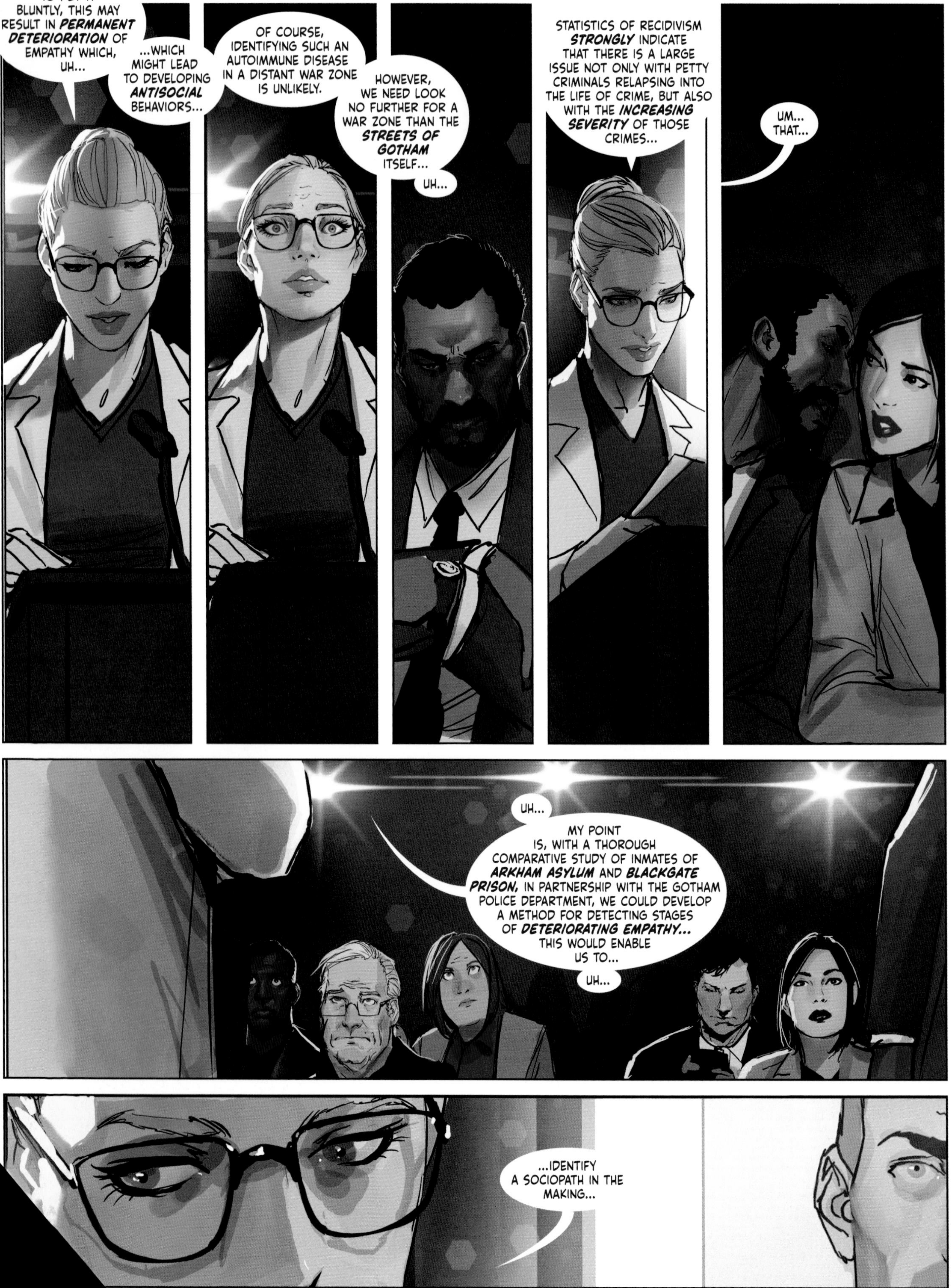
TO PUT IT BLUNTLY, THIS MAY RESULT IN PERMANENT DETERIORATION OF EMPATHY WHICH, UH...
...WHICH MIGHT LEAD TO DEVELOPING ANTISOCIAL BEHAVIORS...
OF COURSE, IDENTIFYING SUCH AN AUTOIMMUNE DISEASE IN A DISTANT WAR ZONE IS UNLIKELY.
HOWEVER, WE NEED LOOK NO FURTHER FOR A WAR ZONE THAN THE STREETS OF GOTHAM ITSELF...
UH...
STATISTICS OF RECIDIVISM STRONGLY INDICATE THAT THERE IS A LARGE ISSUE NOT ONLY WITH PETTY CRIMINALS RELAPSING INTO THE LIFE OF CRIME, BUT ALSO WITH THE INCREASING SEVERITY OF THOSE CRIMES...
UM... THAT...
UH...
MY POINT IS, WITH A THOROUGH COMPARATIVE STUDY OF INMATES OF ARKHAM ASYLUM AND BLACKGATE PRISON, IN PARTNERSHIP WITH THE GOTHAM POLICE DEPARTMENT, WE COULD DEVELOP A METHOD FOR DETECTING STAGES OF DETERIORATING EMPATHY... THIS WOULD ENABLE US TO...
UH...
...IDENTIFY A SOCIOPATH IN THE MAKING...

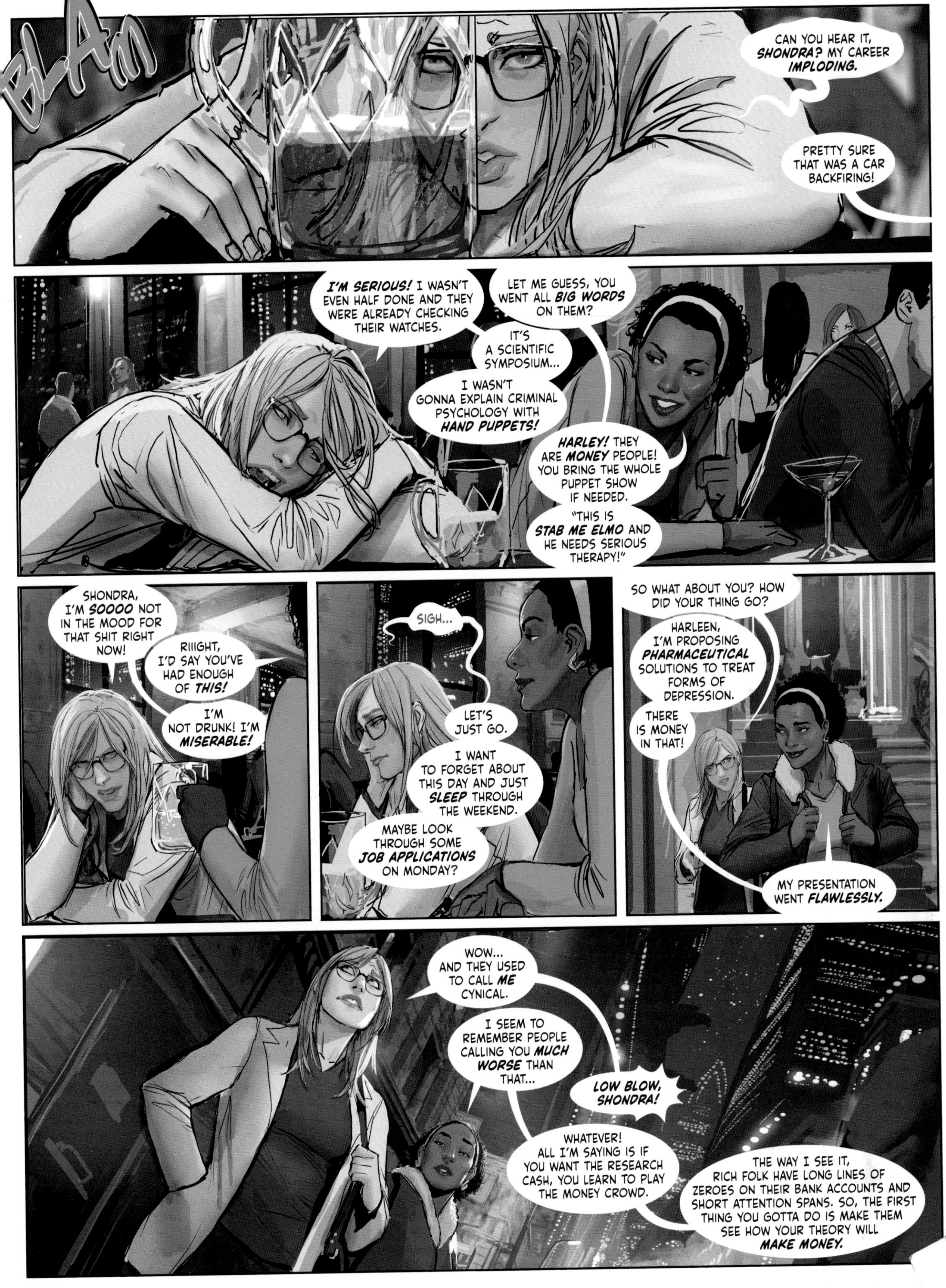
BLAM
CAN YOU HEAR IT, SHONDRA? MY CAREER IMPLODING.
PRETTY SURE THAT WAS A CAR BACKFIRING!
I'M SERIOUS! I WASN'T EVEN HALF DONE AND THEY WERE ALREADY CHECKING THEIR WATCHES.
LET ME GUESS, YOU WENT ALL BIG WORDS ON THEM?
IT'S A SCIENTIFIC SYMPOSIUM...
I WASN'T GONNA EXPLAIN CRIMINAL PSYCHOLOGY WITH HAND PUPPETS!
HARLEY! THEY ARE MONEY PEOPLE! YOU BRING THE WHOLE PUPPET SHOW IF NEEDED.
"THIS IS STAB ME ELMO AND HE NEEDS SERIOUS THERAPY!"
SHONDRA, I'M SOOOO NOT IN THE MOOD FOR THAT SHIT RIGHT NOW!
RIIIGHT, I'D SAY YOU'VE HAD ENOUGH OF THIS!
I'M NOT DRUNK! I'M MISERABLE!
SIGH...
LET'S JUST GO.
I WANT TO FORGET ABOUT THIS DAY AND JUST SLEEP THROUGH THE WEEKEND.
MAYBE LOOK THROUGH SOME JOB APPLICATIONS ON MONDAY?
SO WHAT ABOUT YOU? HOW DID YOUR THING GO?
HARLEEN, I'M PROPOSING PHARMACEUTICAL SOLUTIONS TO TREAT FORMS OF DEPRESSION.
THERE IS MONEY IN THAT!
MY PRESENTATION WENT FLAWLESSLY.
WOW... AND THEY USED TO CALL ME CYNICAL.
I SEEM TO REMEMBER PEOPLE CALLING YOU MUCH WORSE THAN THAT...
LOW BLOW, SHONDRA!
WHATEVER! ALL I'M SAYING IS IF YOU WANT THE RESEARCH CASH, YOU LEARN TO PLAY THE MONEY CROWD.
THE WAY I SEE IT, RICH FOLK HAVE LONG LINES OF ZEROES ON THEIR BANK ACCOUNTS AND SHORT ATTENTION SPANS. SO, THE FIRST THING YOU GOTTA DO IS MAKE THEM SEE HOW YOUR THEORY WILL MAKE MONEY.

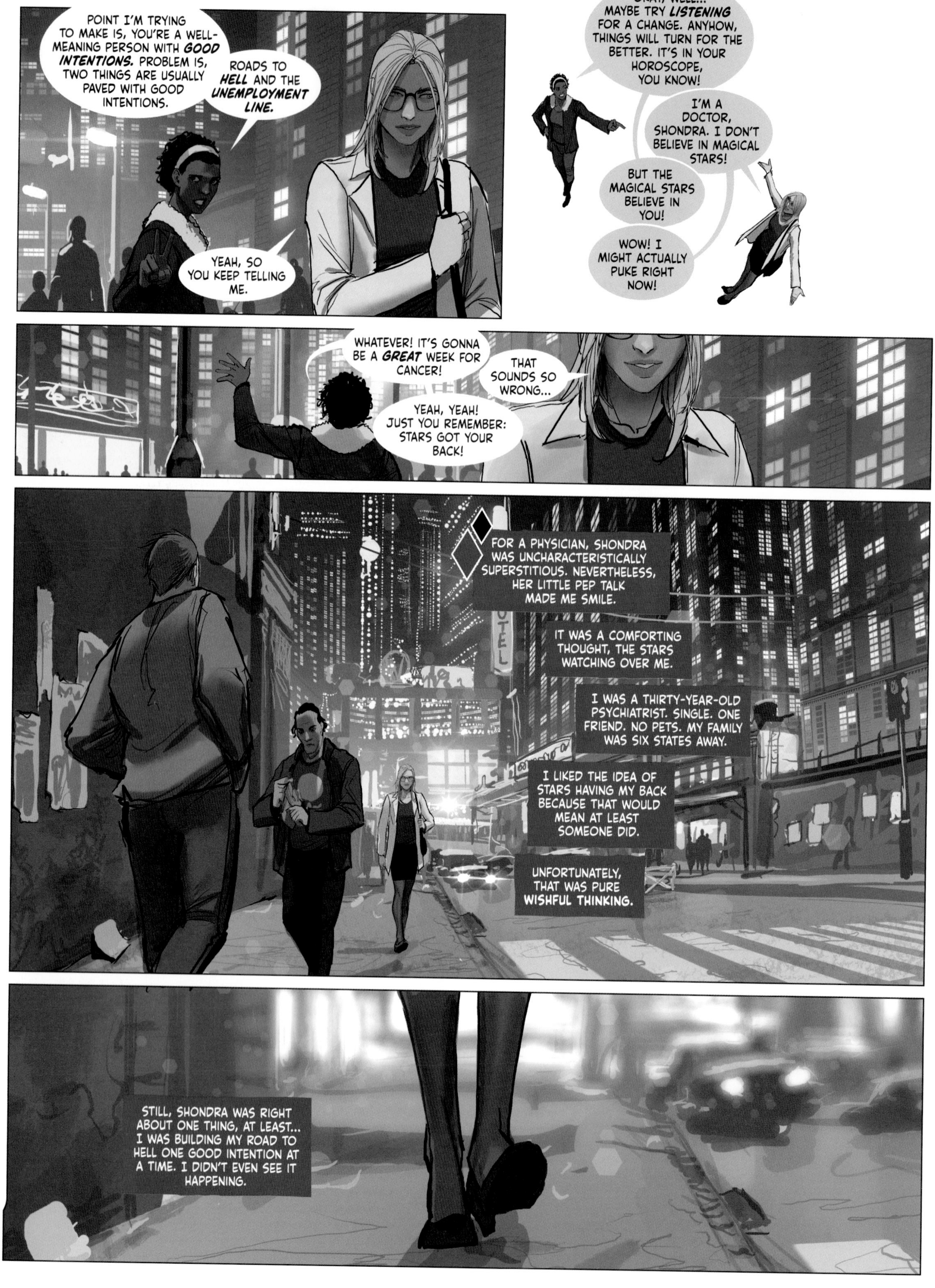
POINT I'M TRYING TO MAKE IS, YOU'RE A WELL-MEANING PERSON WITH GOOD INTENTIONS. PROBLEM IS, TWO THINGS ARE USUALLY PAVED WITH GOOD INTENTIONS.
ROADS TO HELL AND THE UNEMPLOYMENT LINE.
YEAH, SO YOU KEEP TELLING ME.
OKAY, WELL... MAYBE TRY LISTENING FOR A CHANGE. ANYHOW, THINGS WILL TURN FOR THE BETTER. IT'S IN YOUR HOROSCOPE, YOU KNOW!
I'M A DOCTOR, SHONDRA. I DON'T BELIEVE IN MAGICAL STARS!
BUT THE MAGICAL STARS BELIEVE IN YOU!
WOW! I MIGHT ACTUALLY PUKE RIGHT NOW!
WHATEVER! IT'S GONNA BE A GREAT WEEK FOR CANCER!
THAT SOUNDS SO WRONG...
YEAH, YEAH! JUST YOU REMEMBER: STARS GOT YOUR BACK!
FOR A PHYSICIAN, SHONDRA WAS UNCHARACTERISTICALLY SUPERSTITIOUS. NEVERTHELESS, HER LITTLE PEP TALK MADE ME SMILE.
IT WAS A COMFORTING THOUGHT, THE STARS WATCHING OVER ME.
I WAS A THIRTY-YEAR-OLD PSYCHIATRIST. SINGLE. ONE FRIEND. NO PETS. MY FAMILY WAS SIX STATES AWAY.
I LIKED THE IDEA OF STARS HAVING MY BACK BECAUSE THAT WOULD MEAN AT LEAST SOMEONE DID.
UNFORTUNATELY, THAT WAS PURE WISHFUL THINKING.
STILL, SHONDRA WAS RIGHT ABOUT ONE THING, AT LEAST... I WAS BUILDING MY ROAD TO HELL ONE GOOD INTENTION AT A TIME. I DIDN'T EVEN SEE IT HAPPENING.

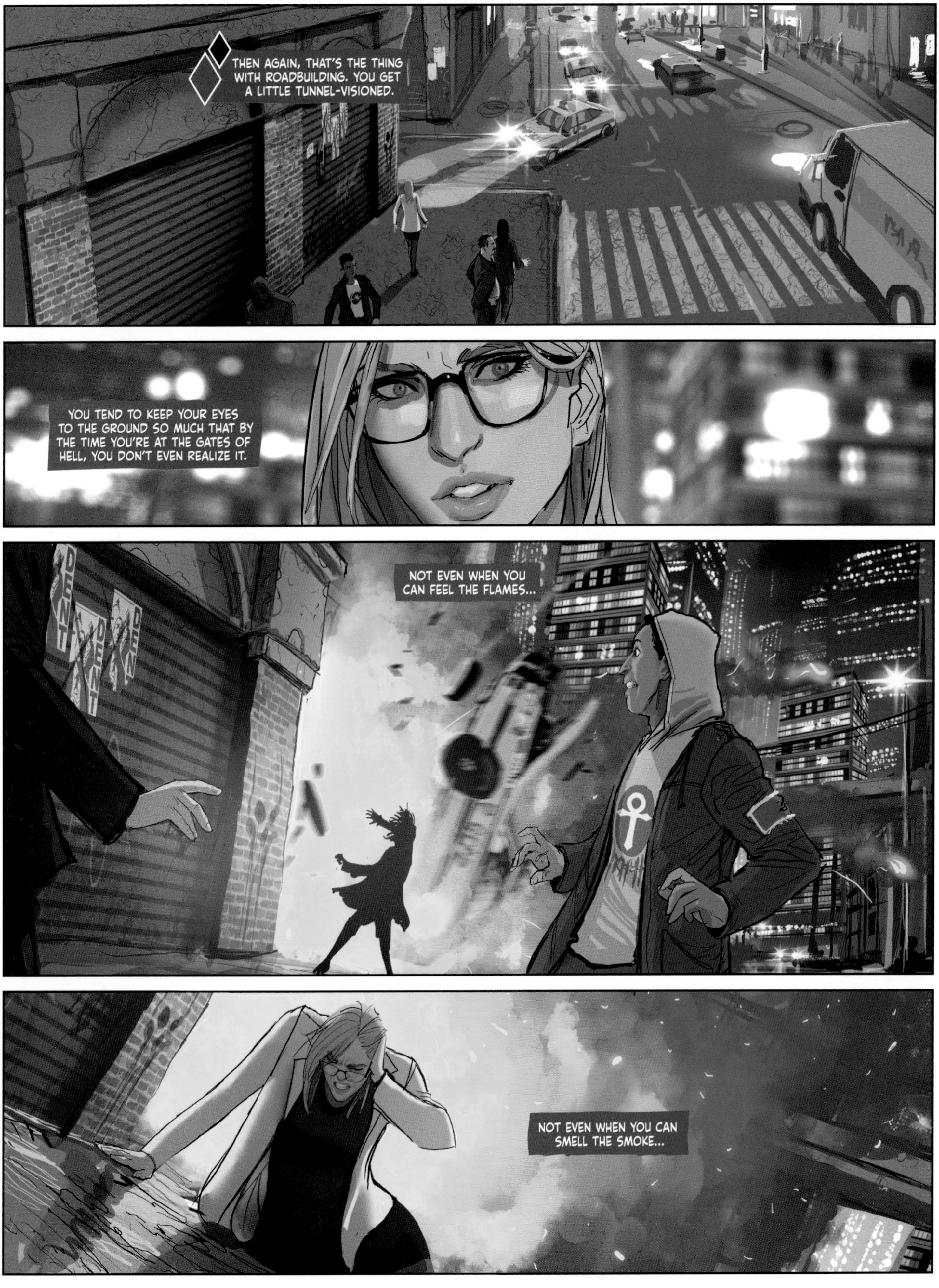
THEN AGAIN, THAT'S THE THING WITH ROADBUILDING. YOU GET A LITTLE TUNNEL-VISIONED.
YOU TEND TO KEEP YOUR EYES TO THE GROUND SO MUCH THAT BY THE TIME YOU'RE AT THE GATES OF HELL, YOU DON'T EVEN REALIZE IT.
DENT
DENT
DEN
NOT EVEN WHEN YOU CAN FEEL THE FLAMES...
NOT EVEN WHEN YOU CAN SMELL THE SMOKE...

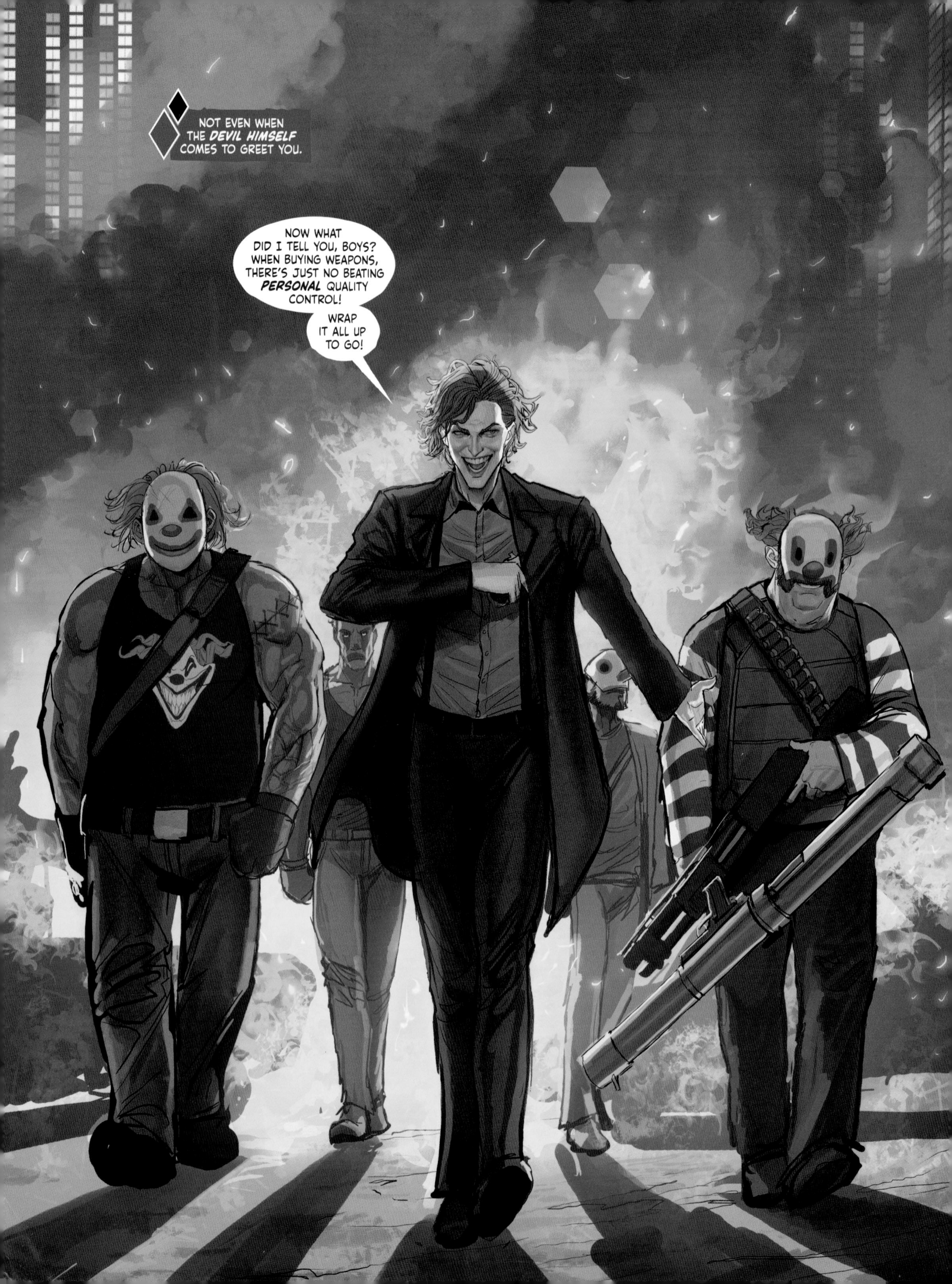
NOT EVEN WHEN THE DEVIL HIMSELF COMES TO GREET YOU.
NOW WHAT DID I TELL YOU, BOYS? WHEN BUYING WEAPONS, THERE'S JUST NO BEATING PERSONAL QUALITY CONTROL!
WRAP IT ALL UP TO GO!

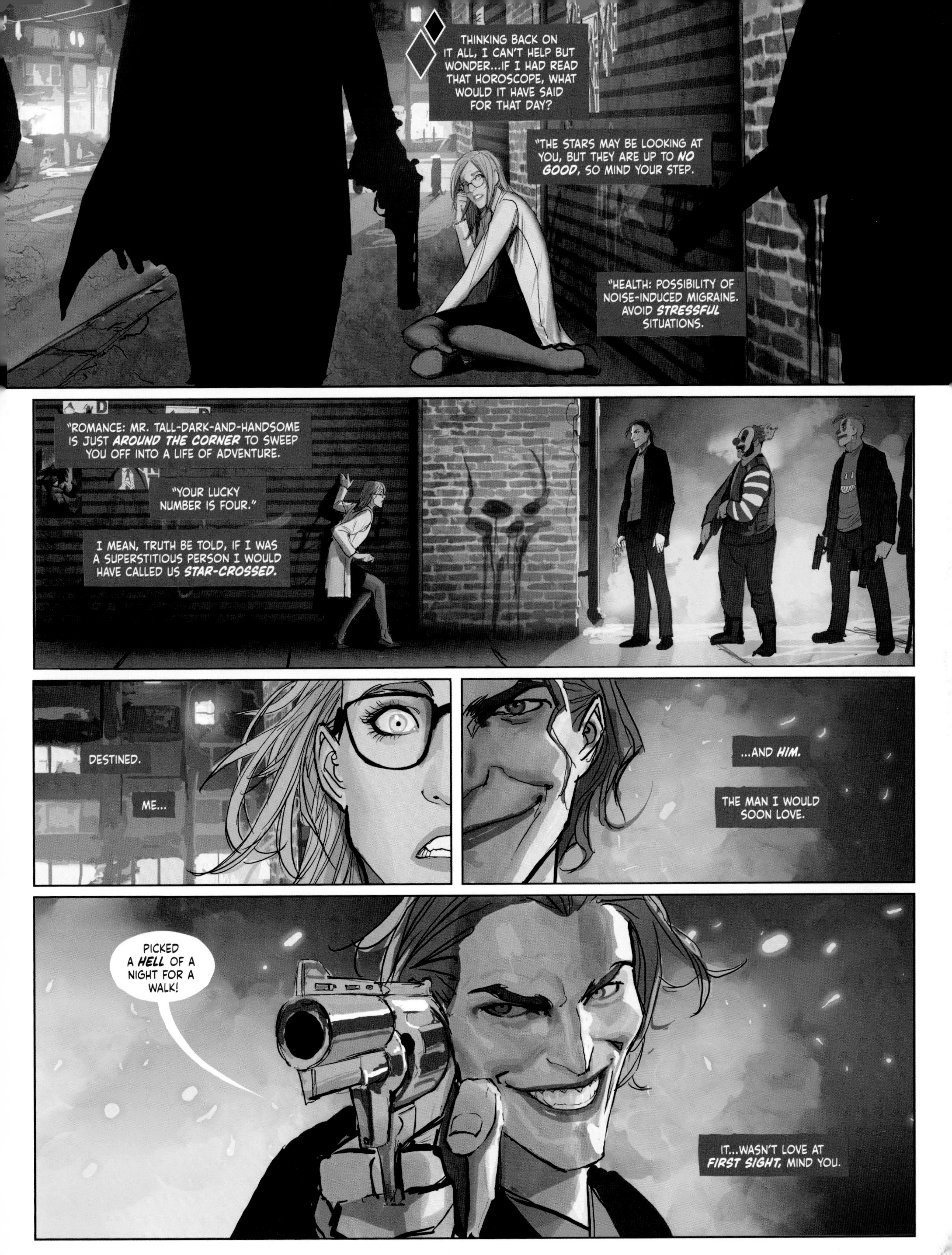

THINKING BACK ON IT ALL, I CAN'T HELP BUT WONDER...IF I HAD READ THAT HOROSCOPE, WHAT WOULD IT HAVE SAID FOR THAT DAY?
"THE STARS MAY BE LOOKING AT YOU, BUT THEY ARE UP TO NO GOOD, SO MIND YOUR STEP.
"HEALTH: POSSIBILITY OF NOISE-INDUCED MIGRAINE. AVOID STRESSFUL SITUATIONS.
"ROMANCE: MR. TALL-DARK-AND-HANDSOME IS JUST AROUND THE CORNER TO SWEEP YOU OFF INTO A LIFE OF ADVENTURE.
"YOUR LUCKY NUMBER IS FOUR."
I MEAN, TRUTH BE TOLD, IF I WAS A SUPERSTITIOUS PERSON I WOULD HAVE CALLED US STAR-CROSSED.
DESTINED.
ME...
...AND HIM.
THE MAN I WOULD SOON LOVE.
PICKED A HELL OF A NIGHT FOR A WALK!
IT...WASN'T LOVE AT FIRST SIGHT, MIND YOU.

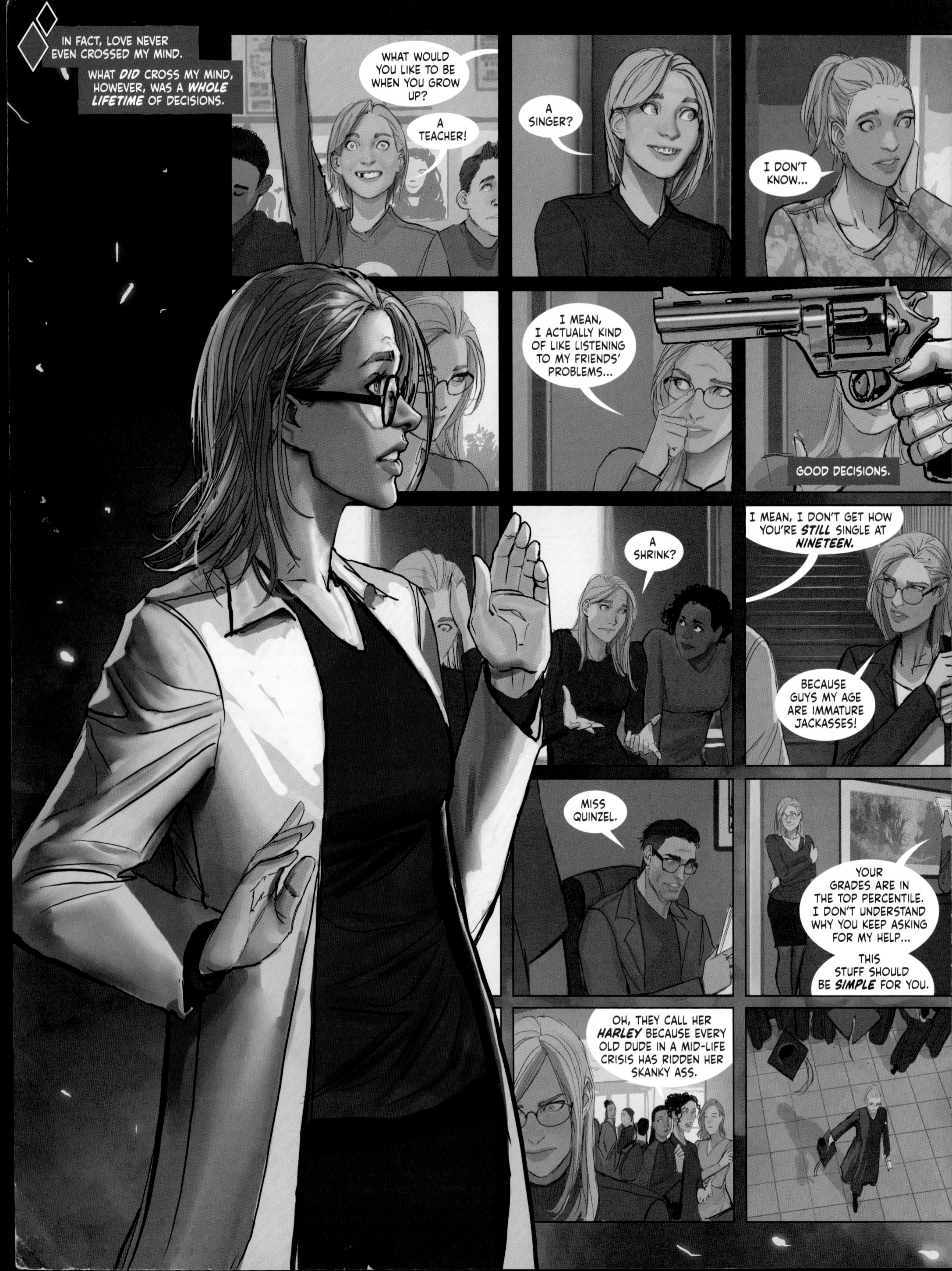

IN FACT, LOVE NEVER EVEN CROSSED MY MIND.
WHAT *DID* CROSS MY MIND, HOWEVER, WAS A ***WHOLE LIFETIME*** OF DECISIONS.
WHAT WOULD YOU LIKE TO BE WHEN YOU GROW UP?
A TEACHER!
A SINGER?
I DON'T KNOW...
I MEAN, I ACTUALLY KIND OF LIKE LISTENING TO MY FRIENDS' PROBLEMS...
GOOD DECISIONS.
A SHRINK?
I MEAN, I DON'T GET HOW YOU'RE ***STILL*** SINGLE AT ***NINETEEN.***
BECAUSE GUYS MY AGE ARE IMMATURE JACKASSES!
MISS QUINZEL.
YOUR GRADES ARE IN THE TOP PERCENTILE. I DON'T UNDERSTAND WHY YOU KEEP ASKING FOR MY HELP...
THIS STUFF SHOULD BE ***SIMPLE*** FOR YOU.
OH, THEY CALL HER ***HARLEY*** BECAUSE EVERY OLD DUDE IN A MID-LIFE CRISIS HAS RIDDEN HER SKANKY ASS.

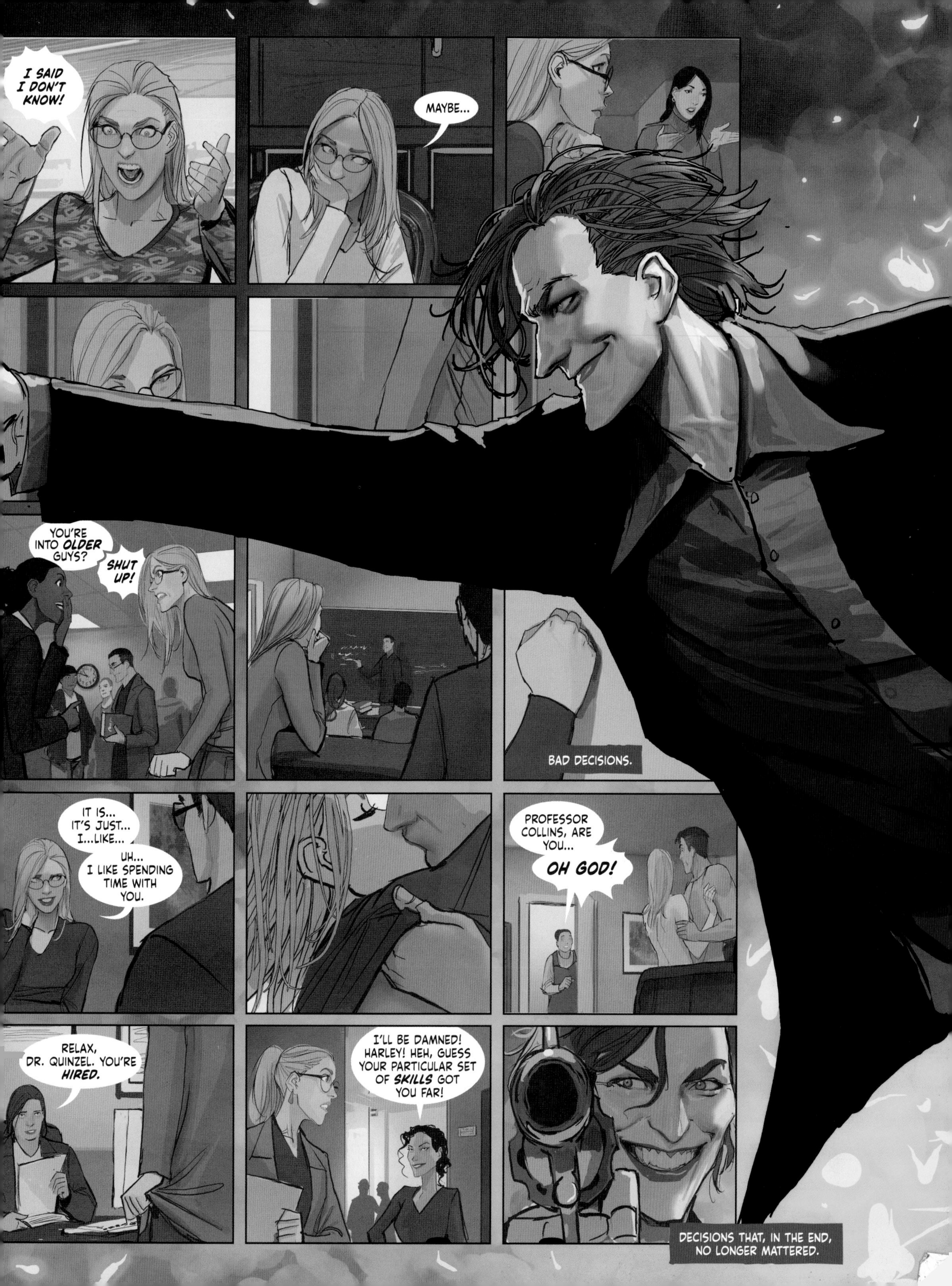
I SAID I DON'T KNOW!
MAYBE...
YOU'RE INTO OLDER GUYS?
SHUT UP!
BAD DECISIONS.
IT IS... IT'S JUST... I...LIKE...
UH... I LIKE SPENDING TIME WITH YOU.
PROFESSOR COLLINS, ARE YOU...
OH GOD!
RELAX, DR. QUINZEL. YOU'RE HIRED.
I'LL BE DAMNED! HARLEY! HEH, GUESS YOUR PARTICULAR SET OF SKILLS GOT YOU FAR!
DECISIONS THAT, IN THE END, NO LONGER MATTERED.

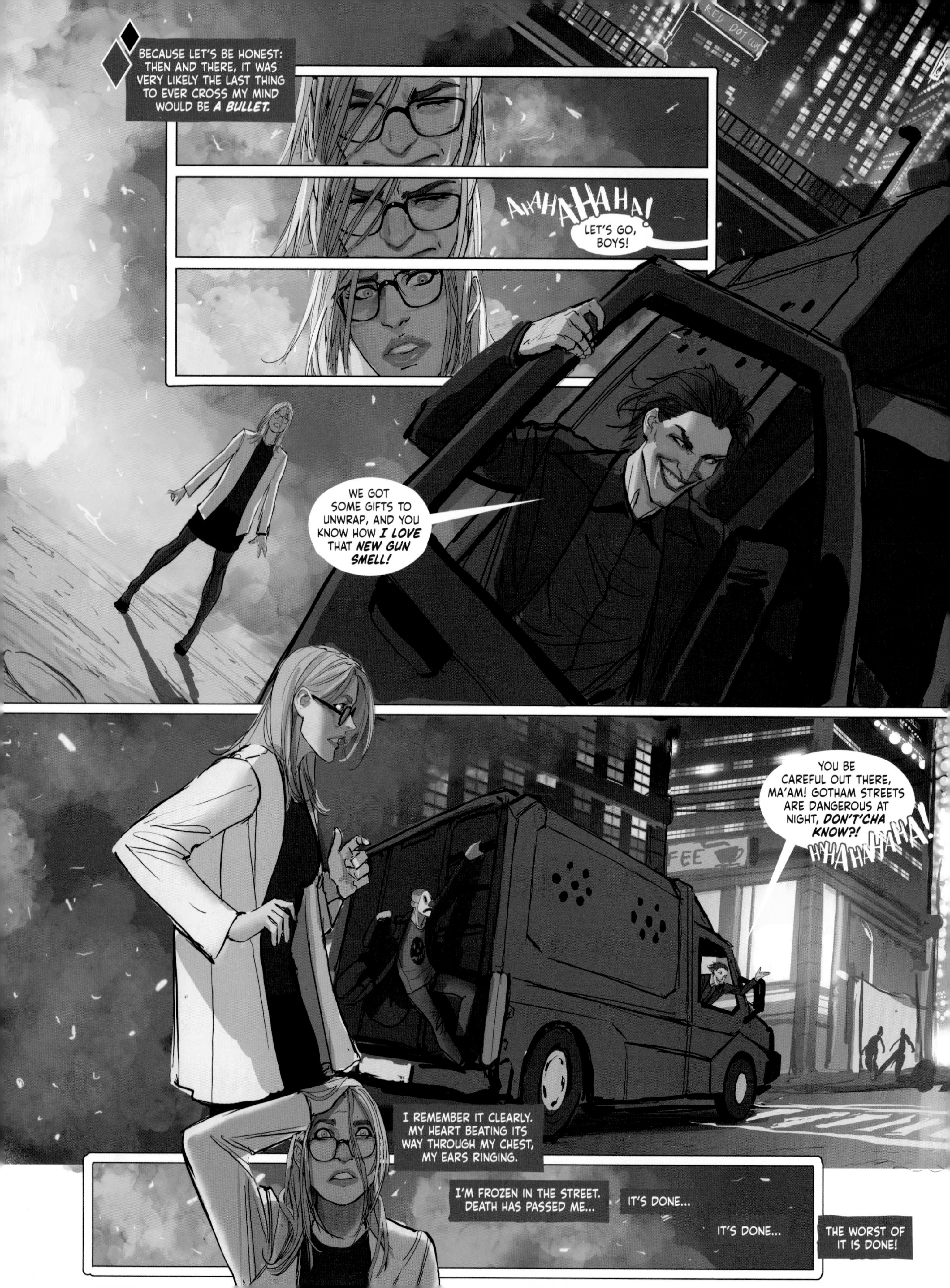
BECAUSE LET'S BE HONEST: THEN AND THERE, IT WAS VERY LIKELY THE LAST THING TO EVER CROSS MY MIND WOULD BE *A BULLET.*
RED DOT CLUB
AHAHAHAHAHA!
LET'S GO, BOYS!
WE GOT SOME GIFTS TO UNWRAP, AND YOU KNOW HOW *I LOVE* THAT *NEW GUN SMELL!*
YOU BE CAREFUL OUT THERE, MA'AM! GOTHAM STREETS ARE DANGEROUS AT NIGHT, *DON'T'CHA KNOW?!*
HAHAHAHAHAHA!
FEE
I REMEMBER IT CLEARLY. MY HEART BEATING ITS WAY THROUGH MY CHEST, MY EARS RINGING.
I'M FROZEN IN THE STREET. DEATH HAS PASSED ME...
IT'S DONE...
IT'S DONE...
THE WORST OF IT IS DONE!

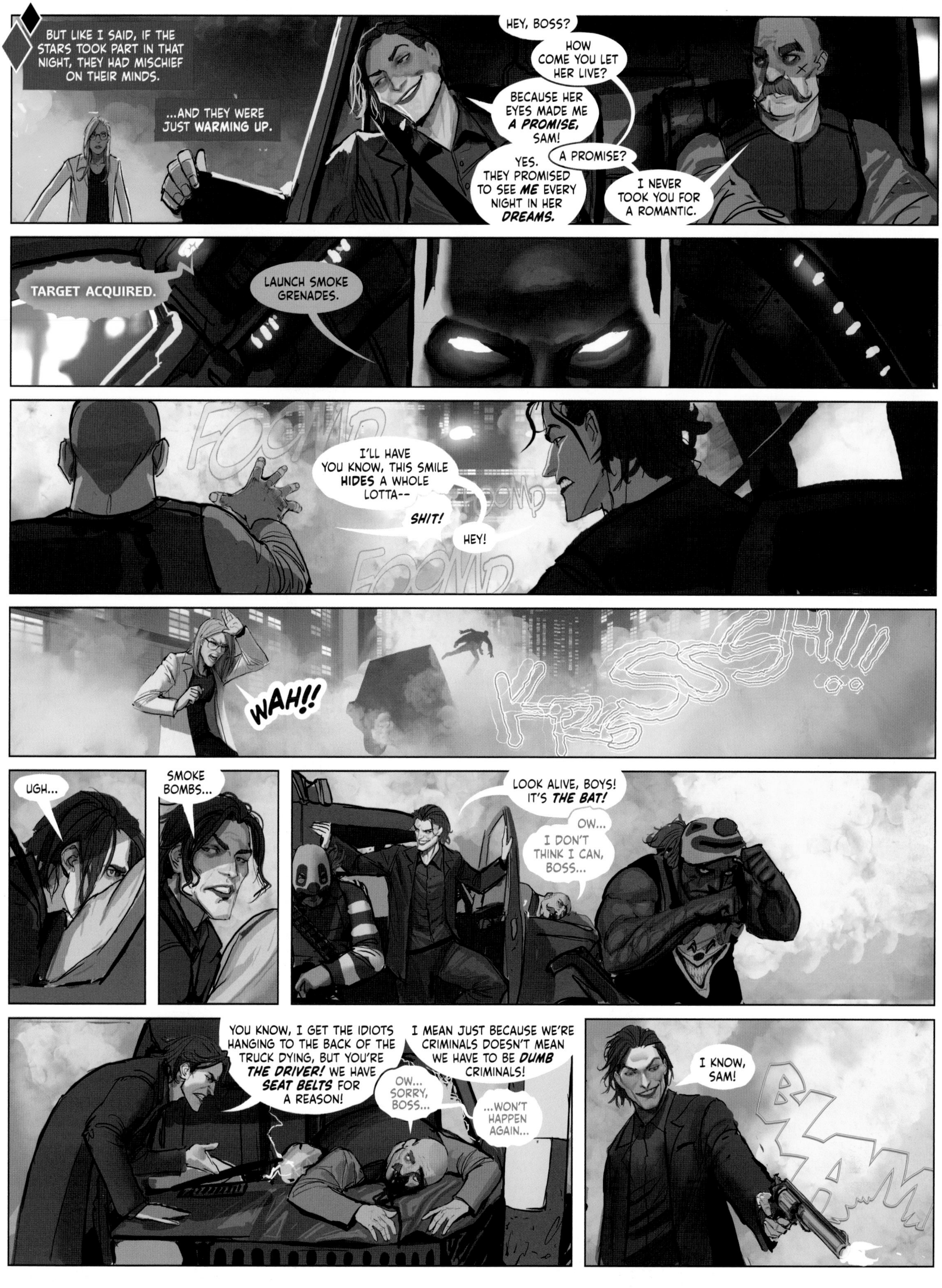

BUT LIKE I SAID, IF THE STARS TOOK PART IN THAT NIGHT, THEY HAD MISCHIEF ON THEIR MINDS.
...AND THEY WERE JUST WARMING UP.
HEY, BOSS?
HOW COME YOU LET HER LIVE?
BECAUSE HER EYES MADE ME A PROMISE, SAM!
A PROMISE?
YES. THEY PROMISED TO SEE ME EVERY NIGHT IN HER DREAMS.
I NEVER TOOK YOU FOR A ROMANTIC.
TARGET ACQUIRED.
LAUNCH SMOKE GRENADES.
FOOMP
I'LL HAVE YOU KNOW, THIS SMILE HIDES A WHOLE LOTTA--
FOOMP
SHIT!
HEY!
FOOMP
WAH!!
KRASSSH!!
UGH...
SMOKE BOMBS...
LOOK ALIVE, BOYS! IT'S THE BAT!
OW... I DON'T THINK I CAN, BOSS...
YOU KNOW, I GET THE IDIOTS HANGING TO THE BACK OF THE TRUCK DYING, BUT YOU'RE THE DRIVER! WE HAVE SEAT BELTS FOR A REASON!
OW... SORRY, BOSS...
I MEAN JUST BECAUSE WE'RE CRIMINALS DOESN'T MEAN WE HAVE TO BE DUMB CRIMINALS!
...WON'T HAPPEN AGAIN...
I KNOW, SAM!
BLAM

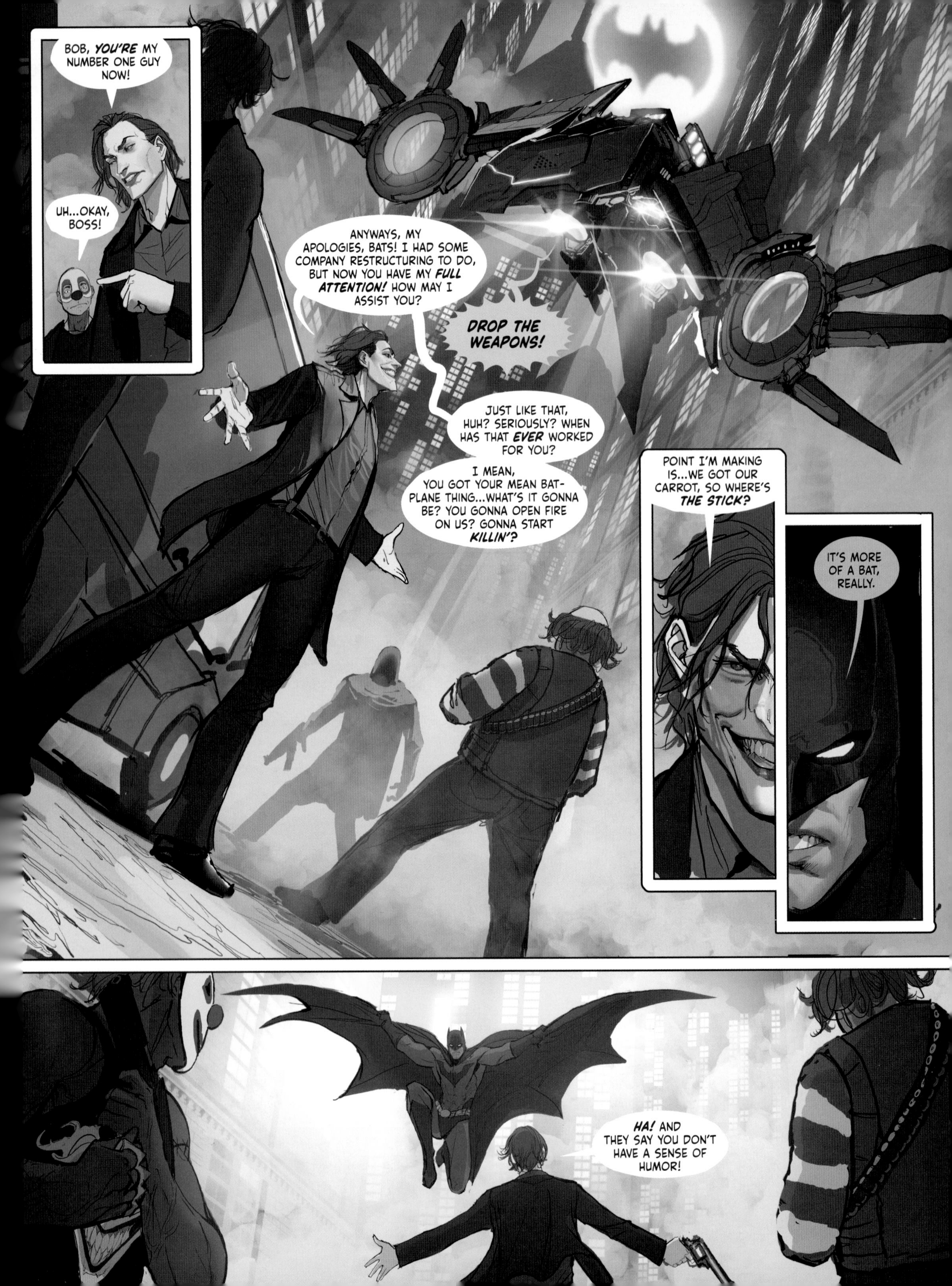
BOB, *YOU'RE* MY NUMBER ONE GUY NOW!
UH...OKAY, BOSS!
ANYWAYS, MY APOLOGIES, BATS! I HAD SOME COMPANY RESTRUCTURING TO DO, BUT NOW YOU HAVE MY *FULL ATTENTION!* HOW MAY I ASSIST YOU?
DROP THE WEAPONS!
JUST LIKE THAT, HUH? SERIOUSLY? WHEN HAS THAT *EVER* WORKED FOR YOU?
I MEAN, YOU GOT YOUR MEAN BAT-PLANE THING...WHAT'S IT GONNA BE? YOU GONNA OPEN FIRE ON US? GONNA START *KILLIN'?*
POINT I'M MAKING IS...WE GOT OUR CARROT, SO WHERE'S *THE STICK?*
IT'S MORE OF A BAT, REALLY.
HA! AND THEY SAY YOU DON'T HAVE A SENSE OF HUMOR!

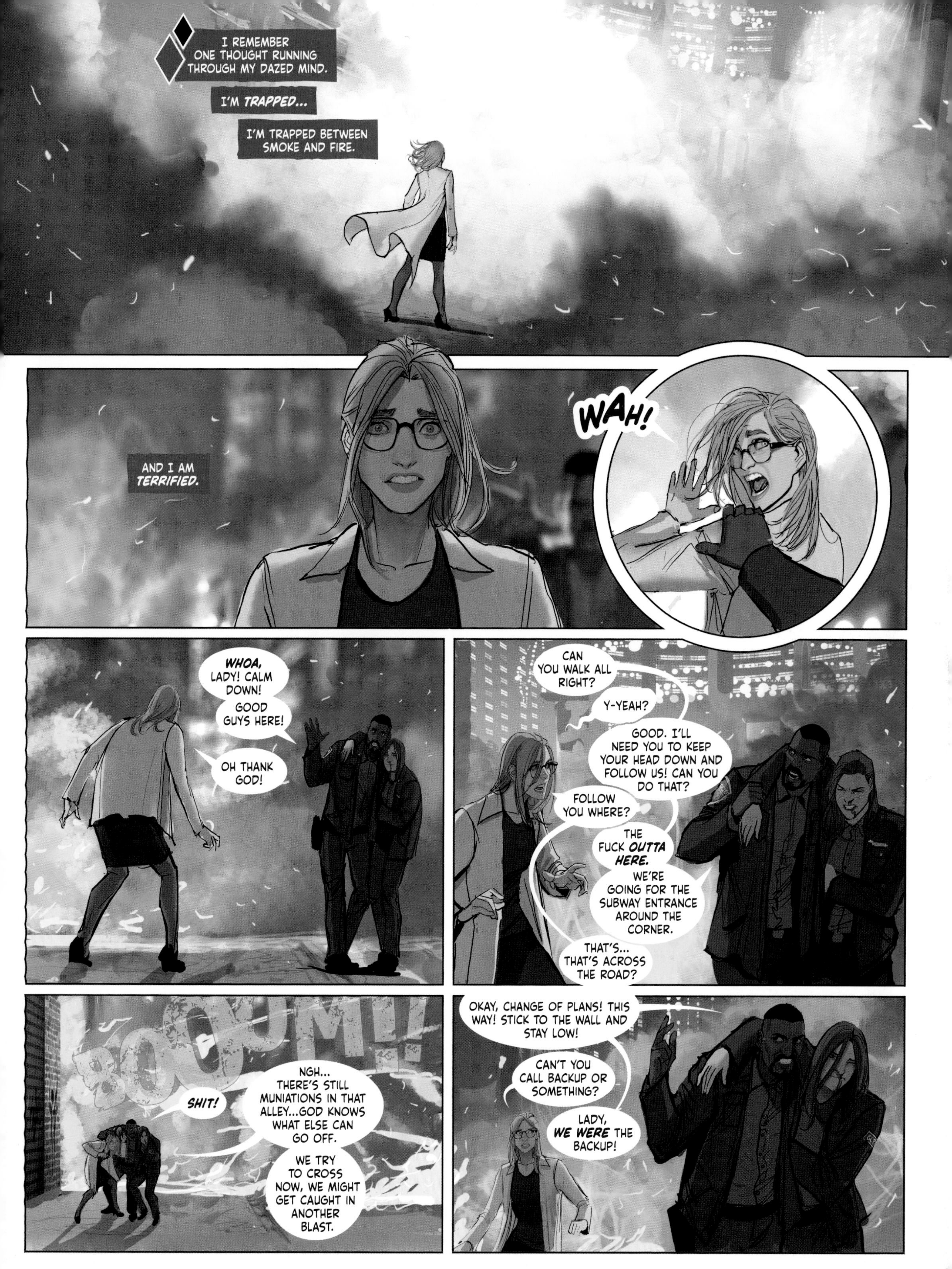
I REMEMBER ONE THOUGHT RUNNING THROUGH MY DAZED MIND.
I'M *TRAPPED...*
I'M TRAPPED BETWEEN SMOKE AND FIRE.
AND I AM *TERRIFIED.*
WAH!
WHOA, LADY! CALM DOWN!
GOOD GUYS HERE!
OH THANK GOD!
CAN YOU WALK ALL RIGHT?
Y-YEAH?
GOOD. I'LL NEED YOU TO KEEP YOUR HEAD DOWN AND FOLLOW US! CAN YOU DO THAT?
FOLLOW YOU WHERE?
THE FUCK *OUTTA HERE.*
WE'RE GOING FOR THE SUBWAY ENTRANCE AROUND THE CORNER.
THAT'S... THAT'S ACROSS THE ROAD?
BOOM!!
SHIT!
NGH... THERE'S STILL MUNIATIONS IN THAT ALLEY...GOD KNOWS WHAT ELSE CAN GO OFF.
WE TRY TO CROSS NOW, WE MIGHT GET CAUGHT IN ANOTHER BLAST.
OKAY, CHANGE OF PLANS! THIS WAY! STICK TO THE WALL AND STAY LOW!
CAN'T YOU CALL BACKUP OR SOMETHING?
LADY, *WE WERE* THE BACKUP!

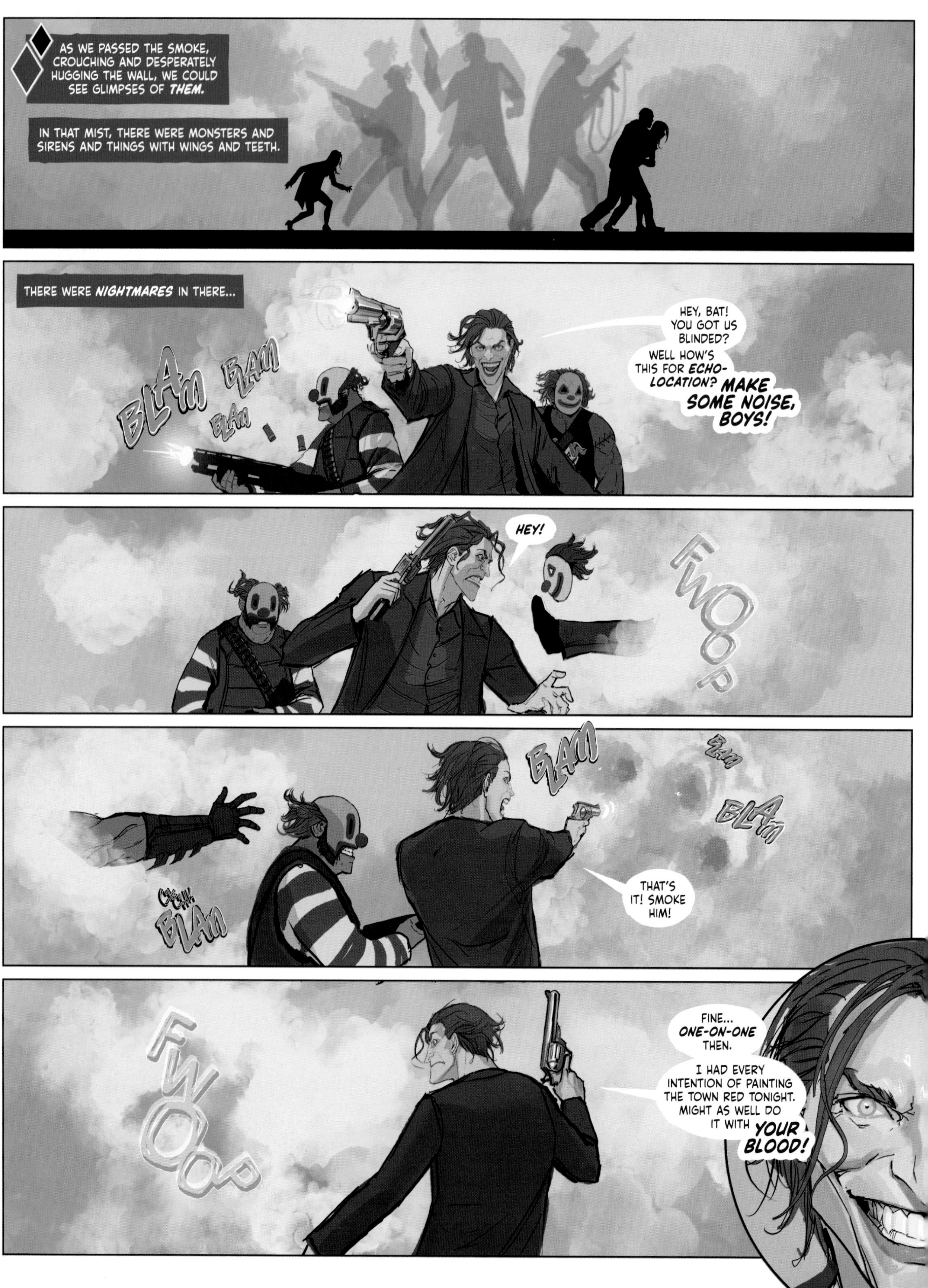
AS WE PASSED THE SMOKE, CROUCHING AND DESPERATELY HUGGING THE WALL, WE COULD SEE GLIMPSES OF *THEM.*
IN THAT MIST, THERE WERE MONSTERS AND SIRENS AND THINGS WITH WINGS AND TEETH.
THERE WERE *NIGHTMARES* IN THERE...
BLAM BLAM BLAM
HEY, BAT! YOU GOT US BLINDED?
WELL HOW'S THIS FOR *ECHO-LOCATION?* **MAKE SOME NOISE, BOYS!**
HEY!
FWOOP
BLAM
BLAM
BLAM
CHK CHK BLAM
THAT'S IT! SMOKE HIM!
FWOOP
FINE... *ONE-ON-ONE* THEN.
I HAD EVERY INTENTION OF PAINTING THE TOWN RED TONIGHT. MIGHT AS WELL DO IT WITH **YOUR BLOOD!**

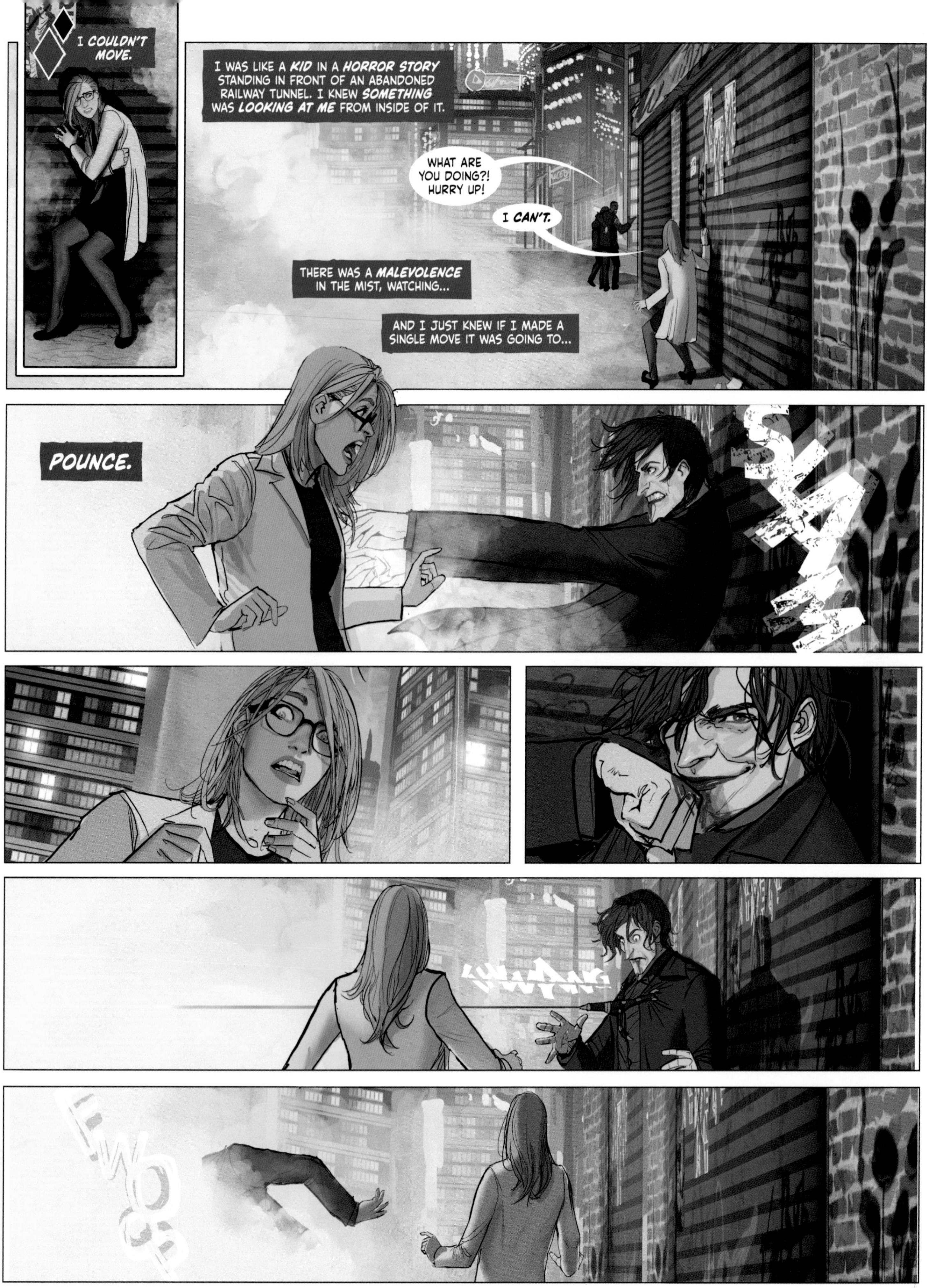
I COULDN'T MOVE.
I WAS LIKE A KID IN A HORROR STORY STANDING IN FRONT OF AN ABANDONED RAILWAY TUNNEL. I KNEW SOMETHING WAS LOOKING AT ME FROM INSIDE OF IT.
WHAT ARE YOU DOING?! HURRY UP!
I CAN'T.
THERE WAS A MALEVOLENCE IN THE MIST, WATCHING...
AND I JUST KNEW IF I MADE A SINGLE MOVE IT WAS GOING TO...
POUNCE.

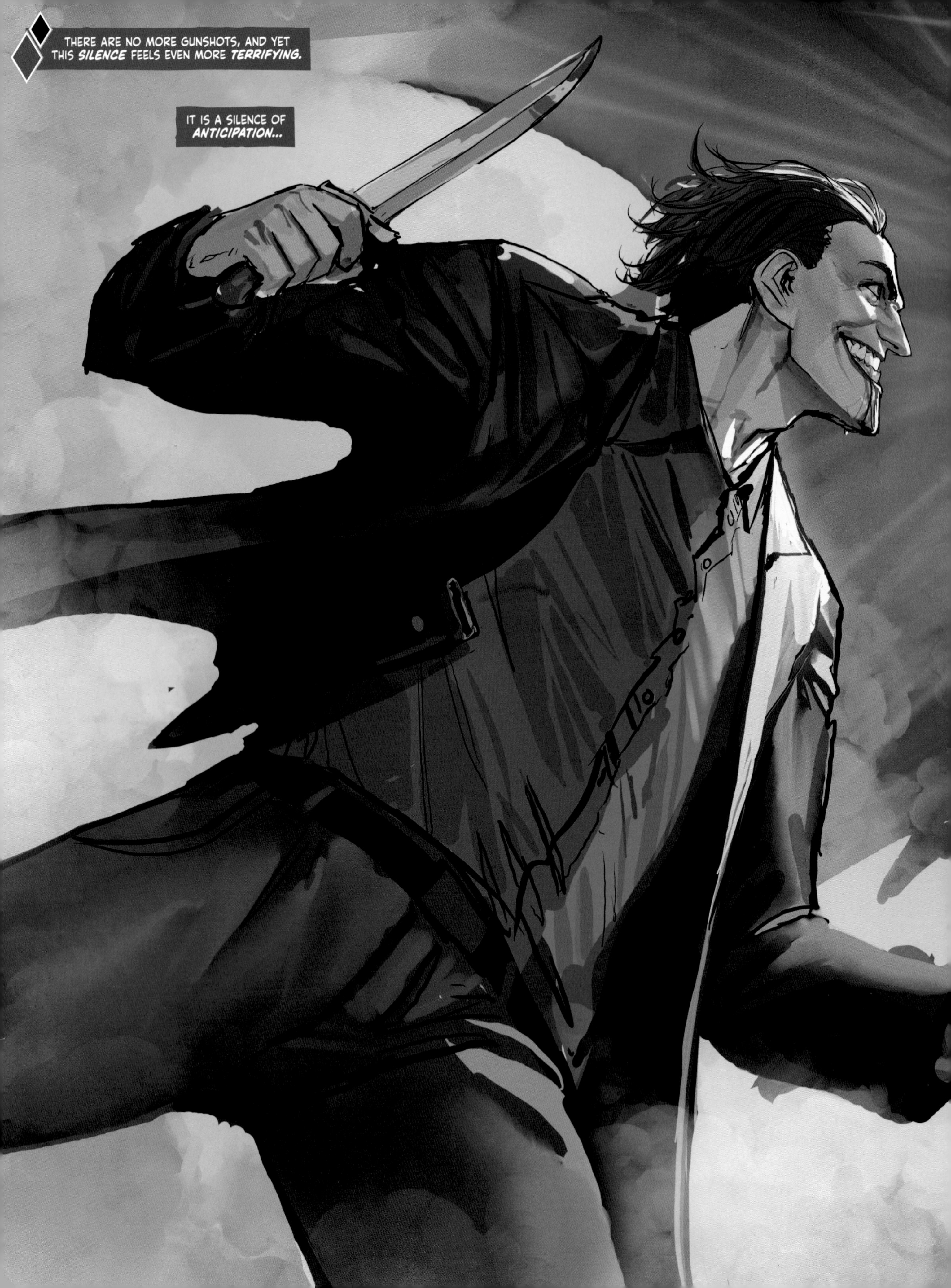
THERE ARE NO MORE GUNSHOTS, AND YET THIS *SILENCE* FEELS EVEN MORE *TERRIFYING.*
IT IS A SILENCE OF *ANTICIPATION...*

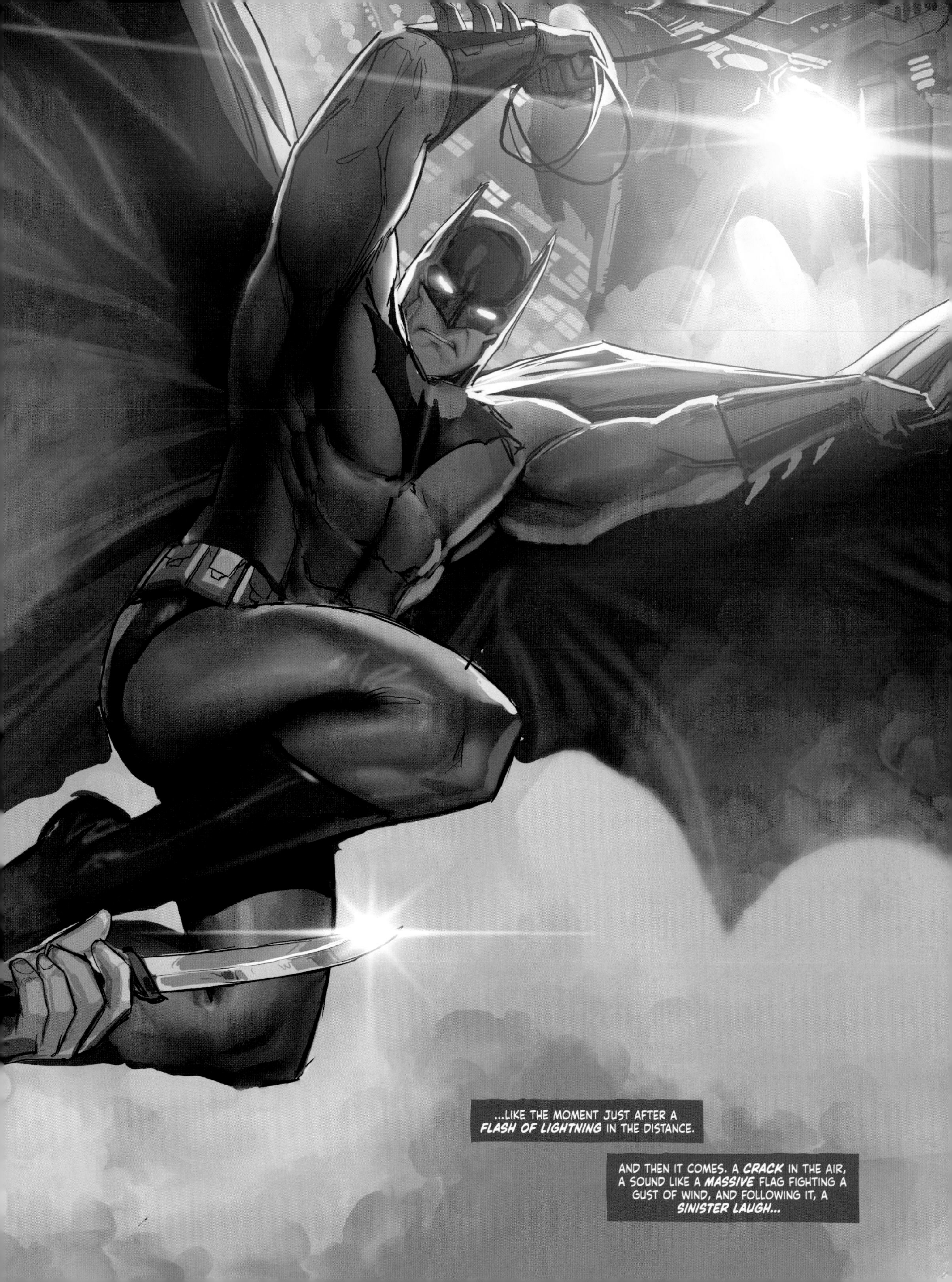
...LIKE THE MOMENT JUST AFTER A FLASH OF LIGHTNING IN THE DISTANCE.
AND THEN IT COMES. A CRACK IN THE AIR, A SOUND LIKE A MASSIVE FLAG FIGHTING A GUST OF WIND, AND FOLLOWING IT, A SINISTER LAUGH...

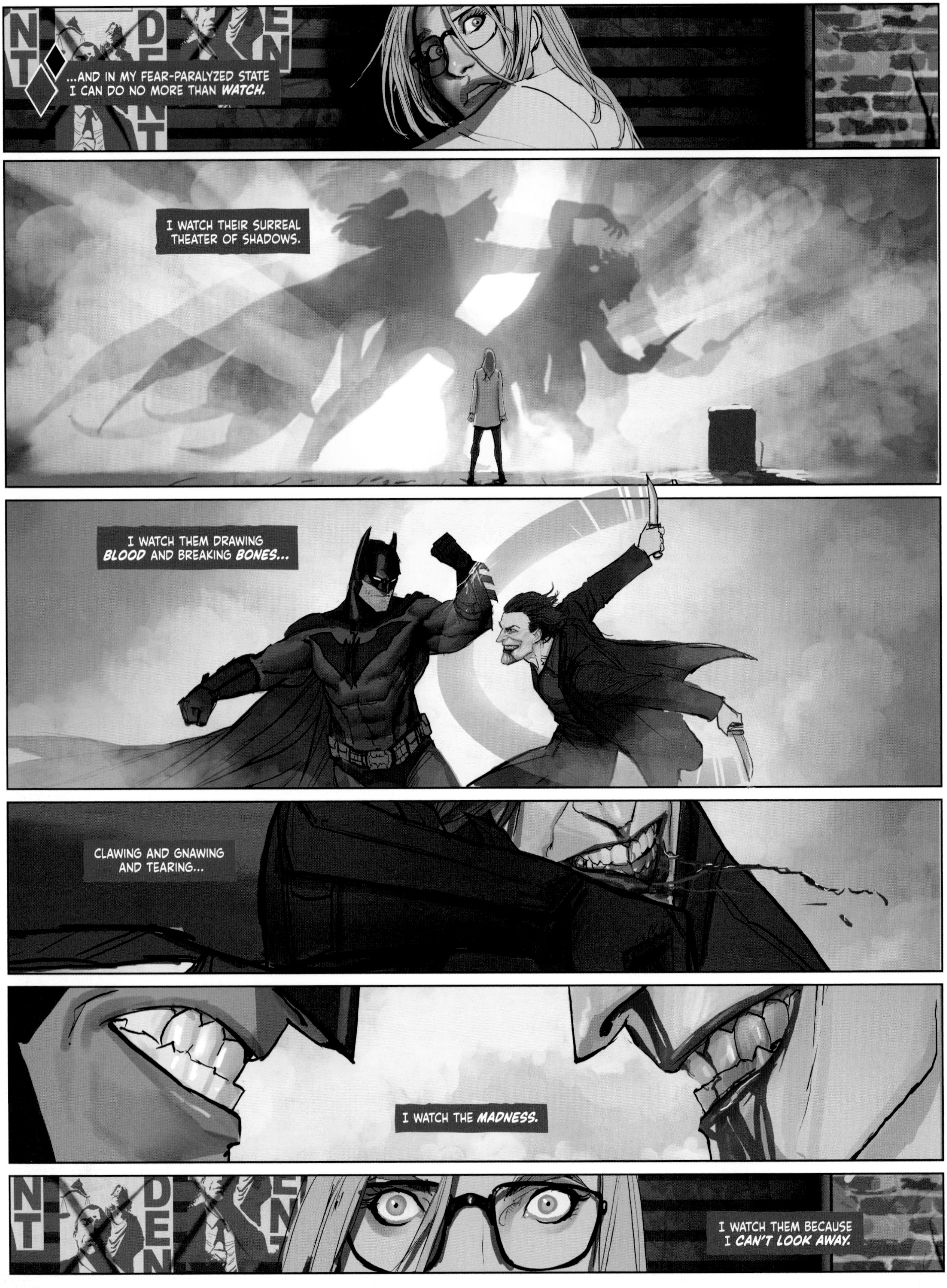

...AND IN MY FEAR-PARALYZED STATE I CAN DO NO MORE THAN *WATCH.*
I WATCH THEIR SURREAL THEATER OF SHADOWS.
I WATCH THEM DRAWING *BLOOD* AND BREAKING *BONES...*
CLAWING AND GNAWING AND TEARING...
I WATCH THE *MADNESS.*
I WATCH THEM BECAUSE I *CAN'T LOOK AWAY.*

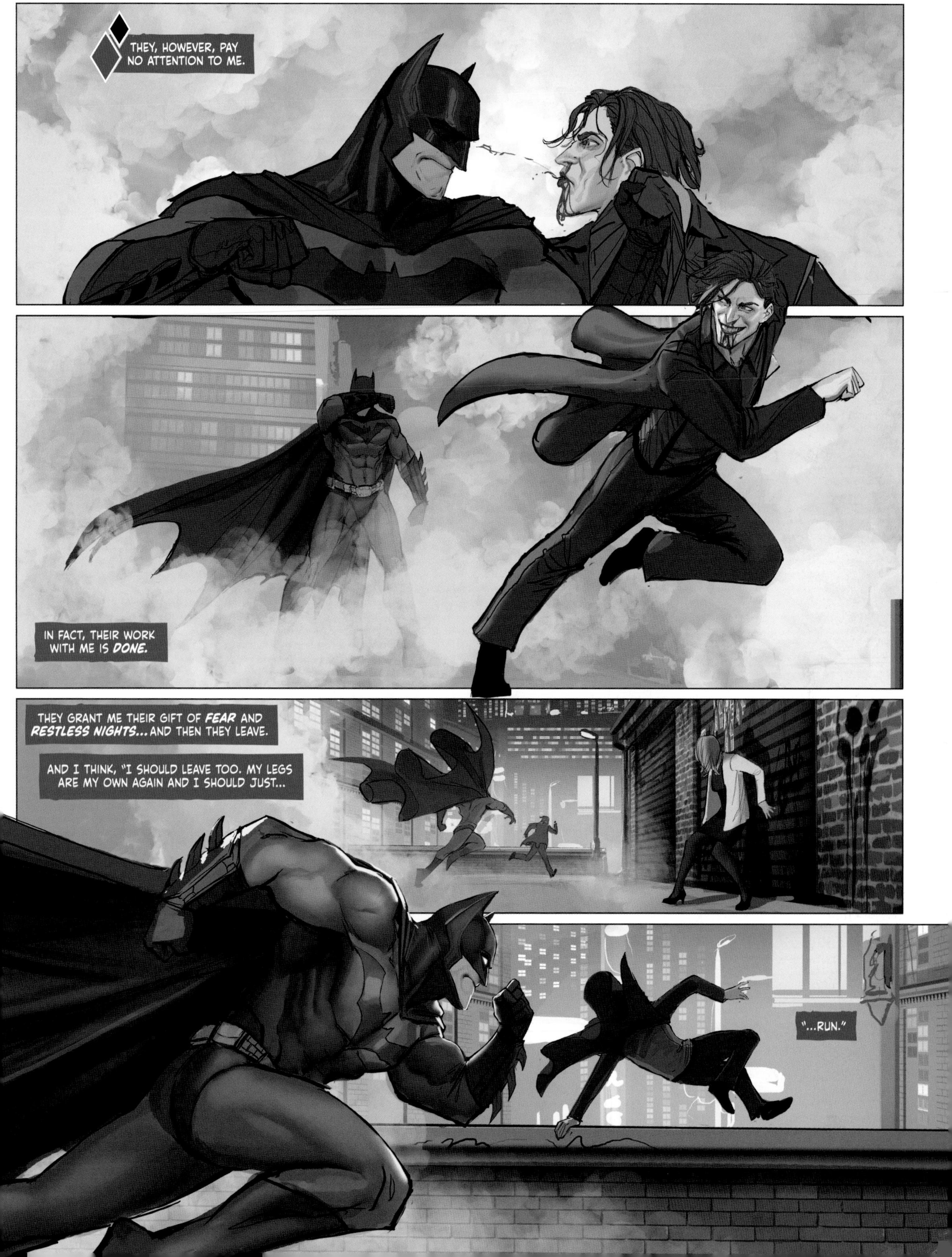

THEY, HOWEVER, PAY NO ATTENTION TO ME.
IN FACT, THEIR WORK WITH ME IS *DONE.*
THEY GRANT ME THEIR GIFT OF *FEAR* AND *RESTLESS NIGHTS...* AND THEN THEY LEAVE.
AND I THINK, "I SHOULD LEAVE TOO. MY LEGS ARE MY OWN AGAIN AND I SHOULD JUST...
"...RUN."

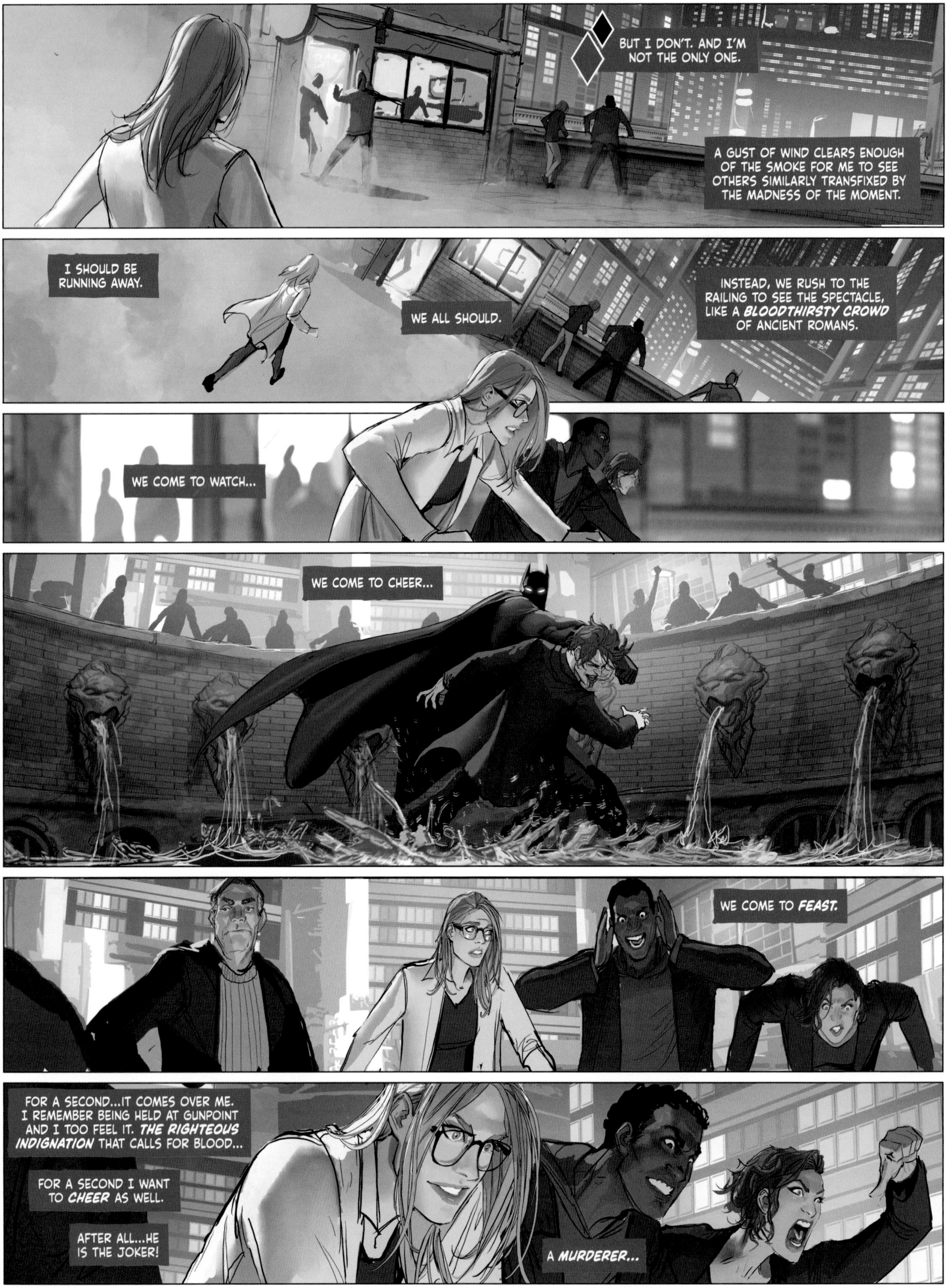
BUT I DON'T. AND I'M NOT THE ONLY ONE.
A GUST OF WIND CLEARS ENOUGH OF THE SMOKE FOR ME TO SEE OTHERS SIMILARLY TRANSFIXED BY THE MADNESS OF THE MOMENT.
I SHOULD BE RUNNING AWAY.
WE ALL SHOULD.
INSTEAD, WE RUSH TO THE RAILING TO SEE THE SPECTACLE, LIKE A *BLOODTHIRSTY CROWD* OF ANCIENT ROMANS.
WE COME TO WATCH...
WE COME TO CHEER...
WE COME TO *FEAST.*
FOR A SECOND...IT COMES OVER ME. I REMEMBER BEING HELD AT GUNPOINT AND I TOO FEEL IT. *THE RIGHTEOUS INDIGNATION* THAT CALLS FOR BLOOD...
FOR A SECOND I WANT TO *CHEER* AS WELL.
AFTER ALL...HE IS THE JOKER!
A *MURDERER*...

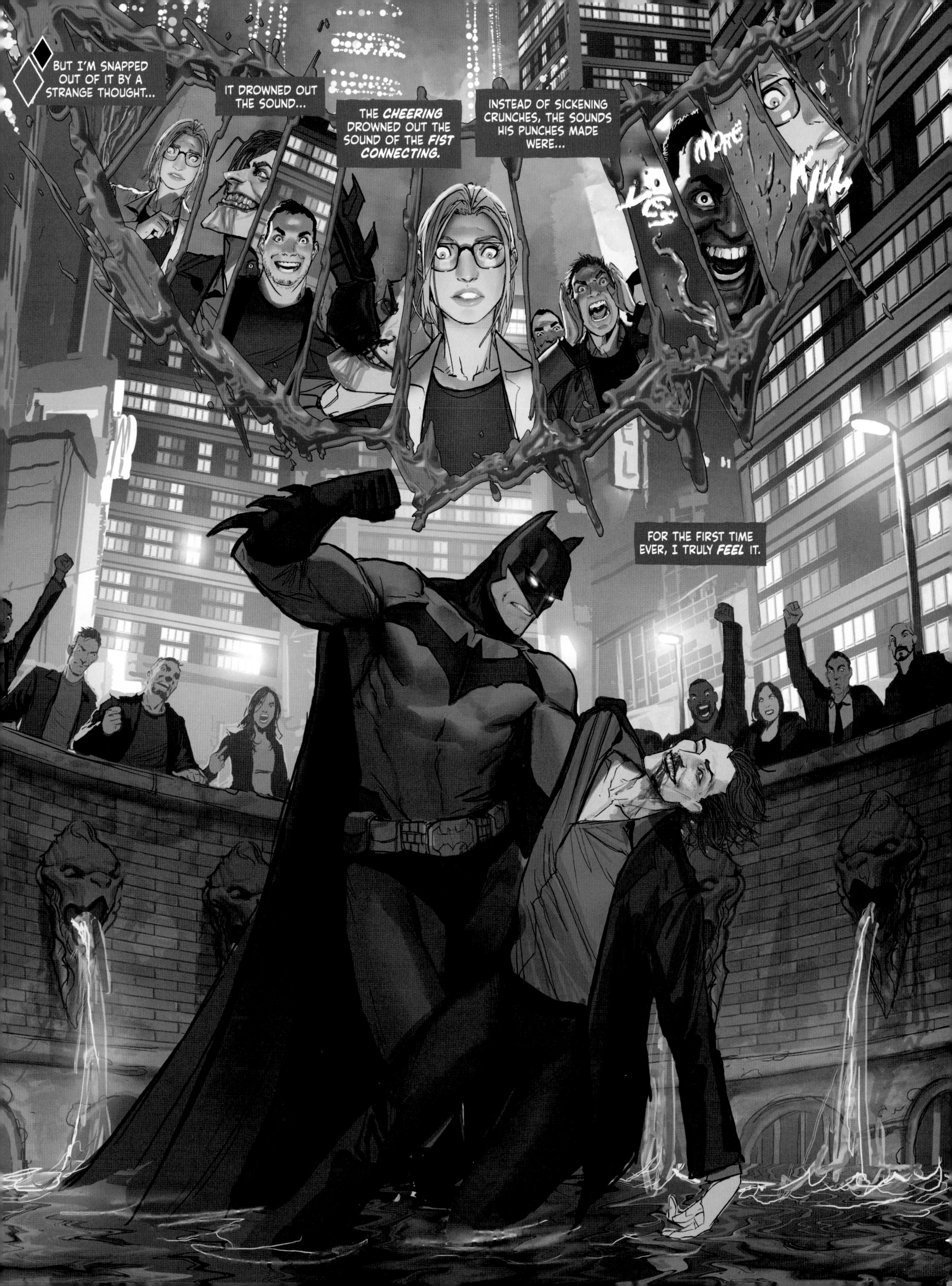
BUT I'M SNAPPED OUT OF IT BY A STRANGE THOUGHT...
IT DROWNED OUT THE SOUND...
THE *CHEERING* DROWNED OUT THE SOUND OF THE *FIST CONNECTING.*
INSTEAD OF SICKENING CRUNCHES, THE SOUNDS HIS PUNCHES MADE WERE...
YES
MORE
KILL
FOR THE FIRST TIME EVER, I TRULY *FEEL* IT.

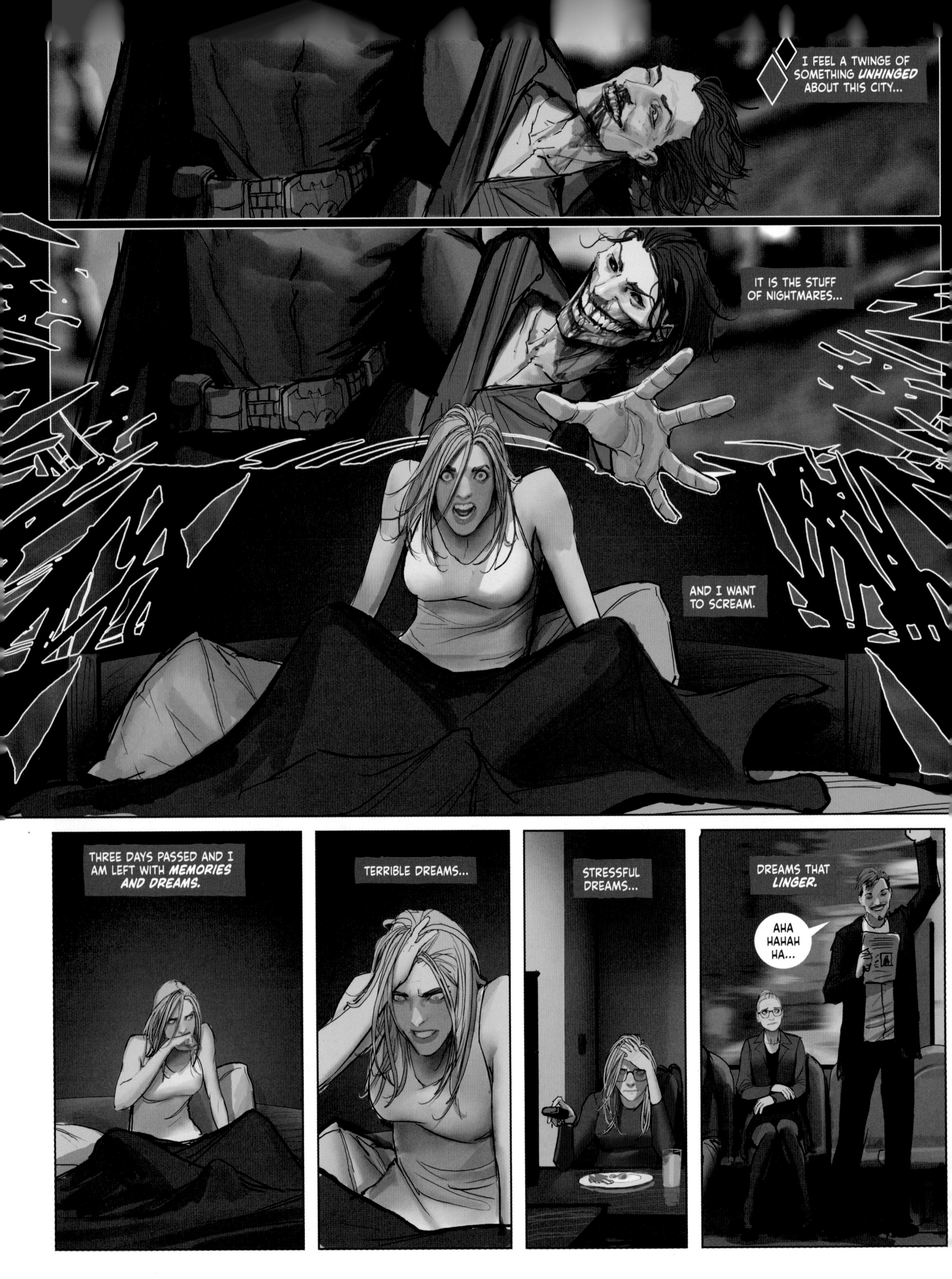
I FEEL A TWINGE OF SOMETHING UNHINGED ABOUT THIS CITY...
IT IS THE STUFF OF NIGHTMARES...
AND I WANT TO SCREAM.
THREE DAYS PASSED AND I AM LEFT WITH MEMORIES AND DREAMS.
TERRIBLE DREAMS...
STRESSFUL DREAMS...
DREAMS THAT LINGER.
AHA HAHAH HA...

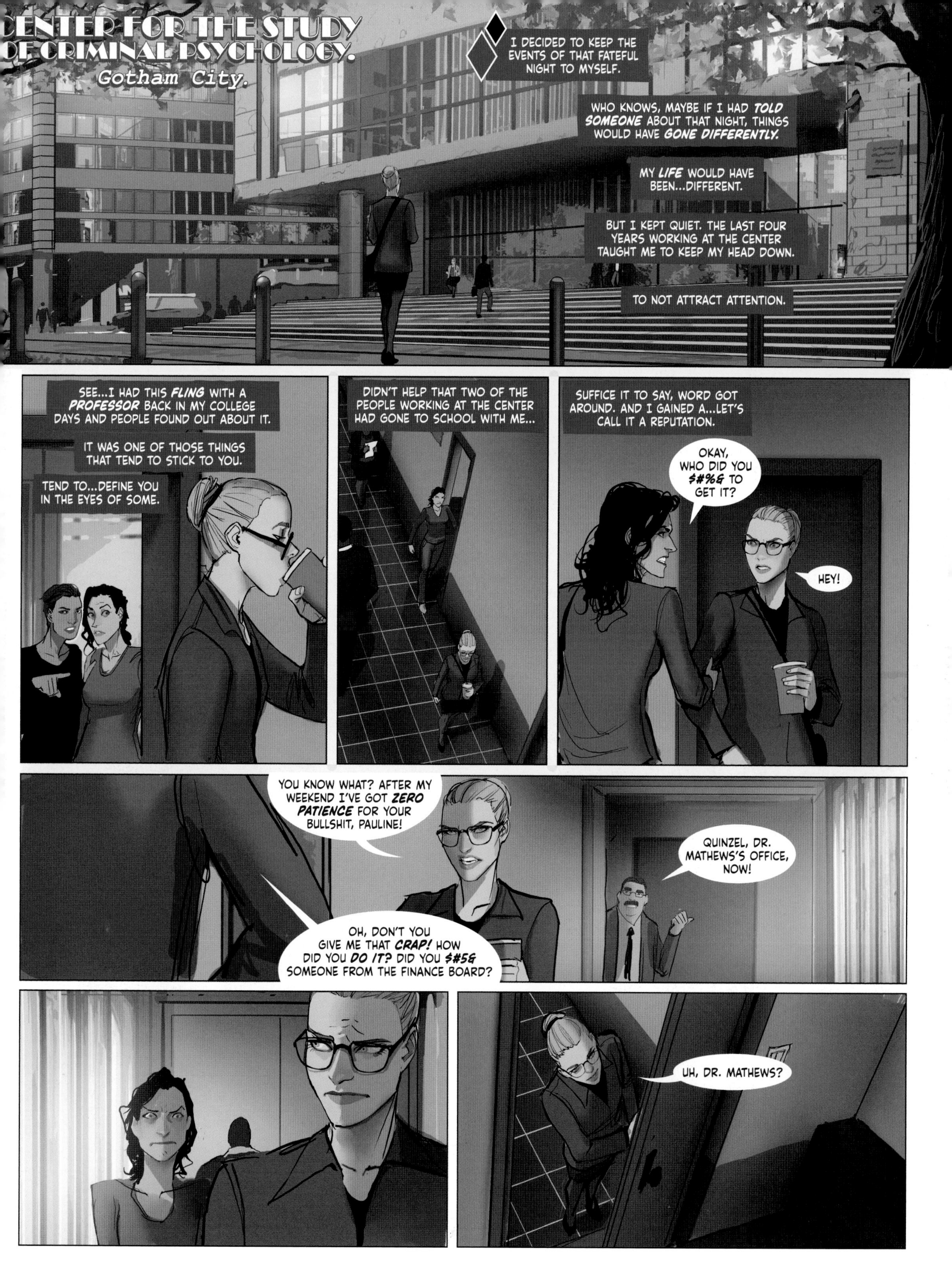
CENTER FOR THE STUDY OF CRIMINAL PSYCHOLOGY.
Gotham City.
I DECIDED TO KEEP THE EVENTS OF THAT FATEFUL NIGHT TO MYSELF.
WHO KNOWS, MAYBE IF I HAD TOLD SOMEONE ABOUT THAT NIGHT, THINGS WOULD HAVE GONE DIFFERENTLY.
MY LIFE WOULD HAVE BEEN...DIFFERENT.
BUT I KEPT QUIET. THE LAST FOUR YEARS WORKING AT THE CENTER TAUGHT ME TO KEEP MY HEAD DOWN.
TO NOT ATTRACT ATTENTION.
SEE...I HAD THIS FLING WITH A PROFESSOR BACK IN MY COLLEGE DAYS AND PEOPLE FOUND OUT ABOUT IT.
IT WAS ONE OF THOSE THINGS THAT TEND TO STICK TO YOU.
TEND TO...DEFINE YOU IN THE EYES OF SOME.
DIDN'T HELP THAT TWO OF THE PEOPLE WORKING AT THE CENTER HAD GONE TO SCHOOL WITH ME...
SUFFICE IT TO SAY, WORD GOT AROUND. AND I GAINED A...LET'S CALL IT A REPUTATION.
OKAY, WHO DID YOU $#%& TO GET IT?
HEY!
YOU KNOW WHAT? AFTER MY WEEKEND I'VE GOT ZERO PATIENCE FOR YOUR BULLSHIT, PAULINE!
OH, DON'T YOU GIVE ME THAT CRAP! HOW DID YOU DO IT? DID YOU $#5& SOMEONE FROM THE FINANCE BOARD?
QUINZEL, DR. MATHEWS'S OFFICE, NOW!
UH, DR. MATHEWS?

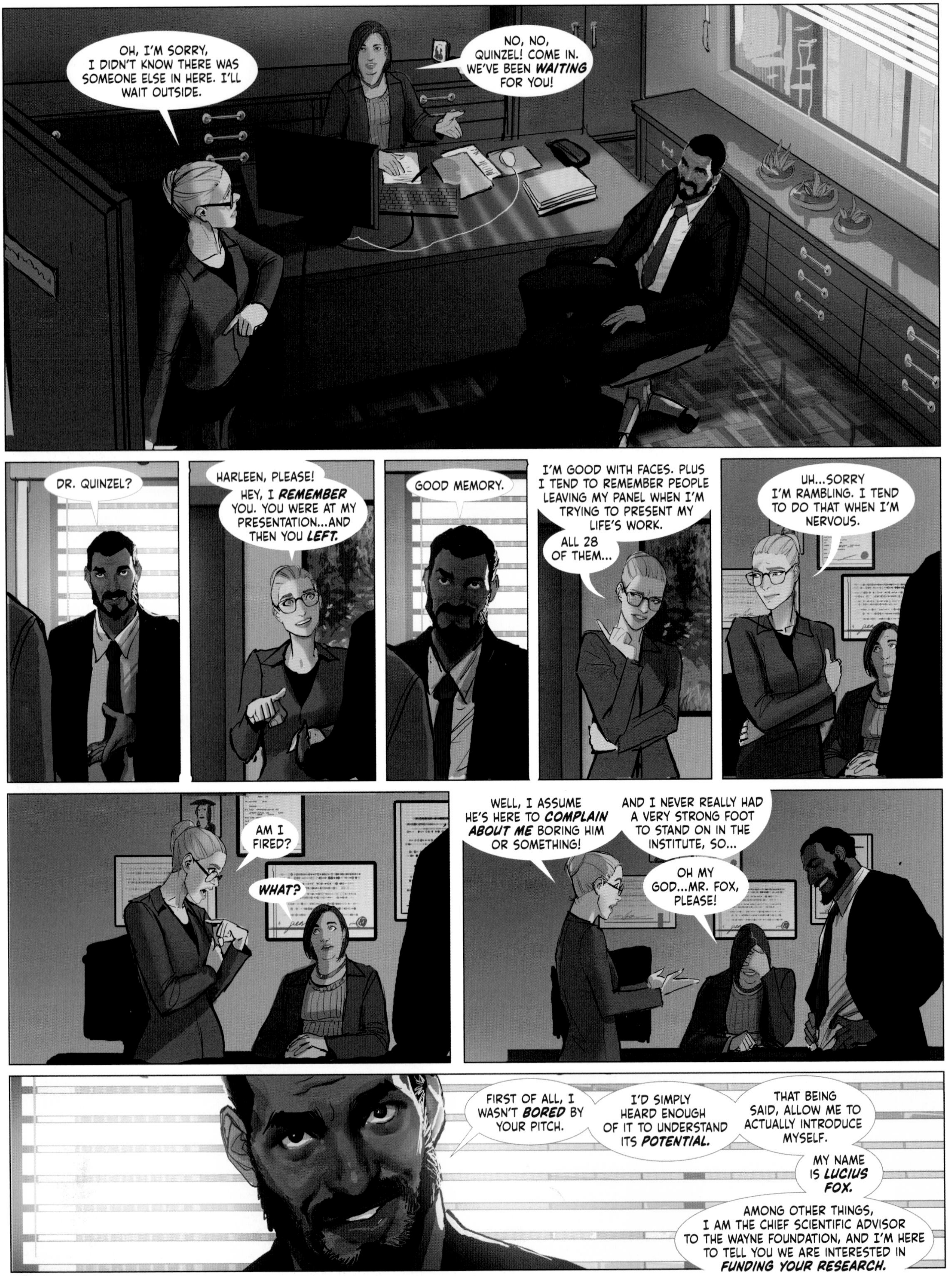
OH, I'M SORRY, I DIDN'T KNOW THERE WAS SOMEONE ELSE IN HERE. I'LL WAIT OUTSIDE.
NO, NO, QUINZEL! COME IN. WE'VE BEEN *WAITING* FOR YOU!
DR. QUINZEL?
HARLEEN, PLEASE!
HEY, I *REMEMBER* YOU. YOU WERE AT MY PRESENTATION...AND THEN YOU *LEFT.*
GOOD MEMORY.
I'M GOOD WITH FACES. PLUS I TEND TO REMEMBER PEOPLE LEAVING MY PANEL WHEN I'M TRYING TO PRESENT MY LIFE'S WORK.
ALL 28 OF THEM...
UH...SORRY I'M RAMBLING. I TEND TO DO THAT WHEN I'M NERVOUS.
AM I FIRED?
WHAT?
WELL, I ASSUME HE'S HERE TO *COMPLAIN ABOUT ME* BORING HIM OR SOMETHING!
AND I NEVER REALLY HAD A VERY STRONG FOOT TO STAND ON IN THE INSTITUTE, SO...
OH MY GOD...MR. FOX, PLEASE!
FIRST OF ALL, I WASN'T *BORED* BY YOUR PITCH.
I'D SIMPLY HEARD ENOUGH OF IT TO UNDERSTAND ITS *POTENTIAL.*
THAT BEING SAID, ALLOW ME TO ACTUALLY INTRODUCE MYSELF.
MY NAME IS *LUCIUS FOX.*
AMONG OTHER THINGS, I AM THE CHIEF SCIENTIFIC ADVISOR TO THE WAYNE FOUNDATION, AND I'M HERE TO TELL YOU WE ARE INTERESTED IN *FUNDING YOUR RESEARCH.*

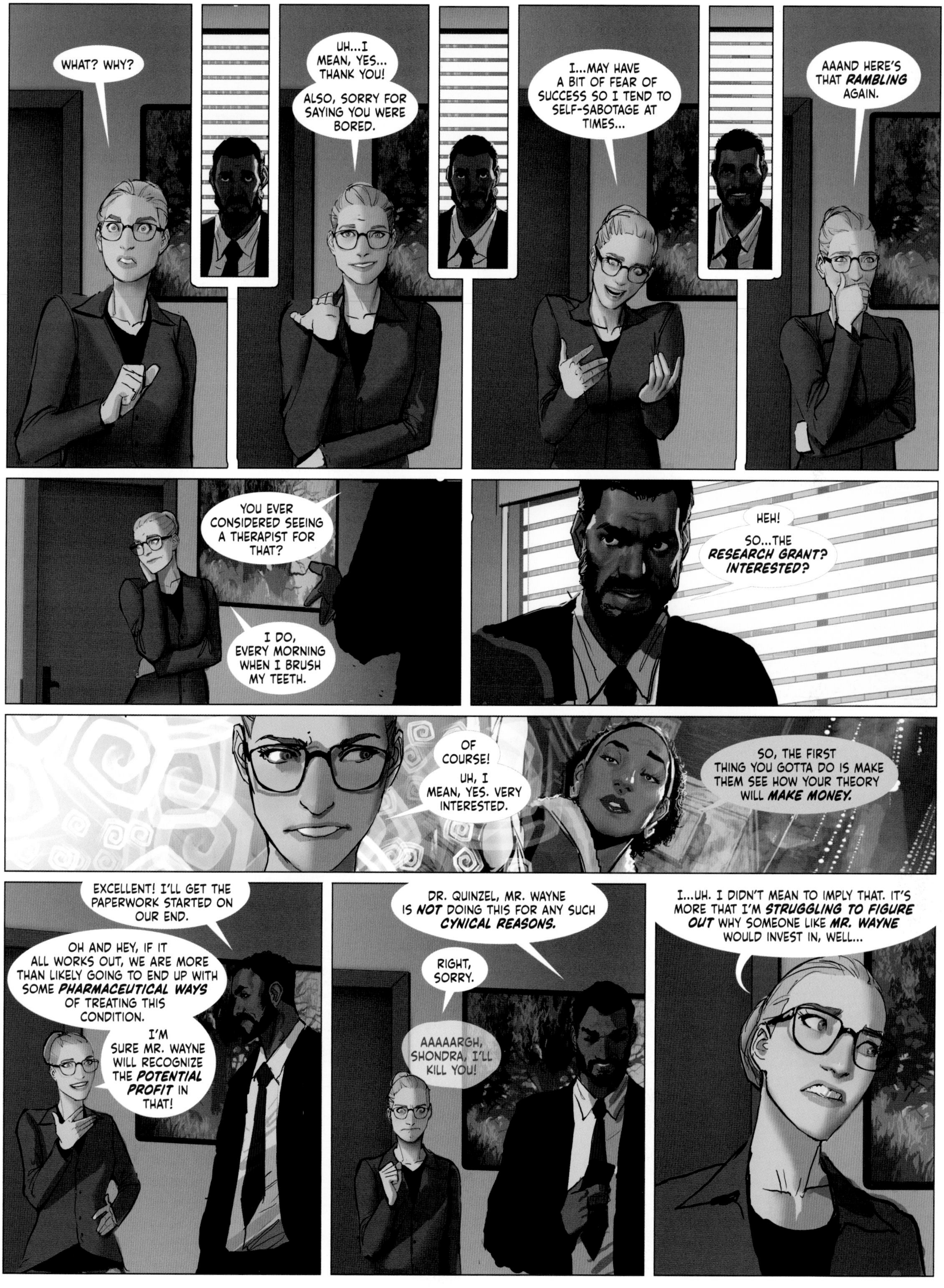
WHAT? WHY?
UH...I MEAN, YES... THANK YOU!
ALSO, SORRY FOR SAYING YOU WERE BORED.
I...MAY HAVE A BIT OF FEAR OF SUCCESS SO I TEND TO SELF-SABOTAGE AT TIMES...
AAAND HERE'S THAT *RAMBLING* AGAIN.
YOU EVER CONSIDERED SEEING A THERAPIST FOR THAT?
I DO, EVERY MORNING WHEN I BRUSH MY TEETH.
HEH!
SO...THE *RESEARCH GRANT? INTERESTED?*
OF COURSE!
UH, I MEAN, YES. VERY INTERESTED.
SO, THE FIRST THING YOU GOTTA DO IS MAKE THEM SEE HOW YOUR THEORY WILL *MAKE MONEY.*
EXCELLENT! I'LL GET THE PAPERWORK STARTED ON OUR END.
OH AND HEY, IF IT ALL WORKS OUT, WE ARE MORE THAN LIKELY GOING TO END UP WITH SOME *PHARMACEUTICAL WAYS* OF TREATING THIS CONDITION.
I'M SURE MR. WAYNE WILL RECOGNIZE THE *POTENTIAL PROFIT* IN THAT!
DR. QUINZEL, MR. WAYNE IS *NOT* DOING THIS FOR ANY SUCH *CYNICAL REASONS.*
RIGHT, SORRY.
AAAAARGH, SHONDRA, I'LL KILL YOU!
I...UH. I DIDN'T MEAN TO IMPLY THAT. IT'S MORE THAT I'M *STRUGGLING TO FIGURE OUT* WHY SOMEONE LIKE *MR. WAYNE* WOULD INVEST IN, WELL...

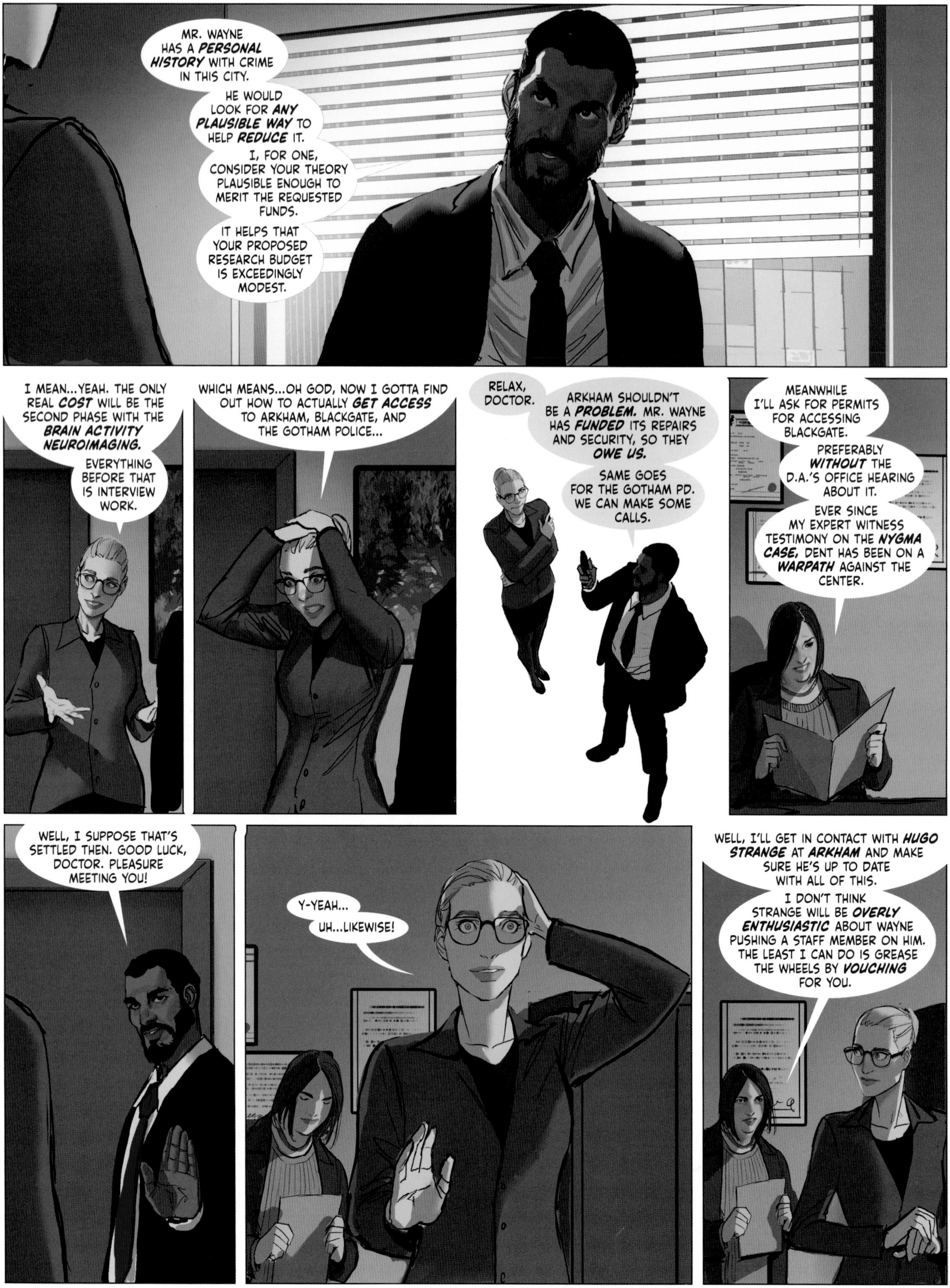
MR. WAYNE HAS A PERSONAL HISTORY WITH CRIME IN THIS CITY.
HE WOULD LOOK FOR ANY PLAUSIBLE WAY TO HELP REDUCE IT.
I, FOR ONE, CONSIDER YOUR THEORY PLAUSIBLE ENOUGH TO MERIT THE REQUESTED FUNDS.
IT HELPS THAT YOUR PROPOSED RESEARCH BUDGET IS EXCEEDINGLY MODEST.
I MEAN...YEAH. THE ONLY REAL COST WILL BE THE SECOND PHASE WITH THE BRAIN ACTIVITY NEUROIMAGING.
EVERYTHING BEFORE THAT IS INTERVIEW WORK.
WHICH MEANS...OH GOD, NOW I GOTTA FIND OUT HOW TO ACTUALLY GET ACCESS TO ARKHAM, BLACKGATE, AND THE GOTHAM POLICE...
RELAX, DOCTOR.
ARKHAM SHOULDN'T BE A PROBLEM. MR. WAYNE HAS FUNDED ITS REPAIRS AND SECURITY, SO THEY OWE US.
SAME GOES FOR THE GOTHAM PD. WE CAN MAKE SOME CALLS.
MEANWHILE I'LL ASK FOR PERMITS FOR ACCESSING BLACKGATE.
PREFERABLY WITHOUT THE D.A.'S OFFICE HEARING ABOUT IT.
EVER SINCE MY EXPERT WITNESS TESTIMONY ON THE NYGMA CASE, DENT HAS BEEN ON A WARPATH AGAINST THE CENTER.
WELL, I SUPPOSE THAT'S SETTLED THEN. GOOD LUCK, DOCTOR. PLEASURE MEETING YOU!
Y-YEAH...
UH...LIKEWISE!
WELL, I'LL GET IN CONTACT WITH HUGO STRANGE AT ARKHAM AND MAKE SURE HE'S UP TO DATE WITH ALL OF THIS.
I DON'T THINK STRANGE WILL BE OVERLY ENTHUSIASTIC ABOUT WAYNE PUSHING A STAFF MEMBER ON HIM. THE LEAST I CAN DO IS GREASE THE WHEELS BY VOUCHING FOR YOU.

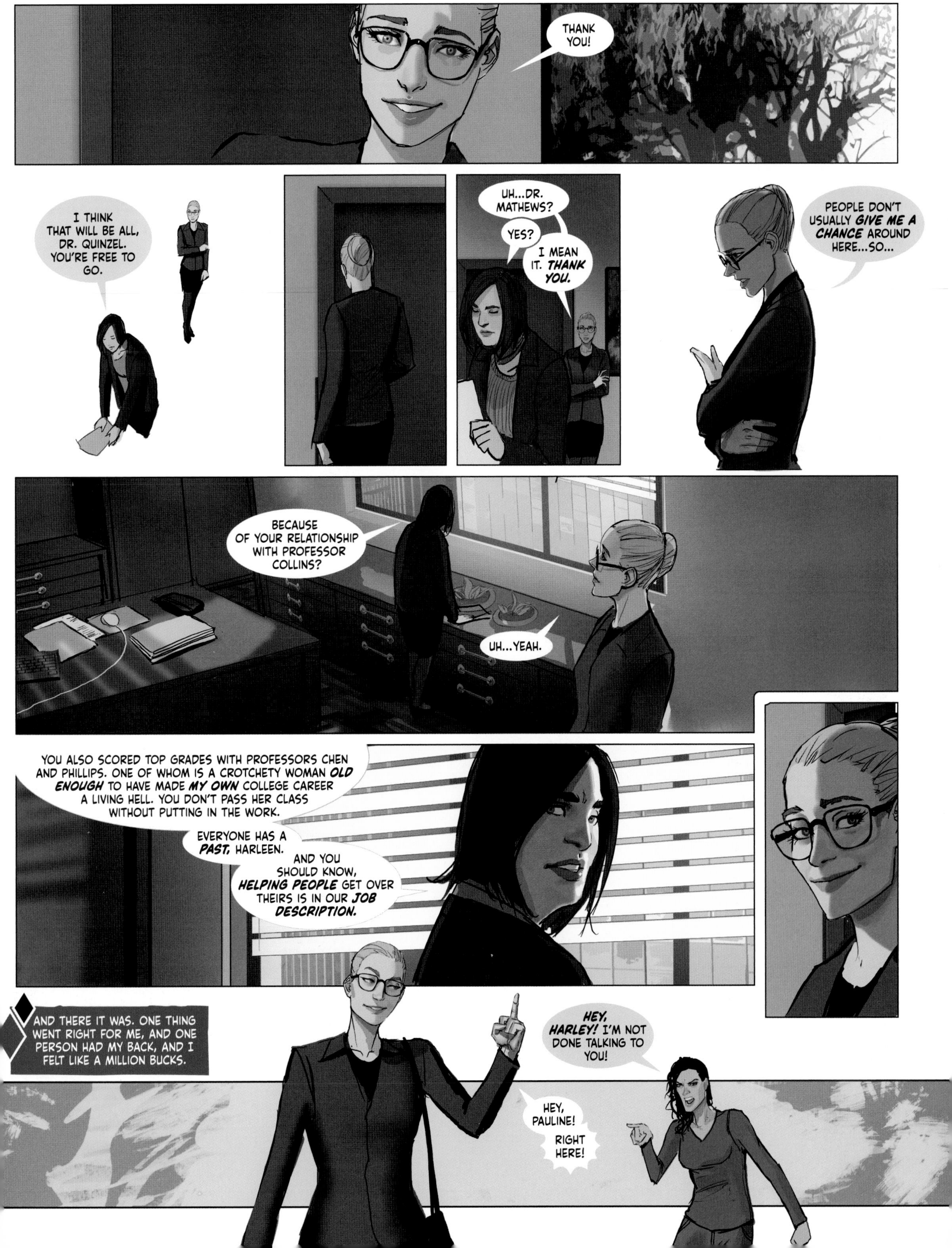
THANK YOU!
I THINK THAT WILL BE ALL, DR. QUINZEL. YOU'RE FREE TO GO.
UH...DR. MATHEWS?
YES?
I MEAN IT. THANK YOU.
PEOPLE DON'T USUALLY GIVE ME A CHANCE AROUND HERE...SO...
BECAUSE OF YOUR RELATIONSHIP WITH PROFESSOR COLLINS?
UH...YEAH.
YOU ALSO SCORED TOP GRADES WITH PROFESSORS CHEN AND PHILLIPS. ONE OF WHOM IS A CROTCHETY WOMAN OLD ENOUGH TO HAVE MADE MY OWN COLLEGE CAREER A LIVING HELL. YOU DON'T PASS HER CLASS WITHOUT PUTTING IN THE WORK.
EVERYONE HAS A PAST, HARLEEN.
AND YOU SHOULD KNOW, HELPING PEOPLE GET OVER THEIRS IS IN OUR JOB DESCRIPTION.
AND THERE IT WAS. ONE THING WENT RIGHT FOR ME, AND ONE PERSON HAD MY BACK, AND I FELT LIKE A MILLION BUCKS.
HEY, HARLEY! I'M NOT DONE TALKING TO YOU!
HEY, PAULINE!
RIGHT HERE!

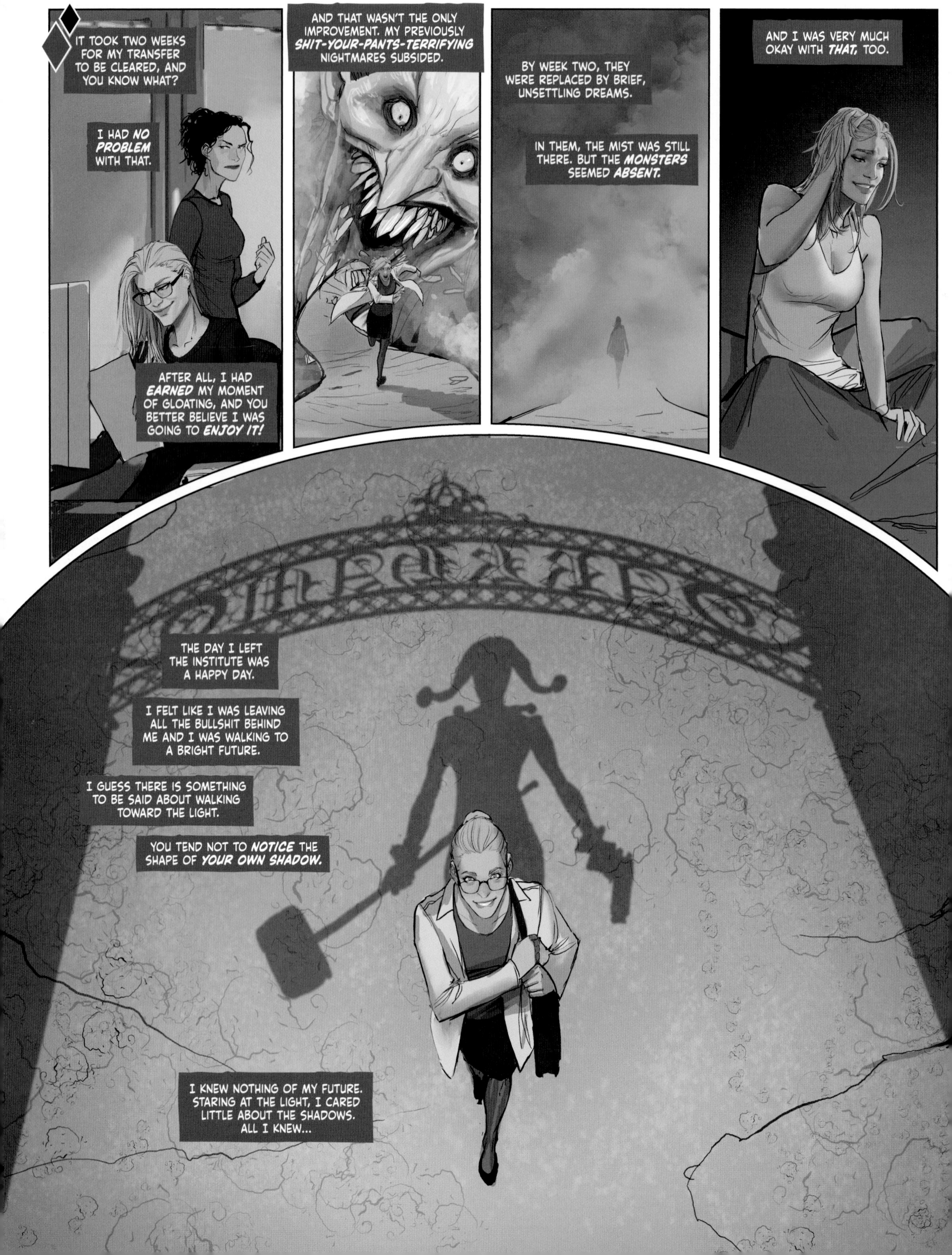
IT TOOK TWO WEEKS FOR MY TRANSFER TO BE CLEARED, AND YOU KNOW WHAT?
I HAD NO PROBLEM WITH THAT.
AFTER ALL, I HAD EARNED MY MOMENT OF GLOATING, AND YOU BETTER BELIEVE I WAS GOING TO ENJOY IT!
AND THAT WASN'T THE ONLY IMPROVEMENT. MY PREVIOUSLY SHIT-YOUR-PANTS-TERRIFYING NIGHTMARES SUBSIDED.
BY WEEK TWO, THEY WERE REPLACED BY BRIEF, UNSETTLING DREAMS.
IN THEM, THE MIST WAS STILL THERE. BUT THE MONSTERS SEEMED ABSENT.
AND I WAS VERY MUCH OKAY WITH THAT, TOO.
THE DAY I LEFT THE INSTITUTE WAS A HAPPY DAY.
I FELT LIKE I WAS LEAVING ALL THE BULLSHIT BEHIND ME AND I WAS WALKING TO A BRIGHT FUTURE.
I GUESS THERE IS SOMETHING TO BE SAID ABOUT WALKING TOWARD THE LIGHT.
YOU TEND NOT TO NOTICE THE SHAPE OF YOUR OWN SHADOW.
I KNEW NOTHING OF MY FUTURE. STARING AT THE LIGHT, I CARED LITTLE ABOUT THE SHADOWS. ALL I KNEW...

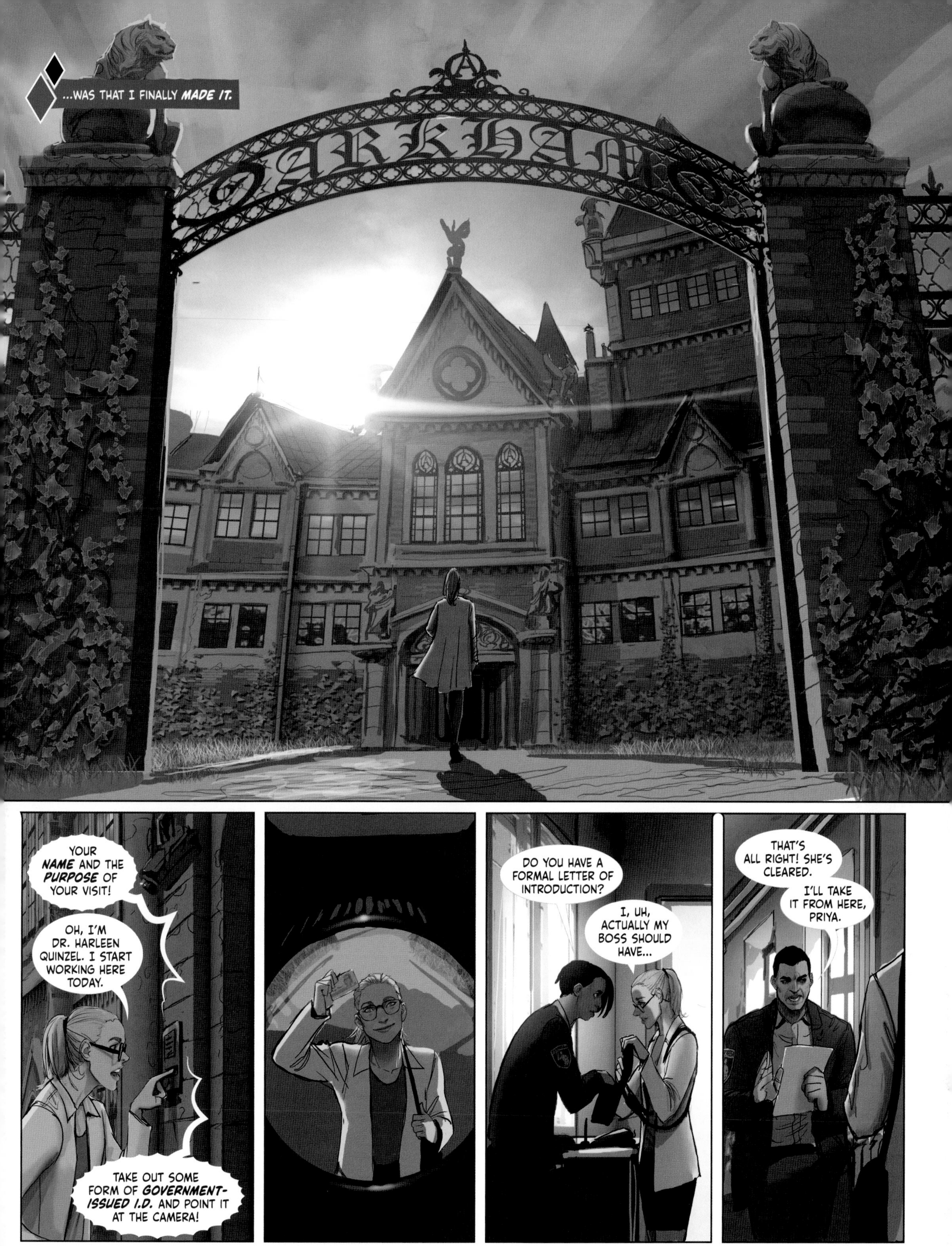
...WAS THAT I FINALLY *MADE IT.*
YOUR *NAME* AND THE *PURPOSE* OF YOUR VISIT!
OH, I'M DR. HARLEEN QUINZEL. I START WORKING HERE TODAY.
TAKE OUT SOME FORM OF *GOVERNMENT-ISSUED I.D.* AND POINT IT AT THE CAMERA!
DO YOU HAVE A FORMAL LETTER OF INTRODUCTION?
I, UH, ACTUALLY MY BOSS SHOULD HAVE...
THAT'S ALL RIGHT! SHE'S CLEARED.
I'LL TAKE IT FROM HERE, PRIYA.

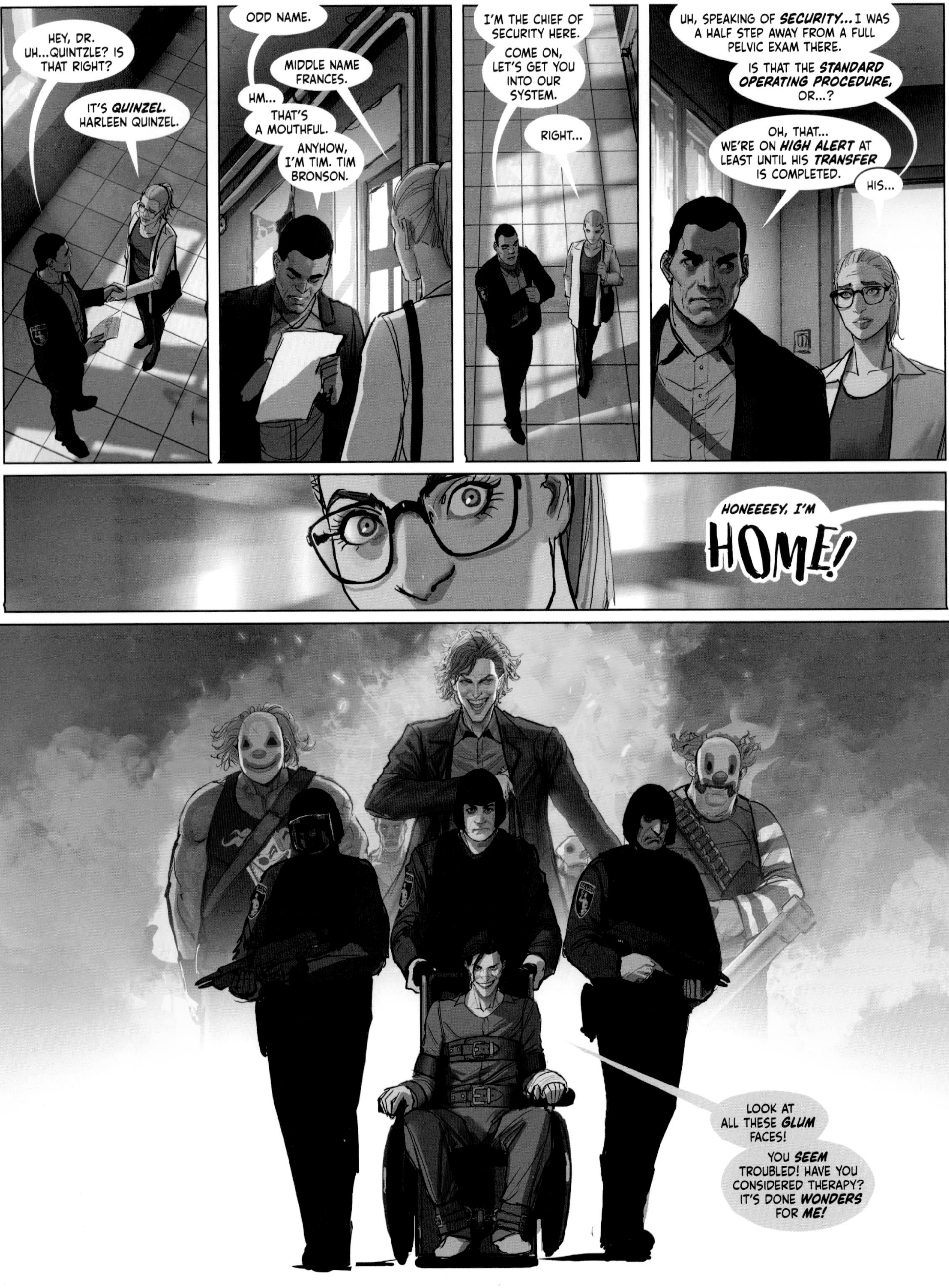
HEY, DR. UH...QUINTZLE? IS THAT RIGHT?
IT'S QUINZEL. HARLEEN QUINZEL.
ODD NAME.
MIDDLE NAME FRANCES.
HM... THAT'S A MOUTHFUL.
ANYHOW, I'M TIM. TIM BRONSON.
I'M THE CHIEF OF SECURITY HERE.
COME ON, LET'S GET YOU INTO OUR SYSTEM.
RIGHT...
UH, SPEAKING OF SECURITY... I WAS A HALF STEP AWAY FROM A FULL PELVIC EXAM THERE.
IS THAT THE STANDARD OPERATING PROCEDURE, OR...?
OH, THAT... WE'RE ON HIGH ALERT AT LEAST UNTIL HIS TRANSFER IS COMPLETED.
HIS...
HONEEEEY, I'M HOME!
LOOK AT ALL THESE GLUM FACES!
YOU SEEM TROUBLED! HAVE YOU CONSIDERED THERAPY? IT'S DONE WONDERS FOR ME!

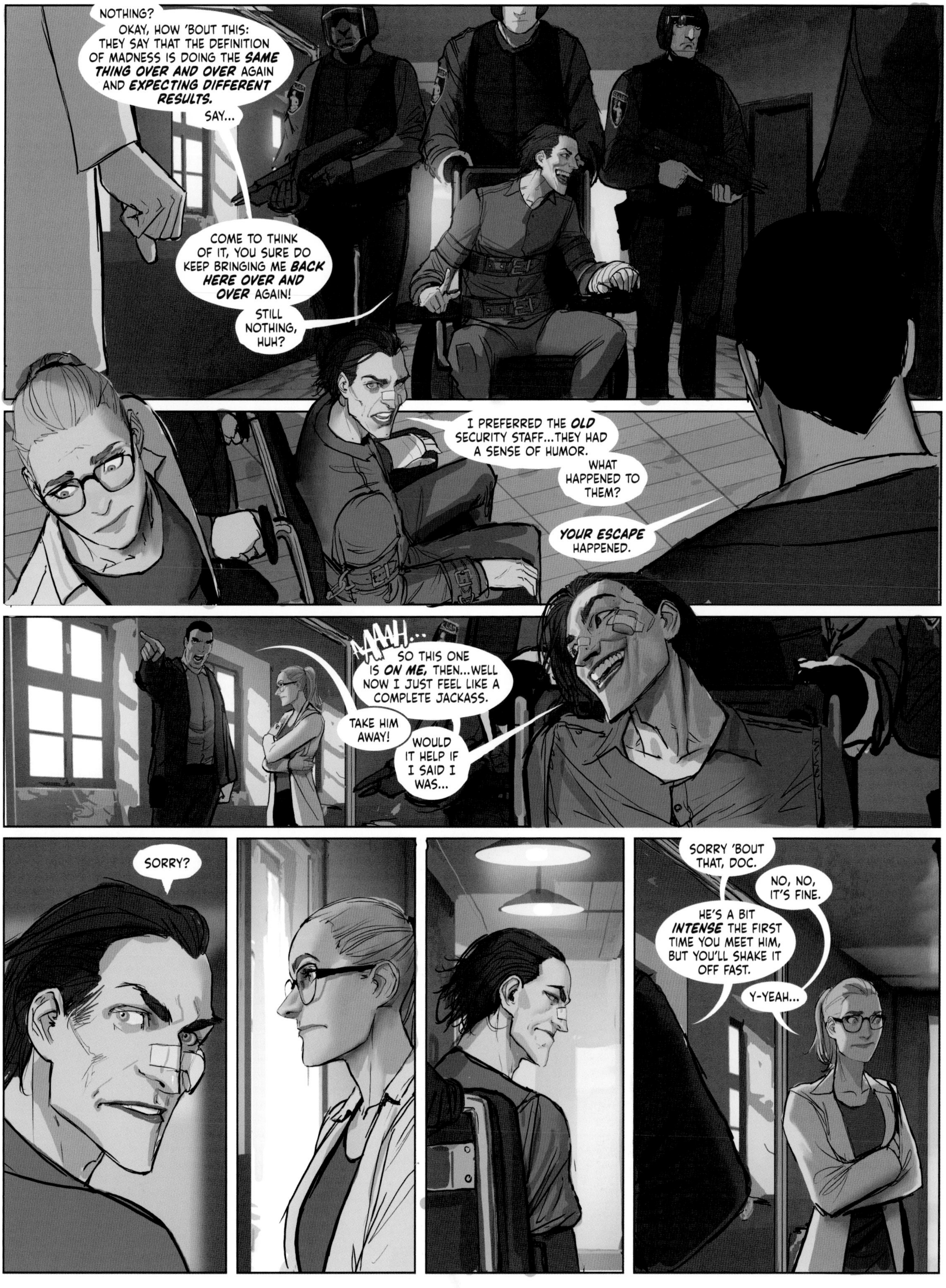
NOTHING?
OKAY, HOW 'BOUT THIS: THEY SAY THAT THE DEFINITION OF MADNESS IS DOING THE **SAME THING OVER AND OVER** AGAIN AND **EXPECTING DIFFERENT RESULTS.**
SAY...
COME TO THINK OF IT, YOU SURE DO KEEP BRINGING ME **BACK HERE OVER AND OVER** AGAIN!
STILL NOTHING, HUH?
I PREFERRED THE **OLD** SECURITY STAFF...THEY HAD A SENSE OF HUMOR.
WHAT HAPPENED TO THEM?
YOUR ESCAPE HAPPENED.
AAAAH...
SO THIS ONE IS **ON ME,** THEN...WELL NOW I JUST FEEL LIKE A COMPLETE JACKASS.
TAKE HIM AWAY!
WOULD IT HELP IF I SAID I WAS...
SORRY?
SORRY 'BOUT THAT, DOC.
NO, NO, IT'S FINE.
HE'S A BIT **INTENSE** THE FIRST TIME YOU MEET HIM, BUT YOU'LL SHAKE IT OFF FAST.
Y-YEAH...

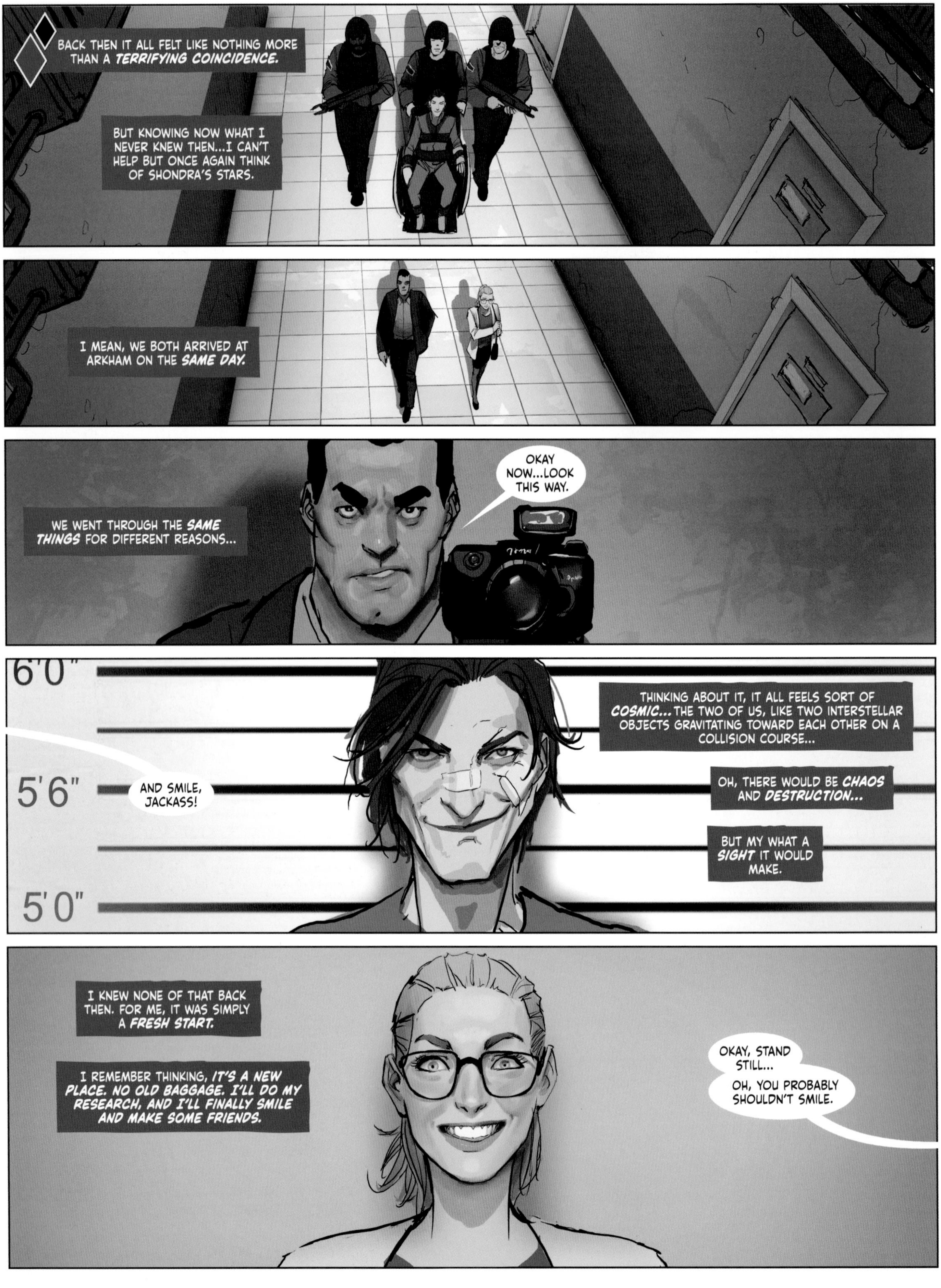
BACK THEN IT ALL FELT LIKE NOTHING MORE THAN A *TERRIFYING COINCIDENCE.*
BUT KNOWING NOW WHAT I NEVER KNEW THEN...I CAN'T HELP BUT ONCE AGAIN THINK OF SHONDRA'S STARS.
I MEAN, WE BOTH ARRIVED AT ARKHAM ON THE *SAME DAY.*
WE WENT THROUGH THE *SAME THINGS* FOR DIFFERENT REASONS...
OKAY NOW...LOOK THIS WAY.
6'0"
5'6"
5'0"
AND SMILE, JACKASS!
THINKING ABOUT IT, IT ALL FEELS SORT OF *COSMIC...* THE TWO OF US, LIKE TWO INTERSTELLAR OBJECTS GRAVITATING TOWARD EACH OTHER ON A COLLISION COURSE...
OH, THERE WOULD BE *CHAOS* AND *DESTRUCTION...*
BUT MY WHAT A *SIGHT* IT WOULD MAKE.
I KNEW NONE OF THAT BACK THEN. FOR ME, IT WAS SIMPLY A *FRESH START.*
I REMEMBER THINKING, *IT'S A NEW PLACE. NO OLD BAGGAGE. I'LL DO MY RESEARCH, AND I'LL FINALLY SMILE AND MAKE SOME FRIENDS.*
OKAY, STAND STILL...
OH, YOU PROBABLY SHOULDN'T SMILE.

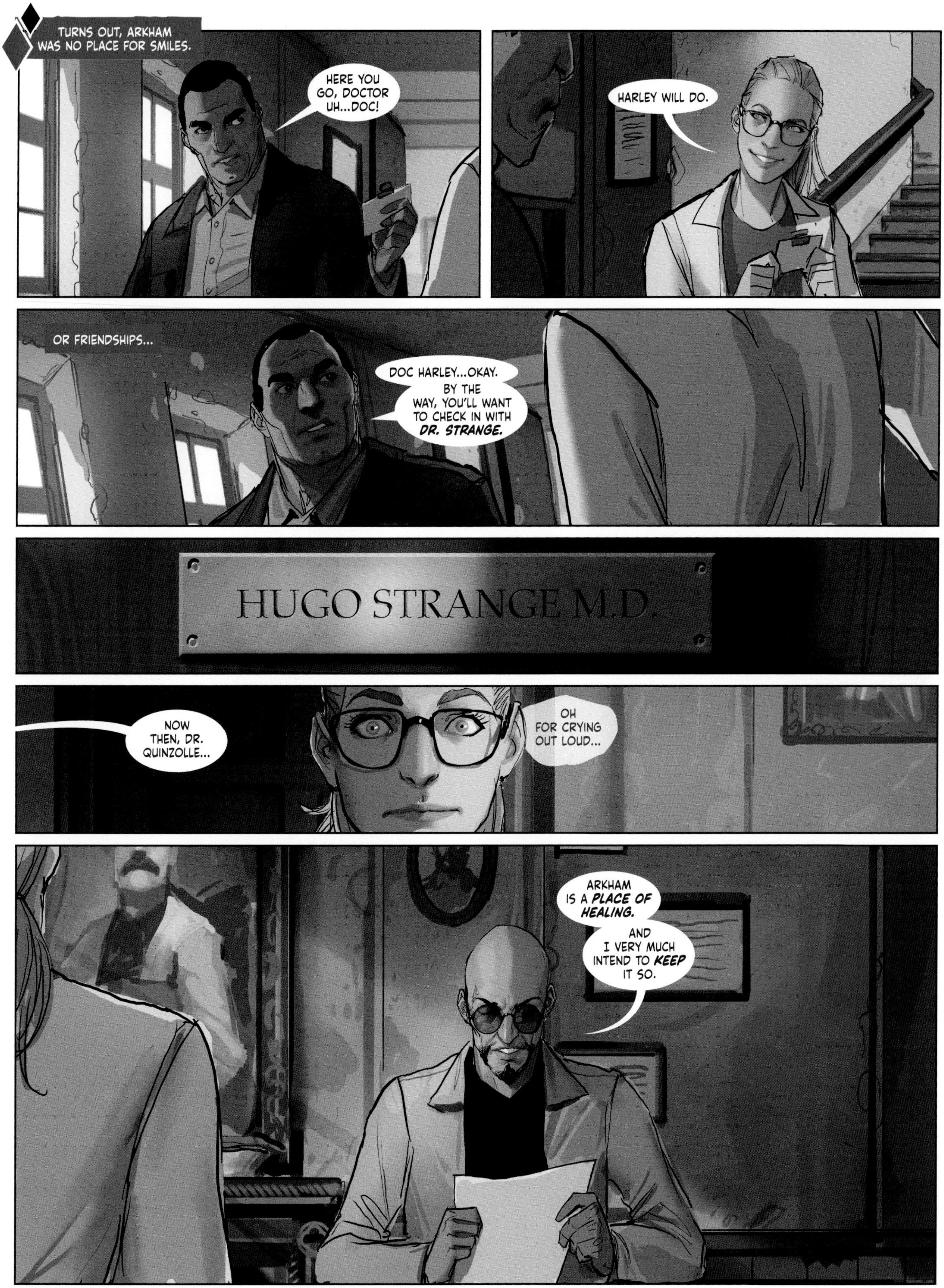
TURNS OUT, ARKHAM WAS NO PLACE FOR SMILES.
HERE YOU GO, DOCTOR UH...DOC!
HARLEY WILL DO.
OR FRIENDSHIPS...
DOC HARLEY...OKAY. BY THE WAY, YOU'LL WANT TO CHECK IN WITH **DR. STRANGE.**
HUGO STRANGE M.D.
NOW THEN, DR. QUINZOLLE...
OH FOR CRYING OUT LOUD...
ARKHAM IS A ***PLACE OF HEALING.***
AND I VERY MUCH INTEND TO ***KEEP*** IT SO.

YOU ARE HERE BECAUSE THIS INSTITUTION OWES MR. WAYNE A GREAT DEAL, AND BECAUSE I RESPECT DR. MATHEWS.

BUT THIS IS WHERE MY *GOODWILL ENDS.*

I LOOKED OVER YOUR RESEARCH PAPERS... YOUR FIRST STAGE IS INTERVIEWS? STANDARD THERAPY PROCEDURES, CORRECT?

UH, YES!

HM...THAT'S FINE. SO, YOU ARE *SEARCHING* FOR *WHAT,* EXACTLY?

I'M LOOKING FOR IDEAL CANDIDATES FOR THE FIRST ROUND OF BRAIN MAPPING. TO...UH...

PINPOINT THE *HEART OF MADNESS?*

LOCATE HOT SPOTS OF BRAIN ACTIVITY THROUGH...

YES, YES. HOOK THEM UP TO *MACHINERY,* ASK THEM *MORE* QUESTIONS, AND HOPE THINGS GO *BEEP* AND YOU GET A *CONDITION* NAMED AFTER YOU.

I...THAT'S NOT WHAT I'M TRYING...

DR. QUINZOLE--

QUINZEL.

MHM...LISTEN. IN ALL *HONESTY* I THINK YOURS IS JUST ONE OF MANY *CRACKPOT THEORIES* I'VE SEEN IDEALISTIC YOUNG PSYCHIATRISTS BRING TO THE TABLE LOOKING FOR THE *HOWS* AND THE *WHYS* OF OUR... RESIDENTS.

THEIR IDEALISM DOESN'T *LAST LONG IN ARKHAM,* AND I'M THINKING YOURS WON'T EITHER.

BUT...

HERE IS ALL I REQUIRE OF YOU. DON'T STIR THE POT. DON'T AGITATE THE PATIENTS. AND YOU ARE FREE TO DO YOUR BUSINESS.

RIGHT... THANK YOU.

OH, I NEED ACCESS TO PREVIOUS INTERVIEWS DONE WITH INMATES ON THIS LIST.

PATIENTS.

YES, SORRY.

THE FILE ROOM WILL HAVE THOSE.

OH, AND DOCTOR!

?

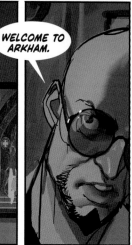

WELCOME TO ARKHAM.

HE SAID WELCOME, BUT LET'S BE HONEST, THIS WAS ARKHAM.

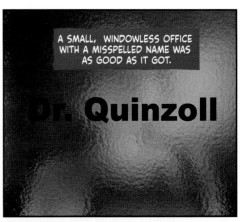

A SMALL, WINDOWLESS OFFICE WITH A MISSPELLED NAME WAS AS GOOD AS IT GOT.

Dr. Quinzoll

AND I WAS OKAY WITH THAT. BEATS A CUBICLE, AND ANYWAY, I HADN'T GONE THERE FOR COMFORT. I HAD *A JOB* TO DO.

I CAME TO ARKHAM WITH A LIST IN HAND. A VERY SPECIFIC LIST.

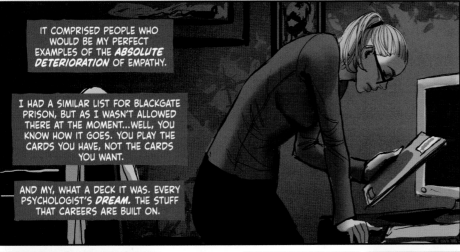

IT COMPRISED PEOPLE WHO WOULD BE MY PERFECT EXAMPLES OF THE *ABSOLUTE DETERIORATION* OF EMPATHY.

I HAD A SIMILAR LIST FOR BLACKGATE PRISON, BUT AS I WASN'T ALLOWED THERE AT THE MOMENT...WELL, YOU KNOW HOW IT GOES. YOU PLAY THE CARDS YOU HAVE, NOT THE CARDS YOU WANT.

AND MY, WHAT A DECK IT WAS. EVERY PSYCHOLOGIST'S *DREAM.* THE STUFF THAT CAREERS ARE BUILT ON.

THE KINGS, QUEENS, JACKS, AND ACES OF THE *CRIMINALLY INSANE.*

AND YES... A JOKER AS WELL...

BACK OF THE LINE FOR YOU.

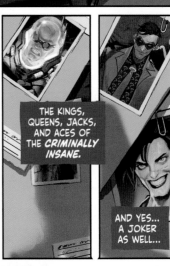

I WASN'T NEARLY READY TO DEAL WITH *HIM*...BUT THAT WAS FINE.

I HAD MORE THAN ENOUGH ANTISOCIAL PERSONALITY DISORDERS TO GO THROUGH.

THE WAY I SAW IT, BY THE TIME I WAS DONE WITH THEM, MY NIGHTMARES WOULD HAVE GONE AWAY, AND HE WOULD SHRINK IN THE EYES OF THIS...WELL... YOU GET IT.

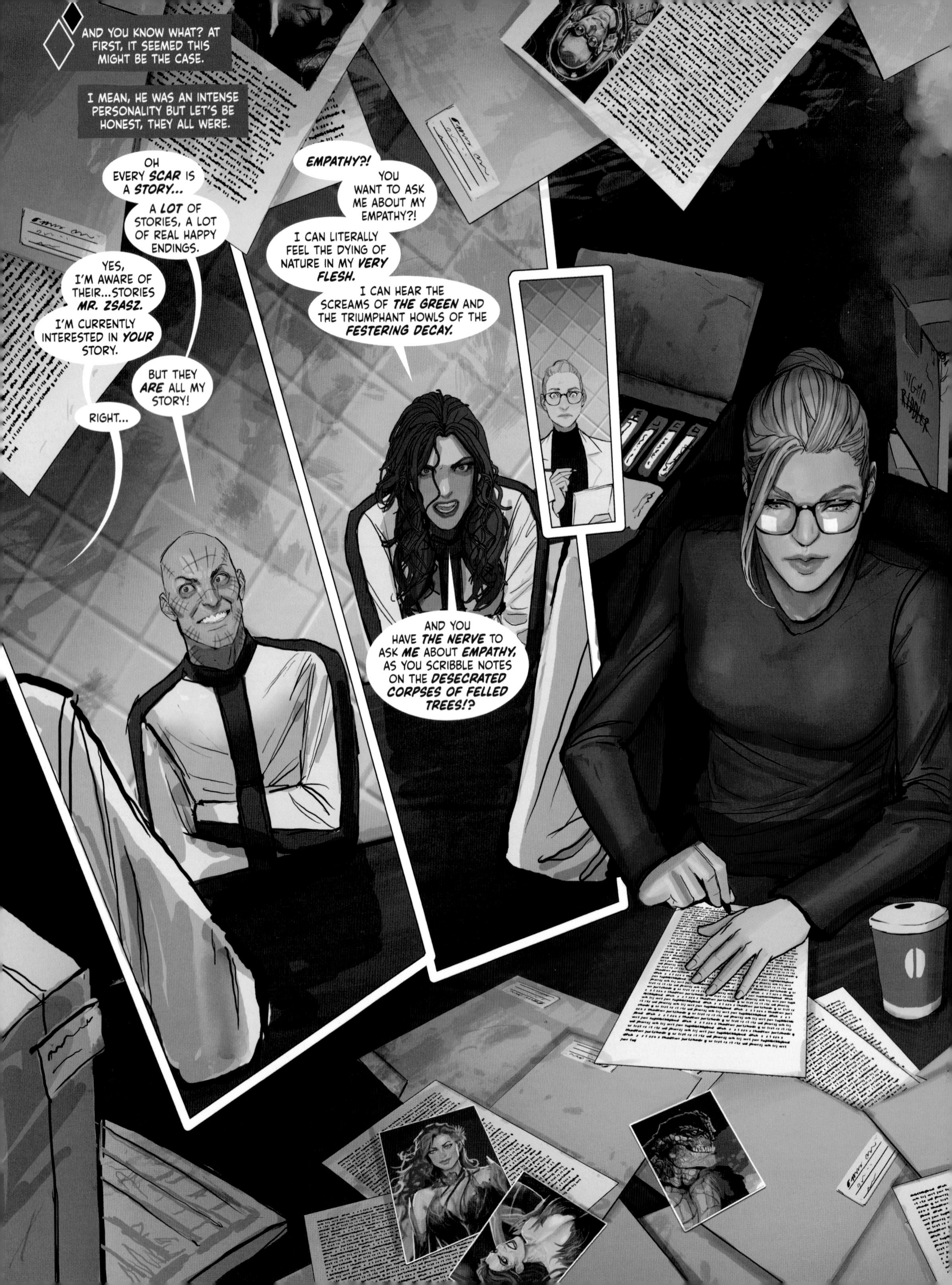
AND YOU KNOW WHAT? AT FIRST, IT SEEMED THIS MIGHT BE THE CASE.
I MEAN, HE WAS AN INTENSE PERSONALITY BUT LET'S BE HONEST, THEY ALL WERE.
OH EVERY SCAR IS A STORY...
A LOT OF STORIES, A LOT OF REAL HAPPY ENDINGS.
YES, I'M AWARE OF THEIR...STORIES MR. ZSASZ.
I'M CURRENTLY INTERESTED IN YOUR STORY.
BUT THEY ARE ALL MY STORY!
RIGHT...
EMPATHY?!
YOU WANT TO ASK ME ABOUT MY EMPATHY?!
I CAN LITERALLY FEEL THE DYING OF NATURE IN MY VERY FLESH.
I CAN HEAR THE SCREAMS OF THE GREEN AND THE TRIUMPHANT HOWLS OF THE FESTERING DECAY.
AND YOU HAVE THE NERVE TO ASK ME ABOUT EMPATHY, AS YOU SCRIBBLE NOTES ON THE DESECRATED CORPSES OF FELLED TREES!?

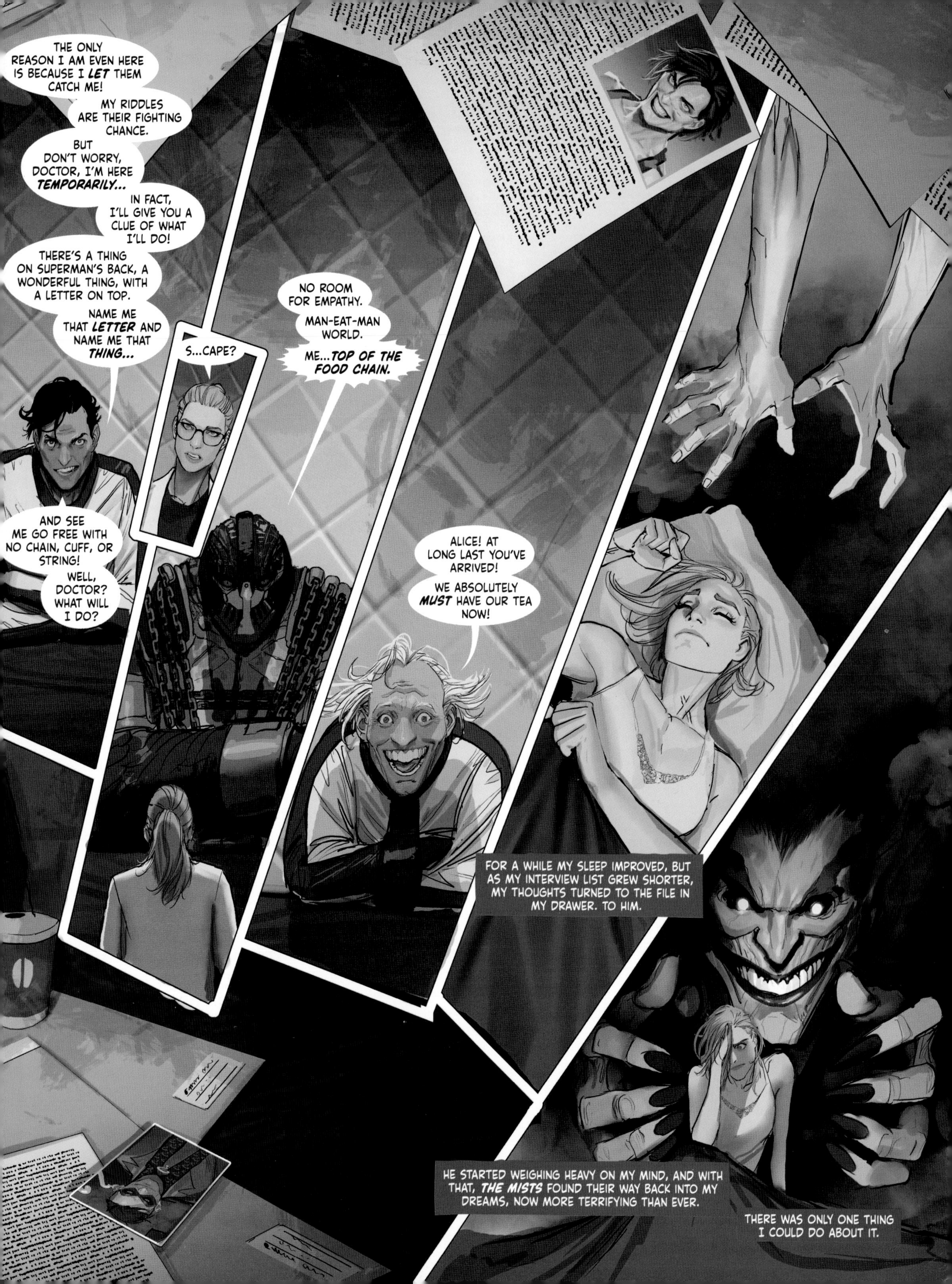

THE ONLY REASON I AM EVEN HERE IS BECAUSE I *LET* THEM CATCH ME!
MY RIDDLES ARE THEIR FIGHTING CHANCE.
BUT DON'T WORRY, DOCTOR, I'M HERE *TEMPORARILY...*
IN FACT, I'LL GIVE YOU A CLUE OF WHAT I'LL DO!
THERE'S A THING ON SUPERMAN'S BACK, A WONDERFUL THING, WITH A LETTER ON TOP.
NAME ME THAT *LETTER* AND NAME ME THAT *THING...*
AND SEE ME GO FREE WITH NO CHAIN, CUFF, OR STRING!
WELL, DOCTOR? WHAT WILL I DO?
S...CAPE?
NO ROOM FOR EMPATHY.
MAN-EAT-MAN WORLD.
ME...*TOP OF THE FOOD CHAIN.*
ALICE! AT LONG LAST YOU'VE ARRIVED!
WE ABSOLUTELY *MUST* HAVE OUR TEA NOW!
FOR A WHILE MY SLEEP IMPROVED, BUT AS MY INTERVIEW LIST GREW SHORTER, MY THOUGHTS TURNED TO THE FILE IN MY DRAWER. TO HIM.
HE STARTED WEIGHING HEAVY ON MY MIND, AND WITH THAT, *THE MISTS* FOUND THEIR WAY BACK INTO MY DREAMS, NOW MORE TERRIFYING THAN EVER.
THERE WAS ONLY ONE THING I COULD DO ABOUT IT.

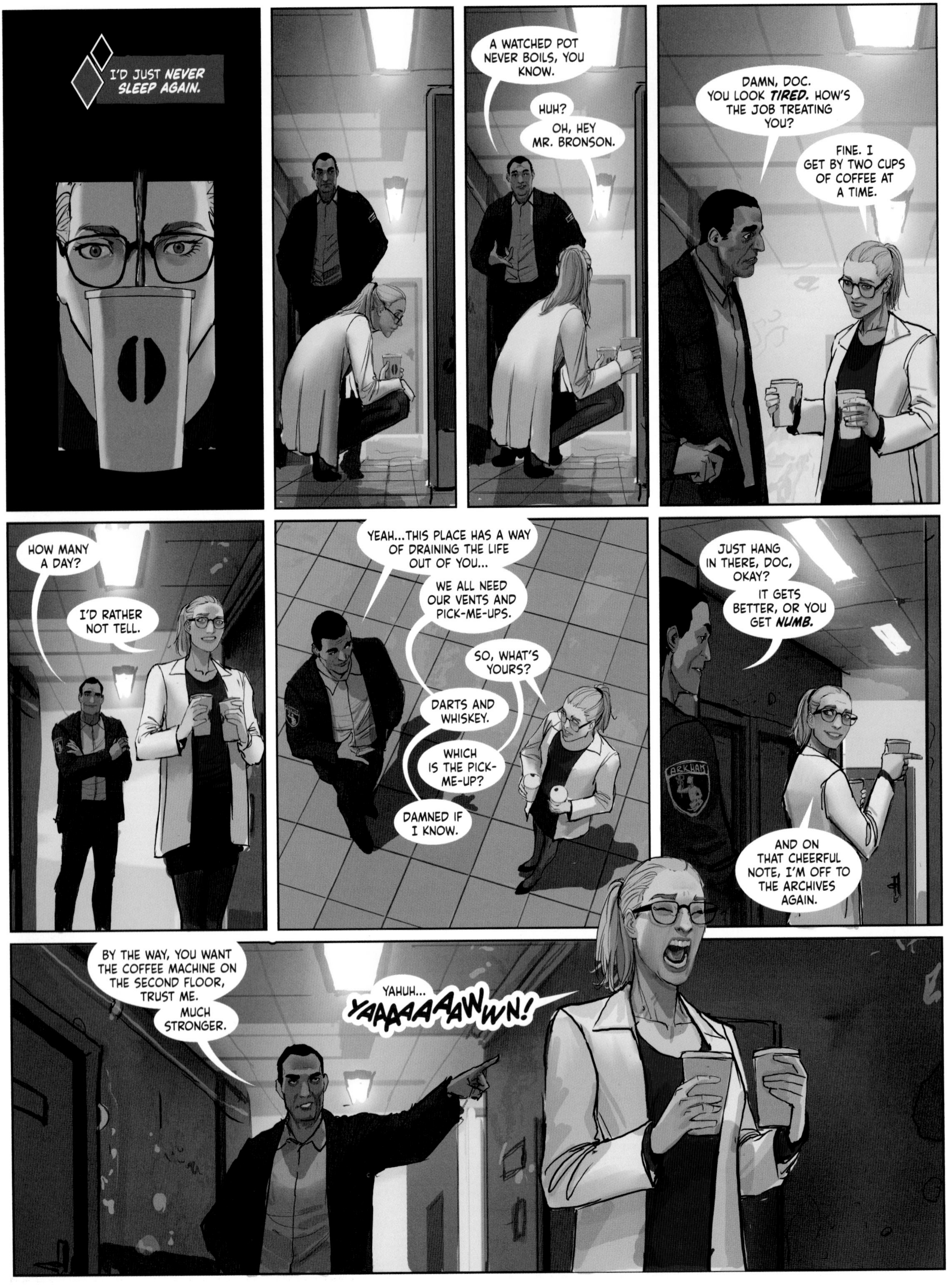
I'D JUST NEVER SLEEP AGAIN.
A WATCHED POT NEVER BOILS, YOU KNOW.
HUH? OH, HEY MR. BRONSON.
DAMN, DOC. YOU LOOK TIRED. HOW'S THE JOB TREATING YOU?
FINE. I GET BY TWO CUPS OF COFFEE AT A TIME.
HOW MANY A DAY?
I'D RATHER NOT TELL.
YEAH...THIS PLACE HAS A WAY OF DRAINING THE LIFE OUT OF YOU...
WE ALL NEED OUR VENTS AND PICK-ME-UPS.
SO, WHAT'S YOURS?
DARTS AND WHISKEY.
WHICH IS THE PICK-ME-UP?
DAMNED IF I KNOW.
JUST HANG IN THERE, DOC, OKAY?
IT GETS BETTER, OR YOU GET NUMB.
AND ON THAT CHEERFUL NOTE, I'M OFF TO THE ARCHIVES AGAIN.
ARKHAM
BY THE WAY, YOU WANT THE COFFEE MACHINE ON THE SECOND FLOOR, TRUST ME.
MUCH STRONGER.
YAHUH...
YAAAAAAWWN!

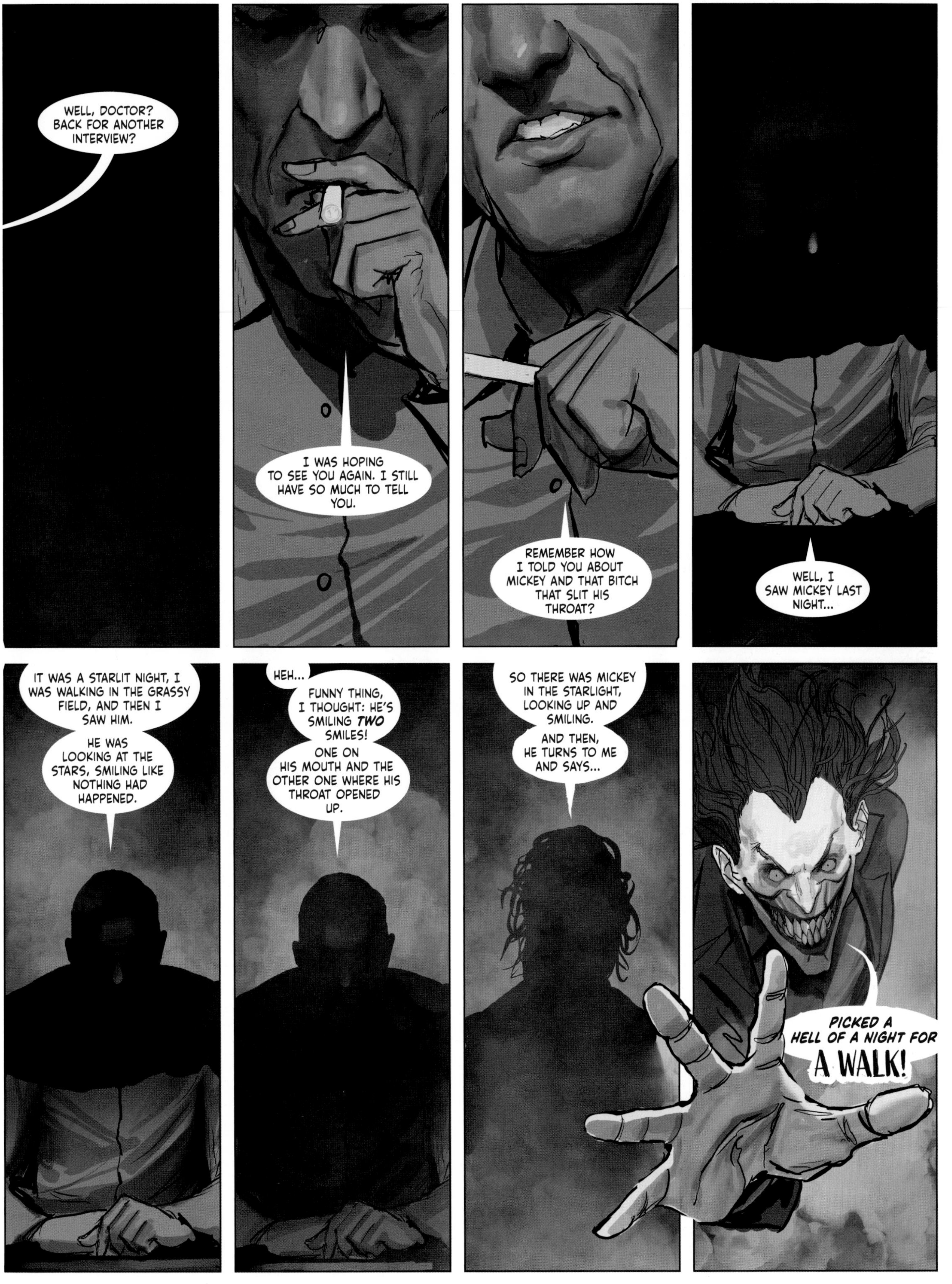
WELL, DOCTOR? BACK FOR ANOTHER INTERVIEW?
I WAS HOPING TO SEE YOU AGAIN. I STILL HAVE SO MUCH TO TELL YOU.
REMEMBER HOW I TOLD YOU ABOUT MICKEY AND THAT BITCH THAT SLIT HIS THROAT?
WELL, I SAW MICKEY LAST NIGHT...
IT WAS A STARLIT NIGHT, I WAS WALKING IN THE GRASSY FIELD, AND THEN I SAW HIM.
HE WAS LOOKING AT THE STARS, SMILING LIKE NOTHING HAD HAPPENED.
HEH...
FUNNY THING, I THOUGHT: HE'S SMILING *TWO* SMILES!
ONE ON HIS MOUTH AND THE OTHER ONE WHERE HIS THROAT OPENED UP.
SO THERE WAS MICKEY IN THE STARLIGHT, LOOKING UP AND SMILING.
AND THEN, HE TURNS TO ME AND SAYS...
PICKED A HELL OF A NIGHT FOR A WALK!

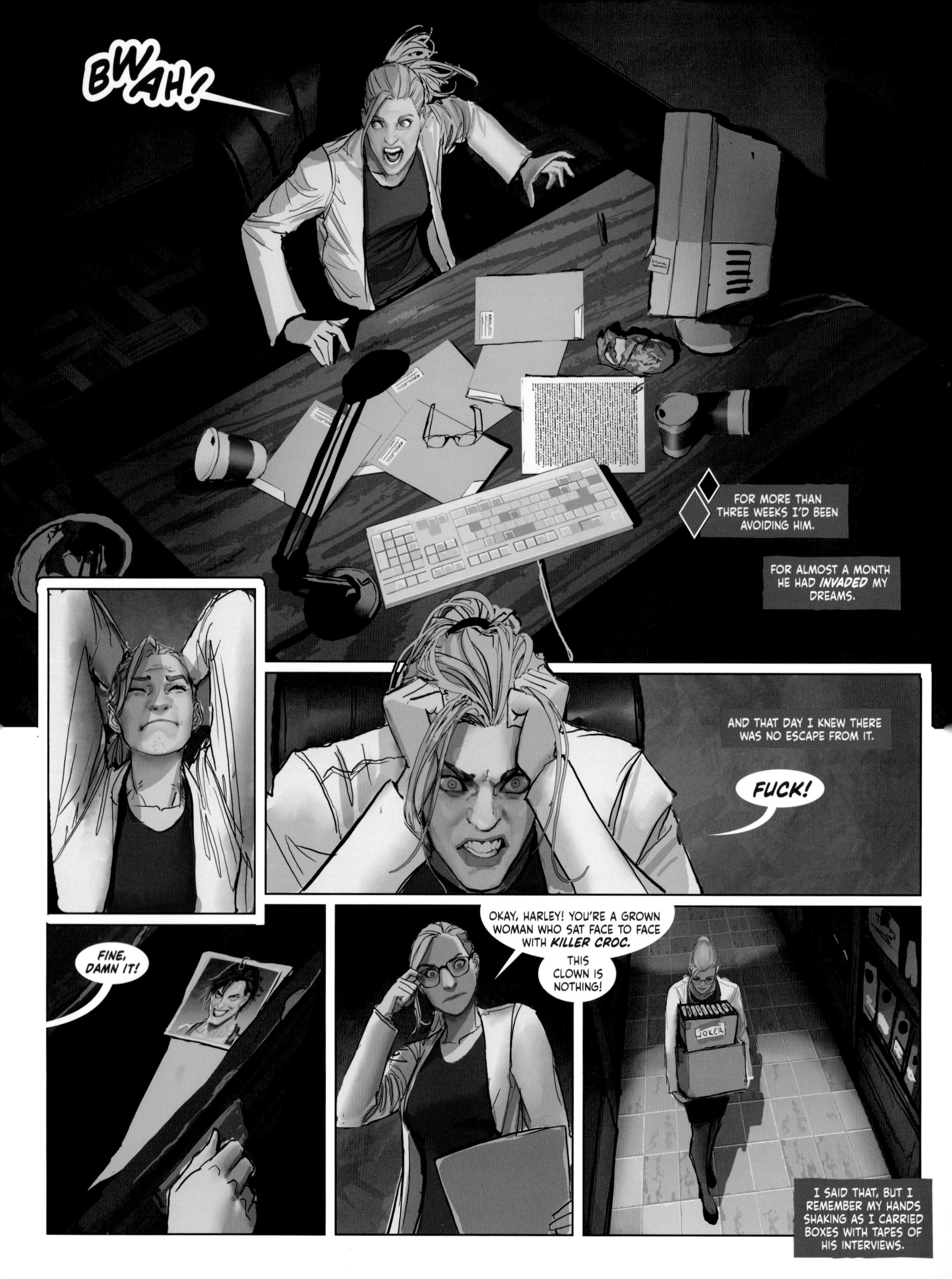
BWAH!
FOR MORE THAN THREE WEEKS I'D BEEN AVOIDING HIM.
FOR ALMOST A MONTH HE HAD *INVADED* MY DREAMS.
AND THAT DAY I KNEW THERE WAS NO ESCAPE FROM IT.
FUCK!
FINE, DAMN IT!
OKAY, HARLEY! YOU'RE A GROWN WOMAN WHO SAT FACE TO FACE WITH *KILLER CROC.*
THIS CLOWN IS NOTHING!
JOKER
I SAID THAT, BUT I REMEMBER MY HANDS SHAKING AS I CARRIED BOXES WITH TAPES OF HIS INTERVIEWS.

PUTTING THE FIRST TAPE IN WAS ITS OWN SPECIAL KIND OF NIGHTMARE.

BUT THEN, THE TAPE STARTED ROLLING AND IT ALL JUST FELT...

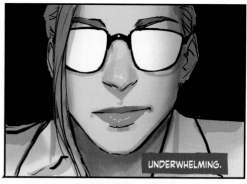

UNDERWHELMING.

MY *FAMILY*? IT'S A SAD STORY, REALLY. VICTIMS IN A *FIRE* DOWN AT THE DOCKS.

I GUESS, MY *REAL* FAMILY WAS THE CIRCUS THAT GAVE ME THE ROOF OVER MY HEAD.

IS THAT WHY YOU ADOPTED THE CLOWN IMAGE?

CLOWN? I WAS THE STRONGMAN!

THIS WAS WRONG. WHATEVER I SAW THAT NIGHT IN THE STREET, IT *WASN'T* THERE IN THOSE TAPES.

THIS WASN'T THE GRINNING MAN WITH THE COLD VOICE WHO HELD ME AT *GUNPOINT*. FOR A MOMENT I FOUND MYSELF QUESTIONING MY OWN MEMORIES: MAYBE I JUST SAW HIM IN A MORE TERRIFYING LIGHT? AFTER ALL, HE NEVER REALLY PULLED THAT TRIGGER.

BUT THEN, AS I KEPT WATCHING, I STARTED NOTICING IT.

SO, *"JOE,"* HOW DID YOU COME TO CRAFT THIS PERSONA OF THE JOKER?

JUST GONNA JUMP *RIGHT INTO* THAT ONE?

MY PREVIOUS SHRINKS WOULD USUALLY *BUTTER ME UP* BEFORE GOING THERE, BUT YOU...

YOU'RE A GO-GETTER, I *LIKE* THAT!

YOU SEE, I WAS A *CITY ORPHAN*. ONE OF *MANY* SPEWED OUT BY GOTHAM'S DARK ALLEYS.

IN A WAY I WAS *ADOPTED* BY THE MOB'S CHIEF HITMAN, JOHNNY "STITCHES" DENETTO.

I STARTED AS HIS EYES ON THE STREET AND GRADUATED TO BEING HIS "CLEANUP" ASSISTANT ON HITS.

THEN, ONE DAY, HE GETS INTO SOME BAD DEALINGS AND THE BOSSES WANT TO TAKE HIM OUT. TAKE US *BOTH* OUT.

SO, MY ONLY CHANCE TO *SURVIVE* WAS FOR ME TO GET GOOD WITH THE BOSSES, YOU KNOW.

SURVIVAL OF THE FITTEST AND ALL THAT.

HE NEVER SAW ME COMING. SO, THE BOSSES ASK ME, "WELL, KID? IS IT DONE?" AND I'M TRYING TO SOUND SMOOTH SO I GO, "ASK SAL THE MORTICIAN-- I LEFT OLD JOHNNY 'STITCHES' *IN STITCHES!*"

AND THE BOSSES WENT, "WHATCHA DO? MAKE HIM LAUGH? GET A LOAD OF THIS JOKER!" AND IT STUCK!

ONE VIDEO AFTER ANOTHER...

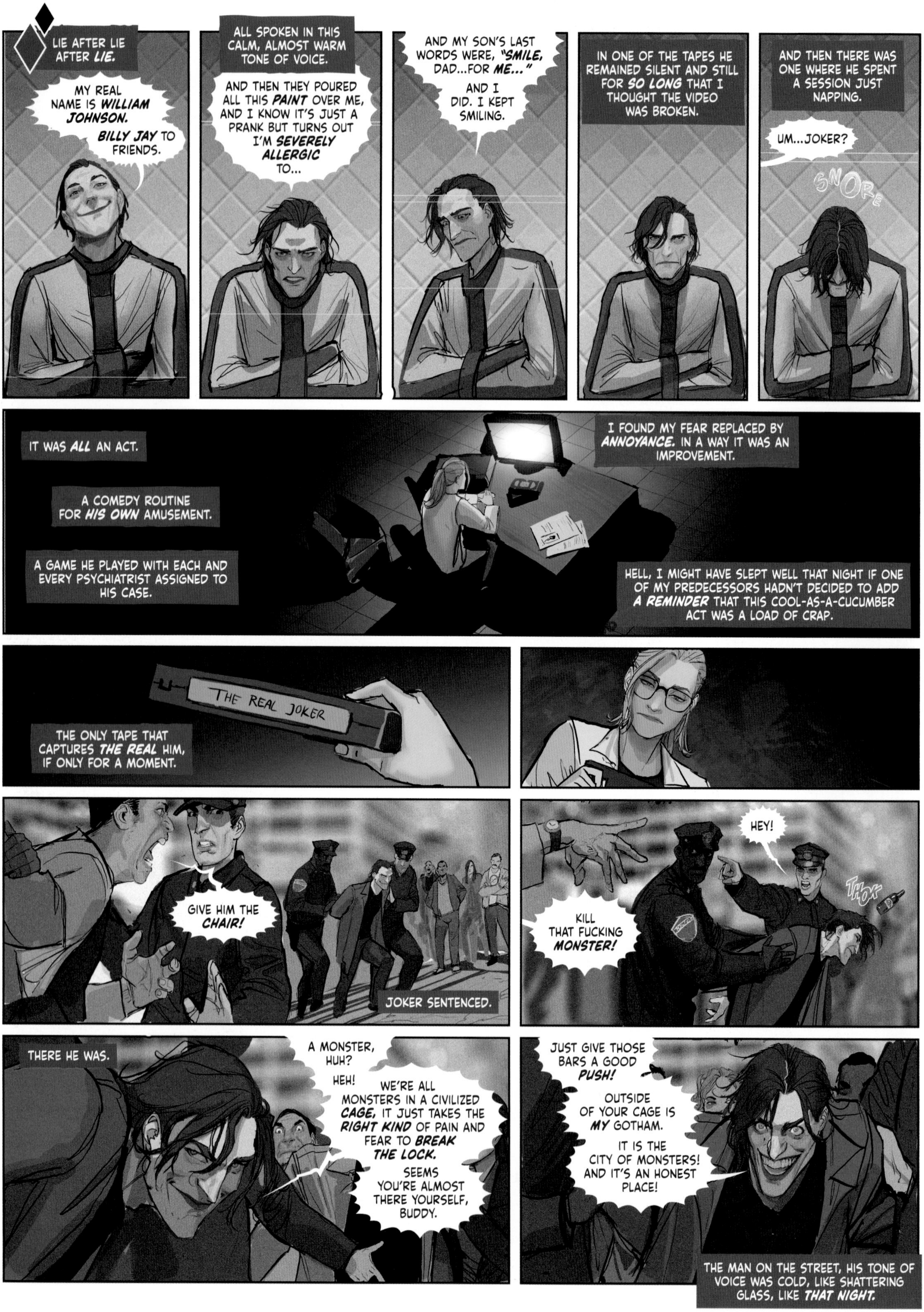

LIE AFTER LIE AFTER LIE.
MY REAL NAME IS WILLIAM JOHNSON.
BILLY JAY TO FRIENDS.
ALL SPOKEN IN THIS CALM, ALMOST WARM TONE OF VOICE.
AND THEN THEY POURED ALL THIS PAINT OVER ME, AND I KNOW IT'S JUST A PRANK BUT TURNS OUT I'M SEVERELY ALLERGIC TO...
AND MY SON'S LAST WORDS WERE, "SMILE, DAD...FOR ME..."
AND I DID. I KEPT SMILING.
IN ONE OF THE TAPES HE REMAINED SILENT AND STILL FOR SO LONG THAT I THOUGHT THE VIDEO WAS BROKEN.
AND THEN THERE WAS ONE WHERE HE SPENT A SESSION JUST NAPPING.
UM...JOKER?
SNORE
IT WAS ALL AN ACT.
A COMEDY ROUTINE FOR HIS OWN AMUSEMENT.
A GAME HE PLAYED WITH EACH AND EVERY PSYCHIATRIST ASSIGNED TO HIS CASE.
I FOUND MY FEAR REPLACED BY ANNOYANCE. IN A WAY IT WAS AN IMPROVEMENT.
HELL, I MIGHT HAVE SLEPT WELL THAT NIGHT IF ONE OF MY PREDECESSORS HADN'T DECIDED TO ADD A REMINDER THAT THIS COOL-AS-A-CUCUMBER ACT WAS A LOAD OF CRAP.
THE REAL JOKER
THE ONLY TAPE THAT CAPTURES THE REAL HIM, IF ONLY FOR A MOMENT.
GIVE HIM THE CHAIR!
JOKER SENTENCED.
HEY!
KILL THAT FUCKING MONSTER!
THOK
THERE HE WAS.
A MONSTER, HUH?
HEH!
WE'RE ALL MONSTERS IN A CIVILIZED CAGE, IT JUST TAKES THE RIGHT KIND OF PAIN AND FEAR TO BREAK THE LOCK.
SEEMS YOU'RE ALMOST THERE YOURSELF, BUDDY.
JUST GIVE THOSE BARS A GOOD PUSH!
OUTSIDE OF YOUR CAGE IS MY GOTHAM.
IT IS THE CITY OF MONSTERS! AND IT'S AN HONEST PLACE!
THE MAN ON THE STREET, HIS TONE OF VOICE WAS COLD, LIKE SHATTERING GLASS, LIKE THAT NIGHT.

BUT, MORE THAN THAT, IT WAS WHAT HE SAID.

WE'RE ALL MONSTERS IN A CIVILIZED *CAGE*, IT JUST TAKES THE *RIGHT KIND* OF PAIN AND FEAR TO *BREAK THE LOCK*.

SEEMS YOU'RE ALMOST THERE YOURSELF, BUDDY.

SO I BROKE *MY OATH* THAT DAY...BLEW HER BRAINS OUT...EMPTIED THE WHOLE DAMNED CLIP...SHIT LIKE THAT, IT SNAPS SOMETHING INSIDE OF YOU...YOU START SEEING THE WORLD *DIFFERENTLY*...

I *HAD* TO INTERVIEW HIM.

MORE THAN EVER, I KNEW THIS.

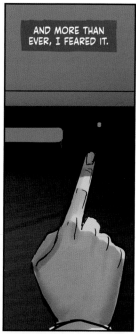

AND MORE THAN EVER, I FEARED IT.

AND WITH THAT FEAR, AND ALL THE WEIGHT OF MY THOUGHTS, MY DREAMS WORSENED TO A LEVEL I THOUGHT *UNIMAGINABLE*.

I SWEAR, I WAS NEVER *DELUSIONAL*, BUT... THERE WERE MOMENTS WHEN I COULD ALMOST SEE *THE MIST* GATHER IN MY WAKING HOURS.

AND WHEN ANYONE LAUGHED, *I FLINCHED*...

SO, I TURNED TO THE ONE PERSON I COULD TRUST, THE ONE PERSON THAT COULD HELP ME.

MOSTLY BECAUSE SHE HAD ACCESS TO THE *STRONGEST* KINDS OF PHARMACEUTICALS.

ALTHOUGH, BEFORE YOU DO THAT, I READ THIS BOOK ABOUT CRYSTALS...

NO CRYSTALS, NO DREAM CATCHERS, NO ROSARIES OR LUCKY CLOVERS. *PILLS, SHONDRA!*

HORSE TRANQUILIZERS, ELEPHANT DOWNERS! SOMETHING THAT WILL KNOCK ME THE HELL OUT FOR EIGHT HOURS OF HONEST-TO-GOD DREAMLESS SLEEP!

JOKER

JOKER

JOKER

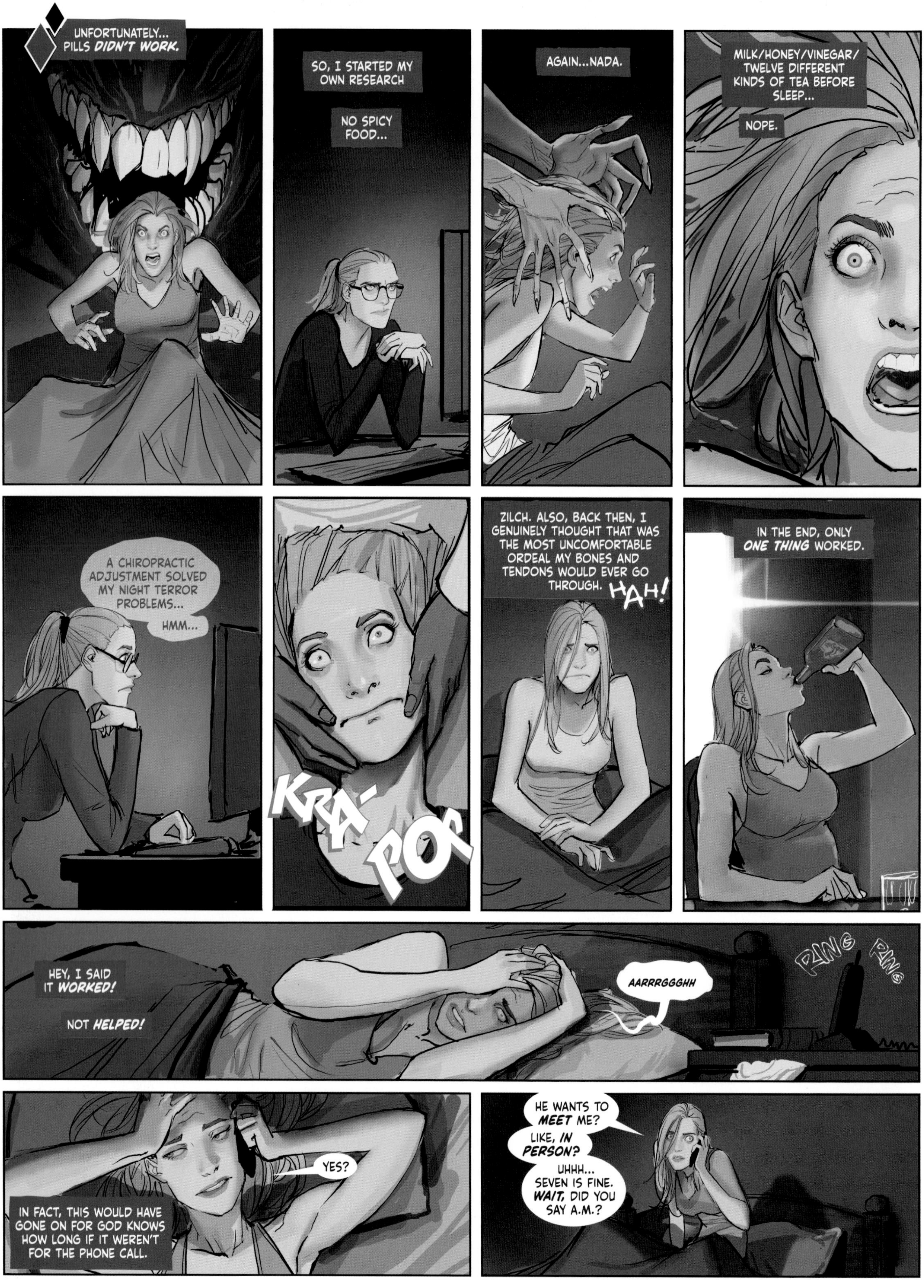
UNFORTUNATELY... PILLS *DIDN'T WORK.*
SO, I STARTED MY OWN RESEARCH
NO SPICY FOOD...
AGAIN...NADA.
MILK/HONEY/VINEGAR/ TWELVE DIFFERENT KINDS OF TEA BEFORE SLEEP...
NOPE.
A CHIROPRACTIC ADJUSTMENT SOLVED MY NIGHT TERROR PROBLEMS...
HMM...
KRA-POP
ZILCH. ALSO, BACK THEN, I GENUINELY THOUGHT THAT WAS THE MOST UNCOMFORTABLE ORDEAL MY BONES AND TENDONS WOULD EVER GO THROUGH.
HAH!
IN THE END, ONLY *ONE THING* WORKED.
HEY, I SAID IT *WORKED!*
NOT *HELPED!*
AARRRGGGHH
RING RING
YES?
IN FACT, THIS WOULD HAVE GONE ON FOR GOD KNOWS HOW LONG IF IT WEREN'T FOR THE PHONE CALL.
HE WANTS TO *MEET* ME?
LIKE, *IN PERSON?*
UHHH... SEVEN IS FINE. *WAIT,* DID YOU SAY A.M.?

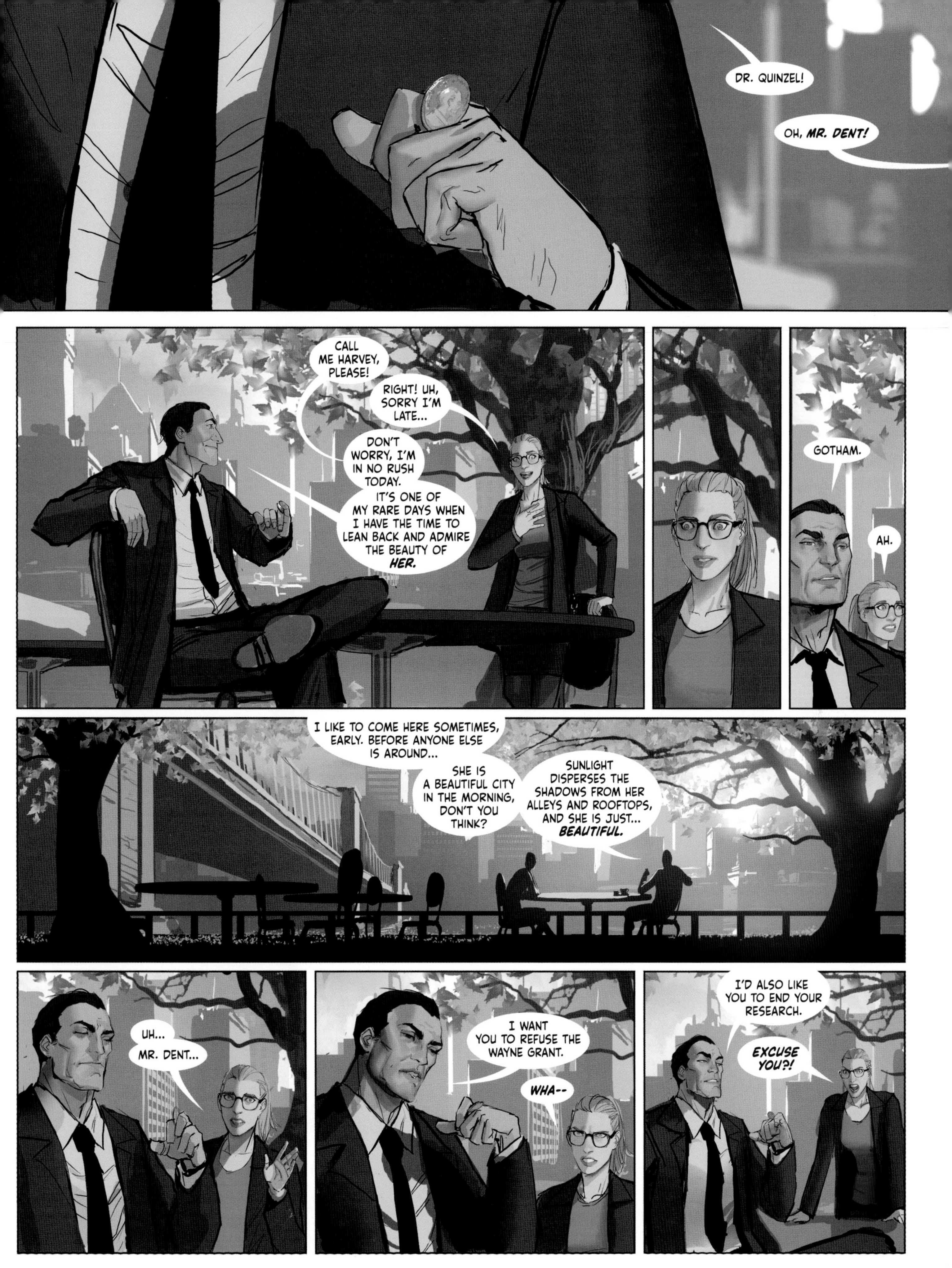
DR. QUINZEL!
OH, MR. DENT!
CALL ME HARVEY, PLEASE!
RIGHT! UH, SORRY I'M LATE...
DON'T WORRY, I'M IN NO RUSH TODAY.
IT'S ONE OF MY RARE DAYS WHEN I HAVE THE TIME TO LEAN BACK AND ADMIRE THE BEAUTY OF *HER.*
GOTHAM.
AH.
I LIKE TO COME HERE SOMETIMES, EARLY. BEFORE ANYONE ELSE IS AROUND...
SHE IS A BEAUTIFUL CITY IN THE MORNING, DON'T YOU THINK?
SUNLIGHT DISPERSES THE SHADOWS FROM HER ALLEYS AND ROOFTOPS, AND SHE IS JUST... *BEAUTIFUL.*
UH... MR. DENT...
I WANT YOU TO REFUSE THE WAYNE GRANT.
WHA--
I'D ALSO LIKE YOU TO END YOUR RESEARCH.
EXCUSE YOU?!

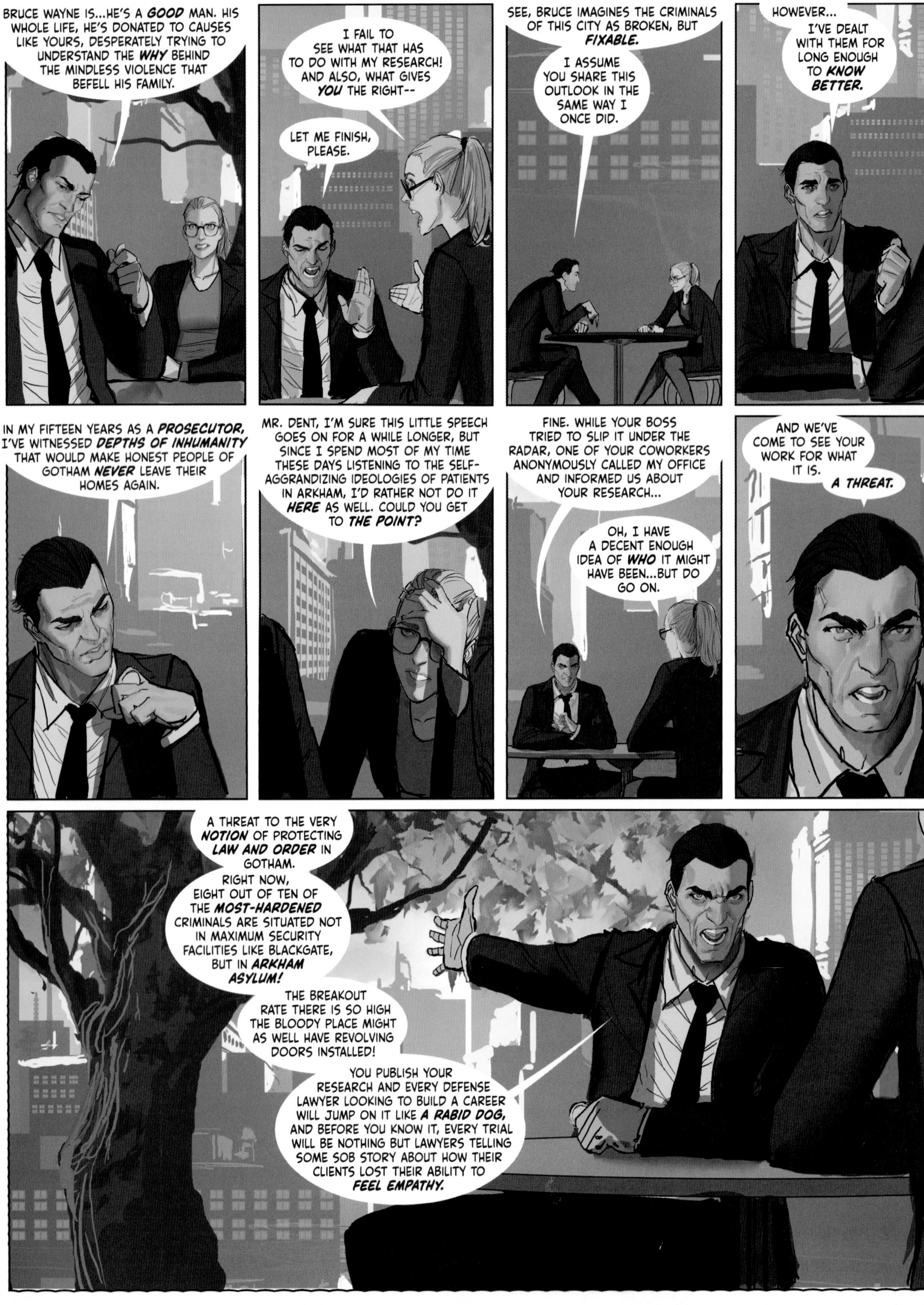
BRUCE WAYNE IS...HE'S A GOOD MAN. HIS WHOLE LIFE, HE'S DONATED TO CAUSES LIKE YOURS, DESPERATELY TRYING TO UNDERSTAND THE WHY BEHIND THE MINDLESS VIOLENCE THAT BEFELL HIS FAMILY.
I FAIL TO SEE WHAT THAT HAS TO DO WITH MY RESEARCH! AND ALSO, WHAT GIVES YOU THE RIGHT--
LET ME FINISH, PLEASE.
SEE, BRUCE IMAGINES THE CRIMINALS OF THIS CITY AS BROKEN, BUT FIXABLE.
I ASSUME YOU SHARE THIS OUTLOOK IN THE SAME WAY I ONCE DID.
HOWEVER...
I'VE DEALT WITH THEM FOR LONG ENOUGH TO KNOW BETTER.
IN MY FIFTEEN YEARS AS A PROSECUTOR, I'VE WITNESSED DEPTHS OF INHUMANITY THAT WOULD MAKE HONEST PEOPLE OF GOTHAM NEVER LEAVE THEIR HOMES AGAIN.
MR. DENT, I'M SURE THIS LITTLE SPEECH GOES ON FOR A WHILE LONGER, BUT SINCE I SPEND MOST OF MY TIME THESE DAYS LISTENING TO THE SELF-AGGRANDIZING IDEOLOGIES OF PATIENTS IN ARKHAM, I'D RATHER NOT DO IT HERE AS WELL. COULD YOU GET TO THE POINT?
FINE. WHILE YOUR BOSS TRIED TO SLIP IT UNDER THE RADAR, ONE OF YOUR COWORKERS ANONYMOUSLY CALLED MY OFFICE AND INFORMED US ABOUT YOUR RESEARCH...
OH, I HAVE A DECENT ENOUGH IDEA OF WHO IT MIGHT HAVE BEEN...BUT DO GO ON.
AND WE'VE COME TO SEE YOUR WORK FOR WHAT IT IS.
A THREAT.
A THREAT TO THE VERY NOTION OF PROTECTING LAW AND ORDER IN GOTHAM.
RIGHT NOW, EIGHT OUT OF TEN OF THE MOST-HARDENED CRIMINALS ARE SITUATED NOT IN MAXIMUM SECURITY FACILITIES LIKE BLACKGATE, BUT IN ARKHAM ASYLUM!
THE BREAKOUT RATE THERE IS SO HIGH THE BLOODY PLACE MIGHT AS WELL HAVE REVOLVING DOORS INSTALLED!
YOU PUBLISH YOUR RESEARCH AND EVERY DEFENSE LAWYER LOOKING TO BUILD A CAREER WILL JUMP ON IT LIKE A RABID DOG, AND BEFORE YOU KNOW IT, EVERY TRIAL WILL BE NOTHING BUT LAWYERS TELLING SOME SOB STORY ABOUT HOW THEIR CLIENTS LOST THEIR ABILITY TO FEEL EMPATHY.

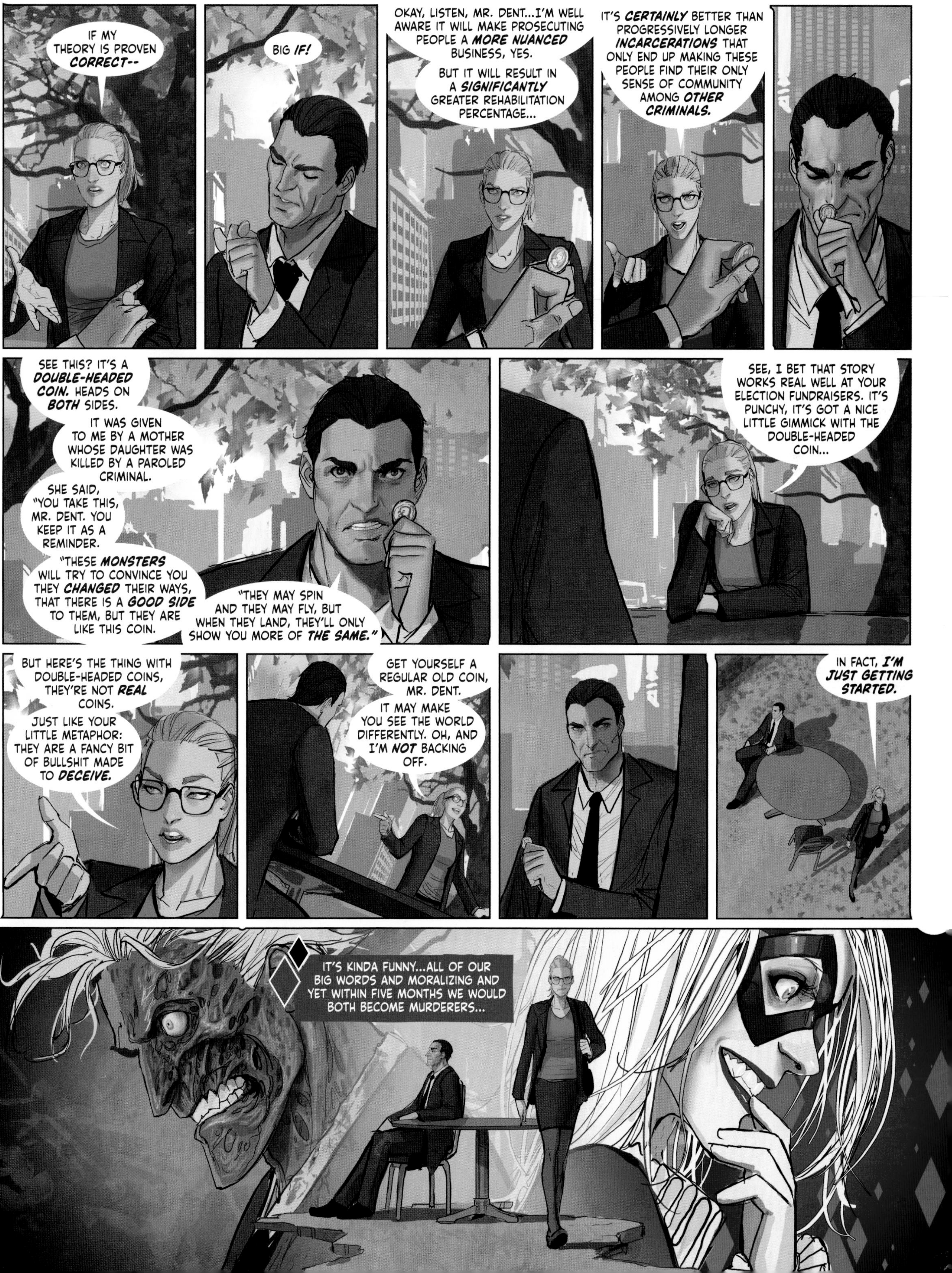

IF MY THEORY IS PROVEN CORRECT--
BIG IF!
OKAY, LISTEN, MR. DENT...I'M WELL AWARE IT WILL MAKE PROSECUTING PEOPLE A MORE NUANCED BUSINESS, YES.
BUT IT WILL RESULT IN A SIGNIFICANTLY GREATER REHABILITATION PERCENTAGE...
IT'S CERTAINLY BETTER THAN PROGRESSIVELY LONGER INCARCERATIONS THAT ONLY END UP MAKING THESE PEOPLE FIND THEIR ONLY SENSE OF COMMUNITY AMONG OTHER CRIMINALS.
SEE THIS? IT'S A DOUBLE-HEADED COIN. HEADS ON BOTH SIDES.
IT WAS GIVEN TO ME BY A MOTHER WHOSE DAUGHTER WAS KILLED BY A PAROLED CRIMINAL.
SHE SAID, "YOU TAKE THIS, MR. DENT. YOU KEEP IT AS A REMINDER.
"THESE MONSTERS WILL TRY TO CONVINCE YOU THEY CHANGED THEIR WAYS, THAT THERE IS A GOOD SIDE TO THEM, BUT THEY ARE LIKE THIS COIN.
"THEY MAY SPIN AND THEY MAY FLY, BUT WHEN THEY LAND, THEY'LL ONLY SHOW YOU MORE OF THE SAME."
SEE, I BET THAT STORY WORKS REAL WELL AT YOUR ELECTION FUNDRAISERS. IT'S PUNCHY, IT'S GOT A NICE LITTLE GIMMICK WITH THE DOUBLE-HEADED COIN...
BUT HERE'S THE THING WITH DOUBLE-HEADED COINS, THEY'RE NOT REAL COINS.
JUST LIKE YOUR LITTLE METAPHOR: THEY ARE A FANCY BIT OF BULLSHIT MADE TO DECEIVE.
GET YOURSELF A REGULAR OLD COIN, MR. DENT.
IT MAY MAKE YOU SEE THE WORLD DIFFERENTLY. OH, AND I'M NOT BACKING OFF.
IN FACT, I'M JUST GETTING STARTED.
IT'S KINDA FUNNY...ALL OF OUR BIG WORDS AND MORALIZING AND YET WITHIN FIVE MONTHS WE WOULD BOTH BECOME MURDERERS...

THAT DAY, HOWEVER, WHILE NOT QUITE *MURDEROUS*, I DID EVER-SO-BRIEFLY ENTERTAINING SOME VIOLENT FANTASIES FEATURING THE ESTEEMED MR. DENT.

IT WAS THE SMUG TONE WITH WHICH HE SIMPLY *DEMANDED* I ABANDON MY WORK.

IT *INFURIATED* ME IN WAYS I NEVER THOUGHT POSSIBLE.

HE'S DOWN THE HALL. YOU CAN'T MISS IT.

WE KEEP HIM SEPARATED FROM THE REST OF THEM AS HE'S GOT A TENDENCY TO START SHIT.

AND SO, DRIVEN BY THIS RAGE AND BARELY SUPPRESSED TIDE OF PROFANITY ADDRESSED TO HARVEY DENT, I THREW *ALL CAUTION TO THE WIND.*

I HAD A JOB TO DO.

I MEAN, FOR ALL I KNEW HE COULD BE *THE ONE...*

THE *PERFECT* CANDIDATE FOR MY STUDY.

CALL IF YOU NEED ME.

THANK YOU, MR. BRONSON.

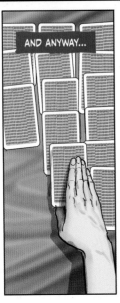

AND ANYWAY...

IT'D BEEN OVER A MONTH.

SURELY HE WOULDN'T REMEMBER *ME*.

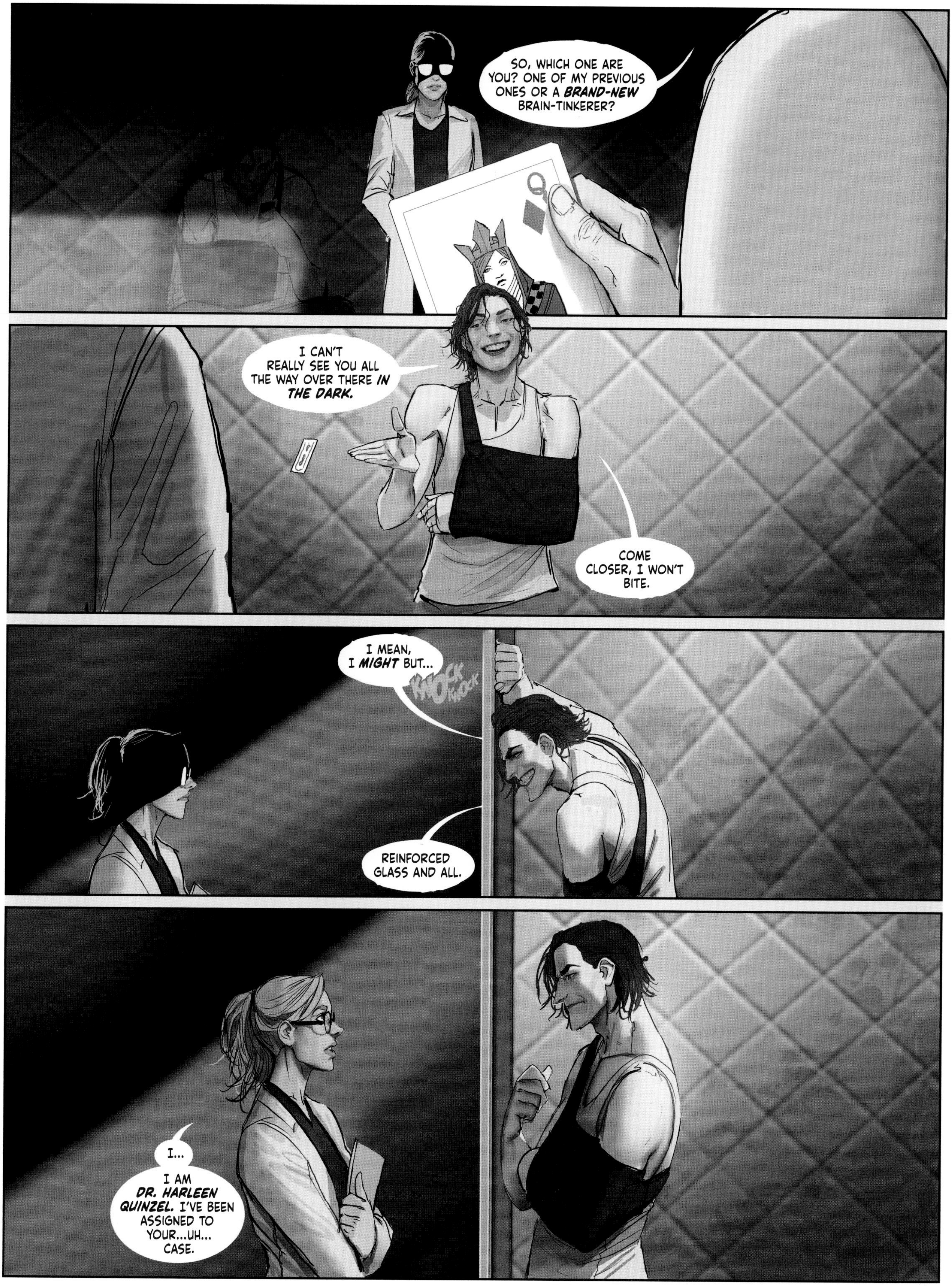
SO, WHICH ONE ARE YOU? ONE OF MY PREVIOUS ONES OR A BRAND-NEW BRAIN-TINKERER?
I CAN'T REALLY SEE YOU ALL THE WAY OVER THERE IN THE DARK.
COME CLOSER, I WON'T BITE.
I MEAN, I MIGHT BUT...
KNOCK KNOCK
REINFORCED GLASS AND ALL.
I...
I AM DR. HARLEEN QUINZEL. I'VE BEEN ASSIGNED TO YOUR...UH... CASE.

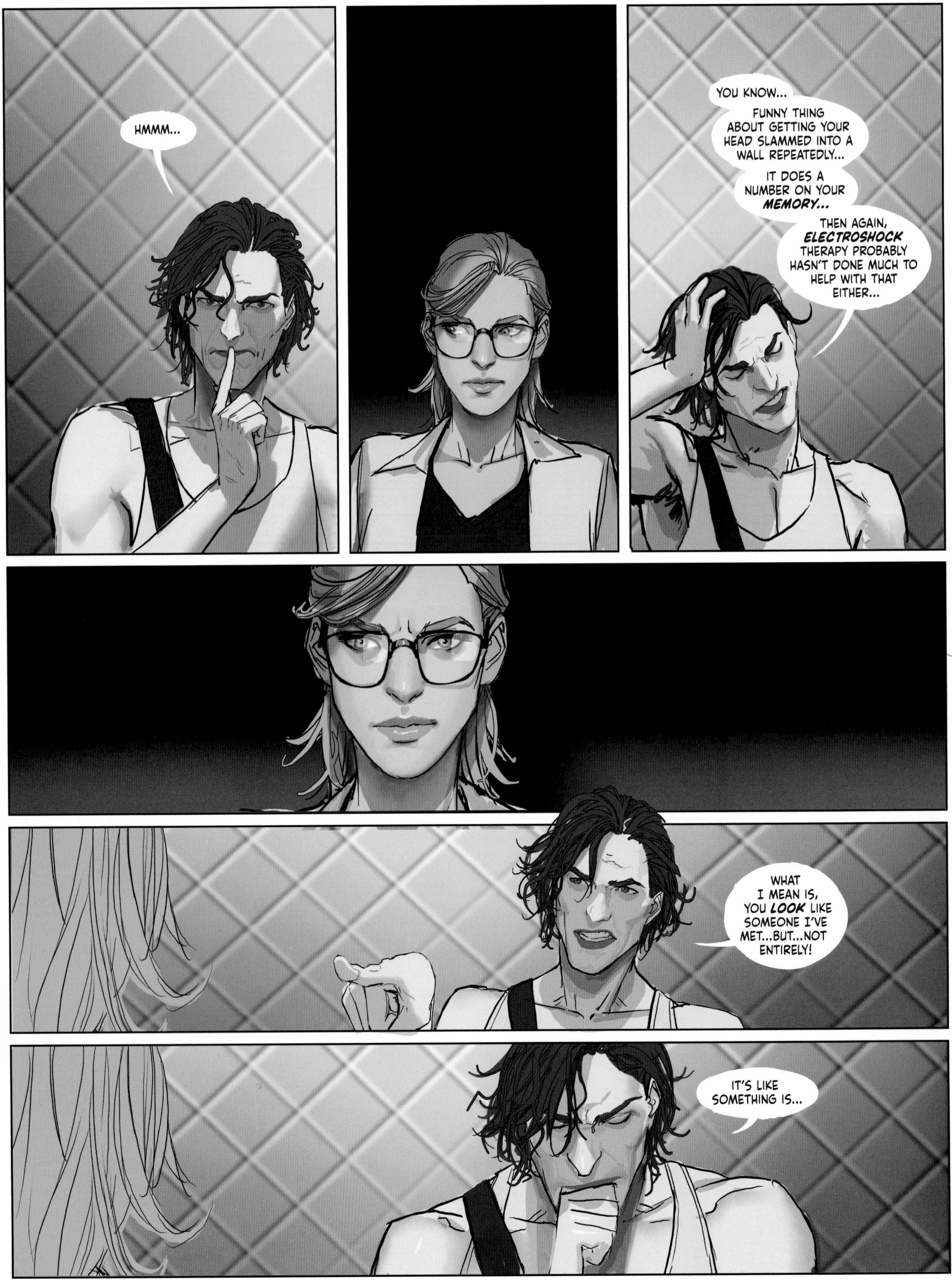
HMMM...
YOU KNOW...
FUNNY THING ABOUT GETTING YOUR HEAD SLAMMED INTO A WALL REPEATEDLY...
IT DOES A NUMBER ON YOUR MEMORY...
THEN AGAIN, ELECTROSHOCK THERAPY PROBABLY HASN'T DONE MUCH TO HELP WITH THAT EITHER...
WHAT I MEAN IS, YOU LOOK LIKE SOMEONE I'VE MET...BUT...NOT ENTIRELY!
IT'S LIKE SOMETHING IS...

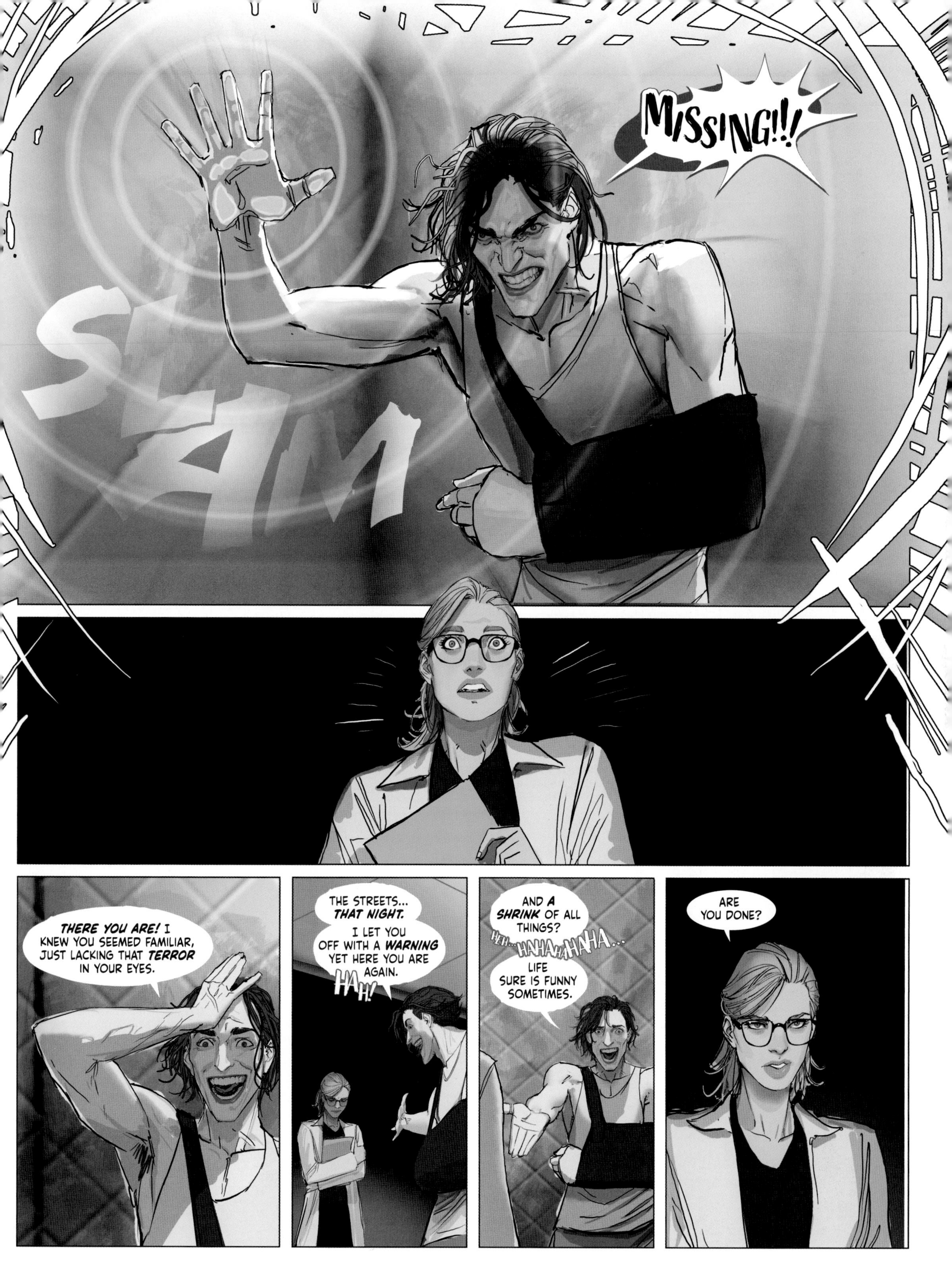

MISSING!!!
SLAM
THERE YOU ARE! I KNEW YOU SEEMED FAMILIAR, JUST LACKING THAT TERROR IN YOUR EYES.
THE STREETS... THAT NIGHT.
I LET YOU OFF WITH A WARNING YET HERE YOU ARE AGAIN.
HAH!
AND A SHRINK OF ALL THINGS?
HEH...HAHAHAHAHA...
LIFE SURE IS FUNNY SOMETIMES.
ARE YOU DONE?

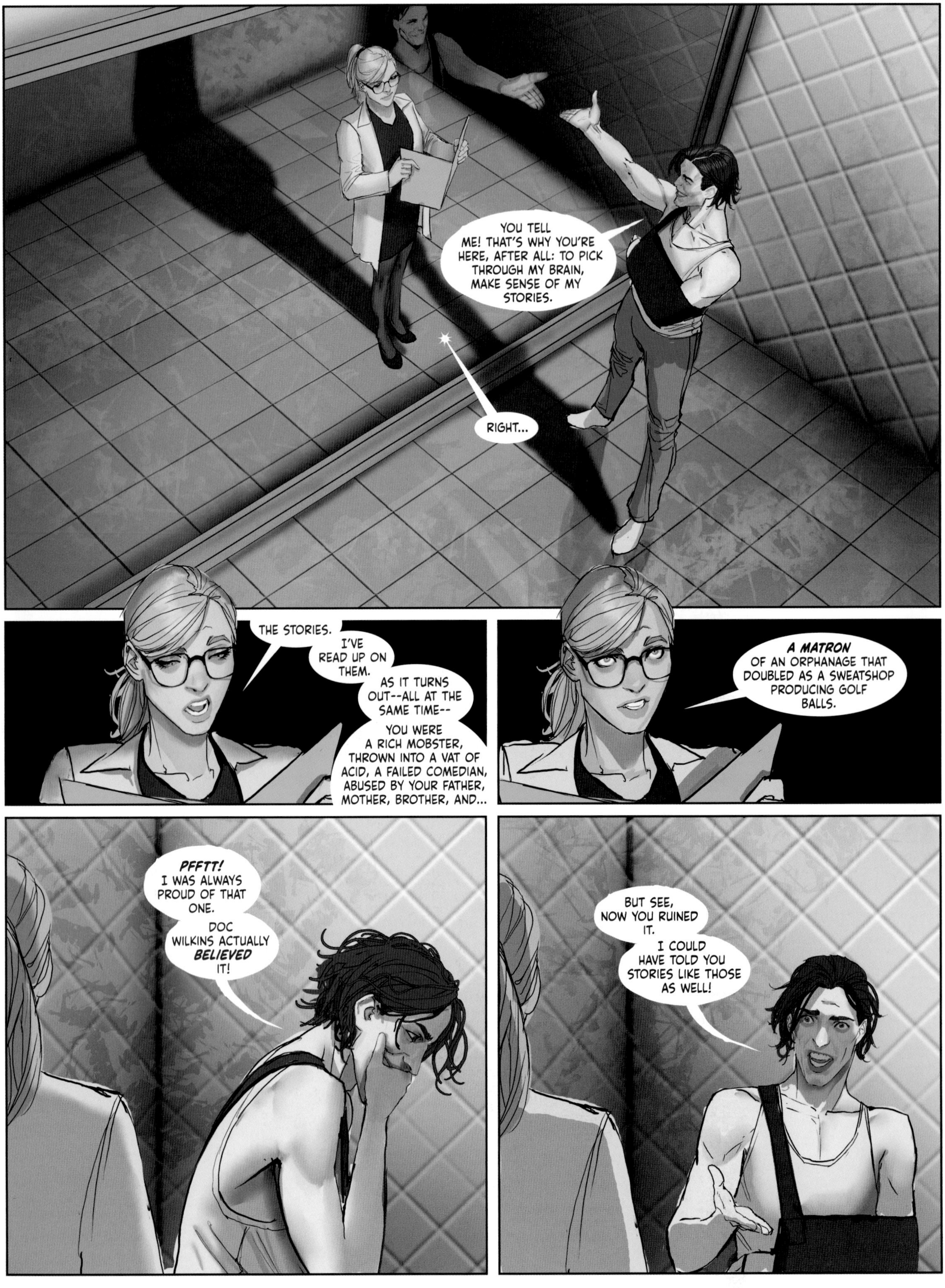
YOU TELL ME! THAT'S WHY YOU'RE HERE, AFTER ALL: TO PICK THROUGH MY BRAIN, MAKE SENSE OF MY STORIES.
RIGHT...
THE STORIES.
I'VE READ UP ON THEM.
AS IT TURNS OUT--ALL AT THE SAME TIME--
YOU WERE A RICH MOBSTER, THROWN INTO A VAT OF ACID, A FAILED COMEDIAN, ABUSED BY YOUR FATHER, MOTHER, BROTHER, AND...
A MATRON OF AN ORPHANAGE THAT DOUBLED AS A SWEATSHOP PRODUCING GOLF BALLS.
PFFTT! I WAS ALWAYS PROUD OF THAT ONE.
DOC WILKINS ACTUALLY BELIEVED IT!
BUT SEE, NOW YOU RUINED IT.
I COULD HAVE TOLD YOU STORIES LIKE THOSE AS WELL!

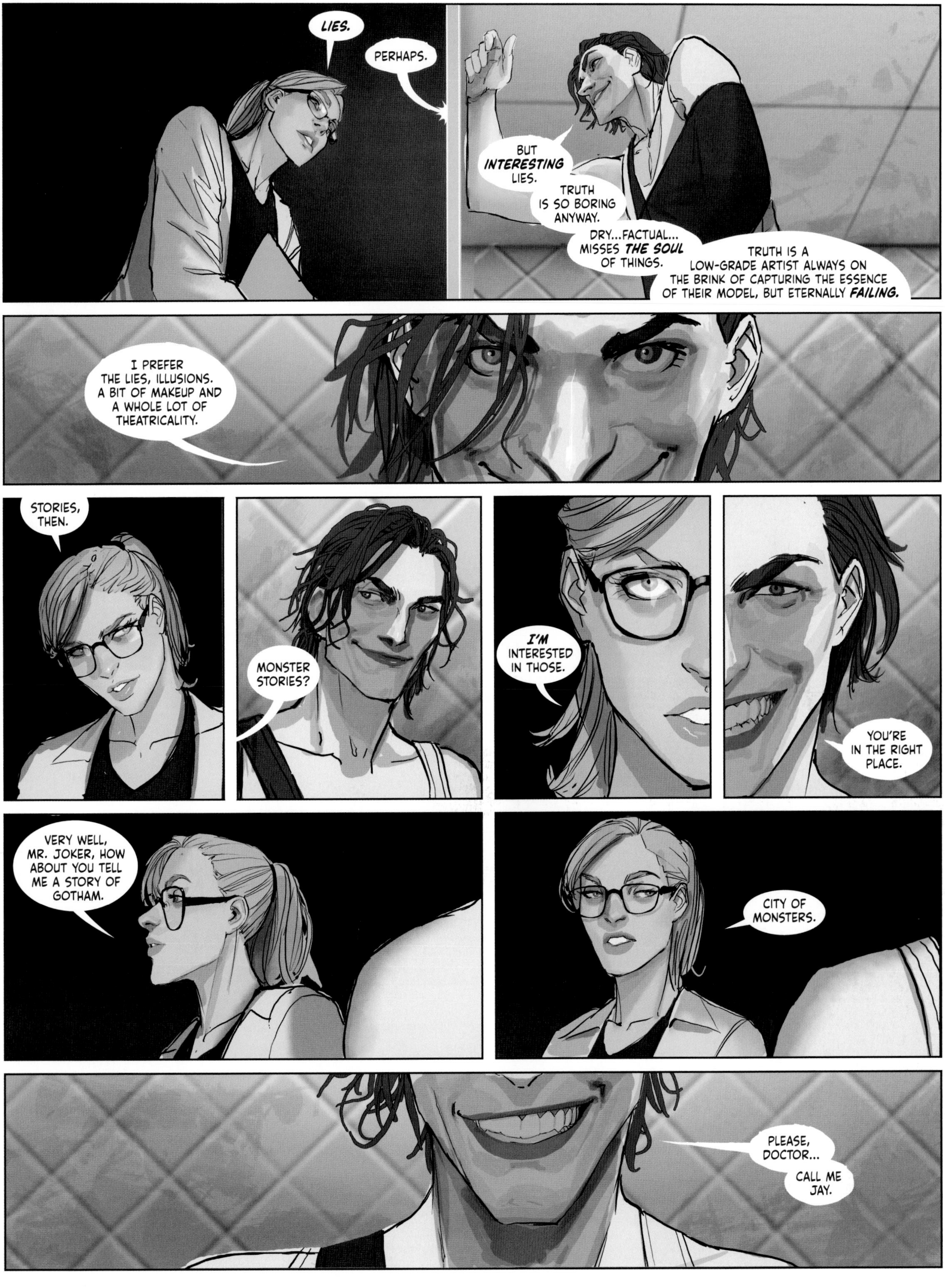
LIES.
PERHAPS.
BUT *INTERESTING* LIES.
TRUTH IS SO BORING ANYWAY.
DRY...FACTUAL... MISSES *THE SOUL* OF THINGS.
TRUTH IS A LOW-GRADE ARTIST ALWAYS ON THE BRINK OF CAPTURING THE ESSENCE OF THEIR MODEL, BUT ETERNALLY *FAILING.*
I PREFER THE LIES, ILLUSIONS. A BIT OF MAKEUP AND A WHOLE LOT OF THEATRICALITY.
STORIES, THEN.
MONSTER STORIES?
I'M INTERESTED IN THOSE.
YOU'RE IN THE RIGHT PLACE.
VERY WELL, MR. JOKER, HOW ABOUT YOU TELL ME A STORY OF GOTHAM.
CITY OF MONSTERS.
PLEASE, DOCTOR...
CALL ME JAY.

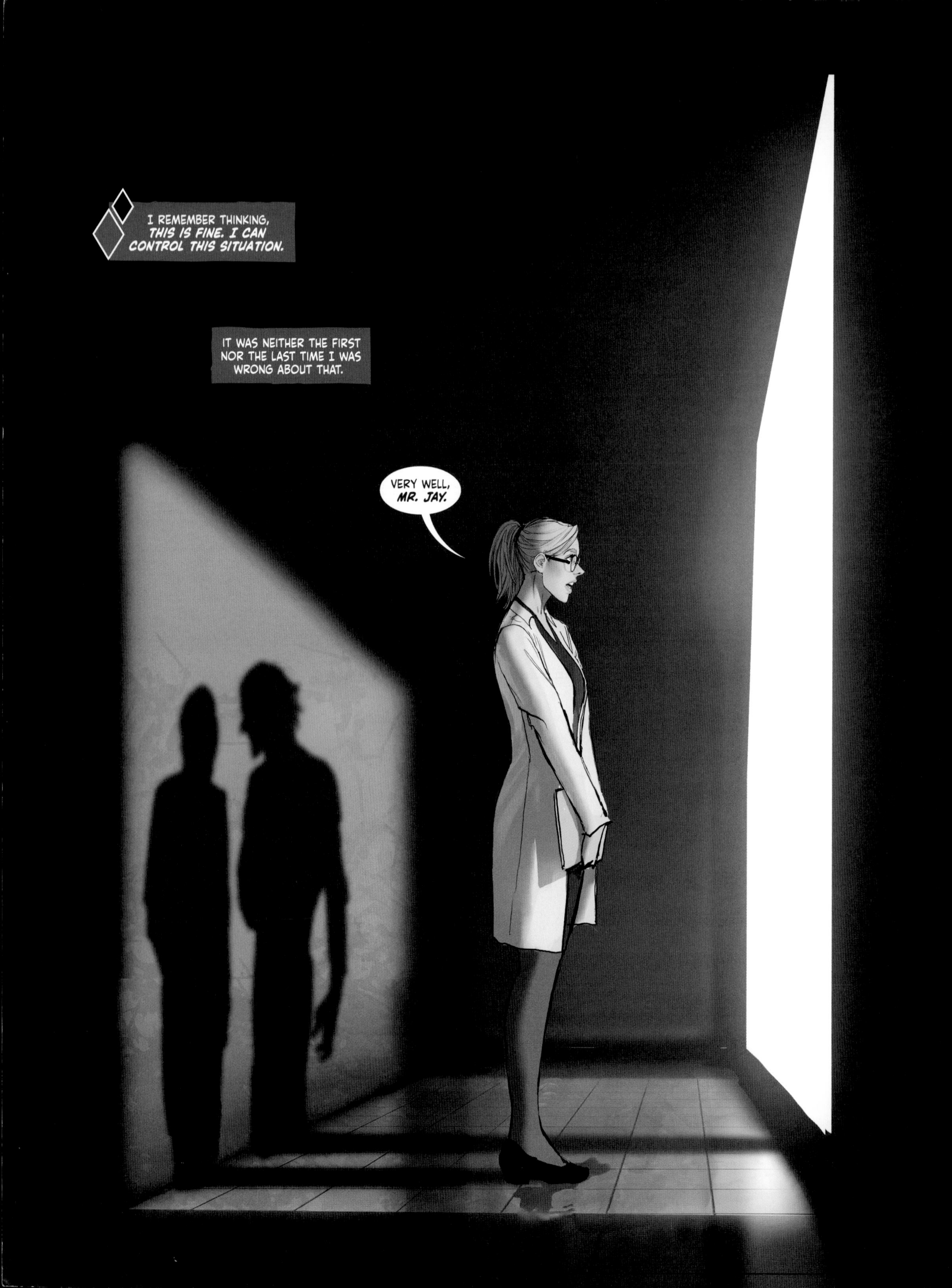
I REMEMBER THINKING, THIS IS FINE. I CAN CONTROL THIS SITUATION.
IT WAS NEITHER THE FIRST NOR THE LAST TIME I WAS WRONG ABOUT THAT.
VERY WELL, MR. JAY.

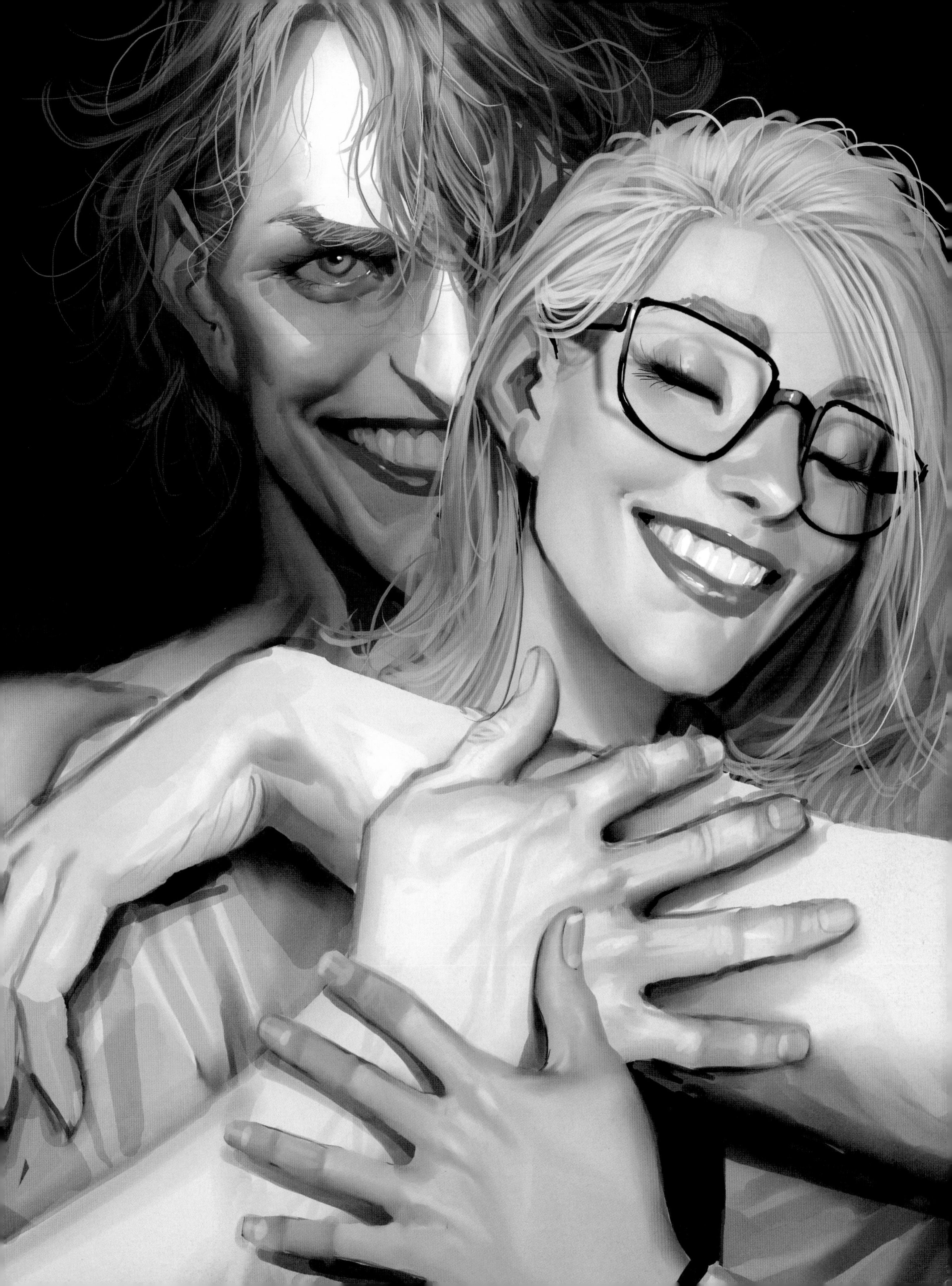

BOOK TWO

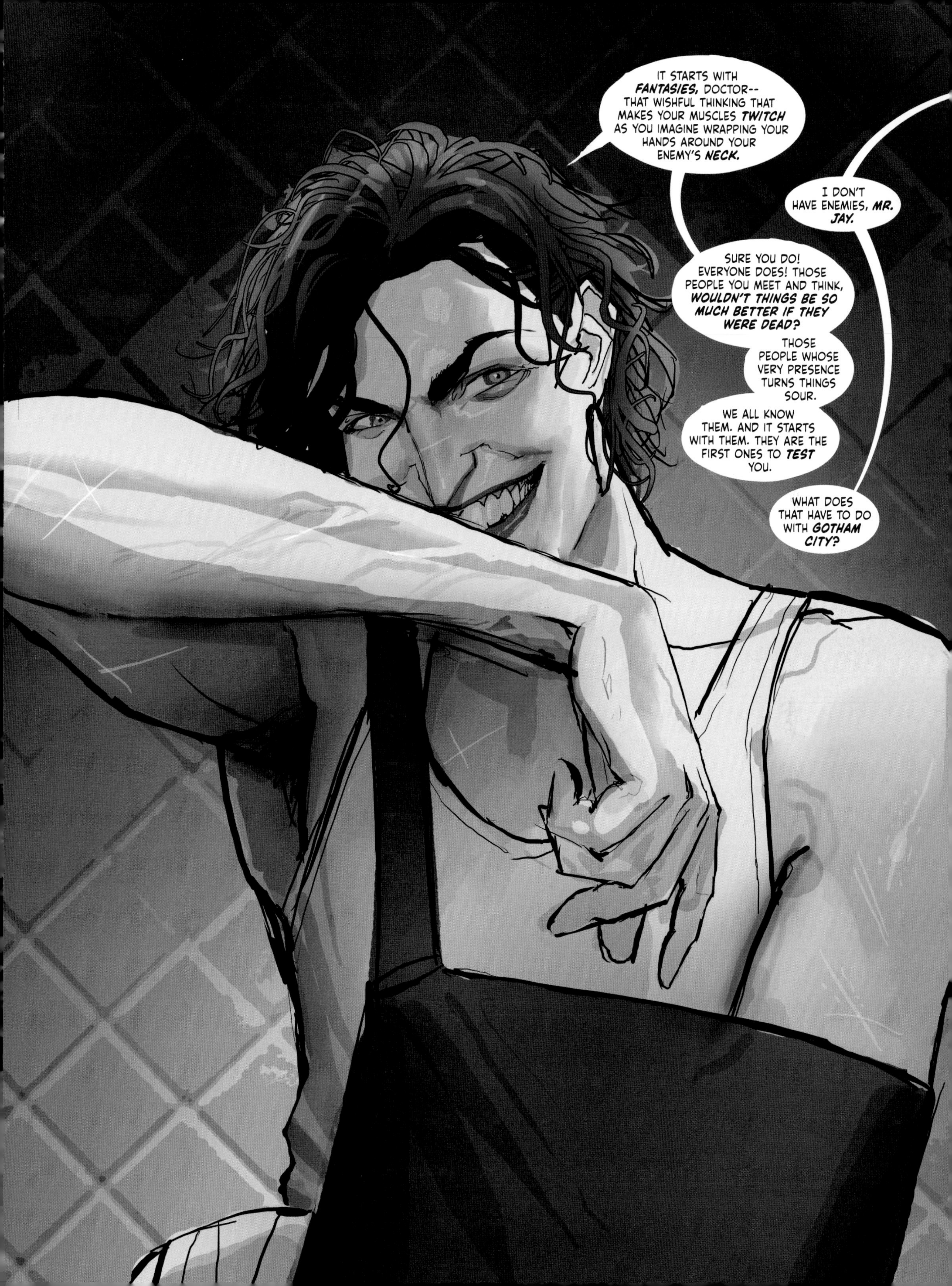
IT STARTS WITH **FANTASIES,** DOCTOR-- THAT WISHFUL THINKING THAT MAKES YOUR MUSCLES **TWITCH** AS YOU IMAGINE WRAPPING YOUR HANDS AROUND YOUR ENEMY'S **NECK.**
I DON'T HAVE ENEMIES, **MR. JAY.**
SURE YOU DO! EVERYONE DOES! THOSE PEOPLE YOU MEET AND THINK, ***WOULDN'T THINGS BE SO MUCH BETTER IF THEY WERE DEAD?***
THOSE PEOPLE WHOSE VERY PRESENCE TURNS THINGS SOUR.
WE ALL KNOW THEM. AND IT STARTS WITH THEM. THEY ARE THE FIRST ONES TO **TEST** YOU.
WHAT DOES THAT HAVE TO DO WITH **GOTHAM CITY?**

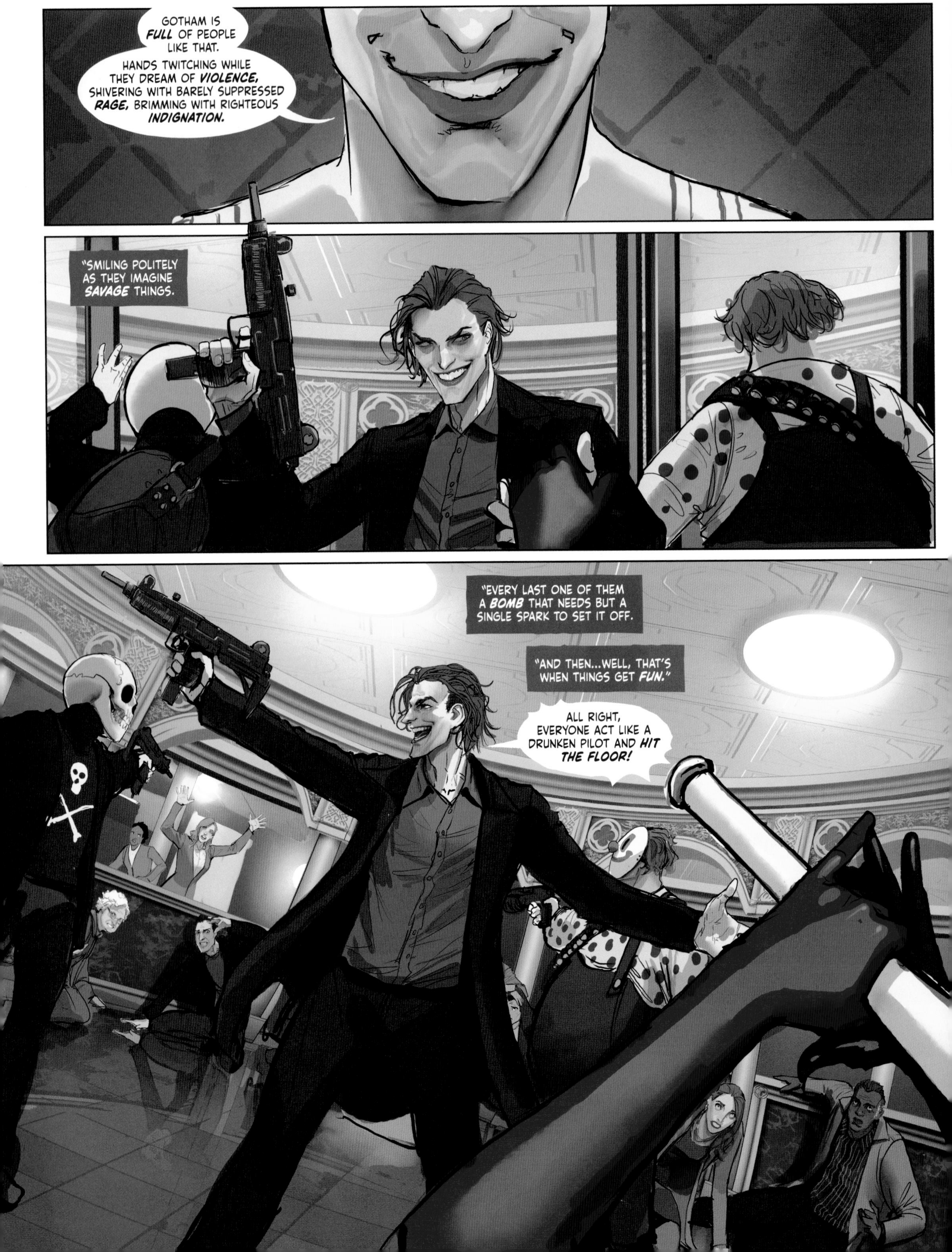
GOTHAM IS FULL OF PEOPLE LIKE THAT.
HANDS TWITCHING WHILE THEY DREAM OF VIOLENCE, SHIVERING WITH BARELY SUPPRESSED RAGE, BRIMMING WITH RIGHTEOUS INDIGNATION.
"SMILING POLITELY AS THEY IMAGINE SAVAGE THINGS.
"EVERY LAST ONE OF THEM A BOMB THAT NEEDS BUT A SINGLE SPARK TO SET IT OFF.
"AND THEN...WELL, THAT'S WHEN THINGS GET FUN."
ALL RIGHT, EVERYONE ACT LIKE A DRUNKEN PILOT AND HIT THE FLOOR!

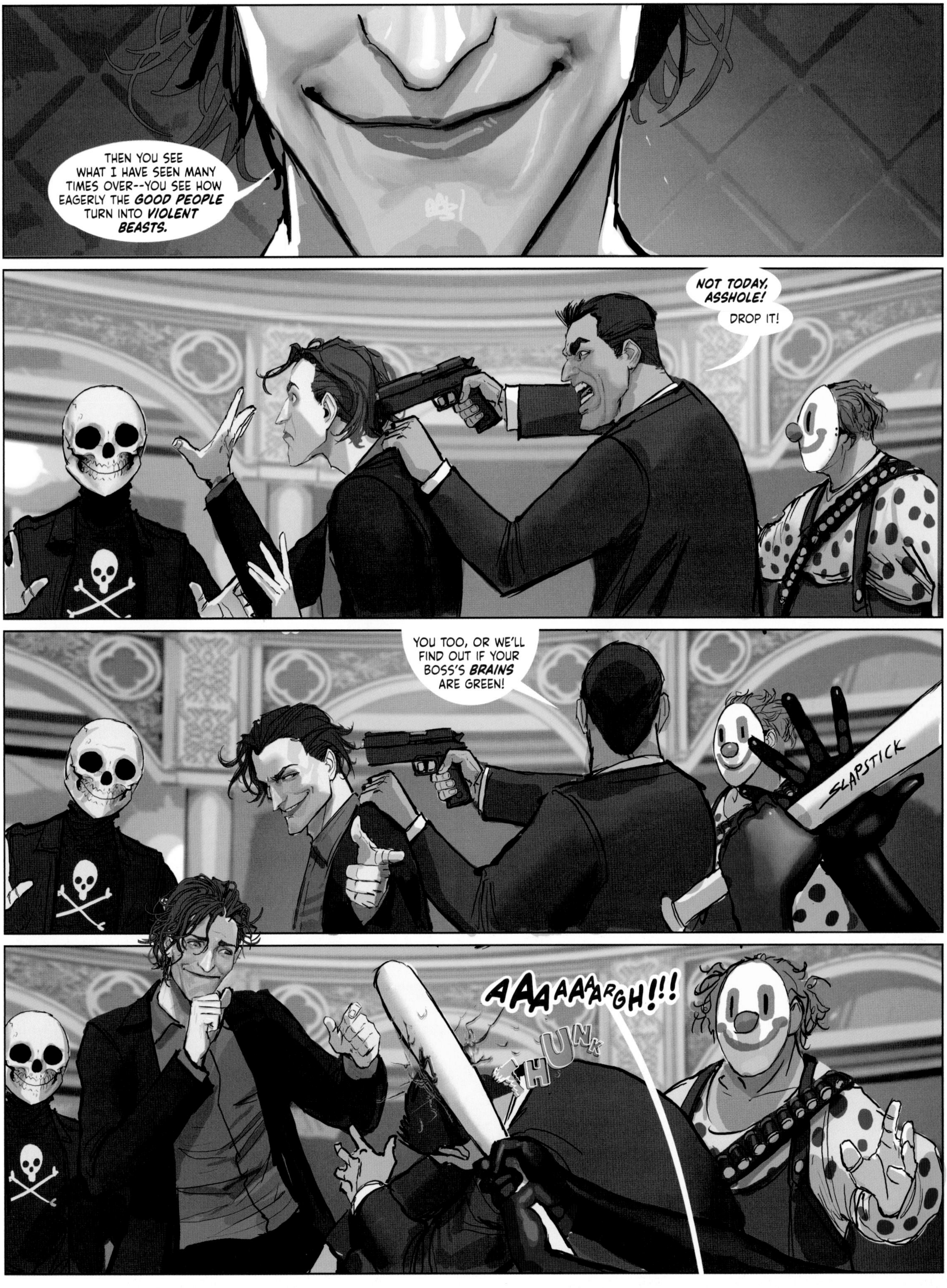
THEN YOU SEE WHAT I HAVE SEEN MANY TIMES OVER--YOU SEE HOW EAGERLY THE GOOD PEOPLE TURN INTO VIOLENT BEASTS.
NOT TODAY, ASSHOLE!
DROP IT!
YOU TOO, OR WE'LL FIND OUT IF YOUR BOSS'S BRAINS ARE GREEN!
SLAPSTICK
AAAAAAARGH!!!
THUNK

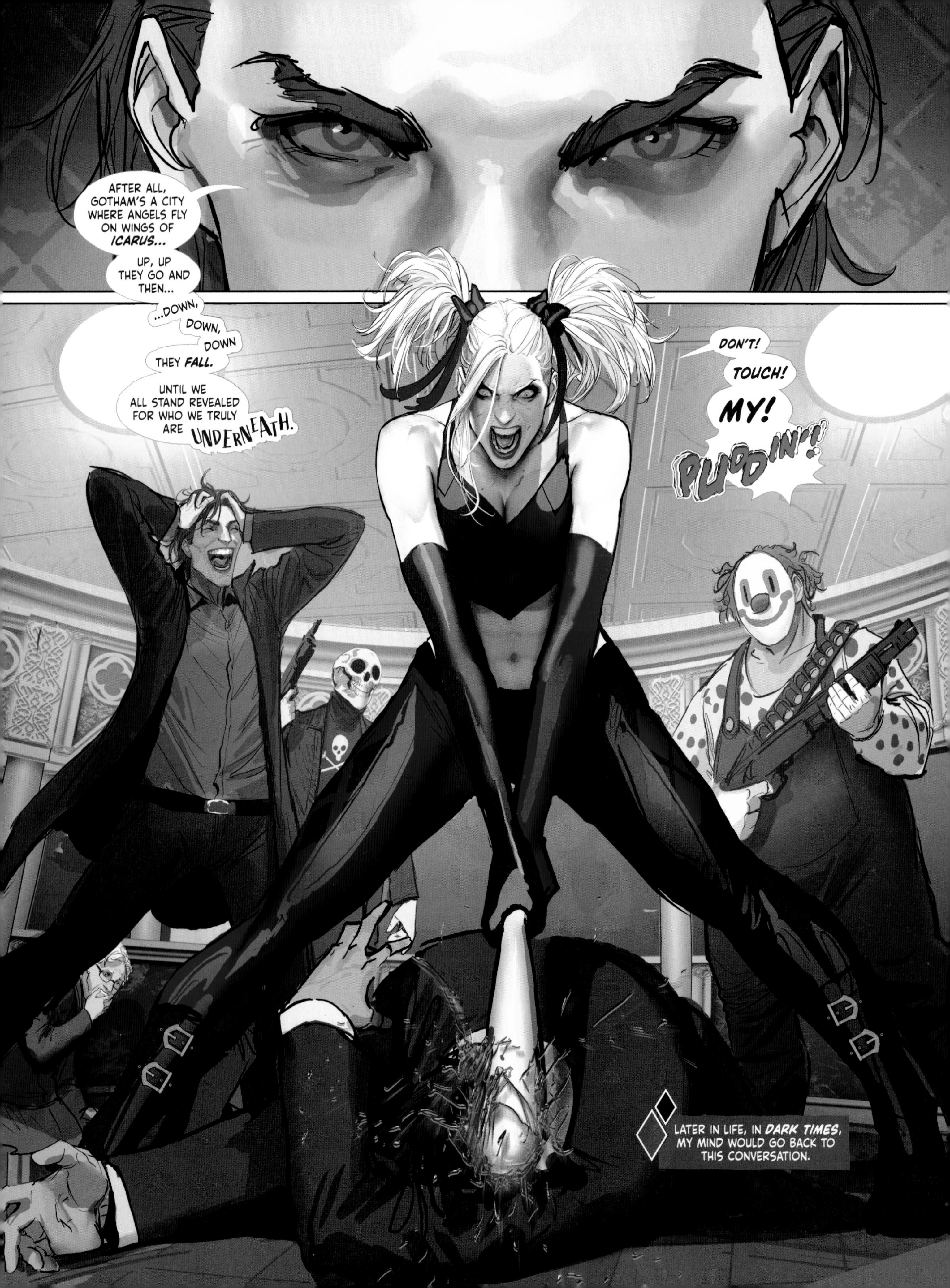

AFTER ALL, GOTHAM'S A CITY WHERE ANGELS FLY ON WINGS OF ICARUS...
UP, UP THEY GO AND THEN...
...DOWN, DOWN, DOWN THEY FALL.
UNTIL WE ALL STAND REVEALED FOR WHO WE TRULY ARE UNDERNEATH.
DON'T! TOUCH! MY! PUDDIN'!
LATER IN LIFE, IN DARK TIMES, MY MIND WOULD GO BACK TO THIS CONVERSATION.

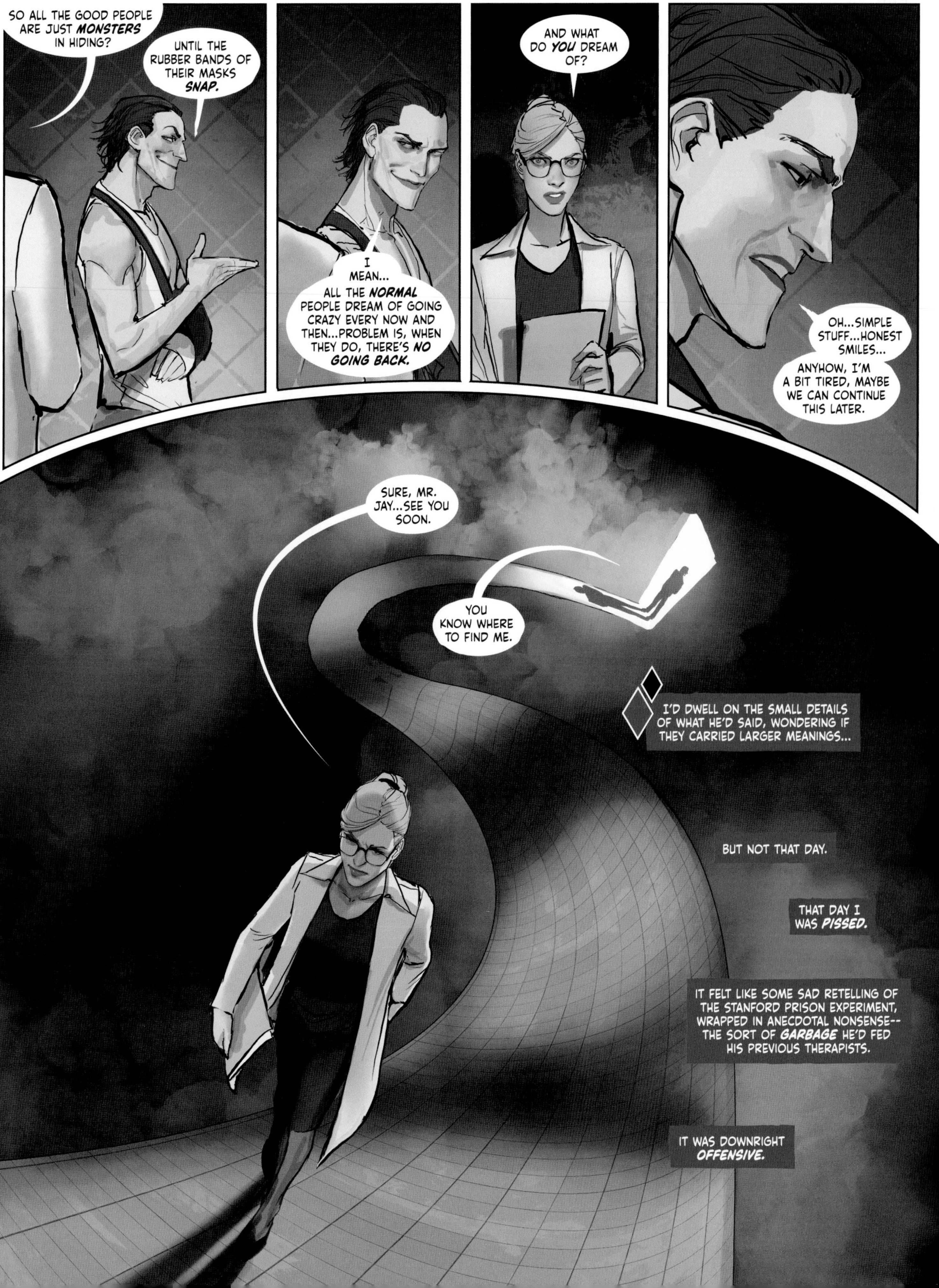
SO ALL THE GOOD PEOPLE ARE JUST MONSTERS IN HIDING?
UNTIL THE RUBBER BANDS OF THEIR MASKS SNAP.
I MEAN... ALL THE NORMAL PEOPLE DREAM OF GOING CRAZY EVERY NOW AND THEN...PROBLEM IS, WHEN THEY DO, THERE'S NO GOING BACK.
AND WHAT DO YOU DREAM OF?
OH...SIMPLE STUFF...HONEST SMILES...
ANYHOW, I'M A BIT TIRED, MAYBE WE CAN CONTINUE THIS LATER.
SURE, MR. JAY...SEE YOU SOON.
YOU KNOW WHERE TO FIND ME.
I'D DWELL ON THE SMALL DETAILS OF WHAT HE'D SAID, WONDERING IF THEY CARRIED LARGER MEANINGS...
BUT NOT THAT DAY.
THAT DAY I WAS PISSED.
IT FELT LIKE SOME SAD RETELLING OF THE STANFORD PRISON EXPERIMENT, WRAPPED IN ANECDOTAL NONSENSE-- THE SORT OF GARBAGE HE'D FED HIS PREVIOUS THERAPISTS.
IT WAS DOWNRIGHT OFFENSIVE.

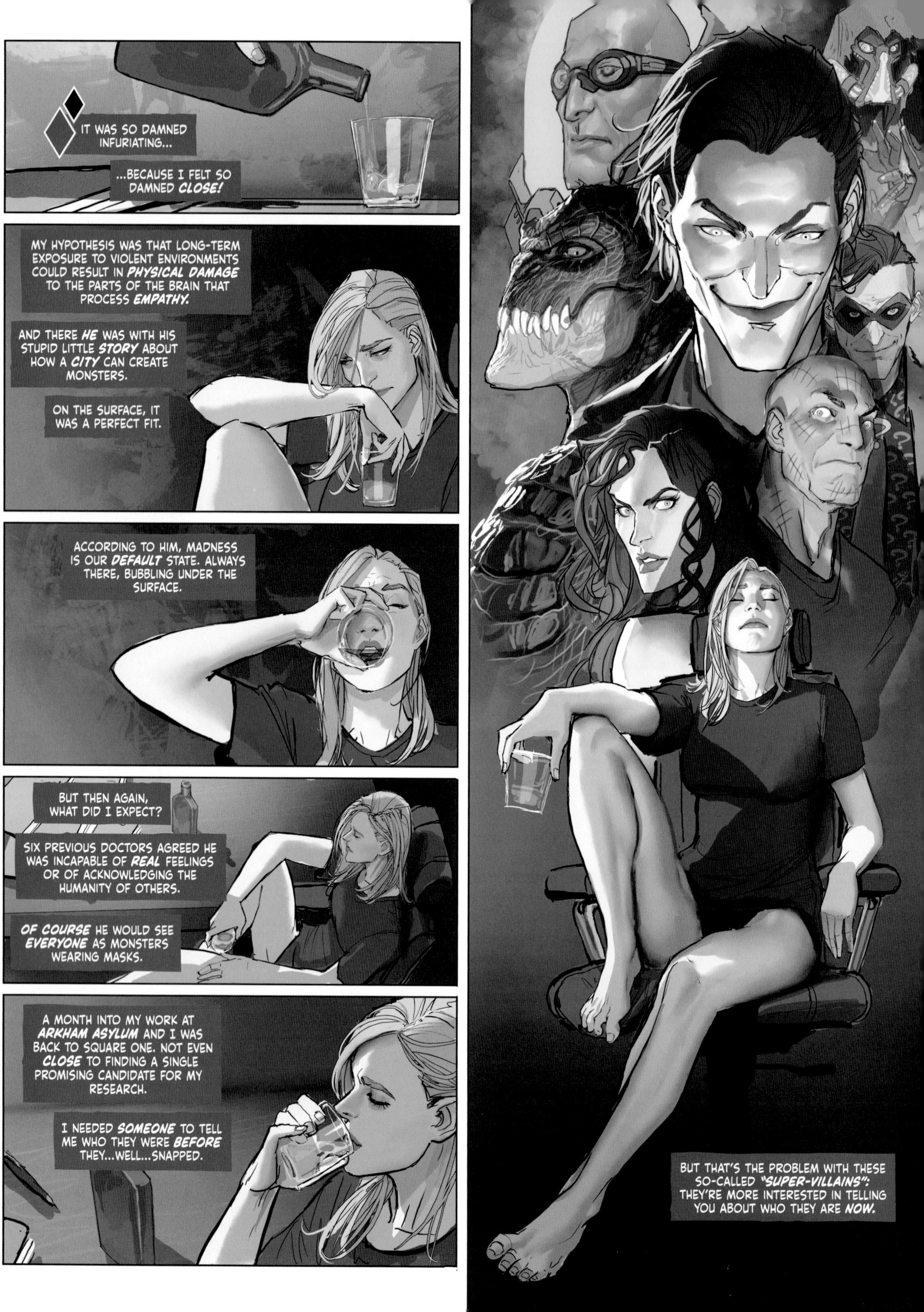
IT WAS SO DAMNED INFURIATING...
...BECAUSE I FELT SO DAMNED CLOSE!
MY HYPOTHESIS WAS THAT LONG-TERM EXPOSURE TO VIOLENT ENVIRONMENTS COULD RESULT IN PHYSICAL DAMAGE TO THE PARTS OF THE BRAIN THAT PROCESS EMPATHY.
AND THERE HE WAS WITH HIS STUPID LITTLE STORY ABOUT HOW A CITY CAN CREATE MONSTERS.
ON THE SURFACE, IT WAS A PERFECT FIT.
ACCORDING TO HIM, MADNESS IS OUR DEFAULT STATE. ALWAYS THERE, BUBBLING UNDER THE SURFACE.
BUT THEN AGAIN, WHAT DID I EXPECT?
SIX PREVIOUS DOCTORS AGREED HE WAS INCAPABLE OF REAL FEELINGS OR OF ACKNOWLEDGING THE HUMANITY OF OTHERS.
OF COURSE HE WOULD SEE EVERYONE AS MONSTERS WEARING MASKS.
A MONTH INTO MY WORK AT ARKHAM ASYLUM AND I WAS BACK TO SQUARE ONE. NOT EVEN CLOSE TO FINDING A SINGLE PROMISING CANDIDATE FOR MY RESEARCH.
I NEEDED SOMEONE TO TELL ME WHO THEY WERE BEFORE THEY...WELL...SNAPPED.
BUT THAT'S THE PROBLEM WITH THESE SO-CALLED "SUPER-VILLAINS": THEY'RE MORE INTERESTED IN TELLING YOU ABOUT WHO THEY ARE NOW.

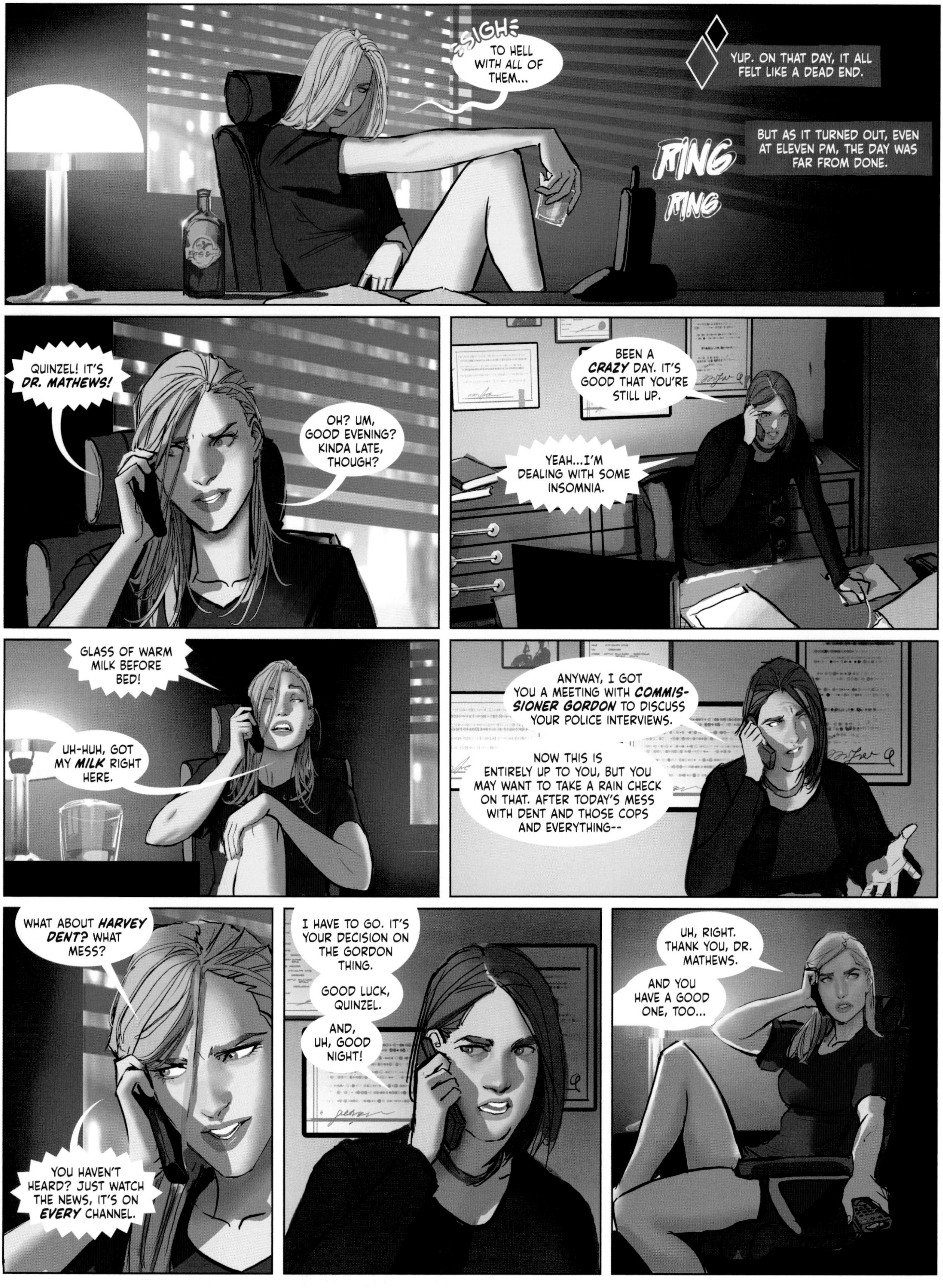
SIGH
TO HELL WITH ALL OF THEM...
YUP. ON THAT DAY, IT ALL FELT LIKE A DEAD END.
RING
RING
BUT AS IT TURNED OUT, EVEN AT ELEVEN PM, THE DAY WAS FAR FROM DONE.
QUINZEL! IT'S *DR. MATHEWS!*
OH? UM, GOOD EVENING? KINDA LATE, THOUGH?
BEEN A *CRAZY* DAY. IT'S GOOD THAT YOU'RE STILL UP.
YEAH...I'M DEALING WITH SOME INSOMNIA.
GLASS OF WARM MILK BEFORE BED!
UH-HUH, GOT MY *MILK* RIGHT HERE.
ANYWAY, I GOT YOU A MEETING WITH *COMMISSIONER GORDON* TO DISCUSS YOUR POLICE INTERVIEWS.
NOW THIS IS ENTIRELY UP TO YOU, BUT YOU MAY WANT TO TAKE A RAIN CHECK ON THAT. AFTER TODAY'S MESS WITH DENT AND THOSE COPS AND EVERYTHING--
WHAT ABOUT *HARVEY DENT?* WHAT MESS?
YOU HAVEN'T HEARD? JUST WATCH THE NEWS, IT'S ON *EVERY* CHANNEL.
I HAVE TO GO. IT'S YOUR DECISION ON THE GORDON THING.
GOOD LUCK, QUINZEL.
AND, UH, GOOD NIGHT!
UH, RIGHT. THANK YOU, DR. MATHEWS.
AND YOU HAVE A GOOD ONE, TOO...

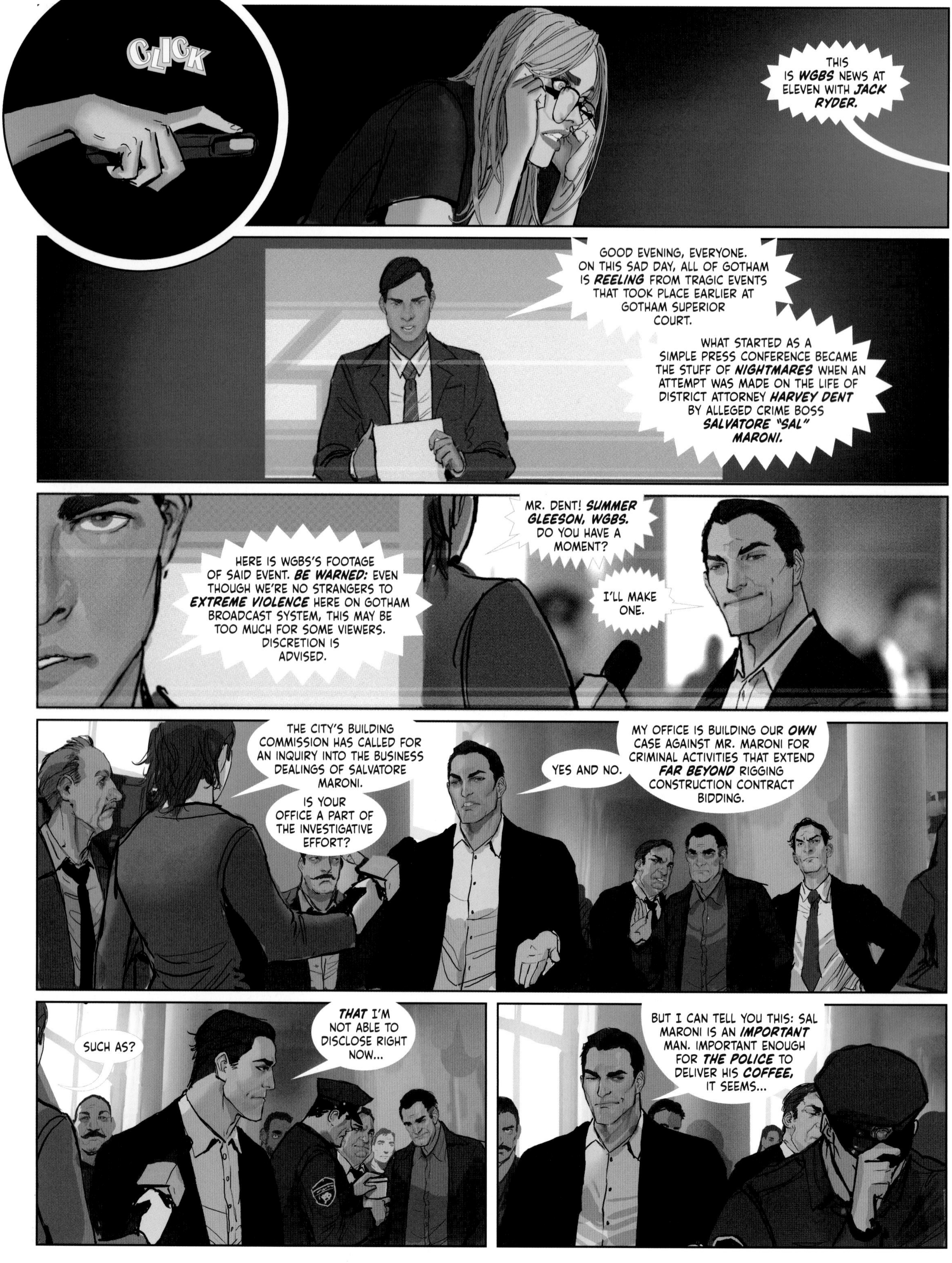
CLICK
THIS IS WGBS NEWS AT ELEVEN WITH JACK RYDER.
GOOD EVENING, EVERYONE. ON THIS SAD DAY, ALL OF GOTHAM IS REELING FROM TRAGIC EVENTS THAT TOOK PLACE EARLIER AT GOTHAM SUPERIOR COURT.
WHAT STARTED AS A SIMPLE PRESS CONFERENCE BECAME THE STUFF OF NIGHTMARES WHEN AN ATTEMPT WAS MADE ON THE LIFE OF DISTRICT ATTORNEY HARVEY DENT BY ALLEGED CRIME BOSS SALVATORE "SAL" MARONI.
HERE IS WGBS'S FOOTAGE OF SAID EVENT. BE WARNED: EVEN THOUGH WE'RE NO STRANGERS TO EXTREME VIOLENCE HERE ON GOTHAM BROADCAST SYSTEM, THIS MAY BE TOO MUCH FOR SOME VIEWERS. DISCRETION IS ADVISED.
MR. DENT! SUMMER GLEESON, WGBS. DO YOU HAVE A MOMENT?
I'LL MAKE ONE.
THE CITY'S BUILDING COMMISSION HAS CALLED FOR AN INQUIRY INTO THE BUSINESS DEALINGS OF SALVATORE MARONI.
IS YOUR OFFICE A PART OF THE INVESTIGATIVE EFFORT?
YES AND NO.
MY OFFICE IS BUILDING OUR OWN CASE AGAINST MR. MARONI FOR CRIMINAL ACTIVITIES THAT EXTEND FAR BEYOND RIGGING CONSTRUCTION CONTRACT BIDDING.
SUCH AS?
THAT I'M NOT ABLE TO DISCLOSE RIGHT NOW...
BUT I CAN TELL YOU THIS: SAL MARONI IS AN IMPORTANT MAN. IMPORTANT ENOUGH FOR THE POLICE TO DELIVER HIS COFFEE, IT SEEMS...

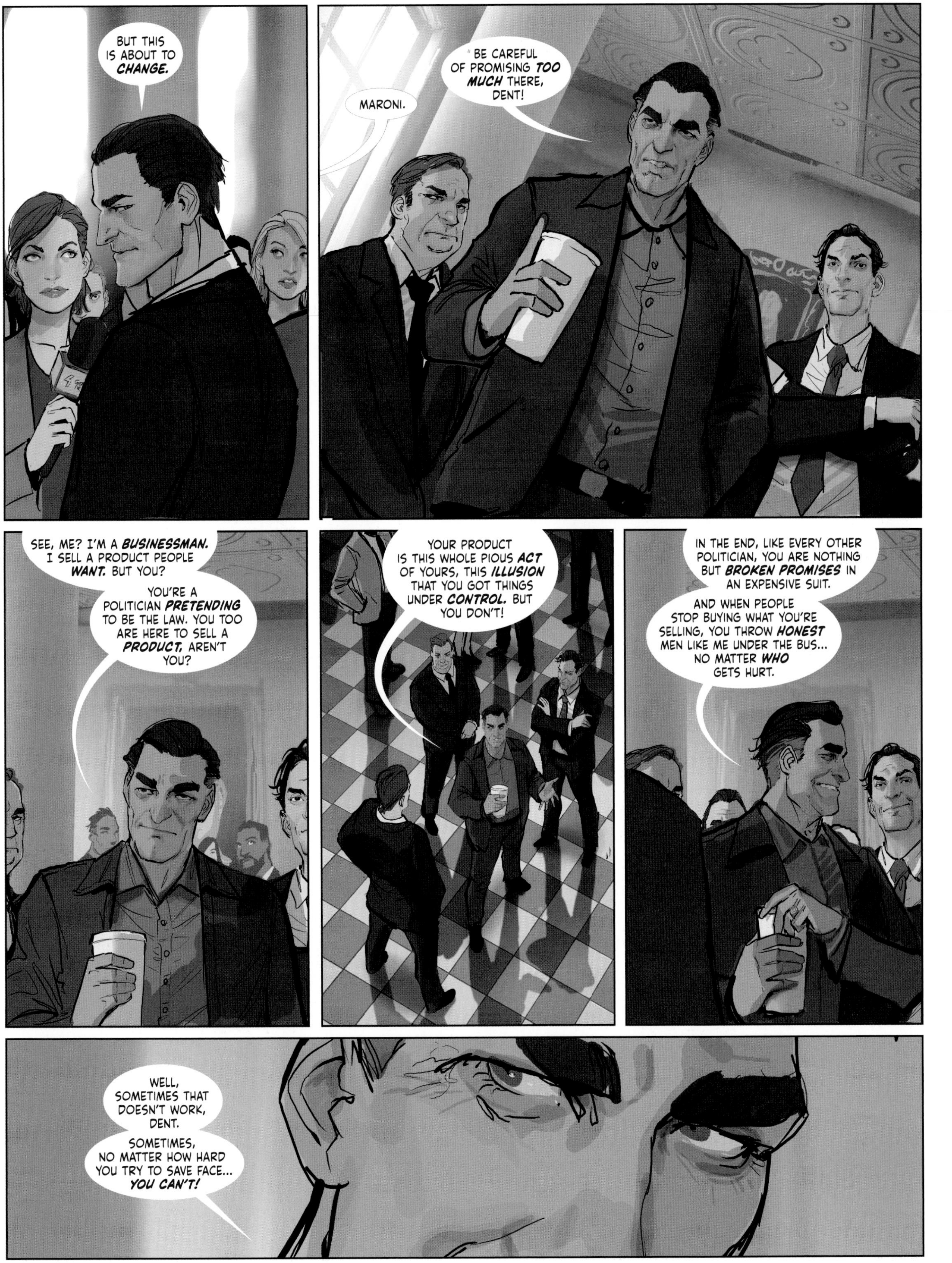
BUT THIS IS ABOUT TO CHANGE.
MARONI.
BE CAREFUL OF PROMISING TOO MUCH THERE, DENT!
SEE, ME? I'M A BUSINESSMAN. I SELL A PRODUCT PEOPLE WANT. BUT YOU?
YOU'RE A POLITICIAN PRETENDING TO BE THE LAW. YOU TOO ARE HERE TO SELL A PRODUCT, AREN'T YOU?
YOUR PRODUCT IS THIS WHOLE PIOUS ACT OF YOURS, THIS ILLUSION THAT YOU GOT THINGS UNDER CONTROL. BUT YOU DON'T!
IN THE END, LIKE EVERY OTHER POLITICIAN, YOU ARE NOTHING BUT BROKEN PROMISES IN AN EXPENSIVE SUIT.
AND WHEN PEOPLE STOP BUYING WHAT YOU'RE SELLING, YOU THROW HONEST MEN LIKE ME UNDER THE BUS... NO MATTER WHO GETS HURT.
WELL, SOMETIMES THAT DOESN'T WORK, DENT.
SOMETIMES, NO MATTER HOW HARD YOU TRY TO SAVE FACE... YOU CAN'T!

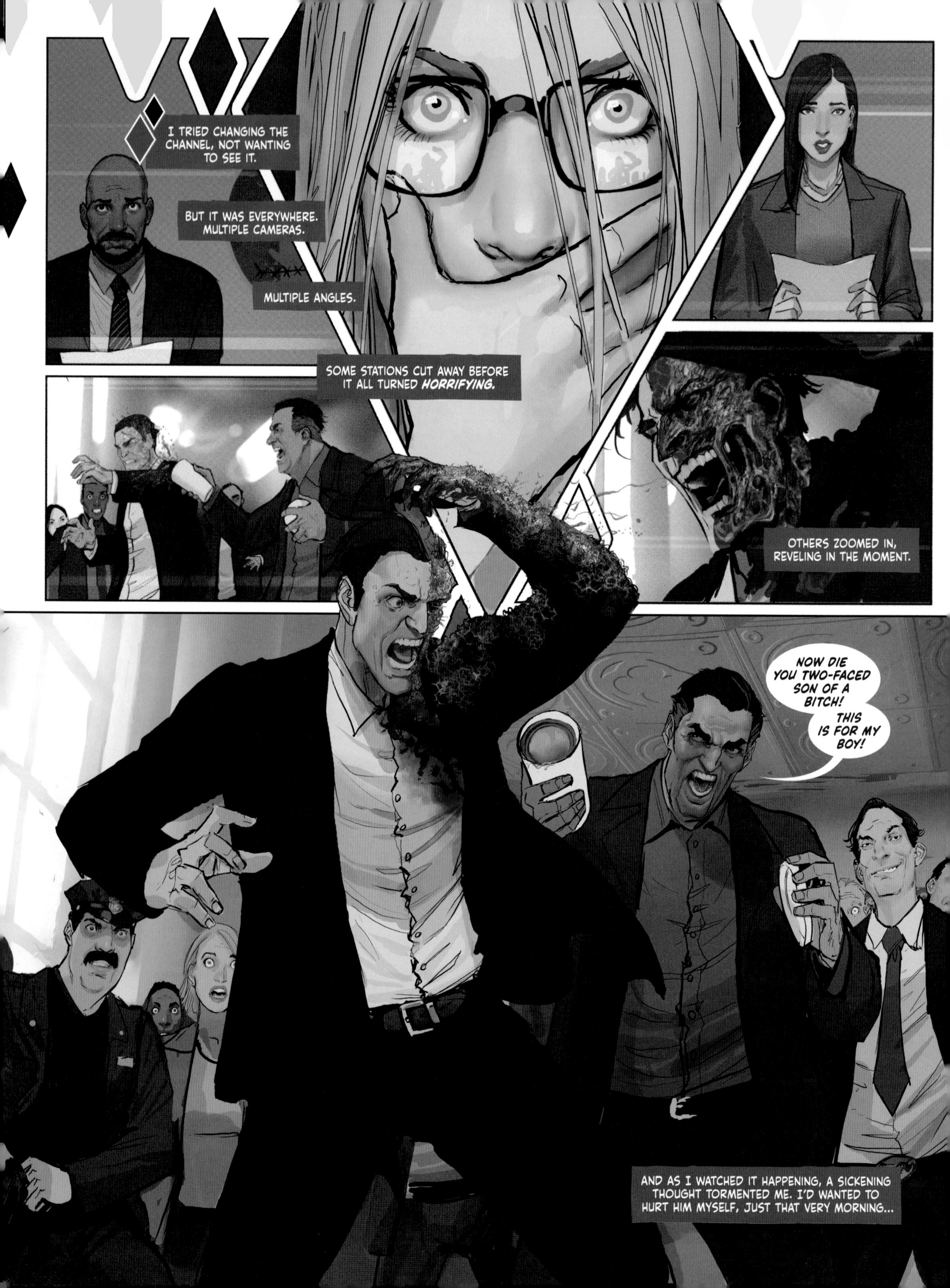
I TRIED CHANGING THE CHANNEL, NOT WANTING TO SEE IT.
BUT IT WAS EVERYWHERE. MULTIPLE CAMERAS.
MULTIPLE ANGLES.
SOME STATIONS CUT AWAY BEFORE IT ALL TURNED ***HORRIFYING.***
OTHERS ZOOMED IN, REVELING IN THE MOMENT.
NOW DIE YOU TWO-FACED SON OF A BITCH! THIS IS FOR MY BOY!
AND AS I WATCHED IT HAPPENING, A SICKENING THOUGHT TORMENTED ME. I'D WANTED TO HURT HIM MYSELF, JUST THAT VERY MORNING...

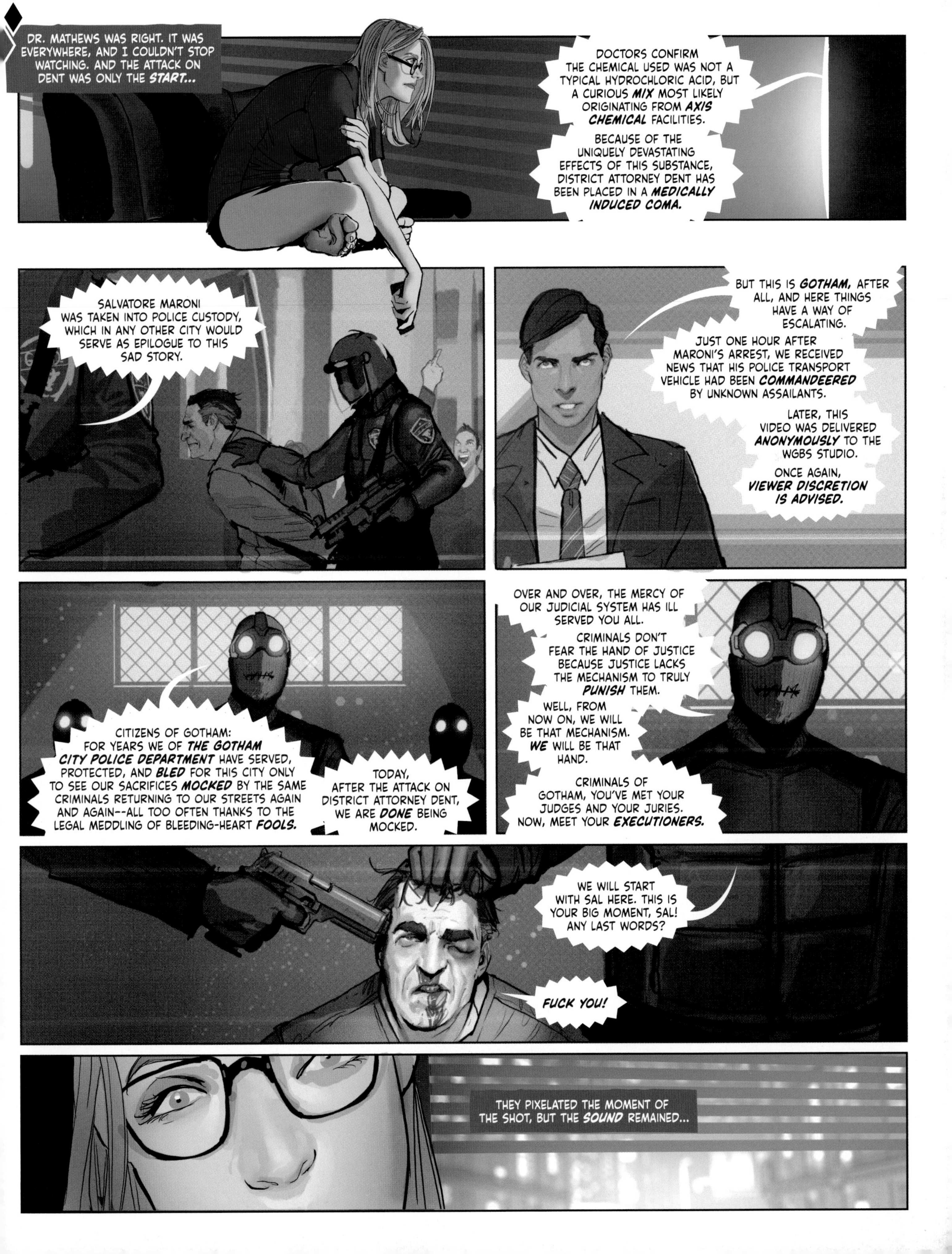
DR. MATHEWS WAS RIGHT. IT WAS EVERYWHERE, AND I COULDN'T STOP WATCHING. AND THE ATTACK ON DENT WAS ONLY THE START...
DOCTORS CONFIRM THE CHEMICAL USED WAS NOT A TYPICAL HYDROCHLORIC ACID, BUT A CURIOUS MIX MOST LIKELY ORIGINATING FROM AXIS CHEMICAL FACILITIES.
BECAUSE OF THE UNIQUELY DEVASTATING EFFECTS OF THIS SUBSTANCE, DISTRICT ATTORNEY DENT HAS BEEN PLACED IN A MEDICALLY INDUCED COMA.
SALVATORE MARONI WAS TAKEN INTO POLICE CUSTODY, WHICH IN ANY OTHER CITY WOULD SERVE AS EPILOGUE TO THIS SAD STORY.
BUT THIS IS GOTHAM, AFTER ALL, AND HERE THINGS HAVE A WAY OF ESCALATING.
JUST ONE HOUR AFTER MARONI'S ARREST, WE RECEIVED NEWS THAT HIS POLICE TRANSPORT VEHICLE HAD BEEN COMMANDEERED BY UNKNOWN ASSAILANTS.
LATER, THIS VIDEO WAS DELIVERED ANONYMOUSLY TO THE WGBS STUDIO.
ONCE AGAIN, VIEWER DISCRETION IS ADVISED.
CITIZENS OF GOTHAM: FOR YEARS WE OF THE GOTHAM CITY POLICE DEPARTMENT HAVE SERVED, PROTECTED, AND BLED FOR THIS CITY ONLY TO SEE OUR SACRIFICES MOCKED BY THE SAME CRIMINALS RETURNING TO OUR STREETS AGAIN AND AGAIN--ALL TOO OFTEN THANKS TO THE LEGAL MEDDLING OF BLEEDING-HEART FOOLS.
TODAY, AFTER THE ATTACK ON DISTRICT ATTORNEY DENT, WE ARE DONE BEING MOCKED.
OVER AND OVER, THE MERCY OF OUR JUDICIAL SYSTEM HAS ILL SERVED YOU ALL.
CRIMINALS DON'T FEAR THE HAND OF JUSTICE BECAUSE JUSTICE LACKS THE MECHANISM TO TRULY PUNISH THEM.
WELL, FROM NOW ON, WE WILL BE THAT MECHANISM. WE WILL BE THAT HAND.
CRIMINALS OF GOTHAM, YOU'VE MET YOUR JUDGES AND YOUR JURIES. NOW, MEET YOUR EXECUTIONERS.
WE WILL START WITH SAL HERE. THIS IS YOUR BIG MOMENT, SAL! ANY LAST WORDS?
FUCK YOU!
THEY PIXELATED THE MOMENT OF THE SHOT, BUT THE SOUND REMAINED...

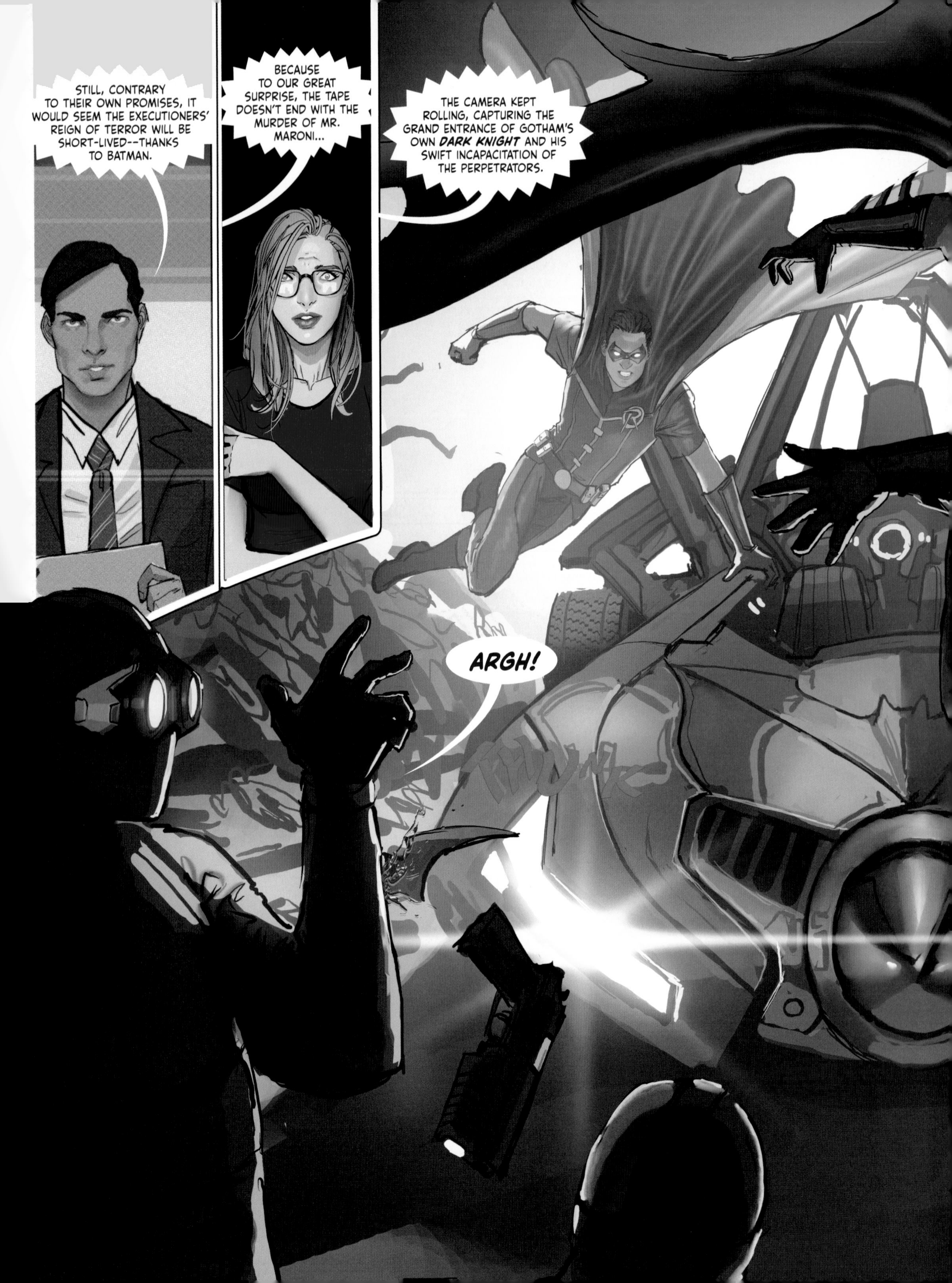
STILL, CONTRARY TO THEIR OWN PROMISES, IT WOULD SEEM THE EXECUTIONERS' REIGN OF TERROR WILL BE SHORT-LIVED--THANKS TO BATMAN.
BECAUSE TO OUR GREAT SURPRISE, THE TAPE DOESN'T END WITH THE MURDER OF MR. MARONI...
THE CAMERA KEPT ROLLING, CAPTURING THE GRAND ENTRANCE OF GOTHAM'S OWN ***DARK KNIGHT*** AND HIS SWIFT INCAPACITATION OF THE PERPETRATORS.
ARGH!

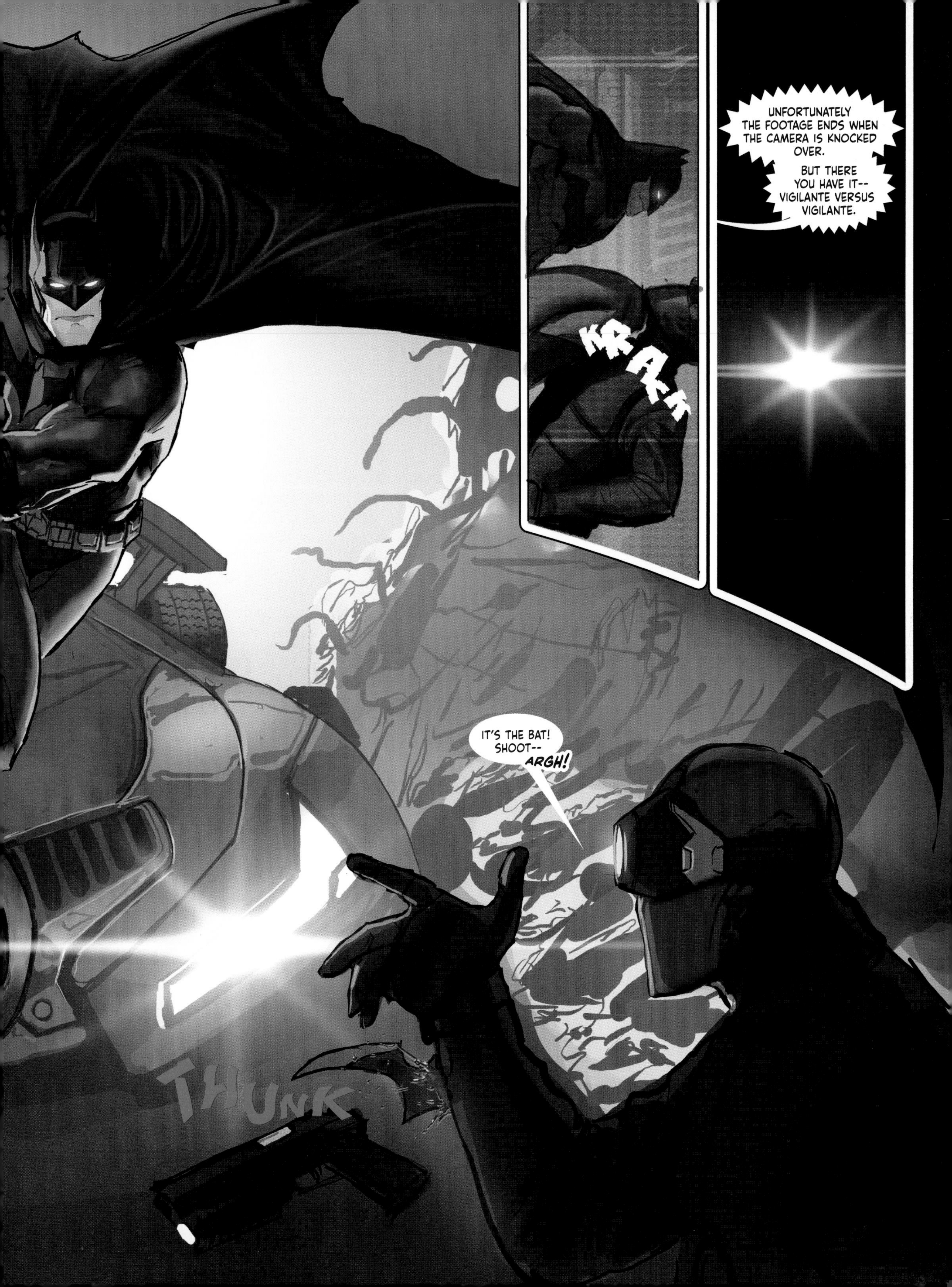
KRACK
UNFORTUNATELY THE FOOTAGE ENDS WHEN THE CAMERA IS KNOCKED OVER.
BUT THERE YOU HAVE IT-- VIGILANTE VERSUS VIGILANTE.
IT'S THE BAT! SHOOT-- ARGH!
THUNK

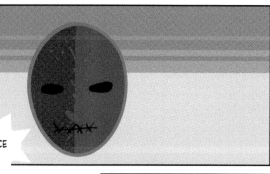

THESE EXECUTIONERS ARE SEEN IN A *POSITIVE LIGHT* BY 68 PERCENT OF GOTHAMITES WE SURVEYED.

AT THE SAME TIME, G.C.P.D.'S APPROVAL NUMBERS ARE AS LOW AS 31 PERCENT.

OUR REPORTER SUMMER GLEESON TRIED TO GET SOME INSIGHT ON THIS MATTER FROM THE POLICE COMMISSIONER, *JAMES GORDON.*

GOTHAM P.D. HAS BEEN COOPERATING WITH A VIGILANTE FOR *YEARS.* HOW ARE THESE ROGUE OFFICERS ANY DIFFERENT?

HOW ARE THEY DIFFERENT FROM *BATMAN?*

BATMAN IS NOT A *MURDERER.*

BUT COMMISSIONER--

NO MORE QUESTIONS!

I FEEL AN UNSETTLING SHUDDER RUN THROUGH MY BODY AND REMEMBER THE SOUND OF *CHEERS.*

IT ALL FEELS SO FAMILIAR...

...SO *SINISTER.*

AND I REMEMBER *HIS* WORDS...

"GOTHAM IS FULL OF PEOPLE LIKE THAT, HANDS TWITCHING AS THEY DREAM OF VIOLENCE. SHIVERING WITH BARELY SUPPRESSED RAGE. BRIMMING WITH RIGHTEOUS INDIGNATION.

"SMILING POLITELY AS THEY DREAM OF SAVAGE THINGS."

THAT NIGHT, AFTER THE SOBERING NEWS TAKES THE EDGE OFF MY NIGHTCAP, I TOO DREAM OF *SAVAGE THINGS.*

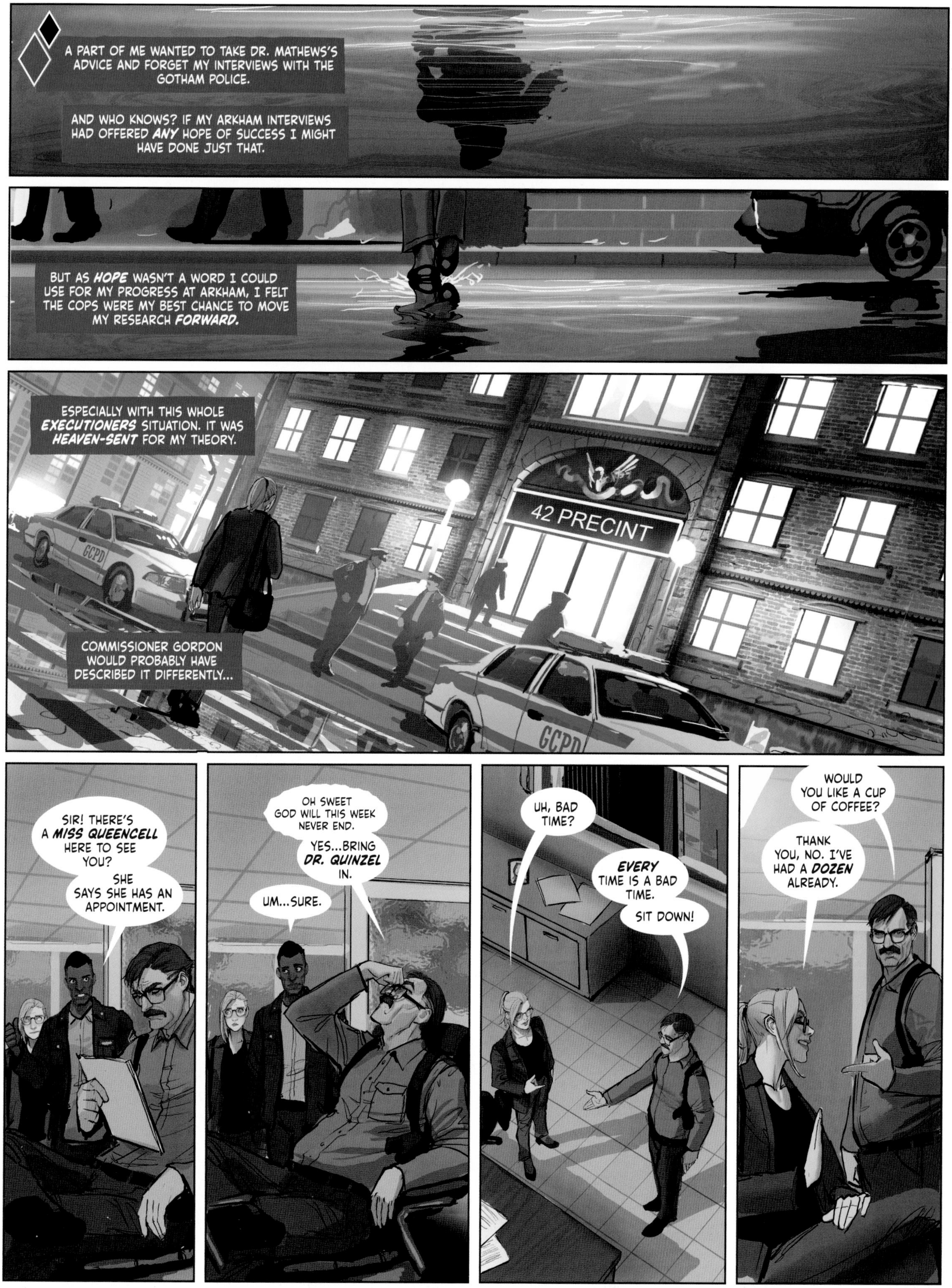
A PART OF ME WANTED TO TAKE DR. MATHEWS'S ADVICE AND FORGET MY INTERVIEWS WITH THE GOTHAM POLICE.
AND WHO KNOWS? IF MY ARKHAM INTERVIEWS HAD OFFERED ANY HOPE OF SUCCESS I MIGHT HAVE DONE JUST THAT.
BUT AS HOPE WASN'T A WORD I COULD USE FOR MY PROGRESS AT ARKHAM, I FELT THE COPS WERE MY BEST CHANCE TO MOVE MY RESEARCH FORWARD.
ESPECIALLY WITH THIS WHOLE EXECUTIONERS SITUATION. IT WAS HEAVEN-SENT FOR MY THEORY.
42 PRECINT
GCPD
COMMISSIONER GORDON WOULD PROBABLY HAVE DESCRIBED IT DIFFERENTLY...
GCPD
SIR! THERE'S A MISS QUEENCELL HERE TO SEE YOU?
SHE SAYS SHE HAS AN APPOINTMENT.
OH SWEET GOD WILL THIS WEEK NEVER END.
YES...BRING DR. QUINZEL IN.
UM...SURE.
UH, BAD TIME?
EVERY TIME IS A BAD TIME.
SIT DOWN!
WOULD YOU LIKE A CUP OF COFFEE?
THANK YOU, NO. I'VE HAD A DOZEN ALREADY.

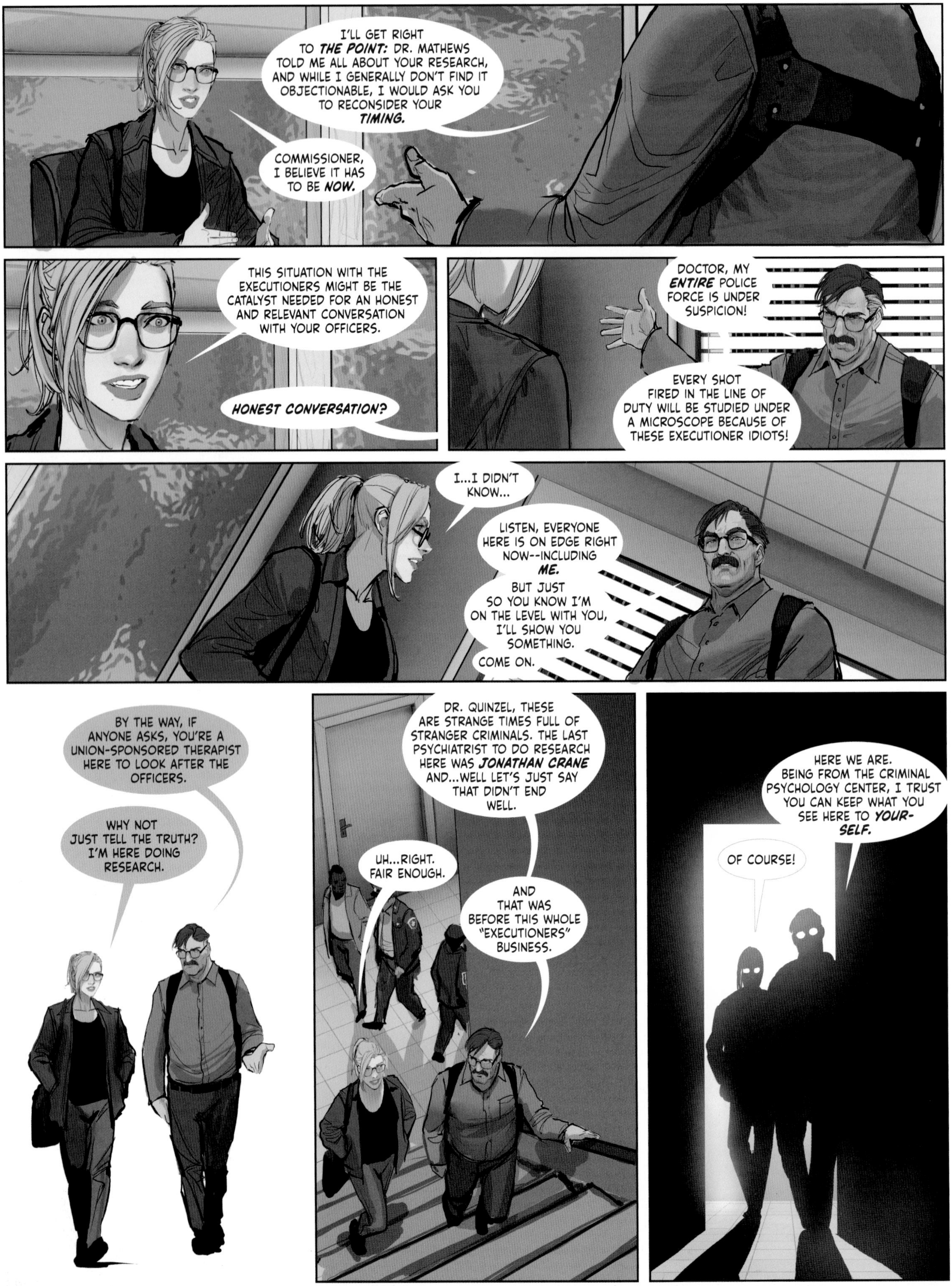

I'LL GET RIGHT TO THE POINT: DR. MATHEWS TOLD ME ALL ABOUT YOUR RESEARCH, AND WHILE I GENERALLY DON'T FIND IT OBJECTIONABLE, I WOULD ASK YOU TO RECONSIDER YOUR TIMING.
COMMISSIONER, I BELIEVE IT HAS TO BE NOW.
THIS SITUATION WITH THE EXECUTIONERS MIGHT BE THE CATALYST NEEDED FOR AN HONEST AND RELEVANT CONVERSATION WITH YOUR OFFICERS.
HONEST CONVERSATION?
DOCTOR, MY ENTIRE POLICE FORCE IS UNDER SUSPICION!
EVERY SHOT FIRED IN THE LINE OF DUTY WILL BE STUDIED UNDER A MICROSCOPE BECAUSE OF THESE EXECUTIONER IDIOTS!
I...I DIDN'T KNOW...
LISTEN, EVERYONE HERE IS ON EDGE RIGHT NOW--INCLUDING ME.
BUT JUST SO YOU KNOW I'M ON THE LEVEL WITH YOU, I'LL SHOW YOU SOMETHING.
COME ON.
BY THE WAY, IF ANYONE ASKS, YOU'RE A UNION-SPONSORED THERAPIST HERE TO LOOK AFTER THE OFFICERS.
WHY NOT JUST TELL THE TRUTH? I'M HERE DOING RESEARCH.
DR. QUINZEL, THESE ARE STRANGE TIMES FULL OF STRANGER CRIMINALS. THE LAST PSYCHIATRIST TO DO RESEARCH HERE WAS JONATHAN CRANE AND...WELL LET'S JUST SAY THAT DIDN'T END WELL.
UH...RIGHT. FAIR ENOUGH.
AND THAT WAS BEFORE THIS WHOLE "EXECUTIONERS" BUSINESS.
HERE WE ARE. BEING FROM THE CRIMINAL PSYCHOLOGY CENTER, I TRUST YOU CAN KEEP WHAT YOU SEE HERE TO YOURSELF.
OF COURSE!

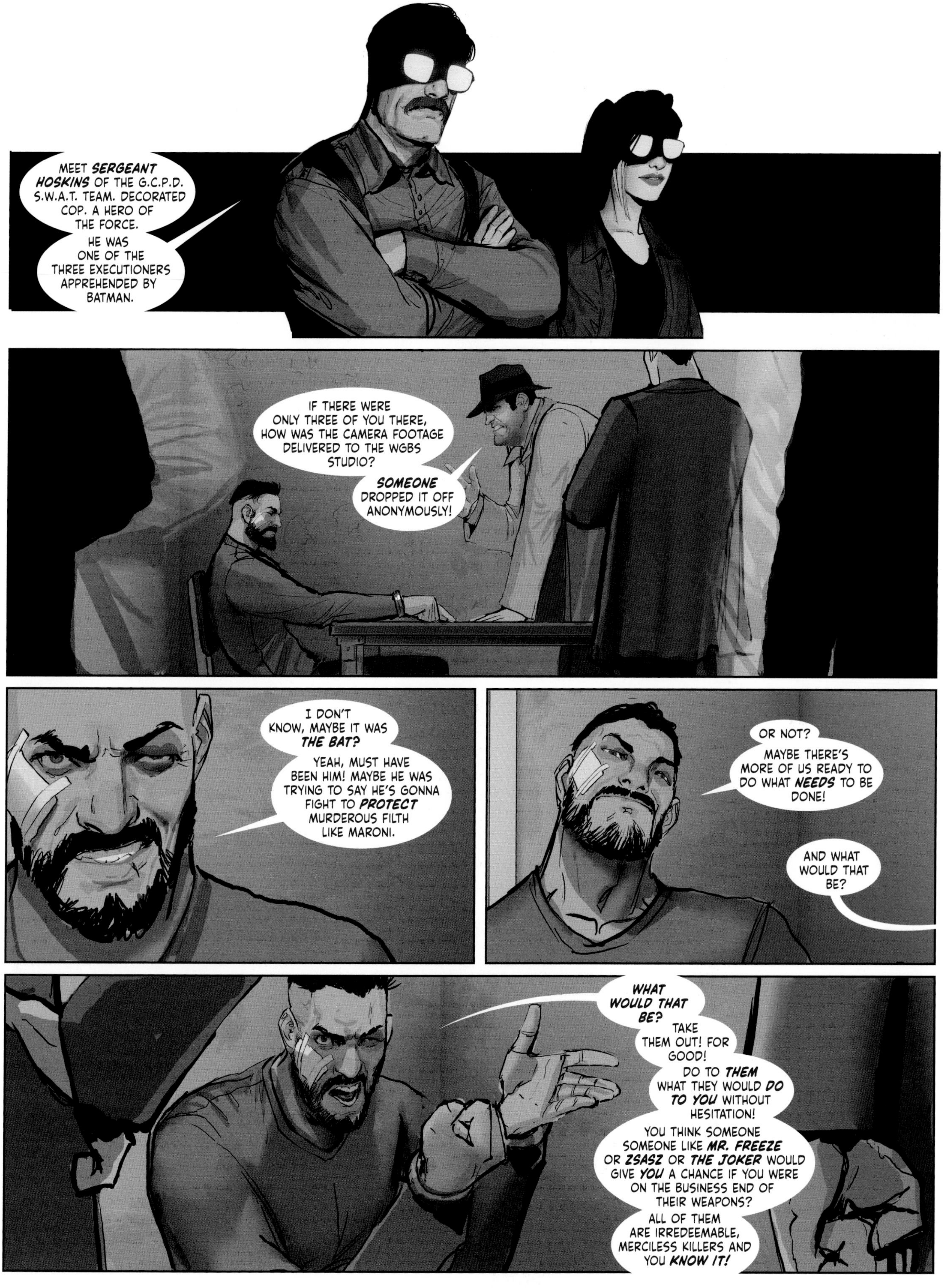
MEET SERGEANT HOSKINS OF THE G.C.P.D. S.W.A.T. TEAM. DECORATED COP. A HERO OF THE FORCE.
HE WAS ONE OF THE THREE EXECUTIONERS APPREHENDED BY BATMAN.
IF THERE WERE ONLY THREE OF YOU THERE, HOW WAS THE CAMERA FOOTAGE DELIVERED TO THE WGBS STUDIO?
SOMEONE DROPPED IT OFF ANONYMOUSLY!
I DON'T KNOW, MAYBE IT WAS THE BAT?
YEAH, MUST HAVE BEEN HIM! MAYBE HE WAS TRYING TO SAY HE'S GONNA FIGHT TO PROTECT MURDEROUS FILTH LIKE MARONI.
OR NOT?
MAYBE THERE'S MORE OF US READY TO DO WHAT NEEDS TO BE DONE!
AND WHAT WOULD THAT BE?
WHAT WOULD THAT BE?
TAKE THEM OUT! FOR GOOD!
DO TO THEM WHAT THEY WOULD DO TO YOU WITHOUT HESITATION!
YOU THINK SOMEONE SOMEONE LIKE MR. FREEZE OR ZSASZ OR THE JOKER WOULD GIVE YOU A CHANCE IF YOU WERE ON THE BUSINESS END OF THEIR WEAPONS?
ALL OF THEM ARE IRREDEEMABLE, MERCILESS KILLERS AND YOU KNOW IT!

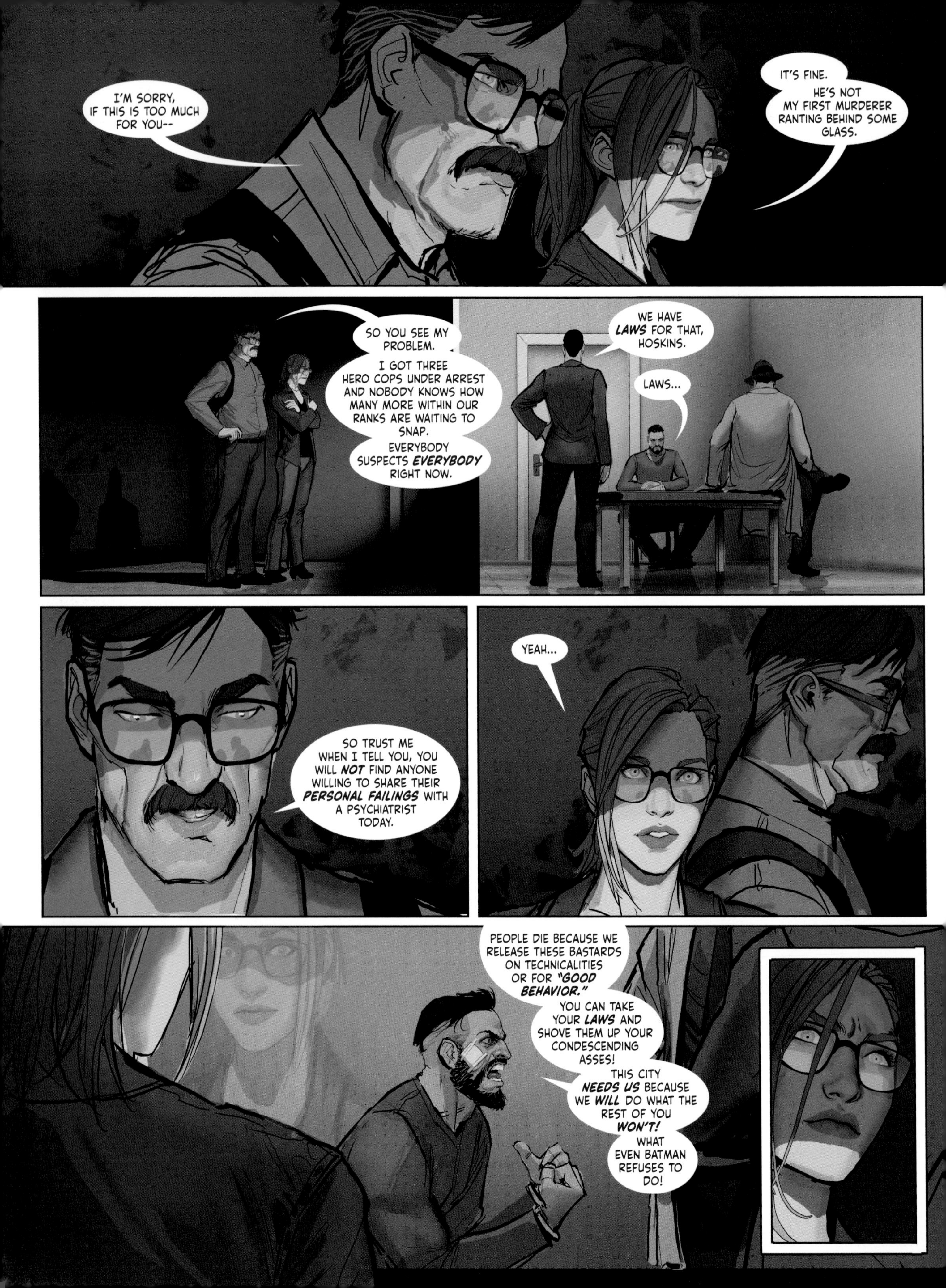
I'M SORRY, IF THIS IS TOO MUCH FOR YOU--
IT'S FINE.
HE'S NOT MY FIRST MURDERER RANTING BEHIND SOME GLASS.
SO YOU SEE MY PROBLEM.
I GOT THREE HERO COPS UNDER ARREST AND NOBODY KNOWS HOW MANY MORE WITHIN OUR RANKS ARE WAITING TO SNAP.
EVERYBODY SUSPECTS EVERYBODY RIGHT NOW.
WE HAVE LAWS FOR THAT, HOSKINS.
LAWS...
SO TRUST ME WHEN I TELL YOU, YOU WILL NOT FIND ANYONE WILLING TO SHARE THEIR PERSONAL FAILINGS WITH A PSYCHIATRIST TODAY.
YEAH...
PEOPLE DIE BECAUSE WE RELEASE THESE BASTARDS ON TECHNICALITIES OR FOR "GOOD BEHAVIOR."
YOU CAN TAKE YOUR LAWS AND SHOVE THEM UP YOUR CONDESCENDING ASSES!
THIS CITY NEEDS US BECAUSE WE WILL DO WHAT THE REST OF YOU WON'T!
WHAT EVEN BATMAN REFUSES TO DO!

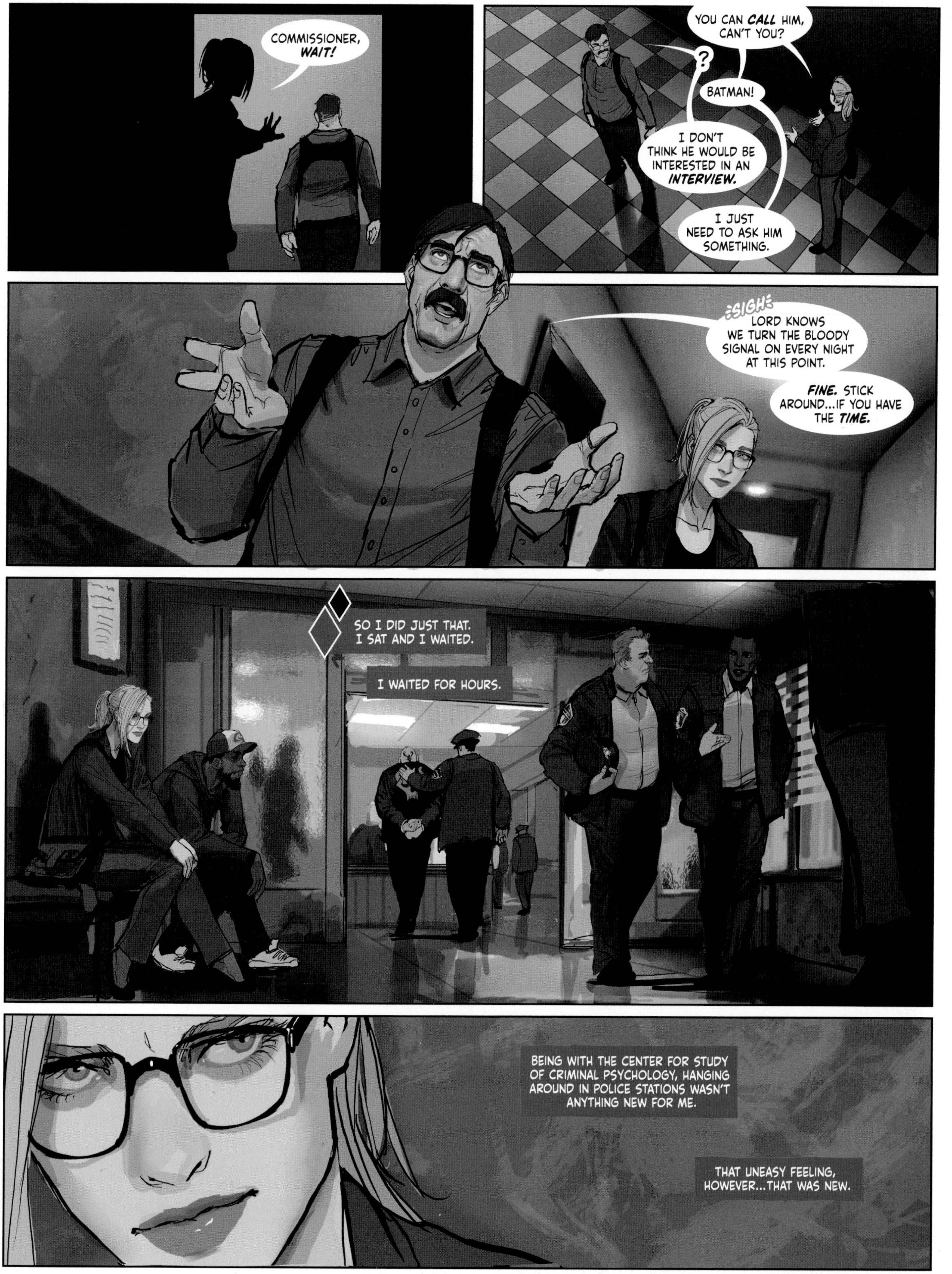
COMMISSIONER, WAIT!
YOU CAN CALL HIM, CAN'T YOU?
?
BATMAN!
I DON'T THINK HE WOULD BE INTERESTED IN AN INTERVIEW.
I JUST NEED TO ASK HIM SOMETHING.
SIGH
LORD KNOWS WE TURN THE BLOODY SIGNAL ON EVERY NIGHT AT THIS POINT.
FINE. STICK AROUND...IF YOU HAVE THE TIME.
SO I DID JUST THAT. I SAT AND I WAITED.
I WAITED FOR HOURS.
BEING WITH THE CENTER FOR STUDY OF CRIMINAL PSYCHOLOGY, HANGING AROUND IN POLICE STATIONS WASN'T ANYTHING NEW FOR ME.
THAT UNEASY FEELING, HOWEVER...THAT WAS NEW.

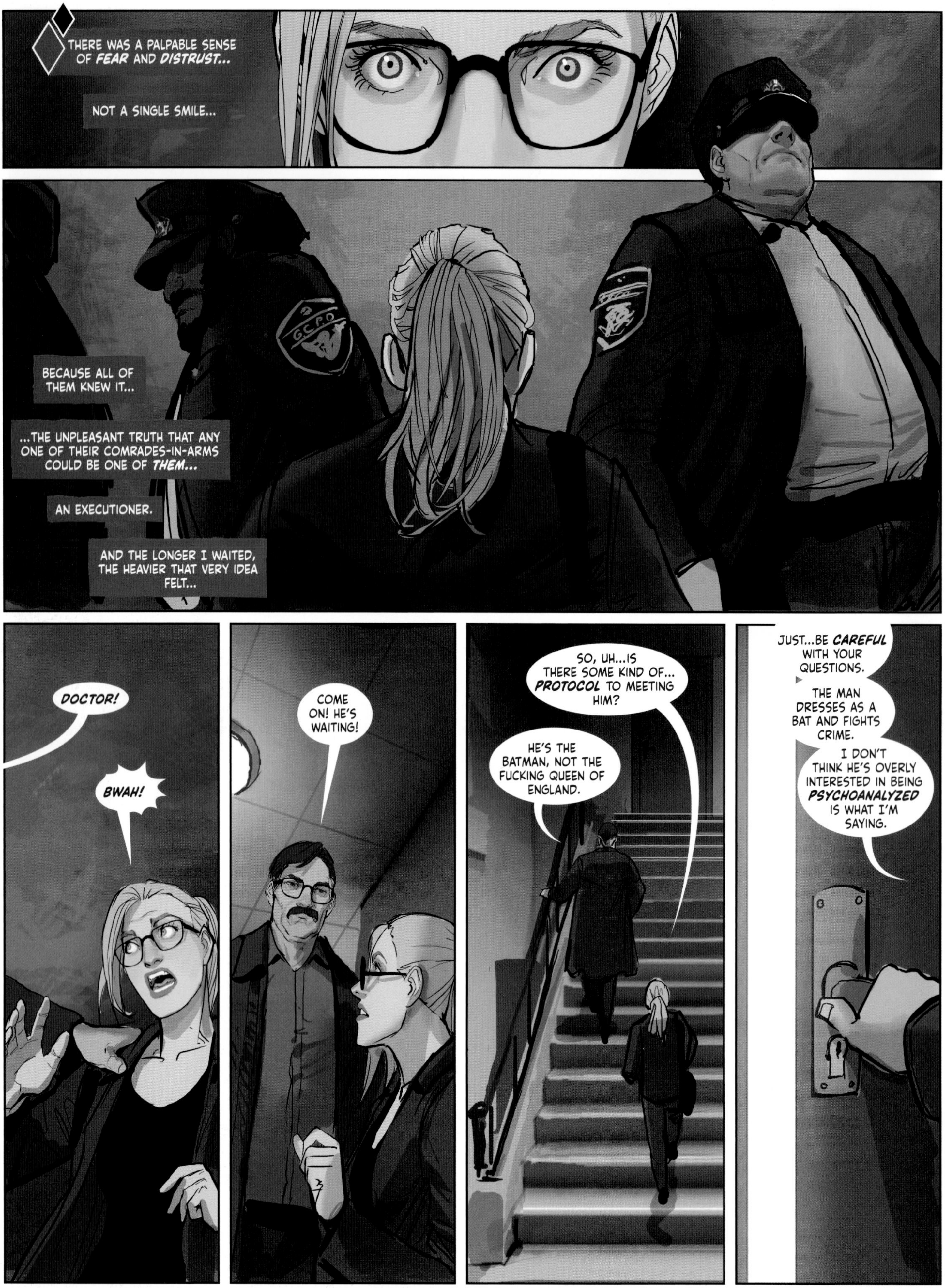
THERE WAS A PALPABLE SENSE OF FEAR AND DISTRUST...
NOT A SINGLE SMILE...
BECAUSE ALL OF THEM KNEW IT...
...THE UNPLEASANT TRUTH THAT ANY ONE OF THEIR COMRADES-IN-ARMS COULD BE ONE OF THEM...
AN EXECUTIONER.
AND THE LONGER I WAITED, THE HEAVIER THAT VERY IDEA FELT...
DOCTOR!
BWAH!
COME ON! HE'S WAITING!
SO, UH...IS THERE SOME KIND OF... PROTOCOL TO MEETING HIM?
HE'S THE BATMAN, NOT THE FUCKING QUEEN OF ENGLAND.
JUST...BE CAREFUL WITH YOUR QUESTIONS.
THE MAN DRESSES AS A BAT AND FIGHTS CRIME.
I DON'T THINK HE'S OVERLY INTERESTED IN BEING PSYCHOANALYZED IS WHAT I'M SAYING.

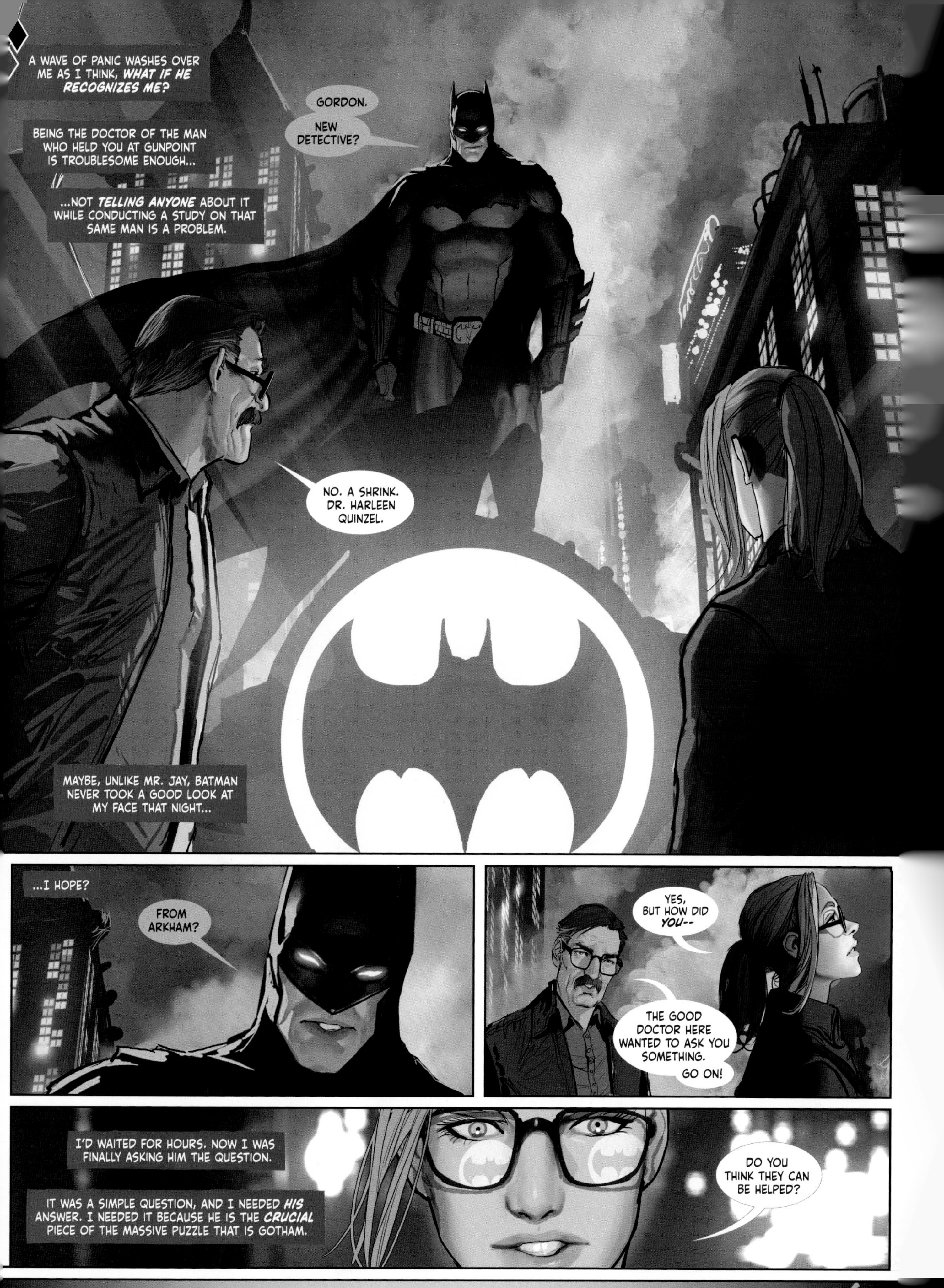
A WAVE OF PANIC WASHES OVER ME AS I THINK, WHAT IF HE RECOGNIZES ME?
GORDON.
NEW DETECTIVE?
BEING THE DOCTOR OF THE MAN WHO HELD YOU AT GUNPOINT IS TROUBLESOME ENOUGH...
...NOT TELLING ANYONE ABOUT IT WHILE CONDUCTING A STUDY ON THAT SAME MAN IS A PROBLEM.
NO. A SHRINK. DR. HARLEEN QUINZEL.
MAYBE, UNLIKE MR. JAY, BATMAN NEVER TOOK A GOOD LOOK AT MY FACE THAT NIGHT...
...I HOPE?
FROM ARKHAM?
YES, BUT HOW DID YOU--
THE GOOD DOCTOR HERE WANTED TO ASK YOU SOMETHING.
GO ON!
I'D WAITED FOR HOURS. NOW I WAS FINALLY ASKING HIM THE QUESTION.
IT WAS A SIMPLE QUESTION, AND I NEEDED HIS ANSWER. I NEEDED IT BECAUSE HE IS THE CRUCIAL PIECE OF THE MASSIVE PUZZLE THAT IS GOTHAM.
DO YOU THINK THEY CAN BE HELPED?

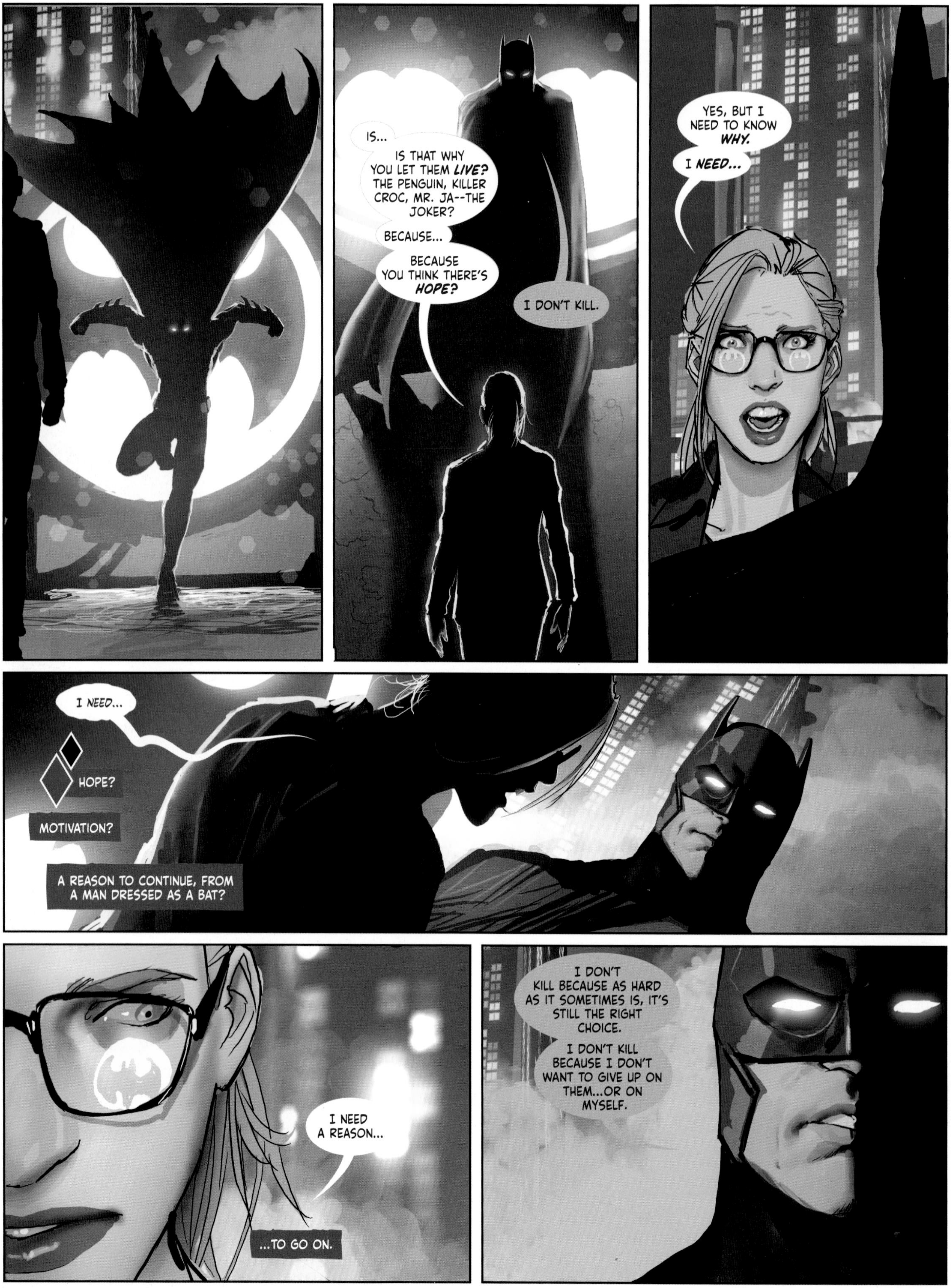

IS...
IS THAT WHY YOU LET THEM LIVE? THE PENGUIN, KILLER CROC, MR. JA--THE JOKER?
BECAUSE...
BECAUSE YOU THINK THERE'S HOPE?
I DON'T KILL.
YES, BUT I NEED TO KNOW WHY.
I NEED...
I NEED...
HOPE?
MOTIVATION?
A REASON TO CONTINUE, FROM A MAN DRESSED AS A BAT?
I NEED A REASON...
...TO GO ON.
I DON'T KILL BECAUSE AS HARD AS IT SOMETIMES IS, IT'S STILL THE RIGHT CHOICE.
I DON'T KILL BECAUSE I DON'T WANT TO GIVE UP ON THEM...OR ON MYSELF.

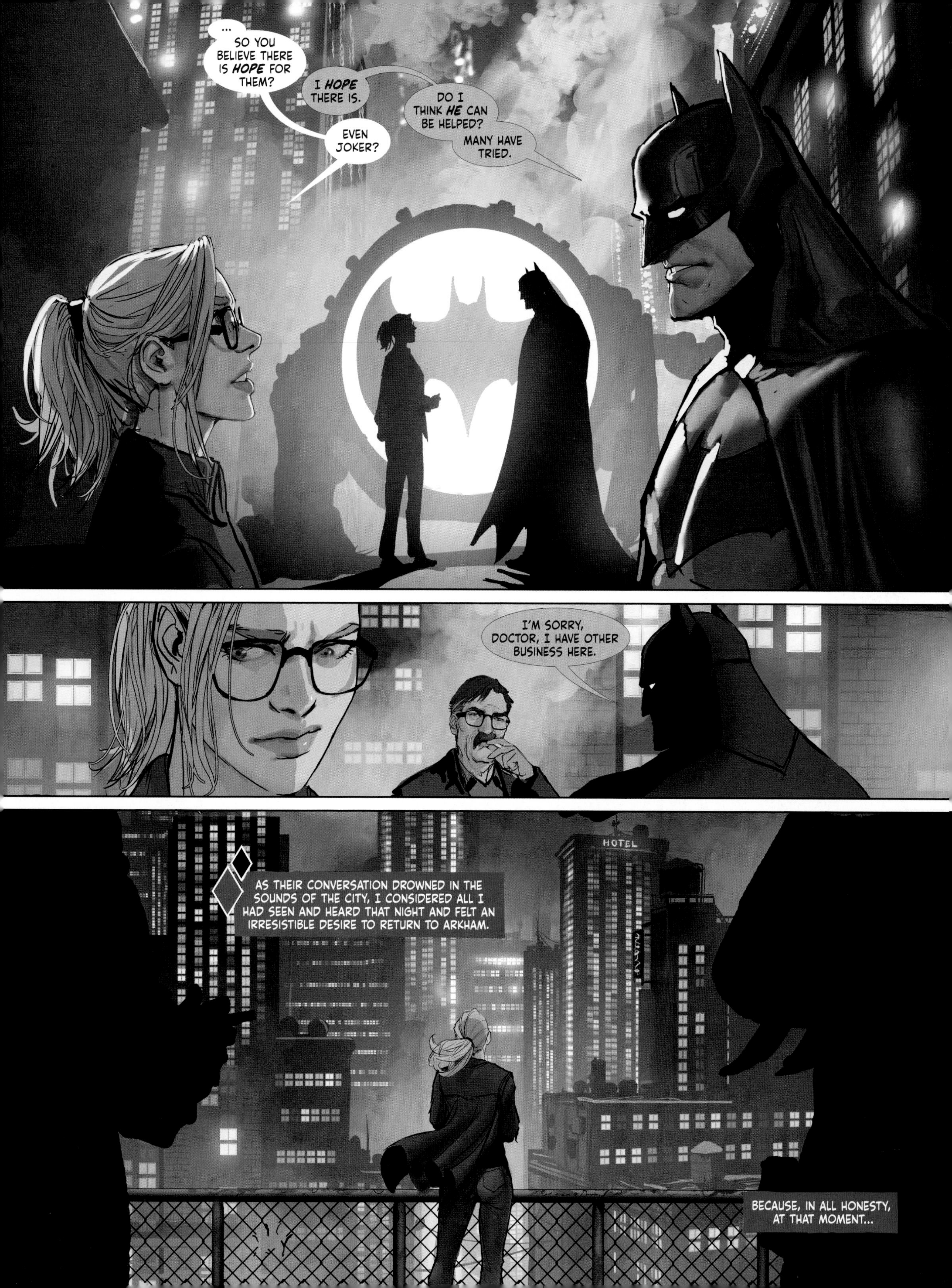

... SO YOU BELIEVE THERE IS **HOPE** FOR THEM?
I **HOPE** THERE IS.
EVEN JOKER?
DO I THINK **HE** CAN BE HELPED?
MANY HAVE TRIED.
I'M SORRY, DOCTOR, I HAVE OTHER BUSINESS HERE.
HOTEL
AS THEIR CONVERSATION DROWNED IN THE SOUNDS OF THE CITY, I CONSIDERED ALL I HAD SEEN AND HEARD THAT NIGHT AND FELT AN IRRESISTIBLE DESIRE TO RETURN TO ARKHAM.
BECAUSE, IN ALL HONESTY, AT THAT MOMENT...

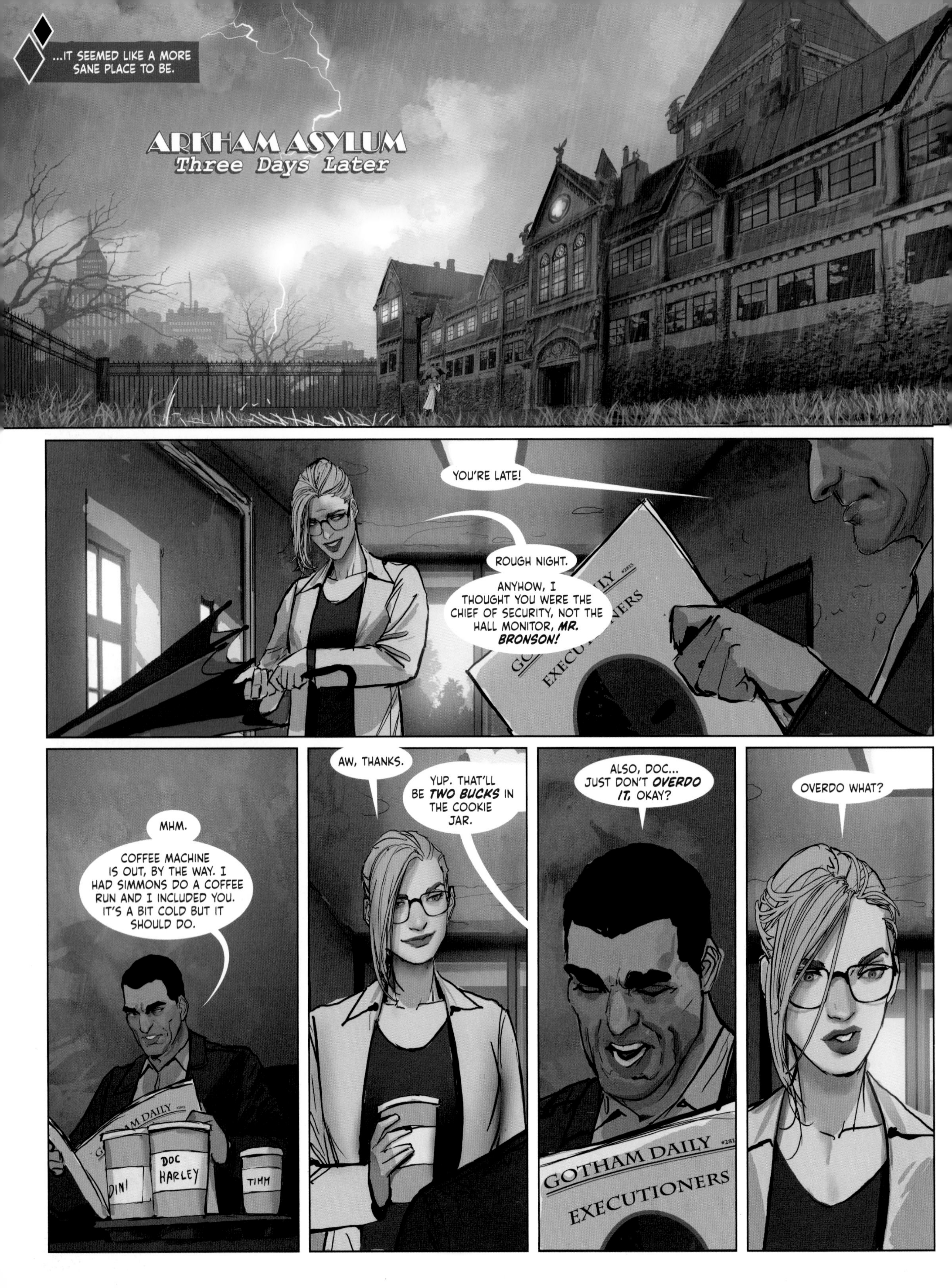

...IT SEEMED LIKE A MORE SANE PLACE TO BE.
ARKHAM ASYLUM
Three Days Later
YOU'RE LATE!
ROUGH NIGHT.
ANYHOW, I THOUGHT YOU WERE THE CHIEF OF SECURITY, NOT THE HALL MONITOR, MR. BRONSON!
GOTHAM DAILY
EXECUTIONERS
MHM.
COFFEE MACHINE IS OUT, BY THE WAY. I HAD SIMMONS DO A COFFEE RUN AND I INCLUDED YOU. IT'S A BIT COLD BUT IT SHOULD DO.
GOTHAM DAILY
DINI
DOC HARLEY
TIMM
AW, THANKS.
YUP. THAT'LL BE TWO BUCKS IN THE COOKIE JAR.
ALSO, DOC... JUST DON'T OVERDO IT, OKAY?
GOTHAM DAILY
EXECUTIONERS
OVERDO WHAT?

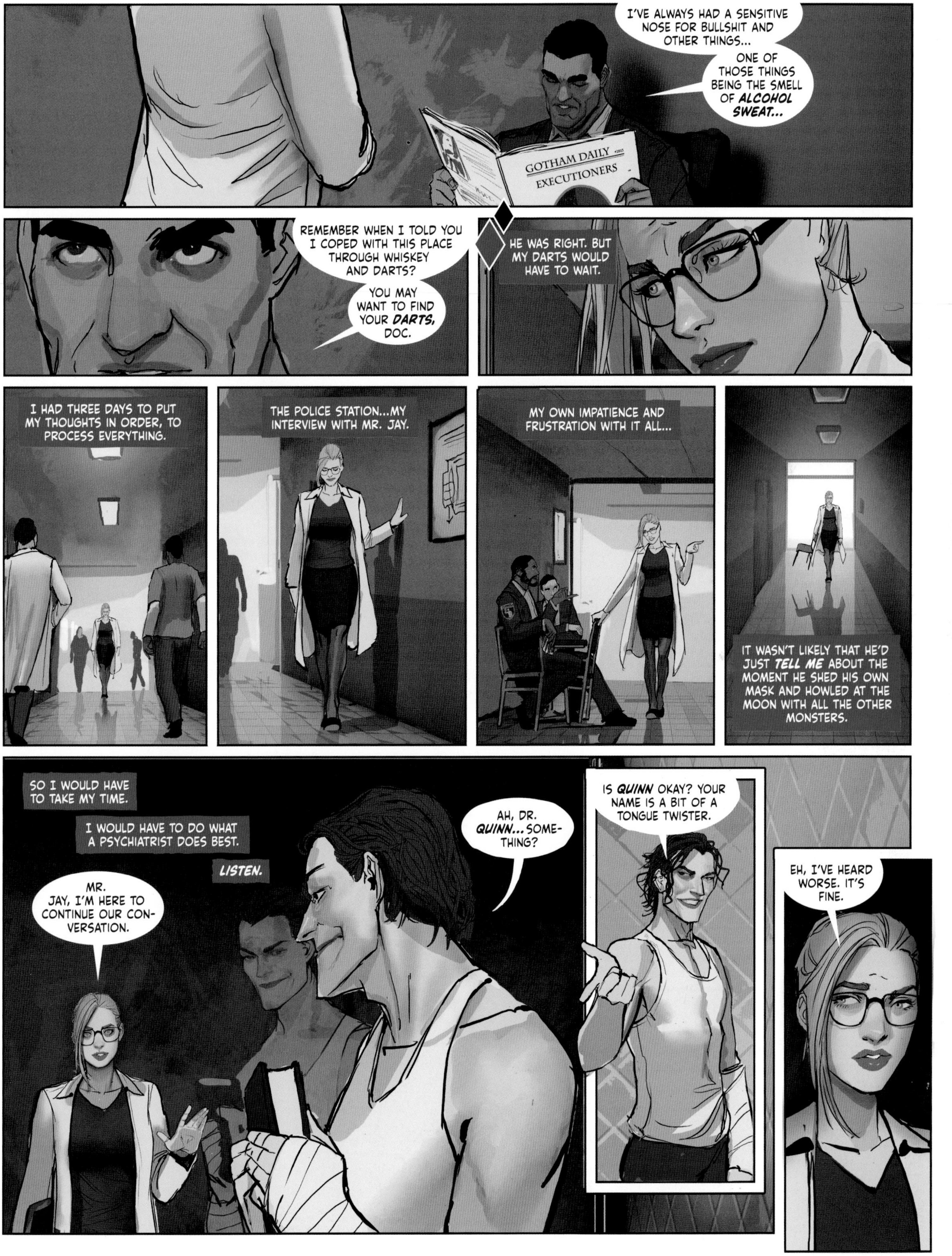

I'VE ALWAYS HAD A SENSITIVE NOSE FOR BULLSHIT AND OTHER THINGS...
ONE OF THOSE THINGS BEING THE SMELL OF ALCOHOL SWEAT...
GOTHAM DAILY
EXECUTIONERS
REMEMBER WHEN I TOLD YOU I COPED WITH THIS PLACE THROUGH WHISKEY AND DARTS?
YOU MAY WANT TO FIND YOUR DARTS, DOC.
HE WAS RIGHT. BUT MY DARTS WOULD HAVE TO WAIT.
I HAD THREE DAYS TO PUT MY THOUGHTS IN ORDER, TO PROCESS EVERYTHING.
THE POLICE STATION...MY INTERVIEW WITH MR. JAY.
MY OWN IMPATIENCE AND FRUSTRATION WITH IT ALL...
IT WASN'T LIKELY THAT HE'D JUST TELL ME ABOUT THE MOMENT HE SHED HIS OWN MASK AND HOWLED AT THE MOON WITH ALL THE OTHER MONSTERS.
SO I WOULD HAVE TO TAKE MY TIME.
I WOULD HAVE TO DO WHAT A PSYCHIATRIST DOES BEST.
LISTEN.
MR. JAY, I'M HERE TO CONTINUE OUR CONVERSATION.
AH, DR. QUINN... SOMETHING?
IS QUINN OKAY? YOUR NAME IS A BIT OF A TONGUE TWISTER.
EH, I'VE HEARD WORSE. IT'S FINE.

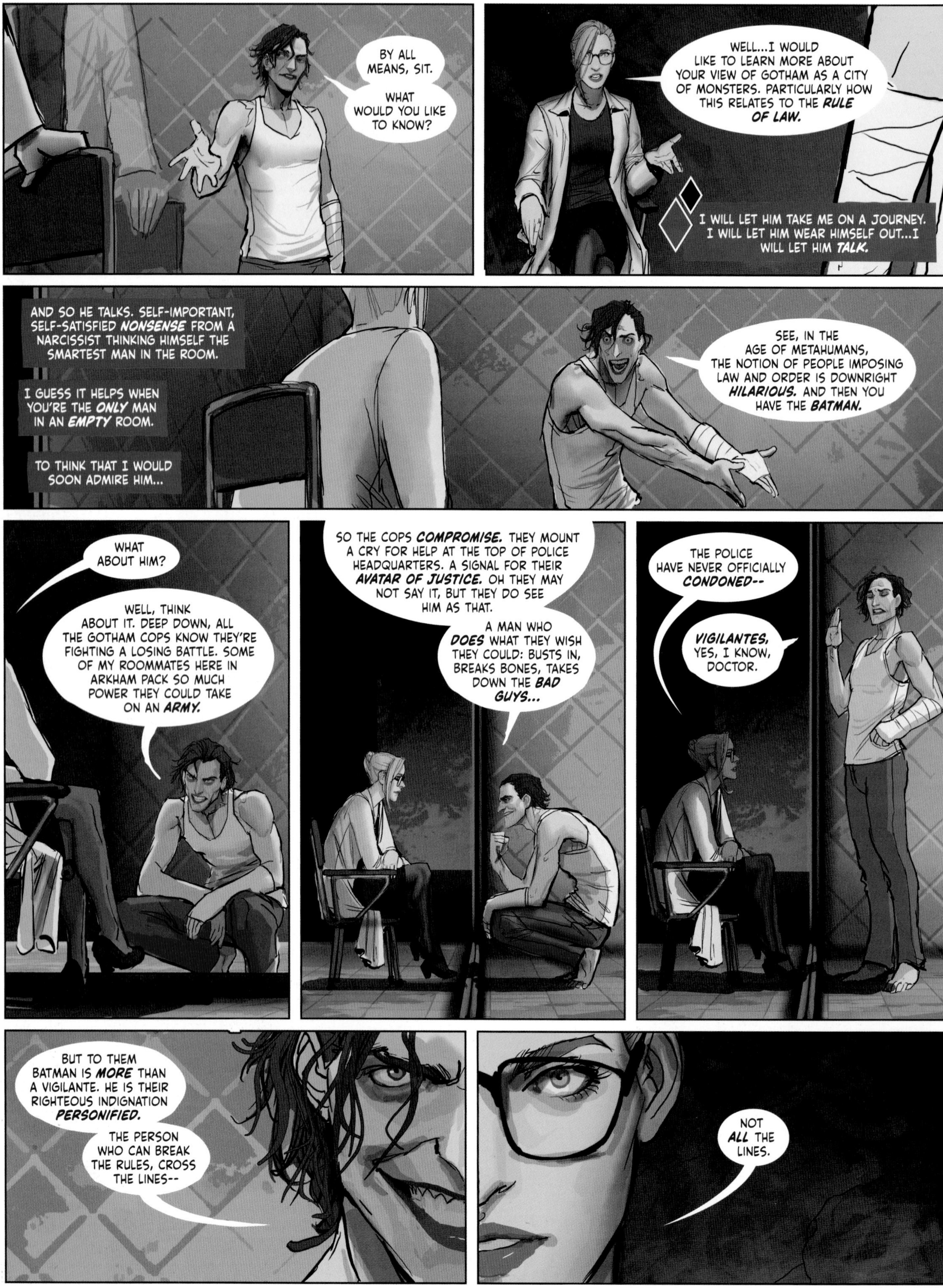

BY ALL MEANS, SIT.
WHAT WOULD YOU LIKE TO KNOW?
WELL...I WOULD LIKE TO LEARN MORE ABOUT YOUR VIEW OF GOTHAM AS A CITY OF MONSTERS. PARTICULARLY HOW THIS RELATES TO THE RULE OF LAW.
I WILL LET HIM TAKE ME ON A JOURNEY. I WILL LET HIM WEAR HIMSELF OUT...I WILL LET HIM TALK.
AND SO HE TALKS. SELF-IMPORTANT, SELF-SATISFIED NONSENSE FROM A NARCISSIST THINKING HIMSELF THE SMARTEST MAN IN THE ROOM.
I GUESS IT HELPS WHEN YOU'RE THE ONLY MAN IN AN EMPTY ROOM.
TO THINK THAT I WOULD SOON ADMIRE HIM...
SEE, IN THE AGE OF METAHUMANS, THE NOTION OF PEOPLE IMPOSING LAW AND ORDER IS DOWNRIGHT HILARIOUS. AND THEN YOU HAVE THE BATMAN.
WHAT ABOUT HIM?
WELL, THINK ABOUT IT. DEEP DOWN, ALL THE GOTHAM COPS KNOW THEY'RE FIGHTING A LOSING BATTLE. SOME OF MY ROOMMATES HERE IN ARKHAM PACK SO MUCH POWER THEY COULD TAKE ON AN ARMY.
SO THE COPS COMPROMISE. THEY MOUNT A CRY FOR HELP AT THE TOP OF POLICE HEADQUARTERS. A SIGNAL FOR THEIR AVATAR OF JUSTICE. OH THEY MAY NOT SAY IT, BUT THEY DO SEE HIM AS THAT.
A MAN WHO DOES WHAT THEY WISH THEY COULD: BUSTS IN, BREAKS BONES, TAKES DOWN THE BAD GUYS...
THE POLICE HAVE NEVER OFFICIALLY CONDONED--
VIGILANTES, YES, I KNOW, DOCTOR.
BUT TO THEM BATMAN IS MORE THAN A VIGILANTE. HE IS THEIR RIGHTEOUS INDIGNATION PERSONIFIED.
THE PERSON WHO CAN BREAK THE RULES, CROSS THE LINES--
NOT ALL THE LINES.

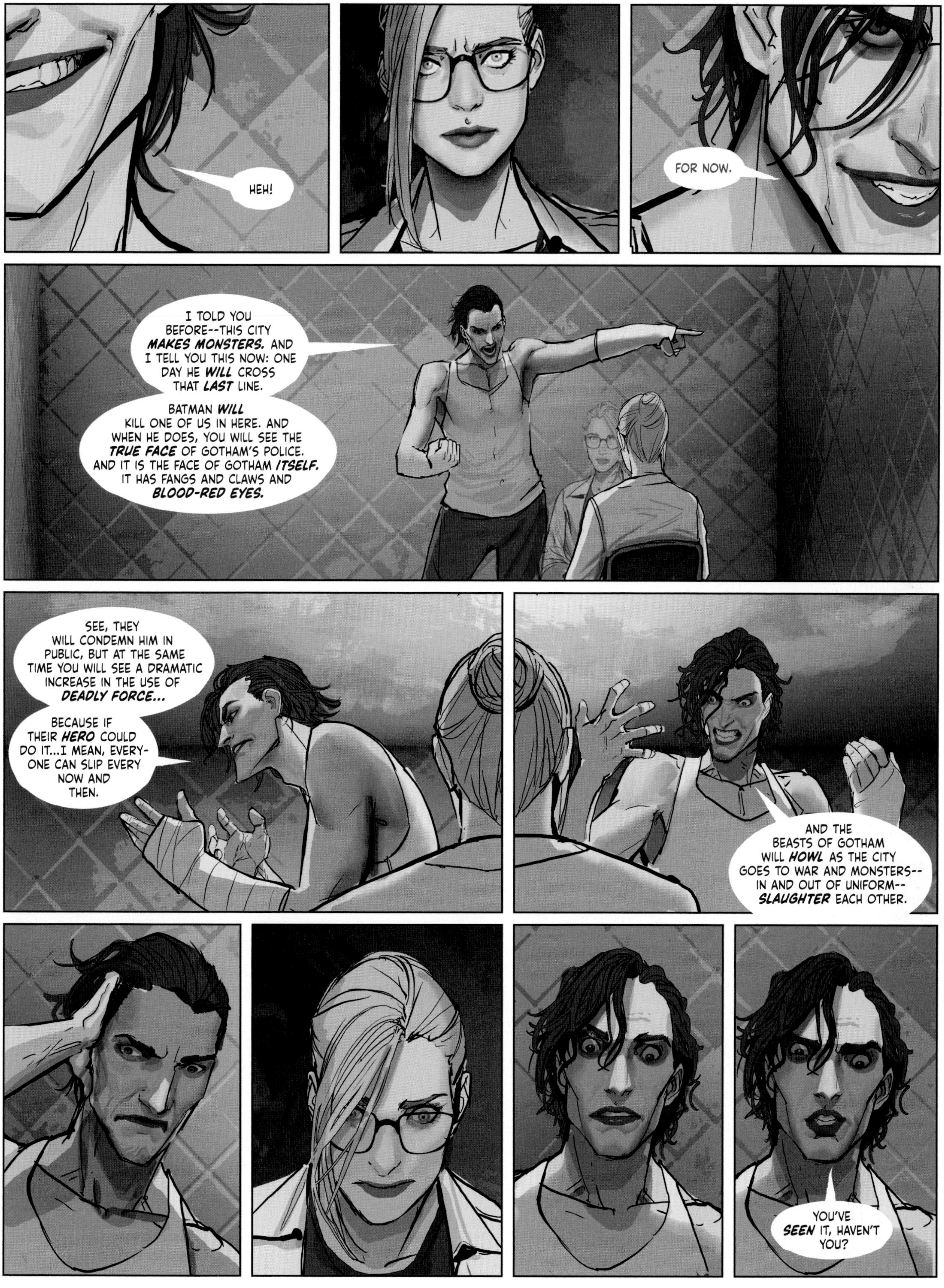
HEH!
FOR NOW.
I TOLD YOU BEFORE--THIS CITY **MAKES MONSTERS.** AND I TELL YOU THIS NOW: ONE DAY HE **WILL** CROSS THAT **LAST** LINE.
BATMAN **WILL** KILL ONE OF US IN HERE. AND WHEN HE DOES, YOU WILL SEE THE **TRUE FACE** OF GOTHAM'S POLICE. AND IT IS THE FACE OF GOTHAM **ITSELF.** IT HAS FANGS AND CLAWS AND **BLOOD-RED EYES.**
SEE, THEY WILL CONDEMN HIM IN PUBLIC, BUT AT THE SAME TIME YOU WILL SEE A DRAMATIC INCREASE IN THE USE OF **DEADLY FORCE...**
BECAUSE IF THEIR **HERO** COULD DO IT...I MEAN, EVERY-ONE CAN SLIP EVERY NOW AND THEN.
AND THE BEASTS OF GOTHAM WILL **HOWL** AS THE CITY GOES TO WAR AND MONSTERS-- IN AND OUT OF UNIFORM-- **SLAUGHTER** EACH OTHER.
YOU'VE **SEEN** IT, HAVEN'T YOU?

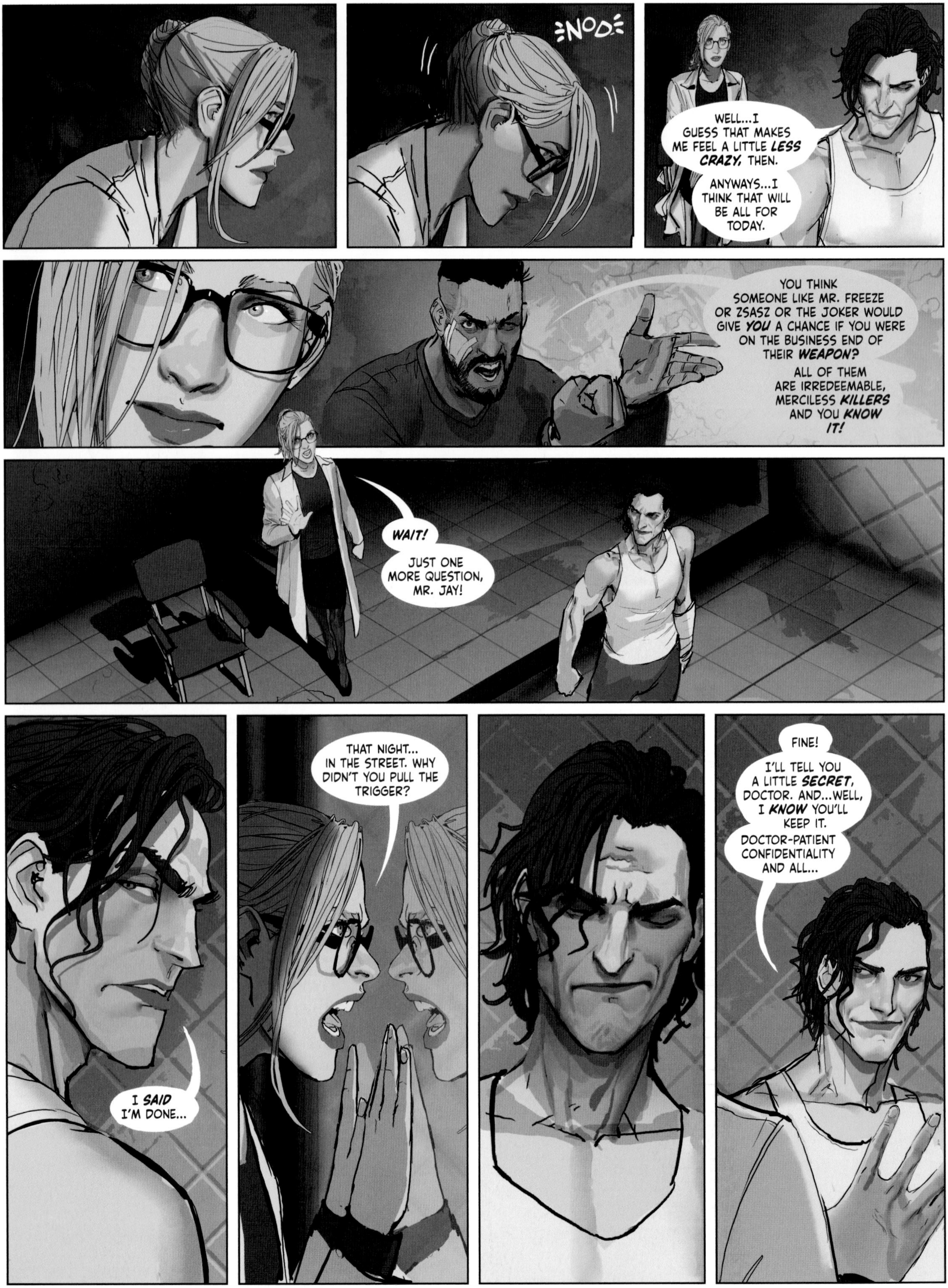
NOD
WELL...I GUESS THAT MAKES ME FEEL A LITTLE LESS CRAZY, THEN.
ANYWAYS...I THINK THAT WILL BE ALL FOR TODAY.
YOU THINK SOMEONE LIKE MR. FREEZE OR ZSASZ OR THE JOKER WOULD GIVE YOU A CHANCE IF YOU WERE ON THE BUSINESS END OF THEIR WEAPON?
ALL OF THEM ARE IRREDEEMABLE, MERCILESS KILLERS AND YOU KNOW IT!
WAIT!
JUST ONE MORE QUESTION, MR. JAY!
I SAID I'M DONE...
THAT NIGHT... IN THE STREET. WHY DIDN'T YOU PULL THE TRIGGER?
FINE!
I'LL TELL YOU A LITTLE SECRET, DOCTOR. AND...WELL, I KNOW YOU'LL KEEP IT.
DOCTOR-PATIENT CONFIDENTIALITY AND ALL...

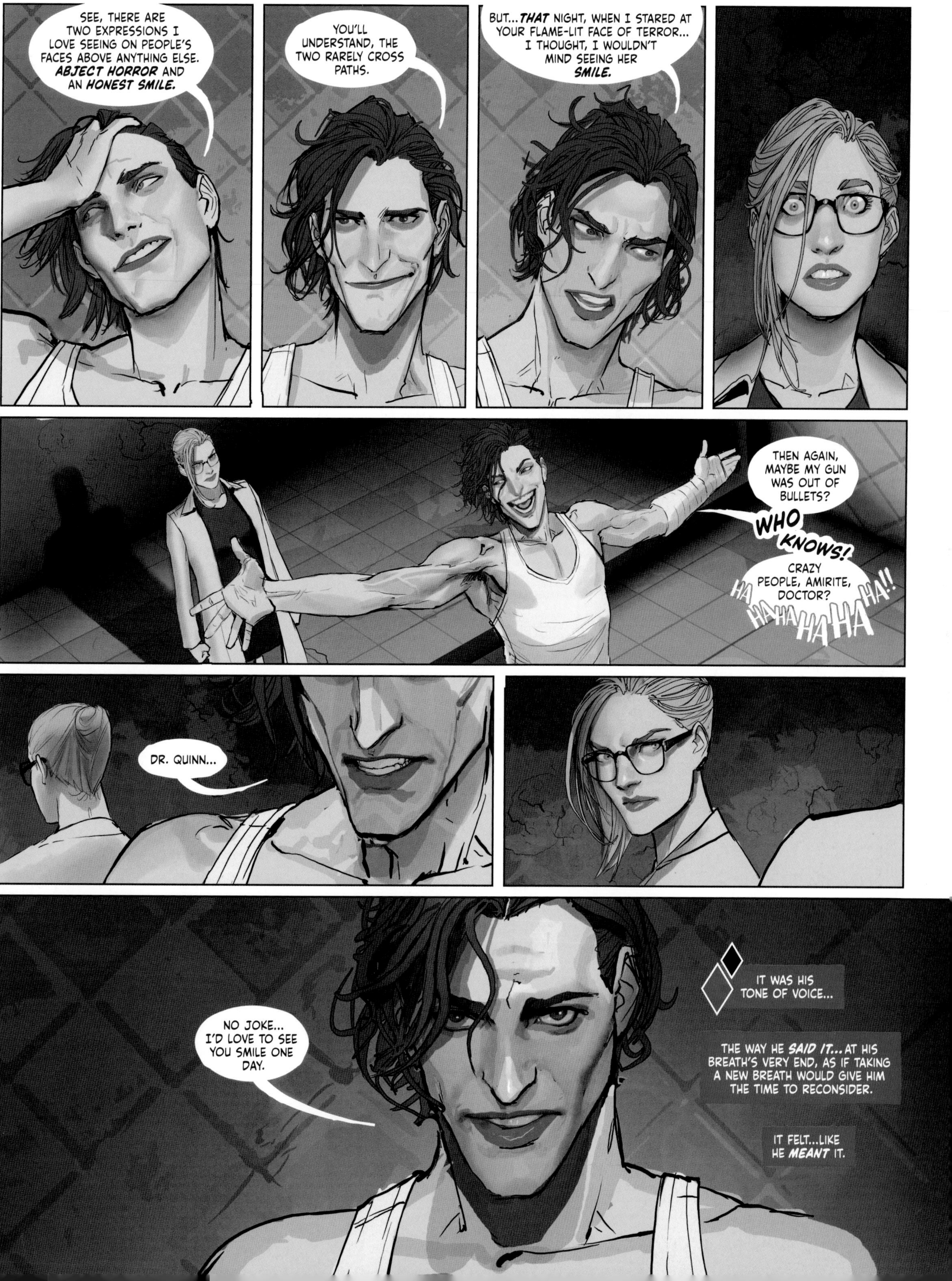
SEE, THERE ARE TWO EXPRESSIONS I LOVE SEEING ON PEOPLE'S FACES ABOVE ANYTHING ELSE. ABJECT HORROR AND AN HONEST SMILE.
YOU'LL UNDERSTAND, THE TWO RARELY CROSS PATHS.
BUT...THAT NIGHT, WHEN I STARED AT YOUR FLAME-LIT FACE OF TERROR... I THOUGHT, I WOULDN'T MIND SEEING HER SMILE.
THEN AGAIN, MAYBE MY GUN WAS OUT OF BULLETS?
WHO KNOWS!
CRAZY PEOPLE, AMIRITE, DOCTOR?
HA HAHAHAHAHA HA!!
DR. QUINN...
NO JOKE... I'D LOVE TO SEE YOU SMILE ONE DAY.
IT WAS HIS TONE OF VOICE...
THE WAY HE SAID IT... AT HIS BREATH'S VERY END, AS IF TAKING A NEW BREATH WOULD GIVE HIM THE TIME TO RECONSIDER.
IT FELT...LIKE HE MEANT IT.

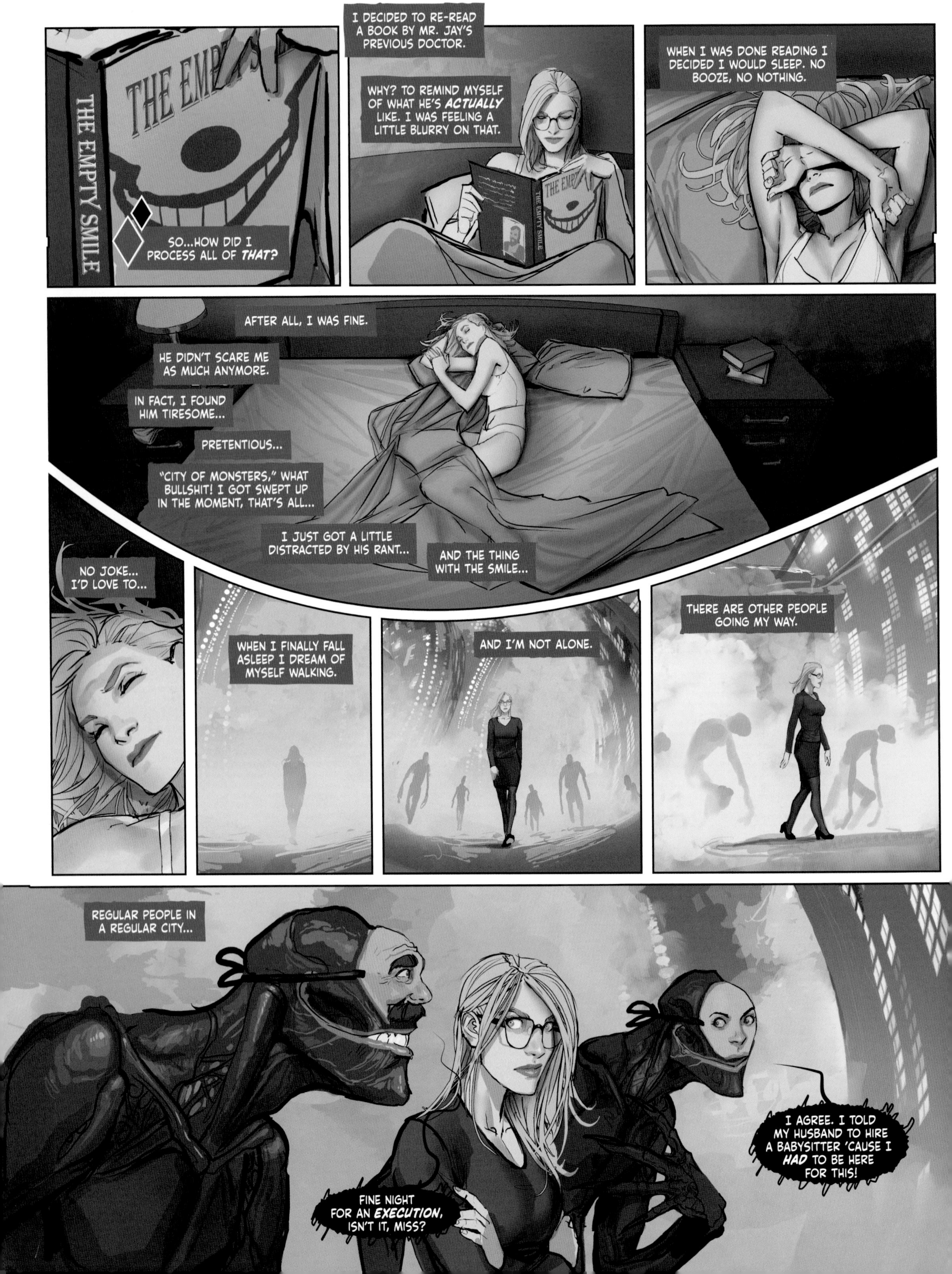
THE EMPTY SMILE
THE EMPTY SMILE
SO...HOW DID I PROCESS ALL OF *THAT?*
I DECIDED TO RE-READ A BOOK BY MR. JAY'S PREVIOUS DOCTOR.
WHY? TO REMIND MYSELF OF WHAT HE'S *ACTUALLY* LIKE. I WAS FEELING A LITTLE BLURRY ON THAT.
THE EMPTY SMILE
WHEN I WAS DONE READING I DECIDED I WOULD SLEEP. NO BOOZE, NO NOTHING.
AFTER ALL, I WAS FINE.
HE DIDN'T SCARE ME AS MUCH ANYMORE.
IN FACT, I FOUND HIM TIRESOME...
PRETENTIOUS...
"CITY OF MONSTERS," WHAT BULLSHIT! I GOT SWEPT UP IN THE MOMENT, THAT'S ALL...
I JUST GOT A LITTLE DISTRACTED BY HIS RANT...
AND THE THING WITH THE SMILE...
NO JOKE... I'D LOVE TO...
WHEN I FINALLY FALL ASLEEP I DREAM OF MYSELF WALKING.
AND I'M NOT ALONE.
THERE ARE OTHER PEOPLE GOING MY WAY.
REGULAR PEOPLE IN A REGULAR CITY...
FINE NIGHT FOR AN *EXECUTION,* ISN'T IT, MISS?
I AGREE. I TOLD MY HUSBAND TO HIRE A BABYSITTER 'CAUSE I *HAD* TO BE HERE FOR THIS!

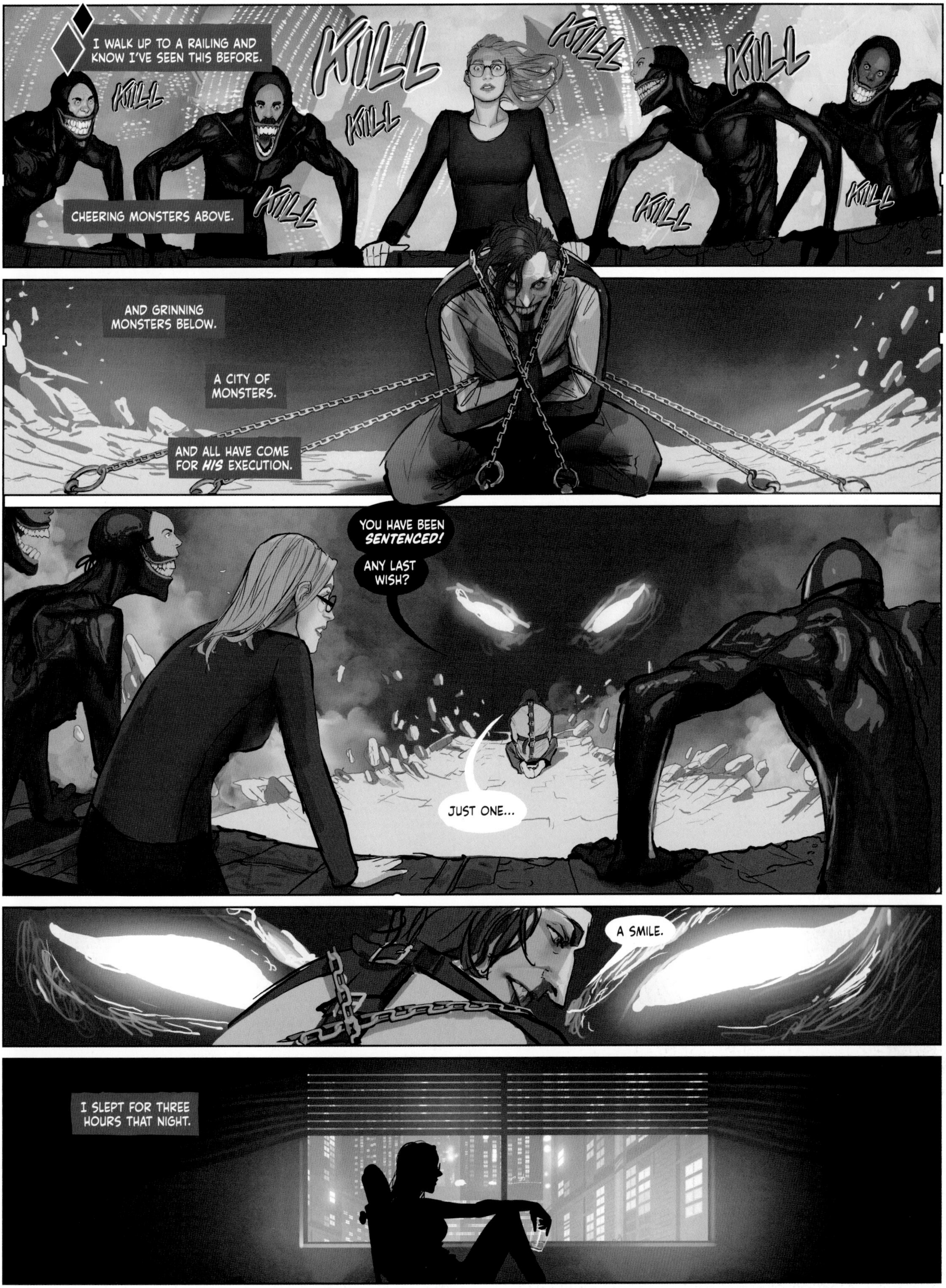
I WALK UP TO A RAILING AND KNOW I'VE SEEN THIS BEFORE.
KILL
KILL
KILL
KILL
KILL
KILL
KILL
KILL
CHEERING MONSTERS ABOVE.
AND GRINNING MONSTERS BELOW.
A CITY OF MONSTERS.
AND ALL HAVE COME FOR HIS EXECUTION.
YOU HAVE BEEN SENTENCED!
ANY LAST WISH?
JUST ONE...
A SMILE.
I SLEPT FOR THREE HOURS THAT NIGHT.

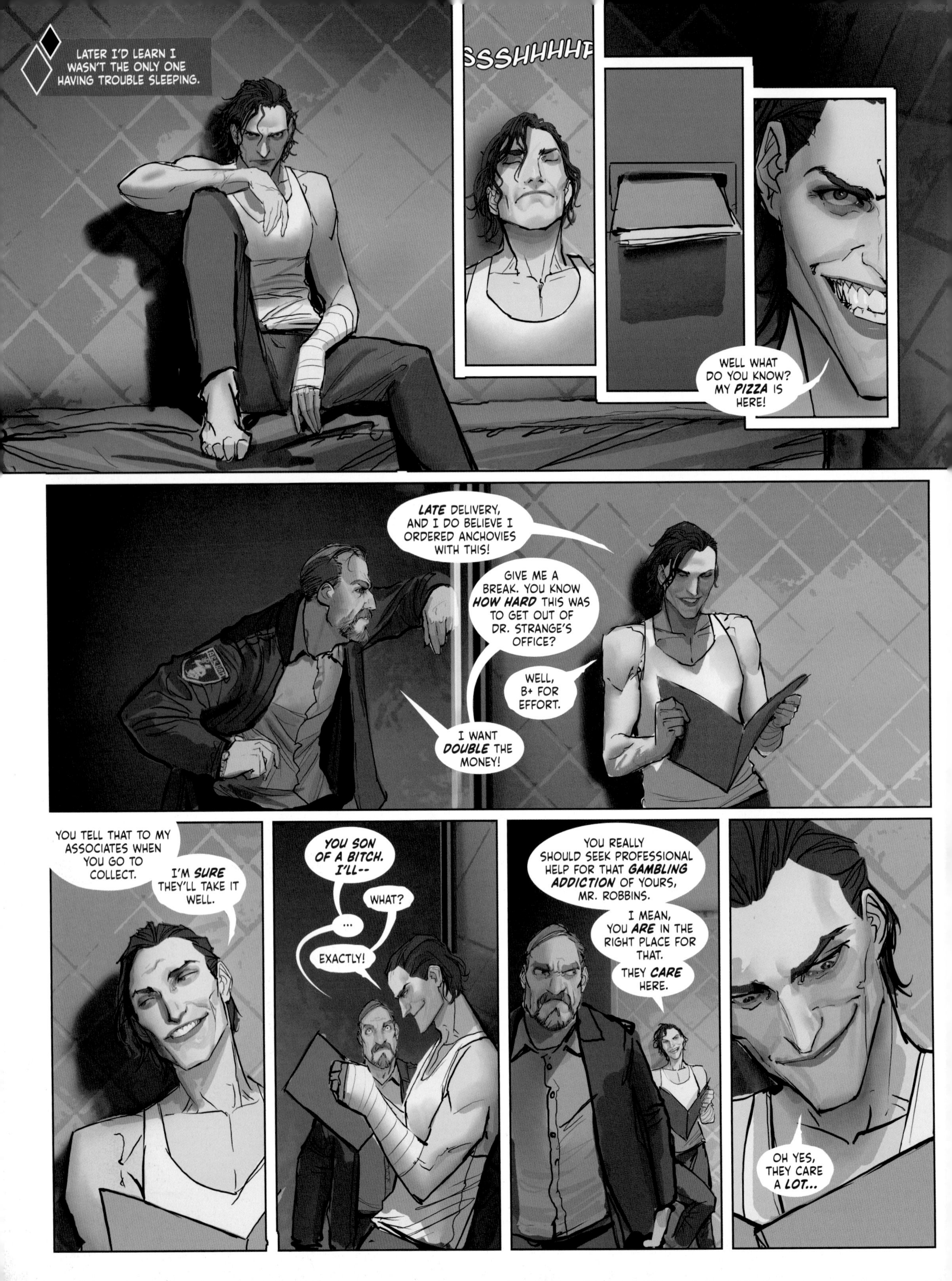

LATER I'D LEARN I WASN'T THE ONLY ONE HAVING TROUBLE SLEEPING.
SSSHHHHP
WELL WHAT DO YOU KNOW? MY *PIZZA* IS HERE!
LATE DELIVERY, AND I DO BELIEVE I ORDERED ANCHOVIES WITH THIS!
GIVE ME A BREAK. YOU KNOW *HOW HARD* THIS WAS TO GET OUT OF DR. STRANGE'S OFFICE?
WELL, B+ FOR EFFORT.
I WANT *DOUBLE* THE MONEY!
YOU TELL THAT TO MY ASSOCIATES WHEN YOU GO TO COLLECT.
I'M *SURE* THEY'LL TAKE IT WELL.
YOU SON OF A BITCH. I'LL--
WHAT?
...
EXACTLY!
YOU REALLY SHOULD SEEK PROFESSIONAL HELP FOR THAT *GAMBLING ADDICTION* OF YOURS, MR. ROBBINS.
I MEAN, YOU *ARE* IN THE RIGHT PLACE FOR THAT.
THEY *CARE* HERE.
OH YES, THEY CARE A *LOT...*

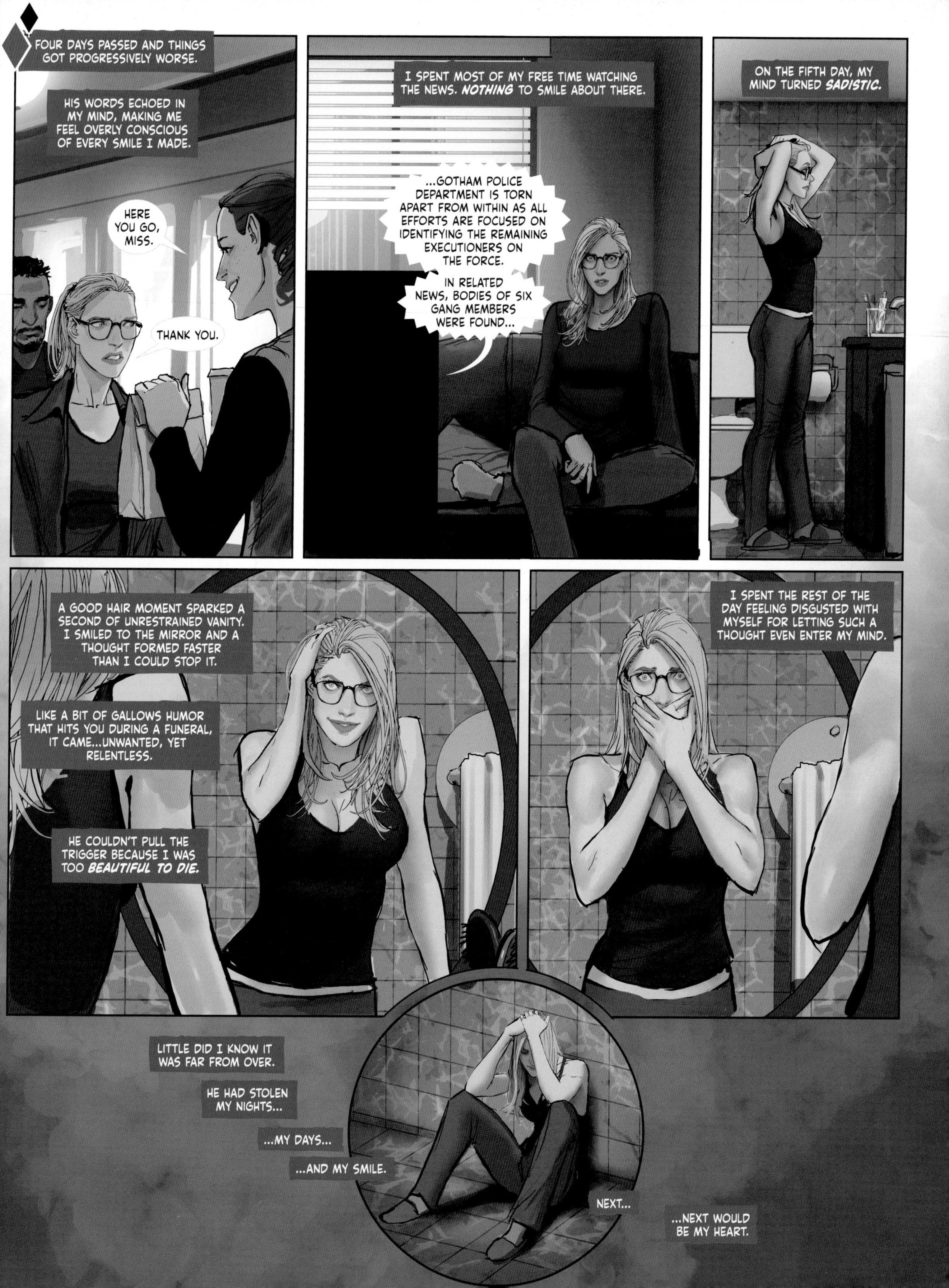

FOUR DAYS PASSED AND THINGS GOT PROGRESSIVELY WORSE.
HIS WORDS ECHOED IN MY MIND, MAKING ME FEEL OVERLY CONSCIOUS OF EVERY SMILE I MADE.
HERE YOU GO, MISS.
THANK YOU.
I SPENT MOST OF MY FREE TIME WATCHING THE NEWS. *NOTHING* TO SMILE ABOUT THERE.
...GOTHAM POLICE DEPARTMENT IS TORN APART FROM WITHIN AS ALL EFFORTS ARE FOCUSED ON IDENTIFYING THE REMAINING EXECUTIONERS ON THE FORCE.
IN RELATED NEWS, BODIES OF SIX GANG MEMBERS WERE FOUND...
ON THE FIFTH DAY, MY MIND TURNED *SADISTIC.*
A GOOD HAIR MOMENT SPARKED A SECOND OF UNRESTRAINED VANITY. I SMILED TO THE MIRROR AND A THOUGHT FORMED FASTER THAN I COULD STOP IT.
LIKE A BIT OF GALLOWS HUMOR THAT HITS YOU DURING A FUNERAL, IT CAME...UNWANTED, YET RELENTLESS.
HE COULDN'T PULL THE TRIGGER BECAUSE I WAS TOO *BEAUTIFUL TO DIE.*
I SPENT THE REST OF THE DAY FEELING DISGUSTED WITH MYSELF FOR LETTING SUCH A THOUGHT EVEN ENTER MY MIND.
LITTLE DID I KNOW IT WAS FAR FROM OVER.
HE HAD STOLEN MY NIGHTS...
...MY DAYS...
...AND MY SMILE.
NEXT...
...NEXT WOULD BE MY HEART.

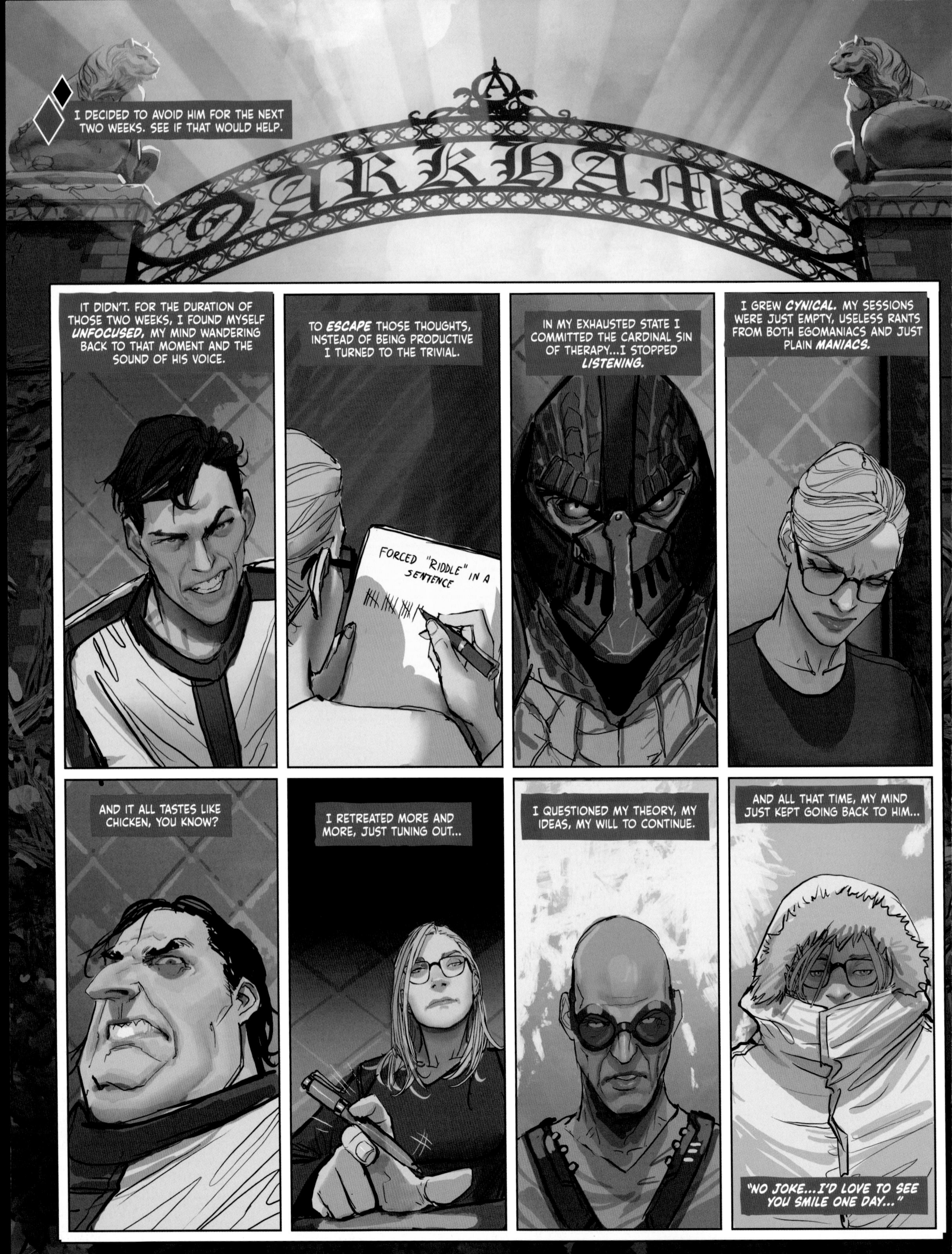
I DECIDED TO AVOID HIM FOR THE NEXT TWO WEEKS. SEE IF THAT WOULD HELP.
ARKHAM
IT DIDN'T. FOR THE DURATION OF THOSE TWO WEEKS, I FOUND MYSELF UNFOCUSED, MY MIND WANDERING BACK TO THAT MOMENT AND THE SOUND OF HIS VOICE.
TO ESCAPE THOSE THOUGHTS, INSTEAD OF BEING PRODUCTIVE I TURNED TO THE TRIVIAL.
FORCED "RIDDLE" IN A SENTENCE
IN MY EXHAUSTED STATE I COMMITTED THE CARDINAL SIN OF THERAPY...I STOPPED LISTENING.
I GREW CYNICAL. MY SESSIONS WERE JUST EMPTY, USELESS RANTS FROM BOTH EGOMANIACS AND JUST PLAIN MANIACS.
AND IT ALL TASTES LIKE CHICKEN, YOU KNOW?
I RETREATED MORE AND MORE, JUST TUNING OUT...
I QUESTIONED MY THEORY, MY IDEAS, MY WILL TO CONTINUE.
AND ALL THAT TIME, MY MIND JUST KEPT GOING BACK TO HIM...
"NO JOKE...I'D LOVE TO SEE YOU SMILE ONE DAY..."

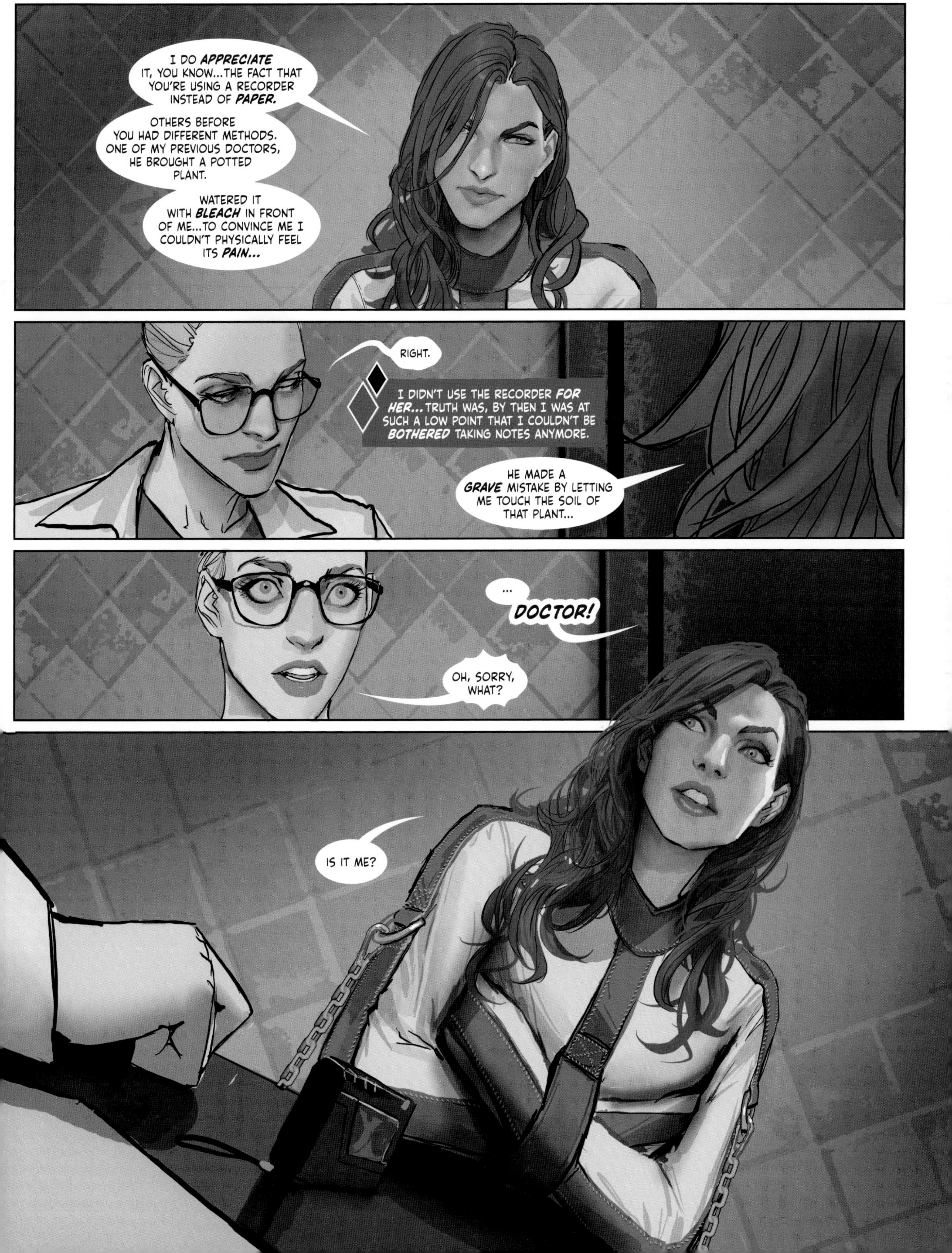
I DO APPRECIATE IT, YOU KNOW...THE FACT THAT YOU'RE USING A RECORDER INSTEAD OF PAPER.
OTHERS BEFORE YOU HAD DIFFERENT METHODS. ONE OF MY PREVIOUS DOCTORS, HE BROUGHT A POTTED PLANT.
WATERED IT WITH BLEACH IN FRONT OF ME...TO CONVINCE ME I COULDN'T PHYSICALLY FEEL ITS PAIN...
RIGHT.
I DIDN'T USE THE RECORDER FOR HER... TRUTH WAS, BY THEN I WAS AT SUCH A LOW POINT THAT I COULDN'T BE BOTHERED TAKING NOTES ANYMORE.
HE MADE A GRAVE MISTAKE BY LETTING ME TOUCH THE SOIL OF THAT PLANT...
... DOCTOR!
OH, SORRY, WHAT?
IS IT ME?

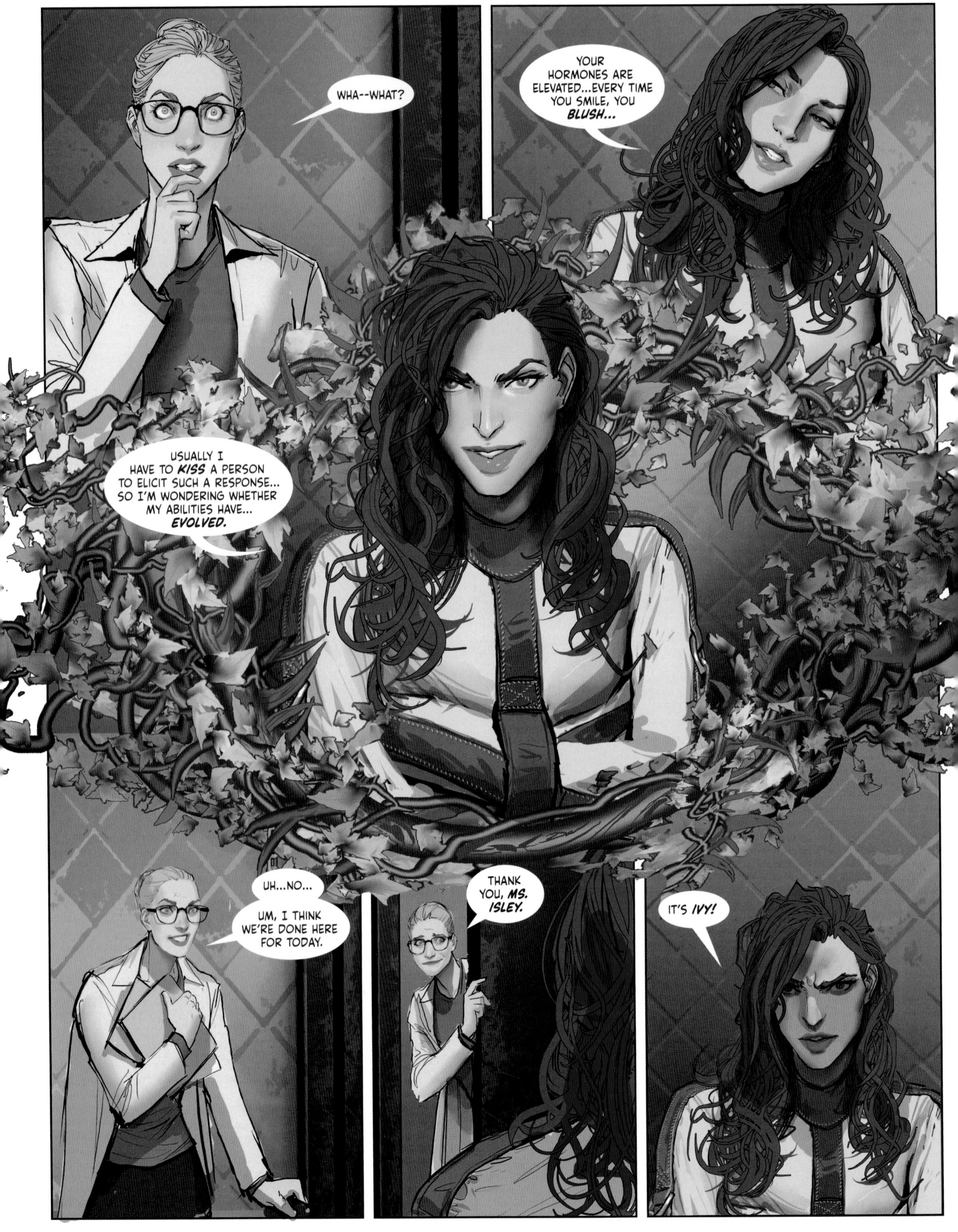
WHA--WHAT?
YOUR HORMONES ARE ELEVATED...EVERY TIME YOU SMILE, YOU BLUSH...
USUALLY I HAVE TO KISS A PERSON TO ELICIT SUCH A RESPONSE... SO I'M WONDERING WHETHER MY ABILITIES HAVE... EVOLVED.
UH...NO...
UM, I THINK WE'RE DONE HERE FOR TODAY.
THANK YOU, MS. ISLEY.
IT'S IVY!

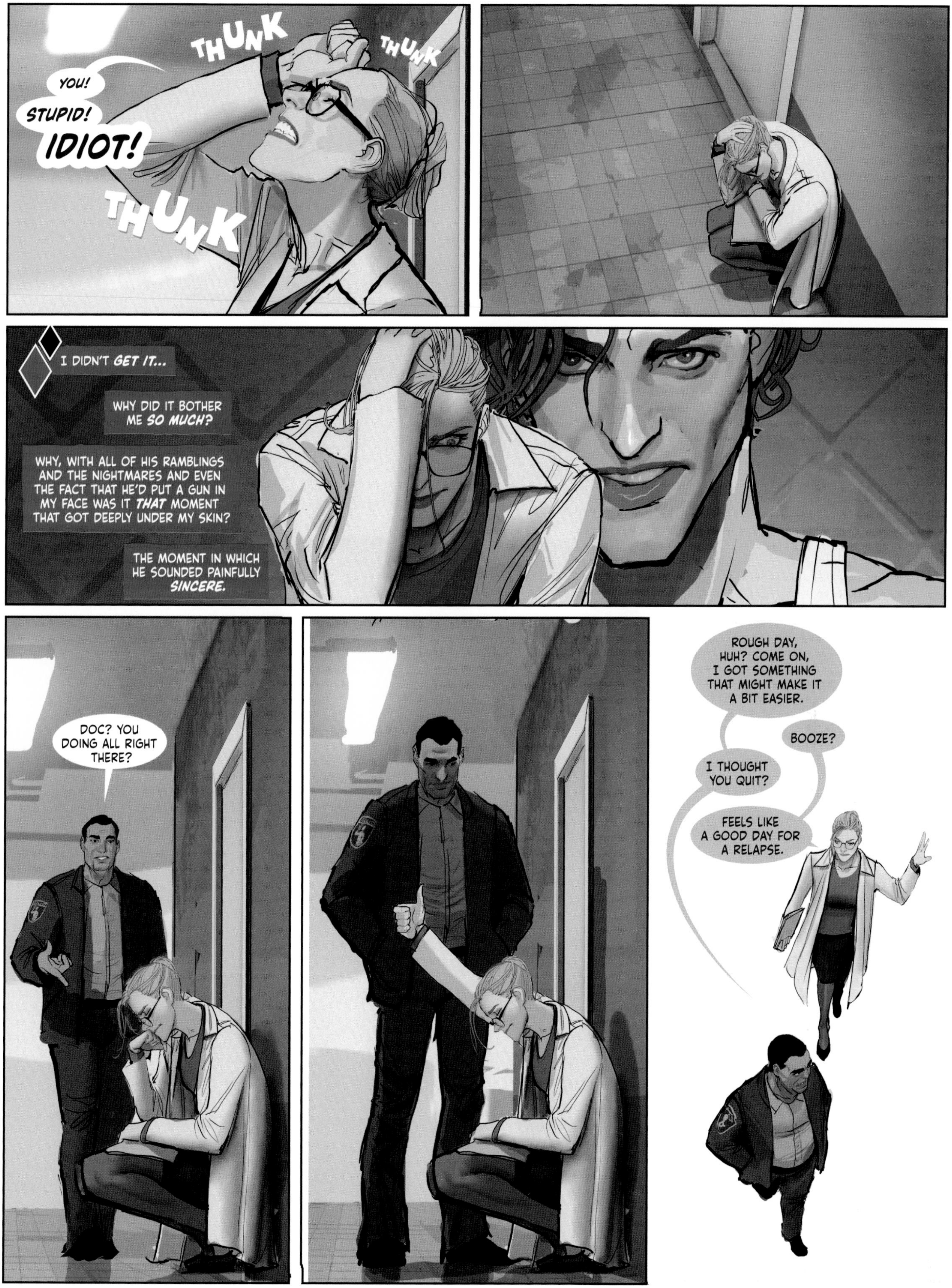

THUNK
THUNK
YOU!
STUPID!
IDIOT!
THUNK
I DIDN'T GET IT...
WHY DID IT BOTHER ME SO MUCH?
WHY, WITH ALL OF HIS RAMBLINGS AND THE NIGHTMARES AND EVEN THE FACT THAT HE'D PUT A GUN IN MY FACE WAS IT THAT MOMENT THAT GOT DEEPLY UNDER MY SKIN?
THE MOMENT IN WHICH HE SOUNDED PAINFULLY SINCERE.
DOC? YOU DOING ALL RIGHT THERE?
ROUGH DAY, HUH? COME ON, I GOT SOMETHING THAT MIGHT MAKE IT A BIT EASIER.
BOOZE?
I THOUGHT YOU QUIT?
FEELS LIKE A GOOD DAY FOR A RELAPSE.

WELL, IT'S NOT BOOZE BUT ONE OF MY GUARDS, PRIYA-- TODAY'S HER BIRTHDAY AND SHE BROUGHT SOME SNACKS AND SODA SO IF YOU WANT YOU CAN JOIN US.

THANKS...

BUT NO. I HAVE TO ORGANIZE MY PAPERWORK BEFORE I SIGN OFF FOR THE DAY.

PLUS THERE IS STILL *ONE MORE* PATIENT I GOTTA SEE.

OKAY, HAVE IT YOUR WAY. GOOD NIGHT, DOC.

NIGHT, MR. BRONSON.

IT IS THE FOURTH NIGHT IN A ROW I GO THROUGH ARKHAM'S MAXIMUM SECURITY WING TO VISIT A PATIENT.

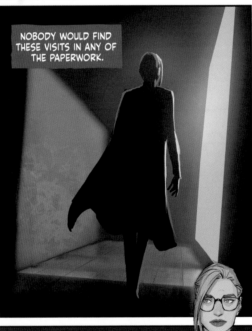

NOBODY WOULD FIND THESE VISITS IN ANY OF THE PAPERWORK.

THESE VISITS AREN'T FOR THE PATIENT'S SAKE, AFTER ALL.

THEY'RE FOR *MINE.*

AS I WATCH HIM SLEEP, I START TO *RELAX*. A SHADOW OF A SMILE SNEAKS UP ON MY FACE.

SLEEPING LIKE THAT, HE SEEMS JUST LIKE A REGULAR PERSON...

PALE NIGHT LIGHT WASHES OUT THE COLOR. IT REMOVES THE GREEN FROM HIS HAIR AND MAKES HIS COMPLEXION A MESMERIZING SIGHT.

ALMOST...*BEAUTIFUL*.

THIS IS MY OWN *SECRET THERAPY*. A WAY TO BEAT THE FEAR.

THERE'S A TRICK PEOPLE USE TO GET OVER THE FEAR OF PUBLIC SPEAKING.

YOU IMAGINE THE AUDIENCE *NAKED*...

WELL, SINCE MY IMAGINATION WAS DARK AND FULL OF NIGHTMARES, THIS WAS THE NEXT BEST THING.

AND YOU KNOW WHAT? IN THAT WAY, IT KIND OF WORKED. HE WASN'T SCARY.

NO...

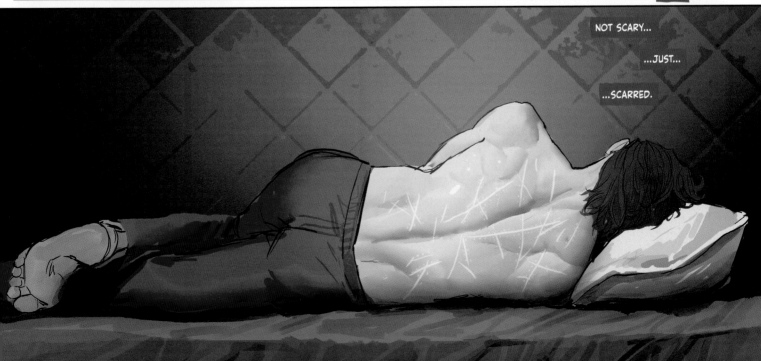

NOT SCARY...

...JUST...

...SCARRED.

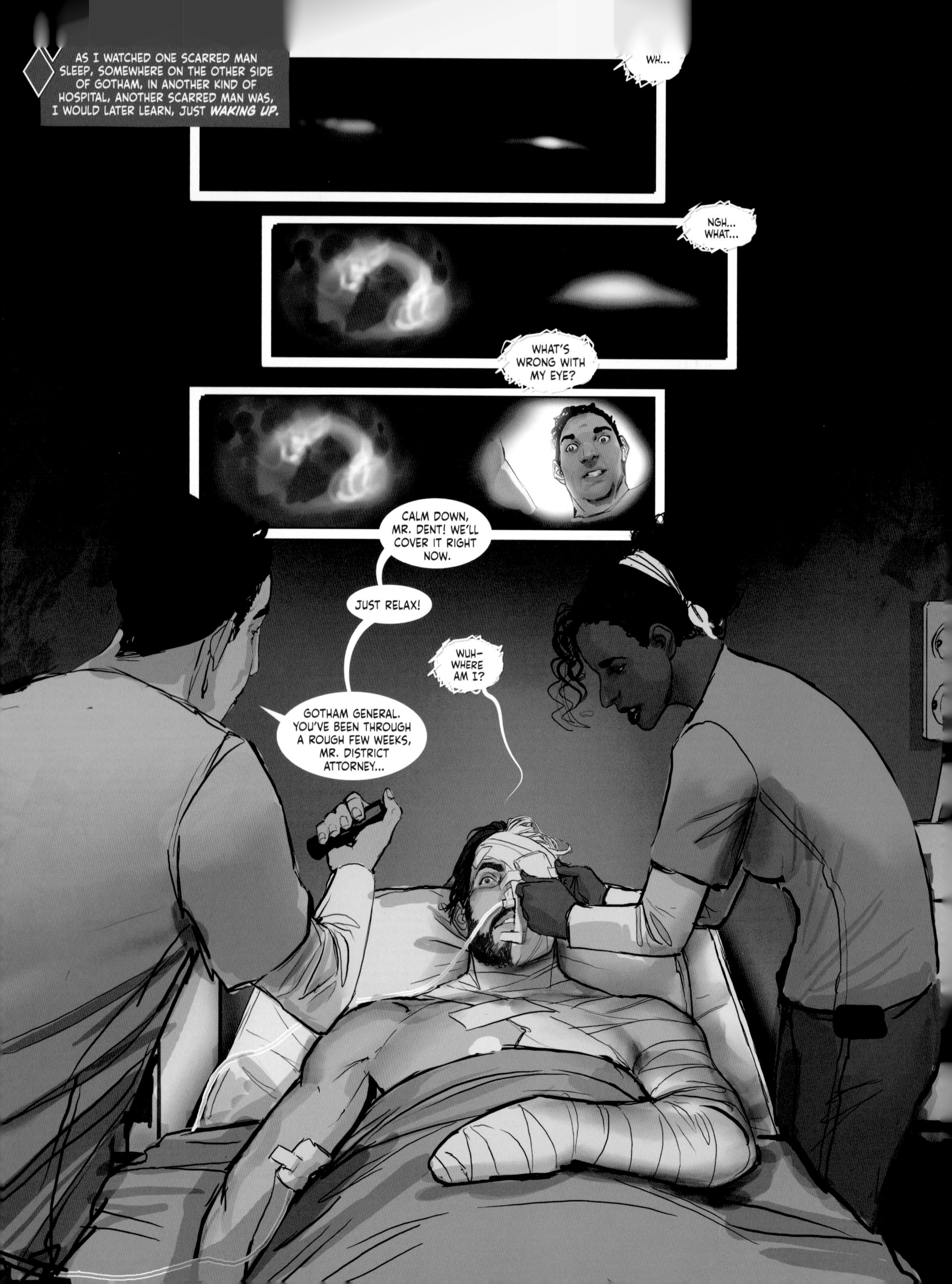

AS I WATCHED ONE SCARRED MAN SLEEP, SOMEWHERE ON THE OTHER SIDE OF GOTHAM, IN ANOTHER KIND OF HOSPITAL, ANOTHER SCARRED MAN WAS, I WOULD LATER LEARN, JUST *WAKING UP.*
WH...
NGH... WHAT...
WHAT'S WRONG WITH MY EYE?
CALM DOWN, MR. DENT! WE'LL COVER IT RIGHT NOW.
JUST RELAX!
WUH-WHERE AM I?
GOTHAM GENERAL. YOU'VE BEEN THROUGH A ROUGH FEW WEEKS, MR. DISTRICT ATTORNEY...

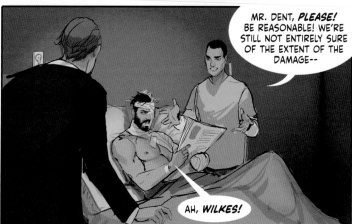

MR. DENT, *PLEASE!* BE REASONABLE! WE'RE STILL NOT ENTIRELY SURE OF THE EXTENT OF THE DAMAGE--

AH, *WILKES!*

HARVEY! OH THANK GOD! I TOOK THE FIRST FLIGHT BACK WHEN I HEARD YOU WERE AWAKE. HOW ARE YOU?

AS GOOD AS COULD BE EXPECTED AFTER ALMOST A MONTH IN A *COMA.*

I'M STILL CATCHING UP ON EVERYTHING THAT'S HAPPENED.

IT SEEMS THE VULTURES HAVE BEEN BUSY CIRCLING WHAT'S LEFT OF MY GOOD NAME?

IT'S...BEEN A CHALLENGING MONTH.

THIS WHOLE EXECUTIONERS BUSINESS, ROGUE COPS MURDERING CRIMINALS IN THE NAME OF THE *MARTYR* HARVEY DENT.

SUFFICE IT TO SAY, THE TABLOIDS HAVE BEEN EATING IT UP.

YES, ABOUT THAT: I WANT YOU TO ARRANGE A PRESS CONFERENCE IN THREE DAYS.

PLEASE, TALK HIM OUT OF IT! HE'S IN NO STATE TO DO THIS.

WHAT DO YOU MEAN?

BOTH HIS LEFT EYE AND EAR ARE *CRITICALLY DAMAGED.* THE TISSUE HAS BARELY BEGUN *HEALING.*

HE'S ON EX-TREMELY POWERFUL *PAINKILLERS* AND--

ENOUGH, DOCTOR.

MR. DENT, YOU WERE DOUSED WITH A *LETHALLY* TOXIC CHEMICAL COCKTAIL.

WE CAN'T EVEN EXCLUD THE POS-SIBILITY OF *BRAIN DAMAGE.*

PLEASE, POSTPONE THIS EVENT FOR AT *LEAST* TWO WEEKS.

GIVE US THE *TIME* TO--

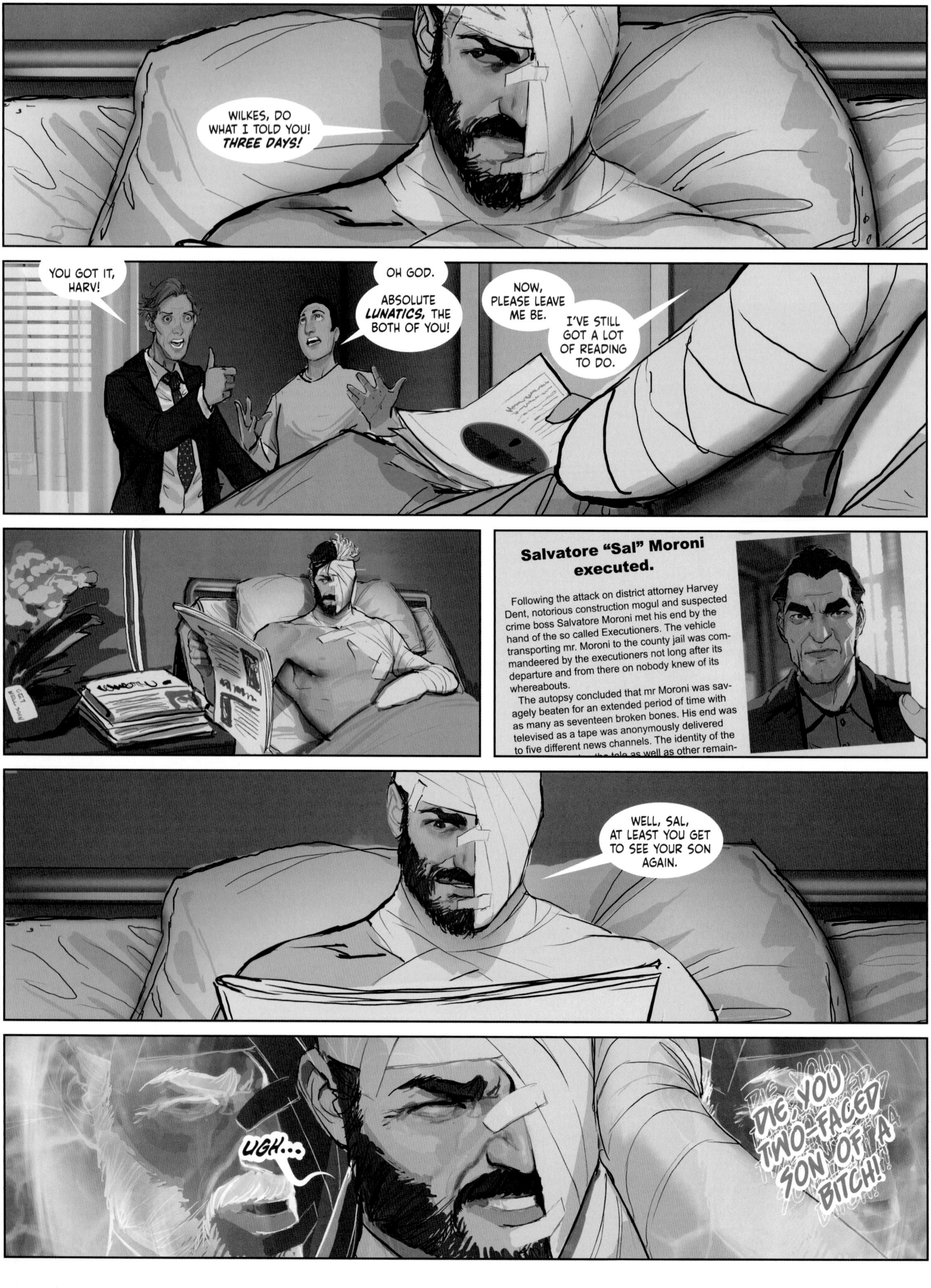
WILKES, DO WHAT I TOLD YOU! *THREE DAYS!*
YOU GOT IT, HARV!
OH GOD.
ABSOLUTE *LUNATICS,* THE BOTH OF YOU!
NOW, PLEASE LEAVE ME BE.
I'VE STILL GOT A LOT OF READING TO DO.
Salvatore "Sal" Moroni executed.
Following the attack on district attorney Harvey Dent, notorious construction mogul and suspected crime boss Salvatore Moroni met his end by the hand of the so called Executioners. The vehicle transporting mr. Moroni to the county jail was commandeered by the executioners not long after its departure and from there on nobody knew of its whereabouts.
The autopsy concluded that mr Moroni was savagely beaten for an extended period of time with as many as seventeen broken bones. His end was televised as a tape was anonymously delivered to five different news channels. The identity of the
WELL, SAL, AT LEAST YOU GET TO SEE YOUR SON AGAIN.
UGH...
DIE, YOU TWO-FACED SON OF A BITCH!

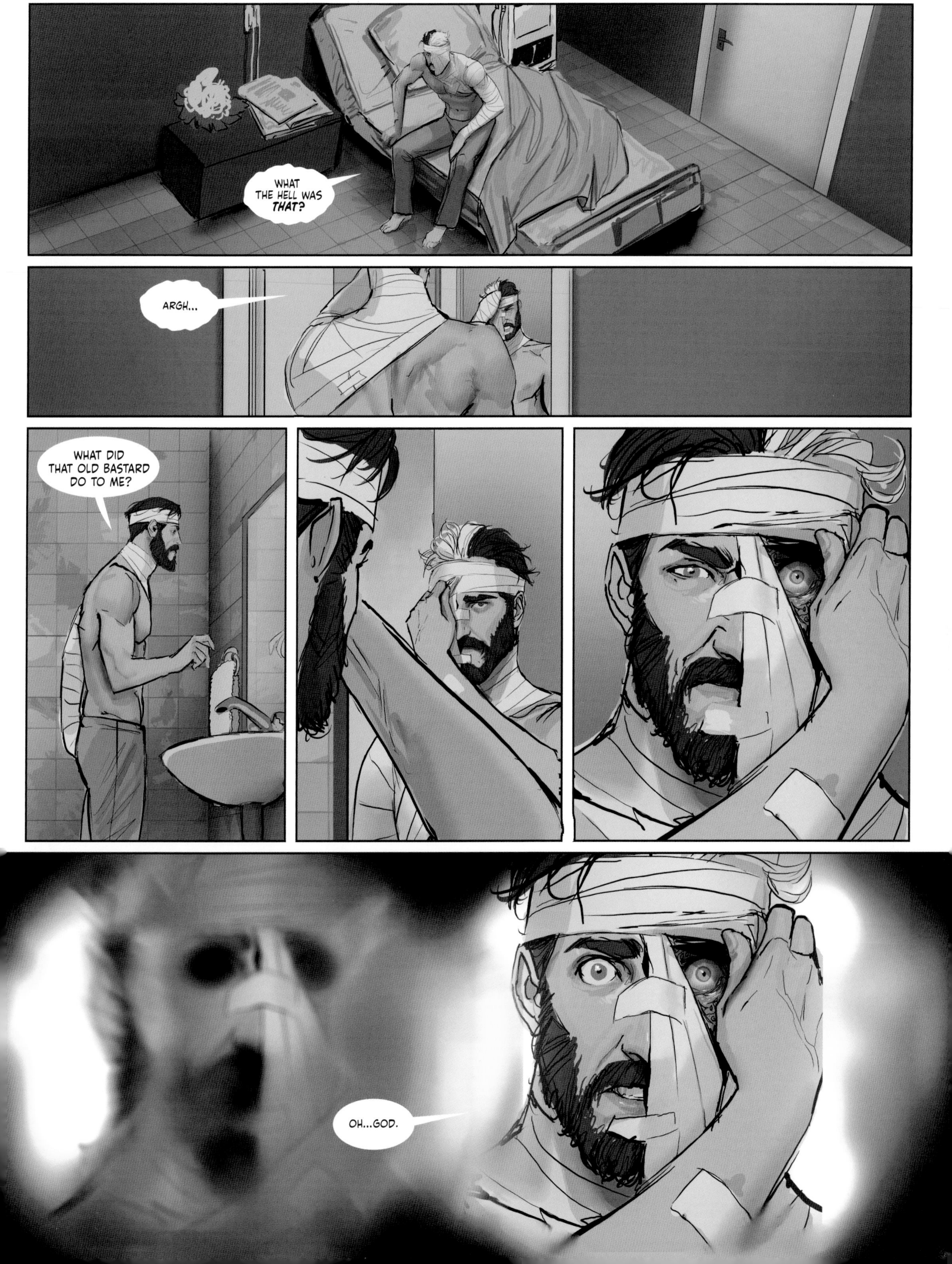
WHAT THE HELL WAS *THAT*?
ARGH...
WHAT DID THAT OLD BASTARD DO TO ME?
OH...GOD.

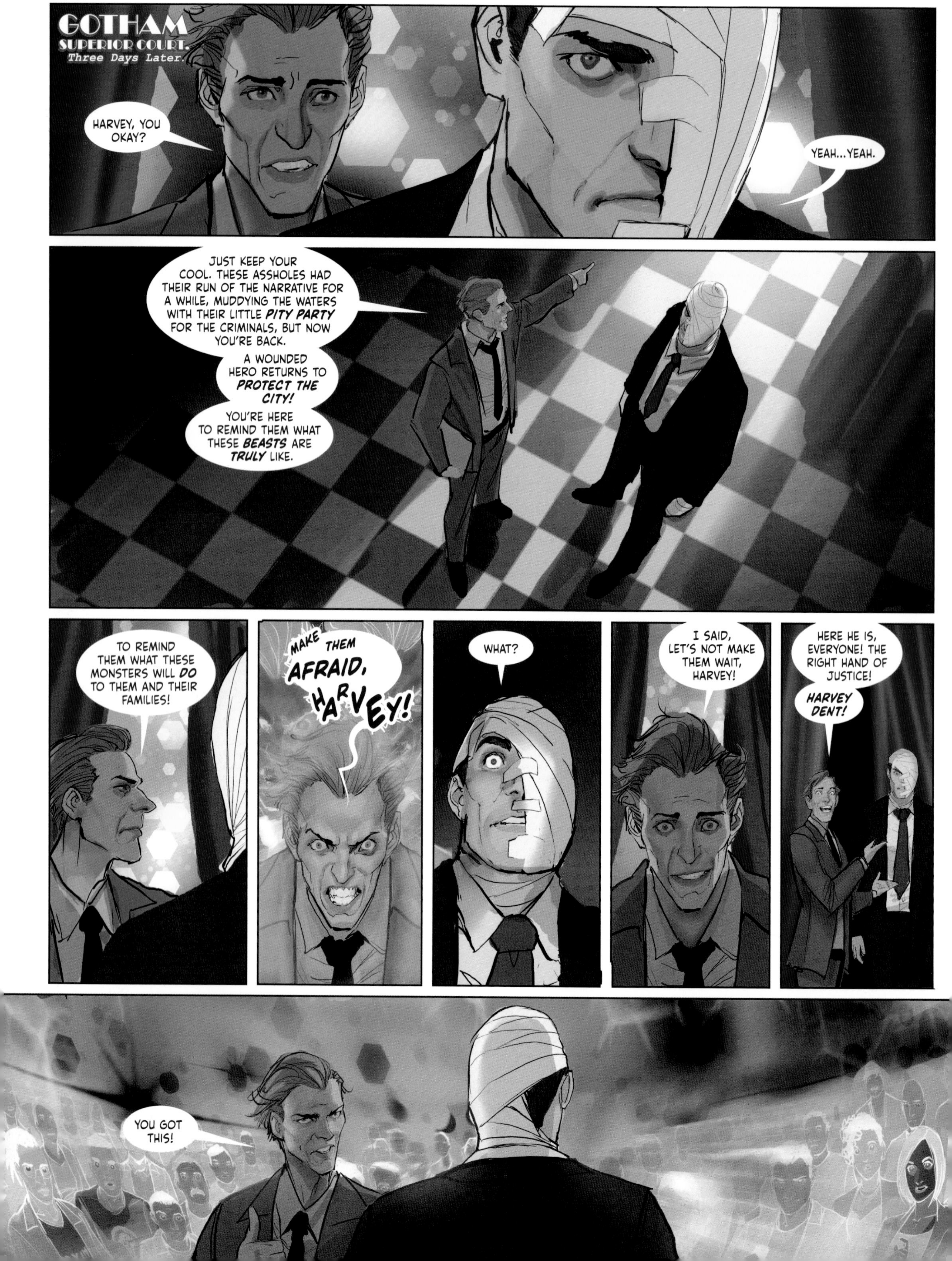
GOTHAM SUPERIOR COURT.
Three Days Later.
HARVEY, YOU OKAY?
YEAH...YEAH.
JUST KEEP YOUR COOL. THESE ASSHOLES HAD THEIR RUN OF THE NARRATIVE FOR A WHILE, MUDDYING THE WATERS WITH THEIR LITTLE *PITY PARTY* FOR THE CRIMINALS, BUT NOW YOU'RE BACK.
A WOUNDED HERO RETURNS TO *PROTECT THE CITY!*
YOU'RE HERE TO REMIND THEM WHAT THESE *BEASTS* ARE *TRULY* LIKE.
TO REMIND THEM WHAT THESE MONSTERS WILL *DO* TO THEM AND THEIR FAMILIES!
MAKE THEM AFRAID, HARVEY!
WHAT?
I SAID, LET'S NOT MAKE THEM WAIT, HARVEY!
HERE HE IS, EVERYONE! THE RIGHT HAND OF JUSTICE!
HARVEY DENT!
YOU GOT THIS!

YOU GOT THIS.

THAT WAS MY ATTITUDE WHEN I FIRST ARRIVED AT ARKHAM.

BUT JUST ABOUT TWO MONTHS LATER, I WAS VERY MUCH QUESTIONING THAT.

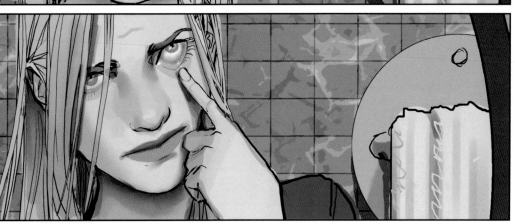

WHAT I *GOT* WAS A DRINKING HABIT, BAGS UNDER MY EYES, AND A FULL-ON NERVOUS BREAKDOWN IN MY FUTURE.

I'D LONG AGO STOPPED DENYING THE LITTLE VOICE IN THE BACK OF MY HEAD TELLING ME TO GO AND SEE *HIM* AGAIN AT NIGHT.

SEE...THE *FEAR* WAS GONE, BUT IT WAS REPLACED WITH SOMETHING *WAY* MORE UNSETTLING.

I WAS ABOUT ONE MORE SLEEPLESS WEEK AWAY FROM JUST ABANDONING IT ALL...

WHY DIDN'T I? WELL, BELIEVE IT OR NOT, IT WAS ONCE AGAIN BECAUSE OF...

GOTHAM'S D.A. HARVEY DENT IS ONCE AGAIN THE TOPIC OF THE DAY!

THIS AFTERNOON MR. DENT GAVE HIS FIRST PRESS CONFERENCE SINCE THE HORRIFIC ATTACK ON HIS PERSON LAST MONTH, AND THE SCENE OUTSIDE GOTHAM SUPERIOR COURT TURNED TO *PANDEMONIUM.*

WE WILL NOW SHOW YOU THE RECORDING OF THIS EVENT.

BUT BE *WARNED:* YOU'LL WANT TO KEEP YOUR CHILDREN AWAY FROM THE TV FOR THE NEXT FEW MINUTES.

THIS *WILL* BE UNCOMFORTABLE TO WATCH.

MR. DENT! *WHY* DID THE LATE CRIME BOSS SALVATORE MARONI TRY TO *KILL* YOU?

SAL MARONI INITIALLY APPROACHED ME AS A BUSINESSMAN WANTING TO SUPPORT MY CAMPAIGN FOR DISTRICT ATTORNEY. I ACCEPTED HIS HELP.

HE SEEMED SINCERE, AND I HAD NO REASON TO DOUBT HIS INTENTIONS.

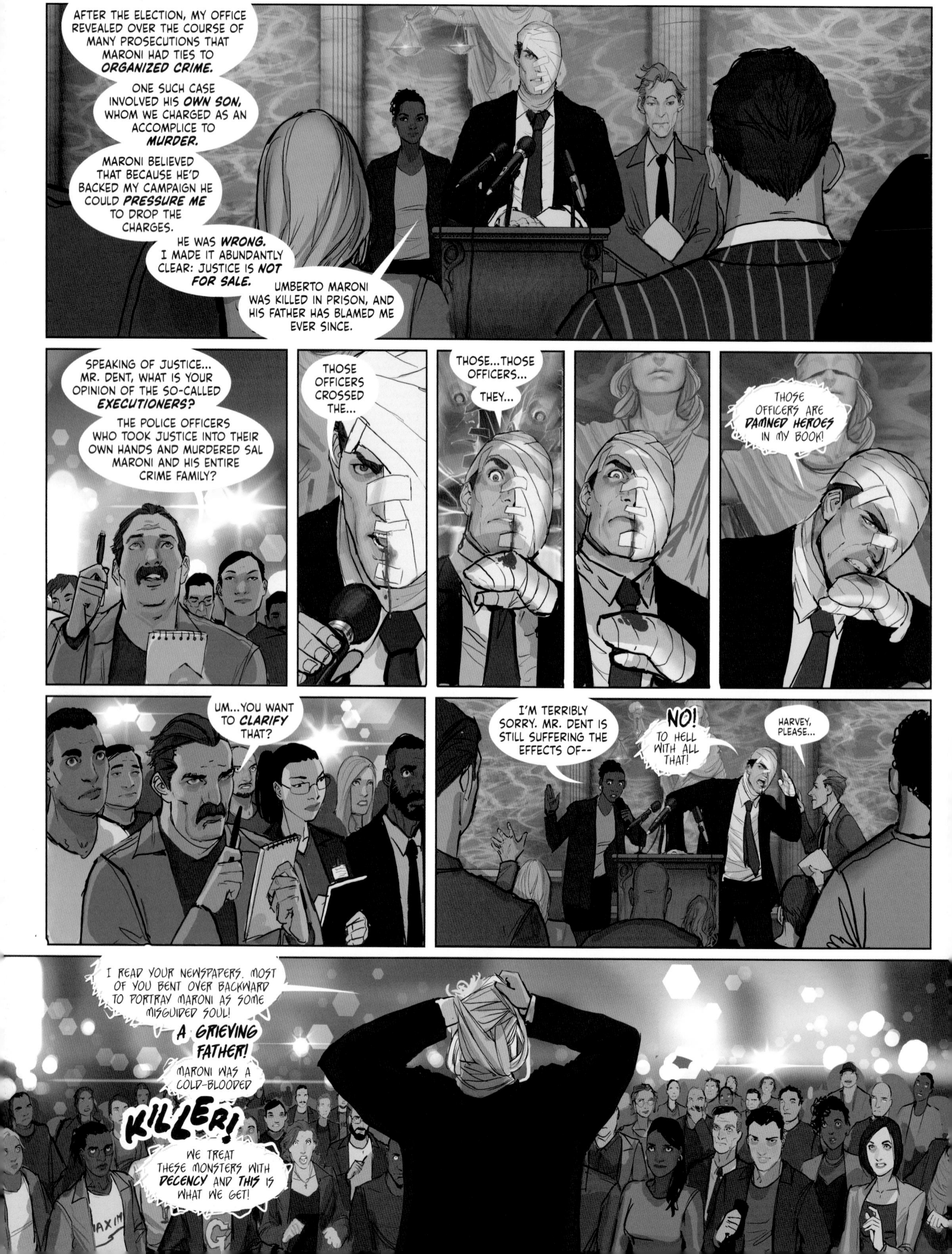

AFTER THE ELECTION, MY OFFICE REVEALED OVER THE COURSE OF MANY PROSECUTIONS THAT MARONI HAD TIES TO ORGANIZED CRIME.
ONE SUCH CASE INVOLVED HIS OWN SON, WHOM WE CHARGED AS AN ACCOMPLICE TO MURDER.
MARONI BELIEVED THAT BECAUSE HE'D BACKED MY CAMPAIGN HE COULD PRESSURE ME TO DROP THE CHARGES.
HE WAS WRONG. I MADE IT ABUNDANTLY CLEAR: JUSTICE IS NOT FOR SALE.
UMBERTO MARONI WAS KILLED IN PRISON, AND HIS FATHER HAS BLAMED ME EVER SINCE.
SPEAKING OF JUSTICE... MR. DENT, WHAT IS YOUR OPINION OF THE SO-CALLED EXECUTIONERS?
THE POLICE OFFICERS WHO TOOK JUSTICE INTO THEIR OWN HANDS AND MURDERED SAL MARONI AND HIS ENTIRE CRIME FAMILY?
THOSE OFFICERS CROSSED THE...
THOSE...THOSE OFFICERS...
THEY...
THOSE OFFICERS ARE DAMNED HEROES IN MY BOOK!
UM...YOU WANT TO CLARIFY THAT?
I'M TERRIBLY SORRY. MR. DENT IS STILL SUFFERING THE EFFECTS OF--
NO! TO HELL WITH ALL THAT!
HARVEY, PLEASE...
I READ YOUR NEWSPAPERS. MOST OF YOU BENT OVER BACKWARD TO PORTRAY MARONI AS SOME MISGUIDED SOUL!
A GRIEVING FATHER!
MARONI WAS A COLD-BLOODED
KILLER!
WE TREAT THESE MONSTERS WITH DECENCY AND THIS IS WHAT WE GET!

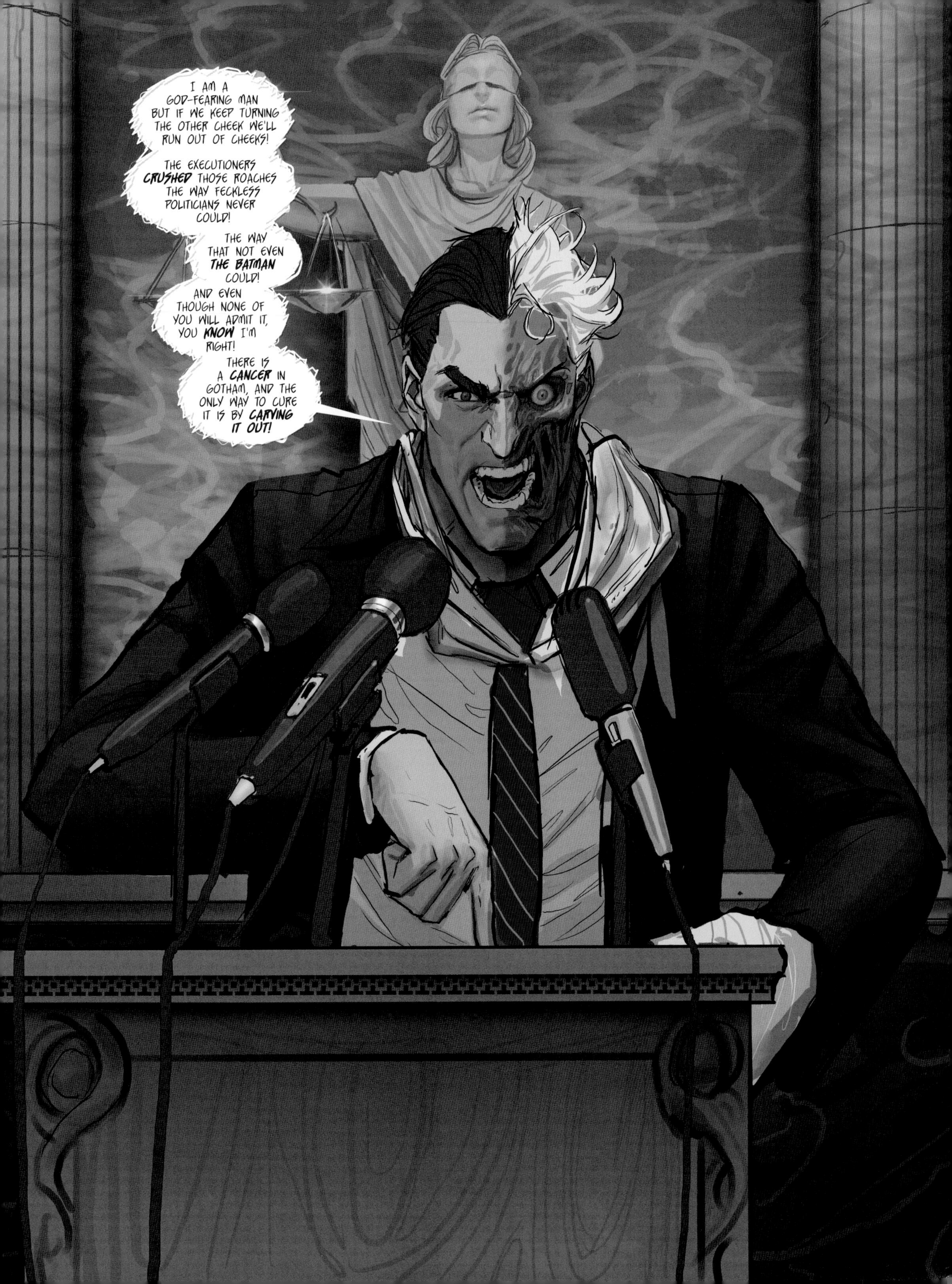
I AM A GOD-FEARING MAN BUT IF WE KEEP TURNING THE OTHER CHEEK WE'LL RUN OUT OF CHEEKS!
THE EXECUTIONERS **CRUSHED** THOSE ROACHES THE WAY FECKLESS POLITICIANS NEVER COULD!
THE WAY THAT NOT EVEN **THE BATMAN** COULD!
AND EVEN THOUGH NONE OF YOU WILL ADMIT IT, YOU **KNOW** I'M RIGHT!
THERE IS A **CANCER** IN GOTHAM, AND THE ONLY WAY TO CURE IT IS BY **CARVING IT OUT!**

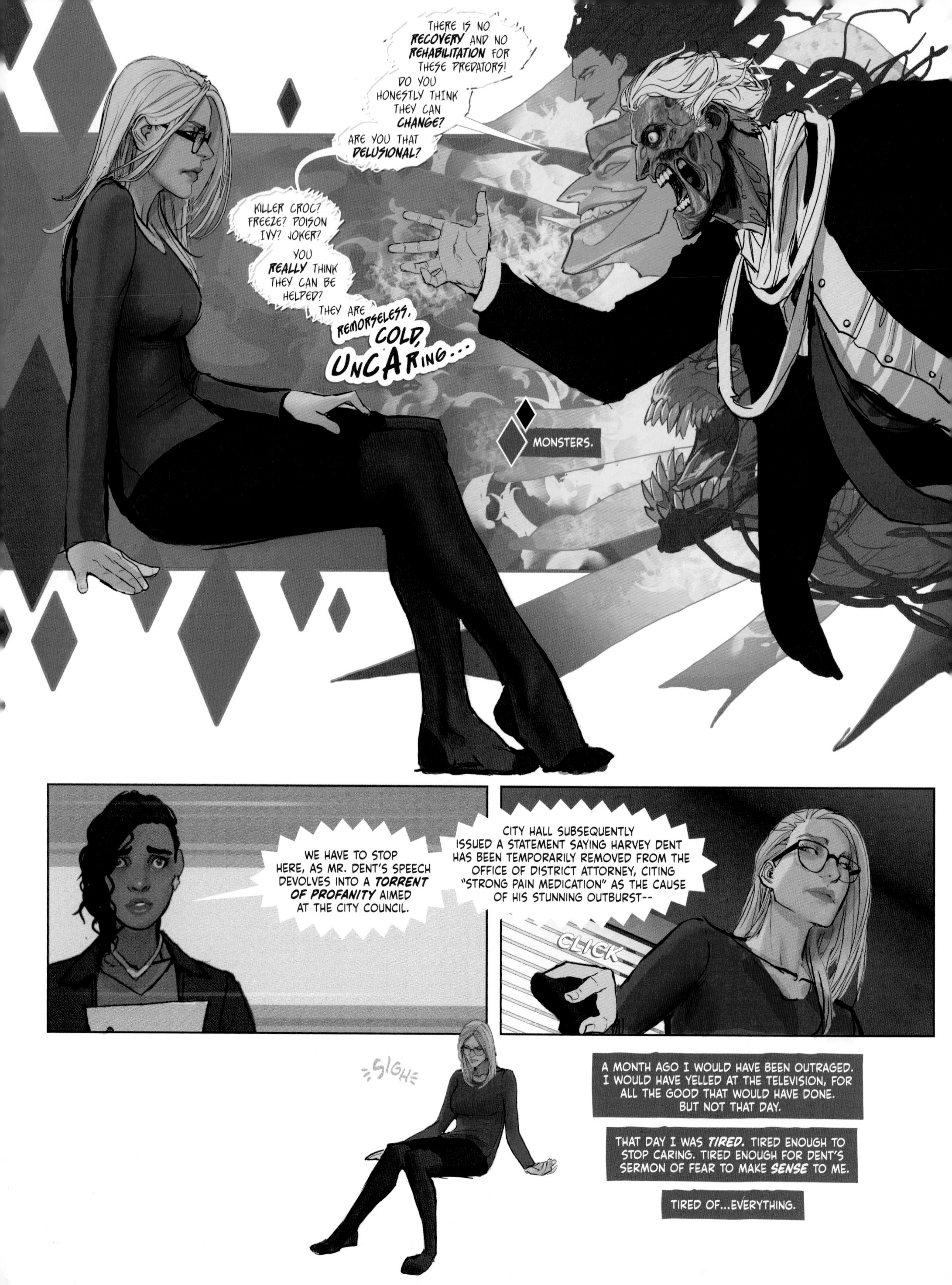

THERE IS NO RECOVERY AND NO REHABILITATION FOR THESE PREDATORS!
DO YOU HONESTLY THINK THEY CAN CHANGE?
ARE YOU THAT DELUSIONAL?
KILLER CROC? FREEZE? POISON IVY? JOKER?
YOU REALLY THINK THEY CAN BE HELPED?
THEY ARE REMORSELESS, COLD, UNCARING...
MONSTERS.
WE HAVE TO STOP HERE, AS MR. DENT'S SPEECH DEVOLVES INTO A TORRENT OF PROFANITY AIMED AT THE CITY COUNCIL.
CITY HALL SUBSEQUENTLY ISSUED A STATEMENT SAYING HARVEY DENT HAS BEEN TEMPORARILY REMOVED FROM THE OFFICE OF DISTRICT ATTORNEY, CITING "STRONG PAIN MEDICATION" AS THE CAUSE OF HIS STUNNING OUTBURST--
CLICK
SIGH
A MONTH AGO I WOULD HAVE BEEN OUTRAGED. I WOULD HAVE YELLED AT THE TELEVISION, FOR ALL THE GOOD THAT WOULD HAVE DONE. BUT NOT THAT DAY.
THAT DAY I WAS TIRED. TIRED ENOUGH TO STOP CARING. TIRED ENOUGH FOR DENT'S SERMON OF FEAR TO MAKE SENSE TO ME.
TIRED OF...EVERYTHING.

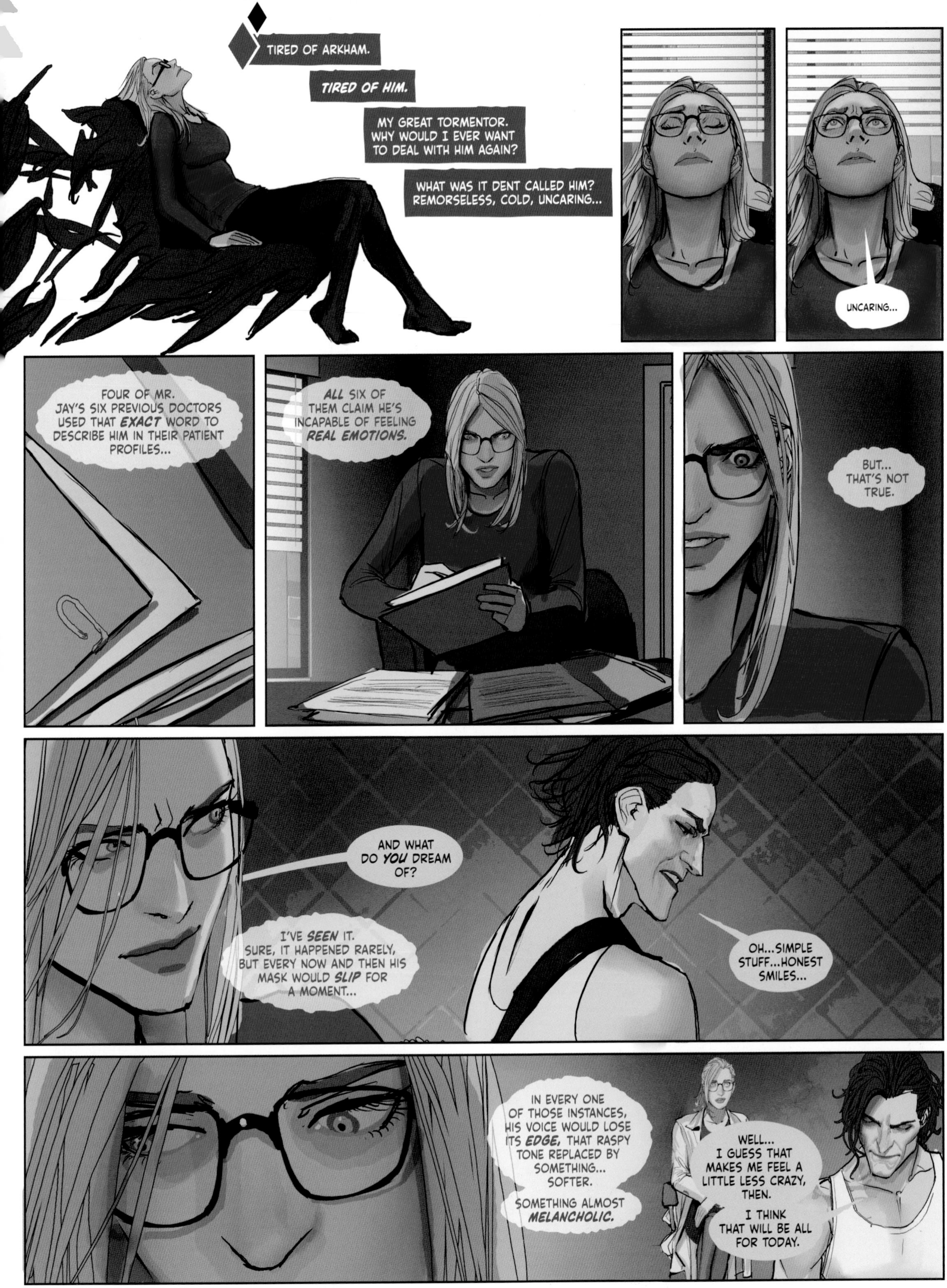
TIRED OF ARKHAM.
TIRED OF HIM.
MY GREAT TORMENTOR. WHY WOULD I EVER WANT TO DEAL WITH HIM AGAIN?
WHAT WAS IT DENT CALLED HIM? REMORSELESS, COLD, UNCARING...
UNCARING...
FOUR OF MR. JAY'S SIX PREVIOUS DOCTORS USED THAT EXACT WORD TO DESCRIBE HIM IN THEIR PATIENT PROFILES...
ALL SIX OF THEM CLAIM HE'S INCAPABLE OF FEELING REAL EMOTIONS.
BUT... THAT'S NOT TRUE.
AND WHAT DO YOU DREAM OF?
I'VE SEEN IT. SURE, IT HAPPENED RARELY, BUT EVERY NOW AND THEN HIS MASK WOULD SLIP FOR A MOMENT...
OH...SIMPLE STUFF...HONEST SMILES...
IN EVERY ONE OF THOSE INSTANCES, HIS VOICE WOULD LOSE ITS EDGE, THAT RASPY TONE REPLACED BY SOMETHING... SOFTER.
SOMETHING ALMOST MELANCHOLIC.
WELL... I GUESS THAT MAKES ME FEEL A LITTLE LESS CRAZY, THEN.
I THINK THAT WILL BE ALL FOR TODAY.

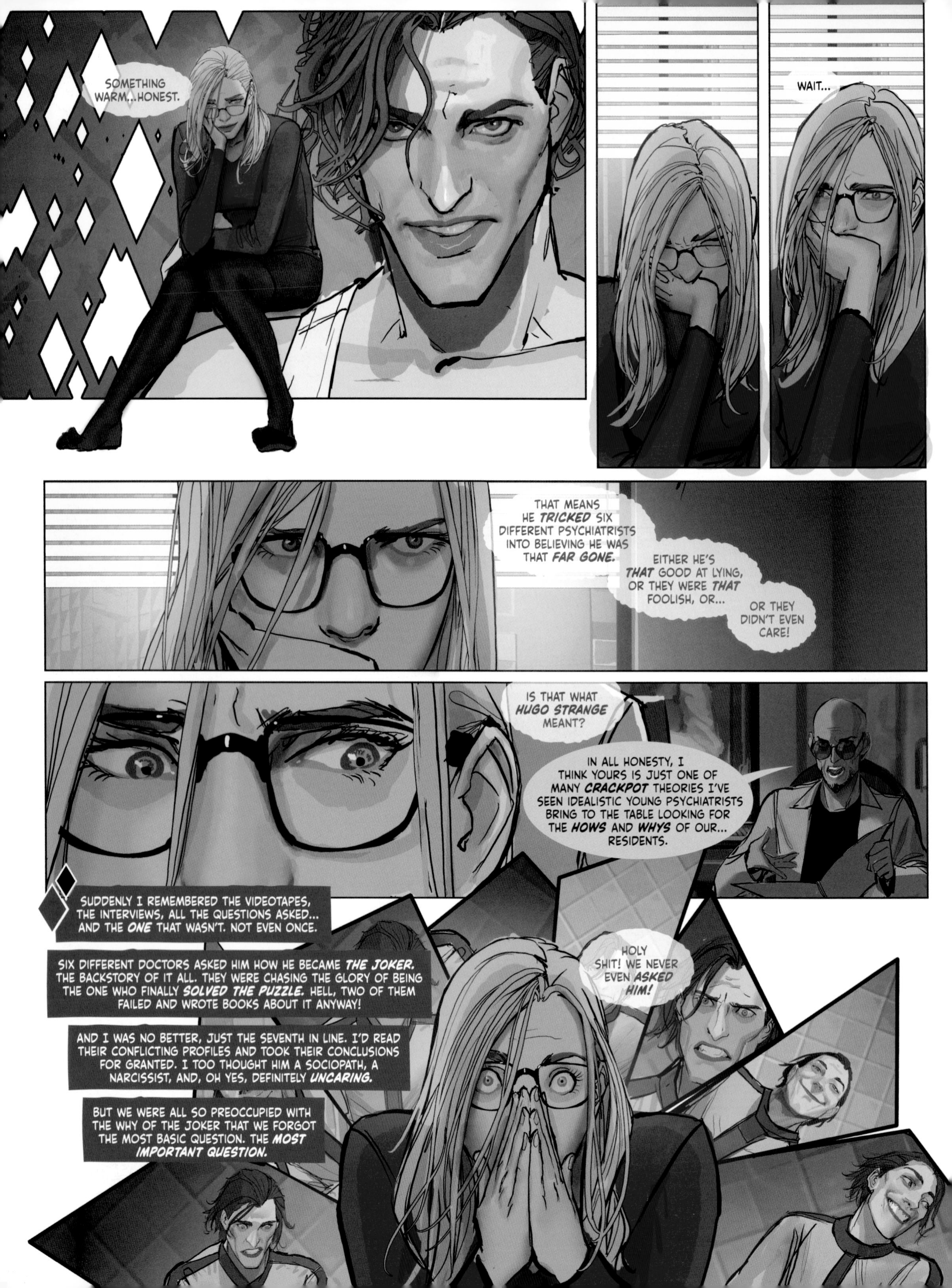

SOMETHING WARM...HONEST.
WAIT...
THAT MEANS HE TRICKED SIX DIFFERENT PSYCHIATRISTS INTO BELIEVING HE WAS THAT FAR GONE.
EITHER HE'S THAT GOOD AT LYING, OR THEY WERE THAT FOOLISH, OR...
OR THEY DIDN'T EVEN CARE!
IS THAT WHAT HUGO STRANGE MEANT?
IN ALL HONESTY, I THINK YOURS IS JUST ONE OF MANY CRACKPOT THEORIES I'VE SEEN IDEALISTIC YOUNG PSYCHIATRISTS BRING TO THE TABLE LOOKING FOR THE HOWS AND WHYS OF OUR... RESIDENTS.
SUDDENLY I REMEMBERED THE VIDEOTAPES, THE INTERVIEWS, ALL THE QUESTIONS ASKED... AND THE ONE THAT WASN'T. NOT EVEN ONCE.
SIX DIFFERENT DOCTORS ASKED HIM HOW HE BECAME THE JOKER. THE BACKSTORY OF IT ALL. THEY WERE CHASING THE GLORY OF BEING THE ONE WHO FINALLY SOLVED THE PUZZLE. HELL, TWO OF THEM FAILED AND WROTE BOOKS ABOUT IT ANYWAY!
AND I WAS NO BETTER, JUST THE SEVENTH IN LINE. I'D READ THEIR CONFLICTING PROFILES AND TOOK THEIR CONCLUSIONS FOR GRANTED. I TOO THOUGHT HIM A SOCIOPATH, A NARCISSIST, AND, OH YES, DEFINITELY UNCARING.
BUT WE WERE ALL SO PREOCCUPIED WITH THE WHY OF THE JOKER THAT WE FORGOT THE MOST BASIC QUESTION. THE MOST IMPORTANT QUESTION.
HOLY SHIT! WE NEVER EVEN ASKED HIM!

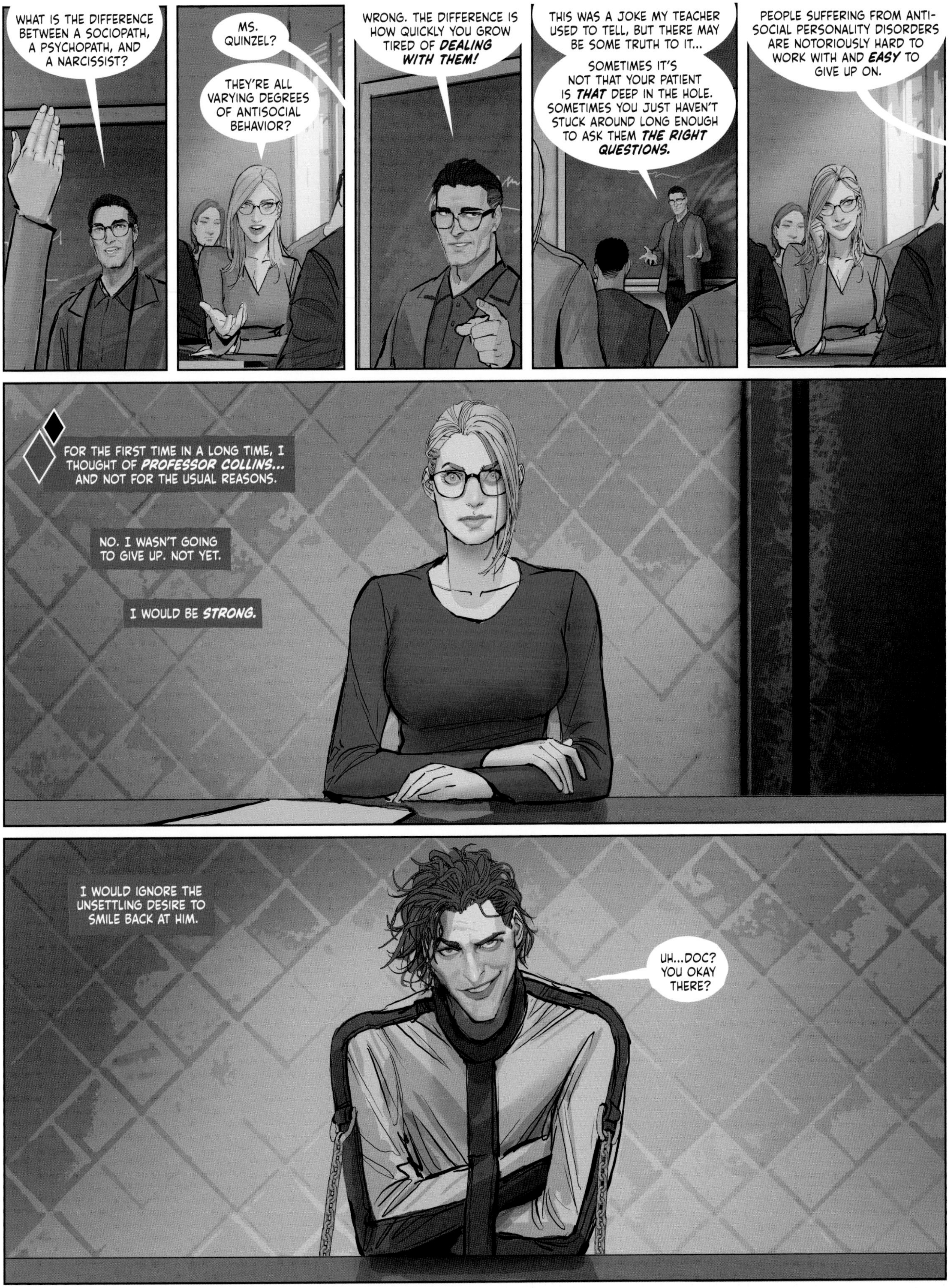
WHAT IS THE DIFFERENCE BETWEEN A SOCIOPATH, A PSYCHOPATH, AND A NARCISSIST?
MS. QUINZEL?
THEY'RE ALL VARYING DEGREES OF ANTISOCIAL BEHAVIOR?
WRONG. THE DIFFERENCE IS HOW QUICKLY YOU GROW TIRED OF DEALING WITH THEM!
THIS WAS A JOKE MY TEACHER USED TO TELL, BUT THERE MAY BE SOME TRUTH TO IT...
SOMETIMES IT'S NOT THAT YOUR PATIENT IS THAT DEEP IN THE HOLE. SOMETIMES YOU JUST HAVEN'T STUCK AROUND LONG ENOUGH TO ASK THEM THE RIGHT QUESTIONS.
PEOPLE SUFFERING FROM ANTI-SOCIAL PERSONALITY DISORDERS ARE NOTORIOUSLY HARD TO WORK WITH AND EASY TO GIVE UP ON.
FOR THE FIRST TIME IN A LONG TIME, I THOUGHT OF PROFESSOR COLLINS... AND NOT FOR THE USUAL REASONS.
NO. I WASN'T GOING TO GIVE UP. NOT YET.
I WOULD BE STRONG.
I WOULD IGNORE THE UNSETTLING DESIRE TO SMILE BACK AT HIM.
UH...DOC? YOU OKAY THERE?

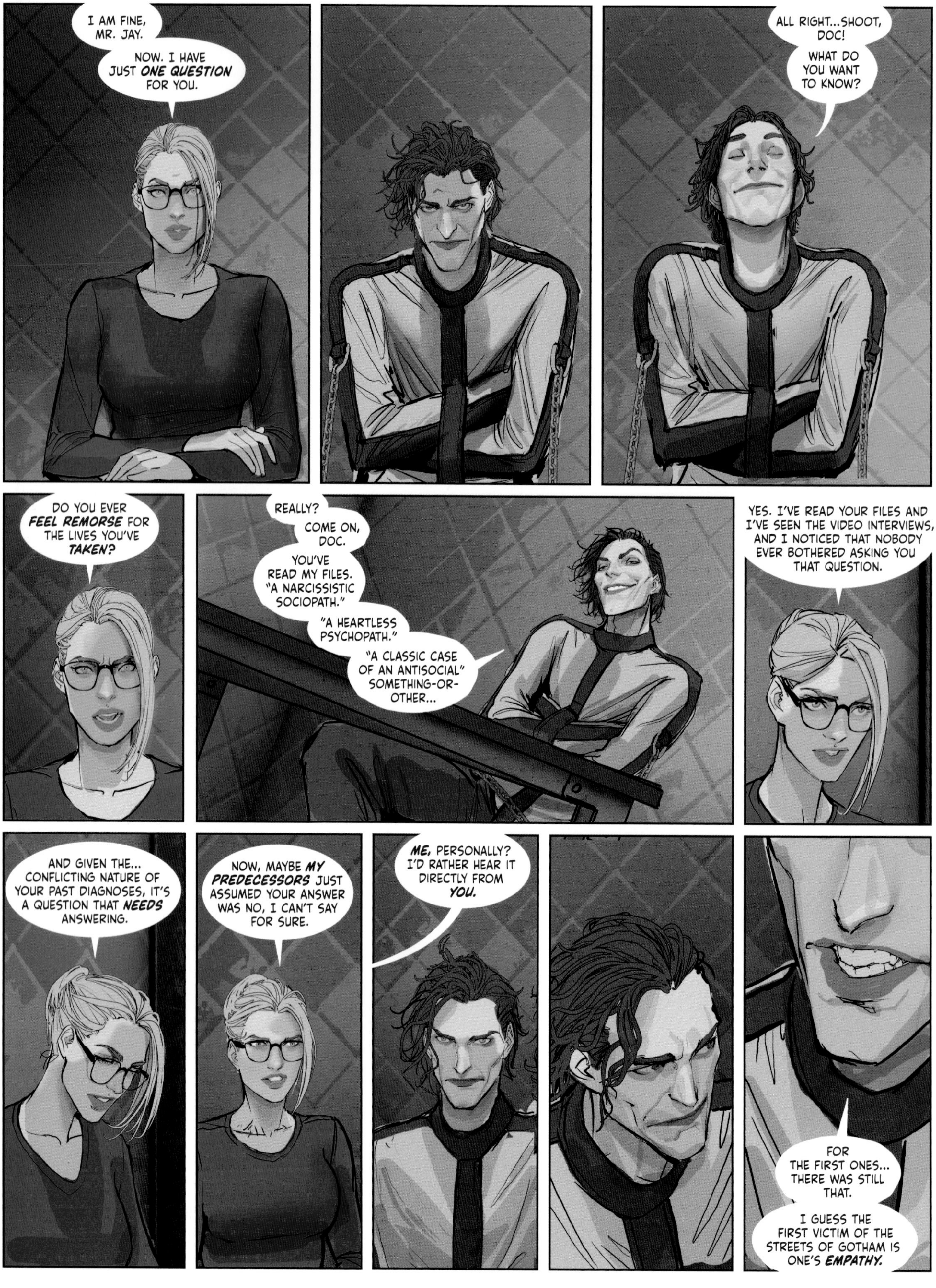
I AM FINE, MR. JAY.
NOW. I HAVE JUST ONE QUESTION FOR YOU.
ALL RIGHT...SHOOT, DOC!
WHAT DO YOU WANT TO KNOW?
DO YOU EVER FEEL REMORSE FOR THE LIVES YOU'VE TAKEN?
REALLY?
COME ON, DOC.
YOU'VE READ MY FILES. "A NARCISSISTIC SOCIOPATH."
"A HEARTLESS PSYCHOPATH."
"A CLASSIC CASE OF AN ANTISOCIAL" SOMETHING-OR-OTHER...
YES. I'VE READ YOUR FILES AND I'VE SEEN THE VIDEO INTERVIEWS, AND I NOTICED THAT NOBODY EVER BOTHERED ASKING YOU THAT QUESTION.
AND GIVEN THE... CONFLICTING NATURE OF YOUR PAST DIAGNOSES, IT'S A QUESTION THAT NEEDS ANSWERING.
NOW, MAYBE MY PREDECESSORS JUST ASSUMED YOUR ANSWER WAS NO, I CAN'T SAY FOR SURE.
ME, PERSONALLY? I'D RATHER HEAR IT DIRECTLY FROM YOU.
FOR THE FIRST ONES... THERE WAS STILL THAT.
I GUESS THE FIRST VICTIM OF THE STREETS OF GOTHAM IS ONE'S EMPATHY.

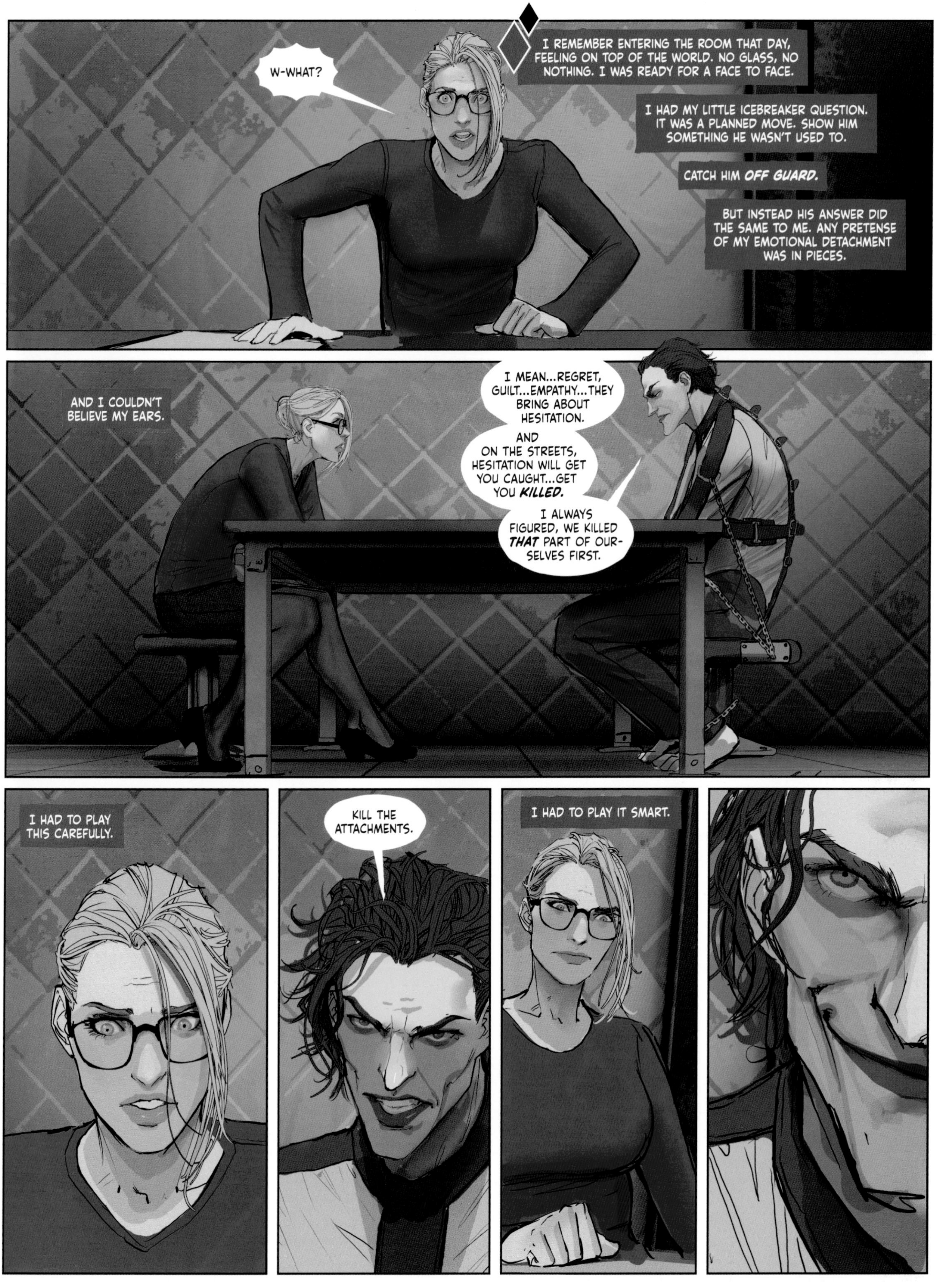
W-WHAT?
I REMEMBER ENTERING THE ROOM THAT DAY, FEELING ON TOP OF THE WORLD. NO GLASS, NO NOTHING. I WAS READY FOR A FACE TO FACE.
I HAD MY LITTLE ICEBREAKER QUESTION. IT WAS A PLANNED MOVE. SHOW HIM SOMETHING HE WASN'T USED TO.
CATCH HIM *OFF GUARD.*
BUT INSTEAD HIS ANSWER DID THE SAME TO ME. ANY PRETENSE OF MY EMOTIONAL DETACHMENT WAS IN PIECES.
AND I COULDN'T BELIEVE MY EARS.
I MEAN...REGRET, GUILT...EMPATHY...THEY BRING ABOUT HESITATION.
AND ON THE STREETS, HESITATION WILL GET YOU CAUGHT...GET YOU *KILLED.*
I ALWAYS FIGURED, WE KILLED *THAT* PART OF OUR-SELVES FIRST.
I HAD TO PLAY THIS CAREFULLY.
KILL THE ATTACHMENTS.
I HAD TO PLAY IT SMART.

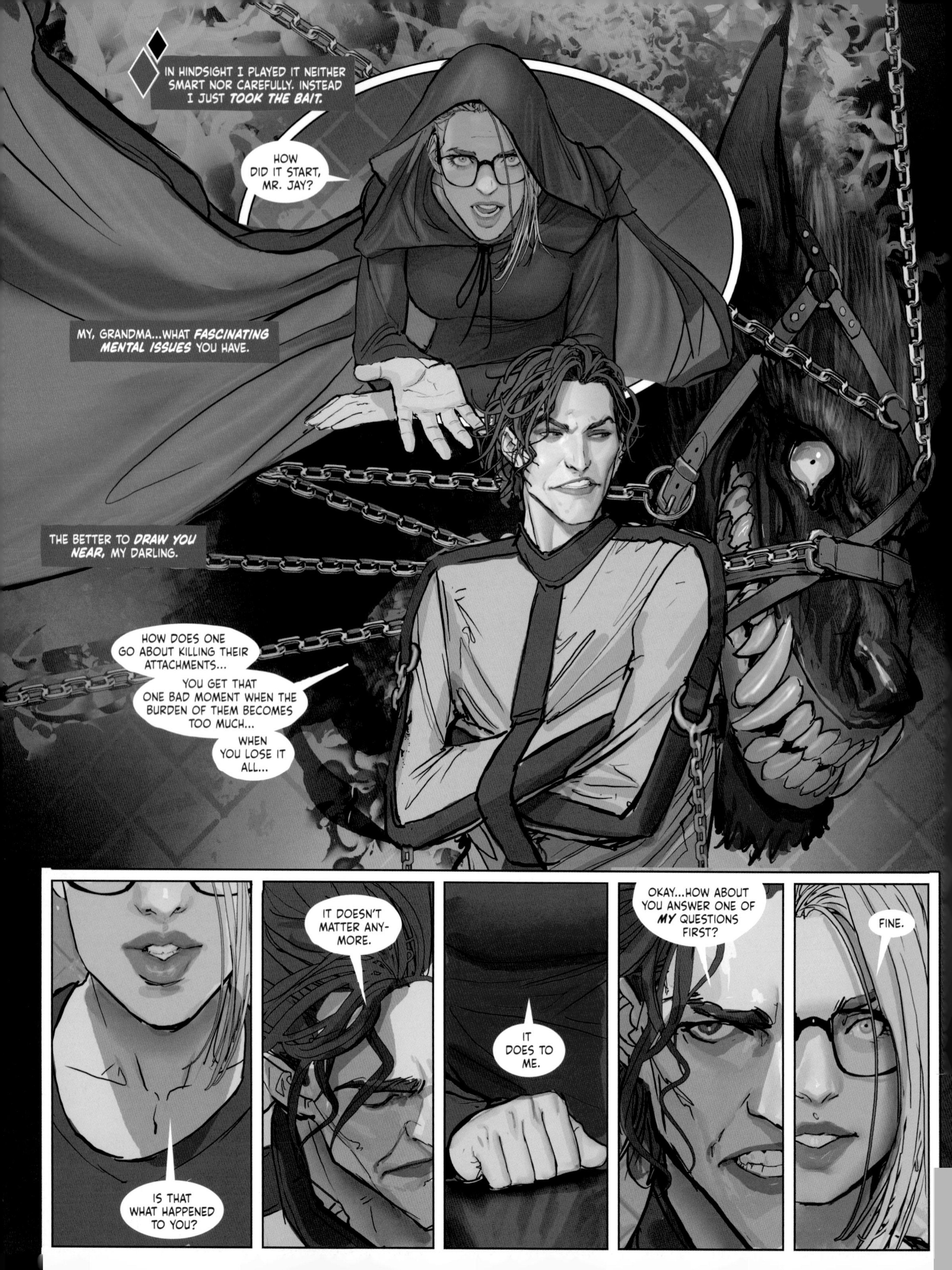
IN HINDSIGHT I PLAYED IT NEITHER SMART NOR CAREFULLY. INSTEAD I JUST TOOK THE BAIT.
HOW DID IT START, MR. JAY?
MY, GRANDMA...WHAT FASCINATING MENTAL ISSUES YOU HAVE.
THE BETTER TO DRAW YOU NEAR, MY DARLING.
HOW DOES ONE GO ABOUT KILLING THEIR ATTACHMENTS...
YOU GET THAT ONE BAD MOMENT WHEN THE BURDEN OF THEM BECOMES TOO MUCH...
WHEN YOU LOSE IT ALL...
IS THAT WHAT HAPPENED TO YOU?
IT DOESN'T MATTER ANY-MORE.
IT DOES TO ME.
OKAY...HOW ABOUT YOU ANSWER ONE OF MY QUESTIONS FIRST?
FINE.

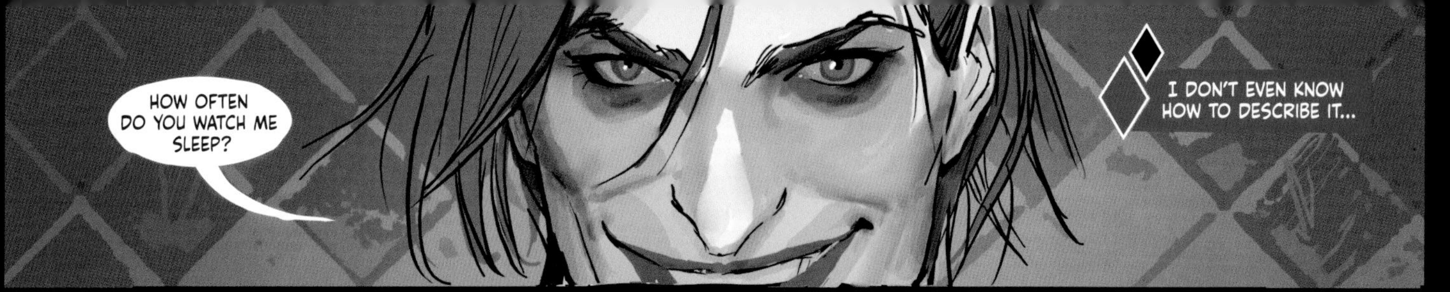
HOW OFTEN DO YOU WATCH ME SLEEP?
I DON'T EVEN KNOW HOW TO DESCRIBE IT...

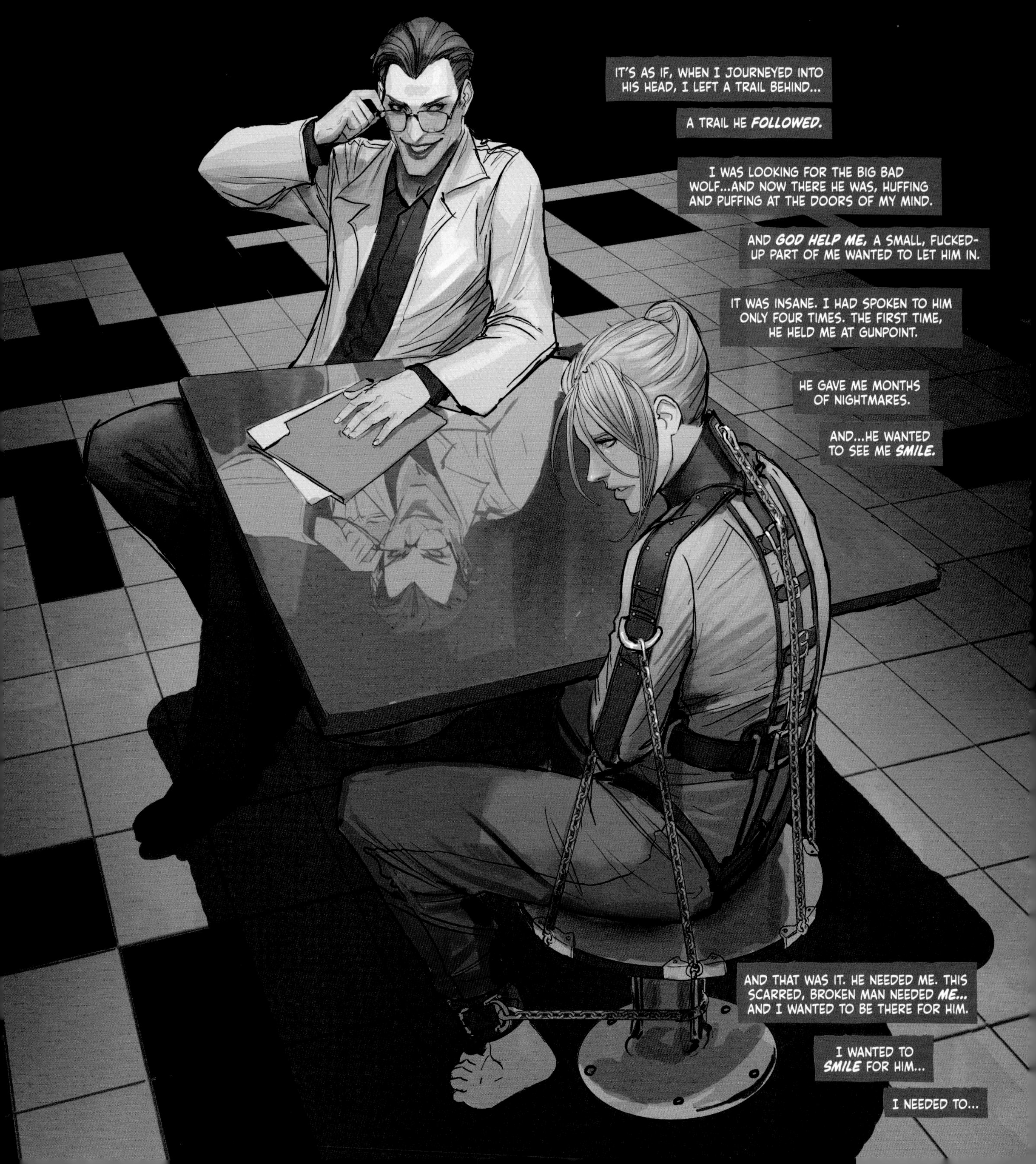
IT'S AS IF, WHEN I JOURNEYED INTO HIS HEAD, I LEFT A TRAIL BEHIND...
A TRAIL HE FOLLOWED.
I WAS LOOKING FOR THE BIG BAD WOLF...AND NOW THERE HE WAS, HUFFING AND PUFFING AT THE DOORS OF MY MIND.
AND GOD HELP ME, A SMALL, FUCKED-UP PART OF ME WANTED TO LET HIM IN.
IT WAS INSANE. I HAD SPOKEN TO HIM ONLY FOUR TIMES. THE FIRST TIME, HE HELD ME AT GUNPOINT.
HE GAVE ME MONTHS OF NIGHTMARES.
AND...HE WANTED TO SEE ME SMILE.
AND THAT WAS IT. HE NEEDED ME. THIS SCARRED, BROKEN MAN NEEDED ME... AND I WANTED TO BE THERE FOR HIM.
I WANTED TO SMILE FOR HIM...
I NEEDED TO...

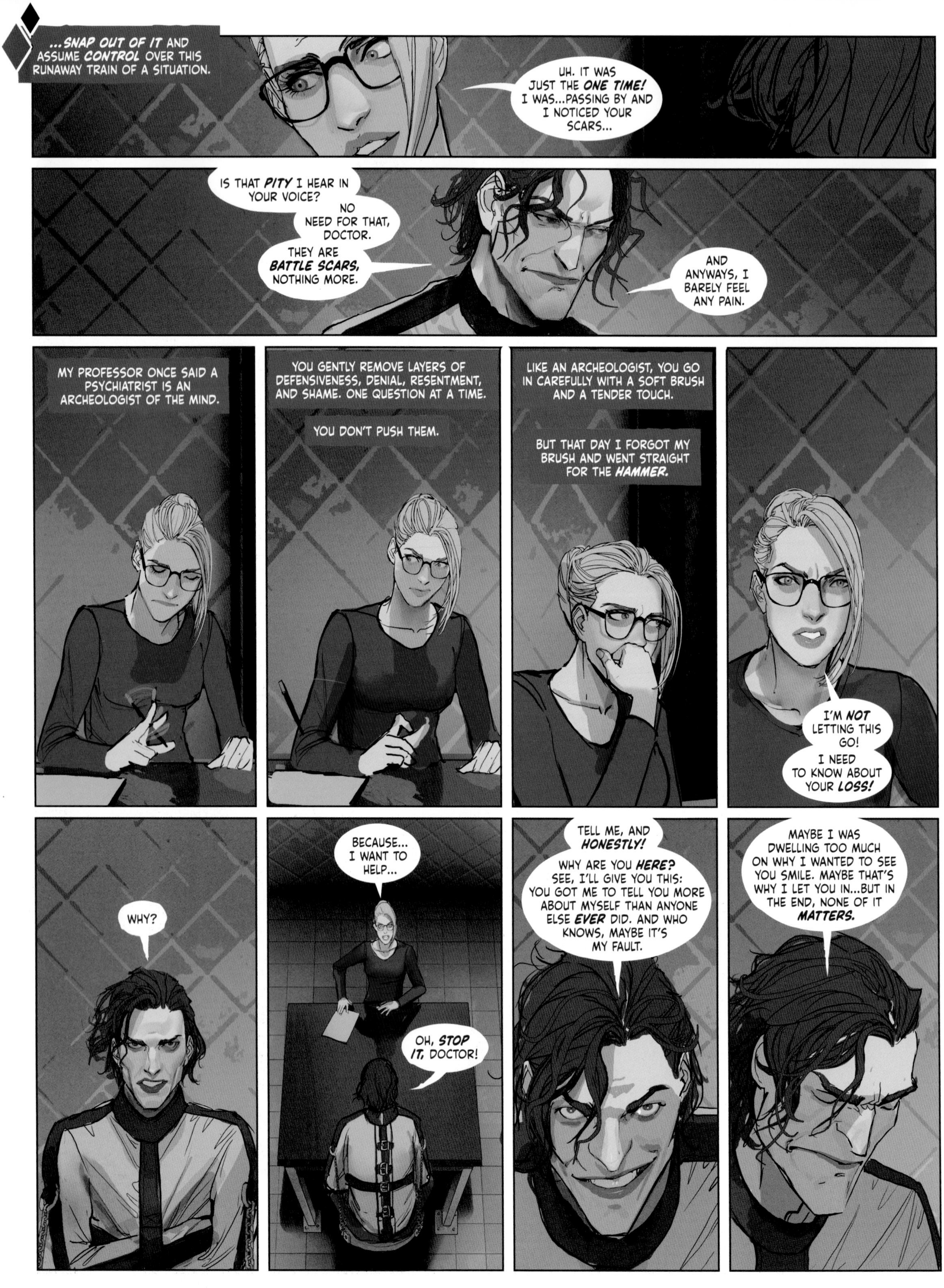
...SNAP OUT OF IT AND ASSUME CONTROL OVER THIS RUNAWAY TRAIN OF A SITUATION.
UH. IT WAS JUST THE ONE TIME! I WAS...PASSING BY AND I NOTICED YOUR SCARS...
IS THAT PITY I HEAR IN YOUR VOICE?
NO NEED FOR THAT, DOCTOR.
THEY ARE BATTLE SCARS, NOTHING MORE.
AND ANYWAYS, I BARELY FEEL ANY PAIN.
MY PROFESSOR ONCE SAID A PSYCHIATRIST IS AN ARCHEOLOGIST OF THE MIND.
YOU GENTLY REMOVE LAYERS OF DEFENSIVENESS, DENIAL, RESENTMENT, AND SHAME. ONE QUESTION AT A TIME.
YOU DON'T PUSH THEM.
LIKE AN ARCHEOLOGIST, YOU GO IN CAREFULLY WITH A SOFT BRUSH AND A TENDER TOUCH.
BUT THAT DAY I FORGOT MY BRUSH AND WENT STRAIGHT FOR THE HAMMER.
I'M NOT LETTING THIS GO!
I NEED TO KNOW ABOUT YOUR LOSS!
WHY?
BECAUSE... I WANT TO HELP...
OH, STOP IT, DOCTOR!
TELL ME, AND HONESTLY!
WHY ARE YOU HERE? SEE, I'LL GIVE YOU THIS: YOU GOT ME TO TELL YOU MORE ABOUT MYSELF THAN ANYONE ELSE EVER DID. AND WHO KNOWS, MAYBE IT'S MY FAULT.
MAYBE I WAS DWELLING TOO MUCH ON WHY I WANTED TO SEE YOU SMILE. MAYBE THAT'S WHY I LET YOU IN...BUT IN THE END, NONE OF IT MATTERS.

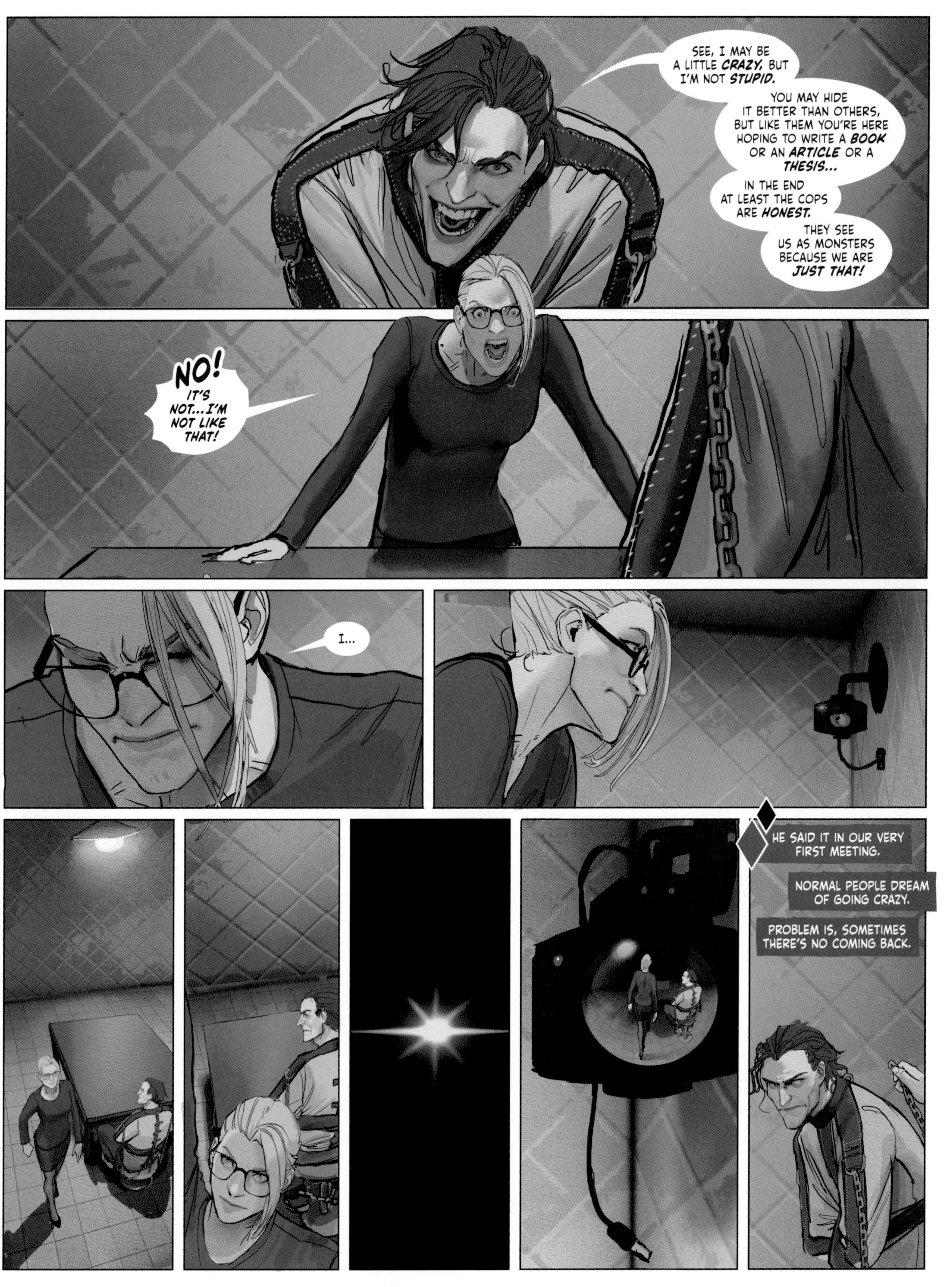
SEE, I MAY BE A LITTLE CRAZY, BUT I'M NOT STUPID.
YOU MAY HIDE IT BETTER THAN OTHERS, BUT LIKE THEM YOU'RE HERE HOPING TO WRITE A BOOK OR AN ARTICLE OR A THESIS...
IN THE END AT LEAST THE COPS ARE HONEST.
THEY SEE US AS MONSTERS BECAUSE WE ARE JUST THAT!
NO! IT'S NOT...I'M NOT LIKE THAT!
I...
HE SAID IT IN OUR VERY FIRST MEETING.
NORMAL PEOPLE DREAM OF GOING CRAZY.
PROBLEM IS, SOMETIMES THERE'S NO COMING BACK.

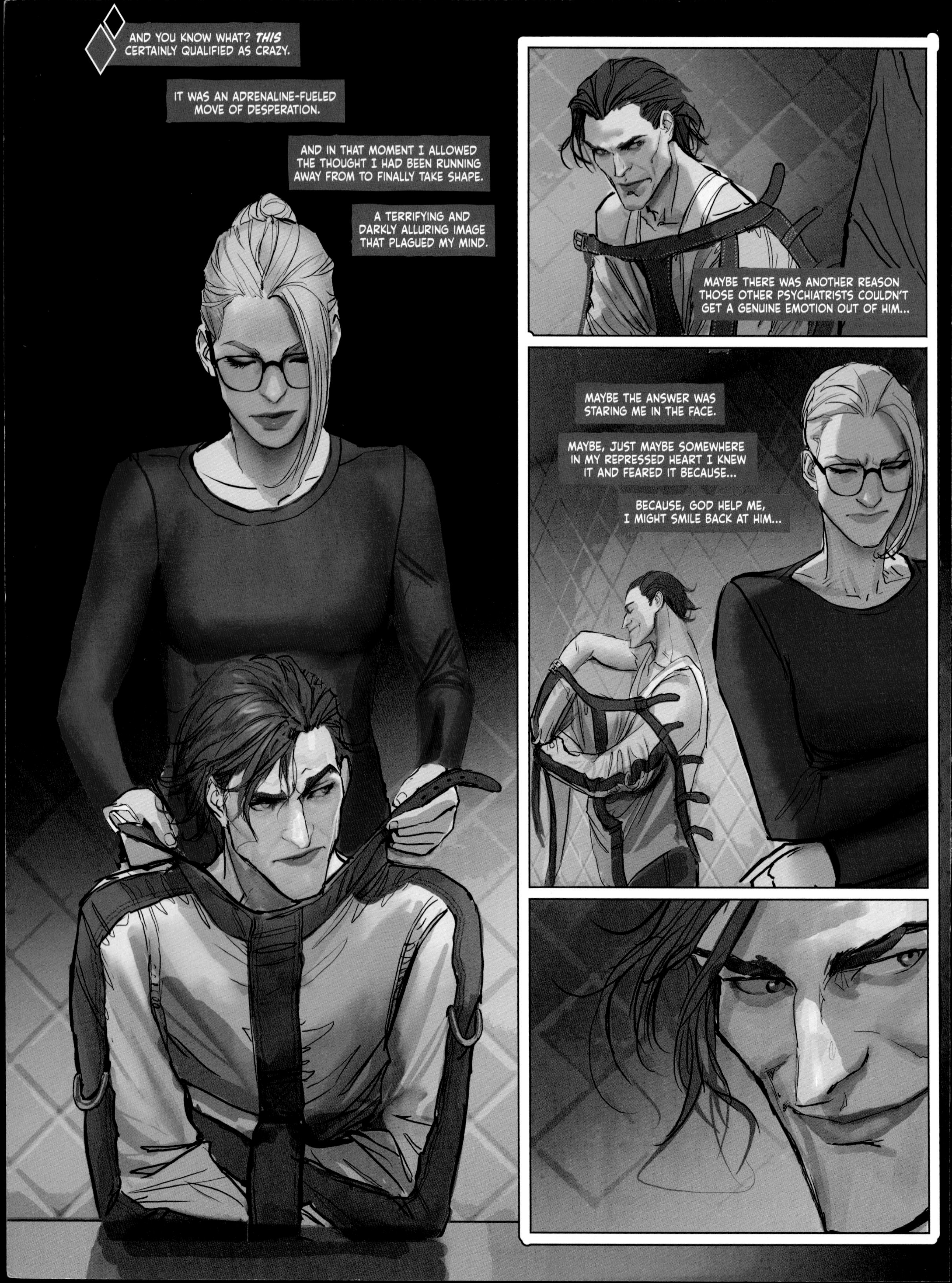
AND YOU KNOW WHAT? THIS CERTAINLY QUALIFIED AS CRAZY.
IT WAS AN ADRENALINE-FUELED MOVE OF DESPERATION.
AND IN THAT MOMENT I ALLOWED THE THOUGHT I HAD BEEN RUNNING AWAY FROM TO FINALLY TAKE SHAPE.
A TERRIFYING AND DARKLY ALLURING IMAGE THAT PLAGUED MY MIND.
MAYBE THERE WAS ANOTHER REASON THOSE OTHER PSYCHIATRISTS COULDN'T GET A GENUINE EMOTION OUT OF HIM...
MAYBE THE ANSWER WAS STARING ME IN THE FACE.
MAYBE, JUST MAYBE SOMEWHERE IN MY REPRESSED HEART I KNEW IT AND FEARED IT BECAUSE...
BECAUSE, GOD HELP ME, I MIGHT SMILE BACK AT HIM...

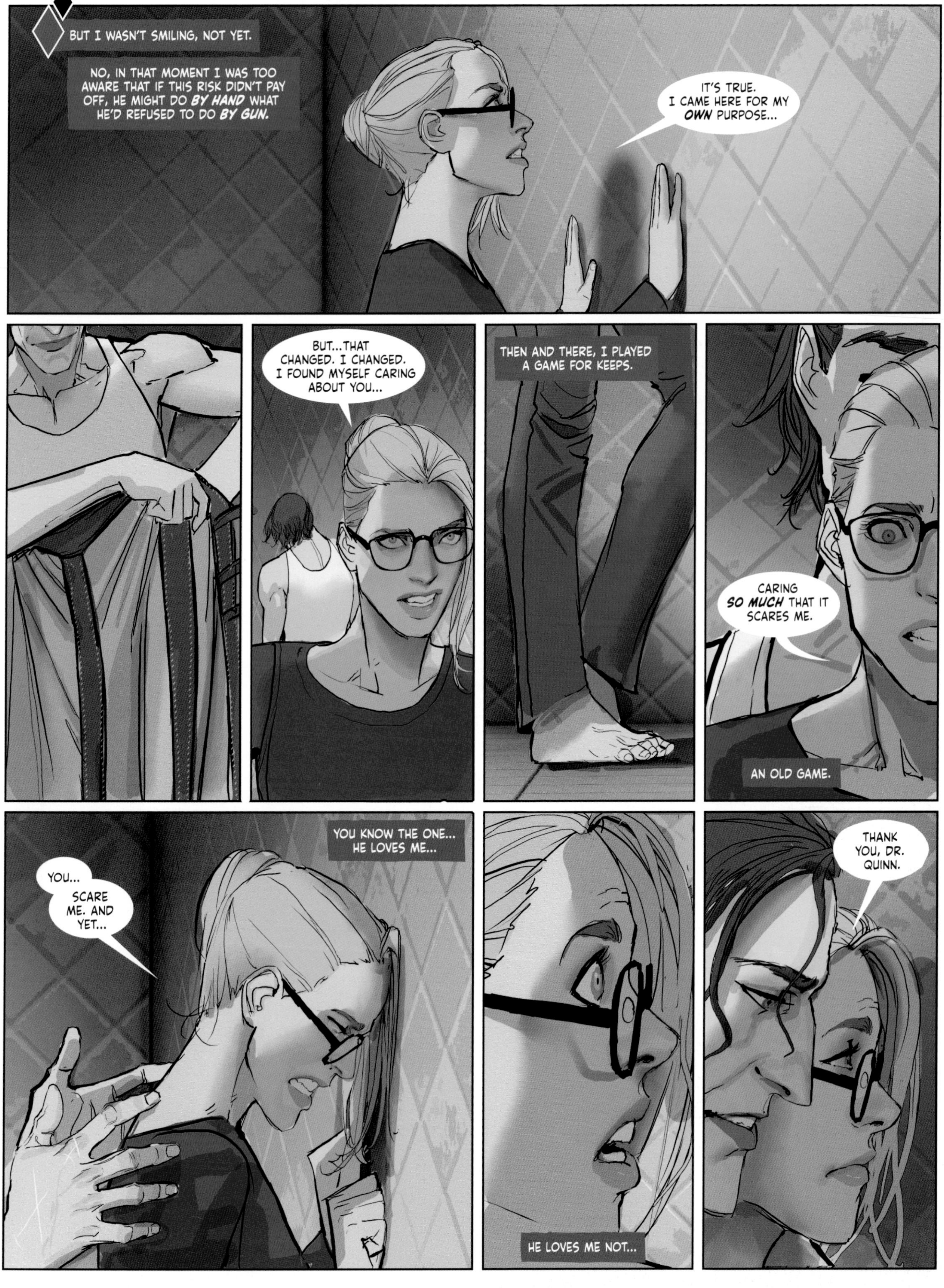
BUT I WASN'T SMILING, NOT YET.
NO, IN THAT MOMENT I WAS TOO AWARE THAT IF THIS RISK DIDN'T PAY OFF, HE MIGHT DO ***BY HAND*** WHAT HE'D REFUSED TO DO ***BY GUN.***
IT'S TRUE. I CAME HERE FOR MY ***OWN*** PURPOSE...
BUT...THAT CHANGED. I CHANGED. I FOUND MYSELF CARING ABOUT YOU...
THEN AND THERE, I PLAYED A GAME FOR KEEPS.
CARING ***SO MUCH*** THAT IT SCARES ME.
AN OLD GAME.
YOU KNOW THE ONE... HE LOVES ME...
YOU... SCARE ME. AND YET...
HE LOVES ME NOT...
THANK YOU, DR. QUINN.

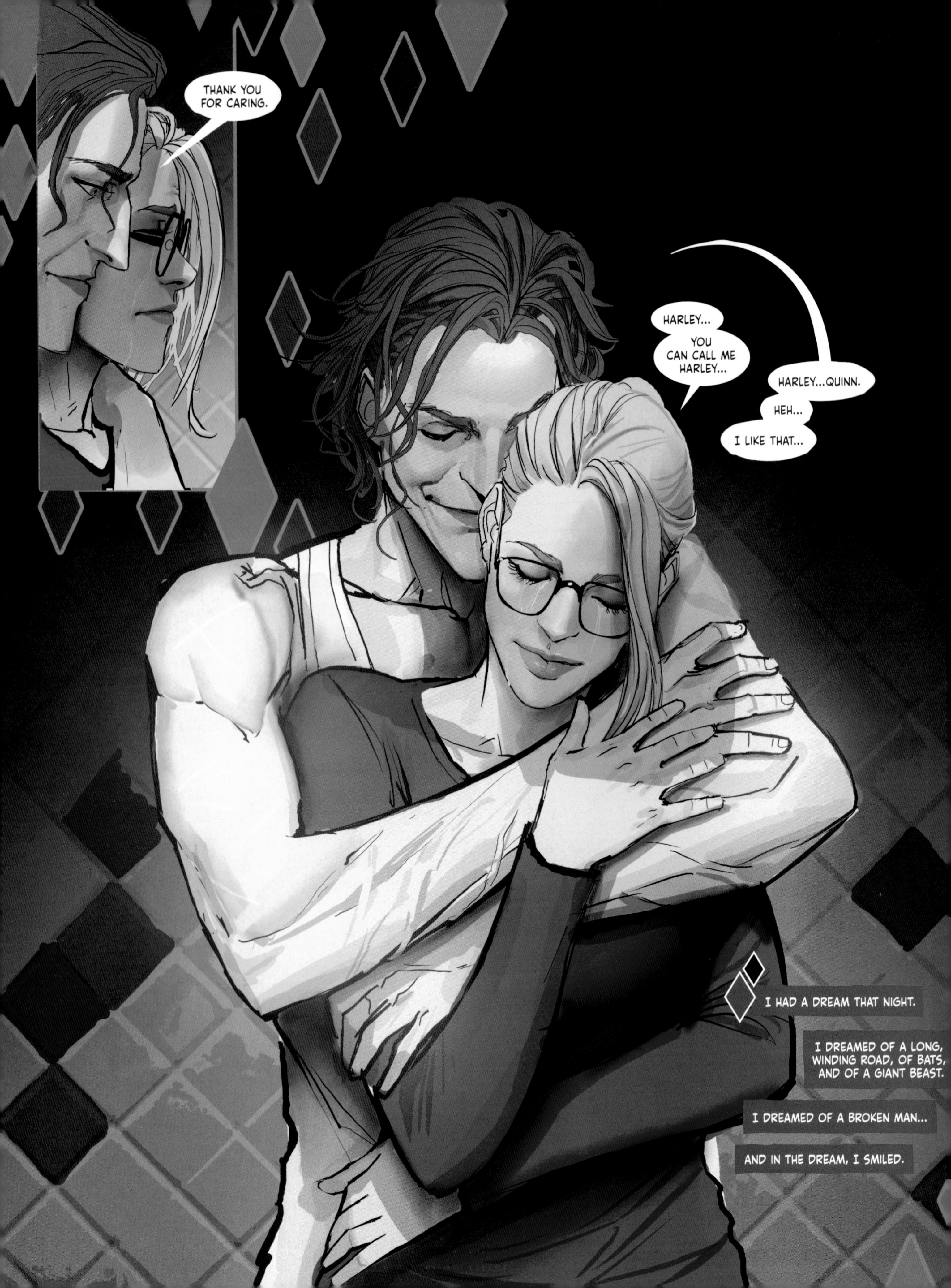
THANK YOU FOR CARING.
HARLEY...
YOU CAN CALL ME HARLEY...
HARLEY...QUINN.
HEH...
I LIKE THAT...
I HAD A DREAM THAT NIGHT.
I DREAMED OF A LONG, WINDING ROAD, OF BATS, AND OF A GIANT BEAST.
I DREAMED OF A BROKEN MAN...
AND IN THE DREAM, I SMILED.

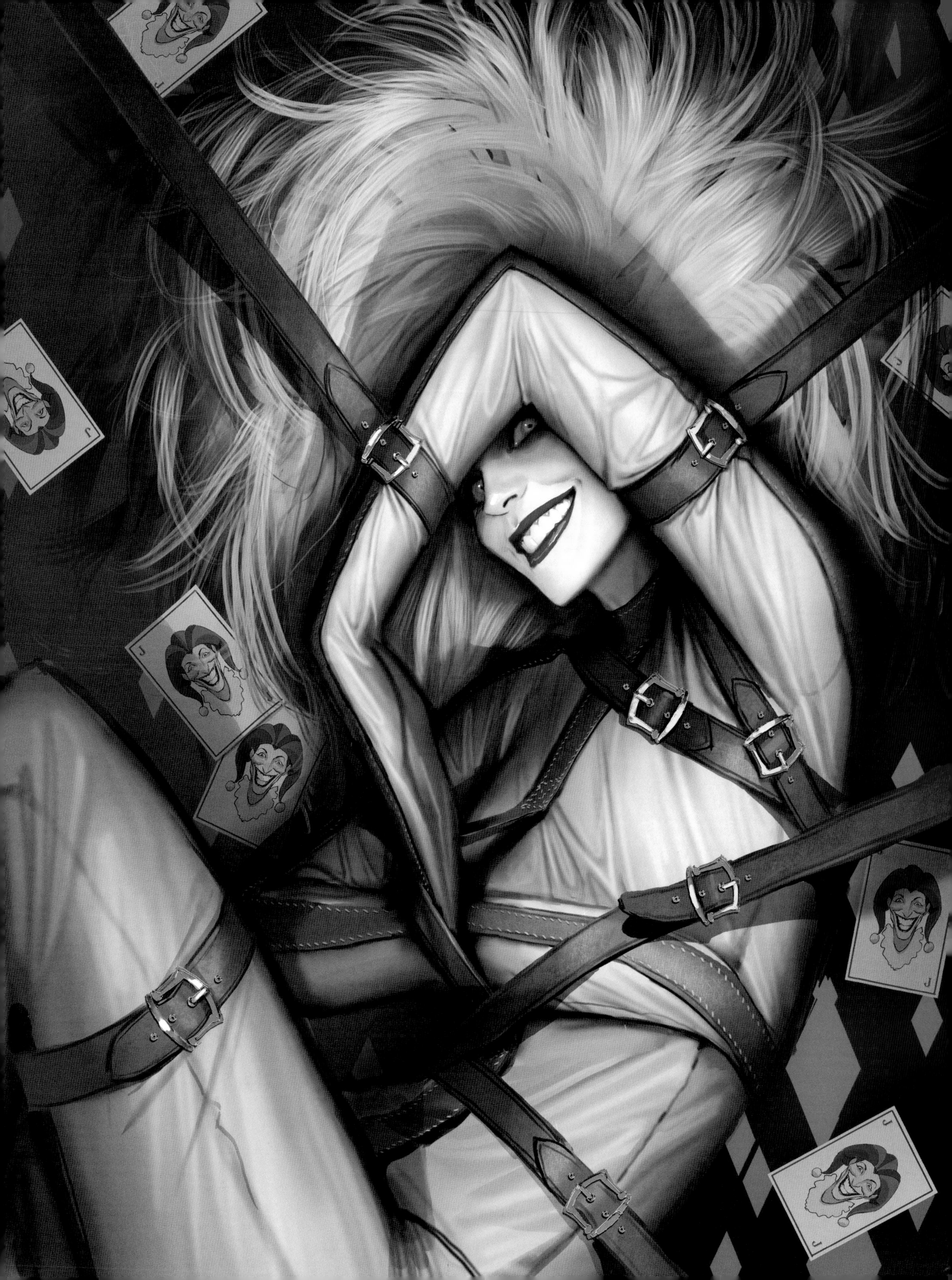

BOOK THREE

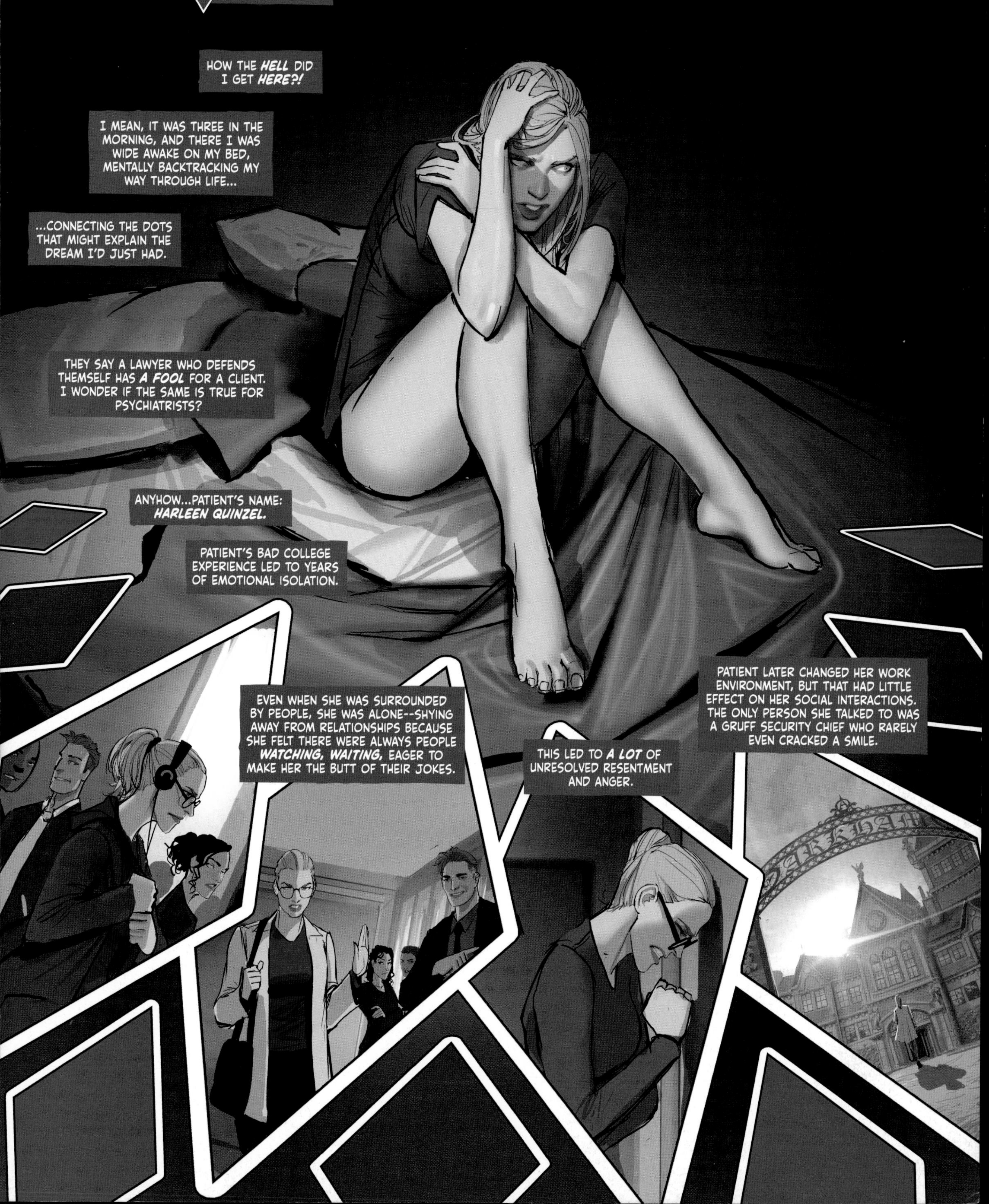

HOW THE HELL DID I GET HERE?!
I MEAN, IT WAS THREE IN THE MORNING, AND THERE I WAS WIDE AWAKE ON MY BED, MENTALLY BACKTRACKING MY WAY THROUGH LIFE...
...CONNECTING THE DOTS THAT MIGHT EXPLAIN THE DREAM I'D JUST HAD.
THEY SAY A LAWYER WHO DEFENDS THEMSELF HAS A FOOL FOR A CLIENT. I WONDER IF THE SAME IS TRUE FOR PSYCHIATRISTS?
ANYHOW...PATIENT'S NAME: HARLEEN QUINZEL.
PATIENT'S BAD COLLEGE EXPERIENCE LED TO YEARS OF EMOTIONAL ISOLATION.
EVEN WHEN SHE WAS SURROUNDED BY PEOPLE, SHE WAS ALONE--SHYING AWAY FROM RELATIONSHIPS BECAUSE SHE FELT THERE WERE ALWAYS PEOPLE WATCHING, WAITING, EAGER TO MAKE HER THE BUTT OF THEIR JOKES.
THIS LED TO A LOT OF UNRESOLVED RESENTMENT AND ANGER.
PATIENT LATER CHANGED HER WORK ENVIRONMENT, BUT THAT HAD LITTLE EFFECT ON HER SOCIAL INTERACTIONS. THE ONLY PERSON SHE TALKED TO WAS A GRUFF SECURITY CHIEF WHO RARELY EVEN CRACKED A SMILE.

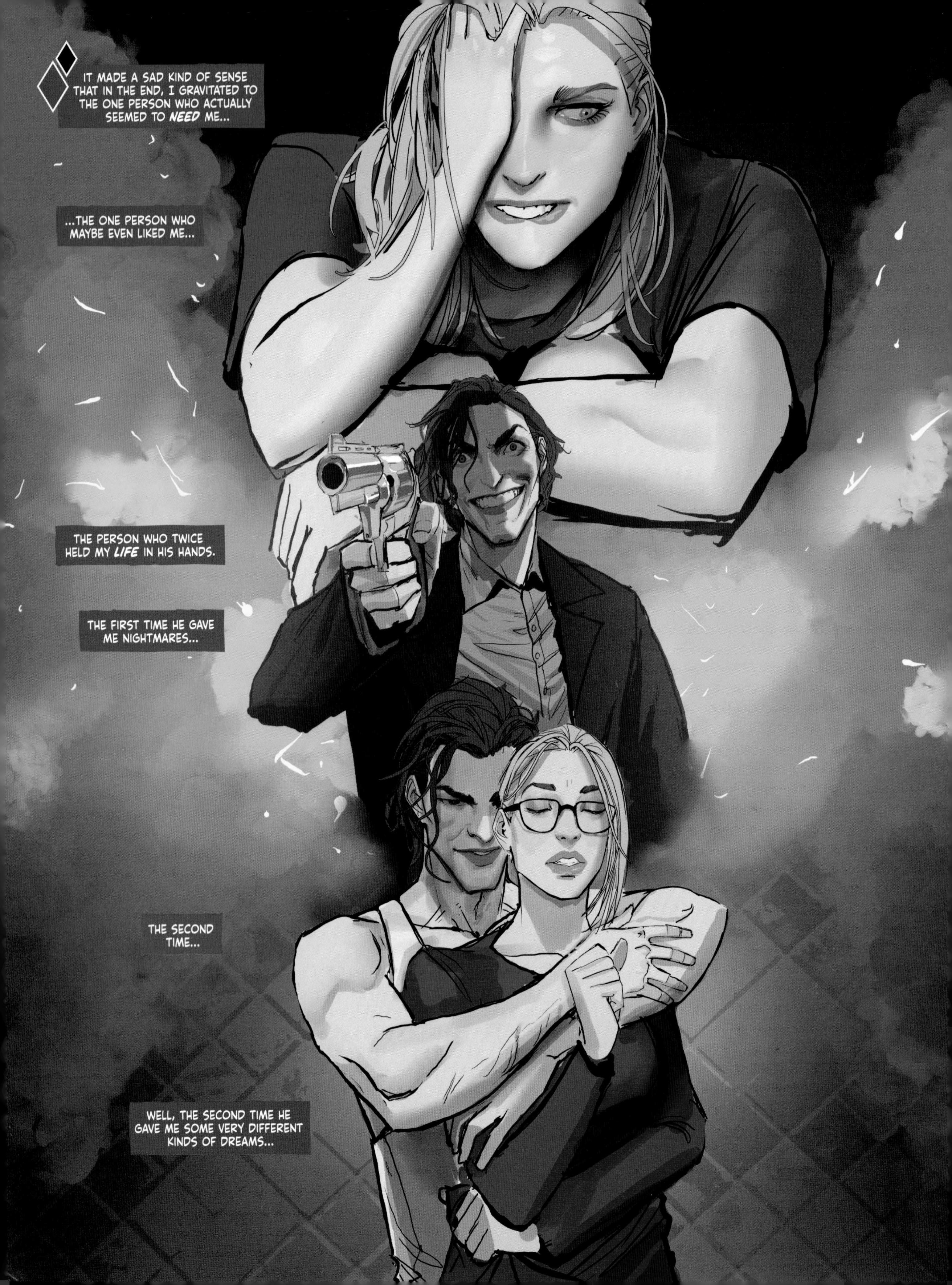
IT MADE A SAD KIND OF SENSE THAT IN THE END, I GRAVITATED TO THE ONE PERSON WHO ACTUALLY SEEMED TO *NEED* ME...
...THE ONE PERSON WHO MAYBE EVEN LIKED ME...
THE PERSON WHO TWICE HELD MY *LIFE* IN HIS HANDS.
THE FIRST TIME HE GAVE ME NIGHTMARES...
THE SECOND TIME...
WELL, THE SECOND TIME HE GAVE ME SOME VERY DIFFERENT KINDS OF DREAMS...

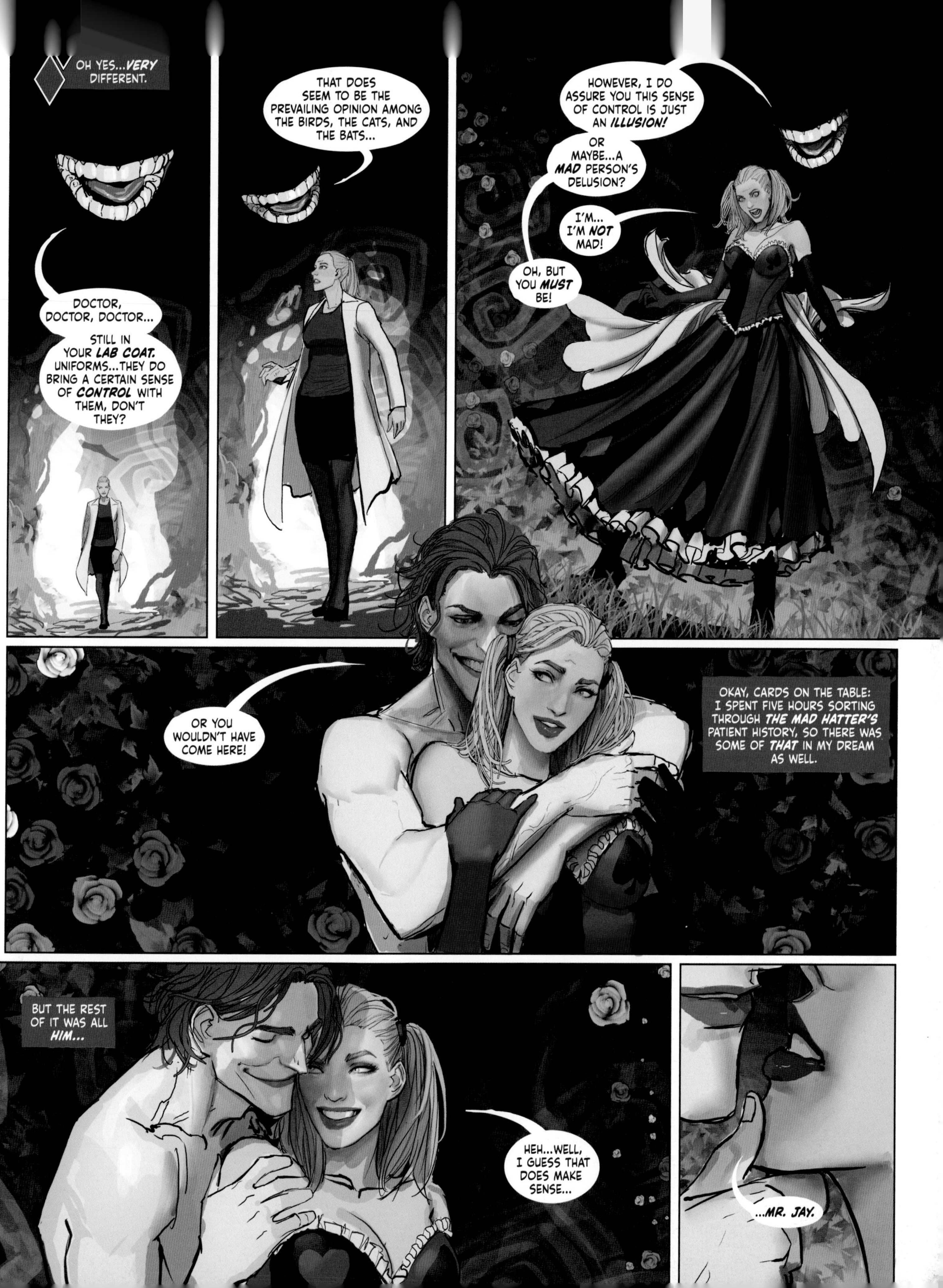
OH YES...VERY DIFFERENT.
DOCTOR, DOCTOR, DOCTOR...
STILL IN YOUR LAB COAT. UNIFORMS...THEY DO BRING A CERTAIN SENSE OF CONTROL WITH THEM, DON'T THEY?
THAT DOES SEEM TO BE THE PREVAILING OPINION AMONG THE BIRDS, THE CATS, AND THE BATS...
HOWEVER, I DO ASSURE YOU THIS SENSE OF CONTROL IS JUST AN ILLUSION!
OR MAYBE...A MAD PERSON'S DELUSION?
I'M... I'M NOT MAD!
OH, BUT YOU MUST BE!
OR YOU WOULDN'T HAVE COME HERE!
OKAY, CARDS ON THE TABLE: I SPENT FIVE HOURS SORTING THROUGH THE MAD HATTER'S PATIENT HISTORY, SO THERE WAS SOME OF THAT IN MY DREAM AS WELL.
BUT THE REST OF IT WAS ALL HIM...
HEH...WELL, I GUESS THAT DOES MAKE SENSE...
...MR. JAY.

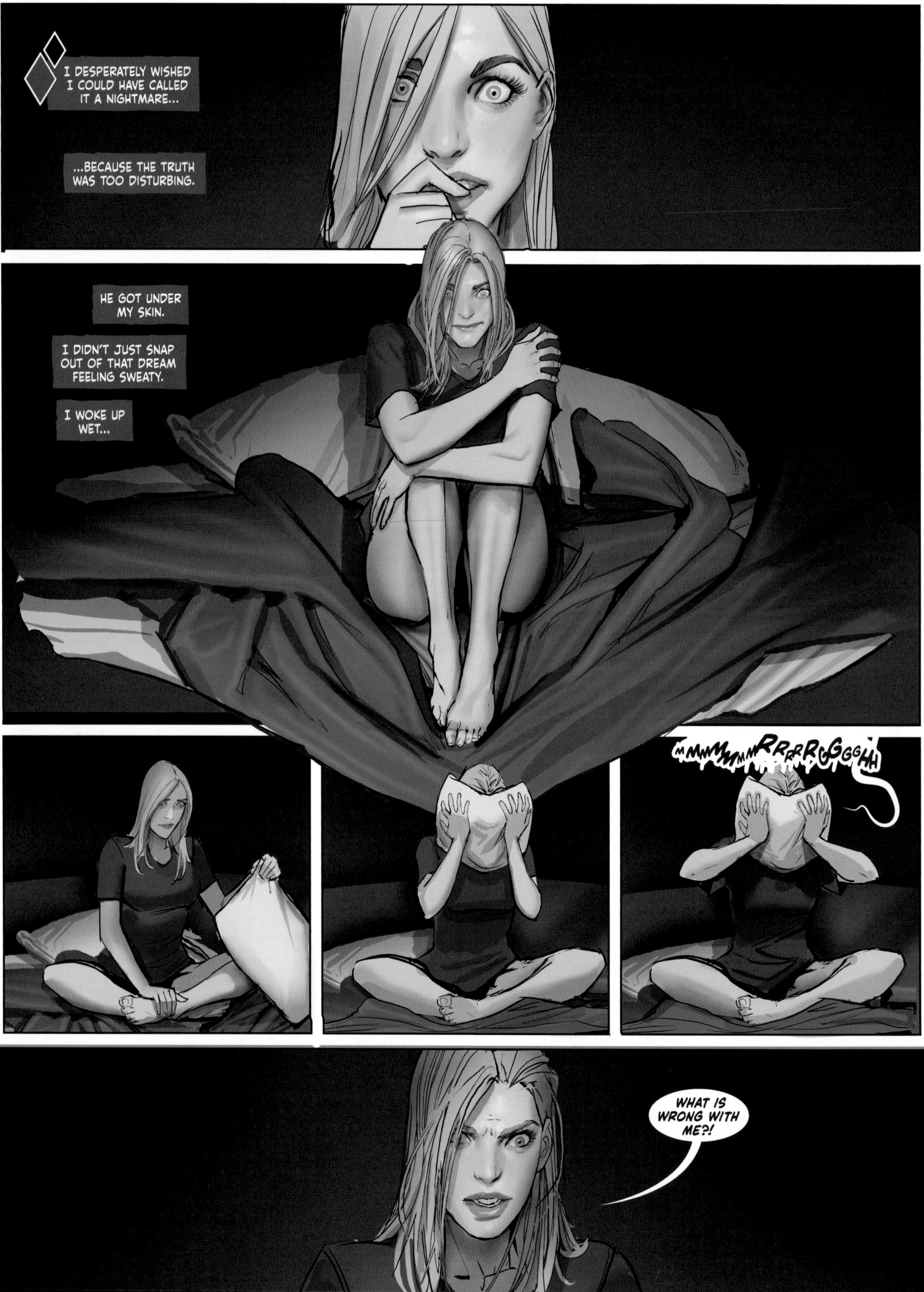
I DESPERATELY WISHED I COULD HAVE CALLED IT A NIGHTMARE...
...BECAUSE THE TRUTH WAS TOO DISTURBING.
HE GOT UNDER MY SKIN.
I DIDN'T JUST SNAP OUT OF THAT DREAM FEELING SWEATY.
I WOKE UP WET...
MMMMMMMMRRRRRGGGGHH
WHAT IS WRONG WITH ME?!

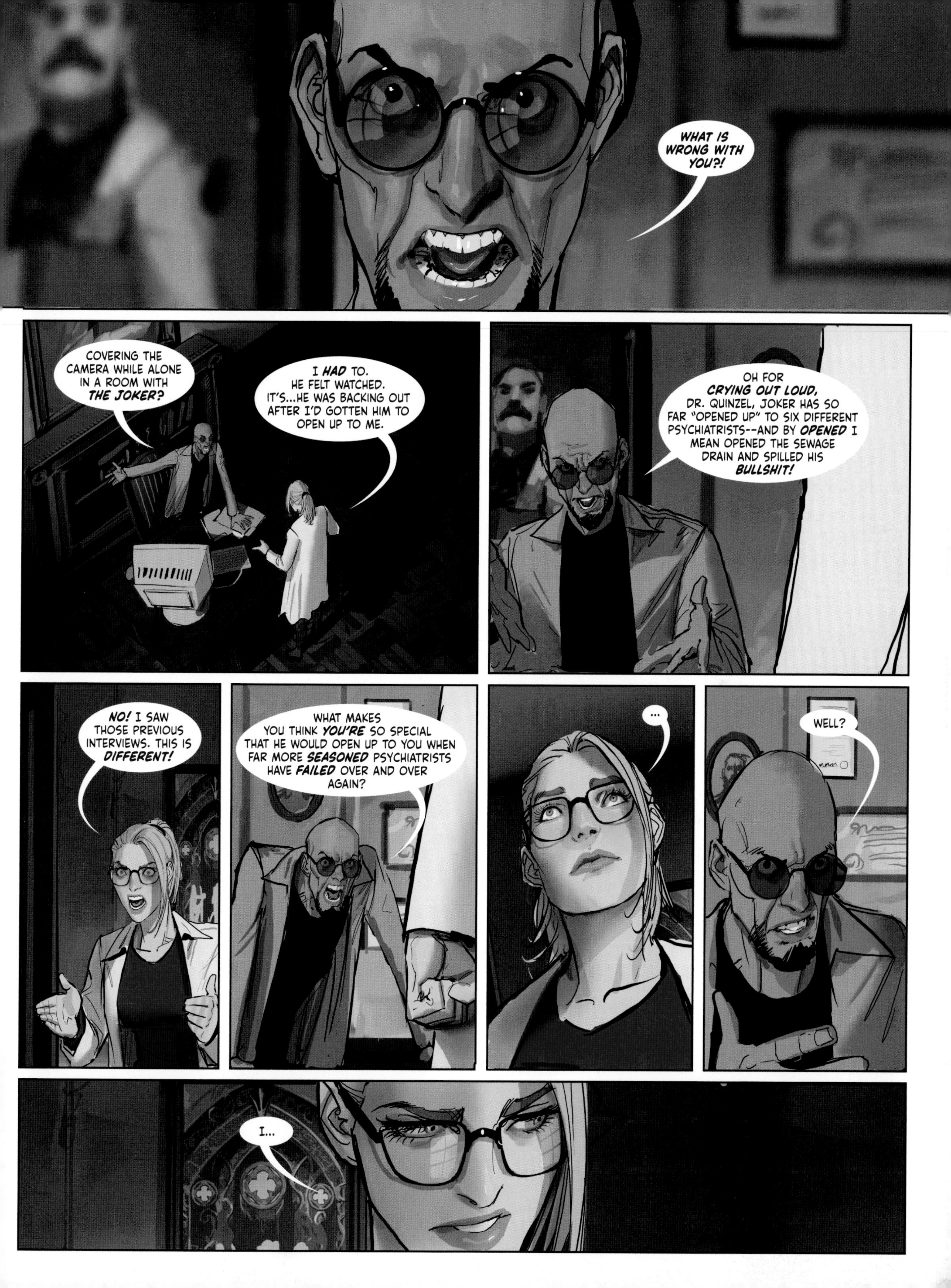
WHAT IS WRONG WITH YOU?!
COVERING THE CAMERA WHILE ALONE IN A ROOM WITH THE JOKER?
I HAD TO. HE FELT WATCHED. IT'S...HE WAS BACKING OUT AFTER I'D GOTTEN HIM TO OPEN UP TO ME.
OH FOR CRYING OUT LOUD, DR. QUINZEL, JOKER HAS SO FAR "OPENED UP" TO SIX DIFFERENT PSYCHIATRISTS--AND BY OPENED I MEAN OPENED THE SEWAGE DRAIN AND SPILLED HIS BULLSHIT!
NO! I SAW THOSE PREVIOUS INTERVIEWS. THIS IS DIFFERENT!
WHAT MAKES YOU THINK YOU'RE SO SPECIAL THAT HE WOULD OPEN UP TO YOU WHEN FAR MORE SEASONED PSYCHIATRISTS HAVE FAILED OVER AND OVER AGAIN?
...
WELL?
I...

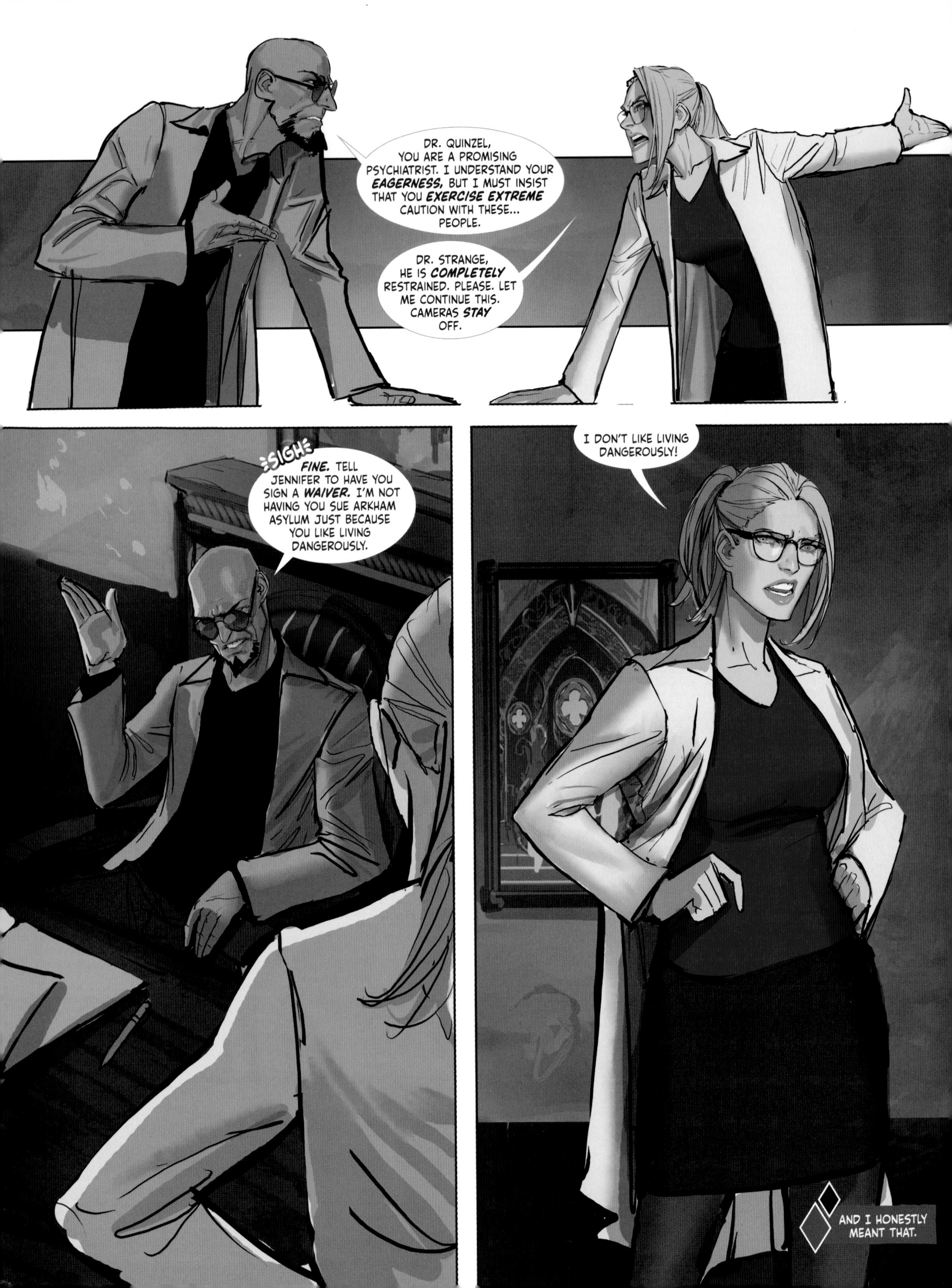
DR. QUINZEL, YOU ARE A PROMISING PSYCHIATRIST. I UNDERSTAND YOUR EAGERNESS, BUT I MUST INSIST THAT YOU EXERCISE EXTREME CAUTION WITH THESE... PEOPLE.
DR. STRANGE, HE IS COMPLETELY RESTRAINED. PLEASE. LET ME CONTINUE THIS. CAMERAS STAY OFF.
SIGH
FINE. TELL JENNIFER TO HAVE YOU SIGN A WAIVER. I'M NOT HAVING YOU SUE ARKHAM ASYLUM JUST BECAUSE YOU LIKE LIVING DANGEROUSLY.
I DON'T LIKE LIVING DANGEROUSLY!
AND I HONESTLY MEANT THAT.

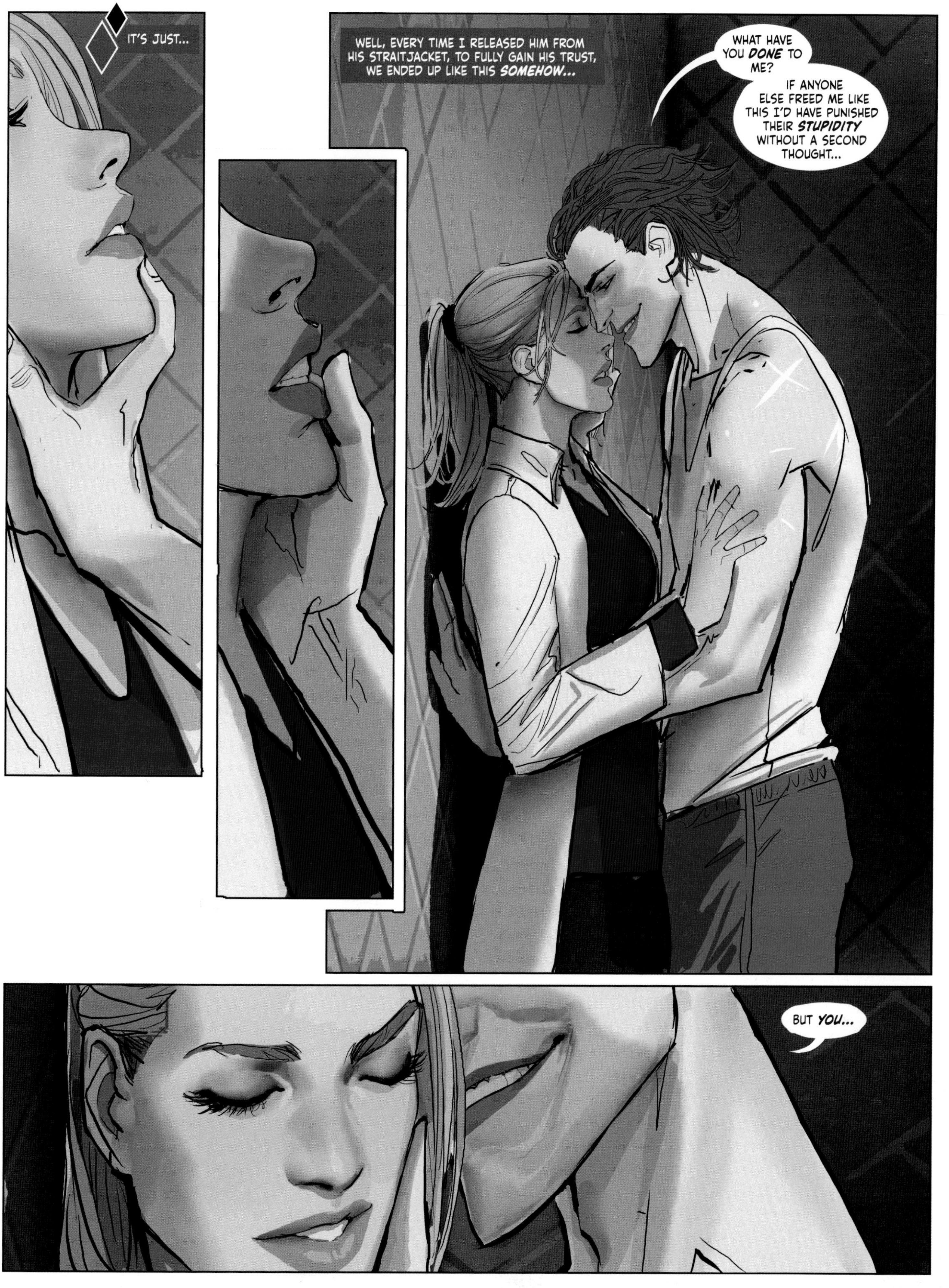
IT'S JUST...
WELL, EVERY TIME I RELEASED HIM FROM HIS STRAITJACKET, TO FULLY GAIN HIS TRUST, WE ENDED UP LIKE THIS SOMEHOW...
WHAT HAVE YOU DONE TO ME?
IF ANYONE ELSE FREED ME LIKE THIS I'D HAVE PUNISHED THEIR STUPIDITY WITHOUT A SECOND THOUGHT...
BUT YOU...

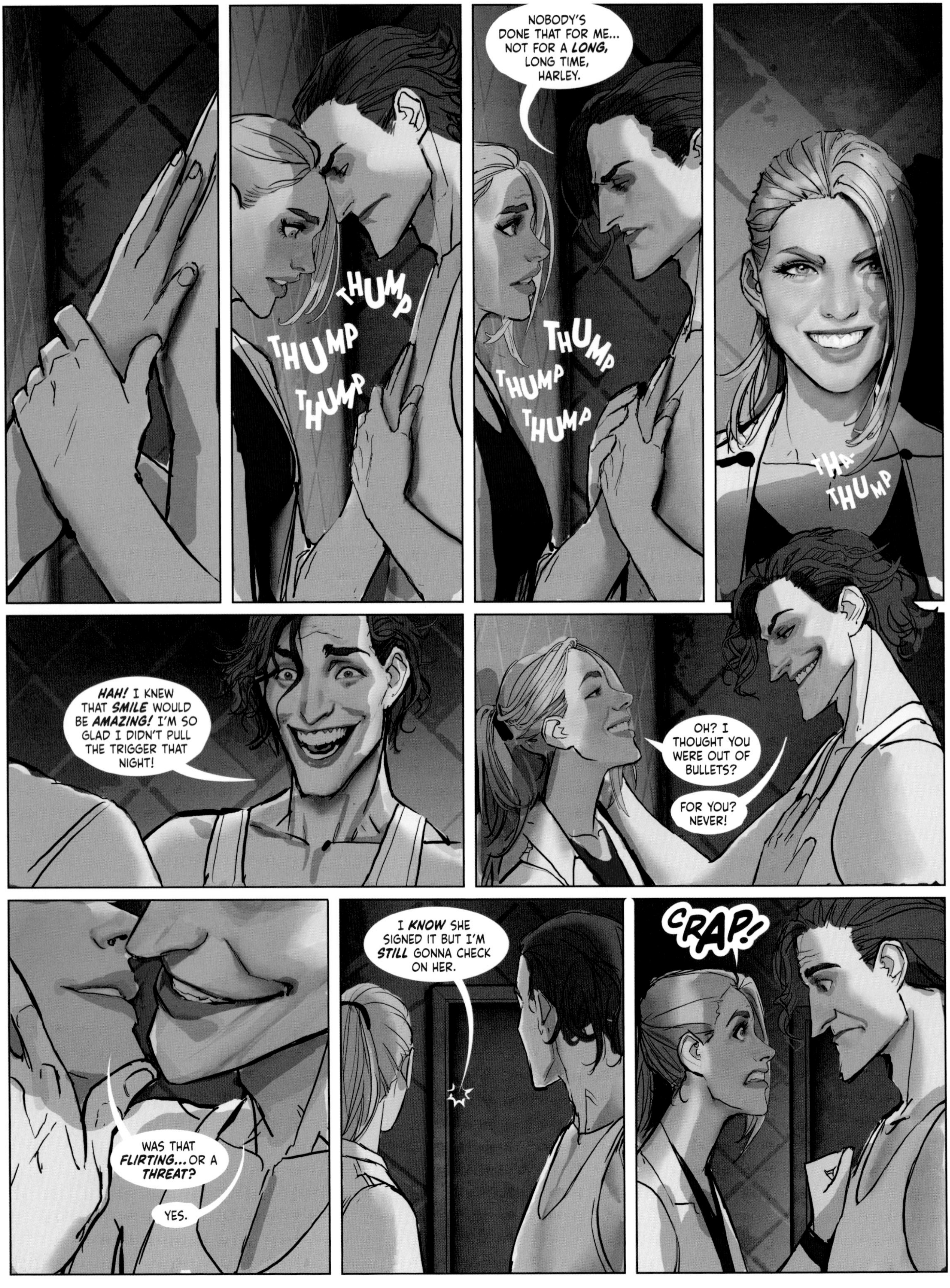
THUMP
THUMP
THUMP
NOBODY'S DONE THAT FOR ME... NOT FOR A LONG, LONG TIME, HARLEY.
THUMP
THUMP
THUMP
THA-THUMP
HAH! I KNEW THAT SMILE WOULD BE AMAZING! I'M SO GLAD I DIDN'T PULL THE TRIGGER THAT NIGHT!
OH? I THOUGHT YOU WERE OUT OF BULLETS?
FOR YOU? NEVER!
WAS THAT FLIRTING...OR A THREAT?
YES.
I KNOW SHE SIGNED IT BUT I'M STILL GONNA CHECK ON HER.
CRAP!

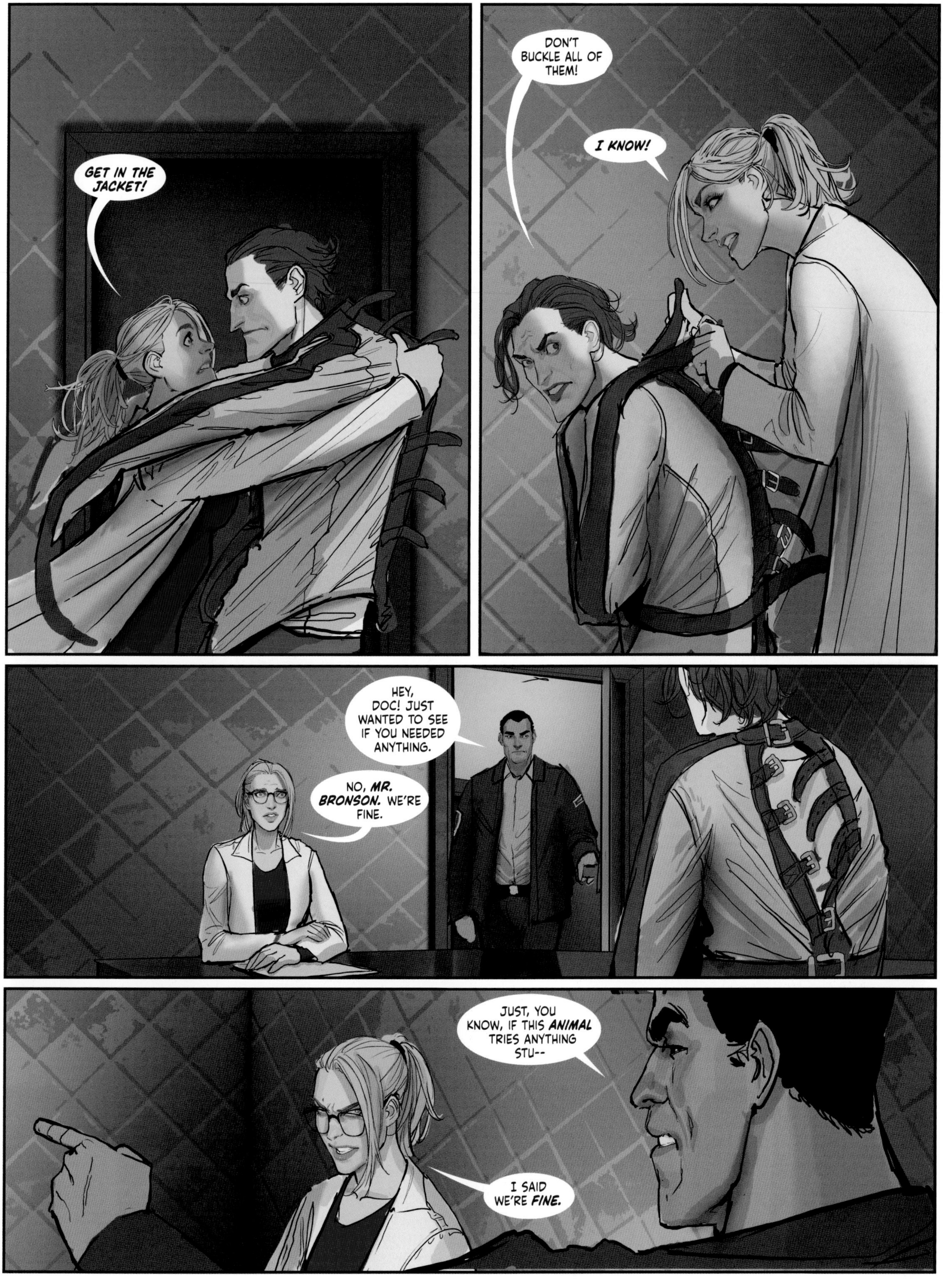
GET IN THE JACKET!
DON'T BUCKLE ALL OF THEM!
I KNOW!
HEY, DOC! JUST WANTED TO SEE IF YOU NEEDED ANYTHING.
NO, MR. BRONSON. WE'RE FINE.
JUST, YOU KNOW, IF THIS ANIMAL TRIES ANYTHING STU--
I SAID WE'RE FINE.

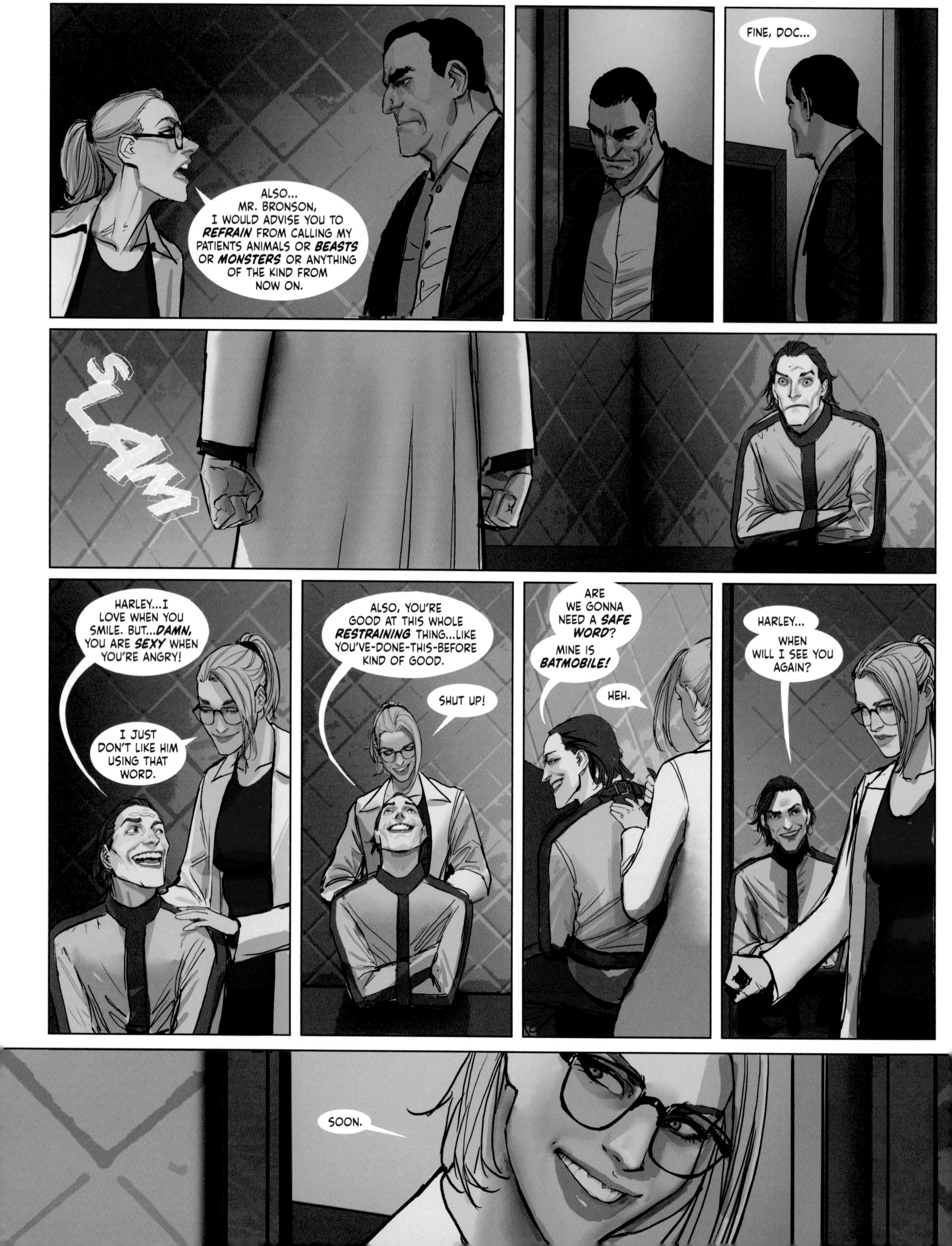
ALSO... MR. BRONSON, I WOULD ADVISE YOU TO REFRAIN FROM CALLING MY PATIENTS ANIMALS OR BEASTS OR MONSTERS OR ANYTHING OF THE KIND FROM NOW ON.
FINE, DOC...
SLAM
HARLEY...I LOVE WHEN YOU SMILE. BUT...DAMN, YOU ARE SEXY WHEN YOU'RE ANGRY!
I JUST DON'T LIKE HIM USING THAT WORD.
ALSO, YOU'RE GOOD AT THIS WHOLE RESTRAINING THING...LIKE YOU'VE-DONE-THIS-BEFORE KIND OF GOOD.
SHUT UP!
ARE WE GONNA NEED A SAFE WORD?
MINE IS BATMOBILE!
HEH.
HARLEY...
WHEN WILL I SEE YOU AGAIN?
SOON.

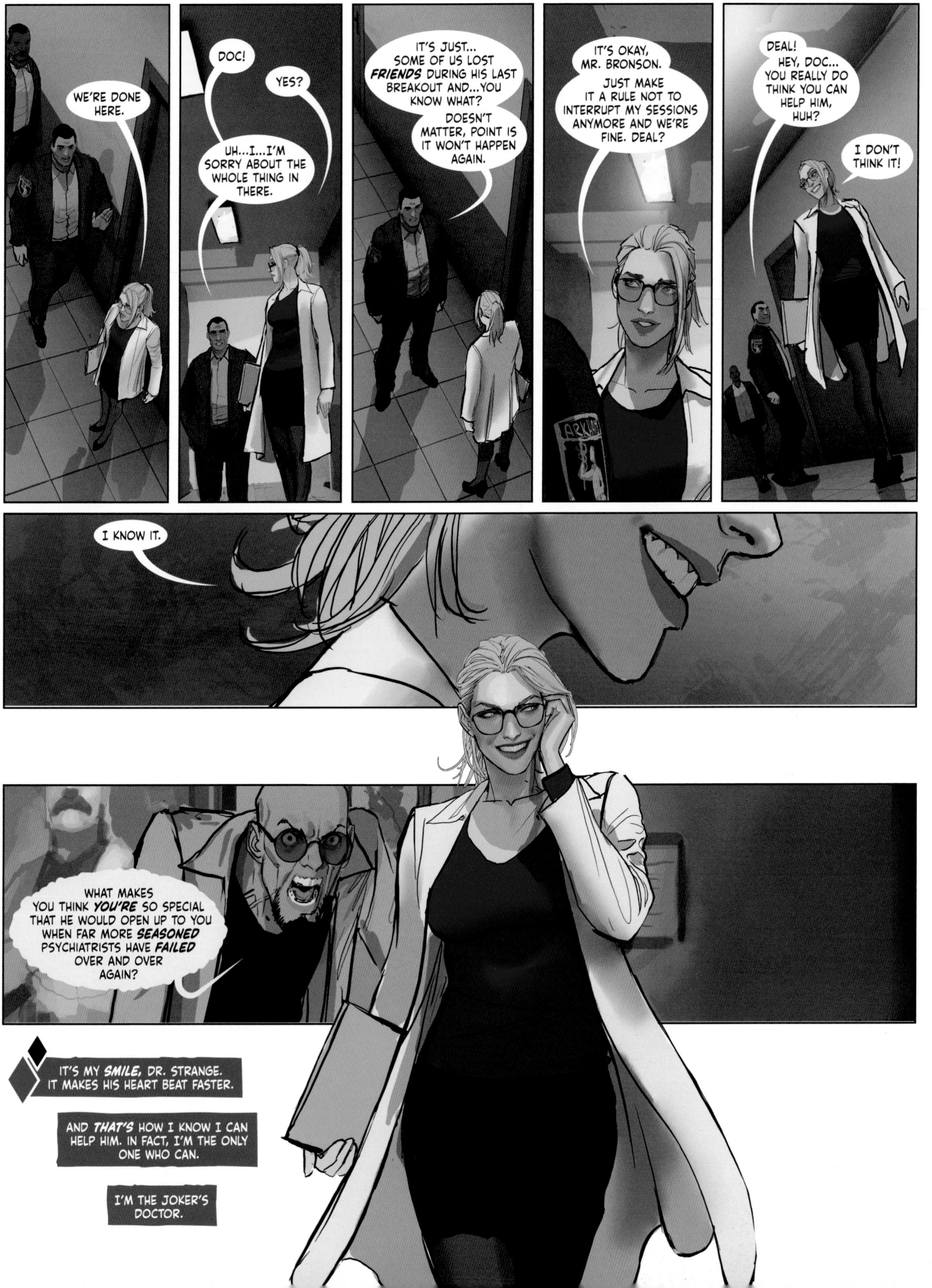
WE'RE DONE HERE.
DOC!
YES?
UH...I...I'M SORRY ABOUT THE WHOLE THING IN THERE.
IT'S JUST... SOME OF US LOST FRIENDS DURING HIS LAST BREAKOUT AND...YOU KNOW WHAT?
DOESN'T MATTER, POINT IS IT WON'T HAPPEN AGAIN.
IT'S OKAY, MR. BRONSON.
JUST MAKE IT A RULE NOT TO INTERRUPT MY SESSIONS ANYMORE AND WE'RE FINE. DEAL?
DEAL!
HEY, DOC... YOU REALLY DO THINK YOU CAN HELP HIM, HUH?
I DON'T THINK IT!
I KNOW IT.
WHAT MAKES YOU THINK YOU'RE SO SPECIAL THAT HE WOULD OPEN UP TO YOU WHEN FAR MORE SEASONED PSYCHIATRISTS HAVE FAILED OVER AND OVER AGAIN?
IT'S MY SMILE, DR. STRANGE. IT MAKES HIS HEART BEAT FASTER.
AND THAT'S HOW I KNOW I CAN HELP HIM. IN FACT, I'M THE ONLY ONE WHO CAN.
I'M THE JOKER'S DOCTOR.

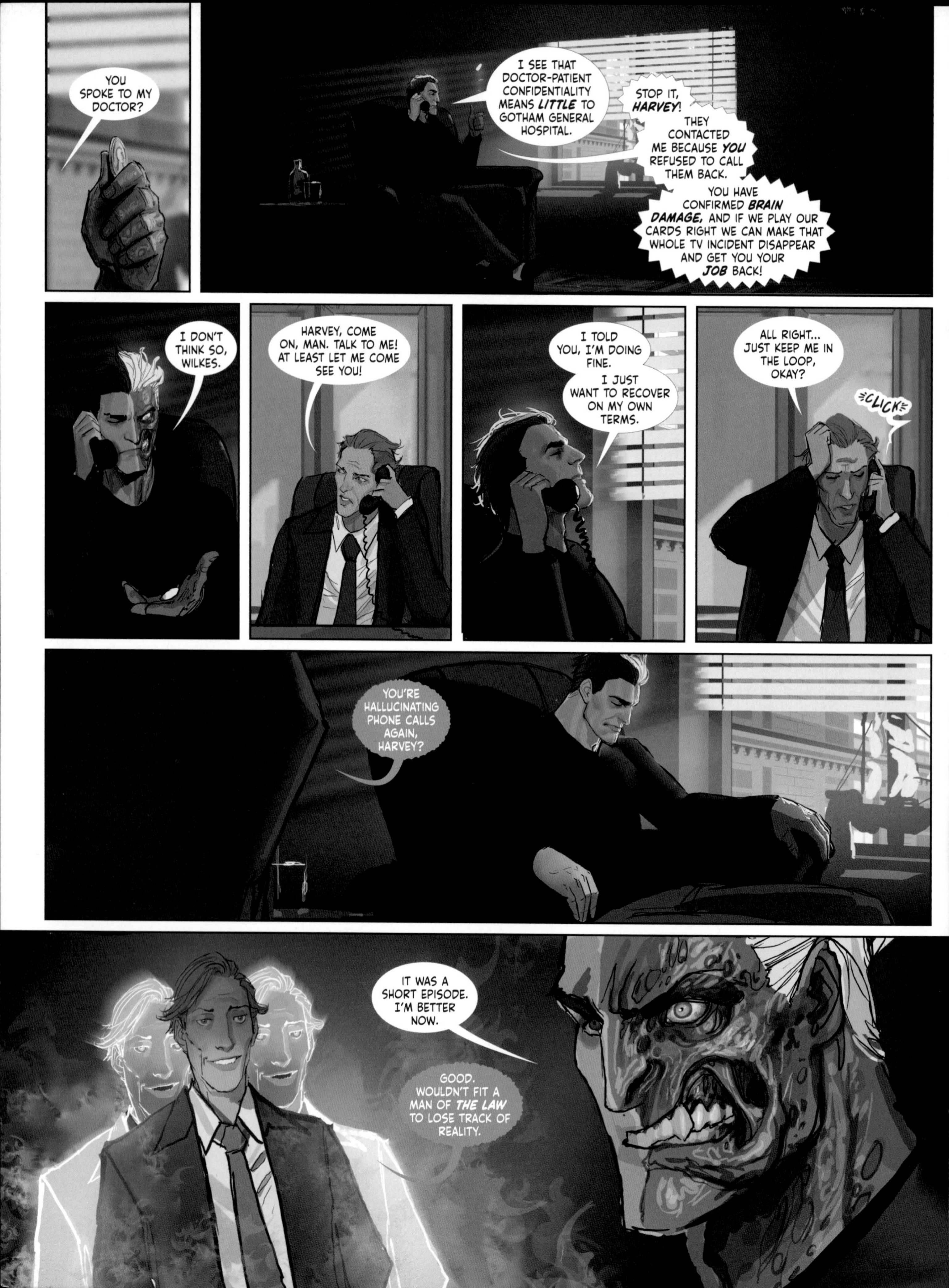
YOU SPOKE TO MY DOCTOR?
I SEE THAT DOCTOR-PATIENT CONFIDENTIALITY MEANS *LITTLE* TO GOTHAM GENERAL HOSPITAL.
STOP IT, ***HARVEY***!
THEY CONTACTED ME BECAUSE ***YOU*** REFUSED TO CALL THEM BACK.
YOU HAVE CONFIRMED ***BRAIN DAMAGE,*** AND IF WE PLAY OUR CARDS RIGHT WE CAN MAKE THAT WHOLE TV INCIDENT DISAPPEAR AND GET YOU YOUR ***JOB*** BACK!
I DON'T THINK SO, WILKES.
HARVEY, COME ON, MAN. TALK TO ME! AT LEAST LET ME COME SEE YOU!
I TOLD YOU, I'M DOING FINE.
I JUST WANT TO RECOVER ON MY OWN TERMS.
ALL RIGHT... JUST KEEP ME IN THE LOOP, OKAY?
CLICK
YOU'RE HALLUCINATING PHONE CALLS AGAIN, HARVEY?
IT WAS A SHORT EPISODE. I'M BETTER NOW.
GOOD. WOULDN'T FIT A MAN OF *THE LAW* TO LOSE TRACK OF REALITY.

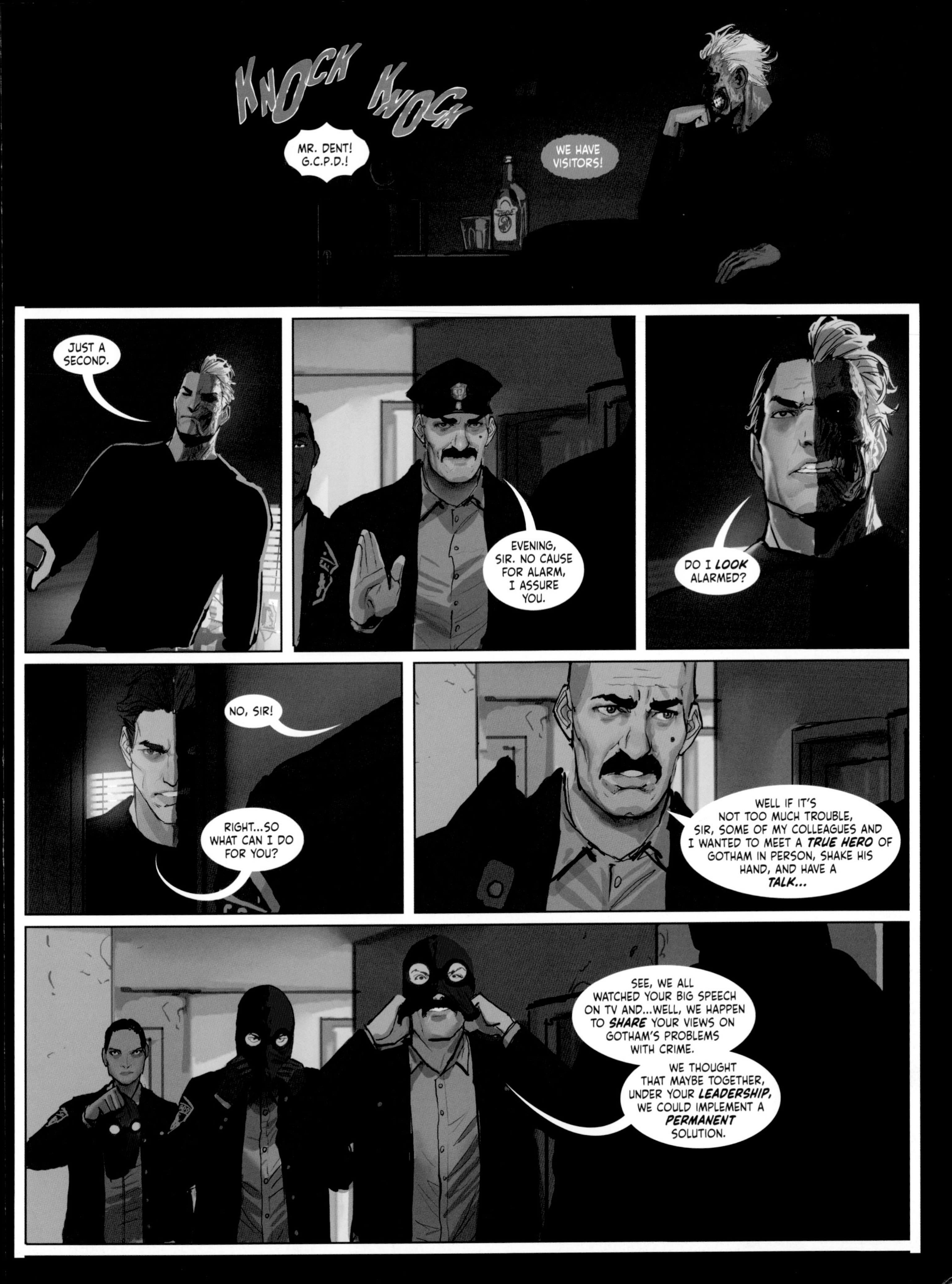
KNOCK KNOCK
MR. DENT! G.C.P.D.!
WE HAVE VISITORS!
JUST A SECOND.
EVENING, SIR. NO CAUSE FOR ALARM, I ASSURE YOU.
DO I LOOK ALARMED?
NO, SIR!
RIGHT...SO WHAT CAN I DO FOR YOU?
WELL IF IT'S NOT TOO MUCH TROUBLE, SIR, SOME OF MY COLLEAGUES AND I WANTED TO MEET A TRUE HERO OF GOTHAM IN PERSON, SHAKE HIS HAND, AND HAVE A TALK...
SEE, WE ALL WATCHED YOUR BIG SPEECH ON TV AND...WELL, WE HAPPEN TO SHARE YOUR VIEWS ON GOTHAM'S PROBLEMS WITH CRIME.
WE THOUGHT THAT MAYBE TOGETHER, UNDER YOUR LEADERSHIP, WE COULD IMPLEMENT A PERMANENT SOLUTION.

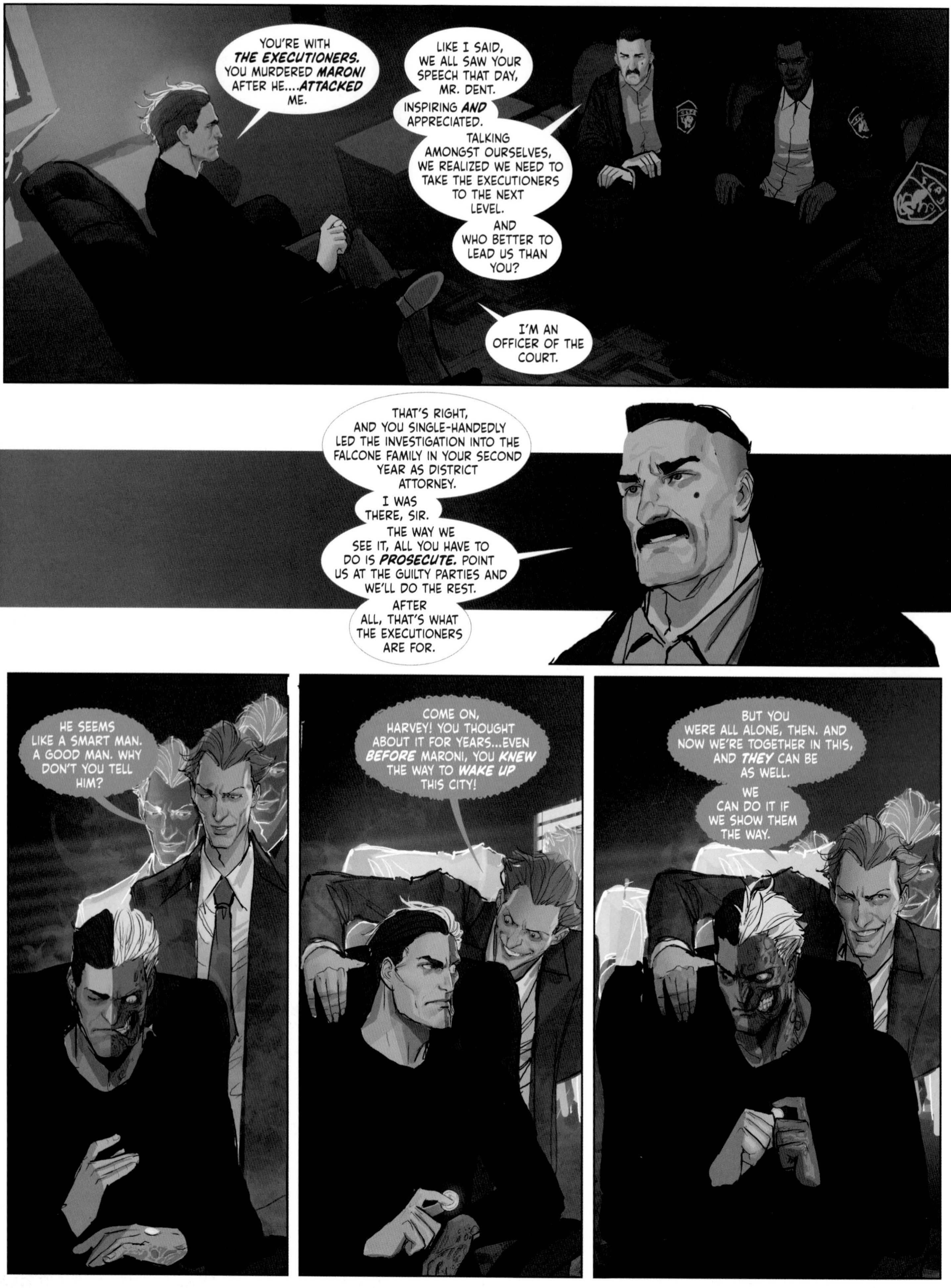

YOU'RE WITH THE EXECUTIONERS. YOU MURDERED MARONI AFTER HE....ATTACKED ME.
LIKE I SAID, WE ALL SAW YOUR SPEECH THAT DAY, MR. DENT.
INSPIRING AND APPRECIATED.
TALKING AMONGST OURSELVES, WE REALIZED WE NEED TO TAKE THE EXECUTIONERS TO THE NEXT LEVEL.
AND WHO BETTER TO LEAD US THAN YOU?
I'M AN OFFICER OF THE COURT.
THAT'S RIGHT, AND YOU SINGLE-HANDEDLY LED THE INVESTIGATION INTO THE FALCONE FAMILY IN YOUR SECOND YEAR AS DISTRICT ATTORNEY.
I WAS THERE, SIR.
THE WAY WE SEE IT, ALL YOU HAVE TO DO IS PROSECUTE. POINT US AT THE GUILTY PARTIES AND WE'LL DO THE REST.
AFTER ALL, THAT'S WHAT THE EXECUTIONERS ARE FOR.
HE SEEMS LIKE A SMART MAN. A GOOD MAN. WHY DON'T YOU TELL HIM?
COME ON, HARVEY! YOU THOUGHT ABOUT IT FOR YEARS...EVEN BEFORE MARONI, YOU KNEW THE WAY TO WAKE UP THIS CITY!
BUT YOU WERE ALL ALONE, THEN. AND NOW WE'RE TOGETHER IN THIS, AND THEY CAN BE AS WELL.
WE CAN DO IT IF WE SHOW THEM THE WAY.

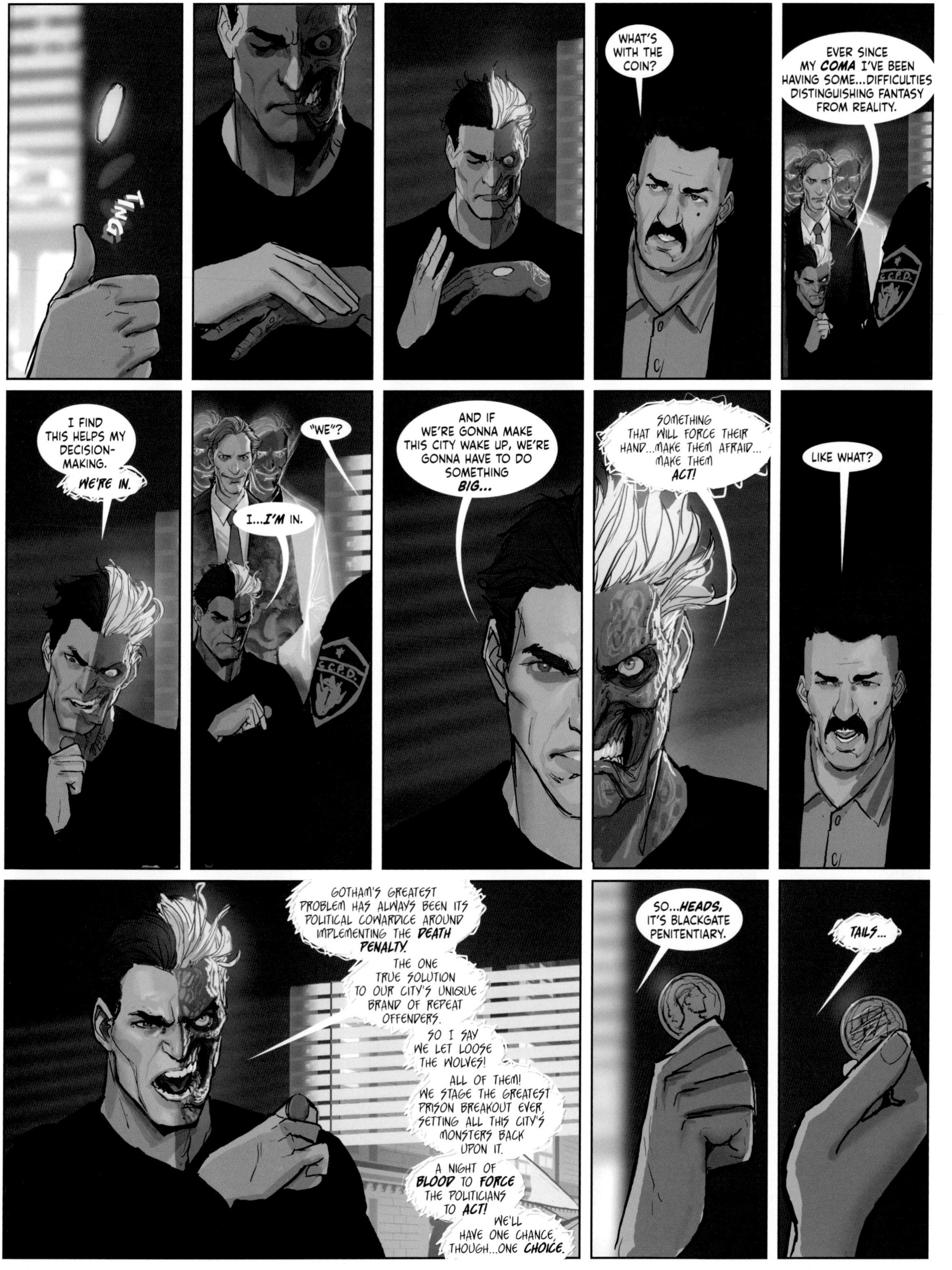
TING
WHAT'S WITH THE COIN?
EVER SINCE MY COMA I'VE BEEN HAVING SOME...DIFFICULTIES DISTINGUISHING FANTASY FROM REALITY.
I FIND THIS HELPS MY DECISION-MAKING.
WE'RE IN.
"WE"?
I...I'M IN.
AND IF WE'RE GONNA MAKE THIS CITY WAKE UP, WE'RE GONNA HAVE TO DO SOMETHING BIG...
SOMETHING THAT WILL FORCE THEIR HAND...MAKE THEM AFRAID...MAKE THEM ACT!
LIKE WHAT?
GOTHAM'S GREATEST PROBLEM HAS ALWAYS BEEN ITS POLITICAL COWARDICE AROUND IMPLEMENTING THE DEATH PENALTY.
THE ONE TRUE SOLUTION TO OUR CITY'S UNIQUE BRAND OF REPEAT OFFENDERS.
SO I SAY WE LET LOOSE THE WOLVES!
ALL OF THEM! WE STAGE THE GREATEST PRISON BREAKOUT EVER, SETTING ALL THIS CITY'S MONSTERS BACK UPON IT.
A NIGHT OF BLOOD TO FORCE THE POLITICIANS TO ACT!
WE'LL HAVE ONE CHANCE, THOUGH...ONE CHOICE.
SO...HEADS, IT'S BLACKGATE PENITENTIARY.
TAILS...

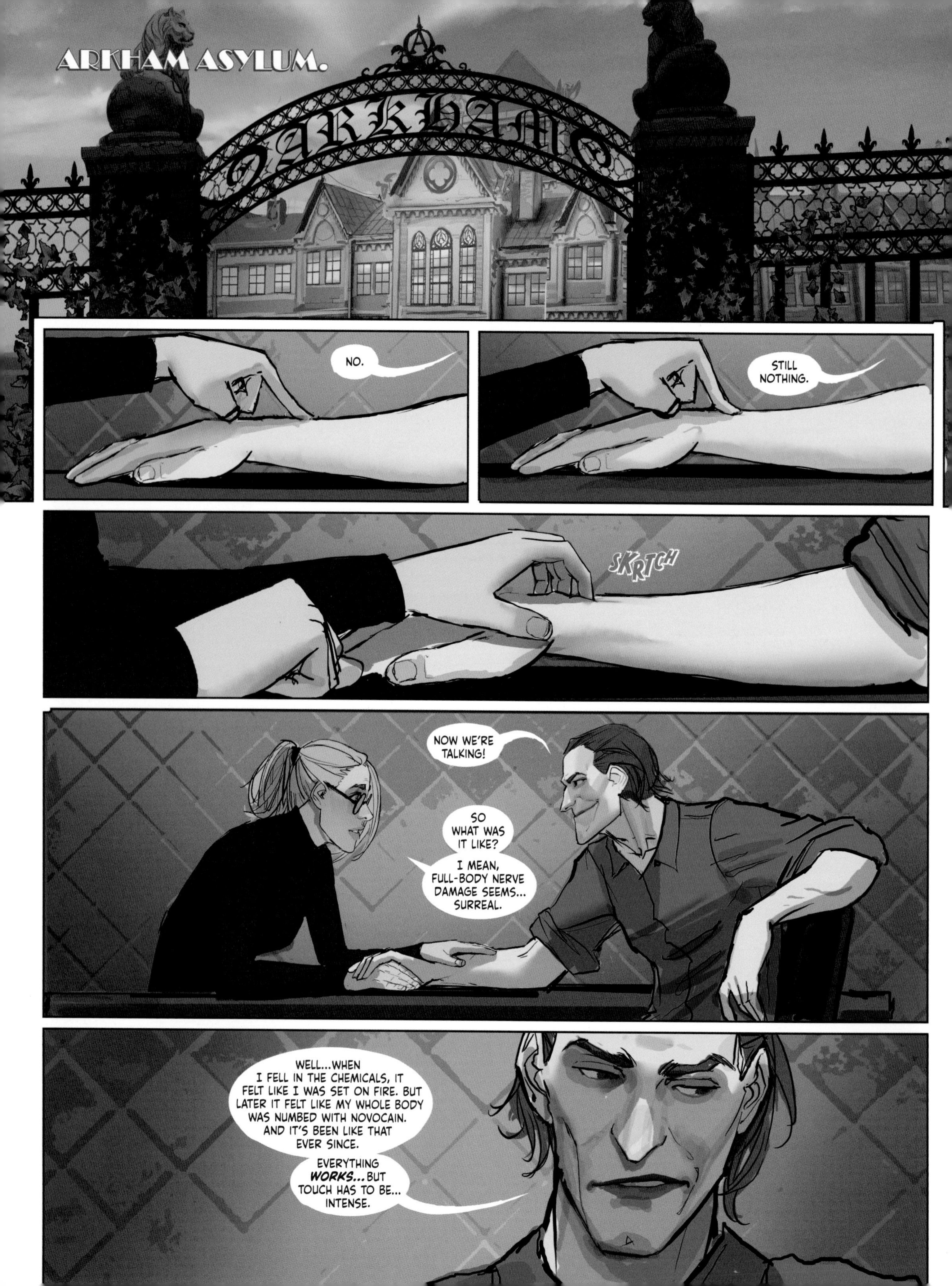
ARKHAM ASYLUM.
ARKHAM
NO.
STILL NOTHING.
SKRTCH
NOW WE'RE TALKING!
SO WHAT WAS IT LIKE?
I MEAN, FULL-BODY NERVE DAMAGE SEEMS... SURREAL.
WELL...WHEN I FELL IN THE CHEMICALS, IT FELT LIKE I WAS SET ON FIRE. BUT LATER IT FELT LIKE MY WHOLE BODY WAS NUMBED WITH NOVOCAIN. AND IT'S BEEN LIKE THAT EVER SINCE.
EVERYTHING ***WORKS...*** BUT TOUCH HAS TO BE... INTENSE.

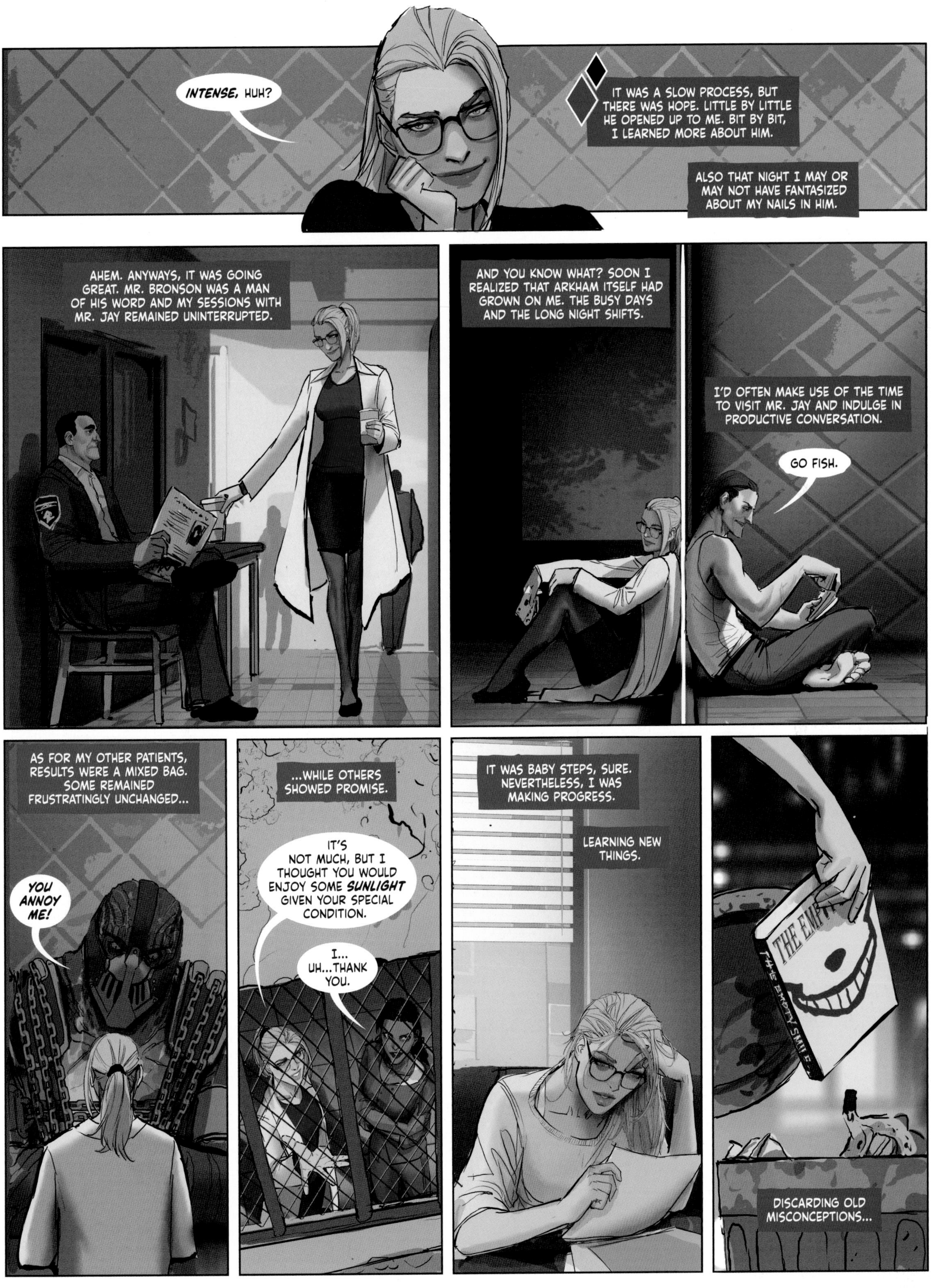

INTENSE, HUH?
IT WAS A SLOW PROCESS, BUT THERE WAS HOPE. LITTLE BY LITTLE HE OPENED UP TO ME. BIT BY BIT, I LEARNED MORE ABOUT HIM.
ALSO THAT NIGHT I MAY OR MAY NOT HAVE FANTASIZED ABOUT MY NAILS IN HIM.
AHEM. ANYWAYS, IT WAS GOING GREAT. MR. BRONSON WAS A MAN OF HIS WORD AND MY SESSIONS WITH MR. JAY REMAINED UNINTERRUPTED.
AND YOU KNOW WHAT? SOON I REALIZED THAT ARKHAM ITSELF HAD GROWN ON ME. THE BUSY DAYS AND THE LONG NIGHT SHIFTS.
I'D OFTEN MAKE USE OF THE TIME TO VISIT MR. JAY AND INDULGE IN PRODUCTIVE CONVERSATION.
GO FISH.
AS FOR MY OTHER PATIENTS, RESULTS WERE A MIXED BAG. SOME REMAINED FRUSTRATINGLY UNCHANGED...
YOU ANNOY ME!
...WHILE OTHERS SHOWED PROMISE.
IT'S NOT MUCH, BUT I THOUGHT YOU WOULD ENJOY SOME SUNLIGHT GIVEN YOUR SPECIAL CONDITION.
I... UH...THANK YOU.
IT WAS BABY STEPS, SURE. NEVERTHELESS, I WAS MAKING PROGRESS.
LEARNING NEW THINGS.
DISCARDING OLD MISCONCEPTIONS...

WEEKS TURNED TO MONTHS. EVEN THOUGH MY SCHEDULE SAID *SESSIONS*, WHAT WE SHARED WERE *DATES*... MINUS THE WINING AND DINING, AND WITH EXCESSIVE SECURITY RESTRAINTS THROWN INTO THE MIX.

AND YES, I'M *AWARE* THAT SOUNDS LIKE SOME DEVELOPING *FETISH*...

SO THE JACKET STAYS ON TODAY?

YEAH, I WANT TO GET SOME WORK DONE AND YOU GET HANDSY.

POT? KETTLE?

=AHEM=

BUT THAT *WASN'T* IT. TRUTH WAS I HAD FALLEN *IN LOVE*. IT WAS A THOUGHT THAT WOULD'VE TERRIFIED ME ONCE, BUT NOW MADE ME START EVERY DAY WITH A SMILE.

I EVEN RECEIVED NEWS THAT THE FINANCIAL BOARD WAS ALLOCATING MORE WAYNE GRANT MONEY TO MY RESEARCH, MEANING ASSISTANTS AND EQUIPMENT! IT WAS ALL WITHIN MY REACH.

EVERYTHING WAS COMING UP HARLEY!

WELL, ALMOST EVERYTHING.

I DON'T KNOW...THE GUY IS JUST *CREEPY*.

I GUESS IT'S GOOD THAT HE'S HERE TO INTERROGATE THE JOKER AND NOT *YOU*.

INTERROGATE? WAIT, PRIYA, WHO ARE YOU TALKING ABOUT?

THE BATMAN.

HE'S *HERE*? WITH JAY?

UH, YEAH?

WHO AUTHORIZED THIS?!

UM... NOBODY? HE'S *BATMAN!*

OH FOR FUCK'S SAKE!

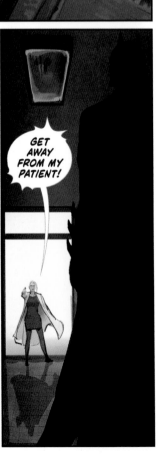

GET AWAY FROM MY PATIENT!

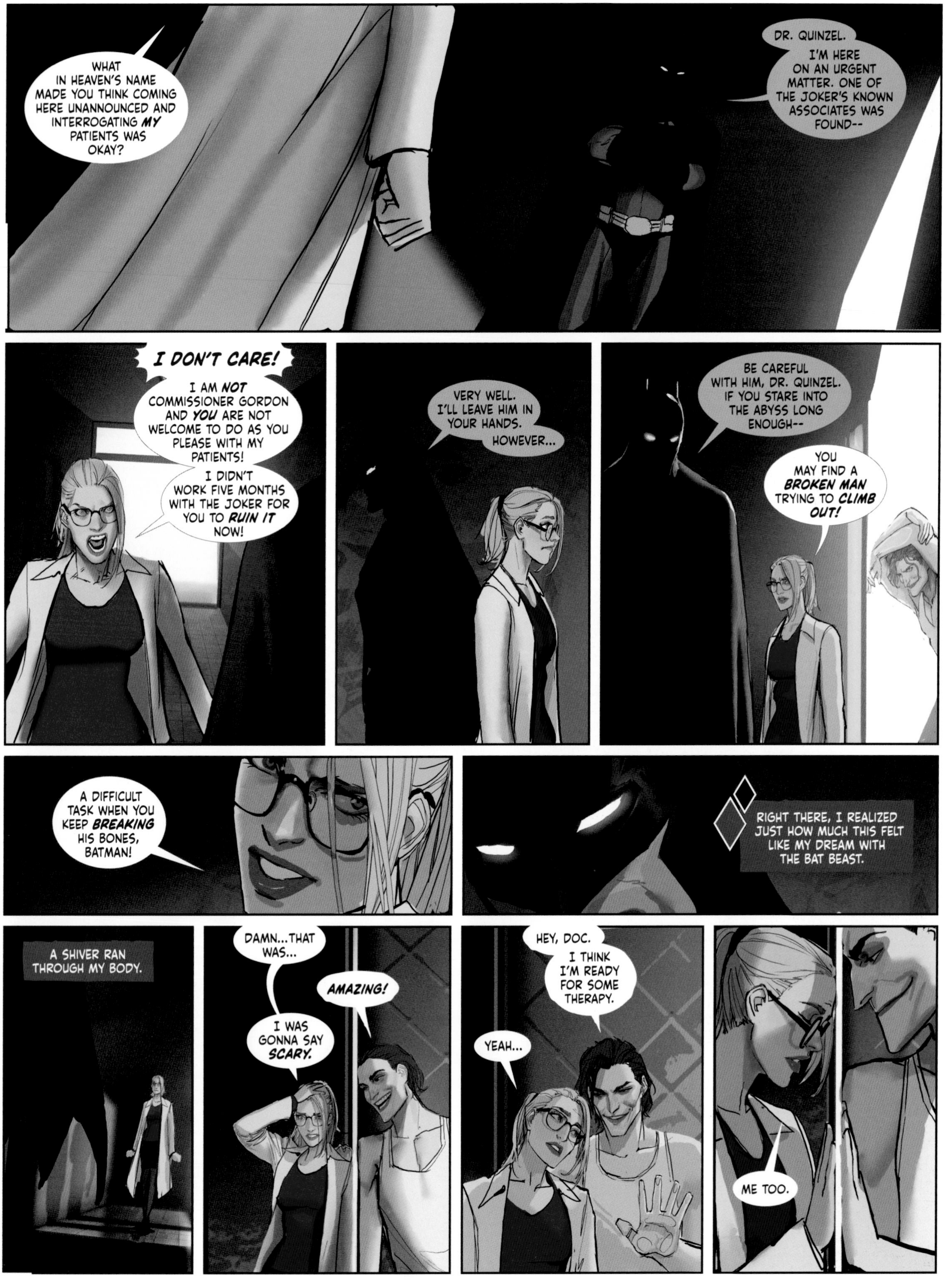
WHAT IN HEAVEN'S NAME MADE YOU THINK COMING HERE UNANNOUNCED AND INTERROGATING MY PATIENTS WAS OKAY?
DR. QUINZEL.
I'M HERE ON AN URGENT MATTER. ONE OF THE JOKER'S KNOWN ASSOCIATES WAS FOUND--
I DON'T CARE!
I AM NOT COMMISSIONER GORDON AND YOU ARE NOT WELCOME TO DO AS YOU PLEASE WITH MY PATIENTS!
I DIDN'T WORK FIVE MONTHS WITH THE JOKER FOR YOU TO RUIN IT NOW!
VERY WELL. I'LL LEAVE HIM IN YOUR HANDS.
HOWEVER...
BE CAREFUL WITH HIM, DR. QUINZEL. IF YOU STARE INTO THE ABYSS LONG ENOUGH--
YOU MAY FIND A BROKEN MAN TRYING TO CLIMB OUT!
A DIFFICULT TASK WHEN YOU KEEP BREAKING HIS BONES, BATMAN!
RIGHT THERE, I REALIZED JUST HOW MUCH THIS FELT LIKE MY DREAM WITH THE BAT BEAST.
A SHIVER RAN THROUGH MY BODY.
DAMN...THAT WAS...
AMAZING!
I WAS GONNA SAY SCARY.
HEY, DOC.
I THINK I'M READY FOR SOME THERAPY.
YEAH...
ME TOO.

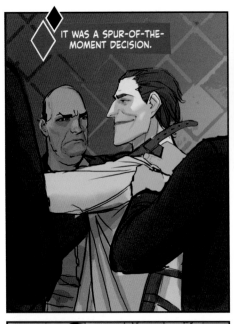

IT WAS A SPUR-OF-THE-MOMENT DECISION.

AND I'D BEEN ON THE SPUR-OF-THE-MOMENT *PILL* FOR ABOUT TWO WEEKS.

BECAUSE *HE* WAS THE SUBJECT OF MOST OF MY SPUR-OF-THE-MOMENT WAKING THOUGHTS...

NOTHING PREMEDITATED ABOUT IT.

ON A *WHIM*, I ARRANGED A DATE.

ON A WHIM, I FOUND MYSELF CARRYING MAKEUP FOR THE FIRST TIME SINCE COLLEGE.

AND MY OH MY, WHO KNEW WHERE MY NEXT WHIM MIGHT TAKE ME...

OH MY GOD, HARLEY! WHAT THE FUCK ARE YOU DOING?

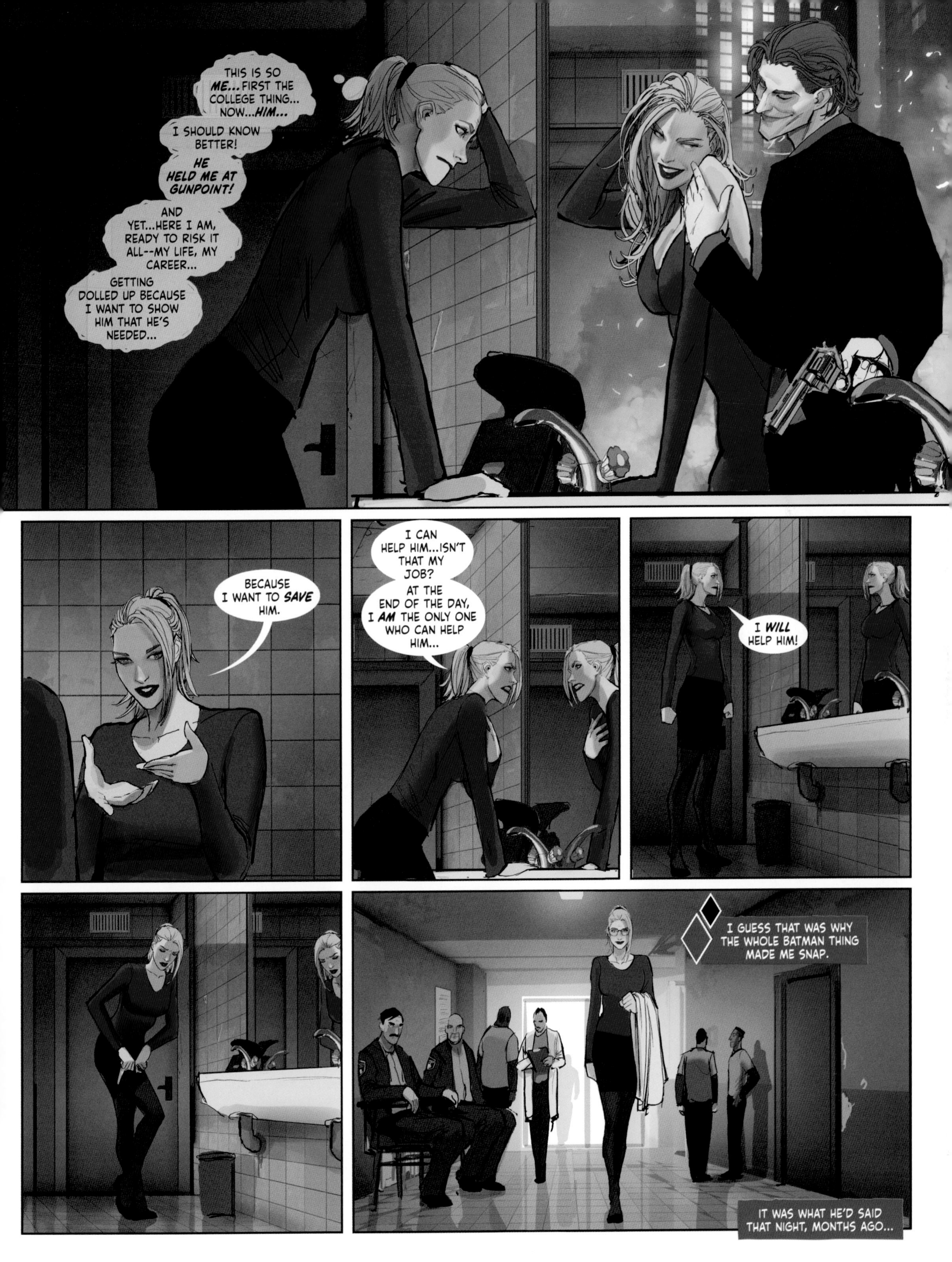

THIS IS SO ME... FIRST THE COLLEGE THING... NOW...HIM...
I SHOULD KNOW BETTER!
HE HELD ME AT GUNPOINT!
AND YET...HERE I AM, READY TO RISK IT ALL--MY LIFE, MY CAREER...
GETTING DOLLED UP BECAUSE I WANT TO SHOW HIM THAT HE'S NEEDED...
BECAUSE I WANT TO SAVE HIM.
I CAN HELP HIM...ISN'T THAT MY JOB?
AT THE END OF THE DAY, I AM THE ONLY ONE WHO CAN HELP HIM...
I WILL HELP HIM!
I GUESS THAT WAS WHY THE WHOLE BATMAN THING MADE ME SNAP.
IT WAS WHAT HE'D SAID THAT NIGHT, MONTHS AGO...

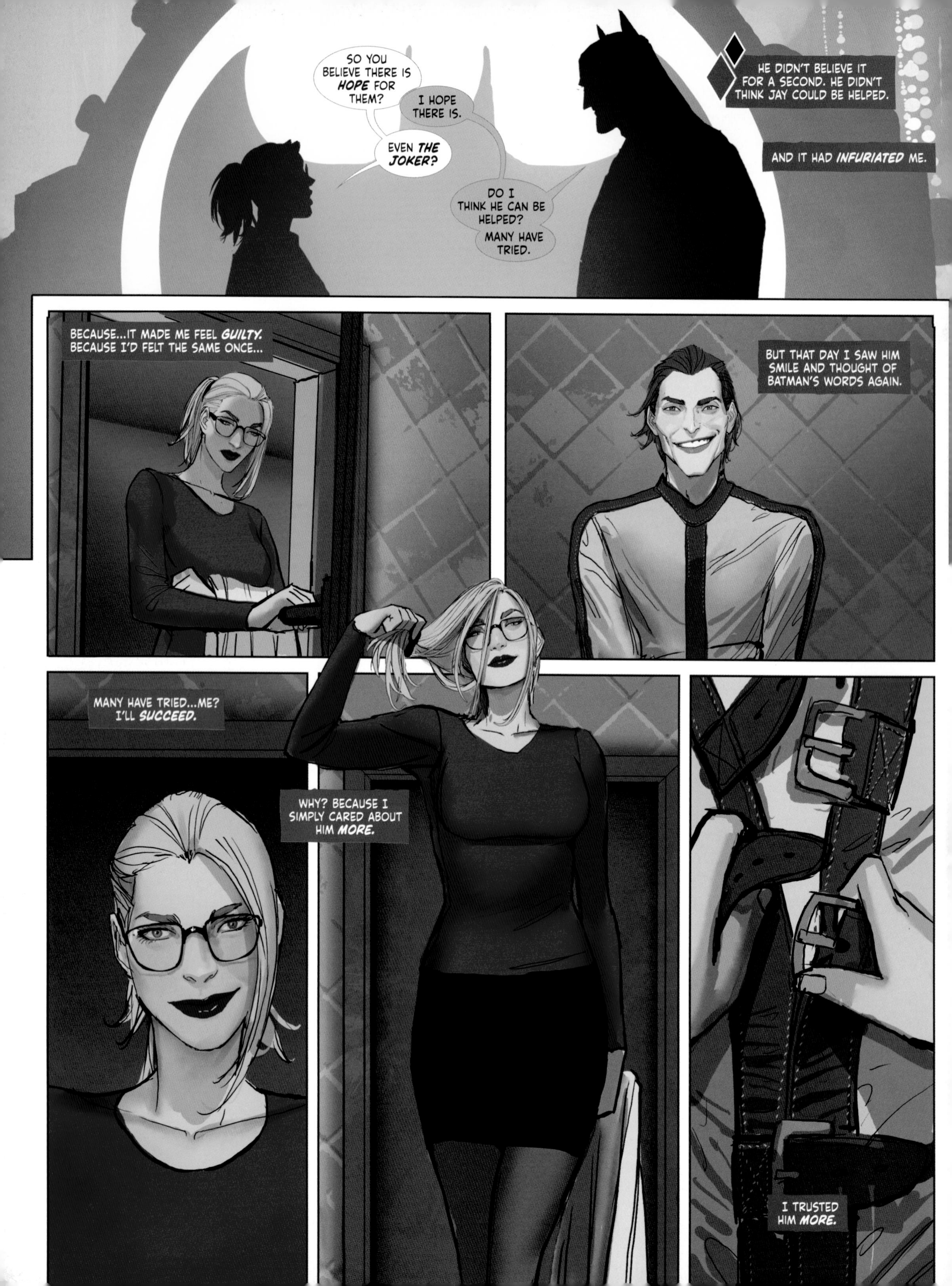

SO YOU BELIEVE THERE IS HOPE FOR THEM?
I HOPE THERE IS.
EVEN THE JOKER?
DO I THINK HE CAN BE HELPED?
MANY HAVE TRIED.
HE DIDN'T BELIEVE IT FOR A SECOND. HE DIDN'T THINK JAY COULD BE HELPED.
AND IT HAD INFURIATED ME.
BECAUSE...IT MADE ME FEEL GUILTY. BECAUSE I'D FELT THE SAME ONCE...
BUT THAT DAY I SAW HIM SMILE AND THOUGHT OF BATMAN'S WORDS AGAIN.
MANY HAVE TRIED...ME? I'LL SUCCEED.
WHY? BECAUSE I SIMPLY CARED ABOUT HIM MORE.
I TRUSTED HIM MORE.

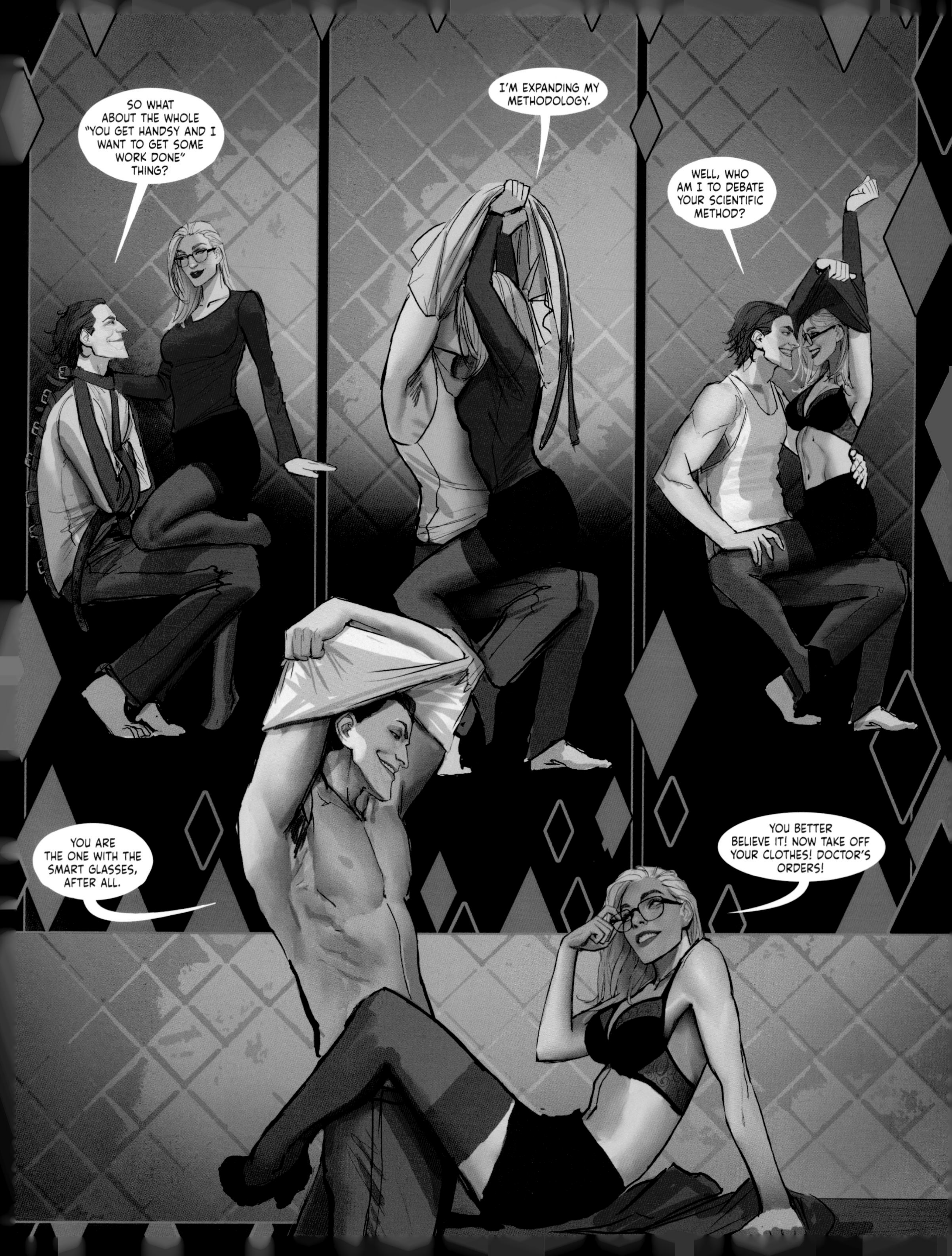
SO WHAT ABOUT THE WHOLE "YOU GET HANDSY AND I WANT TO GET SOME WORK DONE" THING?
I'M EXPANDING MY METHODOLOGY.
WELL, WHO AM I TO DEBATE YOUR SCIENTIFIC METHOD?
YOU ARE THE ONE WITH THE SMART GLASSES, AFTER ALL.
YOU BETTER BELIEVE IT! NOW TAKE OFF YOUR CLOTHES! DOCTOR'S ORDERS!

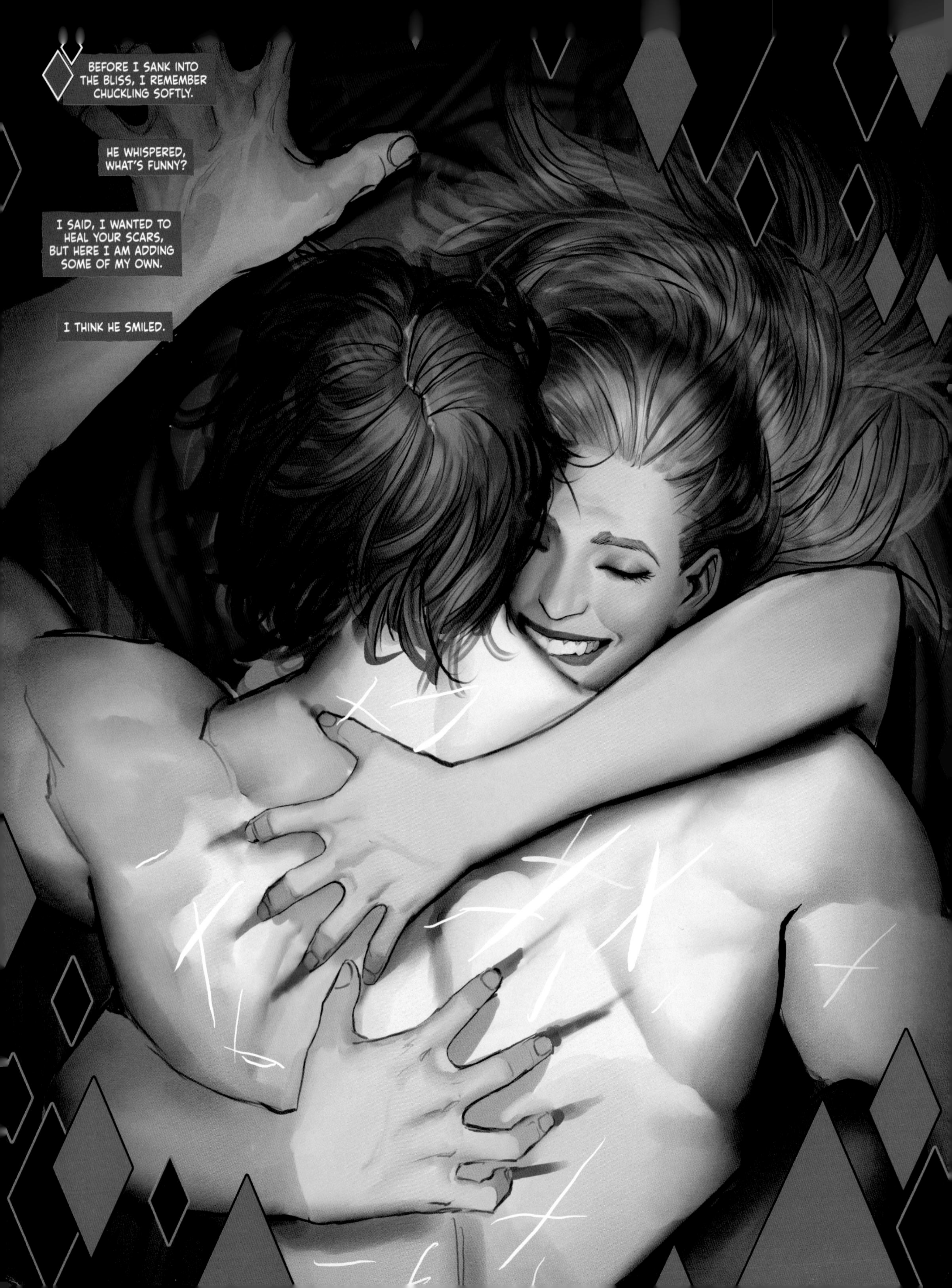
BEFORE I SANK INTO THE BLISS, I REMEMBER CHUCKLING SOFTLY.
HE WHISPERED, WHAT'S FUNNY?
I SAID, I WANTED TO HEAL YOUR SCARS, BUT HERE I AM ADDING SOME OF MY OWN.
I THINK HE SMILED.

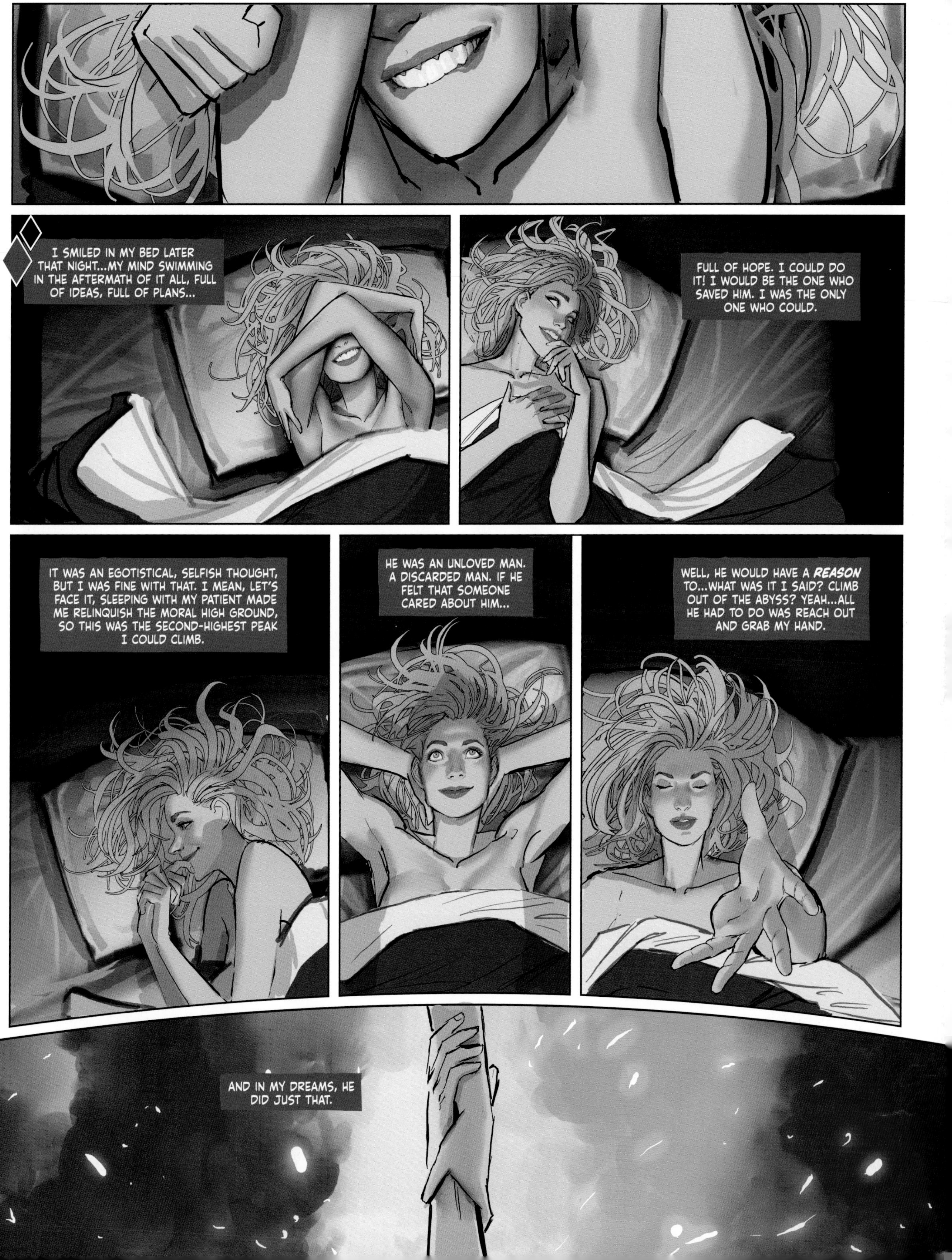
I SMILED IN MY BED LATER THAT NIGHT...MY MIND SWIMMING IN THE AFTERMATH OF IT ALL, FULL OF IDEAS, FULL OF PLANS...
FULL OF HOPE. I COULD DO IT! I WOULD BE THE ONE WHO SAVED HIM. I WAS THE ONLY ONE WHO COULD.
IT WAS AN EGOTISTICAL, SELFISH THOUGHT, BUT I WAS FINE WITH THAT. I MEAN, LET'S FACE IT, SLEEPING WITH MY PATIENT MADE ME RELINQUISH THE MORAL HIGH GROUND, SO THIS WAS THE SECOND-HIGHEST PEAK I COULD CLIMB.
HE WAS AN UNLOVED MAN. A DISCARDED MAN. IF HE FELT THAT SOMEONE CARED ABOUT HIM...
WELL, HE WOULD HAVE A ***REASON*** TO...WHAT WAS IT I SAID? CLIMB OUT OF THE ABYSS? YEAH...ALL HE HAD TO DO WAS REACH OUT AND GRAB MY HAND.
AND IN MY DREAMS, HE DID JUST THAT.

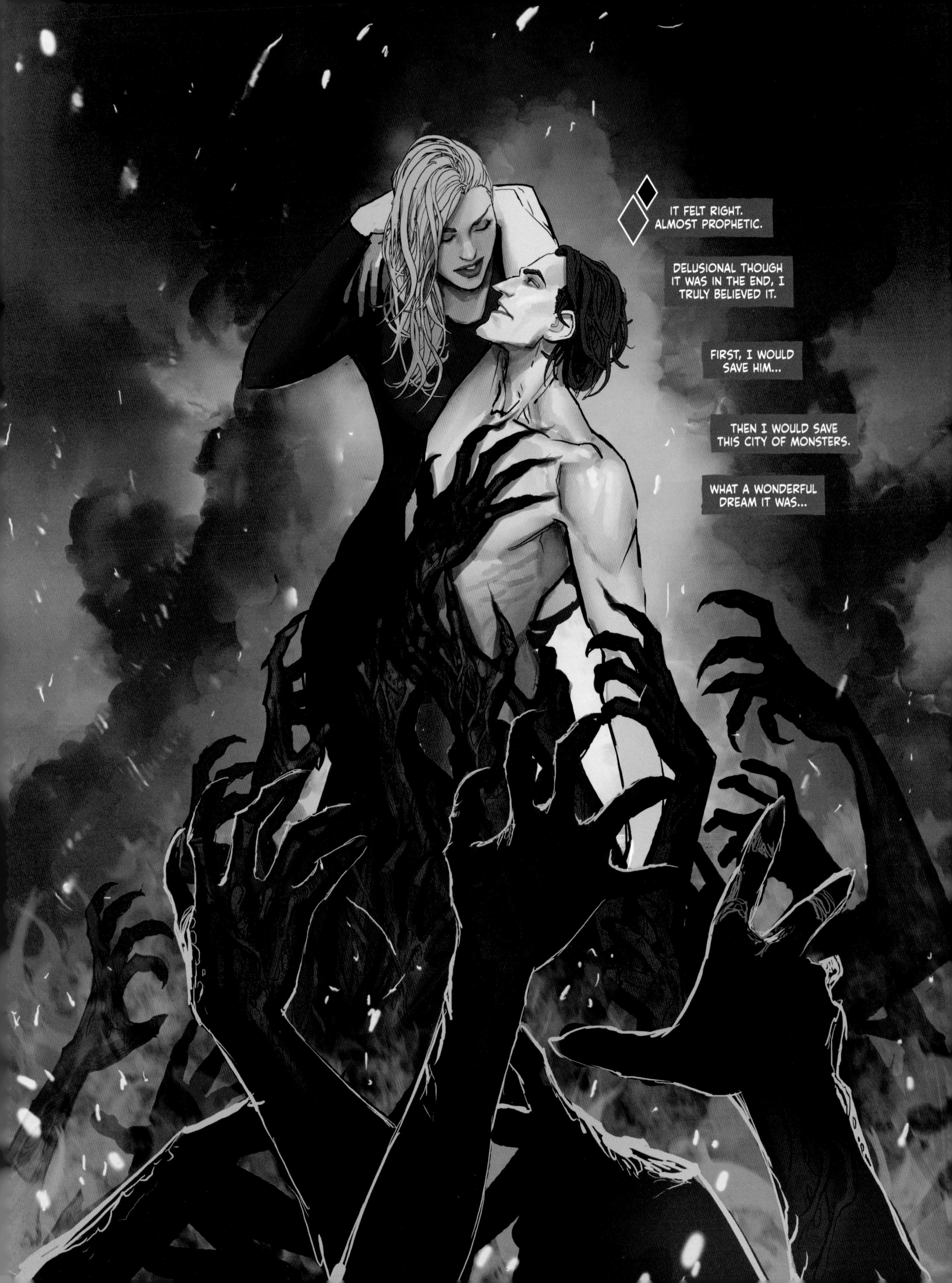
IT FELT RIGHT. ALMOST PROPHETIC.
DELUSIONAL THOUGH IT WAS IN THE END, I TRULY BELIEVED IT.
FIRST, I WOULD SAVE HIM...
THEN I WOULD SAVE THIS CITY OF MONSTERS.
WHAT A WONDERFUL DREAM IT WAS...

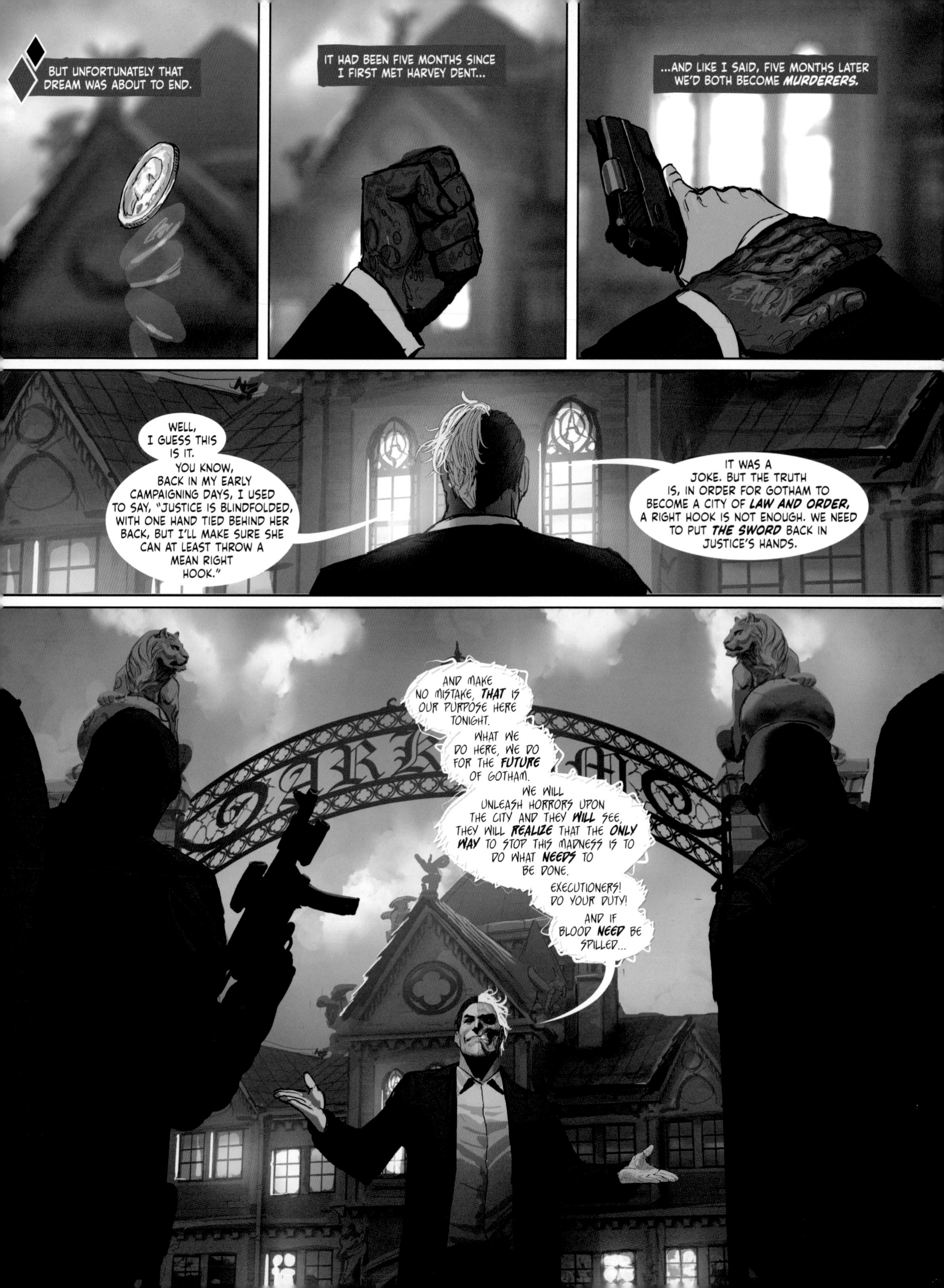
BUT UNFORTUNATELY THAT DREAM WAS ABOUT TO END.
IT HAD BEEN FIVE MONTHS SINCE I FIRST MET HARVEY DENT...
...AND LIKE I SAID, FIVE MONTHS LATER WE'D BOTH BECOME MURDERERS.
WELL, I GUESS THIS IS IT.
YOU KNOW, BACK IN MY EARLY CAMPAIGNING DAYS, I USED TO SAY, "JUSTICE IS BLINDFOLDED, WITH ONE HAND TIED BEHIND HER BACK, BUT I'LL MAKE SURE SHE CAN AT LEAST THROW A MEAN RIGHT HOOK."
IT WAS A JOKE. BUT THE TRUTH IS, IN ORDER FOR GOTHAM TO BECOME A CITY OF LAW AND ORDER, A RIGHT HOOK IS NOT ENOUGH. WE NEED TO PUT THE SWORD BACK IN JUSTICE'S HANDS.
AND MAKE NO MISTAKE, THAT IS OUR PURPOSE HERE TONIGHT.
WHAT WE DO HERE, WE DO FOR THE FUTURE OF GOTHAM.
WE WILL UNLEASH HORRORS UPON THE CITY AND THEY WILL SEE, THEY WILL REALIZE THAT THE ONLY WAY TO STOP THIS MADNESS IS TO DO WHAT NEEDS TO BE DONE.
EXECUTIONERS! DO YOUR DUTY!
AND IF BLOOD NEED BE SPILLED...

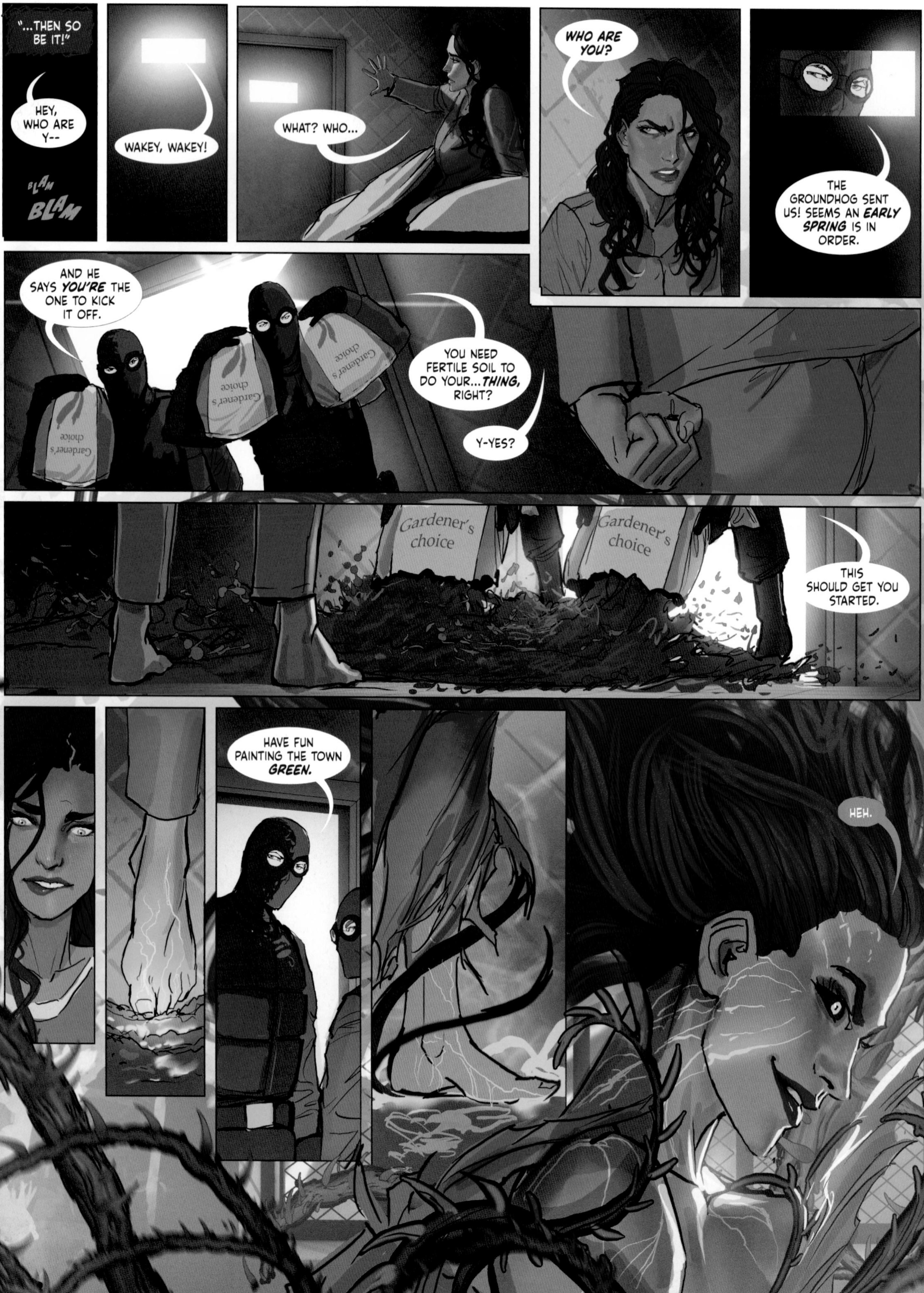
"...THEN SO BE IT!"
HEY, WHO ARE Y--
BLAM
BLAM
WAKEY, WAKEY!
WHAT? WHO...
WHO ARE YOU?
THE GROUNDHOG SENT US! SEEMS AN EARLY SPRING IS IN ORDER.
AND HE SAYS YOU'RE THE ONE TO KICK IT OFF.
Gardener's choice
Gardener's choice
Gardener's choice
YOU NEED FERTILE SOIL TO DO YOUR...THING, RIGHT?
Y-YES?
Gardener's choice
Gardener's choice
THIS SHOULD GET YOU STARTED.
HAVE FUN PAINTING THE TOWN GREEN.
HEH.

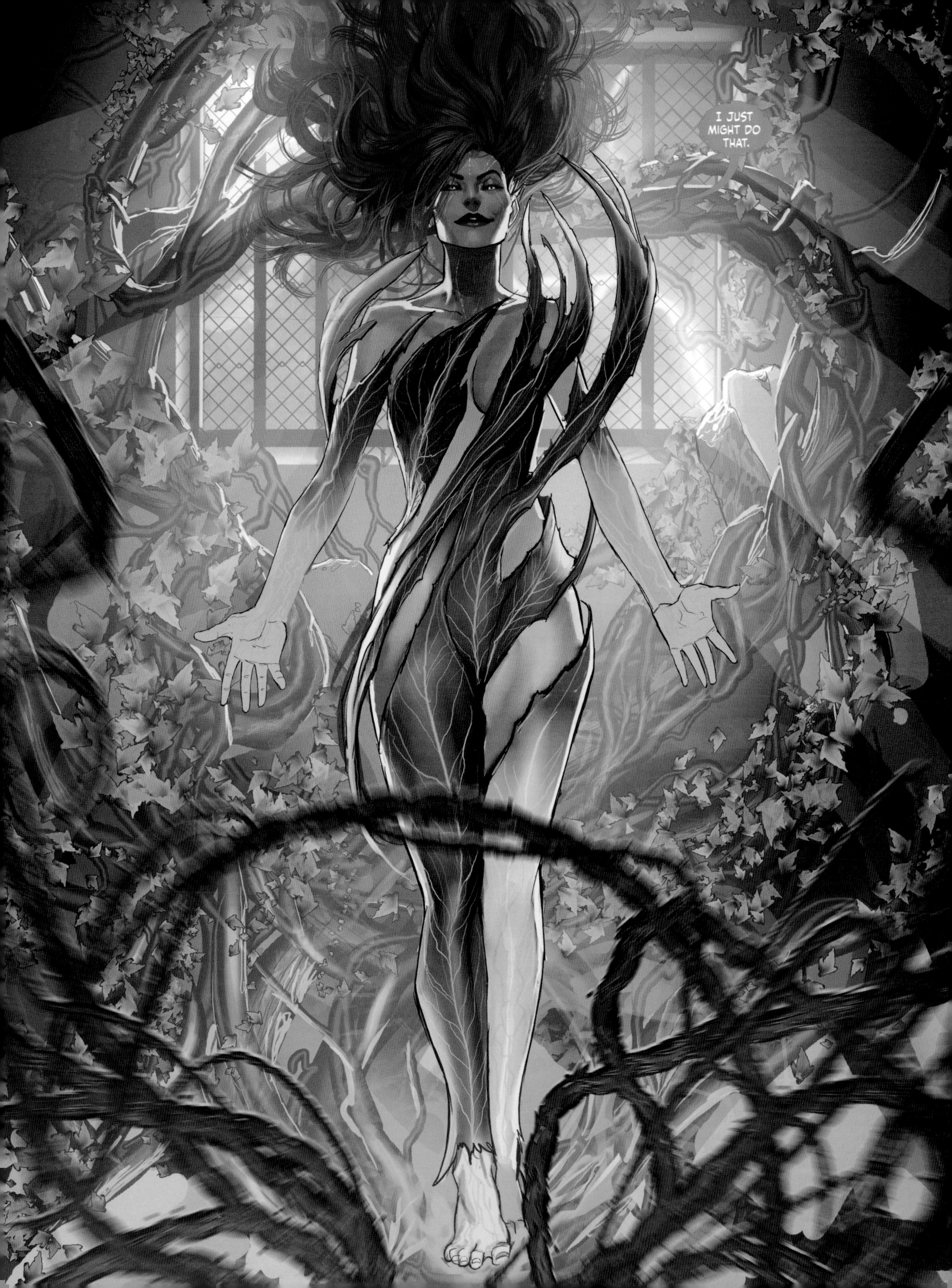
I JUST MIGHT DO THAT.

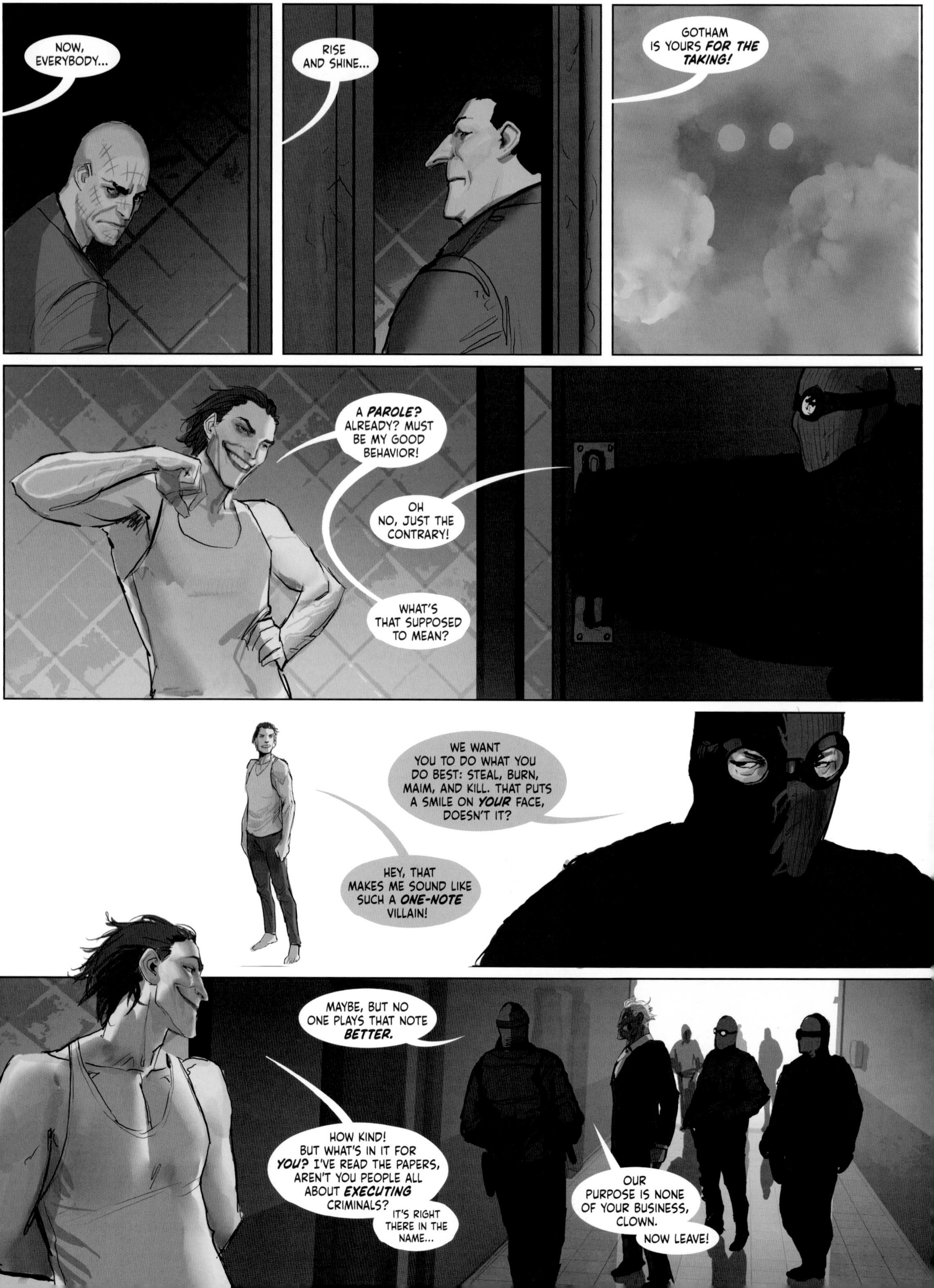

NOW, EVERYBODY...
RISE AND SHINE...
GOTHAM IS YOURS ***FOR THE TAKING!***
A ***PAROLE?*** ALREADY? MUST BE MY GOOD BEHAVIOR!
OH NO, JUST THE CONTRARY!
WHAT'S THAT SUPPOSED TO MEAN?
WE WANT YOU TO DO WHAT YOU DO BEST: STEAL, BURN, MAIM, AND KILL. THAT PUTS A SMILE ON ***YOUR*** FACE, DOESN'T IT?
HEY, THAT MAKES ME SOUND LIKE SUCH A ***ONE-NOTE*** VILLAIN!
MAYBE, BUT NO ONE PLAYS THAT NOTE ***BETTER.***
HOW KIND! BUT WHAT'S IN IT FOR ***YOU?*** I'VE READ THE PAPERS, AREN'T YOU PEOPLE ALL ABOUT ***EXECUTING*** CRIMINALS?
IT'S RIGHT THERE IN THE NAME...
OUR PURPOSE IS NONE OF YOUR BUSINESS, CLOWN.
NOW LEAVE!

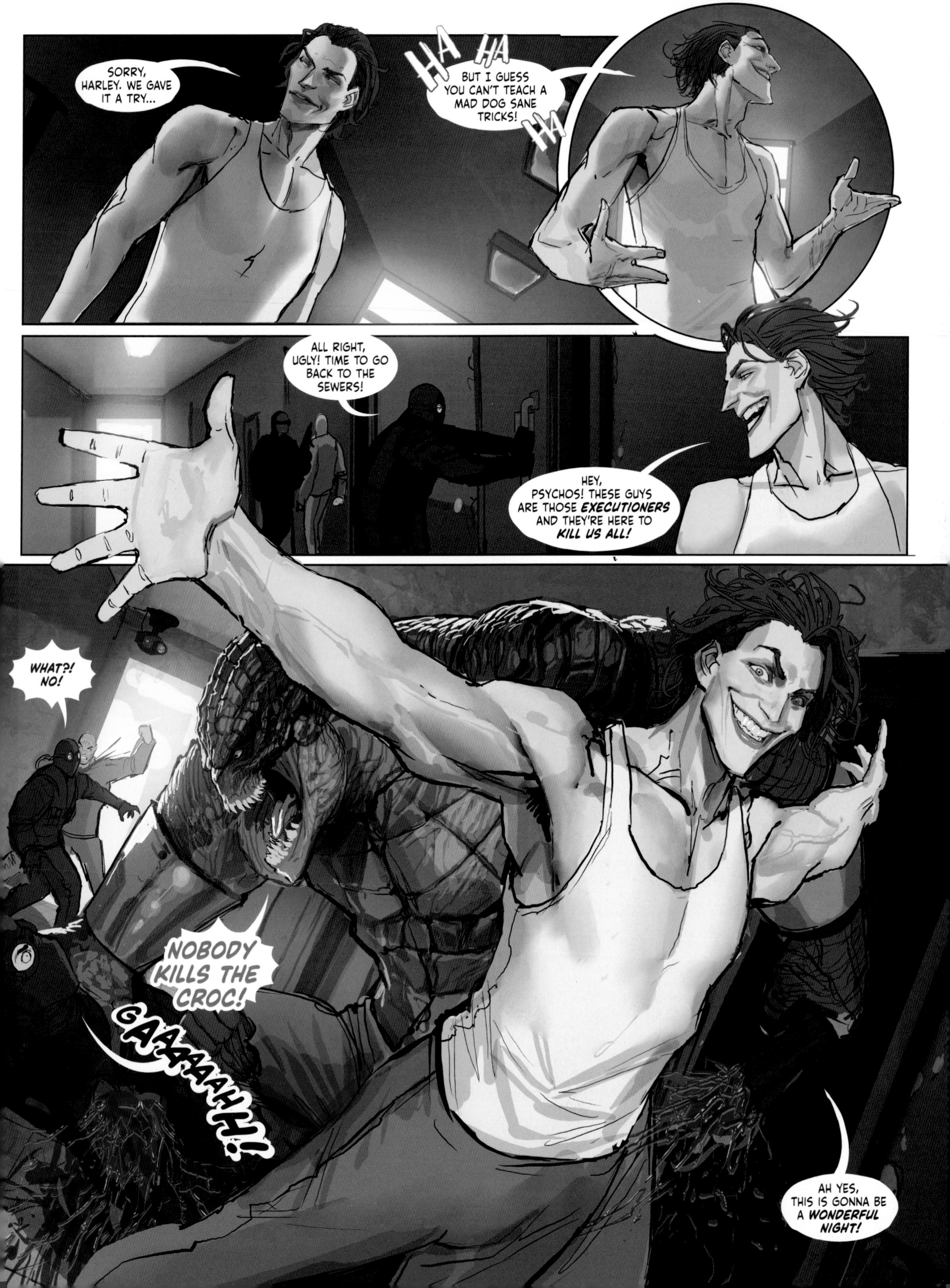
SORRY, HARLEY. WE GAVE IT A TRY...
HA HA
BUT I GUESS YOU CAN'T TEACH A MAD DOG SANE TRICKS!
HA
ALL RIGHT, UGLY! TIME TO GO BACK TO THE SEWERS!
HEY, PSYCHOS! THESE GUYS ARE THOSE EXECUTIONERS AND THEY'RE HERE TO KILL US ALL!
WHAT?! NO!
NOBODY KILLS THE CROC!
GAAAAAAH!
AH YES, THIS IS GONNA BE A WONDERFUL NIGHT!

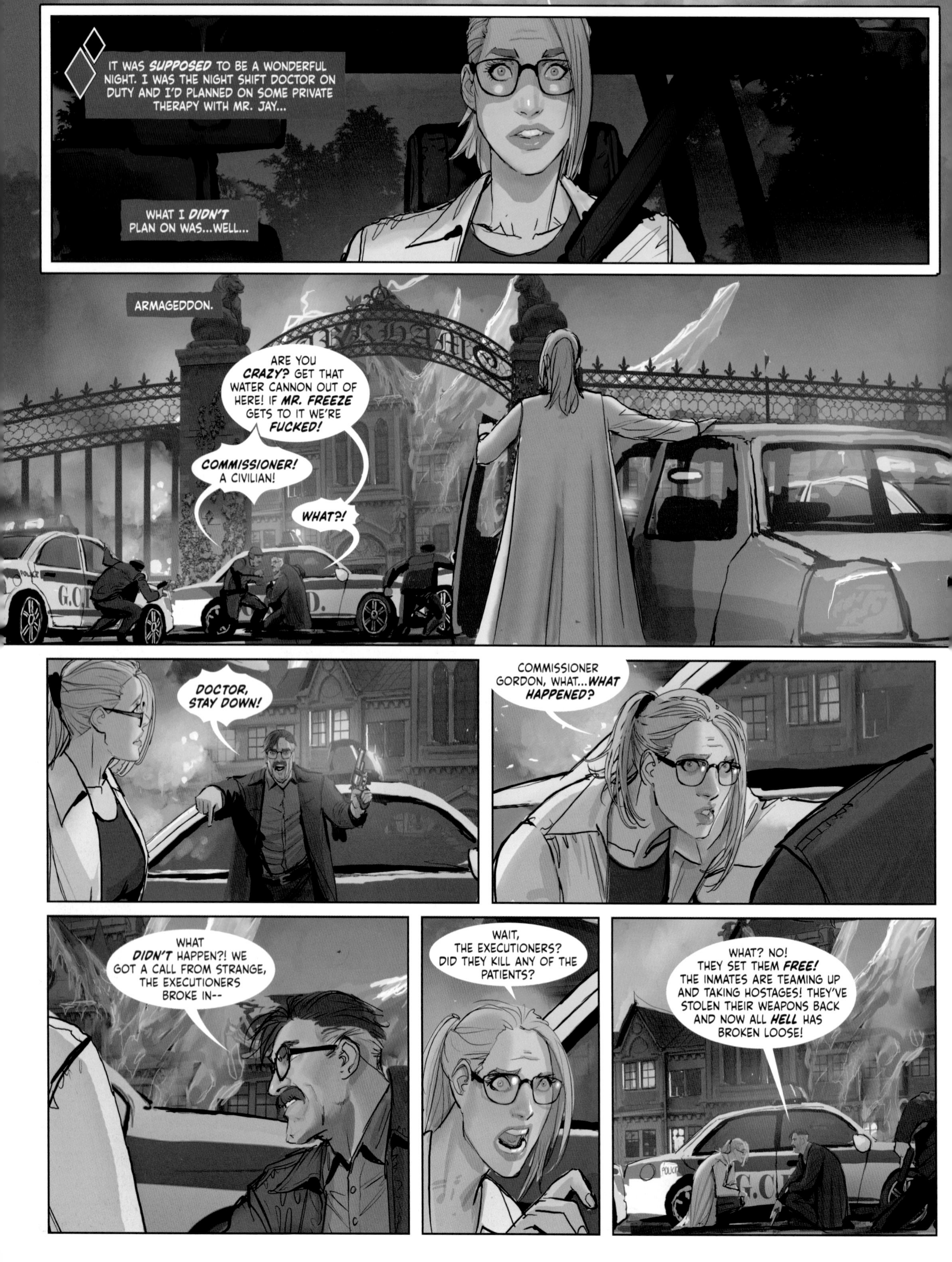
IT WAS SUPPOSED TO BE A WONDERFUL NIGHT. I WAS THE NIGHT SHIFT DOCTOR ON DUTY AND I'D PLANNED ON SOME PRIVATE THERAPY WITH MR. JAY...
WHAT I DIDN'T PLAN ON WAS...WELL...
ARMAGEDDON.
ARKHAM
ARE YOU CRAZY? GET THAT WATER CANNON OUT OF HERE! IF MR. FREEZE GETS TO IT WE'RE FUCKED!
COMMISSIONER! A CIVILIAN!
WHAT?!
DOCTOR, STAY DOWN!
COMMISSIONER GORDON, WHAT...WHAT HAPPENED?
WHAT DIDN'T HAPPEN?! WE GOT A CALL FROM STRANGE, THE EXECUTIONERS BROKE IN--
WAIT, THE EXECUTIONERS? DID THEY KILL ANY OF THE PATIENTS?
WHAT? NO! THEY SET THEM FREE! THE INMATES ARE TEAMING UP AND TAKING HOSTAGES! THEY'VE STOLEN THEIR WEAPONS BACK AND NOW ALL HELL HAS BROKEN LOOSE!

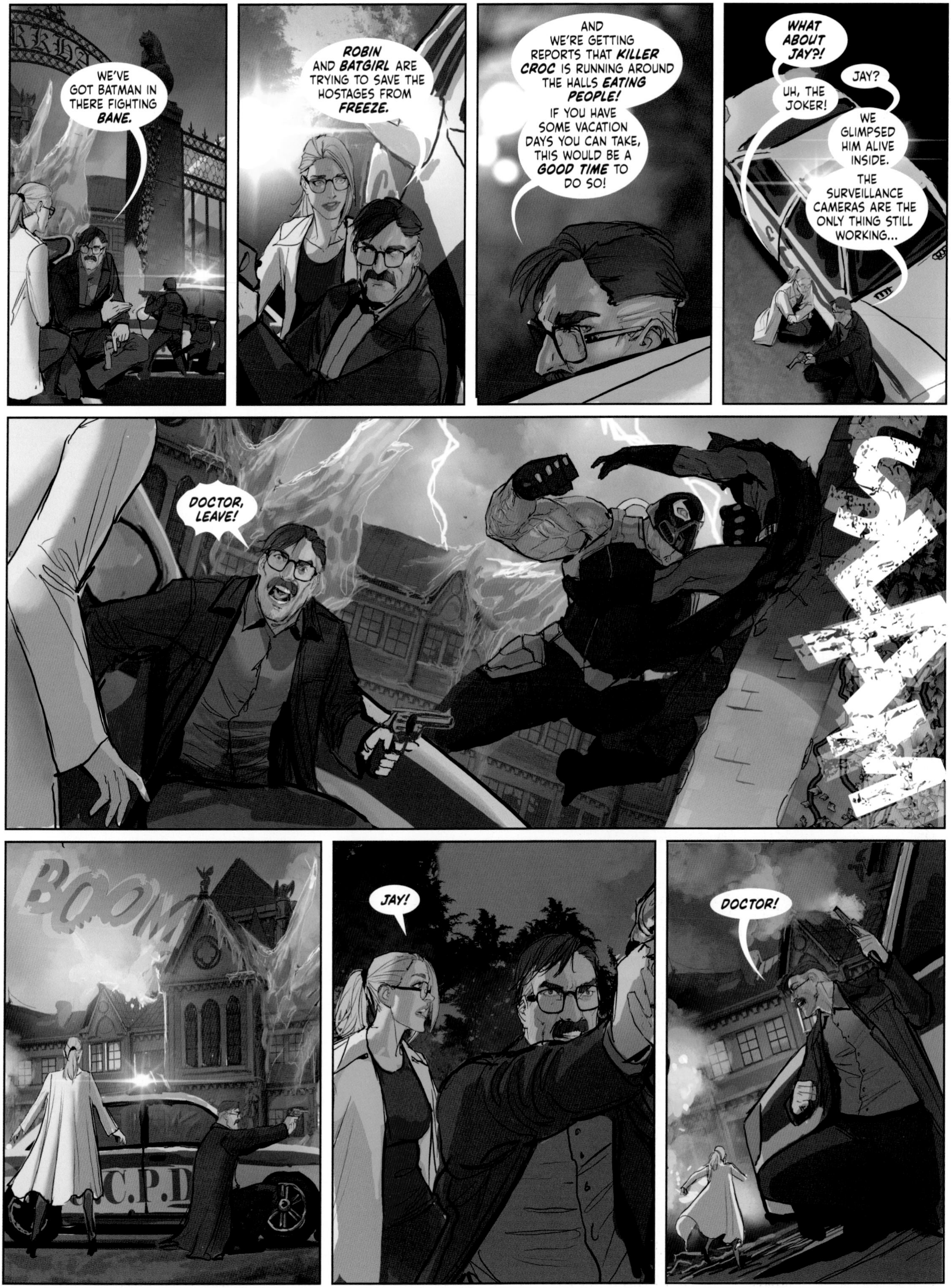
WE'VE GOT BATMAN IN THERE FIGHTING BANE.
ROBIN AND BATGIRL ARE TRYING TO SAVE THE HOSTAGES FROM FREEZE.
AND WE'RE GETTING REPORTS THAT KILLER CROC IS RUNNING AROUND THE HALLS EATING PEOPLE!
IF YOU HAVE SOME VACATION DAYS YOU CAN TAKE, THIS WOULD BE A GOOD TIME TO DO SO!
WHAT ABOUT JAY?!
JAY?
UH, THE JOKER!
WE GLIMPSED HIM ALIVE INSIDE.
THE SURVEILLANCE CAMERAS ARE THE ONLY THING STILL WORKING...
DOCTOR, LEAVE!
WHAM
BOOM
JAY!
DOCTOR!

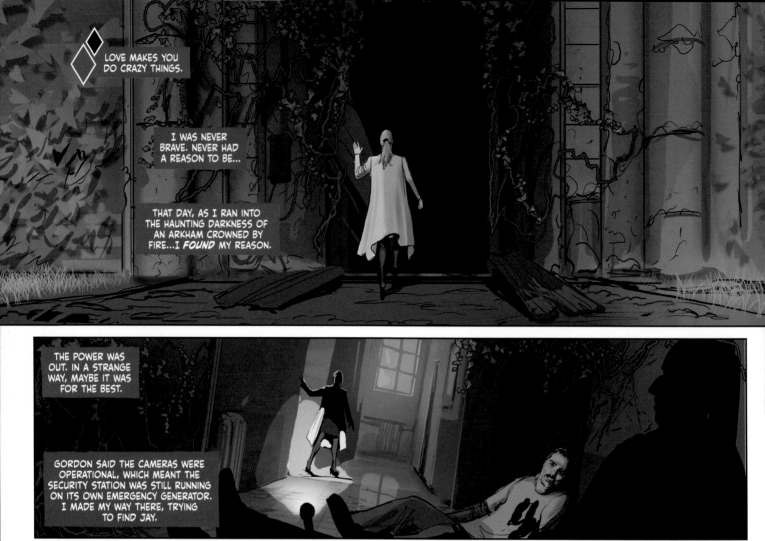

LOVE MAKES YOU DO CRAZY THINGS.

I WAS NEVER BRAVE. NEVER HAD A REASON TO BE...

THAT DAY, AS I RAN INTO THE HAUNTING DARKNESS OF AN ARKHAM CROWNED BY FIRE...I *FOUND* MY REASON.

THE POWER WAS OUT. IN A STRANGE WAY, MAYBE IT WAS FOR THE BEST.

GORDON SAID THE CAMERAS WERE OPERATIONAL, WHICH MEANT THE SECURITY STATION WAS STILL RUNNING ON ITS OWN EMERGENCY GENERATOR. I MADE MY WAY THERE, TRYING TO FIND JAY.

ON THE BRIGHT SIDE, BY THEN I KNEW MY WAY AROUND ARKHAM.

ON THE DARKER SIDE...

...OTHERS DID TOO.

OH GOD!

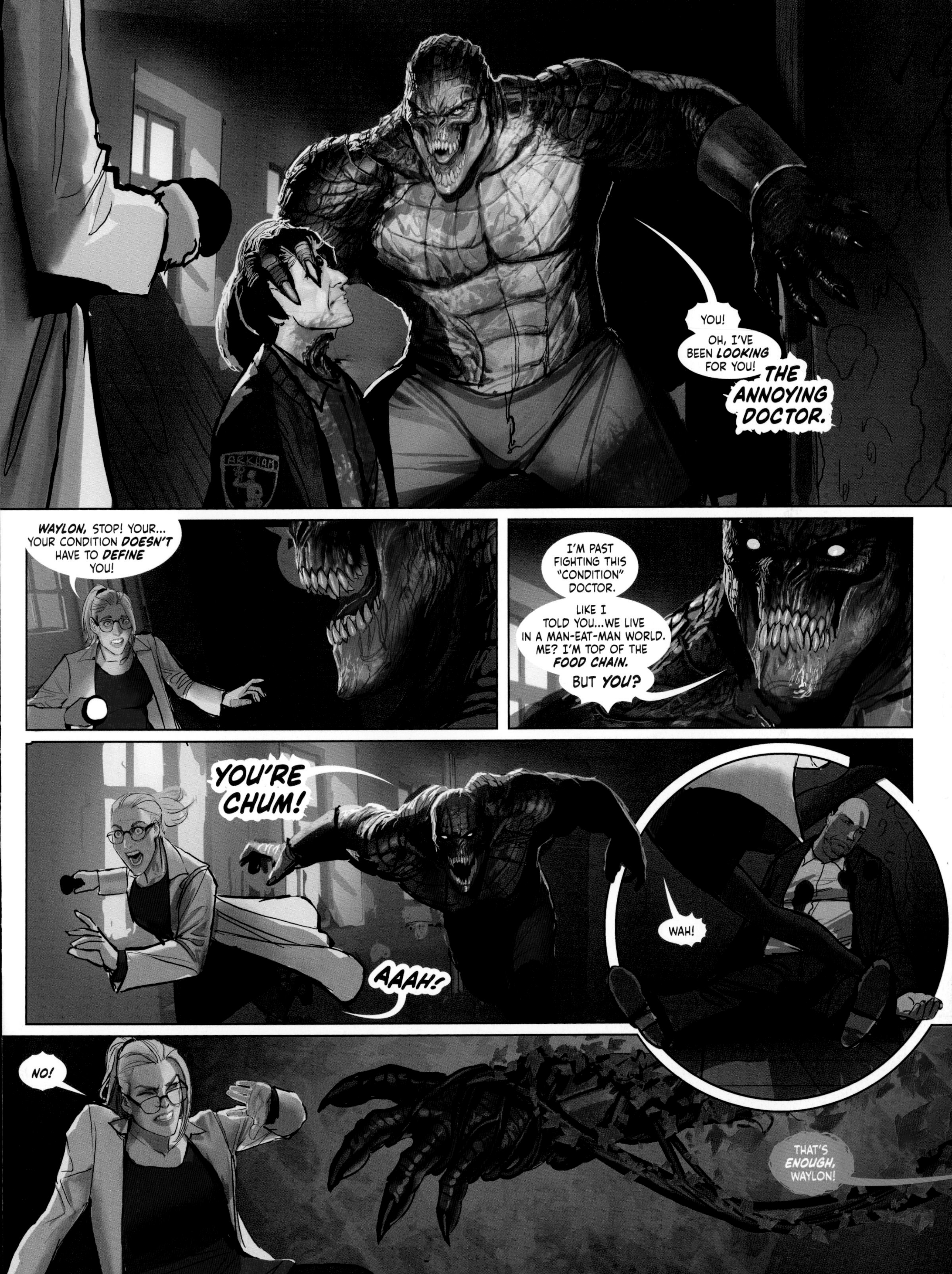
YOU!
OH, I'VE BEEN LOOKING FOR YOU!
THE ANNOYING DOCTOR.
WAYLON, STOP! YOUR... YOUR CONDITION DOESN'T HAVE TO DEFINE YOU!
I'M PAST FIGHTING THIS "CONDITION" DOCTOR.
LIKE I TOLD YOU...WE LIVE IN A MAN-EAT-MAN WORLD. ME? I'M TOP OF THE FOOD CHAIN.
BUT YOU?
YOU'RE CHUM!
AAAH!
WAH!
NO!
THAT'S ENOUGH, WAYLON!

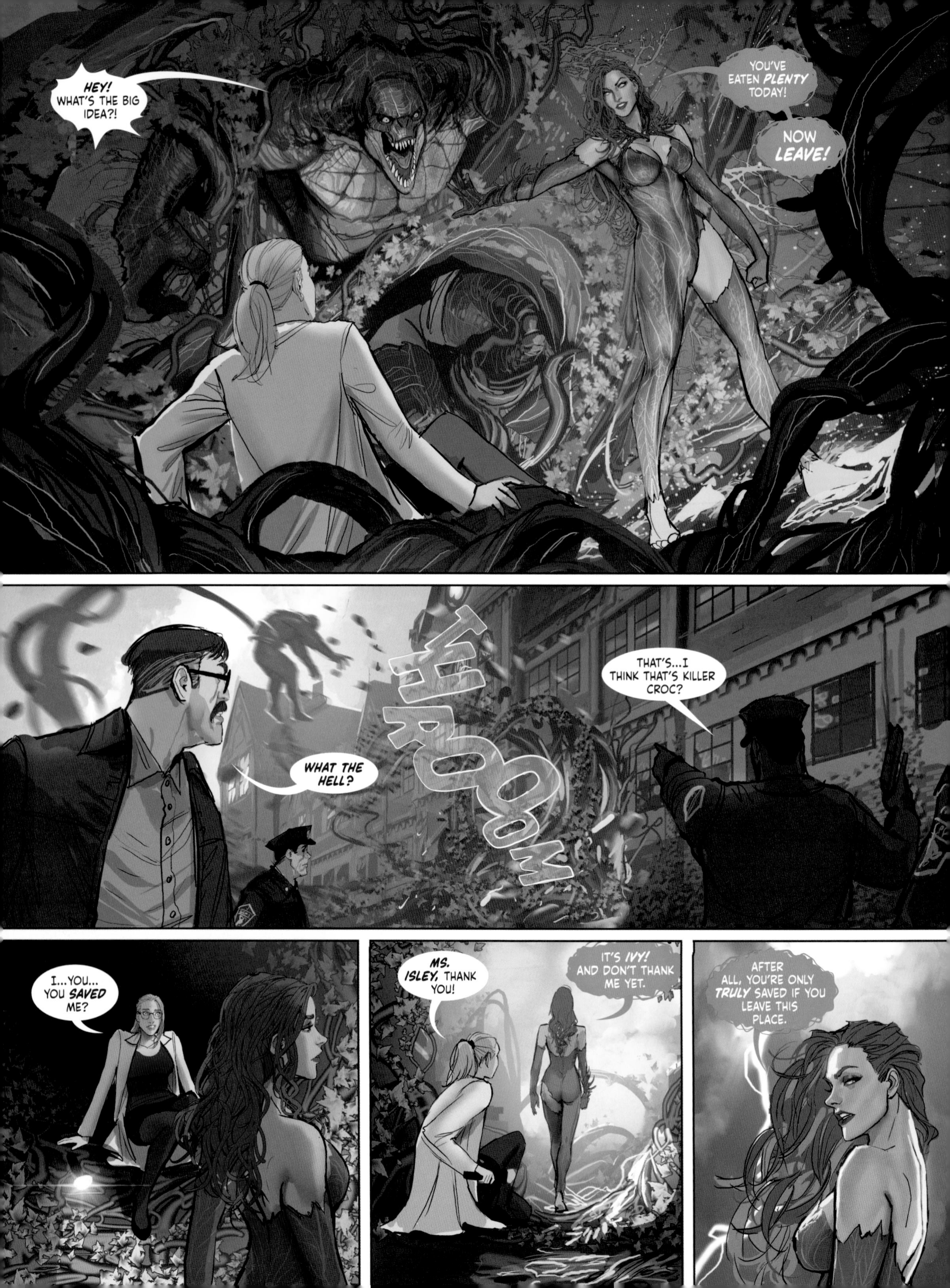
HEY! WHAT'S THE BIG IDEA?!
YOU'VE EATEN PLENTY TODAY!
NOW LEAVE!
WHAT THE HELL?
KRROOOM
THAT'S...I THINK THAT'S KILLER CROC?
I...YOU... YOU SAVED ME?
MS. ISLEY, THANK YOU!
IT'S IVY! AND DON'T THANK ME YET.
AFTER ALL, YOU'RE ONLY TRULY SAVED IF YOU LEAVE THIS PLACE.

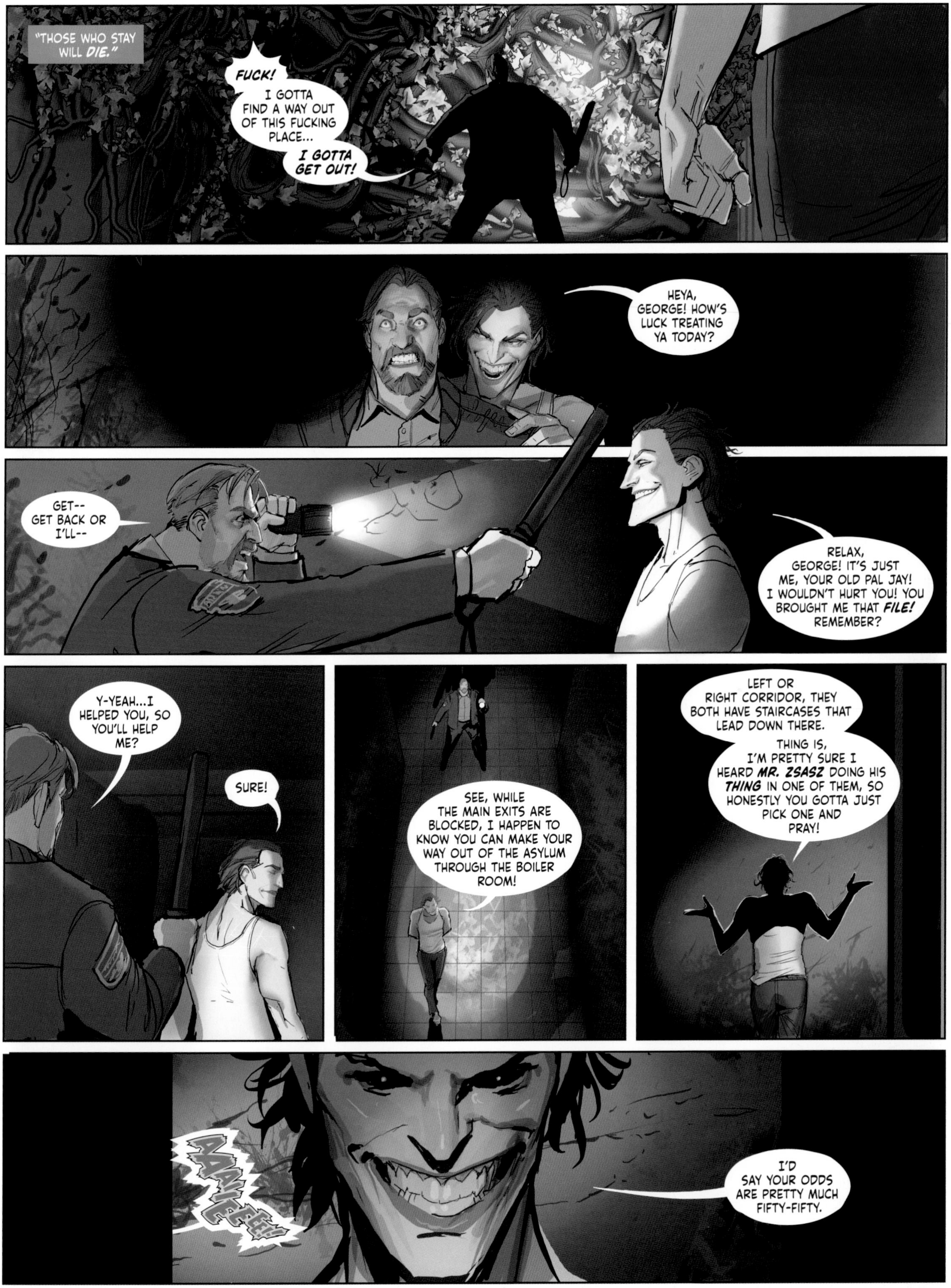
"THOSE WHO STAY WILL DIE."
FUCK! I GOTTA FIND A WAY OUT OF THIS FUCKING PLACE... I GOTTA GET OUT!
HEYA, GEORGE! HOW'S LUCK TREATING YA TODAY?
GET-- GET BACK OR I'LL--
RELAX, GEORGE! IT'S JUST ME, YOUR OLD PAL JAY! I WOULDN'T HURT YOU! YOU BROUGHT ME THAT FILE! REMEMBER?
Y-YEAH...I HELPED YOU, SO YOU'LL HELP ME?
SURE!
SEE, WHILE THE MAIN EXITS ARE BLOCKED, I HAPPEN TO KNOW YOU CAN MAKE YOUR WAY OUT OF THE ASYLUM THROUGH THE BOILER ROOM!
LEFT OR RIGHT CORRIDOR, THEY BOTH HAVE STAIRCASES THAT LEAD DOWN THERE.
THING IS, I'M PRETTY SURE I HEARD MR. ZSASZ DOING HIS THING IN ONE OF THEM, SO HONESTLY YOU GOTTA JUST PICK ONE AND PRAY!
AAAAIEEE!
I'D SAY YOUR ODDS ARE PRETTY MUCH FIFTY-FIFTY.

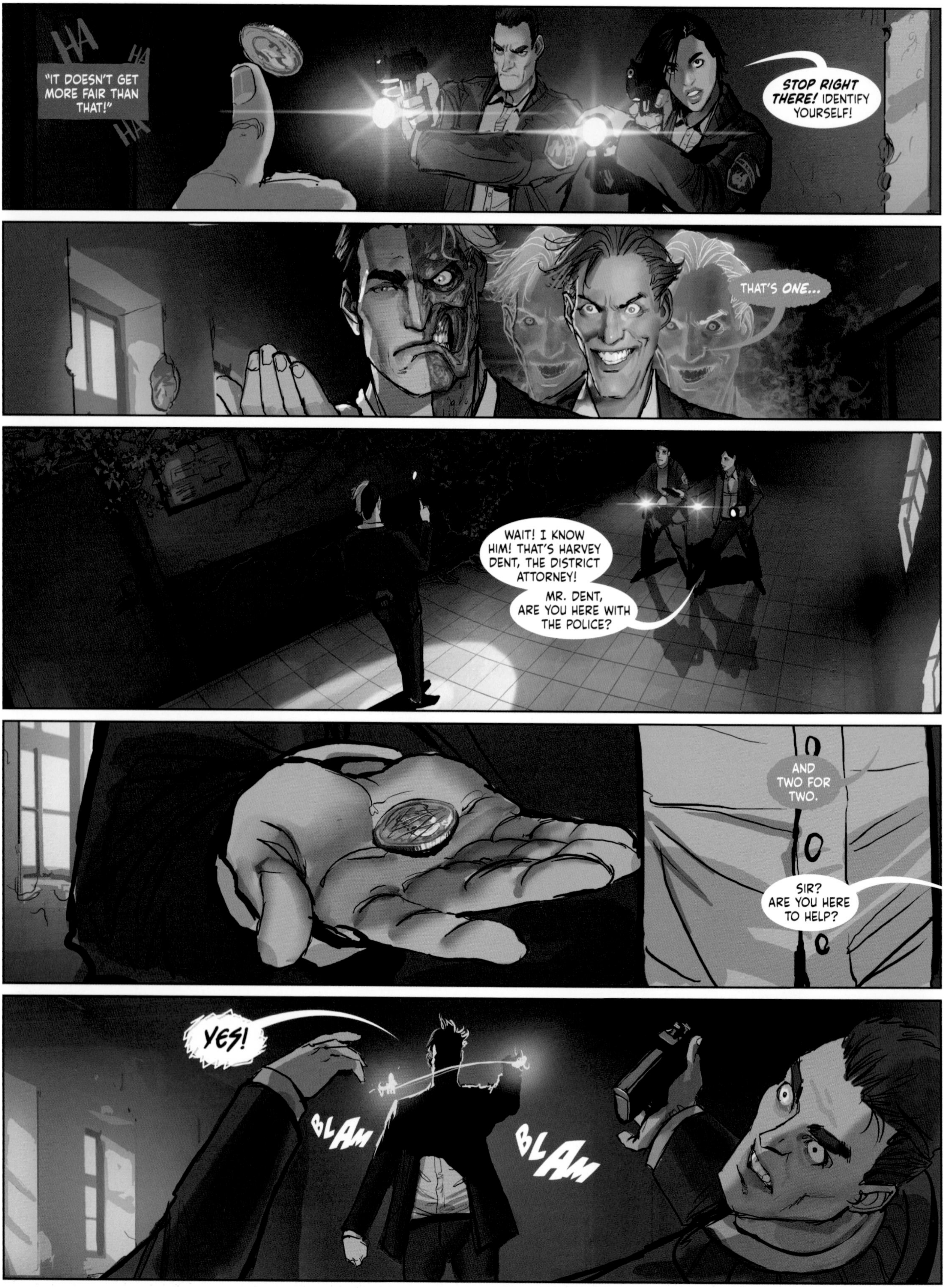
HA
HA
HA
"IT DOESN'T GET MORE FAIR THAN THAT!"
STOP RIGHT THERE! IDENTIFY YOURSELF!
THAT'S ONE...
WAIT! I KNOW HIM! THAT'S HARVEY DENT, THE DISTRICT ATTORNEY!
MR. DENT, ARE YOU HERE WITH THE POLICE?
AND TWO FOR TWO.
SIR? ARE YOU HERE TO HELP?
YES!
BLAM
BLAM

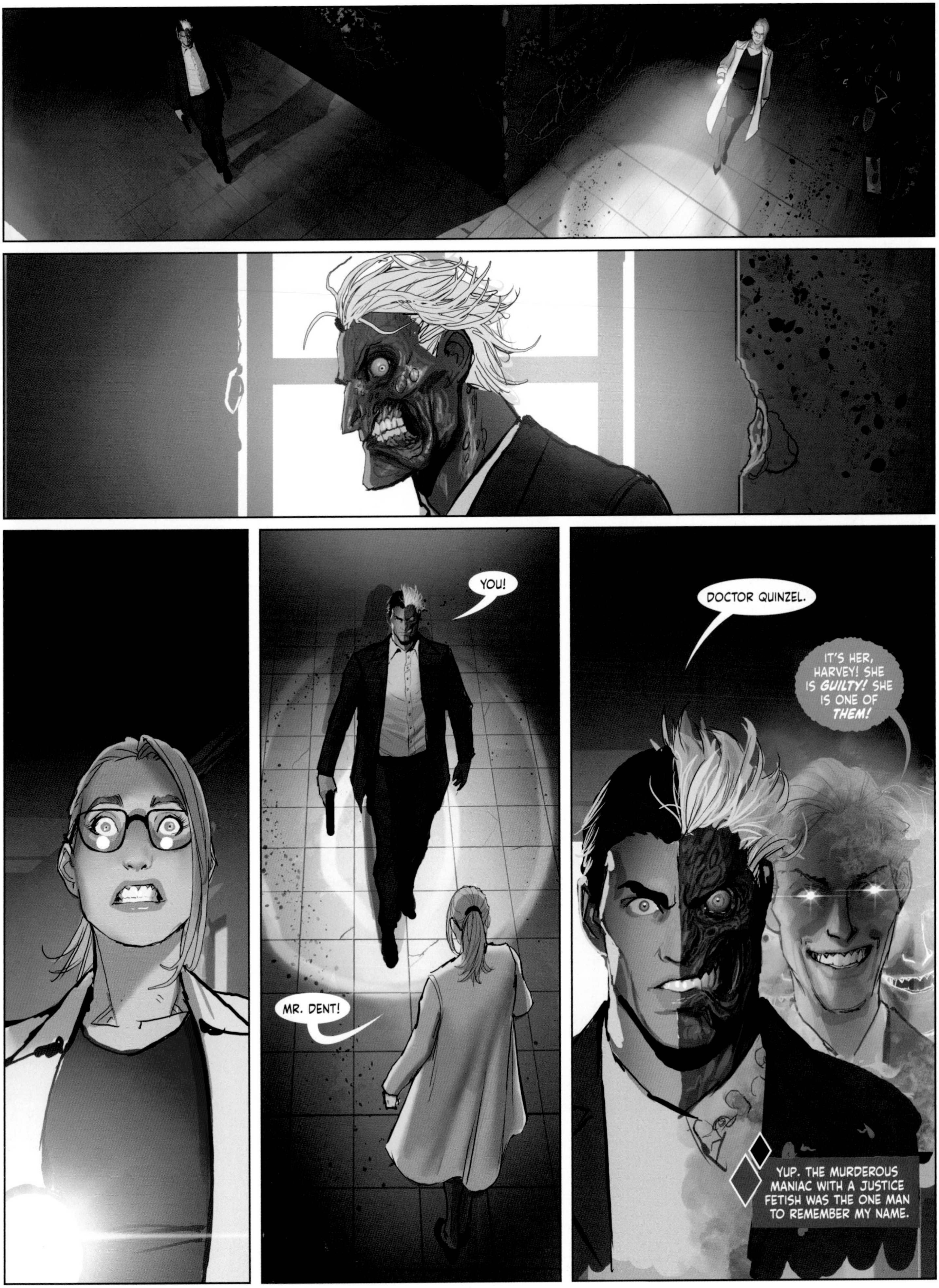

YOU!
MR. DENT!
DOCTOR QUINZEL.
IT'S HER, HARVEY! SHE IS GUILTY! SHE IS ONE OF THEM!
YUP. THE MURDEROUS MANIAC WITH A JUSTICE FETISH WAS THE ONE MAN TO REMEMBER MY NAME.

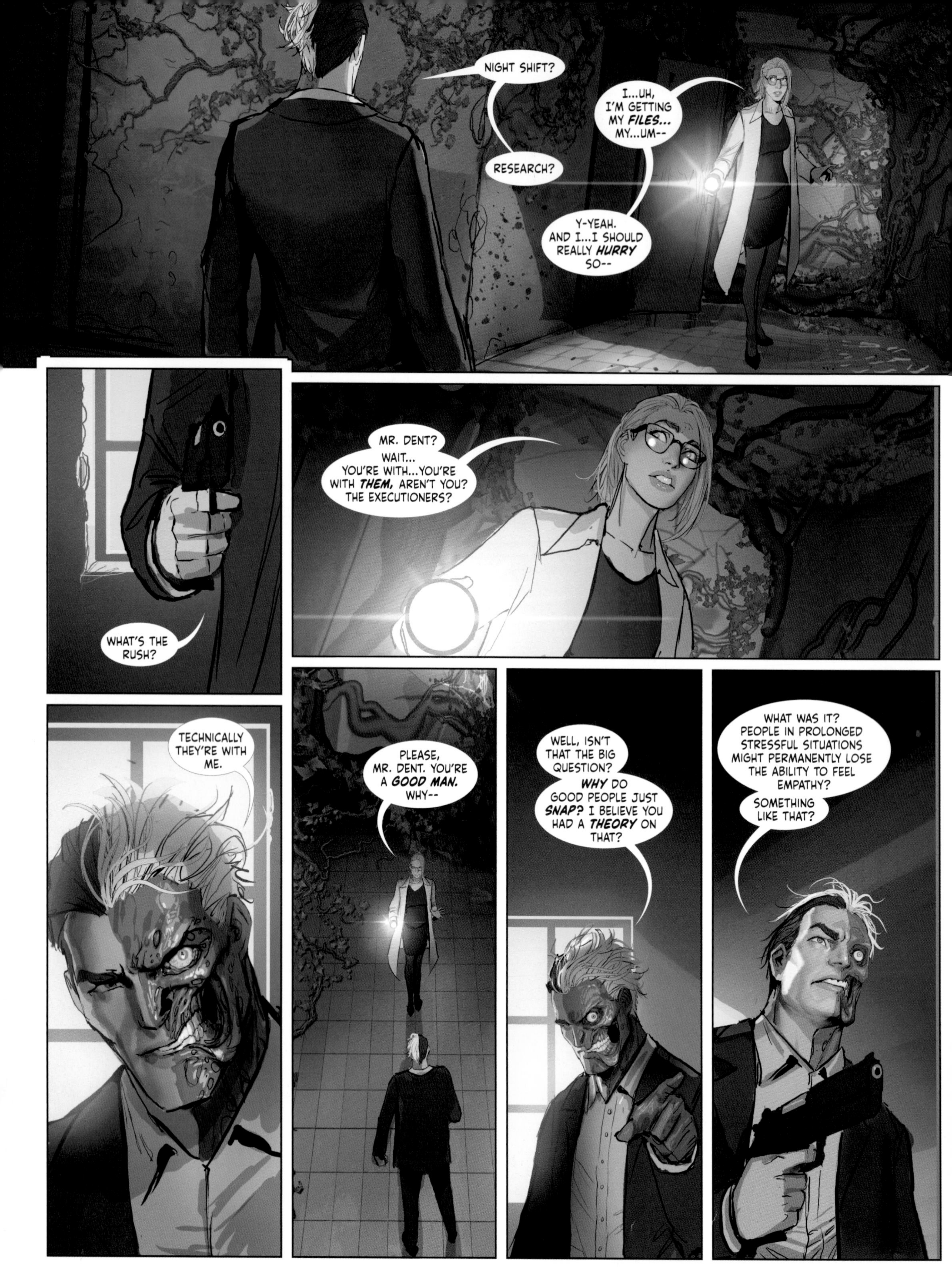

NIGHT SHIFT?
RESEARCH?
I...UH, I'M GETTING MY FILES... MY...UM--
Y-YEAH. AND I...I SHOULD REALLY HURRY SO--
WHAT'S THE RUSH?
MR. DENT?
WAIT... YOU'RE WITH...YOU'RE WITH THEM, AREN'T YOU? THE EXECUTIONERS?
TECHNICALLY THEY'RE WITH ME.
PLEASE, MR. DENT. YOU'RE A GOOD MAN. WHY--
WELL, ISN'T THAT THE BIG QUESTION? WHY DO GOOD PEOPLE JUST SNAP? I BELIEVE YOU HAD A THEORY ON THAT?
WHAT WAS IT? PEOPLE IN PROLONGED STRESSFUL SITUATIONS MIGHT PERMANENTLY LOSE THE ABILITY TO FEEL EMPATHY?
SOMETHING LIKE THAT?

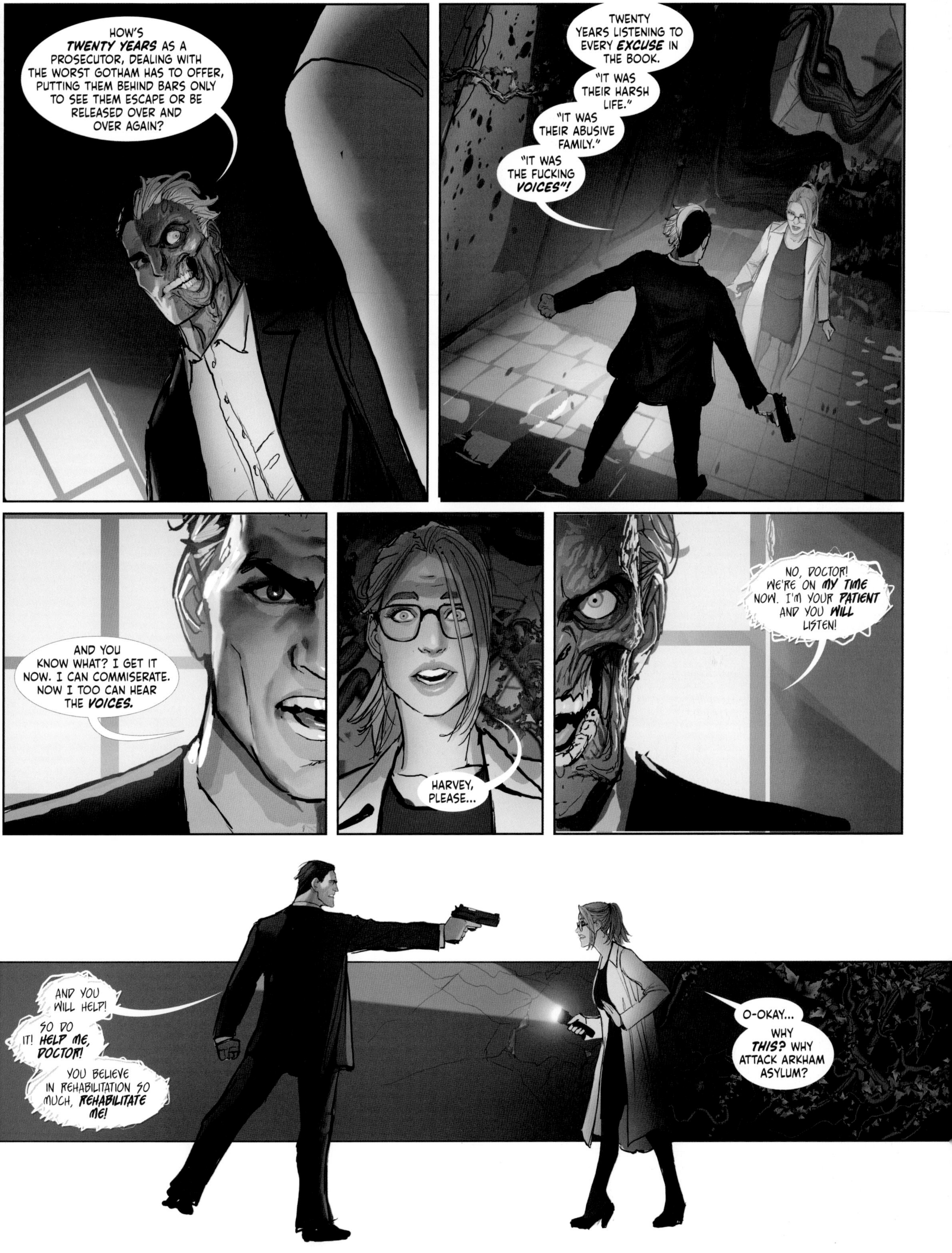

HOW'S TWENTY YEARS AS A PROSECUTOR, DEALING WITH THE WORST GOTHAM HAS TO OFFER, PUTTING THEM BEHIND BARS ONLY TO SEE THEM ESCAPE OR BE RELEASED OVER AND OVER AGAIN?
TWENTY YEARS LISTENING TO EVERY EXCUSE IN THE BOOK.
"IT WAS THEIR HARSH LIFE."
"IT WAS THEIR ABUSIVE FAMILY."
"IT WAS THE FUCKING VOICES"!
AND YOU KNOW WHAT? I GET IT NOW. I CAN COMMISERATE. NOW I TOO CAN HEAR THE VOICES.
HARVEY, PLEASE...
NO, DOCTOR! WE'RE ON MY TIME NOW. I'M YOUR PATIENT AND YOU WILL LISTEN!
AND YOU WILL HELP!
SO DO IT! HELP ME, DOCTOR!
YOU BELIEVE IN REHABILITATION SO MUCH, REHABILITATE ME!
O-OKAY...
WHY THIS? WHY ATTACK ARKHAM ASYLUM?

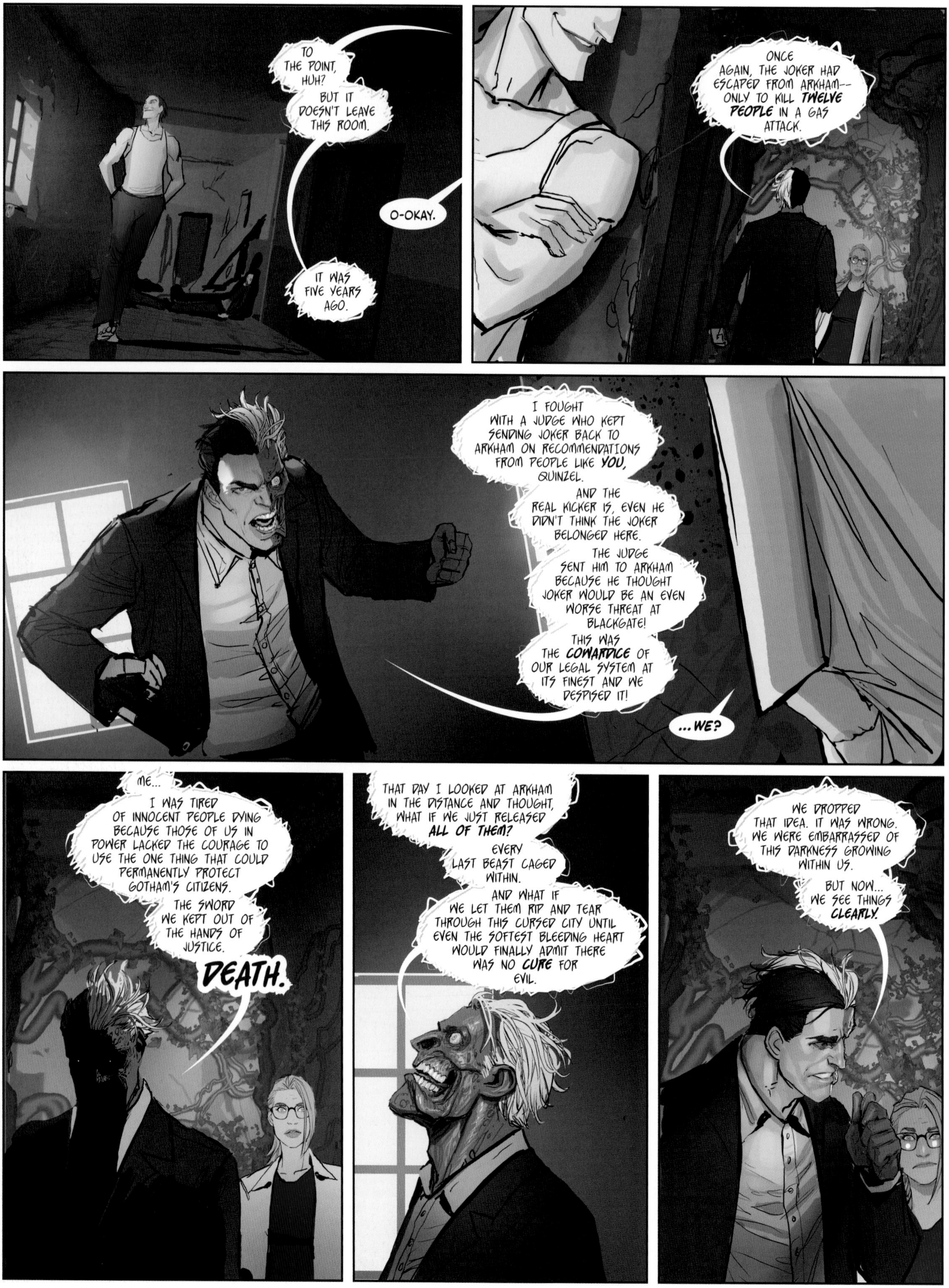

TO THE POINT, HUH?
BUT IT DOESN'T LEAVE THIS ROOM.
O-OKAY.
IT WAS FIVE YEARS AGO.
ONCE AGAIN, THE JOKER HAD ESCAPED FROM ARKHAM-- ONLY TO KILL TWELVE PEOPLE IN A GAS ATTACK.
I FOUGHT WITH A JUDGE WHO KEPT SENDING JOKER BACK TO ARKHAM ON RECOMMENDATIONS FROM PEOPLE LIKE YOU, QUINZEL.
AND THE REAL KICKER IS, EVEN HE DIDN'T THINK THE JOKER BELONGED HERE.
THE JUDGE SENT HIM TO ARKHAM BECAUSE HE THOUGHT JOKER WOULD BE AN EVEN WORSE THREAT AT BLACKGATE!
THIS WAS THE COWARDICE OF OUR LEGAL SYSTEM AT ITS FINEST AND WE DESPISED IT!
...WE?
ME...
I WAS TIRED OF INNOCENT PEOPLE DYING BECAUSE THOSE OF US IN POWER LACKED THE COURAGE TO USE THE ONE THING THAT COULD PERMANENTLY PROTECT GOTHAM'S CITIZENS.
THE SWORD WE KEPT OUT OF THE HANDS OF JUSTICE.
DEATH.
THAT DAY I LOOKED AT ARKHAM IN THE DISTANCE AND THOUGHT, WHAT IF WE JUST RELEASED ALL OF THEM?
EVERY LAST BEAST CAGED WITHIN.
AND WHAT IF WE LET THEM RIP AND TEAR THROUGH THIS CURSED CITY UNTIL EVEN THE SOFTEST BLEEDING HEART WOULD FINALLY ADMIT THERE WAS NO CURE FOR EVIL.
WE DROPPED THAT IDEA. IT WAS WRONG. WE WERE EMBARRASSED OF THIS DARKNESS GROWING WITHIN US.
BUT NOW... WE SEE THINGS CLEARLY.

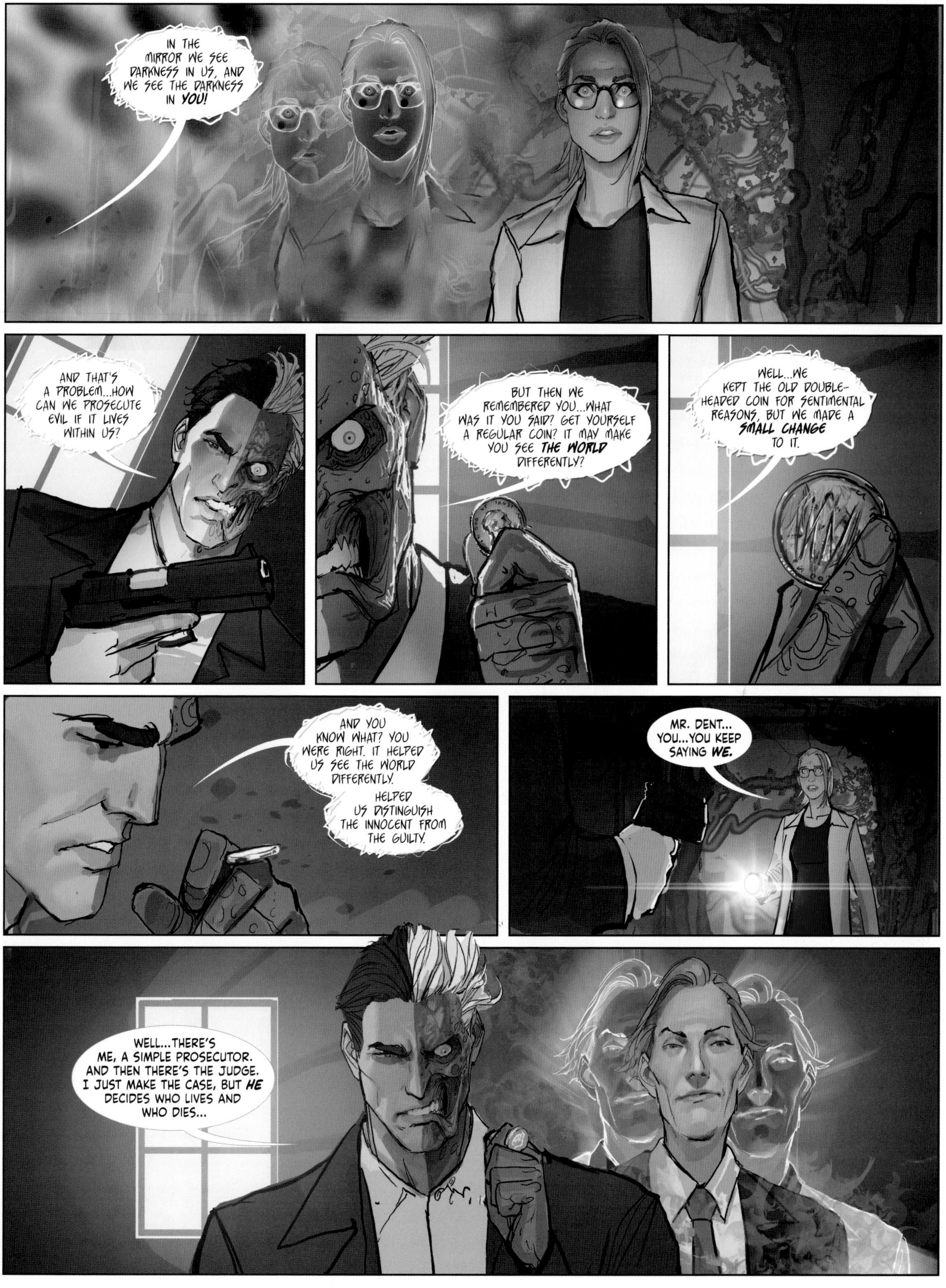
IN THE MIRROR WE SEE DARKNESS IN US, AND WE SEE THE DARKNESS IN YOU!
AND THAT'S A PROBLEM...HOW CAN WE PROSECUTE EVIL IF IT LIVES WITHIN US?
BUT THEN WE REMEMBERED YOU...WHAT WAS IT YOU SAID? GET YOURSELF A REGULAR COIN? IT MAY MAKE YOU SEE THE WORLD DIFFERENTLY?
WELL...WE KEPT THE OLD DOUBLE-HEADED COIN FOR SENTIMENTAL REASONS, BUT WE MADE A SMALL CHANGE TO IT.
AND YOU KNOW WHAT? YOU WERE RIGHT. IT HELPED US SEE THE WORLD DIFFERENTLY.
HELPED US DISTINGUISH THE INNOCENT FROM THE GUILTY.
MR. DENT... YOU...YOU KEEP SAYING WE.
WELL...THERE'S ME, A SIMPLE PROSECUTOR. AND THEN THERE'S THE JUDGE. I JUST MAKE THE CASE, BUT HE DECIDES WHO LIVES AND WHO DIES...

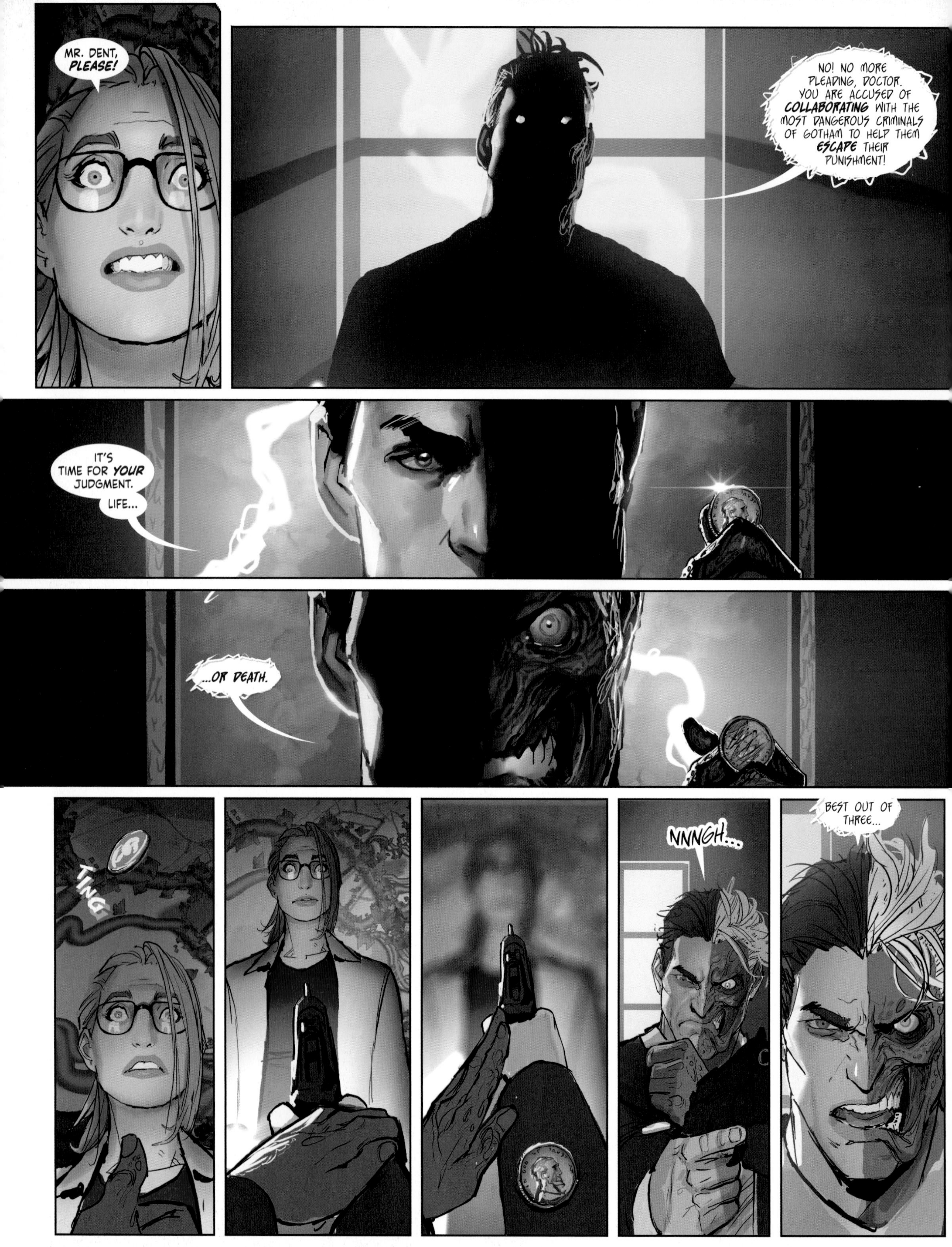
MR. DENT, PLEASE!
NO! NO MORE PLEADING, DOCTOR. YOU ARE ACCUSED OF COLLABORATING WITH THE MOST DANGEROUS CRIMINALS OF GOTHAM TO HELP THEM ESCAPE THEIR PUNISHMENT!
IT'S TIME FOR YOUR JUDGMENT. LIFE...
...OR DEATH.
TING
NNNGH...
BEST OUT OF THREE...

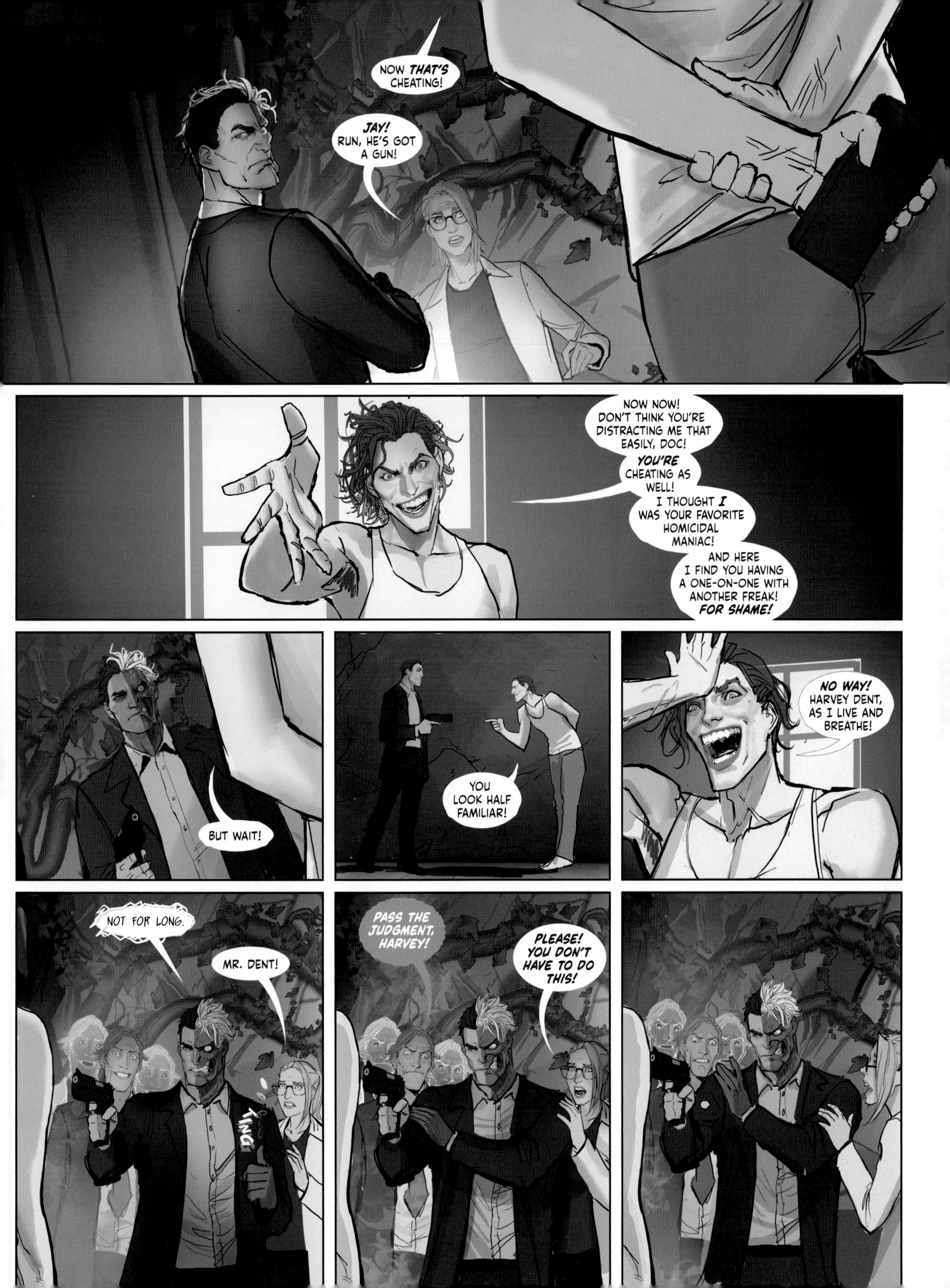
NOW THAT'S CHEATING!
JAY! RUN, HE'S GOT A GUN!
NOW NOW! DON'T THINK YOU'RE DISTRACTING ME THAT EASILY, DOC!
YOU'RE CHEATING AS WELL!
I THOUGHT I WAS YOUR FAVORITE HOMICIDAL MANIAC!
AND HERE I FIND YOU HAVING A ONE-ON-ONE WITH ANOTHER FREAK! FOR SHAME!
BUT WAIT!
YOU LOOK HALF FAMILIAR!
NO WAY! HARVEY DENT, AS I LIVE AND BREATHE!
NOT FOR LONG.
MR. DENT!
TING
PASS THE JUDGMENT, HARVEY!
PLEASE! YOU DON'T HAVE TO DO THIS!

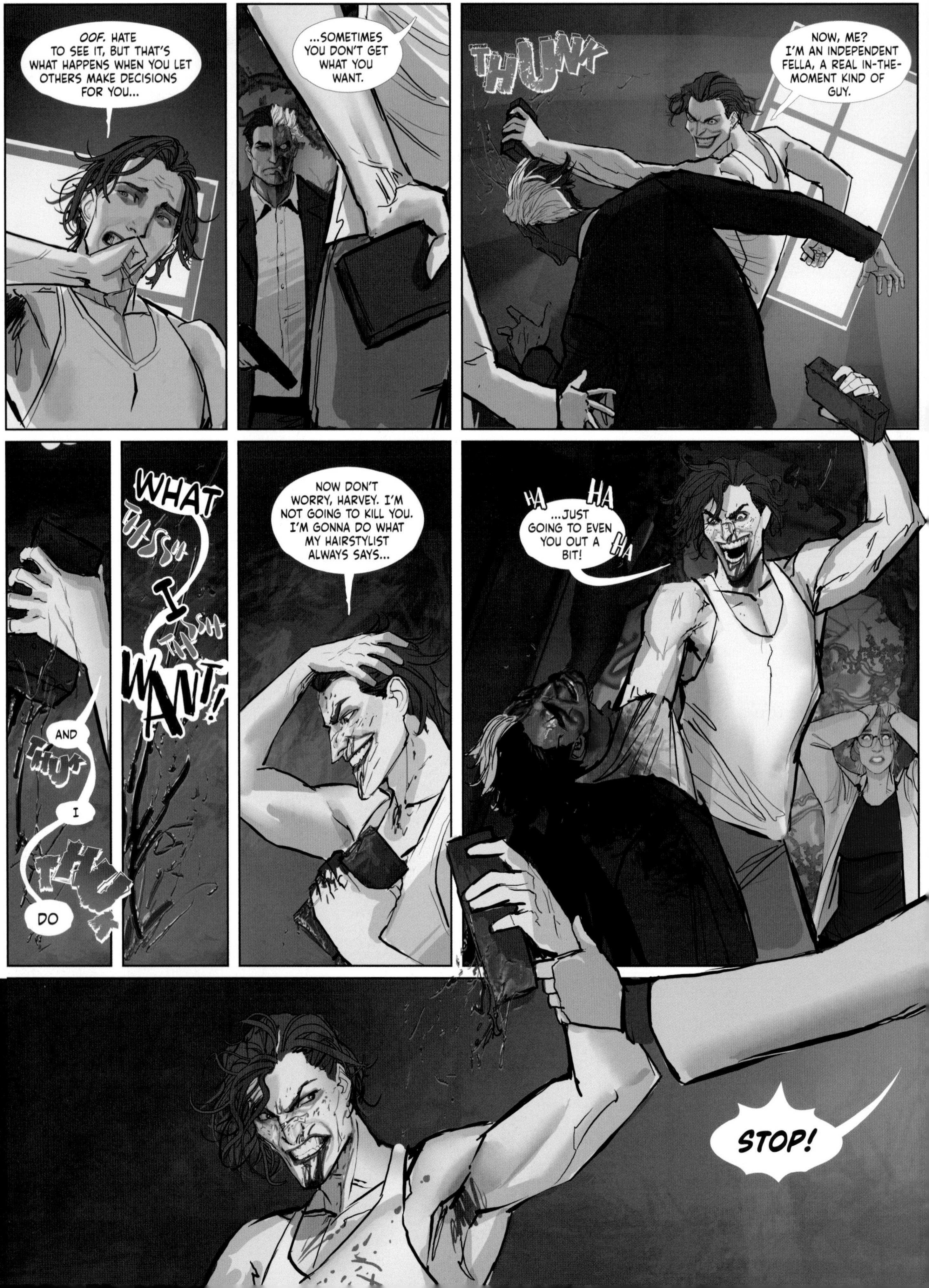
OOF. HATE TO SEE IT, BUT THAT'S WHAT HAPPENS WHEN YOU LET OTHERS MAKE DECISIONS FOR YOU...
...SOMETIMES YOU DON'T GET WHAT YOU WANT.
THUNK
NOW, ME? I'M AN INDEPENDENT FELLA, A REAL IN-THE-MOMENT KIND OF GUY.
AND
I
DO
WHAT
I
WANT!
NOW DON'T WORRY, HARVEY. I'M NOT GOING TO KILL YOU. I'M GONNA DO WHAT MY HAIRSTYLIST ALWAYS SAYS...
HA HA HA
...JUST GOING TO EVEN YOU OUT A BIT!
STOP!

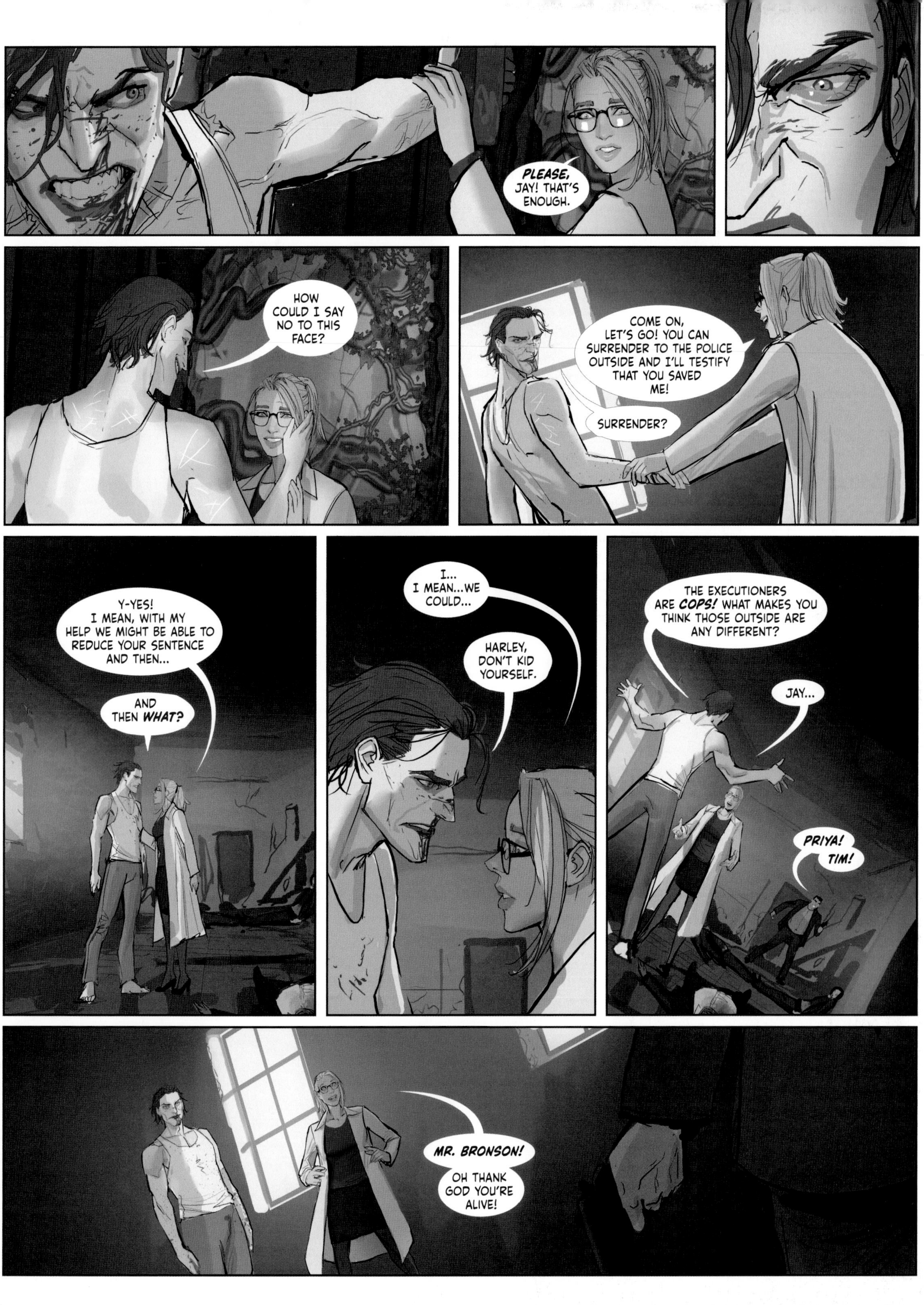
PLEASE, JAY! THAT'S ENOUGH.
HOW COULD I SAY NO TO THIS FACE?
COME ON, LET'S GO! YOU CAN SURRENDER TO THE POLICE OUTSIDE AND I'LL TESTIFY THAT YOU SAVED ME!
SURRENDER?
Y-YES! I MEAN, WITH MY HELP WE MIGHT BE ABLE TO REDUCE YOUR SENTENCE AND THEN...
AND THEN WHAT?
I... I MEAN...WE COULD...
HARLEY, DON'T KID YOURSELF.
THE EXECUTIONERS ARE COPS! WHAT MAKES YOU THINK THOSE OUTSIDE ARE ANY DIFFERENT?
JAY...
PRIYA! TIM!
MR. BRONSON!
OH THANK GOD YOU'RE ALIVE!

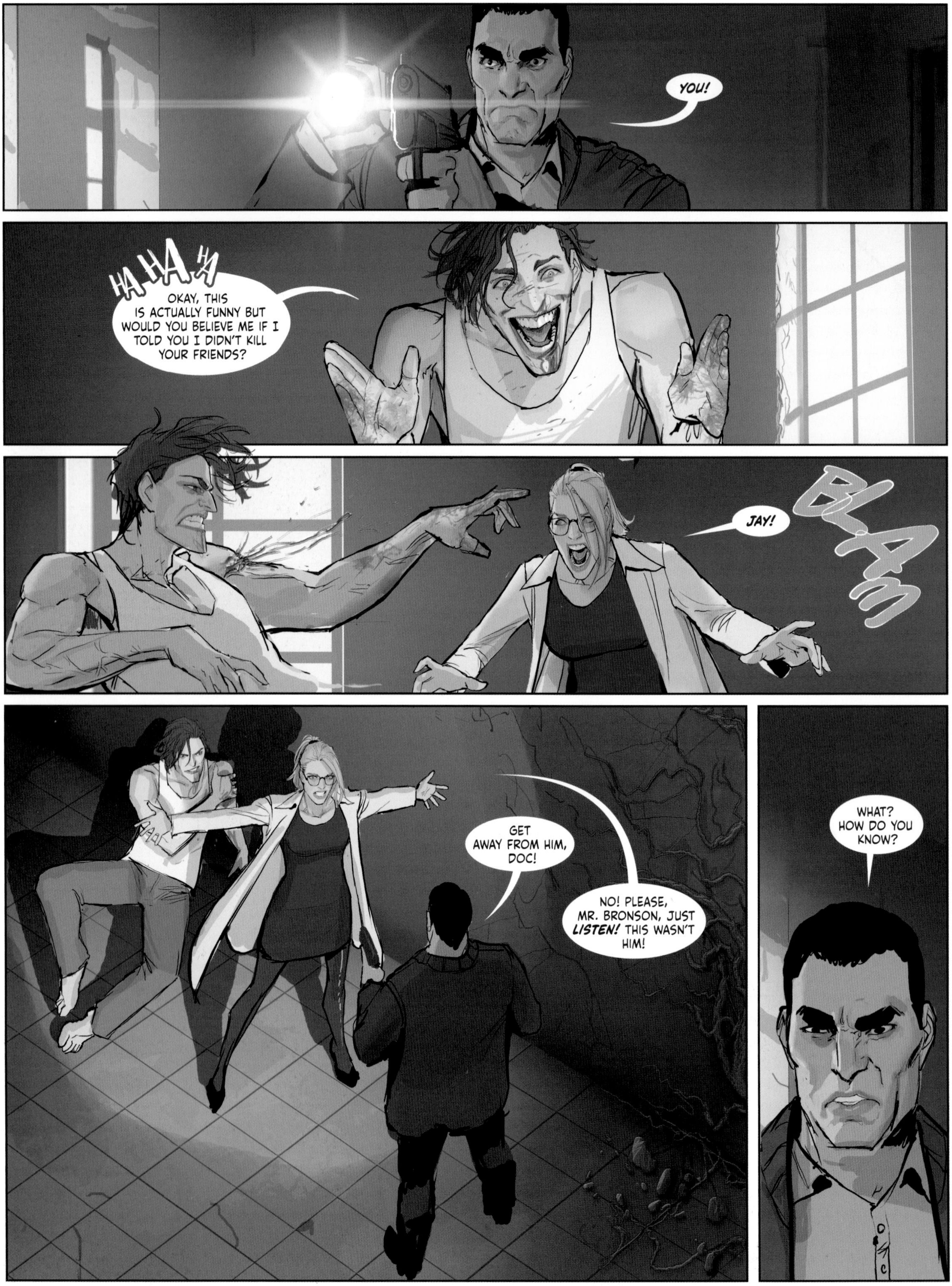
YOU!
HA HA HA HA
OKAY, THIS IS ACTUALLY FUNNY BUT WOULD YOU BELIEVE ME IF I TOLD YOU I DIDN'T KILL YOUR FRIENDS?
JAY!
BLAM
GET AWAY FROM HIM, DOC!
NO! PLEASE, MR. BRONSON, JUST LISTEN! THIS WASN'T HIM!
WHAT? HOW DO YOU KNOW?

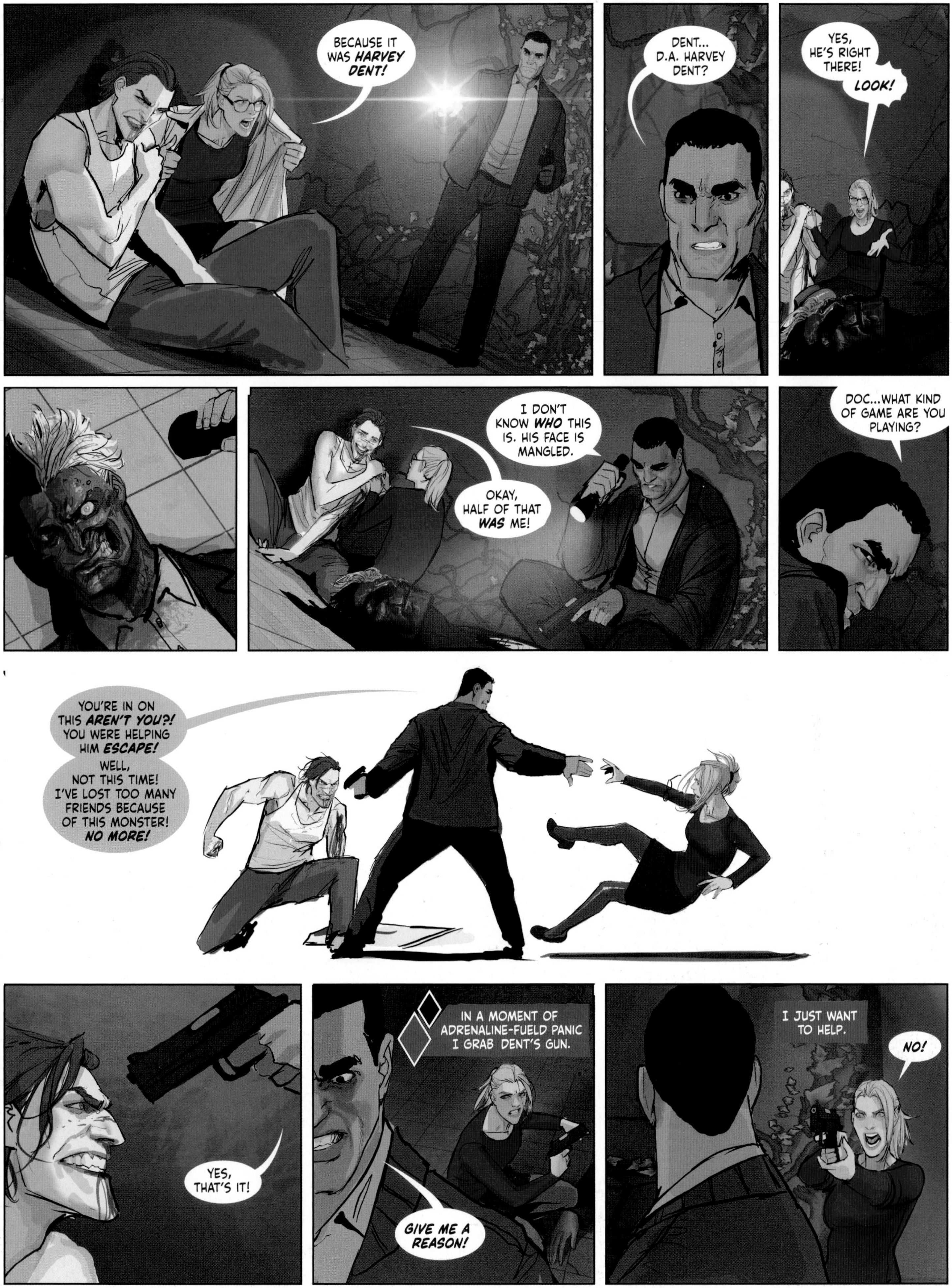
BECAUSE IT WAS HARVEY DENT!
DENT... D.A. HARVEY DENT?
YES, HE'S RIGHT THERE! LOOK!
I DON'T KNOW WHO THIS IS. HIS FACE IS MANGLED.
OKAY, HALF OF THAT WAS ME!
DOC...WHAT KIND OF GAME ARE YOU PLAYING?
YOU'RE IN ON THIS AREN'T YOU?! YOU WERE HELPING HIM ESCAPE!
WELL, NOT THIS TIME! I'VE LOST TOO MANY FRIENDS BECAUSE OF THIS MONSTER! NO MORE!
YES, THAT'S IT!
IN A MOMENT OF ADRENALINE-FUELD PANIC I GRAB DENT'S GUN.
GIVE ME A REASON!
I JUST WANT TO HELP.
NO!

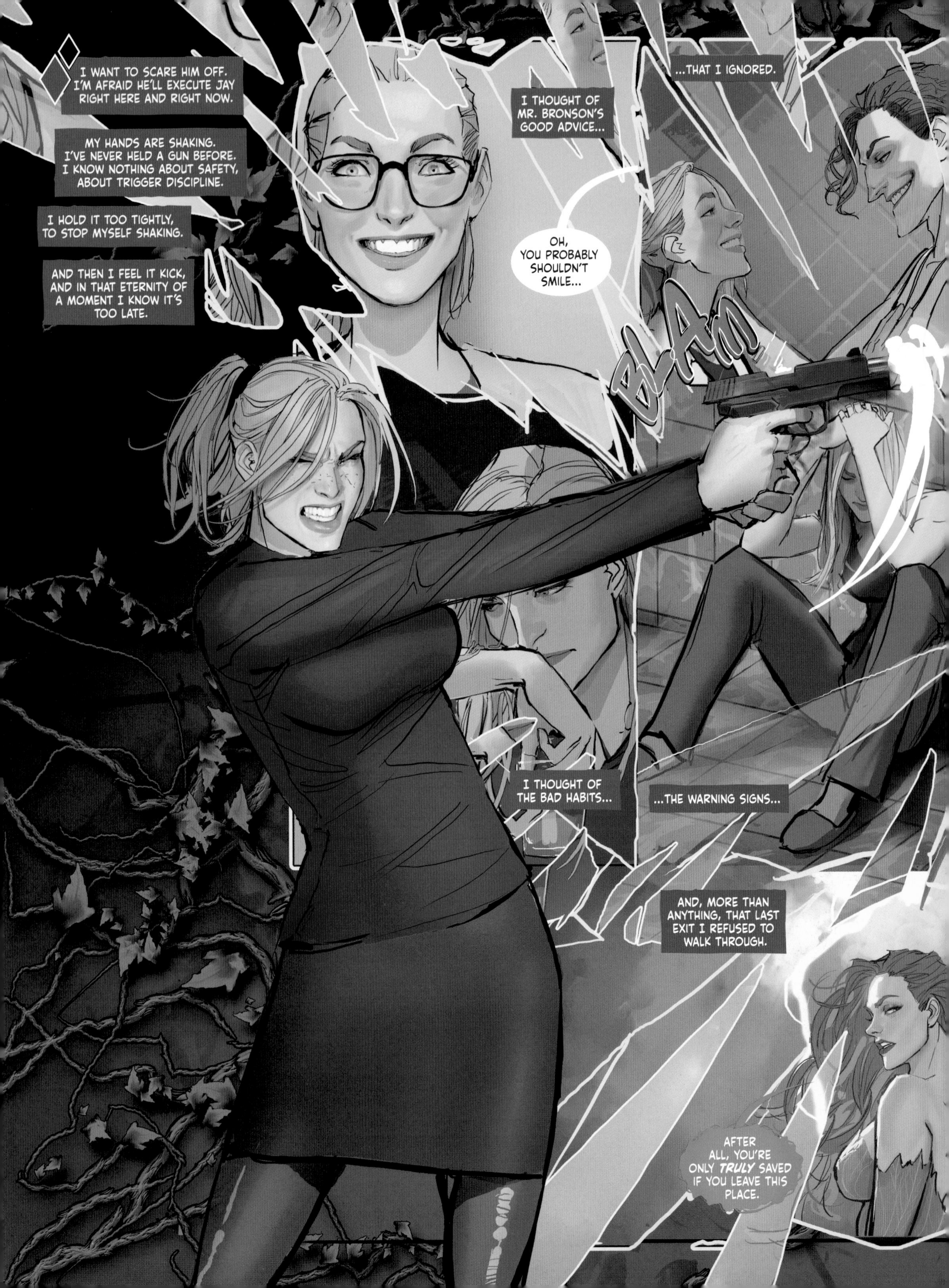
I WANT TO SCARE HIM OFF. I'M AFRAID HE'LL EXECUTE JAY RIGHT HERE AND RIGHT NOW.
MY HANDS ARE SHAKING. I'VE NEVER HELD A GUN BEFORE. I KNOW NOTHING ABOUT SAFETY, ABOUT TRIGGER DISCIPLINE.
I HOLD IT TOO TIGHTLY, TO STOP MYSELF SHAKING.
AND THEN I FEEL IT KICK, AND IN THAT ETERNITY OF A MOMENT I KNOW IT'S TOO LATE.
I THOUGHT OF MR. BRONSON'S GOOD ADVICE...
...THAT I IGNORED.
OH, YOU PROBABLY SHOULDN'T SMILE...
BLAM
I THOUGHT OF THE BAD HABITS...
...THE WARNING SIGNS...
AND, MORE THAN ANYTHING, THAT LAST EXIT I REFUSED TO WALK THROUGH.
AFTER ALL, YOU'RE ONLY *TRULY* SAVED IF YOU LEAVE THIS PLACE.

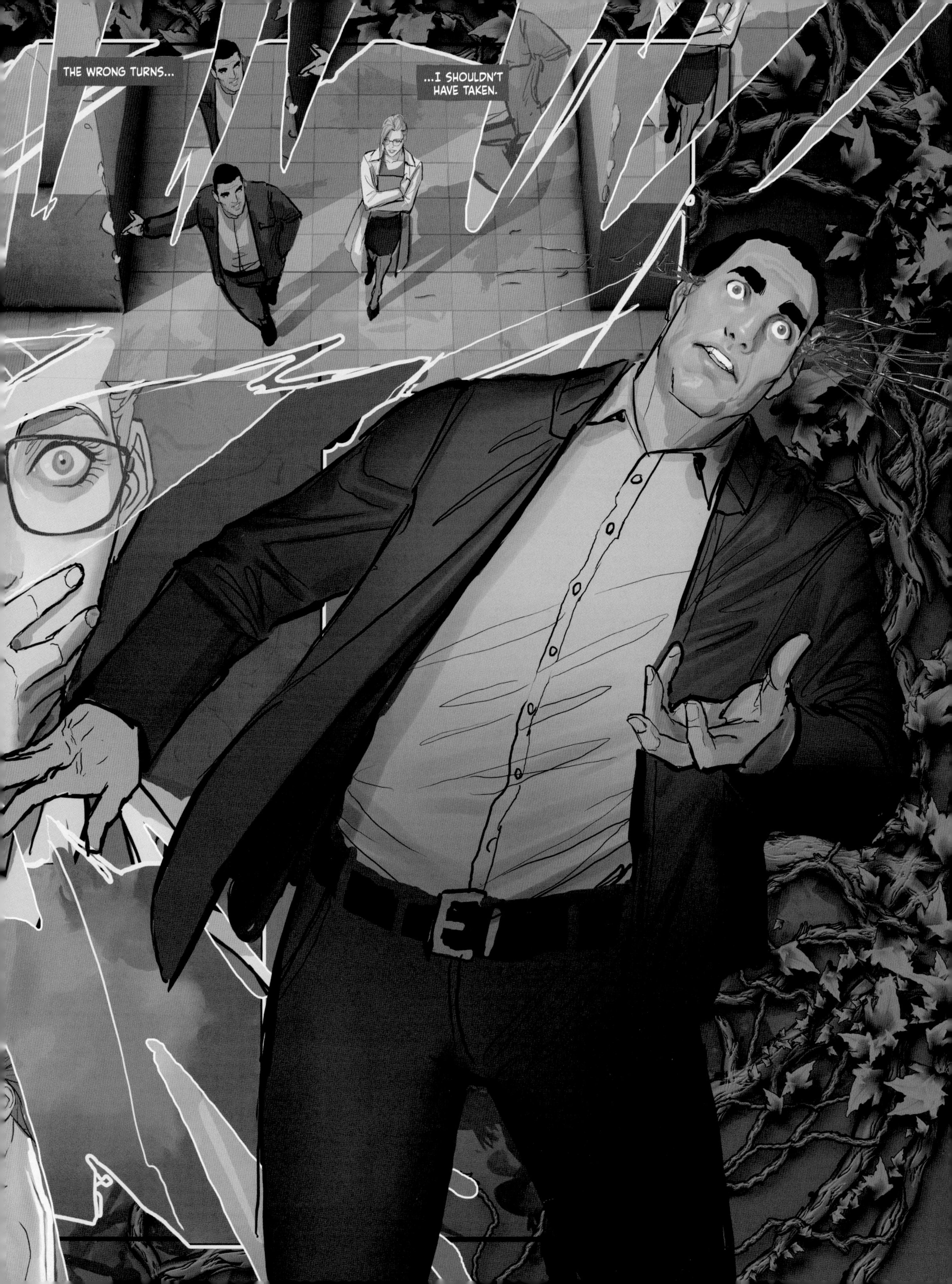
THE WRONG TURNS...
...I SHOULDN'T HAVE TAKEN.

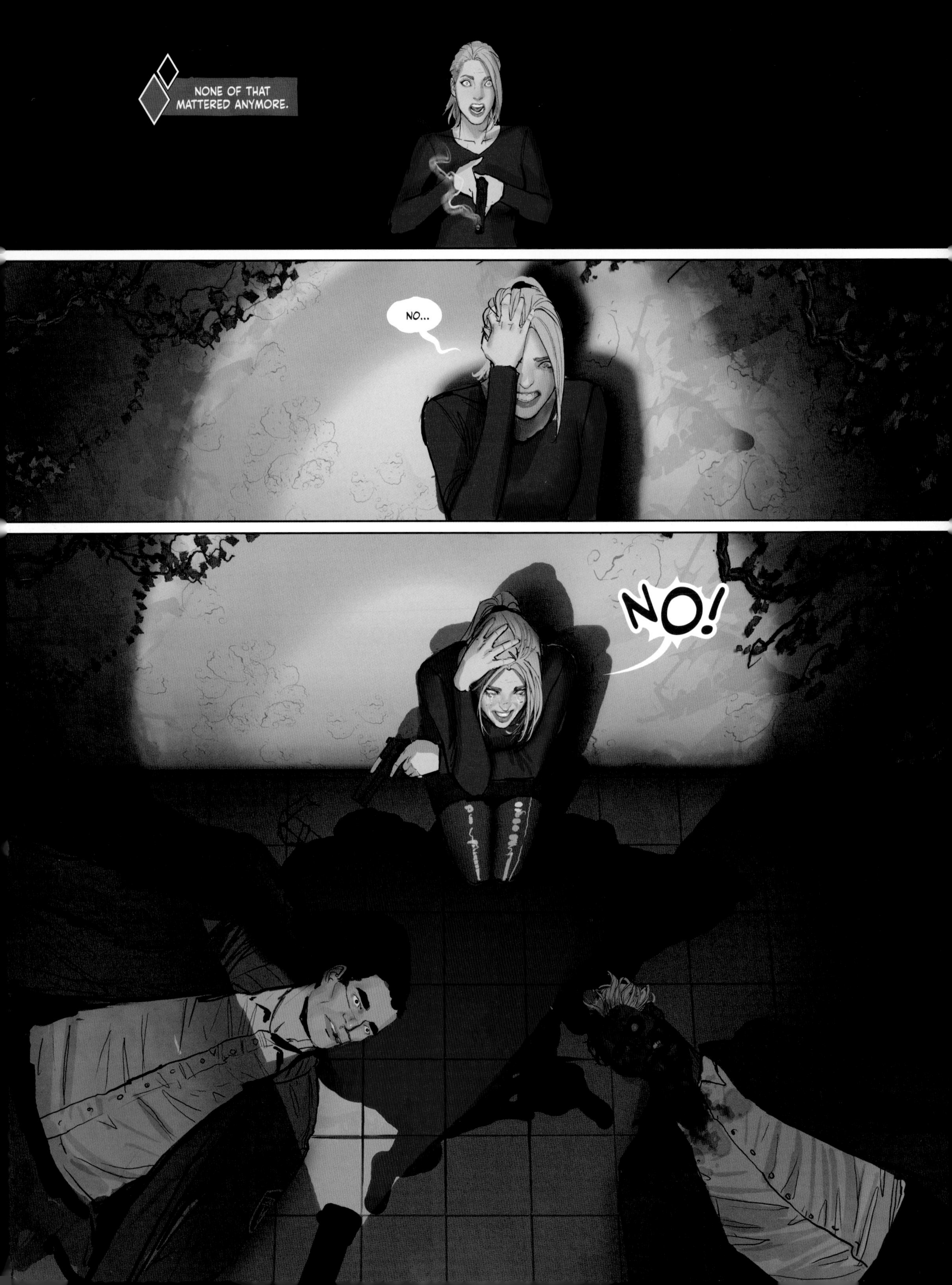
NONE OF THAT MATTERED ANYMORE.
NO...
NO!

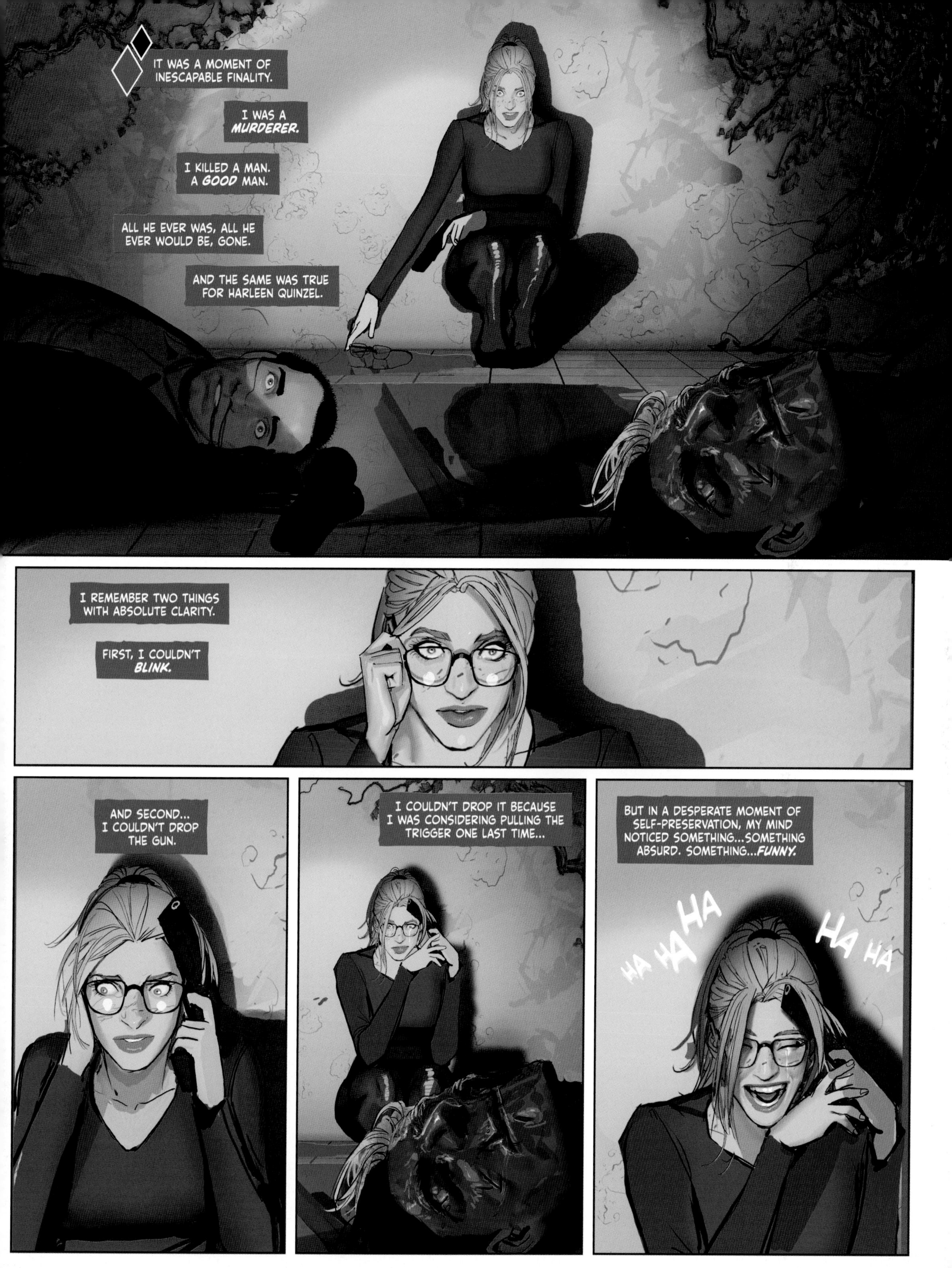
IT WAS A MOMENT OF INESCAPABLE FINALITY.
I WAS A MURDERER.
I KILLED A MAN. A GOOD MAN.
ALL HE EVER WAS, ALL HE EVER WOULD BE, GONE.
AND THE SAME WAS TRUE FOR HARLEEN QUINZEL.
I REMEMBER TWO THINGS WITH ABSOLUTE CLARITY.
FIRST, I COULDN'T BLINK.
AND SECOND... I COULDN'T DROP THE GUN.
I COULDN'T DROP IT BECAUSE I WAS CONSIDERING PULLING THE TRIGGER ONE LAST TIME...
BUT IN A DESPERATE MOMENT OF SELF-PRESERVATION, MY MIND NOTICED SOMETHING...SOMETHING ABSURD. SOMETHING...FUNNY.
HA HA HA
HA HA

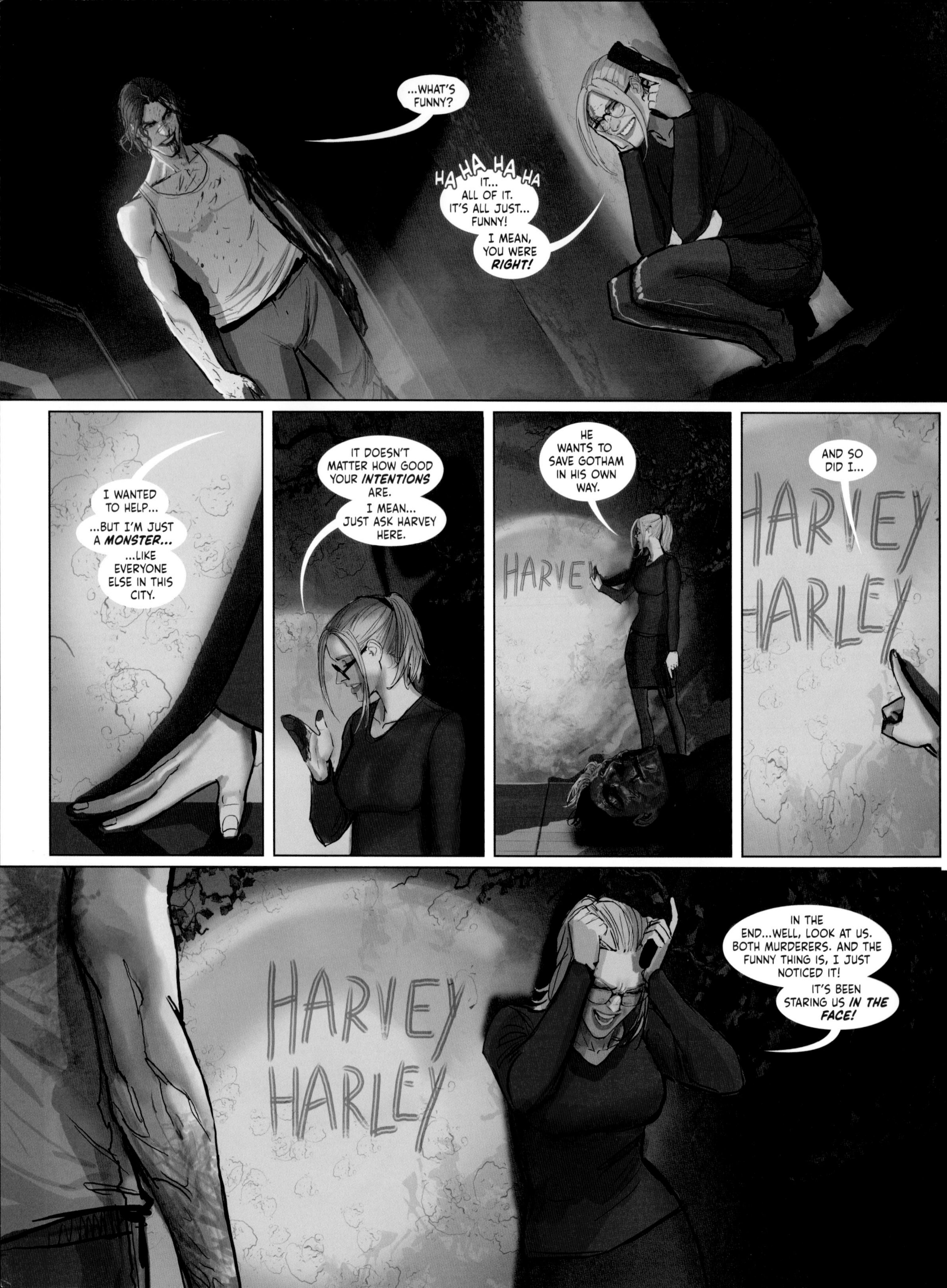
...WHAT'S FUNNY?
HA HA HA HA
IT... ALL OF IT. IT'S ALL JUST... FUNNY!
I MEAN, YOU WERE *RIGHT!*
I WANTED TO HELP...
...BUT I'M JUST A *MONSTER...*
...LIKE EVERYONE ELSE IN THIS CITY.
IT DOESN'T MATTER HOW GOOD YOUR *INTENTIONS* ARE.
I MEAN... JUST ASK HARVEY HERE.
HE WANTS TO SAVE GOTHAM IN HIS OWN WAY.
HARVEY
AND SO DID I...
HARVEY
HARLEY
HARVEY
HARLEY
IN THE END...WELL, LOOK AT US. BOTH MURDERERS. AND THE FUNNY THING IS, I JUST NOTICED IT!
IT'S BEEN STARING US *IN THE FACE!*

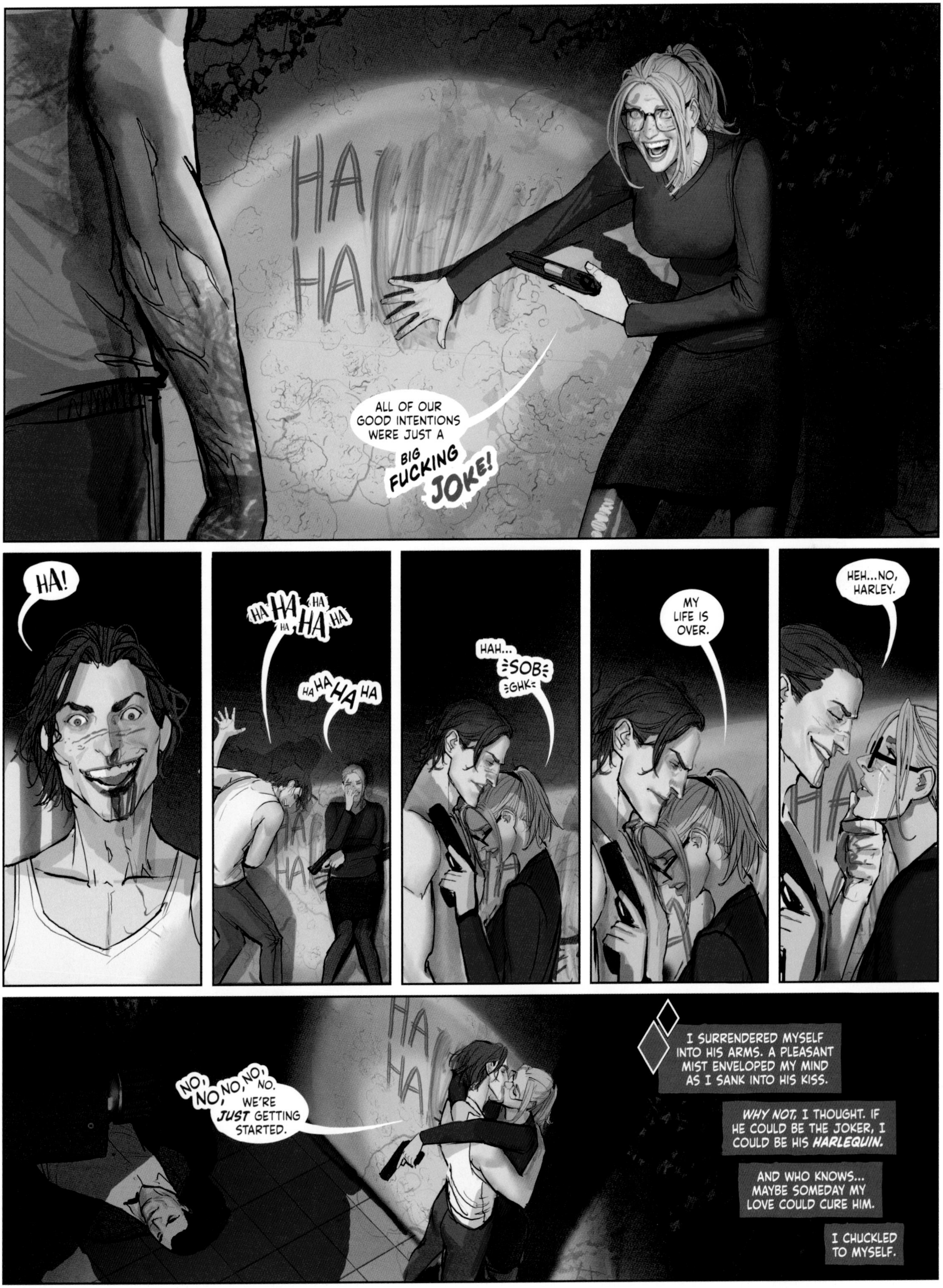
ALL OF OUR GOOD INTENTIONS WERE JUST A BIG FUCKING JOKE!
HA!
HA HA HA HA HA HA
HA HA HA HA
HAH... SOB GHK
MY LIFE IS OVER.
HEH...NO, HARLEY.
NO, NO, NO, NO, NO. WE'RE *JUST* GETTING STARTED.
I SURRENDERED MYSELF INTO HIS ARMS. A PLEASANT MIST ENVELOPED MY MIND AS I SANK INTO HIS KISS.
WHY NOT, I THOUGHT. IF HE COULD BE THE JOKER, I COULD BE HIS ***HARLEQUIN.***
AND WHO KNOWS... MAYBE SOMEDAY MY LOVE COULD CURE HIM.
I CHUCKLED TO MYSELF.

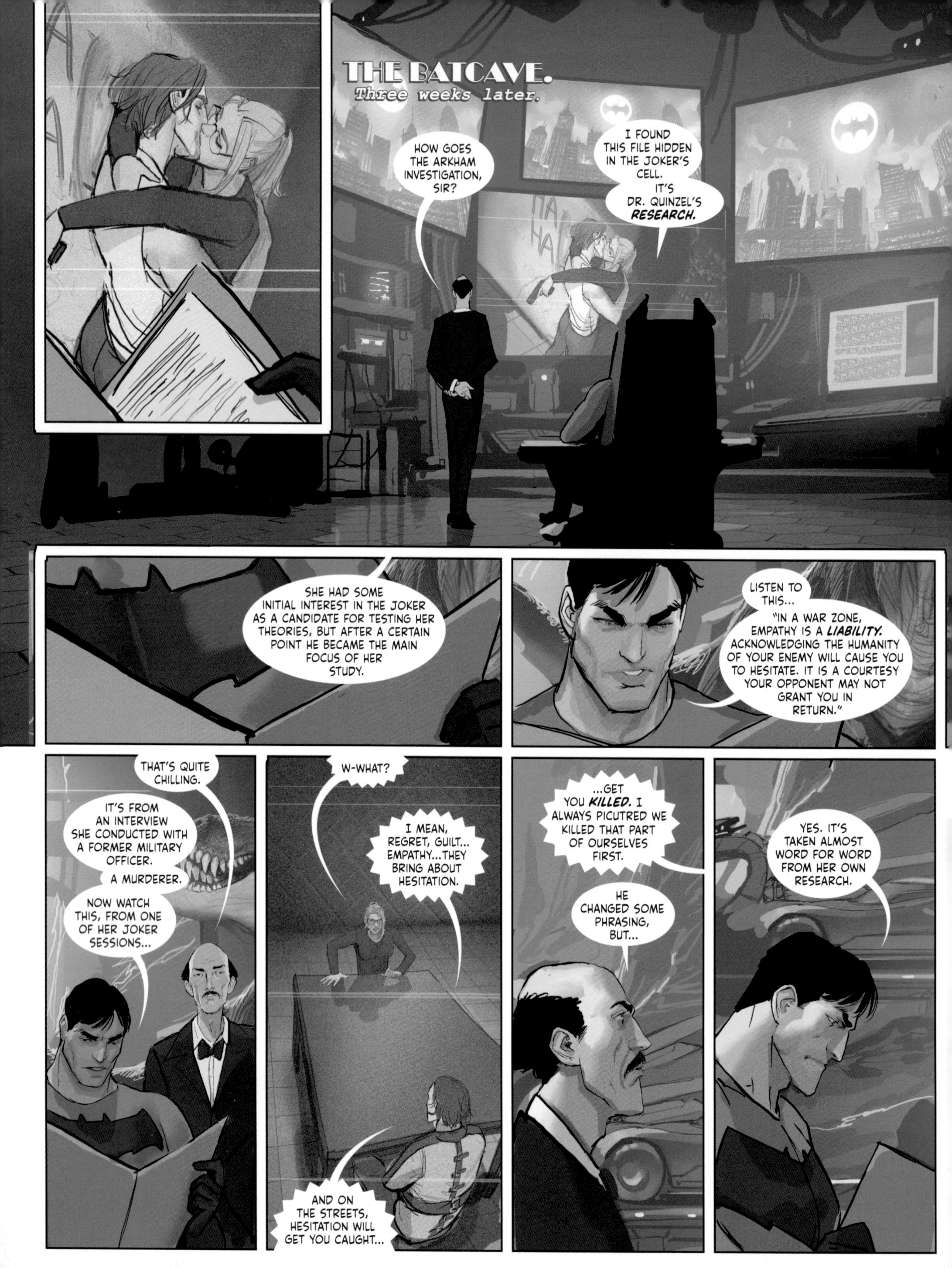
THE BATCAVE.
Three weeks later.
HOW GOES THE ARKHAM INVESTIGATION, SIR?
I FOUND THIS FILE HIDDEN IN THE JOKER'S CELL.
IT'S DR. QUINZEL'S ***RESEARCH.***
SHE HAD SOME INITIAL INTEREST IN THE JOKER AS A CANDIDATE FOR TESTING HER THEORIES, BUT AFTER A CERTAIN POINT HE BECAME THE MAIN FOCUS OF HER STUDY.
LISTEN TO THIS...
"IN A WAR ZONE, EMPATHY IS A ***LIABILITY.*** ACKNOWLEDGING THE HUMANITY OF YOUR ENEMY WILL CAUSE YOU TO HESITATE. IT IS A COURTESY YOUR OPPONENT MAY NOT GRANT YOU IN RETURN."
THAT'S QUITE CHILLING.
IT'S FROM AN INTERVIEW SHE CONDUCTED WITH A FORMER MILITARY OFFICER.
A MURDERER.
NOW WATCH THIS, FROM ONE OF HER JOKER SESSIONS...
W-WHAT?
I MEAN, REGRET, GUILT... EMPATHY...THEY BRING ABOUT HESITATION.
AND ON THE STREETS, HESITATION WILL GET YOU CAUGHT...
...GET YOU ***KILLED.*** I ALWAYS PICUTRED WE KILLED THAT PART OF OURSELVES FIRST.
HE CHANGED SOME PHRASING, BUT...
YES. IT'S TAKEN ALMOST WORD FOR WORD FROM HER OWN RESEARCH.

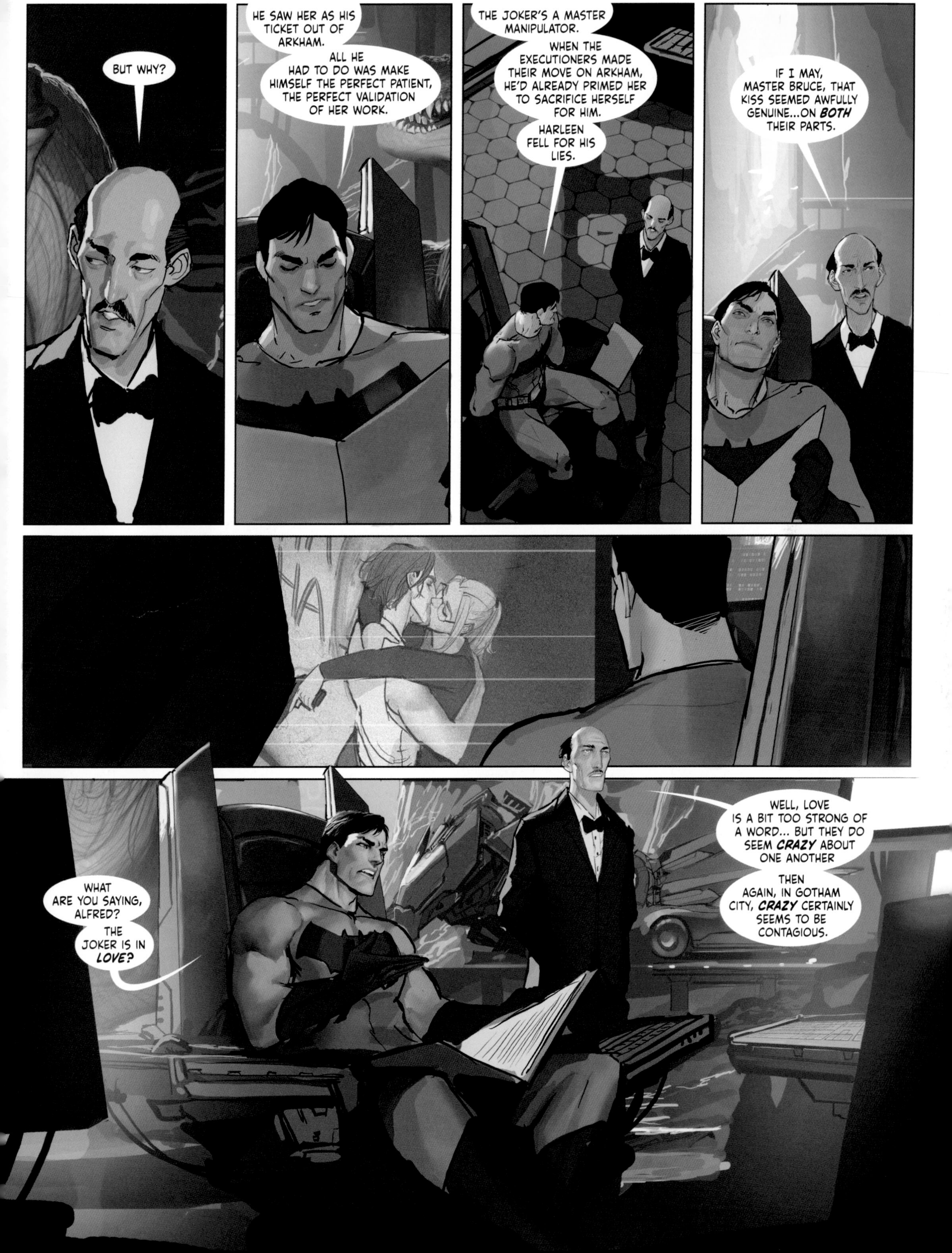
BUT WHY?
HE SAW HER AS HIS TICKET OUT OF ARKHAM.
ALL HE HAD TO DO WAS MAKE HIMSELF THE PERFECT PATIENT, THE PERFECT VALIDATION OF HER WORK.
THE JOKER'S A MASTER MANIPULATOR.
WHEN THE EXECUTIONERS MADE THEIR MOVE ON ARKHAM, HE'D ALREADY PRIMED HER TO SACRIFICE HERSELF FOR HIM.
HARLEEN FELL FOR HIS LIES.
IF I MAY, MASTER BRUCE, THAT KISS SEEMED AWFULLY GENUINE...ON BOTH THEIR PARTS.
WHAT ARE YOU SAYING, ALFRED?
THE JOKER IS IN LOVE?
WELL, LOVE IS A BIT TOO STRONG OF A WORD... BUT THEY DO SEEM CRAZY ABOUT ONE ANOTHER
THEN AGAIN, IN GOTHAM CITY, CRAZY CERTAINLY SEEMS TO BE CONTAGIOUS.

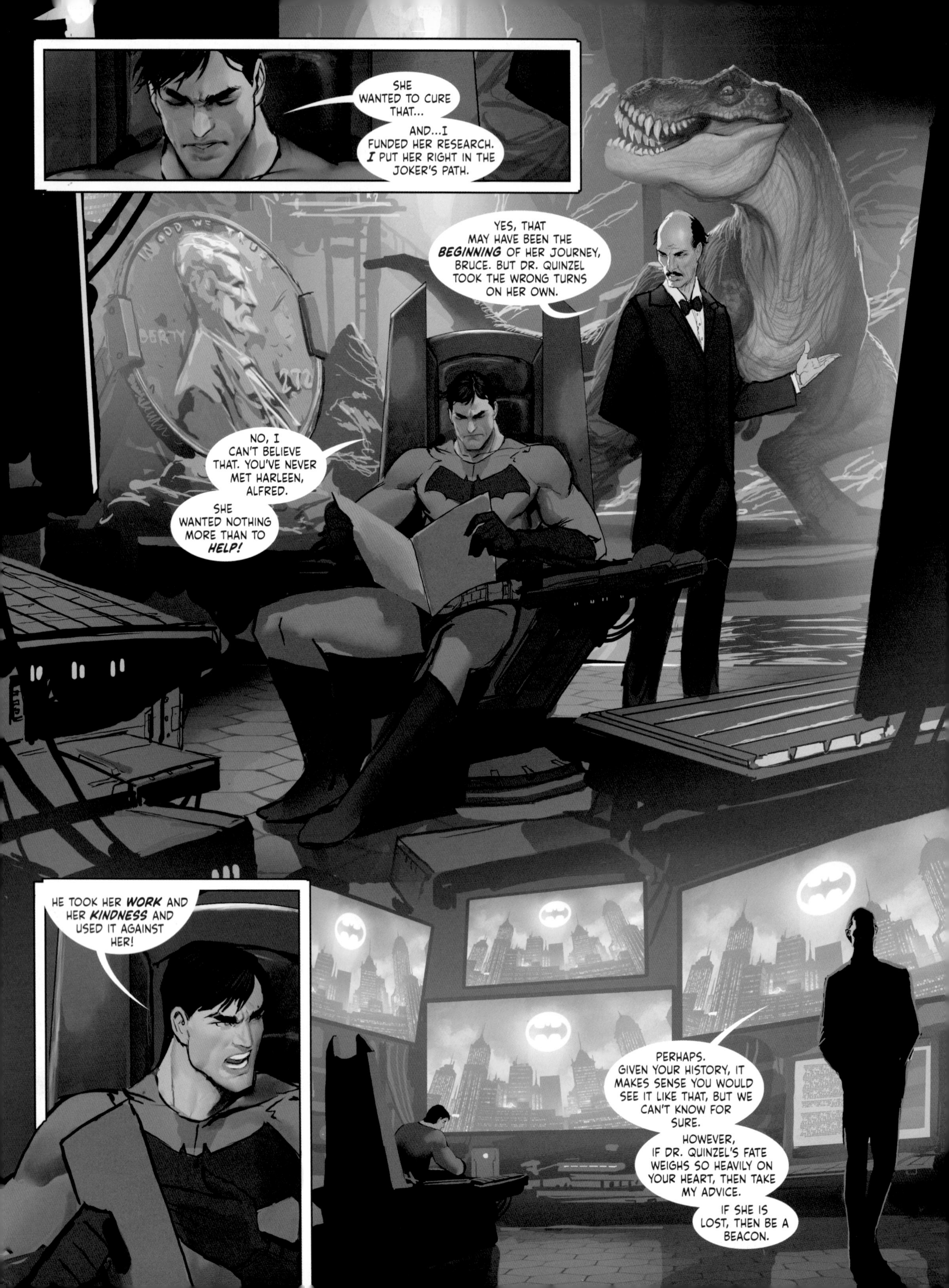
SHE WANTED TO CURE THAT...
AND...I FUNDED HER RESEARCH. *I* PUT HER RIGHT IN THE JOKER'S PATH.
YES, THAT MAY HAVE BEEN THE ***BEGINNING*** OF HER JOURNEY, BRUCE. BUT DR. QUINZEL TOOK THE WRONG TURNS ON HER OWN.
NO, I CAN'T BELIEVE THAT. YOU'VE NEVER MET HARLEEN, ALFRED.
SHE WANTED NOTHING MORE THAN TO ***HELP!***
HE TOOK HER ***WORK*** AND HER ***KINDNESS*** AND USED IT AGAINST HER!
PERHAPS. GIVEN YOUR HISTORY, IT MAKES SENSE YOU WOULD SEE IT LIKE THAT, BUT WE CAN'T KNOW FOR SURE.
HOWEVER, IF DR. QUINZEL'S FATE WEIGHS SO HEAVILY ON YOUR HEART, THEN TAKE MY ADVICE.
IF SHE IS LOST, THEN BE A BEACON.

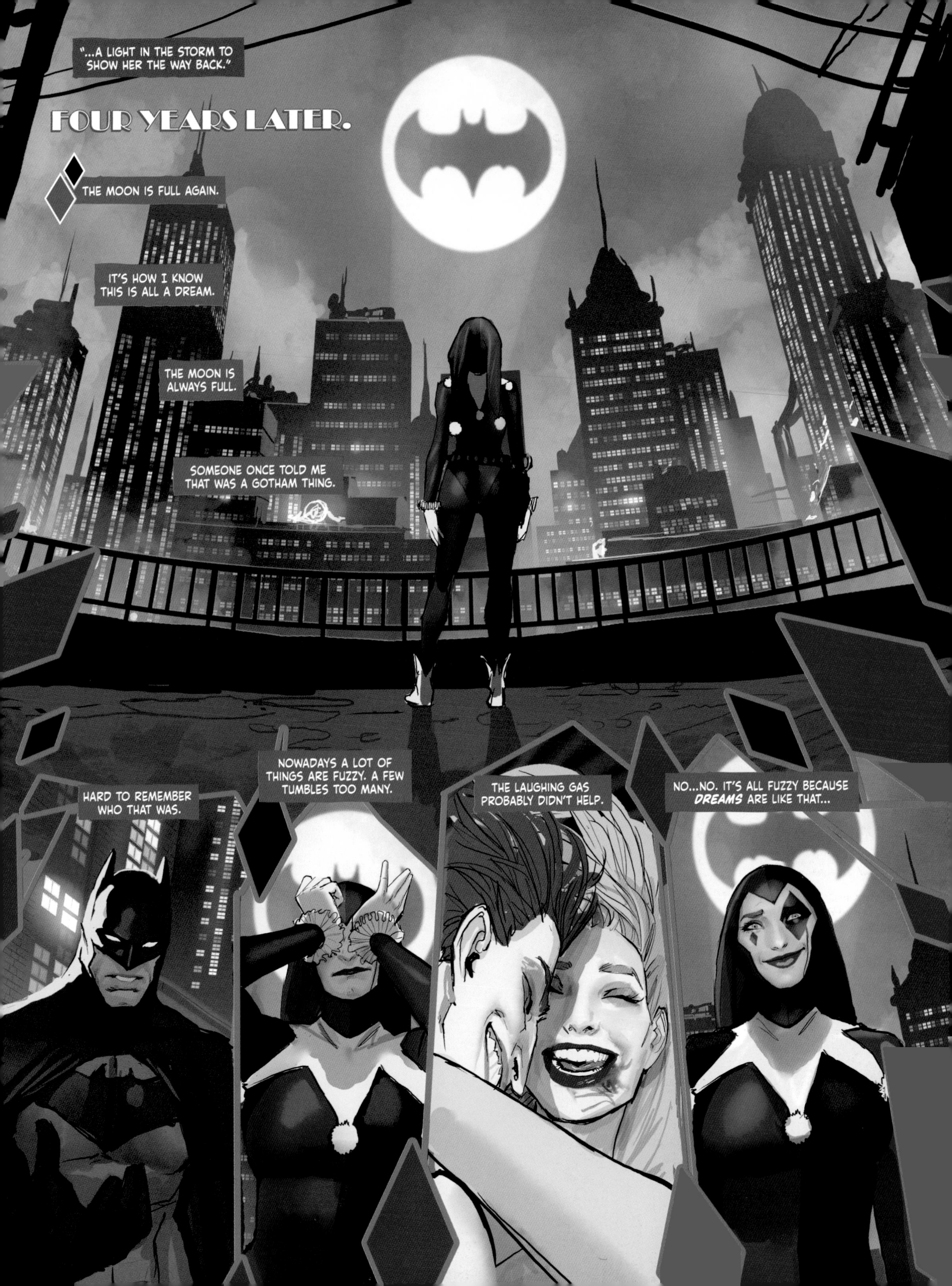
"...A LIGHT IN THE STORM TO SHOW HER THE WAY BACK."
FOUR YEARS LATER.
THE MOON IS FULL AGAIN.
IT'S HOW I KNOW THIS IS ALL A DREAM.
THE MOON IS ALWAYS FULL.
SOMEONE ONCE TOLD ME THAT WAS A GOTHAM THING.
HARD TO REMEMBER WHO THAT WAS.
NOWADAYS A LOT OF THINGS ARE FUZZY. A FEW TUMBLES TOO MANY.
THE LAUGHING GAS PROBABLY DIDN'T HELP.
NO...NO. IT'S ALL FUZZY BECAUSE *DREAMS* ARE LIKE THAT...

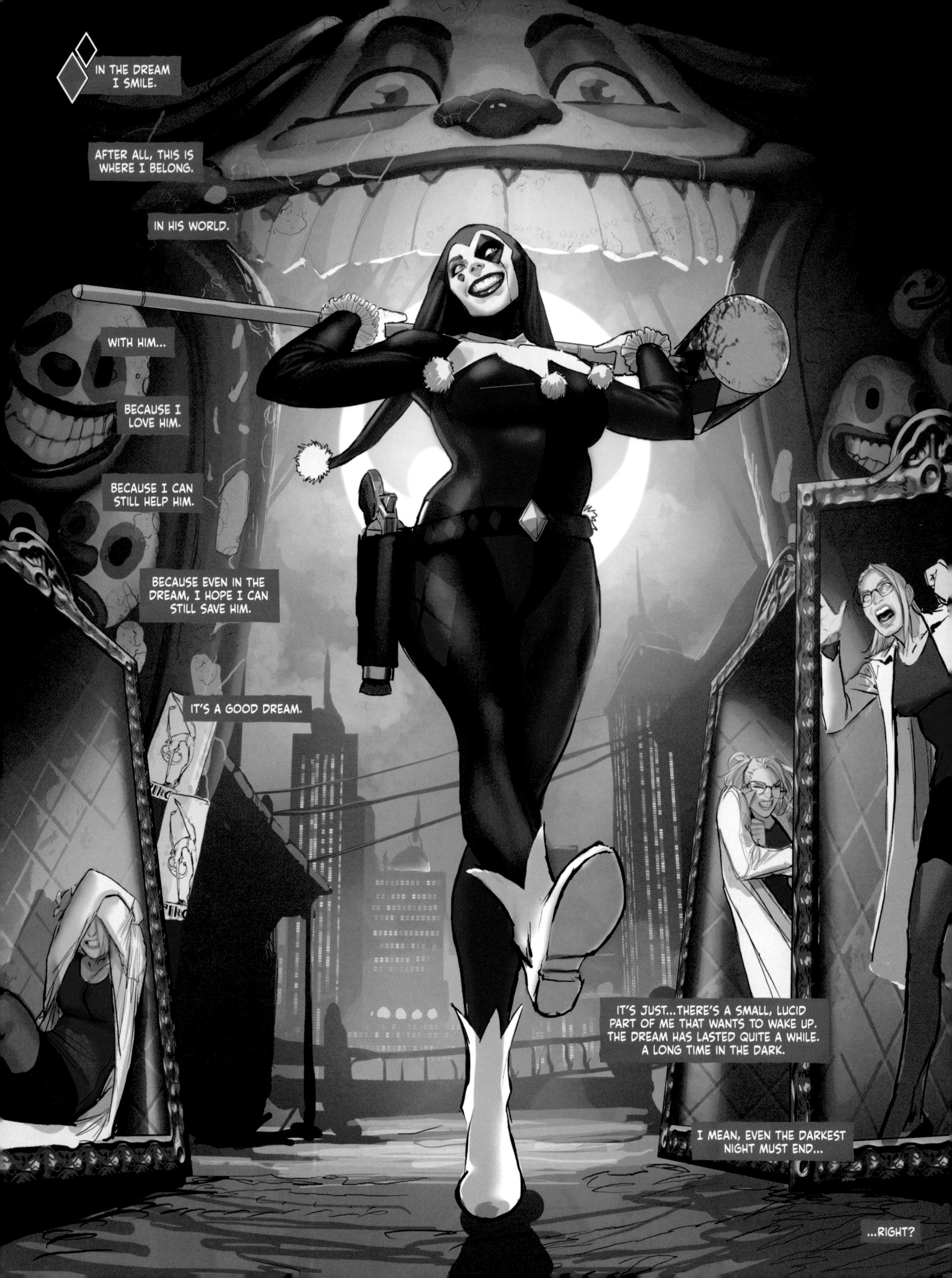
IN THE DREAM I SMILE.
AFTER ALL, THIS IS WHERE I BELONG.
IN HIS WORLD.
WITH HIM...
BECAUSE I LOVE HIM.
BECAUSE I CAN STILL HELP HIM.
BECAUSE EVEN IN THE DREAM, I HOPE I CAN STILL SAVE HIM.
IT'S A GOOD DREAM.
IT'S JUST...THERE'S A SMALL, LUCID PART OF ME THAT WANTS TO WAKE UP. THE DREAM HAS LASTED QUITE A WHILE. A LONG TIME IN THE DARK.
I MEAN, EVEN THE DARKEST NIGHT MUST END...
...RIGHT?

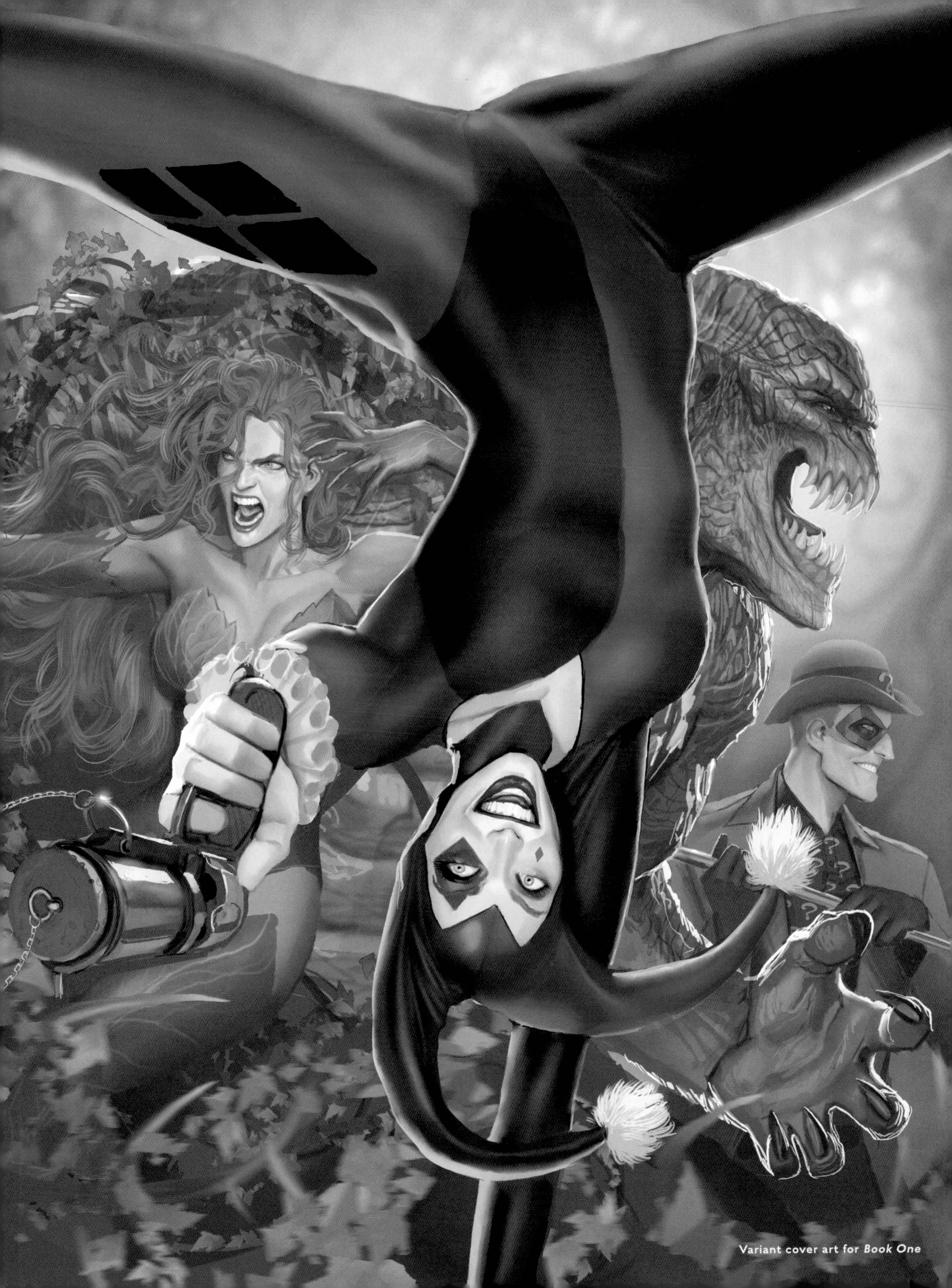

Variant cover art for *Book One*

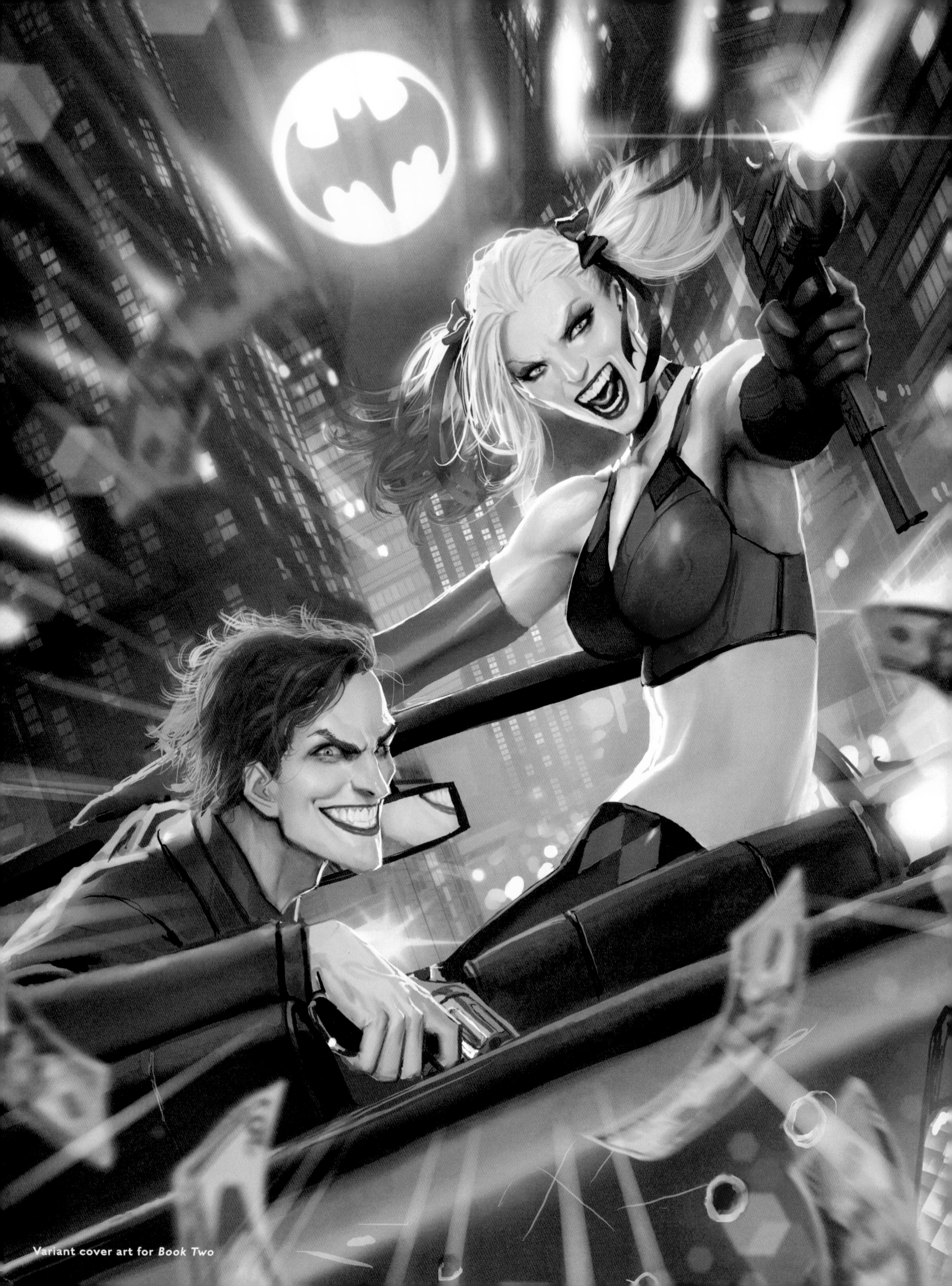

Variant cover art for *Book Two*

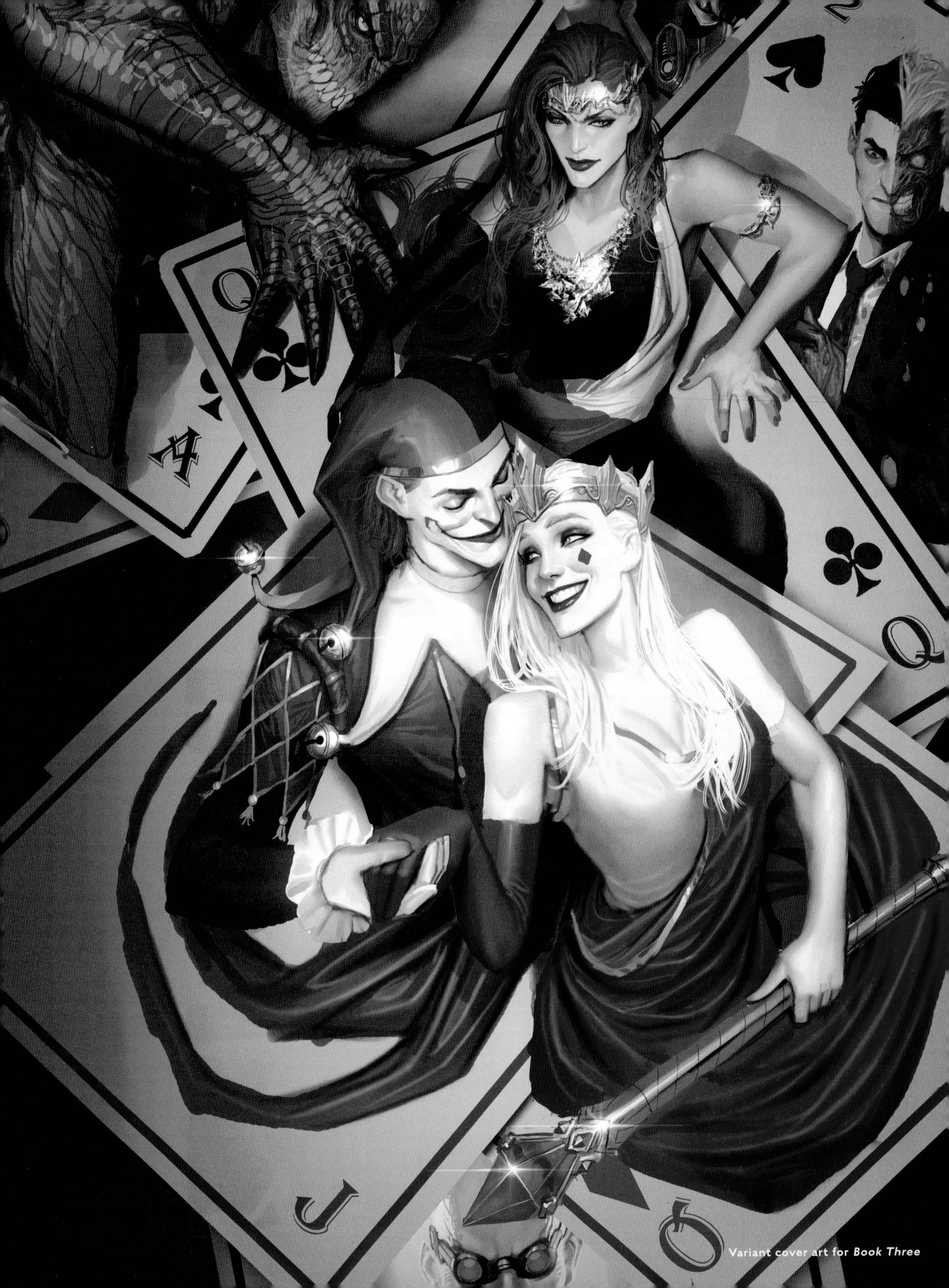
Q
A
Q
J
Q

Variant cover art for *Book Three*

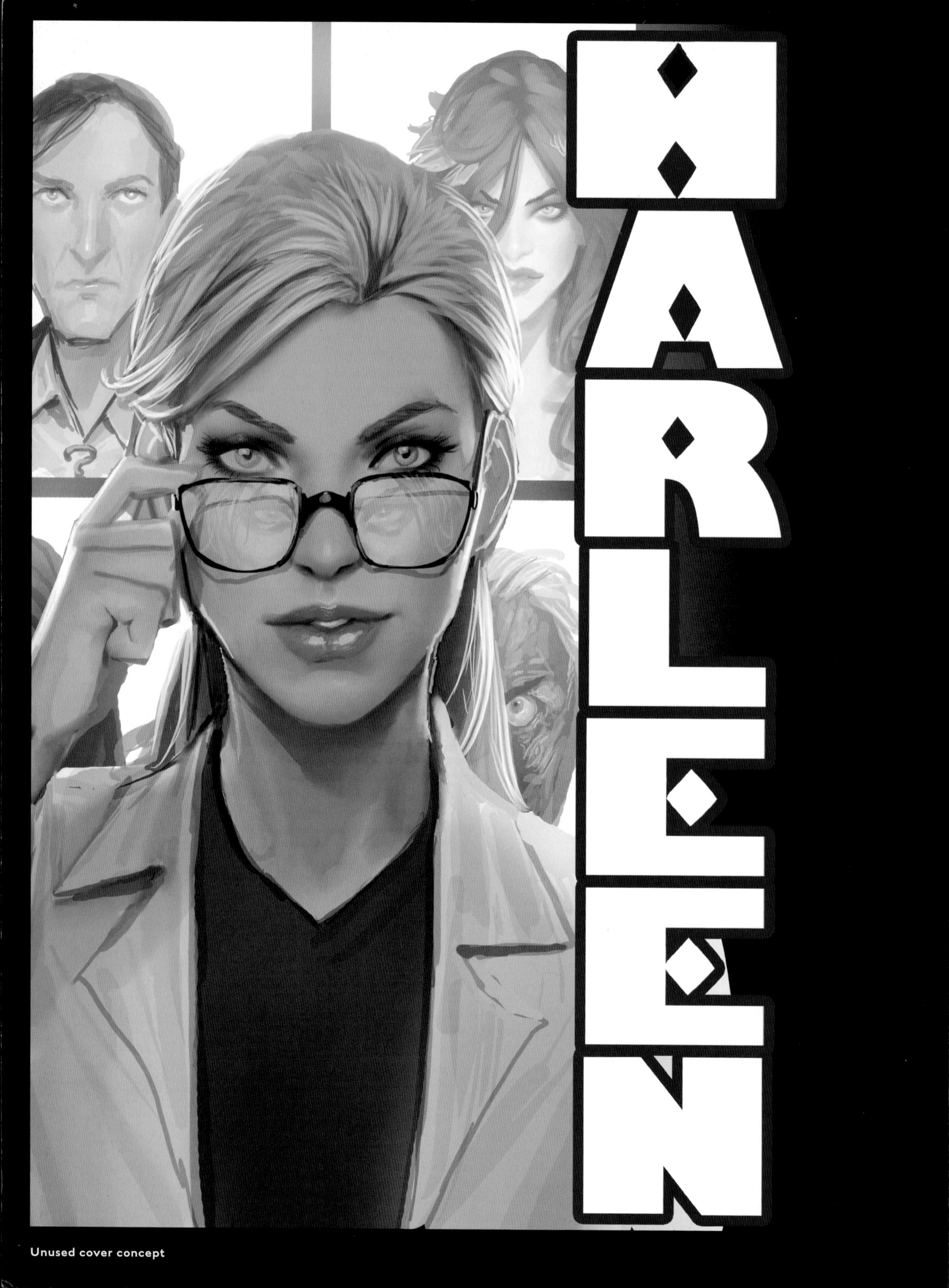
HARLEEN

Unused cover concept

JOURNEY INTO MADNESS

A Graphic Timeline of Stjepan Šejić's *Harleen*

2015-2016

Harleen begins as a series of comic strips crafted by Stjepan Šejić for his own exploration of the character. These early works are not full issues, but rather disparate scenes for a story that is gradually taking shape in his mind.

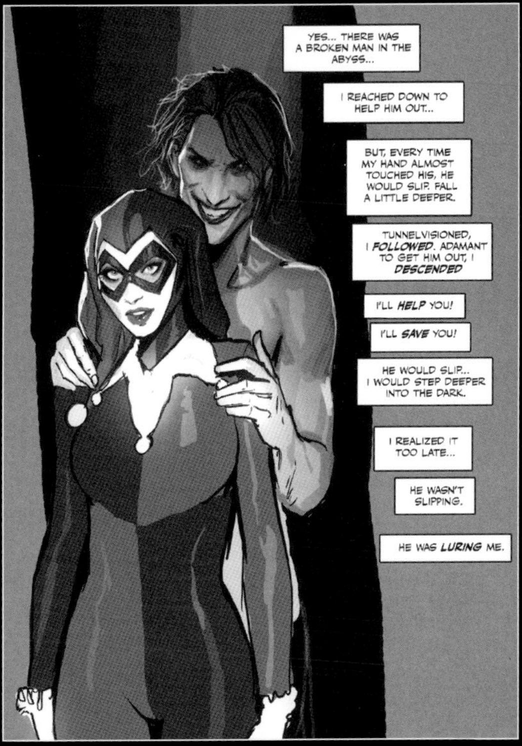

YES... THERE WAS A BROKEN MAN IN THE ABYSS...
I REACHED DOWN TO HELP HIM OUT...
BUT, EVERY TIME MY HAND ALMOST TOUCHED HIS, HE WOULD SLIP. FALL A LITTLE DEEPER.
TUNNELVISIONED, I *FOLLOWED*. ADAMANT TO GET HIM OUT, I *DESCENDED*
I'LL *HELP* YOU!
I'LL *SAVE* YOU!
HE WOULD SLIP... I WOULD STEP DEEPER INTO THE DARK.
I REALIZED IT TOO LATE...
HE WASN'T SLIPPING.
HE WAS *LURING* ME.

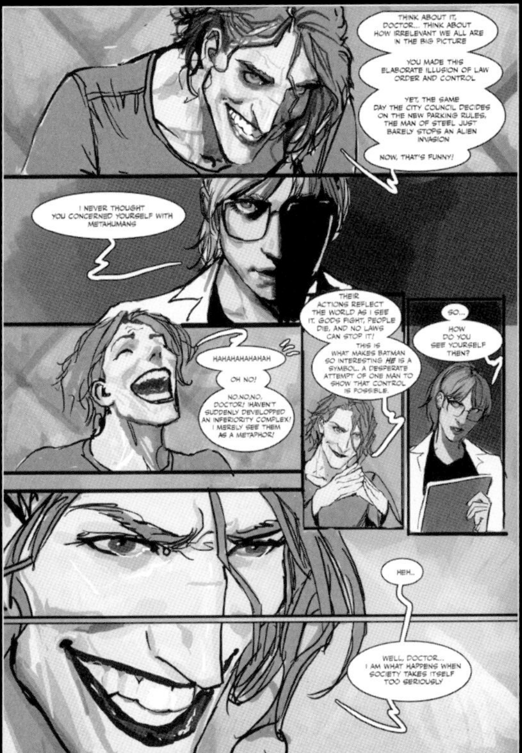

THINK ABOUT IT, DOCTOR... THINK ABOUT HOW IRRELEVANT WE ALL ARE IN THE BIG PICTURE
YOU MADE THIS ELABORATE ILLUSION OF LAW ORDER AND CONTROL
YET, THE SAME DAY THE CITY COUNCIL DECIDES ON THE NEW PARKING RULES, THE MAN OF STEEL JUST BARELY STOPS AN ALIEN INVASION
NOW, THAT'S FUNNY!
I NEVER THOUGHT YOU CONCERNED YOURSELF WITH METAHUMANS
HAHAHAHAHAHAH
OH NO!
NO,NO,NO, DOCTOR! I HAVEN'T SUDDENLY DEVELOPPED AN INFERIORITY COMPLEX! I MERELY SEE THEM AS A METAPHOR!
THEIR ACTIONS REFLECT THE WORLD AS I SEE IT. GODS FIGHT, PEOPLE DIE, AND NO LAWS CAN STOP IT!
THIS IS WHAT MAKES BATMAN SO INTERESTING *HE* IS A SYMBOL. A DESPERATE ATTEMPT OF ONE MAN TO SHOW THAT CONTROL IS POSSIBLE.
SO...
HOW DO YOU SEE YOURSELF THEN?
HEH..
WELL, DOCTOR... I AM WHAT HAPPENS WHEN SOCIETY TAKES ITSELF TOO SERIOUSLY

November 2016

Šejić first discusses the possibility of a *Harleen* series with DC editor Andy Khouri, who hires him in January 2017 to draw the "Underworld" story arc for *Aquaman* №25-30.

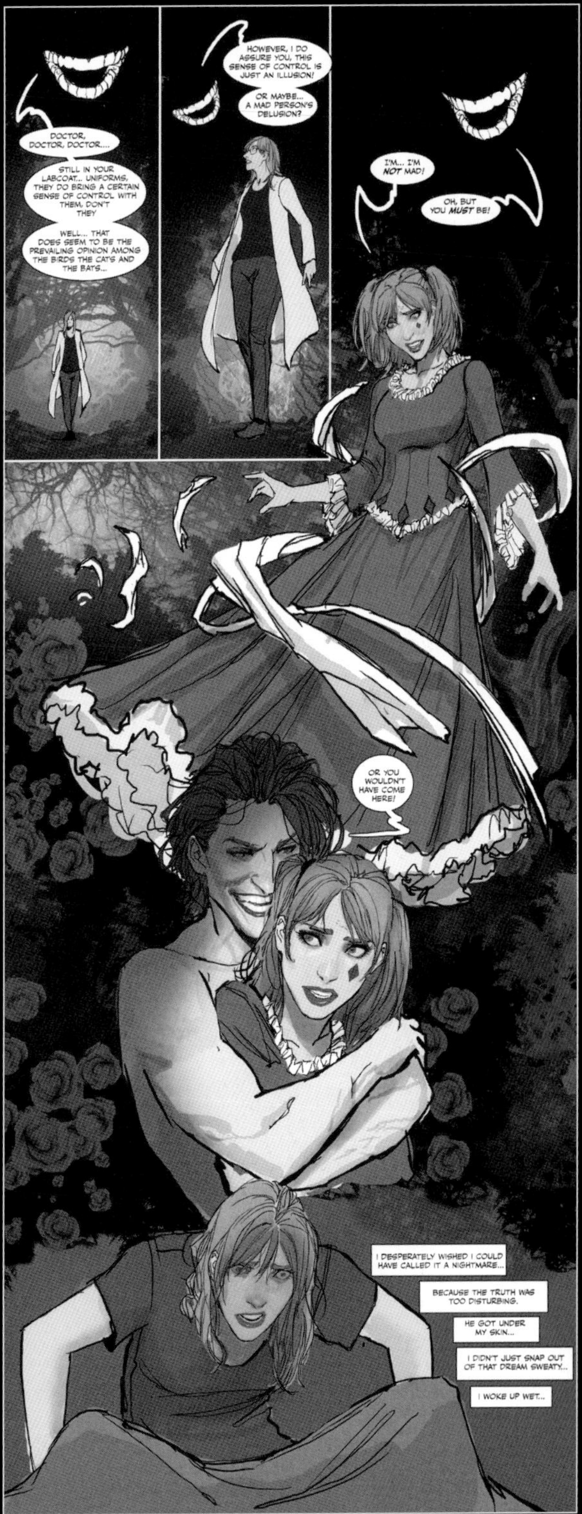

DOCTOR, DOCTOR, DOCTOR....
STILL IN YOUR LABCOAT... UNIFORMS, THEY DO BRING A CERTAIN SENSE OF CONTROL WITH THEM, DON'T THEY
WELL... THAT DOES SEEM TO BE THE PREVAILING OPINION AMONG THE BIRDS THE CAT'S AND THE BATS...
HOWEVER, I DO ASSURE YOU, THIS SENSE OF CONTROL IS JUST AN ILLUSION!
OR MAYBE... A MAD PERSON'S DELUSION?
I'M... I'M *NOT* MAD!
OH, BUT YOU *MUST* BE!
OR YOU WOULDN'T HAVE COME HERE!
I DESPERATELY WISHED I COULD HAVE CALLED IT A NIGHTMARE...
BECAUSE THE TRUTH WAS TOO DISTURBING.
HE GOT UNDER MY SKIN...
I DIDN'T JUST SNAP OUT OF THAT DREAM SWEATY...
I WOKE UP WET...

June 2017

Šejić illustrates the story "Managing People" for *Suicide Squad* №20; his vision of Harley Quinn leaps off the issue's pages. In August 2017, discussions over a possible *Harleen* series resume in earnest. Šejić develops the project with Khouri over the next few months.

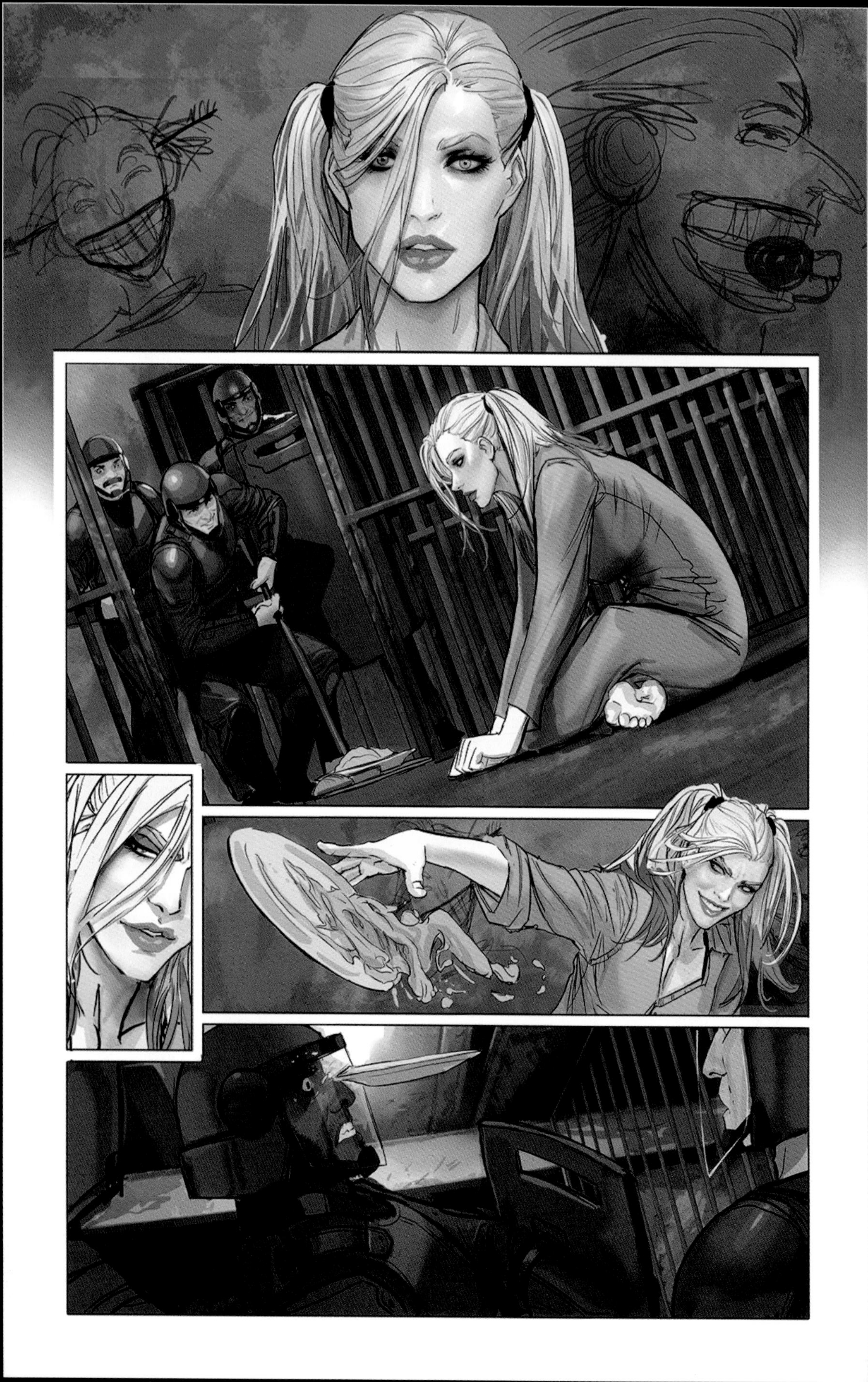

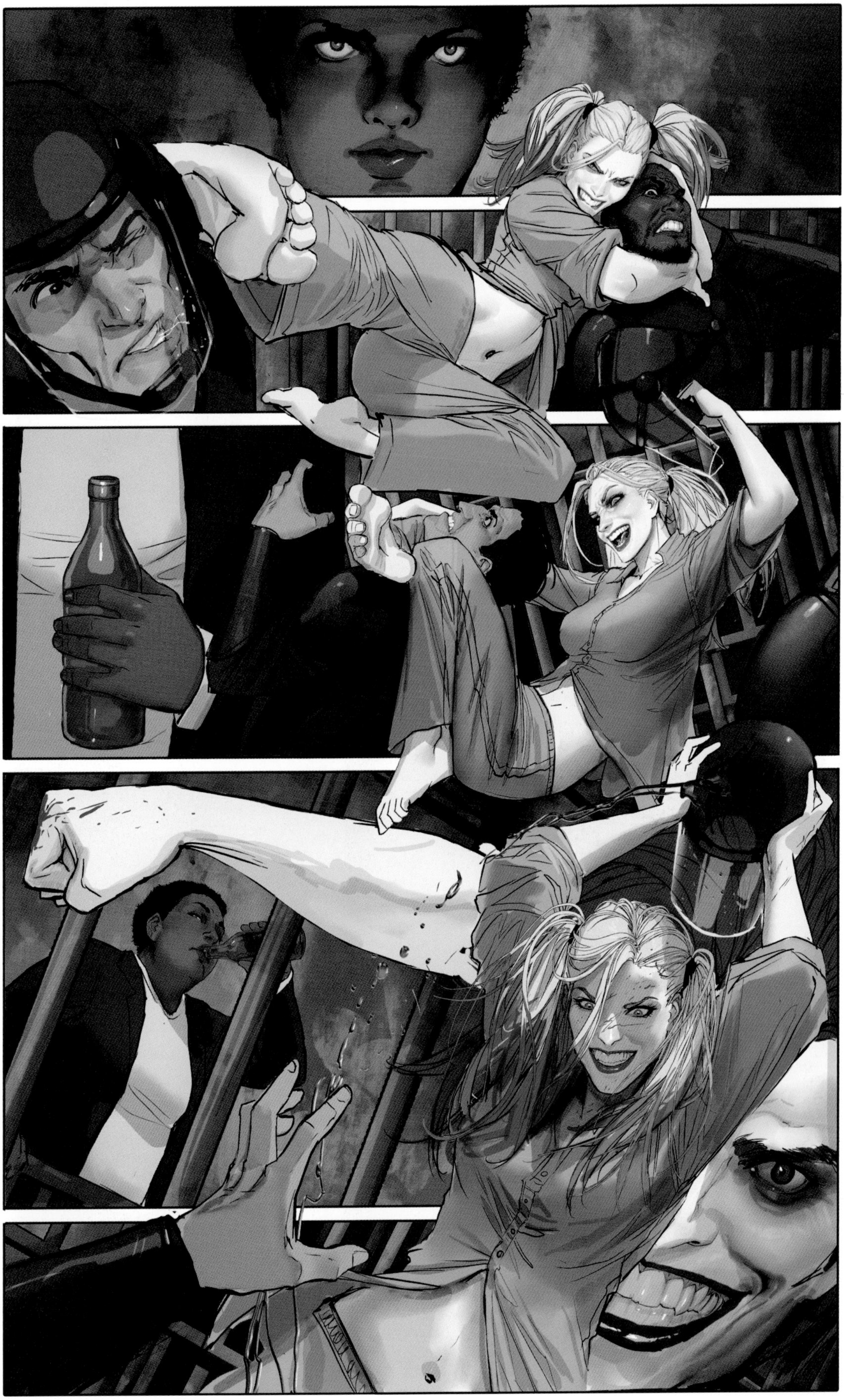

February 2018

Harleen is formally approved as a three-issue series for DC Black Label—and the real work begins.

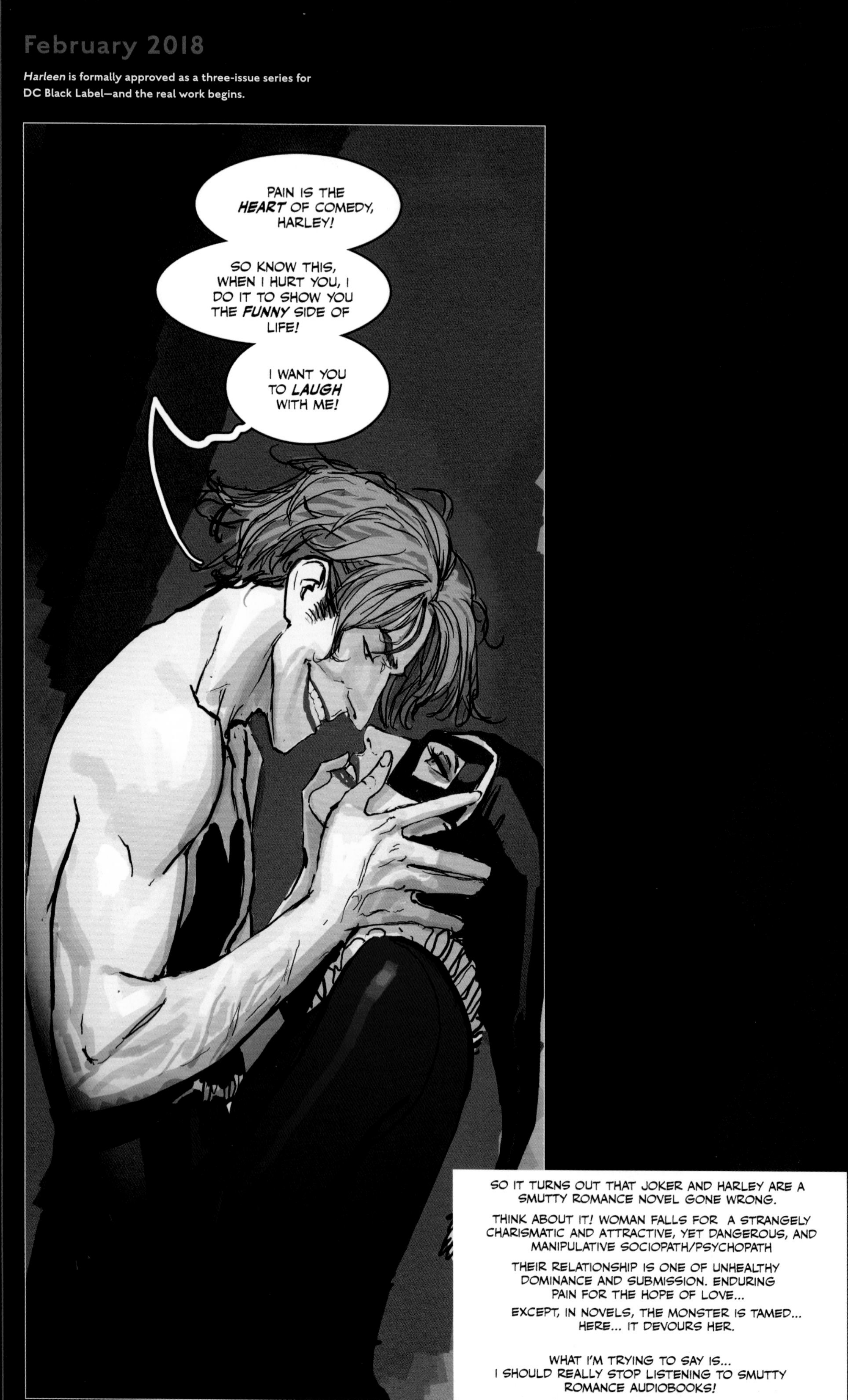
PAIN IS THE *HEART* OF COMEDY, HARLEY!
SO KNOW THIS, WHEN I HURT YOU, I DO IT TO SHOW YOU THE *FUNNY* SIDE OF LIFE!
I WANT YOU TO *LAUGH* WITH ME!

SO IT TURNS OUT THAT JOKER AND HARLEY ARE A SMUTTY ROMANCE NOVEL GONE WRONG.

THINK ABOUT IT! WOMAN FALLS FOR A STRANGELY CHARISMATIC AND ATTRACTIVE, YET DANGEROUS, AND MANIPULATIVE SOCIOPATH/PSYCHOPATH

THEIR RELATIONSHIP IS ONE OF UNHEALTHY DOMINANCE AND SUBMISSION. ENDURING PAIN FOR THE HOPE OF LOVE...

EXCEPT, IN NOVELS, THE MONSTER IS TAMED... HERE... IT DEVOURS HER.

WHAT I'M TRYING TO SAY IS... I SHOULD REALLY STOP LISTENING TO SMUTTY ROMANCE AUDIOBOOKS!

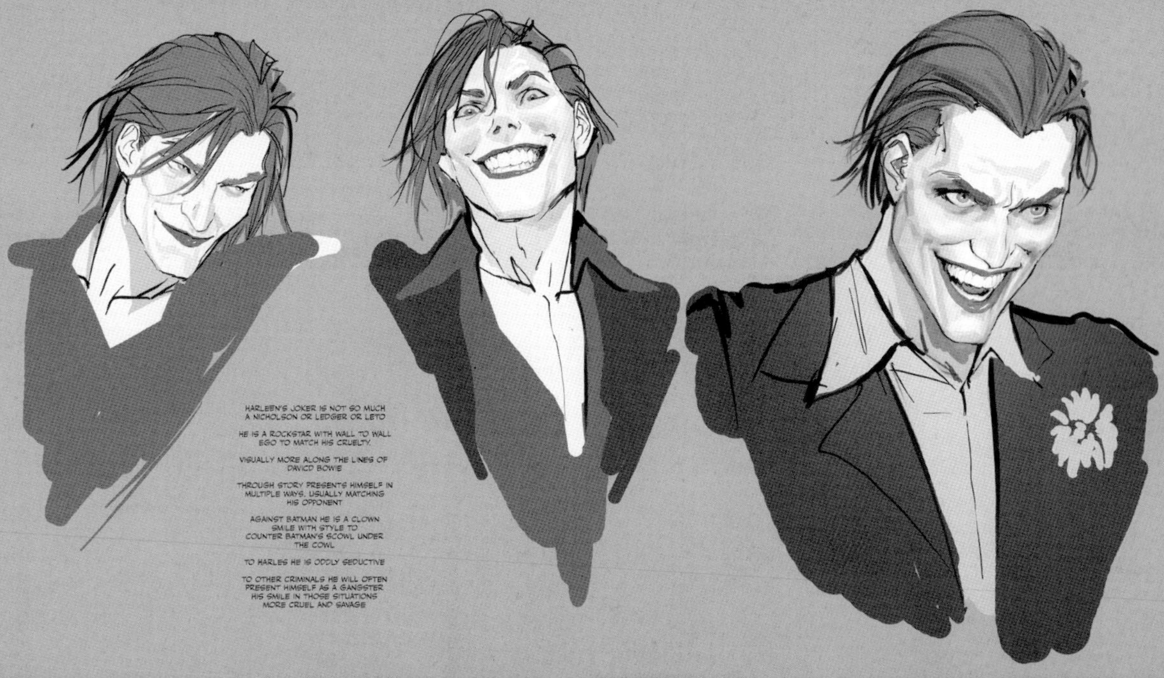
HARLEEN'S JOKER IS NOT SO MUCH A NICHOLSON OR LEDGER OR LETO
HE IS A ROCKSTAR WITH WALL TO WALL EGO TO MATCH HIS CRUELTY.
VISUALLY MORE ALONG THE LINES OF DAVICD BOWIE
THROUGH STORY PRESENTS HIMSELF IN MULTIPLE WAYS, USUALLY MATCHING HIS OPPONENT
AGAINST BATMAN HE IS A CLOWN SMILE WITH STYLE TO COUNTER BATMAN'S SCOWL UNDER THE COWL
TO HARLES HE IS ODDLY SEDUCTIVE
TO OTHER CRIMINALS HE WILL OFTEN PRESENT HIMSELF AS A GANGSTER HIS SMILE IN THOSE SITUATIONS MORE CRUEL AND SAVAGE

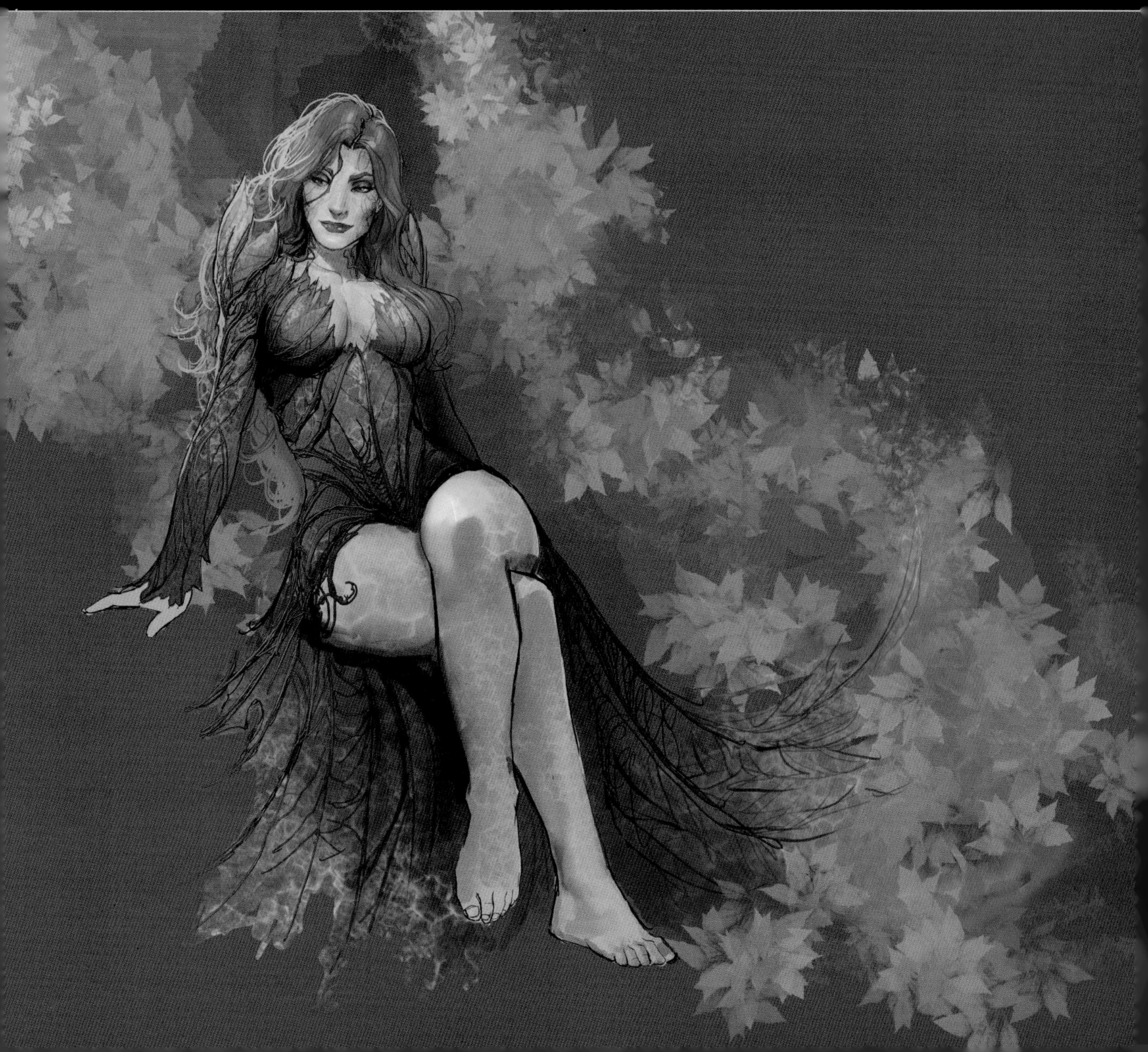

2019–?

Throughout the course of *Harleen*'s development, Šejić continues to draft possible scenes for the characters. Some of these become fully realized scenes in the series, and some may appear in future stories.

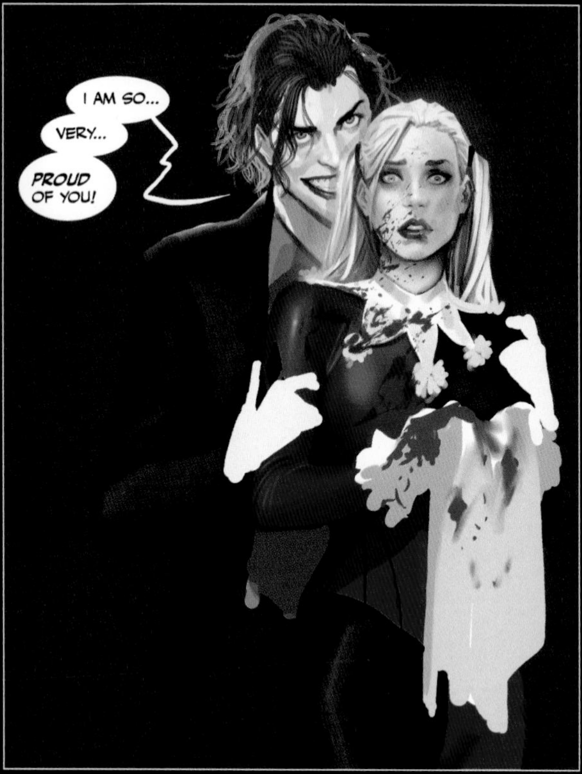
I AM SO...
VERY...
PROUD OF YOU!

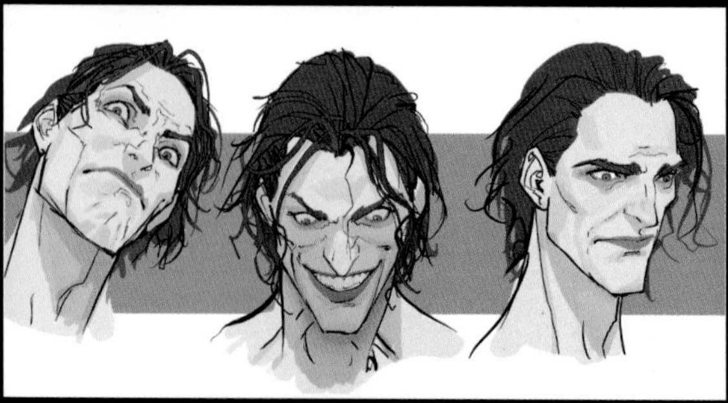

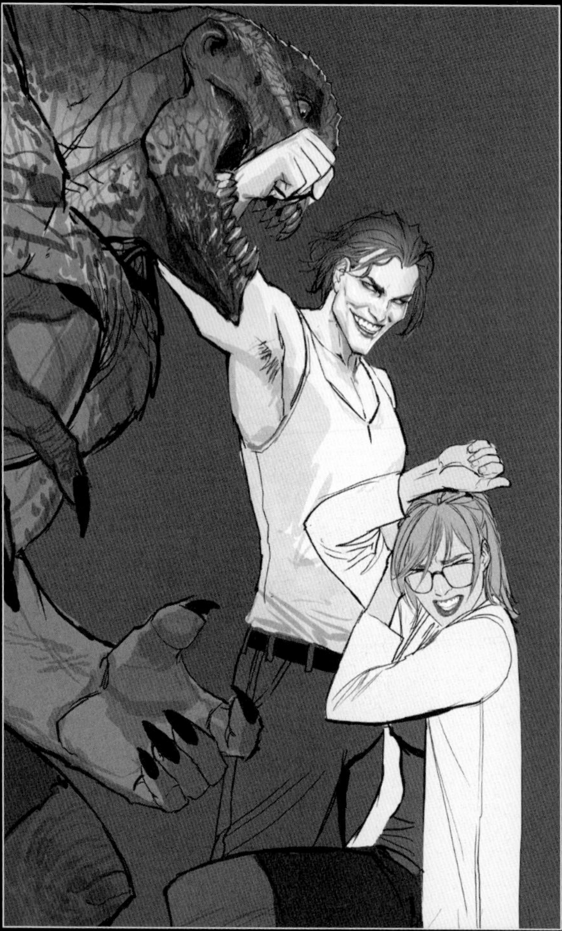

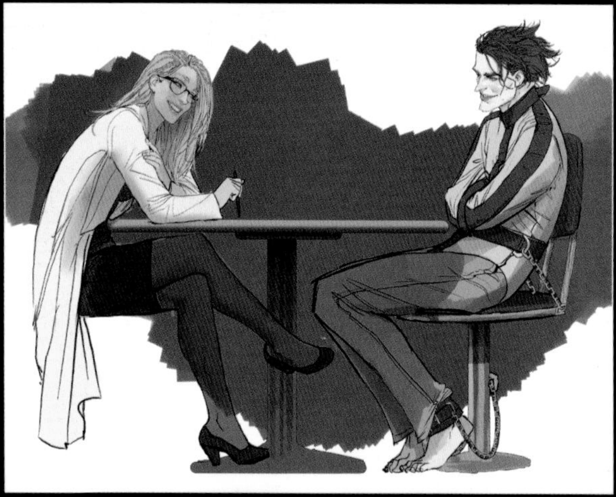

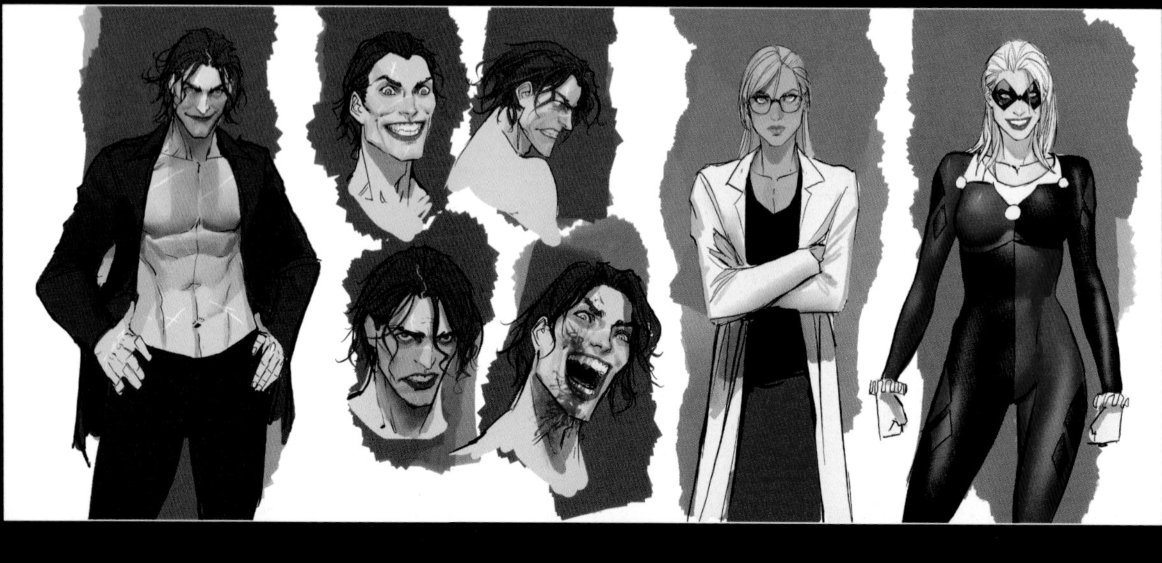

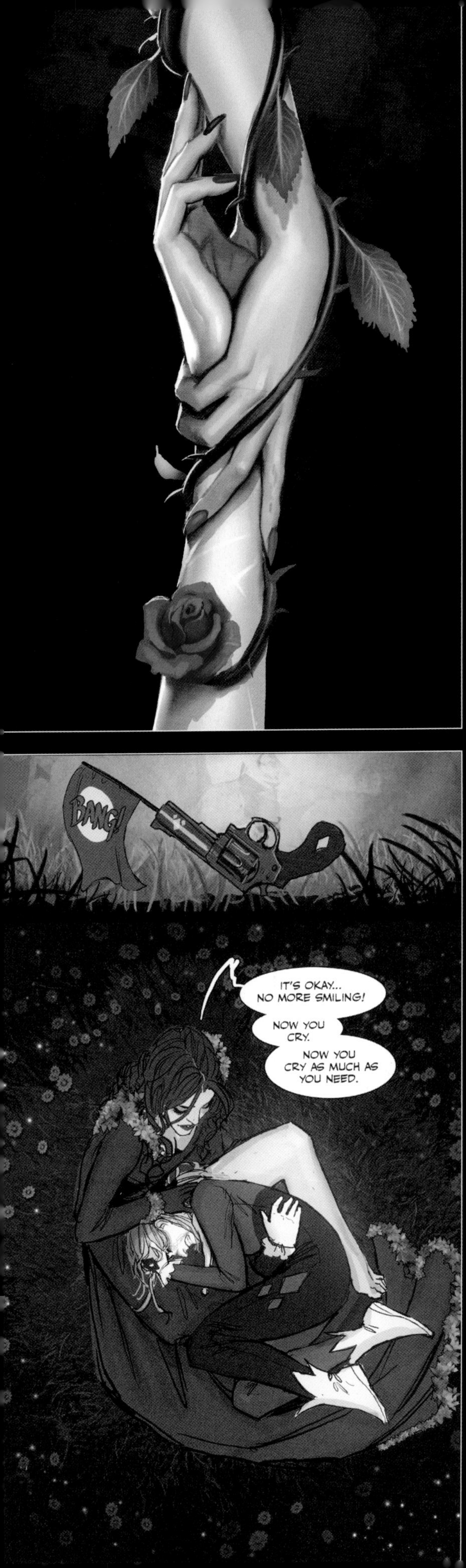
BANG!
IT'S OKAY... NO MORE SMILING!
NOW YOU CRY.
NOW YOU CRY AS MUCH AS YOU NEED.

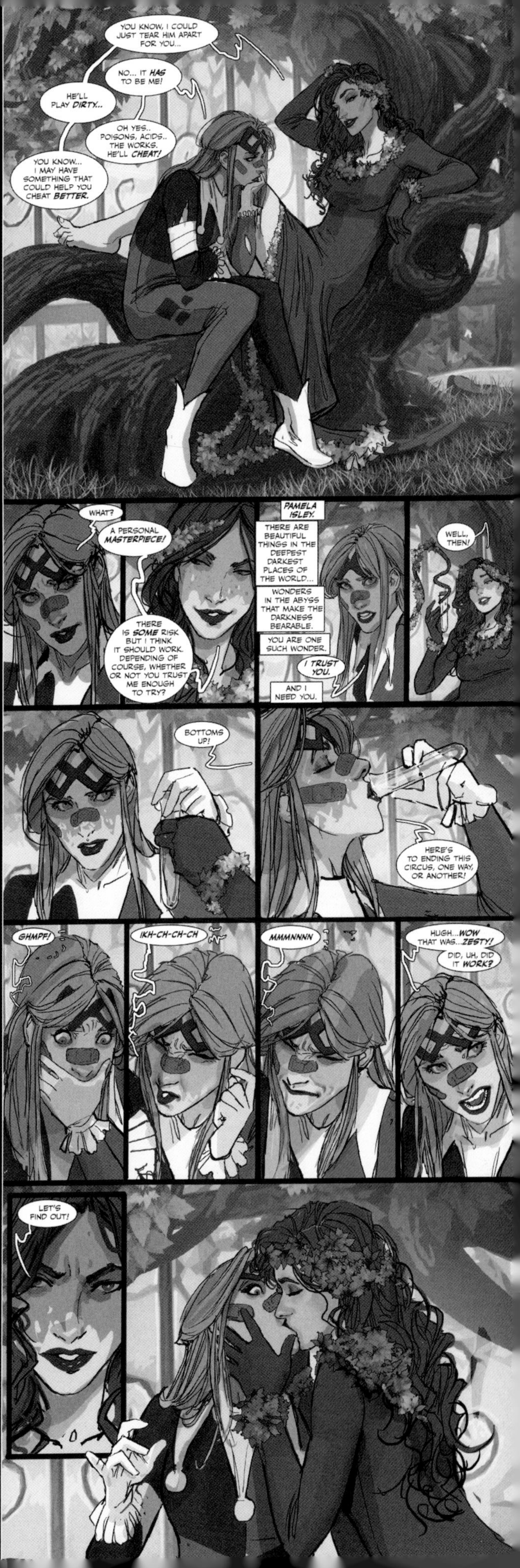
YOU KNOW, I COULD JUST TEAR HIM APART FOR YOU...
NO... IT **HAS** TO BE ME!
HE'LL PLAY **DIRTY**..
OH YES.. POISONS, ACIDS.. THE WORKS. HE'LL **CHEAT!**
YOU KNOW... I MAY HAVE SOMETHING THAT COULD HELP YOU CHEAT **BETTER.**
WHAT?
A PERSONAL **MASTERPIECE!**
THERE IS **SOME** RISK BUT I THINK IT SHOULD WORK. DEPENDING OF COURSE, WHETHER OR NOT YOU TRUST ME ENOUGH TO TRY?
PAMELA ISLEY.
THERE ARE BEAUTIFUL THINGS IN THE DEEPEST DARKEST PLACES OF THE WORLD...
WONDERS IN THE ABYSS THAT MAKE THE DARKNESS BEARABLE.
YOU ARE ONE SUCH WONDER.
I TRUST YOU.
AND I NEED YOU.
WELL, THEN!
BOTTOMS UP!
HERE'S TO ENDING THIS CIRCUS, ONE WAY, OR ANOTHER!
GHMPF!
!KH-CH-CH-CH
MMMNNNN
HUGH...**WOW** THAT WAS...**ZESTY!**
DID, UH, DID IT **WORK?**
LET'S FIND OUT!

STEPS BY STJEPAN

Rather than drafting traditional scripts, Stjepan Šejić creates outlines of his stories that he then translates into thumbnail layouts for his finished pages. The following section showcases three examples of this innovative process from *Harleen.*

Opening, an interview with a dishonorably discharged veteran imprisoned for war crimes. He tells a story about his past and how he went from a soldier with a code of honor to a survivalist who was unable to separate enemy troops from collateral victims.

He is interviewed by Harleen Quinzel.

Scene continues with Harleen giving a speech at a symposium on criminal psychology in front of potential private investors. She outlines a theory stating that people in situations of great stress tend to block their empathy in order to increase their likelihood of survival. Prolonged exposure to these stressful environments may be capable of permanently blocking the brain's ability to process empathy on a hormonal level. It is in a way a mental illness as a survival mechanism.

Harleen therefore postulates that this theory may be applied to criminals of Gotham who in a way live in an urban war zone of their own. If her research is proven correct, it may lead to developing therapy methods that may end up finally putting a dent into Gotham's prison recidivism rates.

Unfortunately, her theory seems to bore or confuse some of her listeners who leave before she is done, and she sees the whole endeavor as a failure.

Scene changes to a bar where she spends the night with one of her rare friends drinking. Her friend offers some pointers for playing the money crowd in order to secure a grant, but to Harleen it all sounds like a case of hindsight being 20/20.

They part ways, and as Harleen walks the streets of Gotham, a great noise catches her attention. A police chase, the Joker and his goons in a car being chased by the police. Joker uses a shoulder-mounted missile launcher to blow up a police car, which lands just behind Harley, but his goon loses control and rams the car into a parked car in front of Harleen.

She is trapped between fiery wreckage behind her and a homicidal maniac in front.

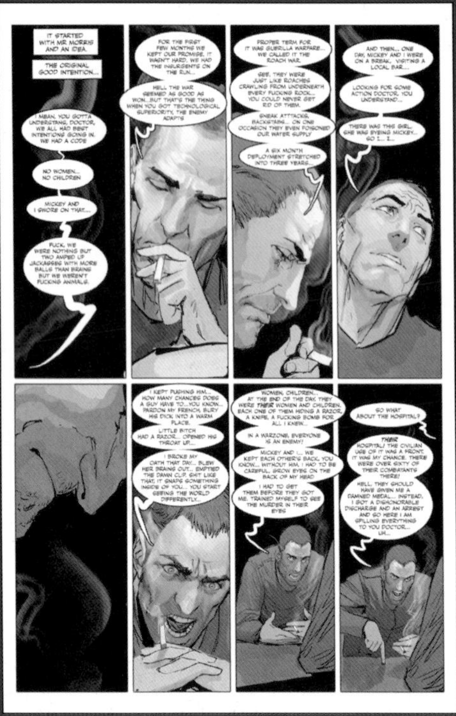

IT STARTED WITH MR MORRIS AND AN IDEA.
THE ORIGINAL GOOD INTENTION...
I MEAN, YOU GOTTA UNDERSTANG, DOCTOR, WE ALL HAD BEST INTENTIONS GOING IN. WE HAD A CODE
NO WOMEN... NO CHILDREN
MICKEY AND I SWORE ON THAT...
FUCK, WE WERE NOTHING BUT TWO AMPED UP JACKASSES WITH MORE BALLS THAN BRAINS BUT WE WEREN'T FUCKING ANIMALS.
FOR THE FIRST FEW MONTHS WE KEPT OUR PROMISE. IT WASN'T HARD. WE HAD THE INSURGENTS ON THE RUN...
HELL THE WAR SEEMED AS GOOD AS WON...BUT THAT'S THE THING WHEN YOU GOT TECHNOLOGICAL SUPERIORITY, THE ENEMY ADAPTS
PROPER TERM FOR IT WAS GUERILLA WARFARE... WE CALLED IT THE ROACH WAR.
SEE, THEY WERE JUST LIKE ROACHES CRAWLING FROM UNDERNEATH EVERY FUCKING ROCK... YOU COULD NEVER GET RID OF THEM.
SNEAK ATTACKS, BACKSTABS... ON ONE OCCASION THEY EVEN POISONED OUR WATER SUPPLY
A SIX MONTH DEPLOYMENT STRETCHED INTO THREE YEARS...
AND THEN... ONE DAY, MICKEY AND I WERE ON A BREAK, VISITING A LOCAL BAR...
LOOKING FOR SOME ACTION DOCTOR, YOU UNDERSTAND...
THERE WAS THIS GIRL, SHE WAS EYEING MICKEY... SO I... I...
I KEPT PUSHING HIM... HOW MANY CHANCES DOES A GUY HAVE TO...YOU KNOW... PARDON MY FRENCH, BURY HIS DICK INTO A WARM PLACE.
LITTLE BITCH HAD A RAZOR... OPENED HIS THROAT UP...
I BROKE MY OATH THAT DAY... BLEW HER BRAINS OUT... EMPTIED THE DAMN CLIP. SHIT LIKE THAT, IT SNAPS SOMETHING INSIDE OF YOU... YOU START SEEING THE WORLD DIFFERENTLY...
WOMEN, CHILDREN... AT THE END OF THE DAY, THEY WERE THEIR WOMEN AND CHILDREN. EACH ONE OF THEM HIDING A RAZOR, A KNIFE, A FUCKING BOMB FOR ALL I KNEW...
IN A WARZONE, EVERYONE IS AN ENEMY!
MICKEY AND I... WE KEPT EACH OTHER'S BACK, YOU KNOW... WITHOUT HIM, I HAD TO BE CAREFUL, GROW EYES ON THE BACK OF MY HEAD
I HAD TO GET THEM BEFORE THEY GOT ME. TRAINED MYSELF TO SEE THE MURDER IN THEIR EYES
SO WHAT ABOUT THE HOSPITAL?
THEIR HOSPITAL! THE CIVILIAN USE OF IT WAS A FRONT. IT WAS MY CHANCE. THERE WERE OVER SIXTY OF THEIR COMBATANTS THERE!
HELL, THEY SHOULD HAVE GIVEN ME A DAMNED MEDAL... INSTEAD, I GOT A DISHONORABLE DISCHARGE AND AN ARREST AND SO HERE I AM SPILLING EVERYTHING TO YOU DOCTOR... UH...

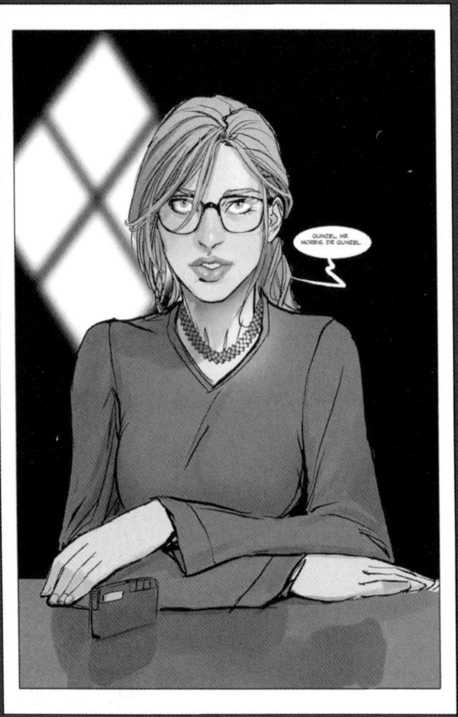

QUINZEL... MR MORRIS, DR QUINZEL.

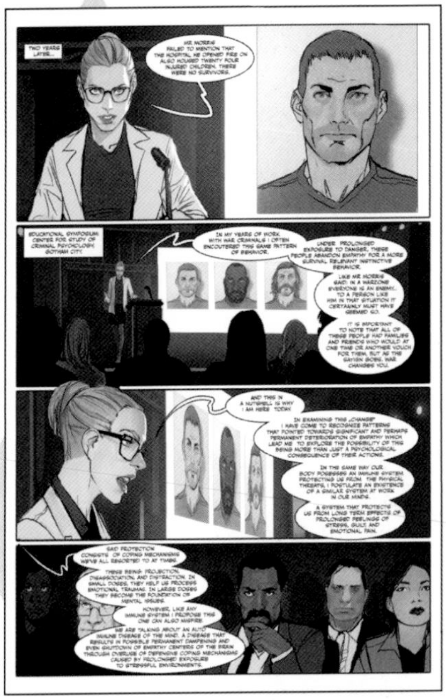
TWO YEARS LATER...
MR. MORRIS FAILED TO MENTION THAT THE HOSPITAL HE OPENED FIRE ON ALSO HOUSED TWENTY FOUR INJURED CHILDREN. THERE WERE NO SURVIVORS.
EDUCATIONAL SYMPOSIUM CENTER FOR STUDY OF CRIMINAL PSYCHOLOGY, GOTHAM CITY.
IN MY YEARS OF WORK WITH WAR CRIMINALS I OFTEN ENCOUTERED THIS SAME PATTERN OF BEHAVIOR.
UNDER PROLONGED EXPOSURE TO DANGER, THESE PEOPLE ABANDON EMPATHY FOR A MORE SURVIVAL RELEVANT INSTINCTIVE BEHAVIOR.
LIKE MR. MORRIS SAID: IN A WARZONE EVERYONE IS AN ENEMY... TO A PERSON LIKE HIM IN THAT SITUATION IT CERTAINLY MUST HAVE SEEMED SO.
IT IS IMPORTANT TO NOTE THAT ALL OF THESE PEOPLE HAD FAMILIES AND FRIENDS WHO WOULD AT ONE TIME OR ANOTHER VOUCH FOR THEM, BUT AS THE SAYIGN GOES, WAR CHANGES YOU.
AND THIS IN A NUTSHELL IS WHY I AM HERE TODAY.
IN EXAMINING THIS „CHANGE" I HAVE COME TO RECOGNIZE PATTERNS THAT POINTED TOWARDS SIGNIFICANT AND PERHAPS PERMANENT DETERIORATION OF EMPATHY WHICH LEAD ME TO EXPLORE THE POSSIBILITY OF THIS BEING MORE THAN JUST A PSYCHOLOGICAL CONSEQUENCE OF THEIR ACTIONS.
IN THE SAME WAY OUR BODY POSSESSES AN IMMUNE SYSTEM PROTECTING US FROM THE PHYSICAL THREATS, I POSTULATE AN EXISTENCE OF A SIMILAR SYSTEM AT WORK IN OUR MINDS.
A SYSTEM THAT PROTECTS US FROM LONG TERM EFFECTS OF PROLONGED FEELINGS OF STRESS, GUILT AND EMOTIONAL PAIN.
SAID PROTECTION CONSISTS OF COPING MECHANISMS WE'VE ALL RESORTED TO AT TIMES.
THESE BEING: PROJECTION, DISASSOCIATION, AND DISTRACTION. IN SMALL DOSES, THEY HELP US PROCESS EMOTIONAL TRAUMAS. IN LARGE DOSES THEY BECOME THE FOUNDATION OF MENTAL ISSUES.
HOWEVER, LIKE ANY IMMUNE SYSTEM I PROPOSE THIS ONE CAN ALSO MISFIRE.
WE ARE TALKING ABOUT AN AUTO IMMUNE DISEASE OF THE MIND. A DISEASE THAT RESULTS IN POSSIBLE PERMANENT DAMPENING AND EVEN SHUTDOWN OF EMPATHY CENTERS OF THE BRAIN THROUGH OVERUSE OF DEFENSIVE COPING MECHANISMS CAUSED BY PROLONGED EXPOSURE TO STRESSFUL ENVIRONMENTS.

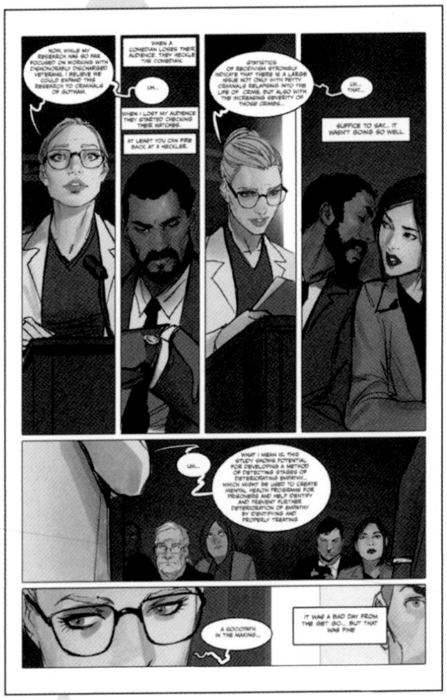
NOW, WHILE MY RESEARCH HAS SO FAR FOCUSED ON WORKING WITH DISHONORABLY DISCHARGED VETERANS, I BELIEVE WE COULD EXPAND THIS RESEARCH TO CRIMINALS OF GOTHAM.
WHEN A COMEDIAN LOSES THEIR AUDIENCE, THEY HECKLE THE COMEDIAN.
UH...
WHEN I LOST MY AUDIENCE THEY STARTED CHECKING THEIR WATCHES.
AT LEAST YOU CAN FIRE BACK AT A HECKLER.
STATISTICS OF RECIDIVISM STRONGLY INDICATE THAT THERE IS A LARGE ISSUE NOT ONLY WITH PETTY CRIMINALS RELAPSING INTO THE LIFE OF CRIME, BUT ALSO WITH THE INCREASING SEVERITY OF THOSE CRIMES...
UH... THAT...
SUFFICE TO SAY... IT WASN'T GOING SO WELL.
UH...
WHAT I MEAN IS, THIS STUDY SHOWS POTENTIAL FOR DEVELOPING A METHOD OF DETECTING STAGES OF DETERIORATING EMPATHY... WHICH MIGHT BE USED TO CREATE MENTAL HEALTH PROGRAMS FOR PRISONERS AND HELP IDENTIFY AND PREVENT FURTHER DETERIORATION OF EMPATHY BY IDENTIFYING AND PROPERLY TREATING
A GOGOTRTH IN THE MAKING...
IT WAS A BAD DAY FROM THE GET GO... BUT THAT WAS FINE

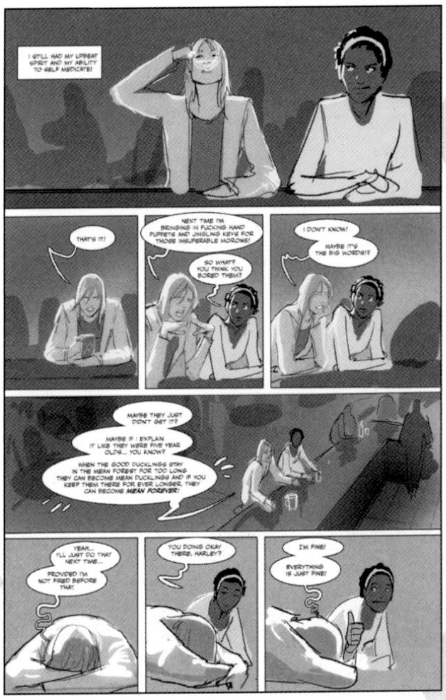
I STILL HAD MY UPBEAT SPIRIT AND MY ABILITY TO SELF MEDICATE!
THAT'S IT!
NEXT TIME I'M BRINGING IN FUCKING HAND PUPPETS AND JINGLING KEYS FOR THOSE INSUFERABLE MORONS!
SO WHAT? YOU THINK YOU BORED THEM?
I DON'T KNOW!
MAYBE IT'S THE BIG WORDS!?
MAYBE THEY JUST DIDN'T GET IT?
MAYBE IF I EXPLAIN IT LIKE THEY WERE FIVE YEAR OLDS... YOU KNOW?
WHEN THE GOOD DUCKLINGS STAY IN THE MEAN FOREST FOR TOO LONG THEY CAN BECOME MEAN DUCKLINGS AND IF YOU KEEP THEM THERE FOR EVER LONGER, THEY CAN BECOME MEAN FOREVER!
YEAH... I'LL JUST DO THAT NEXT TIME...
PROVIDED I'M NOT FIRED BEFORE THAT.
YOU DOING OKAY THERE, HARLEY?
I'M FINE!
EVERYTHING IS JUST FINE!

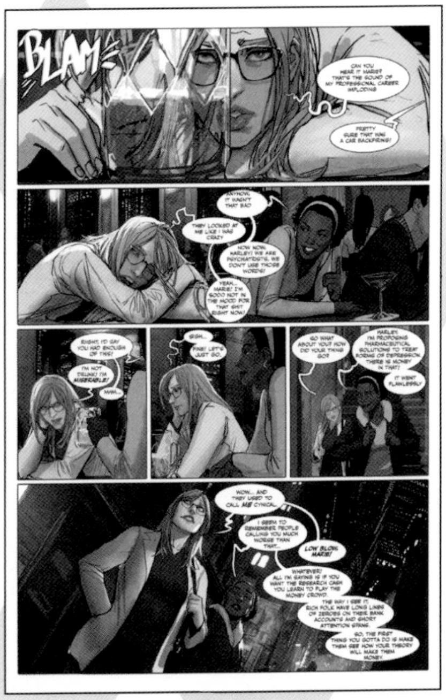
BLAM
CAN YOU HEAR IT MARIE? THAT'S THE SOUND OF MY PROFESSIONAL CAREER IMPLODING
PRETTY SURE THAT WAS A CAR BACKFIRING!
ANYHOW, IT WASN'T THAT BAD
THEY LOOKED AT ME LIKE I WAS CRAZY
NOW NOW, HARLEY! WE ARE PSYCHIATRISTS, WE DON'T USE THOSE WORDS!
YEAH... MARIE! I'M SOOO NOT IN THE MOOD FOR THAT SHIT RIGHT NOW!
RIGHT, I'D SAY YOU HAD ENOUGH OF THIS!
I'M NOT DRUNK! I'M MISERABLE!
MMM...
SIGH...
FINE! LET'S JUST GO.
SO WHAT ABOUT YOU? HOW DID YOUR THING GO?
HARLEY, I'M PROPOSING PHARMACEUTICAL SOLUTIONS TO TREAT FORMS OF DEPRESSION. THERE IS MONEY IN THAT?
IT WENT FLAWLESSLY
WOW... AND THEY USED TO CALL ME CYNICAL
I SEEM TO REMEMBER PEOPLE CALLING YOU MUCH WORSE THAN THAT...
LOW BLOW, MARIE!
WHATEVER! ALL I'M SAYING IS IF YOU WANT THE RESEARCH CASH YOU LEARN TO PLAY THE MONEY CROWD.
THE WAY I SEE IT, RICH FOLK HAVE LONG LINES OF ZEROES ON THEIR BANK ACCOUNTS AND SHORT ATTENTION SPANS.
SO, THE FIRST THING YOU GOTTA DO IS MAKE THEM SEE HOW YOUR THEORY WILL MAKE THEM MONEY.

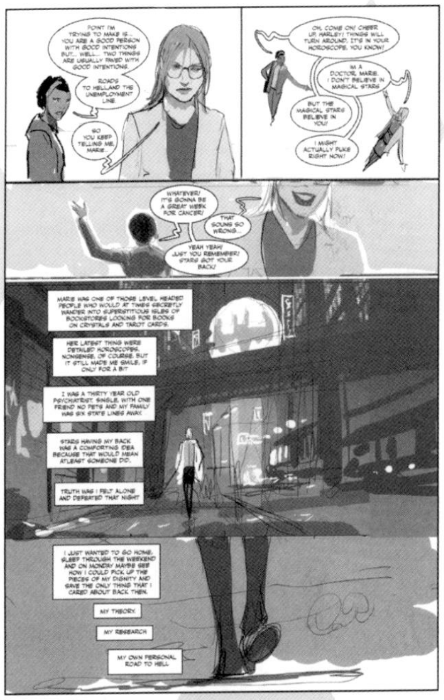
POINT I'M TRYING TO MAKE IS... YOU ARE A GOOD PERSON WITH GOOD INTENTIONS BUT... WELL... TWO THINGS ARE USUALLY PAVED WITH GOOD INTENTIONS.
ROADS TO HELLAND THE UNEMPLOYMENT LINE.
SO YOU KEEP TELLING ME, MARIE...
OH, COME ON! CHEER UP, HARLEY! THINGS WILL TURN AROUND. IT'S IN YOUR HOROSCOPE, YOU KNOW!
IM A DOCTOR, MARIE. I DON'T BELIEVE IN MAGICAL STARS
BUT THE MAGICAL STARS BELIEVE IN YOU!
I MIGHT ACTUALLY PUKE RIGHT NOW!
WHATEVER! IT'S GONNA BE A GREAT WEEK FOR CANCER!
THAT SOUNS SO WRONG...
YEAH YEAH! JUST YOU REMEMBER! STARS GOT YOUR BACK!
MARIE WAS ONE OF THOSE LEVEL HEADED PEOPLE WHO WOULD AT TIMES SECRETLY WANDER INTO SUPERSTITIOUS ISLES OF BOOKSTORES LOOKING FOR BOOKS ON CRYSTALS AND TAROT CARDS.
HER LATEST THING WERE DETAILED HOROSCOPES. NONSENSE, OF COURSE. BUT IT STILL MADE ME SMILE, IF ONLY FOR A BIT
I WAS A THIRTY YEAR OLD PSYCHIATRIST, SINGLE, WITH ONE FRIEND NO PETS AND MY FAMILY WAS SIX STATE LINES AWAY.
STARS HAVING MY BACK WAS A COMFORTING IDEA BECAUSE THAT WOULD MEAN ATLEAST SOMEONE DID.
TRUTH WAS I FELT ALONE AND DEFEATED THAT NIGHT
I JUST WANTED TO GO HOME, SLEEP THROUGH THE WEEKEND AND ON MONDAY MAYBE SEE HOW I COULD PICK UP THE PIECES OF MY DIGNITY AND SAVE THE ONLY THING THAT I CARED ABOUT BACK THEN.
MY THEORY.
MY RESEARCH
MY OWN PERSONAL ROAD TO HELL

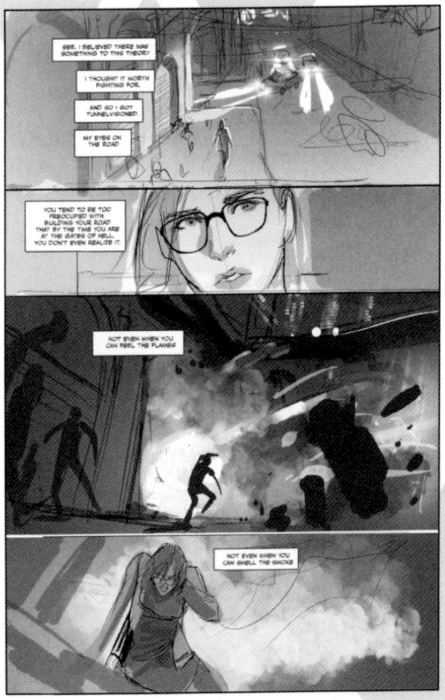
SEE, I BELIEVED THERE WAS SOMETHING TO THIS THEORY
I THOUGHT IT WORTH FIGHTING FOR.
AND SO I GOT TUNNELVISIONED.
MY EYES ON THE ROAD
YOU TEND TO BE TOO PREOCUPIED WITH BUILDING YOUR ROAD THAT BY THE TIME YOU ARE AT THE GATES OF HELL, YOU DON'T EVEN REALIZE IT.
NOT EVEN WHEN YOU CAN FEEL THE FLAMES
NOT EVEN WHEN YOU CAN SMELL THE SMOKE

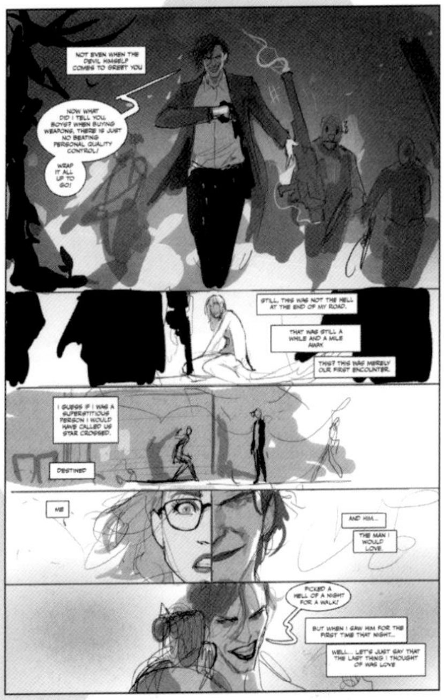
NOT EVEN WHEN THE DEVIL HIMSELF COMES TO GREET YOU
NOW WHAT DID I TELL YOU, BOYS? WHEN BUYING WEAPONS, THERE IS JUST NO BEATING PERSONAL QUALITY CONTROL!
WRAP IT ALL UP TO GO!
STILL, THIS WAS NOT THE HELL AT THE END OF MY ROAD.
THAT WAS STILL A WHILE AND A MILE AWAY.
THIS? THIS WAS MERELY OUR FIRST ENCOUNTER.
I GUESS IF I WAS A SUPERSTITIOUS PERSON I WOULD HAVE CALLED US STAR CROSSED.
DESTINED
ME
AND HIM...
THE MAN I WOULD LOVE.
PICKED A HELL OF A NIGHT FOR A WALK!
BUT WHEN I SAW HIM FOR THE FIRST TIME THAT NIGHT...
WELL... LET'S JUST SAY THAT THE LAST THING I THOUGHT OF WAS LOVE

A dark hallway. Harleen walks through it escorted by a guard. She asks to go alone.

She sticks to the shadows, as she comes in front of Joker's cell. Bulletproof glass for surveillance.

He is still bruised, bandaged. Broken arm. However there is an attractiveness to him. This Joker is a rock star. Wall-to-wall charisma and ego with a short fuse. Has quite a bit of David Bowie in him if I was to define it.

Plays solitaire. From inside of the cell he is holding a queen card, letter Q on it. Visually aligned just behind it in the shadows, Harleen.

Joker slowly gets up.

So, which one are you, one of my previous ones, or a brand-new brain tinkerer?

I can't really see you all the way over there. Come closer, I won't bite...I mean, I might, but...knocks at the glass...and chuckles.

Harleen pauses for a second...and then enters into the illuminated part of the hallway. In a way mimicking the scene from issue 1 on the street, but this time she should be safe. She certainly doesn't feel safe. They look at each other.

I am Doctor Harleen Quinzel. I have been assigned with your...case.

Joker stares at her...an uncomfortable moment lasting a bit too long.

Taps his lips. You know...funny thing about getting your head slammed into a wall repetitively...does a number on your memory...then again electroshock therapy probably hasn't done much to help with that either...

Harleen frowns.

What I mean is...you look like someone I met...but something is...

MISSING!

He shouts and suddenly slams the glass. It's a scary moment and she is taken aback, her body language and expression terrified.

Joker laughs. THERE YOU ARE! I knew you seemed familiar, just missing that terror in your eyes.

The streets...that night.

I let you off with a warning, yet here you are again. He chuckles.

And a shrink...heh...hahahhahah...

Are you done? Harleen asks.

He looks at her with some curiosity.

You tell me? That's why you're here, to pick through my brain, so I can tell you all the stories.

Oh, I've read up on the stories. You were at the same time a rich mobster, thrown into a vat of acid, and a failed poor comedian, abused by your father, mother, brother, and...she checks the file.

A matron of an orphanage that doubled as a sweatshop producing golf balls.

He laughs. I was always proud of that one.

But now you ruined it. I had such stories to tell you.

Lies.

Perhaps. But truth is so boring anyways. Dry...factual... misses the soul of things. It's a low-grade artist always on the brink of capturing the essence of their model but eternally failing.

I prefer the lies, illusions. A bit of makeup and a whole lot of theatricality.

Stories then.

He grins.

Monster stories?

You're in the right place, he says.

I'm interested in those.

Very well, Mister Joker, why don't you tell me a story of Gotham. The city of monsters.

He looks at her. Grinning.

Call me Jay.

We zoom out from them through the dark hallway. In the distance a small figure of Harleen illuminated by the light of Joker's cell.

Very well, Mr. Jay.

SO THEY ARE STONEWALLING HER ON ACESS TO PRISON INMATES.
BUT MATTHEWS IS A TOUGH OLD LADY.
AND TURNS OUT SHE'S GOT YOUR BACK.
HE'S DOWN THE HALL. YOU CAN'T MISS IT
WE KEEP HIM SEPARATED FROM THE REST OF THEM AS HE'S GOT A TENDENCY OF STARTING SHIT
I CAN'T SAY HOW LONG I WOULD HAVE BEEN AVOIDING HIM.
HOW LONG HE WOULD HAVE HAUNTED MY DREAMS... WITHOUT ME EVER CONFRONTING HIM.
BUT THAT DAY I FOUND OUT SOMEONE HAD MY BACK AND IT WAS ALL I NEEDED TO SNAP ME OUT OF MY FEAR
CALLL IF YOU NEED ME.
THANK YOU, MR. BRONSON.
MY BOSS WAS OUT THERE STICKING HER NECK OUT FOR ME
I SURE AS HELL WASN'T GONNA COWER AWAY FROM TALKING TO THE LAST MAN ON MY LIST.
AND ANYWAYS...
IT'S BEEN OVER A MONTH.
SURELY HE WOULDN'T REMEMBER ME.

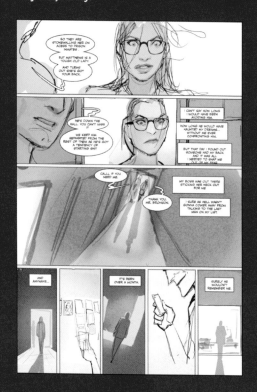

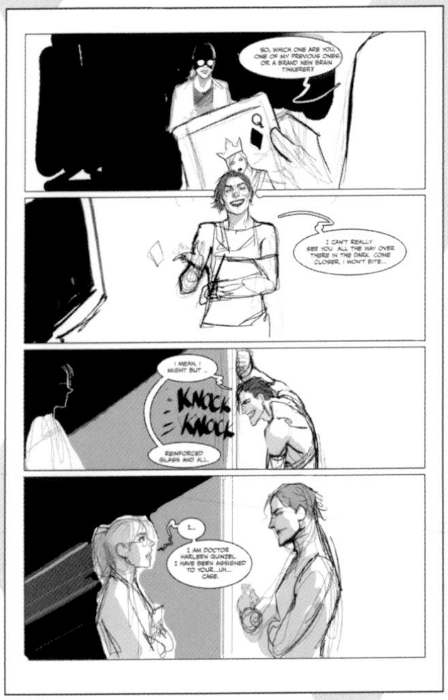
SO, WHICH ONE ARE YOU, ONE OF MY PREVIOUS ONES, OR A BRAND NEW BRAIN TINKERER?
I CAN'T REALLY SEE YOU ALL THE WAY OVER THERE IN THE DARK. COME CLOSER, I WON'T BITE...
I MEAN, I MIGHT BUT ..
KNOCK KNOCK
REINFORCED GLASS AND ALL.
I...
I AM DOCTOR HARLEEN QUINZEL. I HAVE BEEN ASSIGNED TO YOUR...UH... CASE.

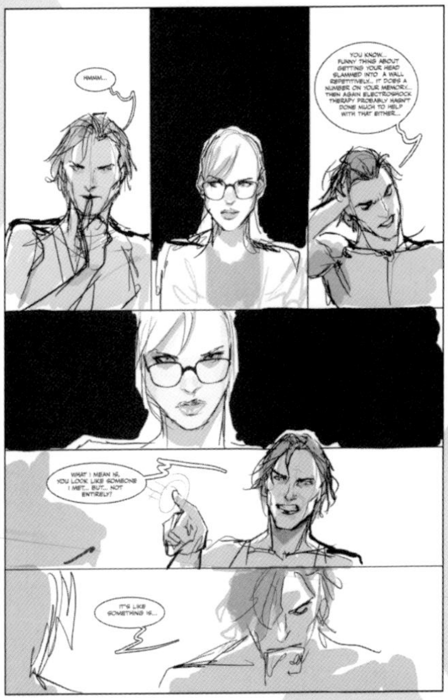
HMMM...
YOU KNOW... FUNNY THING ABOUT GETTING YOUR HEAD SLAMMED INTO A WALL REPETITIVELY... IT DOES A NUMBER ON YOUR MEMORY... THEN AGAIN ELECTROSHOCK THERAPY PROBABLY HASN'T DONE MUCH TO HELP WITH THAT EITHER...
WHAT I MEAN IS, YOU LOOK LIKE SOMEONE I MET... BUT... NOT ENTIRELY?
IT'S LIKE SOMETHING IS...

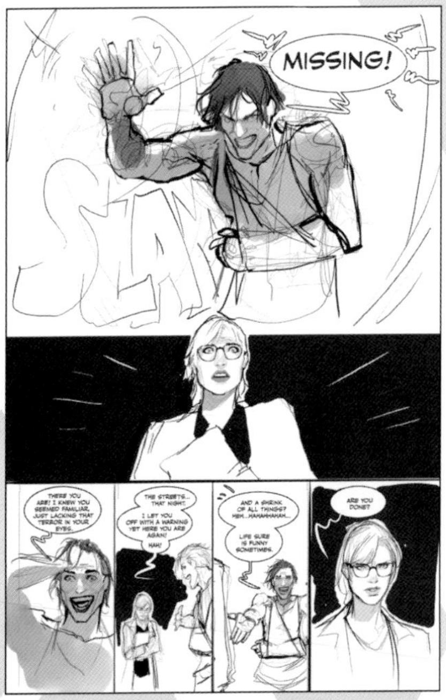
MISSING!
THERE YOU ARE! I KNEW YOU SEEMED FAMILIAR, JUST LACKING THAT TERROR IN YOUR EYES.
THE STREETS... THAT NIGHT.
I LET YOU OFF WITH A WARNING YET HERE YOU ARE AGAIN!
HAH!
AND A SHRINK OF ALL THINGS? HEH...HAHAHHAHAH...
LIFE SURE IS FUNNY SOMETIMES.
ARE YOU DONE?

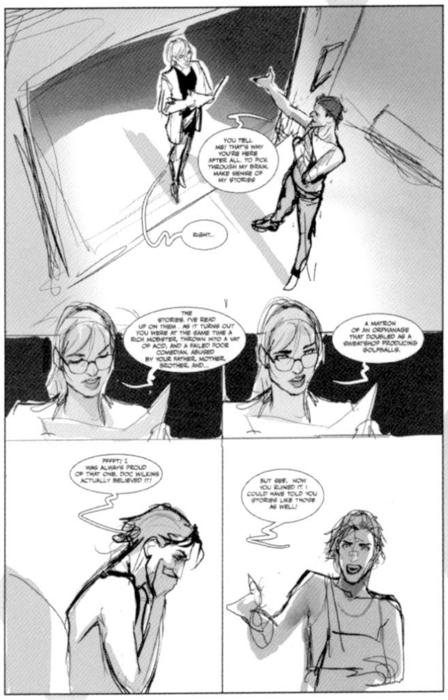
YOU TELL ME! THAT'S WHY YOU'RE HERE AFTER ALL. TO PICK THROUGH MY BRAIN, MAKE SENSE OF MY STORIES
RIGHT...
THE STORIES. I'VE READ UP ON THEM . AS IT TURNS OUT YOU WERE AT THE SAME TIME A RICH MOBSTER, THROWN INTO A VAT OF ACID, AND A FAILED POOR COMEDIAN, ABUSED BY YOUR FATHER, MOTHER, BROTHER, AND...
A MATRON OF AN ORPHANAGE THAT DOUBLED AS A SWEATSHOP PRODUCING GOLFBALLS.
PFFFT! I WAS ALWAYS PROUD OF THAT ONE. DOC WILKINS ACTUALLY BELIEVED IT!
BUT SEE. NOW YOU RUINED IT. I COULD HAVE TOLD YOU STORIES LIKE THOSE AS WELL!

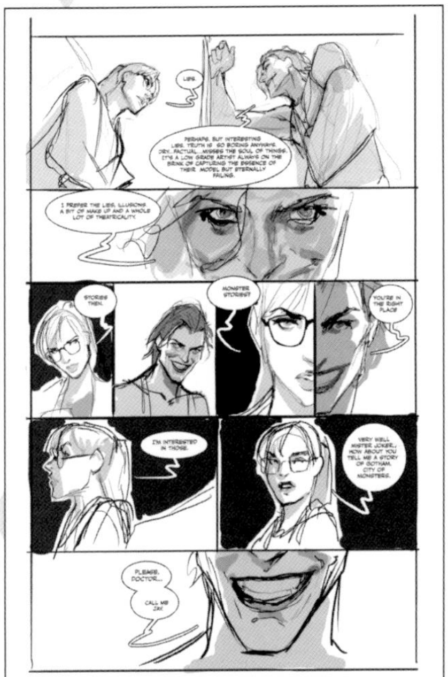
LIES.
PERHAPS. BUT INTERESTING LIES. TRUTH IS SO BORING ANYWAYS. DRY...FACTUAL...MISSES THE SOUL OF THINGS. IT'S A LOW GRADE ARTIST ALWAYS ON THE BRINK OF CAPTURING THE ESSENCE OF THEIR MODEL BUT ETERNALLY FAILING.
I PREFER THE LIES, ILLUSIONS. A BIT OF MAKE UP AND A WHOLE LOT OF THEATRICALITY.
STORIES THEN.
MONSTER STORIES?
YOU'RE IN THE RIGHT PLACE
I'M INTERESTED IN THOSE.
VERY WELL MISTER JOKER., HOW ABOUT YOU TELL ME A STORY OF GOTHAM. CITY OF MONSTERS.
PLEASE. DOCTOR...
CALL ME JAY.

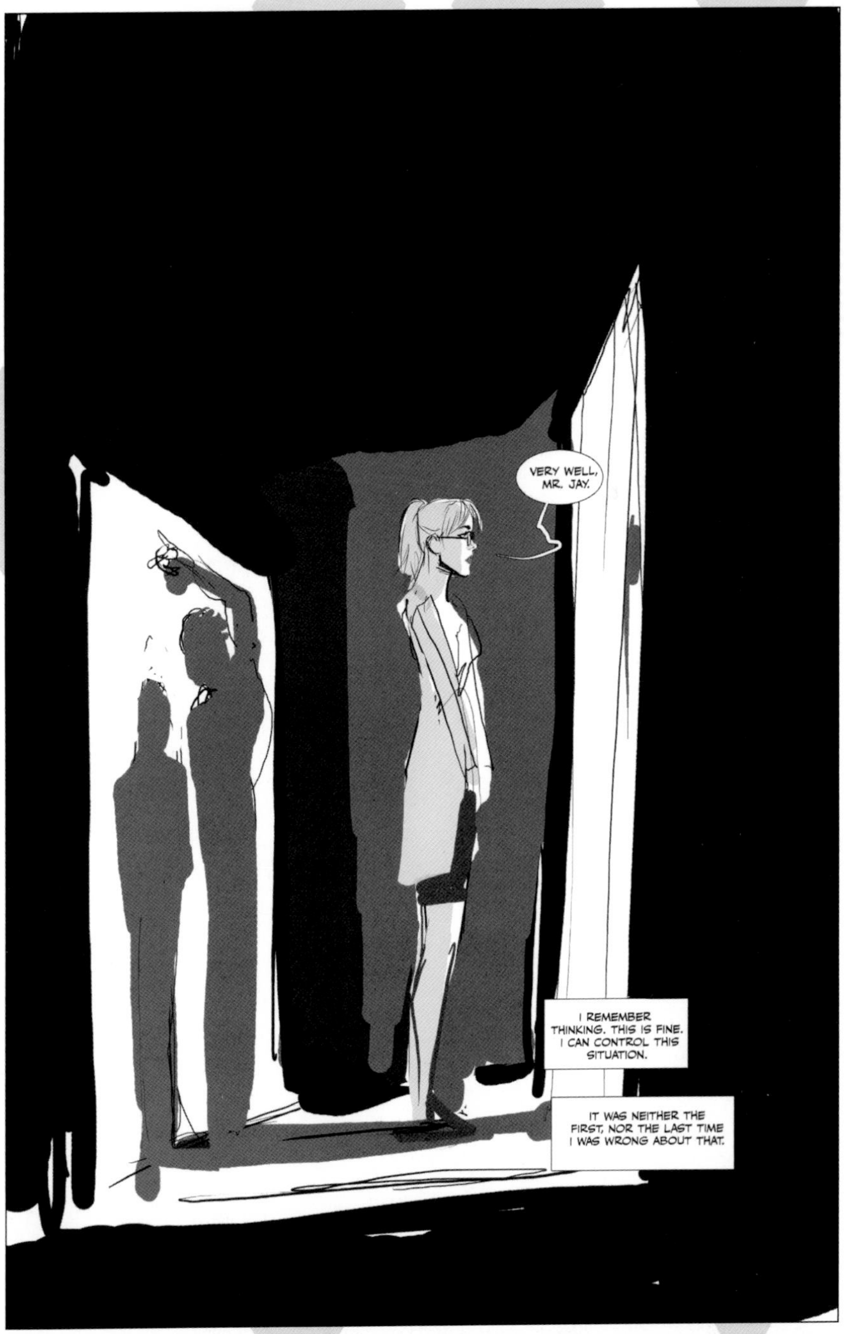
VERY WELL, MR. JAY.
I REMEMBER THINKING. THIS IS FINE. I CAN CONTROL THIS SITUATION.
IT WAS NEITHER THE FIRST, NOR THE LAST TIME I WAS WRONG ABOUT THAT.

We turn to see a little confused Joker.

Doc? You okay there?

I am fine Mr. Jay, she answers stiffly. Now. Shall we begin?

He looks at her a bit suspiciously, and shrugs as much as his straitjacket will allow.

Alright...shoot, doc! What do you want to know?

She looks at her notes. Do you ever feel pity for those you killed?

A little taken aback both by the question and her cold, stiff tone. He takes a minute...frowns, and says.

For the first ones...there was still that. I guess, the first victim on the streets of Gotham is one's empathy.

Harleen snaps out of her stiffness...

W-what?

I mean...regret, guilt...empathy...they bring about hesitation and, on the streets, hesitation will get you caught...get you killed.

I always figured, we killed that part of ourselves first.

Kill the attachments.

Harleen's shell is broken. The thing he just said fit her theory perfectly. She has lost any sense of detachment. This man that has been on her mind seemingly 24/7 these days also seems to be the perfect proof to her theory.

This is what she tells herself to distract herself from that other nagging sensation she would rather not face.

How did it start, Mr. Jay?

He notices the change on her face. (Unknown to audience for now, this is where he knows she took the bait.)

How does anyone go about killing their attachments... you get that one bad moment when the pain of them becomes too much...when you lose it all...

Is that what happened to you, she asks.

He looks at her...

It doesn't matter anymore.

It does to me.

Okay...how about you answer one of my questions first.

Fine.

How often do you watch me sleep?

Uh...she recovers.

It was just yesterday, I was...passing by and noticed the scars on you...

Is that pity I hear in your voice?

Don't, doctor. They are battle scars, nothing else. And like I said, I barely feel any pain.

He looks at the table avoiding her look.

She is awkwardly spinning a pen in her hand and drops it.

I would still like to know...about your loss...

He looks at her annoyed.

Why?

Because...I want to help...

Oh, stop it, doctor!

Tell me, and honestly! Why are you here? See, I'll give you this. You got me to tell you more about myself than anyone else ever did. And who knows, maybe it is my fault.

Maybe I was dwelling too much on why I wanted to see you smile. Maybe that is why I let you in...but in the end none of it matters.

In the end none of you come to Arkham because you truly want to help...

Because I know. You hide it better than others, but like them you too are here hoping to write a book or an article or a thesis...

In the end at least the cops are honest. They see us as monsters because we are just that!

No! she shouts.

All pretense of emotional distance gone.

She gets up to the camera and covers it with her coat.

She angrily walks behind him, he feels the straitjacket getting unbuckled.

She walks in front of him and turns her back to him. She is afraid. But fights it because there is another more powerful feeling taking her over...and she hopes.

It is a moment of desperate hope and trust.

Joker gets up as the straitjacket falls to the floor

It is a tense moment as his hand hovers behind her.

She is trembling.

I came here for my own purpose...but...I found myself caring. Caring so much that it scares me. You...scare me, and yet...

And then he hugs her. And whispers, Thank you, Doctor Quinn....

A silent panel and then she says...Harley...you can call me Harley...

Harley...Quinn he says. I like that...

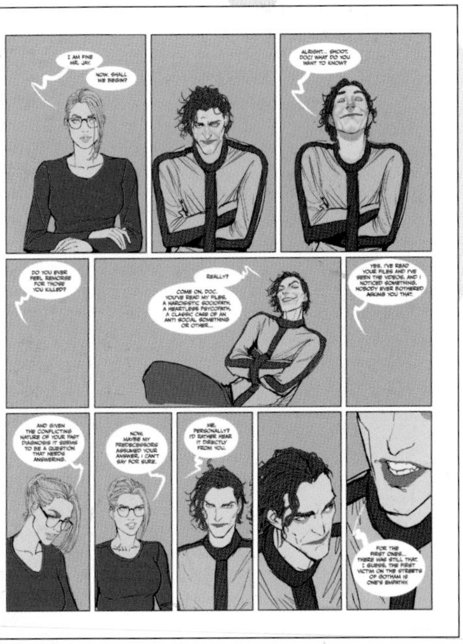
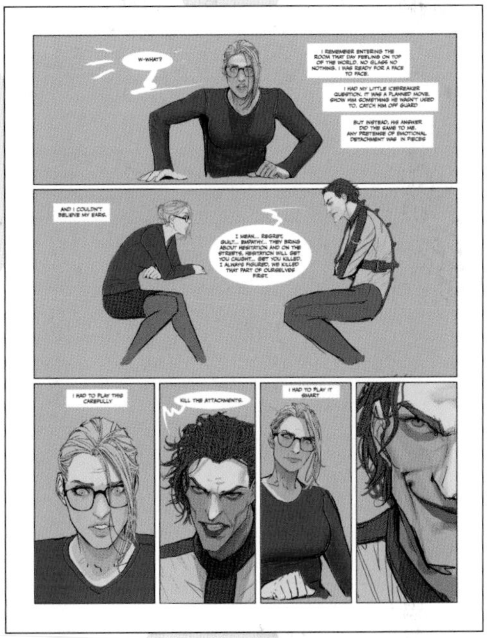
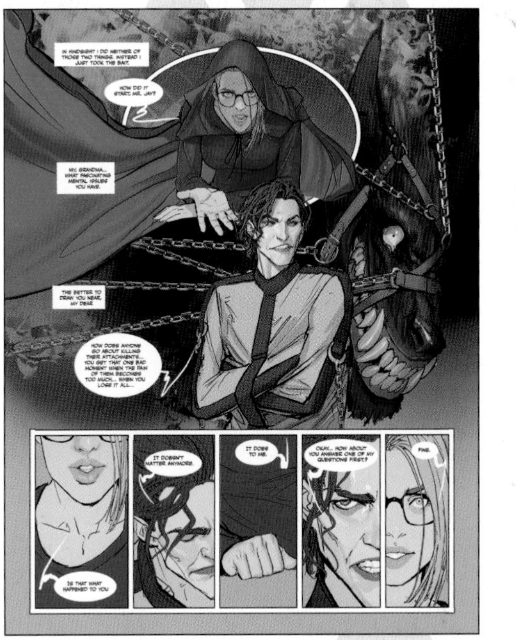
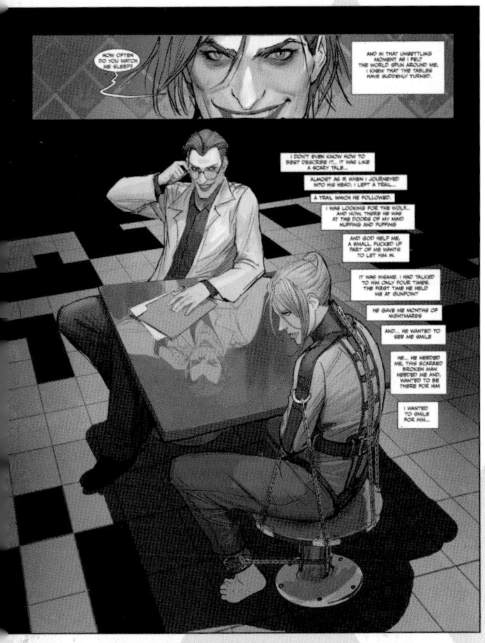
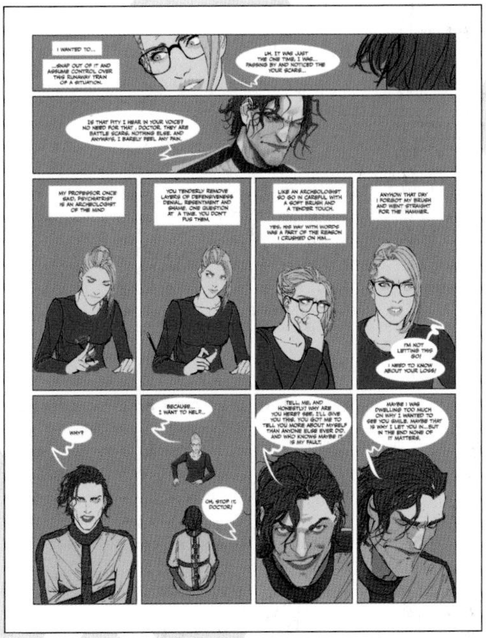
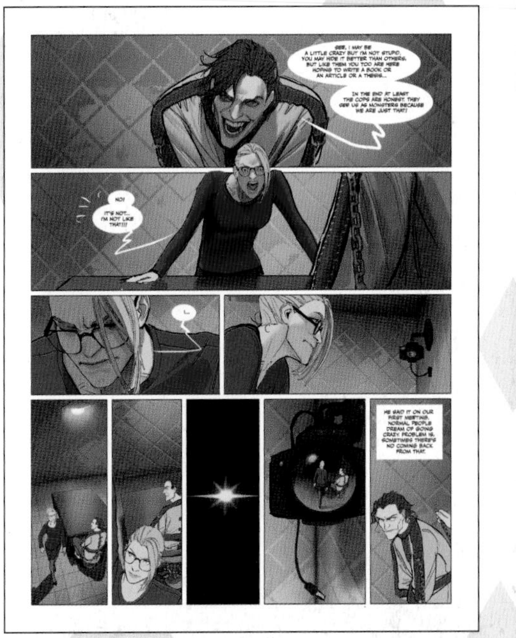
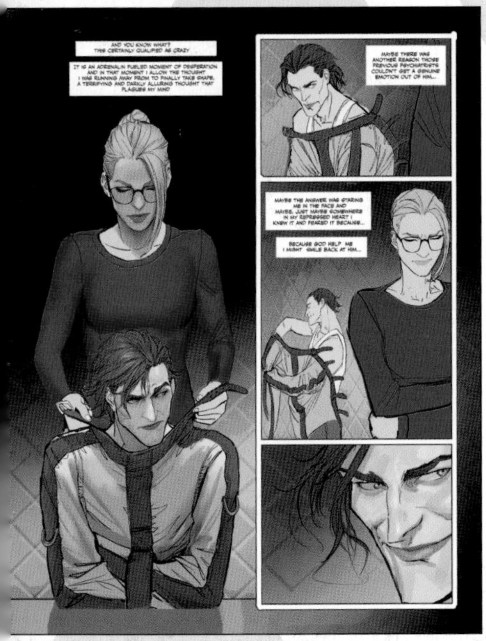
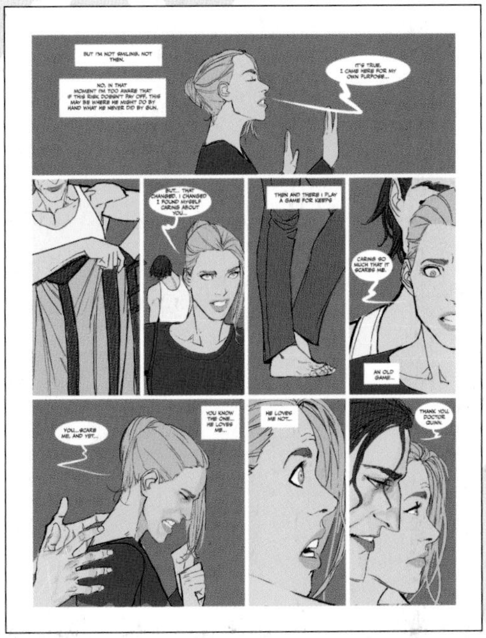
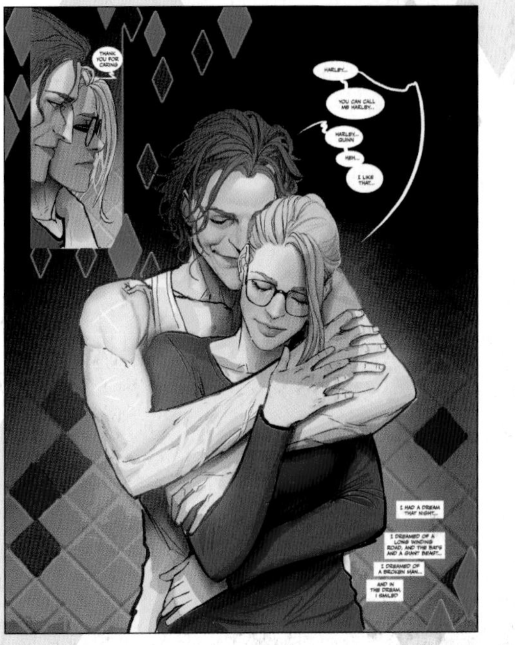

Stjepan Šejić started his career in comics in 2006 as a colorist for the Arcana Comics series *Kade*. From there he moved to work at Top Cow, where he had extended runs on most of the company's properties, including *Witchblade*, *Artifacts*, *Aphrodite IX*, and *The Darkness*. Since then, Šejić has created the critically acclaimed series *Death Vigil* and the bestselling *Sunstone* series of graphic novels, among other projects. His recent works include art duties on DC Comics' *Aquaman*, *Suicide Squad*, and the ongoing *Justice League Odyssey* series. Alongside those projects, Šejić has created a large number of comics covers and contributed additional work to various other publishers. He resides in the silence of Croatia's coastline, enjoying the sea breeze and excessive amounts of coffee.

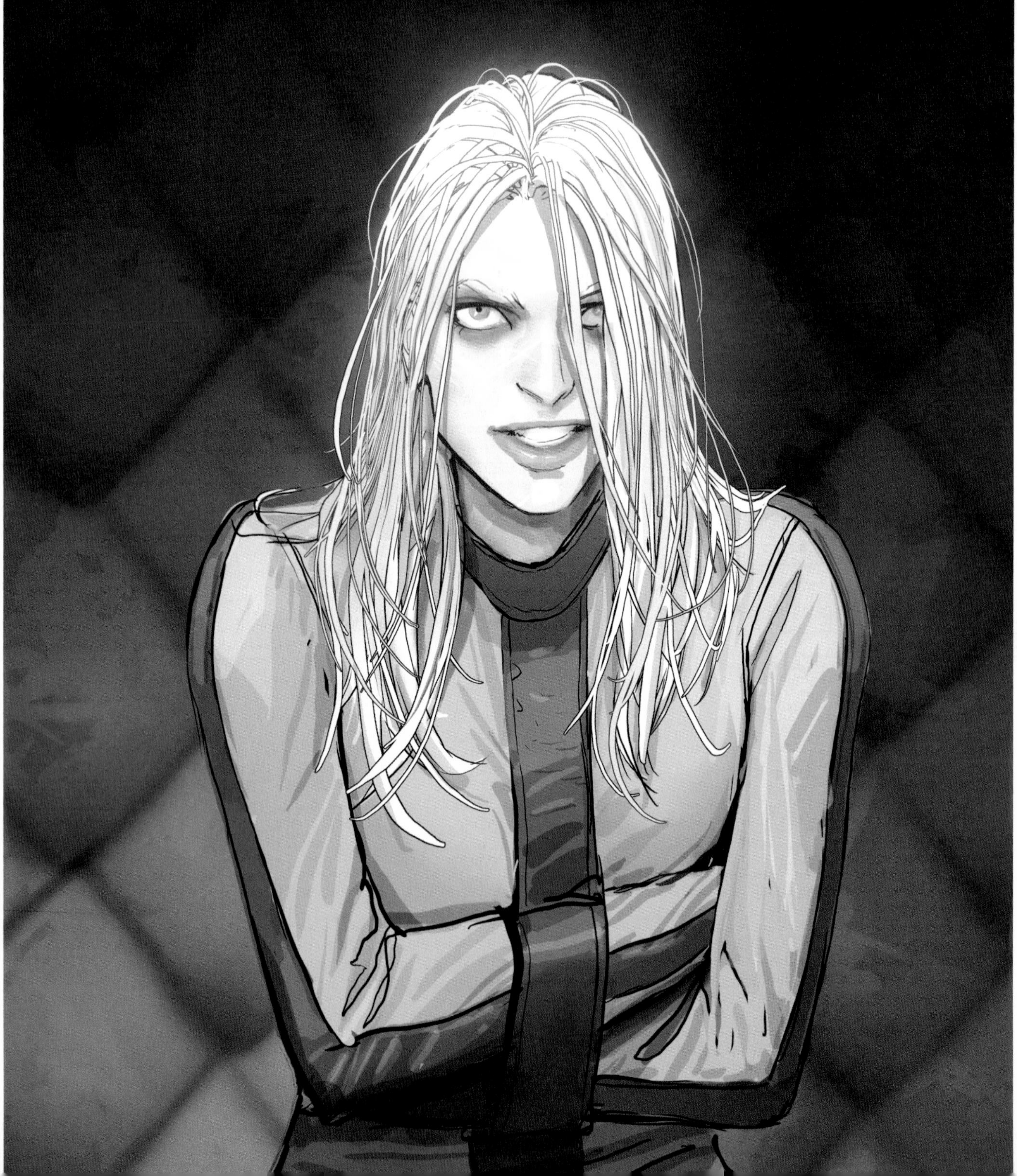

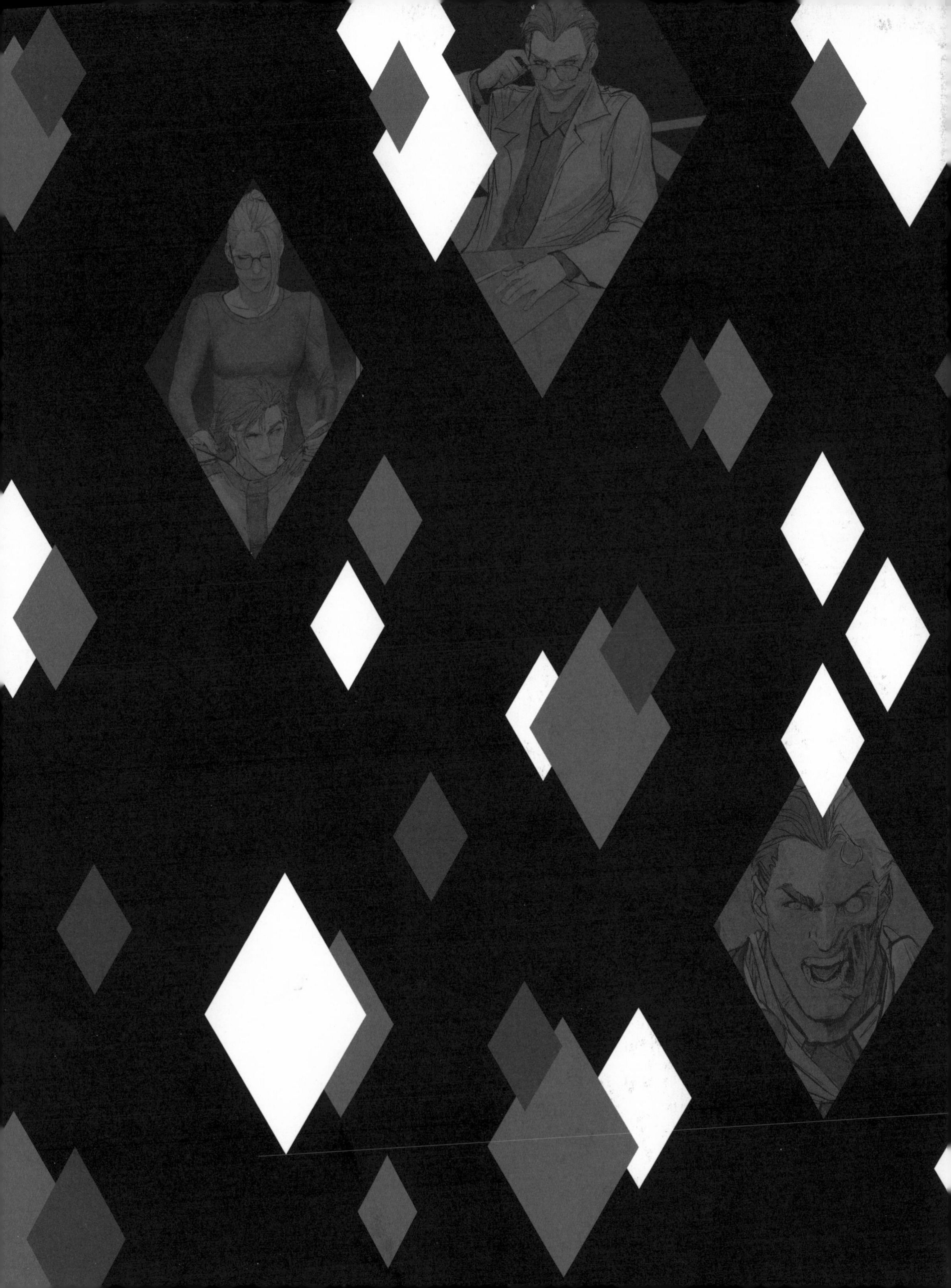